MUSICALS

THE DEFINITIVE ILLUSTRATED STORY

MUSICALS

THE DEFINITIVE ILLUSTRATED STORY

CONTENTS

1

THE MODERN MUSICAL
TO 1939

From *Show Boat* to *The Wizard of Oz*:
The first truly "modern" musicals evolve, mature, and then flourish amid the turbulent times of World War I, the Roaring Twenties, and the Great Depression.

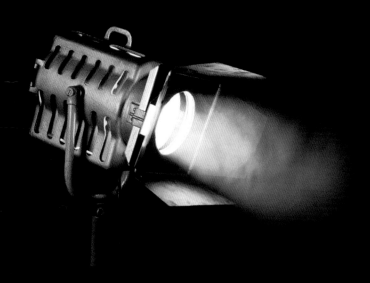

2

A GOLDEN AGE
1940–1969

From *Pal Joey* to *Oh! Calcutta!*:
A time of great creativity as musical theatre and cinema productions thrive in post-Depression America and London's West End comes to life.

 Penguin Random House

Project Art Editor
Duncan Turner

Project Editor
Miezan van Zyl

Designers
Paul Drislane, Alex Lloyd,
Shahid Mahmood, Francis Wong

Editors
Kaiya Shang, Helen
Fewster, Andy Szudek

Jacket designer
Natalie Godwin

Jacket Editor
Claire Gell

Managing Art Editor
Michael Duffy

Managing Editor
Angeles Gavira Guerrero

Jacket Design Development Manager
Sophia MTT

Art Director
Karen Self

Design Director
Phil Ormerod

Pre-production
Luca Frassinetti

Producer
Mary Slater

Publisher
Liz Wheeler

Publishing Director
Jonathan Metcalf

SCHERMULY DESIGN CO. LTD

Art Director
Hugh Schermuly

Project Editor
Cathy Meeus

Designers
Jane McKenna,
Keith Miller,
Louise Turpin,
Kathryn Gammon

Editors
Constance Novis,
John Andrews

GUY CROTON PUBLISHING SERVICES, TONBRIDGE, KENT

Art Director
Neil Adams

Project Director
Guy Croton

Designer
Heather McMillan

3
NEW INVENTIONS
1970–1999

From *Jesus Christ Superstar* to *Mamma Mia!*:
The genre is reinvented with rock musicals and the rise
of spectacular "mega musicals" that bring musicals to
new audiences around the world.

4
A MUSICAL REVIVAL
2000–PRESENT

From *The Producers* to *Into the Woods*:
Musicals continue to entertain, with big budget shows,
"jukebox" shows, popular revivals, and small-scale
productions ensuring that the show does go on.

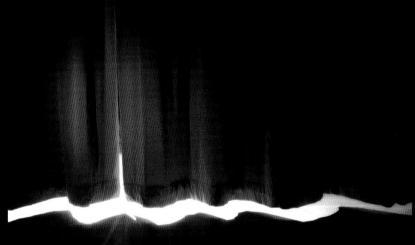

First published in Great Britain in 2015 by
Dorling Kindersley Limited
80 Strand, London, WC2R 0RL

Copyright © 2015 Dorling Kindersley Limited
A Penguin Random House Company
15 16 17 18 19 10 9 8 7 6 5 4 3
005–275080–Oct/2015

A CIP catalogue record for this book
is available from the British Library.
ISBN: 978-0-2412-1456-5

Printed in China

A WORLD OF IDEAS:
SEE ALL THERE IS TO KNOW

www.dk.com

FOREWORD

Turning page after page of this enjoyable book reminded me why I had to tread "the boards". It was seeing the musical film of *West Side Story* that was my inspiration and ignited in me a passion for this unique art form – musical theatre.

Included here are over 200 musicals ranging from the traditional American classic *Show Boat* (1927) to the renaissance of the British musical of the 70s and 80s (Andrew Lloyd Webber and Tim Rice), which I had the good fortune to be part of, through to the present day.

There is something here for everyone who loves musical theatre. This highly visual, photographic factual book contains a timeline of original artwork of posters, stage sets, stills and biographies – a treasure trove of information beautifully presented.

If you are fascinated to know the facts of the composers and lyricists, the designers and directors, the choreographers and casts, a team of writers have compiled here a book that enlightens, enriches, and entertains readers of all ages from the novice to the all time fan and celebrates the excitement that musical theatre has to offer both on stage and on screen.

And hopefully it will encourage you to pick up the phone, buy a ticket, and discover the magic of the musical live.

Elaine Paige

▶ **Curtain up!**
Whether performed live on stage or filmed for the silver screen, musicals have the ability to entertain and uplift.

THE MODERN MUSICAL

TO 1939

From Tin Pan Alley and Broadway to Hollywood and the silver screen, new musical productions captivate audiences with their catchy melodies, witty lyrics, and engaging plots.

MUSIC AND THEATRE

▲ The Beggar's Opera
In Gay's satire, popular tunes provided the soundtrack for his bawdy characters and their topical jokes about the government of the day.

Although musical theatre has ancient origins, the form of the musical as we recognize it today only began to flourish during the late 19th century.

The infusion of music, dance, and drama into uniquely engaging entertainment has probably existed as long as drama itself. Greek comedies and tragedies of the 5th and 3rd centuries BCE are known to have incorporated choreographed movement and song, often devised by the dramatists themselves. Entertainment provided by travelling performers during the Middle Ages consisted of a mixture of songs and physical comedy, whilst medieval religious dramas and biblical Mystery Plays featured chanting and melodized poetry.

A LIGHTER TONE
In 17th-century France, there emerged *comédie en vaudeville*, a light theatrical entertainment featuring comedic lyrics set to the tunes of popular songs. During the early 18th century, the *Singspiel* ("sing-play") materialized in Germany, while in England the "ballad opera" appeared, notably in the form of John Gay's popular and still-performed *The Beggar's Opera*

(1728). All these forms of musical entertainment featured spoken dialogue between musical numbers and were romantic, comedic, or satirical in manner.

These styles were, to some extent, a reaction against the prevalence of heroic grandeur in classical opera – as indeed was Italian *opera buffa* (or comic opera), which featured a lighter tone, plainer language, and stock characters from the Italian *commedia dell'arte* tradition. However, it was the 19th-century French "operette" that helped to pave the way for modern musical theatre, with the works of Hervé (1825–92) and especially the *opéra bouffe* of Jacques Offenbach (1819–80) setting the tone; "true comic opera", as Offenbach himself described it, "gay, bright, spirited music with real life in it".

SENSATIONAL SUCCESSES
The show that is regarded by some as the first modern musical – *The Black Crook*, by American playwright Charles Barras (1826–73) – opened in New

GEORGE M. COHAN 1878–1942
BIOGRAPHY

Born in Providence, Rhode Island, Cohan was a child performer in the family vaudeville act The Four Cohans, where he also developed his writing and compositional skills. He produced his first show for the act in 1901 before going on to create more than three dozen musicals, several straight plays, and over 300 songs, including "Give My Regards to Broadway", "Mary is a Grand Old Name", and one of the most popular songs of World War I, "Over There". He was portrayed by James Cagney in the highly-regarded musical biopic *Yankee Doodle Dandy* (1942).

York's burgeoning Broadway theatre district in 1866. It was a melodrama interspersed with adapted and original songs – such as "You Naughty, Naughty Men" – by George Bickwell and others. However, it was perhaps the inclusion of a large, scantily-dressed chorus of female dancers that ensured the show's runaway success. It ran for 474 performances and was revived in 1870, and again in 1872. Meanwhile, in 19th-century England "Victorian burlesque" (or "travesty") – a pastiche of established operas with a risqué and parodic tone – was gaining popularity. Among the many authors working in the form was W.S. Gilbert (1836–1911) who, with the composer Arthur Sullivan (1842–1900), became hugely influential in the development of the musical. Between 1874 and

▲ Entertainment for everyone
"Vaudeville" came to describe shows without an overall story featuring a variety of different acts, often, but not always, including musical numbers.

1898, Gilbert and Sullivan wrote 14 comic operas, most of which were staged in producer Richard D'Oyly Carte's Savoy Theatre in London. Works such as *H.M.S. Pinafore* (1878), *The Pirates Of Penzance* (1879), and *The Mikado* (1885) feature absurd, satirical plots integrated with witty, memorable songs that remain popular today.

VAUDEVILLE SHOWS AND MUSIC HALLS
Gilbert and Sullivan operas tended to appeal to middle-class audiences, but the lower classes were drawn to earthier musical entertainment – bawdy translations of French operettas,

music hall revues, vaudeville acts, and minstrel shows. The latter, despite presenting racial stereotypes, brought black musical traditions to a wider audience, which had an immeasurable impact on the development of both the American popular song, and consequently musical theatre. Edward Harrigan (1844–1911), the American comedian and writer, together with his performing partner, Tony Hart (1855–91), and father-in-law, the composer David Braham (1834–1905), are credited with bringing the liveliness of vaudeville into a coherent narrative structure. Their shows, including *The Mulligan Guards' Ball* (1879) and *The Mulligans'*

Silver Wedding (1883), featured sketches and comic songs that gently lampooned the various imigrant communities – whether Irish, Italian, German, or Jewish. The Harrigan and Hart social and ethnic satires were set in New York and performed on Broadway with great success.

NEW STYLES EMERGE

American composers like Reginald Dekoven (1859–1920) and John Philip Sousa (1854–1932) took their cue from the Gilbert and Sullivan style for their respective Broadway hits *Robin Hood* (1891) and *El Capitan* (1896), but ragtime and other black music styles also started to make an

appearance, notably in *Clorindy, or the Origin of the Cakewalk* (1898) and *In Dahomey* (1903), both composed by Will Marion Cook (1869–1944).

Meanwhile, back in London's West End, former D'Oyly Carte manager George Edwardes (1855–1915) had taken over the Gaiety Theatre in the 1880s. He initally specialized in "new burlesques" like *Frankenstein, or the Vampire's Victim* (1887) and *Faust up to Date* (1888), with original music by Meyer Lutz (1829–1903), but from the 1890s onwards, he presented "light, bright and enjoyable" refined new shows that he called "musical comedies" featuring variations on a shopgirl-made-good plotline as well as dancing, songs, and witty banter. This particularly English version of the musical form produced the hits *The Orchid* (1903) and *Our Miss Gibbs* (1909), among many other shows that, despite their historical influence, are rarely performed today.

Another highly popular form of musical theatre was translated European romantic operetta, many of which were also produced by the canny Edwardes. Enduring works of the period include *The Merry Widow* (1907), composed by Austro-Hungarian Franz Lehár (1870–1948), and *Naughty Marietta* (1910), by the Irish-German-American Victor Herbert (1859–1924).

THE AMERICAN MUSICAL

Gilbert and Sullivan's light operas, Edwardes' musical comedies, and European operetta all contributed to the development of the musical, but it was the vaudeville-flavoured shows of the actor/songwriter/playwright/producer George M. Cohan (see opposite) that introduced a distinctly American energy to the musical. Shows such as *Little Johnny Jones* (1904) and *Forty-five Minutes from Broadway* (1906) brought all the vitality of Tin Pan Alley – as New York's songwriters and popular music publishers were known – to the theatre stage and threaded a literate and engaging narrative through them. These qualities ensure Cohan's reputation as the founding father of the American musical.

THE MODERN MUSICAL

In the early 20th century, musical theatre was approaching maturity with the ongoing popularity of revues and operetta, the evolution of the book musical, and the influence of jazz.

Musical revues – plotless, variety-style presentations of singers, dancers, and comedians, with elaborate production numbers that often featured glamorous, scantily-clad showgirls – became popular in in the 1910s and 20s. Theatrical impresario Florenz Ziegfeld (see opposite) was king of the revue and, inspired by the risqué Parisian cabaret *Folies Bergère*, produced his annual show *Ziegfeld Follies* from 1907 to 1931, "glorifying", as he put it, "the American girl". Ziegfeld's success encouraged George White (1891–1968) to produce his *Scandals* (1919–39) and led Earl Carroll (1893–1948) to push the salacious boundaries with his *Vanities* (1923–32). The films *The Great Ziegfeld* (1936) and *Ziegfeld Follies* (1946) provide a toned-down flavour of these spectacles.

PLOTTING BROADWAY SUCCESS
The years 1915–18 were a key period in the development of the musical, as intimate venues too small to support lavish spectacles sought new ways to attract audiences. Written by British-American playright Guy Bolton (1884–1979), with later collaboration

▼ Landmark show
Show Boat was so well received by Broadway critics that this London production followed within five months, and achieved similar critical acclaim.

by British writer P.G. Wodehouse (1881–1975), and composed by Jerome Kern (1885–1945), the shows presented at Broadway's Princess Theatre featured original music that integrated with, and naturally flowed from, the plot situations and characters. Praised for their wit, intimate charm, and beguiling music, productions like *Oh, Boy!* (1917) and *Oh, Lady! Lady!!* (1918) set the standard that others would follow. "I like the way they go about a musical comedy," wrote American critic Dorothy Parker in 1918. "I like the way the action slides casually into the songs. I like the deft rhyming."

RAGTIME AND JAZZ

It was Kern, along with songwriter Irving Berlin (see pp.76–77), who popularized the lively, vernacular American musical styles of ragtime and jazz on the stage, giving Broadway shows a fresh, modern musical palette. Taking their cue from the popular songs of Tin Pan Alley, the songwriting brothers George and Ira Gershwin (see pp.24–25) had a string of hit shows including *Lady, Be Good* (1924), *Oh, Kay!* (1926), and *Funny Face* (1927). The similarly inspired composer Richard Rodgers (see pp.70–71) and lyricist Lorenz Hart (1895–1943) had comparable successes with *The Girl Friend* (1926), *A Connecticut Yankee* (1927), and *Ever Green* (1930).

Light-hearted in tone and largely frivolous of plot, the Gershwin and Rodgers and Hart musicals from this period, along with those of Cole Porter (see pp.84–85) and Vincent Youmans (1898–1946), are rarely revived without major revisions to their book,

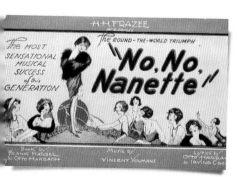

▲ "I Want To Be Happy"
Songs from musical comedies like Youmans' *No, No, Nanette* (1925) struck a chord with audiences looking for light-hearted entertainment.

while the scores are often augmented by songs from the composers' other shows. However, these musicals introduced dozens of popular songs that have endured down the years, outliving the shows by decades. The

songs became known as "standards" and are still performed and recorded by jazz and pop vocalists to this day.

OPERETTA

European operetta largely disappeared from the Broadway stage during the war years 1914–18, but it re-emerged in the 1920s, proving that the theatre-going public still had an appetite for exotic romance, sweeping Viennese rhythms, and soaring melody.

▲ Key players
Jack Donahue (left) and Marilyn Miller rehearse for *Rosalie* (1928) with George Gershwin at the piano, Sigmund Romberg behind him, and Florenz Ziegfeld (right).

Rose-Marie (1924) and *The Vagabond King* (1925) by Czech composer Rudolf Friml (1879–1972), along with *The Student Prince* (1924) and *The New Moon* (1928) by the Hungarian-American composer Sigmund Romberg (1887–1951), exemplified the style. The popular films of singer-actors Jeanette MacDonald and Nelson Eddy in the 1930s and 40s kept the operetta alive in the cinema, even as it once again faded from Broadway.

Unaffected by the jazz-fuelled revolution in the American popular song, London-based composer-actor Ivor Novello (1893–1951) wrote several operetta-style musicals, including wartime hit *Theodore & Co* (1916). Although Novello's last show, *Gay's the Word* (1951), did acknowledge modern musical developments, his work can be seen as a parochial parallel rather than a core development of the musical.

The same is true of the work of playwright-actor-composer Nöel Coward (1899–1973), who created a series of popular revues and musicals including *Bitter Sweet* (1929) and *Words and Music* (1932). The scripts were sharp, and the songs lyrically witty, but the shows remain distinct from developments in the musical,

belonging rather to the European and Gilbert and Sullivan operetta tradition (see pp.10–11).

BOOK MUSICALS

Setting the bar for Broadway musicals in 1927 was *Show Boat* (see pp.14–17), with songs by Jerome Kern and lyricist Oscar Hammerstein (see p.99). Dubbed a "musical play" to distinguish it from its more lightweight predecessors, its crafted "book" (the dialogue and plot), serious themes, and sensitive integration of the thoughtful, lyrical songs – such as "Ol' Man River" and "Can't Help Lovin' Dat Man" – became a benchmark for serious-minded book musicals. Irving Berlin's *As Thousands Cheer* (1933) had similarly powerful moments, including "Supper Time", a song sung by a woman whose husband had been lynched. However, when it comes to solemn tone and artistic prowess, George Gershwin's "folk-opera" *Porgy and Bess* (see p.32) is considered by many to be in a league of its own.

Although it foreshadowed the ambition of later through-sung musicals such as Stephen Sondheim's *Sweeney Todd* (see pp.216–19), the opera-musical was not immediately adopted as a Broadway style. In the grip of the Great Depression, there remained an appetite for escapist, upbeat entertainment, albeit sometimes informed by the ground-breaking advances of *Show Boat*. Romantic musical comedies of the 1930s that fitted the bill included Cole Porter's *Anything Goes* (1934) and Rodgers and Hart's *On Your Toes* (1936), as well as the political satire *Knickerbocker Holiday* (1938) by German composer Kurt Weill (see p.21) and Maxwell Anderson (1888–1959).

MOVIE MUSICALS

The 1930s also saw an explosion of interest in movies of musicals, whether adaptations of existing shows like *No, No, Nanette* (released in 1930) and *Anything Goes* (1936), or shows written especially for cinema such as Fred Astaire/Ginger Rogers vehicles *Top Hat* (1935) and *Swing Time* (1936). These popular films allowed the increasingly sophisticated work of

BIOGRAPHY

FLORENZ ZIEGFELD
(1867–1932)

A unique blend of the tacky and the transporting, the *Ziegfeld Follies* produced some enduring musical repertory – thanks to the work of contemporary composers like Irving Berlin, George Gershwin, and Jerome Kern, and performers such as Fanny Brice, W.C. Fields, and Eddie Cantor. In addition to the *Follies*, the Chicago-born Broadway impresario produced over 50 shows in New York including Kern and Grey's *Sally* (1920), Kern and Hammerstein's *Show Boat* (1927), Gershwin and Romberg's *Rosalie* (1928), and Coward's *Bitter Sweet* (1929).

the composer, performer, and choreographer to be enjoyed not just on the New York or London stage, but on the silver screen throughout the world. The musical had become a global phenomenon.

▲ Kaleidoscopic fantasies
Choreographer Busby Berkeley made the most of the special effects available to movie musicals. His showgirls created amazing geometric displays in film extravaganzas like *Footlight Parade* (1933).

SHOW BOAT

{ **1927** }

Considered one of the most influential musicals of the early 20th century, *Show Boat* steered the Broadway musical in an entirely new direction by exploring subject matter such as unhappy marriages and racial tension.

▼ **Robeson as "Joe"**
Paul Robeson, lawyer, football player, civil rights activist, and renowned bass singer, reprised the part of Joe that he had first played in the London production in the hugely successful 1936 film.

The 1926 novel *Show Boat* by American writer Edna Ferber fascinated composer Jerome Kern (see below) almost from the moment he began to read it. Oscar Hammerstein II (see p.99), Kern's writing partner, shared his enthusiasm. Both were sure that *Show Boat* was just the vehicle they needed to enable them to create a new type of musical play that differed from the fast-moving, but lightweight, musical comedies and flamboyant operettas that had long been the bread and butter of the Broadway stage. With *Show Boat*'s exceptionally strong storyline, they could create well-defined characters. In addition, Kern also had the chance he had long been looking for – the opportunity to craft expressive songs and music that would drive the drama forward, so becoming an integral part of the overall tale. Racial intolerance forms a key subplot of *Show Boat*. The tragic figure of Julie is secretly of mixed race. She is married to a white man, a crime in the Mississippi of the time. In fact, interracial marriage remained illegal through much of the American South until 1967. In addition, it was decades before a black American actress was finally cast to play Julie, rather than a white one.

> *"The book in present shape has not got a chance except with critics."*

FLORENZ ZIEGFELD JR, *SHOW BOAT'S* PRODUCER, IN A TELEGRAM SENT DURING PRODUCTION, 1926

JEROME KERN (1885–1945)   BIOGRAPHY

Born in New York City, Kern began his Broadway career before World War I; he was still active in 1945, when he collapsed with a cerebral haemorrhage and died. He wrote more than 700 songs and worked with the leading lyricists of the time to create Broadway musical hits and major Hollywood movies. While his songs are still recorded widely, *Show Boat* is the only one of his musicals that is regularly revived.

DELAYS AND DOUBTS

Kern and Hammerstein got to work quickly (they began writing even before the initially reluctant Ferber had sold them the rights to adapt her work). But it took far longer than they originally had hoped to get *Show Boat* on stage. The opening had been announced for 1 April 1927, but it did not premiere in New York until 27 December of that year, and the continued delays had caused three of the original stars to withdraw from the production.

There were various reasons why *Show Boat* fell behind schedule. Kern was involved simultaneously with a new show, a spectacular being mounted by impresario Charles B. Dillingham. Florenz Ziegfeld Jr, *Show Boat*'s producer, was also expressing doubts about Hammerstein's work. Hammerstein would have to revise the book to meet Ziegfeld's objections or someone else would need to be called in to fix it. The "present lay-out", Ziegfeld warned, was "too serious". He wanted more comedy and stronger love interest.

Casting, too, was problematic. American singer and actress Helen Morgan, whom Kern desperately wanted to play Julie, did not return to New York from a London engagement until 6 September. She was signed the following day. *Show Boat* finally went into rehearsal a week later. The rehearsals, too, lasted for longer than was customary. It was not until mid November that the show was ready for its out-of-town try-outs.

SMASH-HIT PREMIERE

Even though its running time stretched to nearly four and a half hours, *Show Boat* was an immediate success at the try-out in Washington, D.C. Critic Harold Phillips predicted that "Can't

KEY FACTS

🎭 **STAGE**

🎬 **Director** Oscar Hammerstein II

📖 **Book** Edna Ferber

🎵 **Music** Jerome Kern

🎼 **Lyrics** Oscar Hammerstein II

🎭 **Venue** Ziegfeld Theatre, New York

📅 **Date** 27 December 1927

◉ **Key information**

The original Broadway show ran for 572 performances (the longest run Kern's shows ever achieved during his lifetime). It was made into a movie three times. The 1994 Broadway revival won five Tony Awards.

Help Lovin' Dat Man", "Make Believe", and "Ol' Man River" would be instant hits. The Pittsburgh try-outs were even more successful. Another local critic, Karl B. Krug, wrote, "This musical marks a milestone in musical comedy production." The production moved on to Cleveland and Philadelphia with equal success.

Three weeks later, the show opened in the Ziegfeld Theatre in New York. Success was instantaneous, even though, despite the cuts that had been made on tour, the show did not end until 20 minutes before midnight. *The New York Times* was particularly effusive. It commended the "exceptional tuneful score – the most lilting and satisfactory that the wily Jerome Kern has contrived in several seasons". As for Hammerstein's stage direction (though, for some unknown reason, he was not given a credit on the programme), Joseph Urban's scenic design, John Harkrider's costumes, and Sammy Lee's choreography, all were given unstinting praise. Ziegfeld had a smash hit show on his hands.

The story was the same in London, where British theatre impresario Alfred Butt mounted *Show Boat* at the Theatre Royal, Drury Lane, in May 1928. Singer and actor Paul Robeson joined the cast as Joe, singing the part that originally had been conceived specifically for him. The curtain came down on the show's last night after 350 performances.

Show Boat was a smash hit, and Ziegfeld revived it on Broadway in 1932, and again in 1946. Despite the Great Depression years that followed the 1929 Wall Street Crash, the show undertook an extensive national tour. It was filmed in 1929 as a part-talkie; in 1936; and by MGM in 1951.

On stage, the 1994 Broadway revival directed by Harold Prince (see pp.210–11) ran for 947 performances. There were also notable West End revivals of *Show Boat* in 1971, 1990, and the Harold Prince production in 1998.

▲ **Hit music**
The sheet music cover for "Ol' Man River", the show's crowd-pulling hit number, incorporating the poster artwork for the original Broadway production.

STORYLINE

An epic tribute to the power of undying love and a demonstration of how human sufferings and triumphs fade away as time passes, the plot is centred around a troupe of travelling performers on a "show boat". It focuses on the evolving relationship between Magnolia and Gaylord as they move from life on the Mississippi to a seedy existence in Chicago. A subplot follows the fortunes of the mixed-race performer Julie and her husband Steve.

CAST	
Norma Terris Magnolia	**Edna May Oliver** Parthy
Howard Marsh Gaylord	**Tess Gardella** Queenie
Charles Winninger Cap'n Andy Hawks	**Eva Puck** Ellie
Helen Morgan Julie LaVerne	**Sammy White** Frank
Jules Bledsoe Joe	**Charles Ellis** Steve

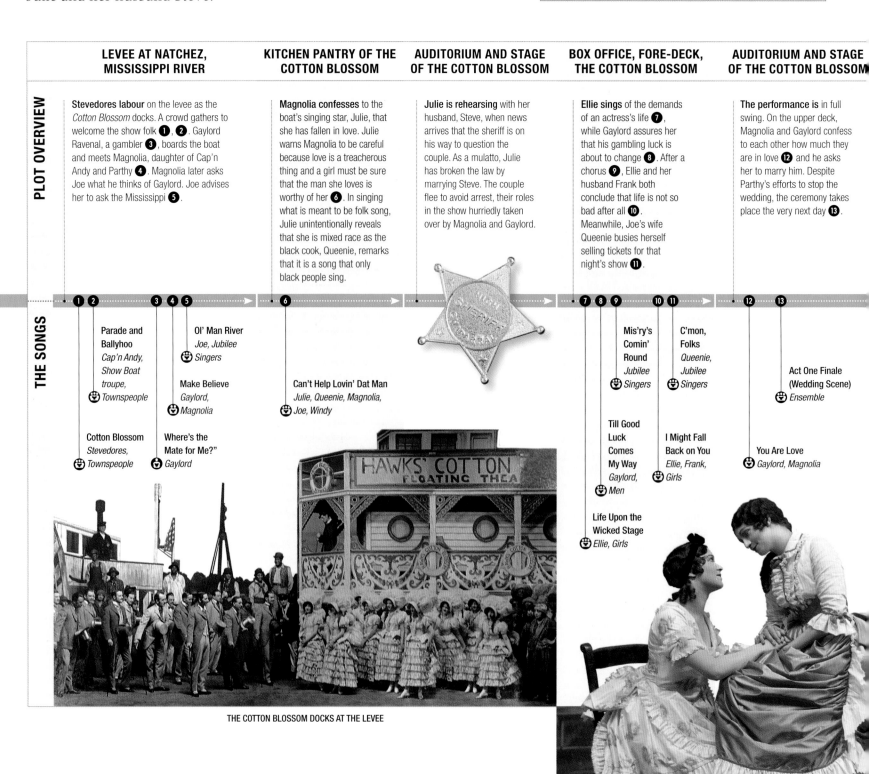

PLOT OVERVIEW

LEVEE AT NATCHEZ, MISSISSIPPI RIVER

Stevedores labour on the levee as the *Cotton Blossom* docks. A crowd gathers to welcome the show folk ❶, ❷. Gaylord Ravenal, a gambler ❸, boards the boat and meets Magnolia, daughter of Cap'n Andy and Parthy ❹. Magnolia later asks Joe what he thinks of Gaylord. Joe advises her to ask the Mississippi ❺.

KITCHEN PANTRY OF THE COTTON BLOSSOM

Magnolia confesses to the boat's singing star, Julie, that she has fallen in love. Julie warns Magnolia to be careful because love is a treacherous thing and a girl must be sure that the man she loves is worthy of her ❻. In singing what is meant to be folk song, Julie unintentionally reveals that she is mixed race as the black cook, Queenie, remarks that it is a song that only black people sing.

AUDITORIUM AND STAGE OF THE COTTON BLOSSOM

Julie is rehearsing with her husband, Steve, when news arrives that the sheriff is on his way to question the couple. As a mulatto, Julie has broken the law by marrying Steve. The couple flee to avoid arrest, their roles in the show hurriedly taken over by Magnolia and Gaylord.

BOX OFFICE, FORE-DECK, THE COTTON BLOSSOM

Ellie sings of the demands of an actress's life ❼, while Gaylord assures her that his gambling luck is about to change ❽. After a chorus ❾, Ellie and her husband Frank both conclude that life is not so bad after all ❿. Meanwhile, Joe's wife Queenie busies herself selling tickets for that night's show ⓫.

AUDITORIUM AND STAGE OF THE COTTON BLOSSOM

The performance is in full swing. On the upper deck, Magnolia and Gaylord confess to each other how much they are in love ⓬ and he asks her to marry him. Despite Parthy's efforts to stop the wedding, the ceremony takes place the very next day ⓭.

THE SONGS

❶ ❷ ❸ ❹ ❺ ❻ ❼ ❽ ❾ ❿ ⓫ ⓬ ⓭

Parade and Ballyhoo
Cap'n Andy, Show Boat troupe,
☺ *Townspeople*

Cotton Blossom
Stevedores,
☺ *Townspeople*

Ol' Man River
Joe, Jubilee
☺ *Singers*

Make Believe
Gaylord,
☺ *Magnolia*

Where's the Mate for Me?"
☺ *Gaylord*

Can't Help Lovin' Dat Man
Julie, Queenie, Magnolia,
☺ *Joe, Windy*

Mis'ry's Comin' Round
Jubilee
☺ *Singers*

Till Good Luck Comes My Way
Gaylord,
☺ *Men*

Life Upon the Wicked Stage
☺ *Ellie, Girls*

C'mon, Folks
*Queenie,
Jubilee*
☺ *Singers*

I Might Fall Back on You
Ellie, Frank,
☺ *Girls*

You Are Love
☺ *Gaylord, Magnolia*

Act One Finale (Wedding Scene)
☺ *Ensemble*

THE COTTON BLOSSOM DOCKS AT THE LEVEE

MAGNOLIA AND JULIE CONFIDE IN EACH OTHER

"Next time ... we'll all charter a show boat and just drift down the rivers."

WINTHROP AMES, PRODUCER, COMMENTING AFTER THE *SHOW BOAT* PREVIEWS, 1927

EDITH DAY
AS MAGNOLIA
IN THE LONDON
PRODUCTION

CHICAGO WORLD FAIR	ONTARIO STREET, CHICAGO	TROCADERO CLUB REHEARSAL ROOM	ST AGATHA'S CONVENT	NEW YEAR'S EVE, TROCADERO CLUB	COTTON BLOSSOM, NATCHEZ
Magnolia and Gaylord now live in Chicago with Kim, their young daughter. Cap'n Andy, in town for the World Fair **14**, **15**, **16**, visits them. Magnolia reveals to him that Gaylord's constant gambling has lost them all their money and ruined their relationship. Yet, she still loves him **17**.	**Frank and Ellie,** seeking lodgings, find Magnolia and Gaylord about to be thrown out for rent arrears. Frank offers to get Magnolia a singing job at the nightclub where he and Ellie appear. A note from Gaylord arrives with money for Kim's convent-school fees but telling Magnolia he is leaving her.	**Julie, resident signer** at the Trocadero Club and now on her own, is about to be fired for missing performances due to her heavy drinking. She is rehearsing **18**, **19** when Magnolia arrives to audition **20**. Julie announces she is leaving the club so Magnolia can take her place.	**The scene shifts** to the convent **21**, where Gaylord tells Kim he has to leave Chicago on a long business trip.	**The club is buzzing** as the orchestra and dancers perform **22**, followed by Ellie and Frank **23**. Then Magnolia makes her debut, singing a sweetly sentimental waltz **24**. As a standing ovation erupts, she falls into her father's arms.	**Joe reprises** his song about the Mississippi **25** and Queenie makes a final attempt to get him to make up his mind about her **26**. The story moves forward to the 1920s. Magnolia and Kim are now both Broadway stars **27**–**31**. They decide to revisit the *Cotton Blossom*, where they find Gaylord waiting for them. He begs Magnolia for forgiveness and the family is reunited as Joe's voice is heard once again singing behind the scenes **32**.

14 15 16   **17**   **18 19**   **20**   **21**   **22 23 24**   **25 26 27 28 29 30 31**   **32**

Dandies on Parade
Sightseers, Barkers,
😇 *Dandies*

Why Do I Love You?
Magnolia, Cap'n Andy, Parthy,
😇 *Company*

Adagio Dance
Sidell
😇 *Sisters*

At the Fair
Sightseers, Barkers,
😇 *Dandies*

Bill
😇 *Julie*

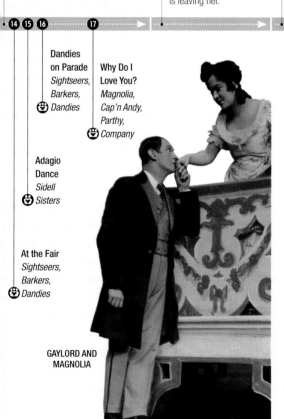

GAYLORD AND MAGNOLIA

⭐ *Finding a suitable song to reintroduce Julie into Act II was a problem until Kern thought of using "Bill", which he had written with British writer P.G. Wodehouse in 1918. It became one of the great hits of the show.*

😇 **In Dahomey**
Jubilee Singers, Dahomey Dancers

Can't Help Lovin' Dat Man (reprise)
😇 *Magnolia*

Service and Scene Music, St Agatha's Convent
😇 *Nuns*

After the Ball
Magnolia,
😇 *Ensemble*

Goodbye, My Lady Love
😇 *Frank, Ellie*

Apache Dance
😇 *Sidell Sisters*

Tap Dance
😇 *Una, Val*

Kim's Imitations
😇 *Kim*

😇 **Eccentric Dance**

Why Do I Love You? (Reprise)
😇 *Kim, Flappers*

You Are Love (reprise)
😇 *Magnolia*

Hey, Feller
😇 *Queenie, Jubilee Singers*

Ol' Man River (reprise)
😇 *Joe*

Finale
😇 *Company*

GAYLORD IN CHICAGO

LONDON'S
WEST END

The West End is the loosely defined district in central London where most of the city's mainstream commercial theatres can be found.

London's 450-year-old West End district is home to hotels, restaurants, nightclubs, bars, and also most of the major professional theatres in London. In all, 40 theatres reside in the West End, many of which will feature musicals at any given time.

The first theatre in the West End was the simply named Drury Lane. It opened in 1663, but nine years later it burned down and was replaced by the current Theatre Royal, Drury Lane. The two next oldest West End theatres are the Haymarket Theatre, which opened in 1720, and the Theatre Royal (now the Royal Opera House), which opened in 1732 in Covent Garden. By the early 1800s, many smaller theatres had opened in the area, establishing it as the centre of theatrical activity.

After the Restoration of Charles II in 1660, only two theatres in London were licensed to perform spoken drama, all other theatres had to offer comedy, musical entertainments, or pantomime. This forced producers and theatre owners to offer music hall entertainments and melodramas (literally "music-drama"). Parliament lifted this law in 1843, but by then the public taste for musical forms of theatre had firmly taken hold.

THRIVING BUSINESS
The Society of London Theatres reports overall box office grosses on a yearly basis. Figures indicate that the theatre is thriving; both attendance and revenues seem to be increasing every year. The West End has also become a big draw for visitors and tourists, with tickets for shows often bought in advance.

Successful musicals of the West End have had people queuing up for years. West End theatres have seen some long runs, with a number of musicals running for more than 15 years. The shows with impressively long runs include: *Les Misérables* (over 30 years, see pp.246–49), *The Phantom of the Opera* (over 29 years, see pp.252–53), *Blood Brothers* (24 years), *Cats* (21 years, see pp.228–31), *Mamma Mia!* (over 16 years, see pp.284–85), and *The Lion King* (over 16 years, see pp.276–79).

◀ **Waiting for the show**
Theatregoers wait outside the Theatre Royal, Drury Lane, in 1928 for *Show Boat*. People queued for a long time and chairs could be rented for the wait.

"The musical is the one area of the theatre that can give you the biggest buzz of all."

SIR CAMERON MACKINTOSH, BRITISH PRODUCER, *THE NEW YORK TIMES*, 1990

THE THREEPENNY OPERA

{ 1928 }

Brecht and Weill's subversive and intense masterpiece is an influential cornerstone in the development of the musical, while remaining a dazzling one-off achievement. Its worldwide popularity with audiences and critics endures to this day.

◀ Scenes of the underworld
Audiences were intrigued and entranced by the seedy and cynical themes of *The Threepenny Opera*, as reflected in the art of this poster.

German theatre director and playwright Bertolt Brecht was intrigued by British dramatist John Gay's *The Beggar's Opera* from 1728, which Brecht's assistant Elisabeth Hauptmann had introduced him to, translating the English libretto into German. In 1920, *The Beggar's Opera* had been successfully revived in London for a year-long run, and its themes of poverty, injustice, and corruption were exactly what interested Brecht. He adapted the piece to his own purposes over the course of six months to create *Die Dreigroschenoper (The Threepenny Opera)*, which follows the sordid exploits of the womanizing bandit Mackie Messer (Macheath or Mack the Knife) in the beggar-ridden Soho of 1830s London.

WIDE-RANGING INFLUENCES

Brecht drew on sources beyond Gay, including Rudyard Kipling and the French medieval poet François Villon. Ultimately, Brecht sacrificed a proportion of his royalties to the German translator of *Villon* when verbatim excerpts were identified in some songs.

Ernst Josef Aufricht, producer at Berlin's Theater am Schiffbauerdamm became excited about Brecht's idea, but was nervous at his choice of composer, Kurt Weill (see opposite).

In Germany in 1927, Kurt Weill and Bertolt Brecht had already collaborated on *Mahagonny-Songspiel*, a short-form song cycle intended as a precursor to their epic political-satirical opera *Rise and Fall of the City of Mahagonny* – which they would complete in 1930, causing scandal among the Nazis. At the same time, Weill had a reputation as a challenging modernist whose music was not especially audience-friendly. Aufricht even went to the trouble of locating the original *Beggar's Opera* music as insurance, but his fears were allayed upon hearing the composer's work for the first time.

AN UNUSUAL COMBINATION

Weill had fashioned German oompah and jazz, dance-band, cabaret, and mock-Baroque classical music into an acrid, sinister, and thoroughly compelling whole. He also ingeniously orchestrated the score of the musical for only seven musicians to play as many as 23 instruments (including banjo, trombone, trumpet, harmonium, bassoon,

◀ Breaking new ground
Weill and Brecht's contentious new production proved a huge hit, despite a shaky start. This is the first scene of the play, set in Peachum's shop.

"*Weill's* Threepenny Opera ... *presented the perfect image of that hopeless and stressful time in Berlin.*"

AARON COPLAND, AMERICAN COMPOSER

and various saxophones), creating a meticulous *Klangbild,* or soundworld, that is as intractable a part of the character of the show as the songs or libretto.

Rehearsals were frenzied, with creative arguments, last-minute cast and score changes, and a dress rehearsal that dragged on until 5am. The mood was gloomy, not helped when the opening-night programs arrived without the name of Weill's wife, Lotte Lenya, who was playing Jenny—a mistake that nearly prevented Lenya appearing at all. In the event, the show was a brilliant hit, with 46 stage productions of the piece appearing throughout Europe within a year of the August 1928 Berlin premiere. In 1931, the film *Die 3-Groschenoper* was released, making an international star of Lenya.

Although he sympathized with socialism, Weill became unhappy with Brecht's extreme Marxist tendencies, and so withdrew from the collaboration. All Weill/Brecht works were banned from the German stage by the time Weill fled Nazi Germany for Paris in 1933, ultimately settling in New York in 1935. By this time, *The Threepenny Opera* had already been produced 130 times worldwide, though it was years before a significant American production appeared, and by then Weill was dead.

BROADWAY PRODUCTION

In 1954, American composer and lyricist Marc Blitzstein (see p.45) translated *Die Dreigroschenoper* into English and this Off-Broadway production of *The Threepenny Opera* at the Theatre de Lys ran for 2,707 performances.

The originally menacing, rather horrific opening number "Moritat", which details Macheath's worst crimes, was turned into "Ballad of Mack the Knife". This became a toe-tapping hit for jazz singers Louis Armstrong, Bobby Darin, Ella Fitzgerald, and others. While popularizing and publicizing the show like a hit song should, it also served to somewhat dilute the original menacing flavour of the piece, with its accessible lyrics and distinctive, catchy melody.

This 1950s Broadway run ensured the enduring influence of this singular German piece on the musical in general, not least on John Kander and Fred Ebb's *Cabaret* (see p.166) and *Chicago* (see pp.196–99).

Several songs from *The Threepenny Opera* have been widely covered and have become international standards, performed in many different versions.

Apart from the enduring stage musical, at least three film versions of *The Threepenny Opera* have been made. The first came out in 1931 in German and French, the second in 1962 in German, and the third in English, as *Mack the Knife*, in 1989.

◀ **Celebrating their wedding**
Tim Curry as Macheath and Sally Dexter as Polly Peachum, dancing together in a 1996 production at the National Theatre, London.

BIOGRAPHY

KURT WEILL (1900–50)

A member of the *Novembergruppe* (November Group), a community of Berlin-based left-wing artists with a social and political agenda in the 1920s, Weill divided his efforts between modernistic orchestral and chamber works and abrasive, jazz-influenced vocal/opera/musical theatre, notably with dramatists Georg Kaiser and Bertolt Brecht. Further success was achieved with Brecht–Weill's epic opera parody *Rise and Fall of the City of Mahagonny* (1930), from which comes "Alabama Song", famously covered by the American rock group, The Doors.

CAST LIST

Harald Paulsen Macheath
Roma Bahn Polly
Erich Ponto Mr Peachum
Rosa Valetti Mrs Peachum
Lotte Lenya Jenny
Kate Kühl Lucy

OF THEE I SING

{ 1931 }

Written during the Great Depression, *Of Thee I Sing* gleefully lampooned presidential elections and the governing that followed. Its zany premise and memorable songs made this the Gershwin brothers' most successful musical.

Playwright George S. Kaufman was reunited with George and Ira Gershwin, writing partner Morrie Ryskind, and choreographer George Hale for *Of Thee I Sing*. They had collaborated on another satire in 1930, *Strike Up the Band*, the first in a politically themed trilogy. The show had a respectable run but nothing like *Of Thee I Sing*, one of the most popular stage shows of the 1930s. At 441 performances, it was at the time the longest-running musical for the Gershwins (see pp.24–25). *Let 'Em Eat Cake*, the third of the three, featuring the same leading characters, ran for 89 performances. Kaufman and Ryskind originally envisioned a story that pitted two national anthems against each other to replace the "Star-Spangled Banner". The two writers, who had worked together before for the Marx Brothers, among others, decided the comedy was too impersonal and transformed it into a love story about a presidential campaign. The show came together very quickly: the script took only 17 days to write. Before the preview in Boston, a nervous Kaufman worried that the show might not be the laugh riot he had hoped for. He needn't have. When *Of Thee I Sing* opened on 26 December 1931 at the Music Box Theatre, the critics loved it and so did ticket buyers. Not only was it the first musical to win the Pulitzer Prize for Drama – although George Gershwin was not included in the award until after his death – it was the first musical to be published as a hardcover book, which appeared the following year.

he and his party operatives mull over a campaign strategy, a chambermaid freshens up their hotel room. When asked what is most important to her, she answers: money. Her second choice is love and a political slogan is born: "Love Is Sweeping the Country". From here, the plot follows the wacky travails of the politician from his candidacy to his impeachment. John P. Wintergreen, a bachelor, needs a

"A biting and true satire on American politics."

PULITZER PRIZE FOR DRAMA CITATION, 1932

KEY FACTS

STAGE

📽 **Director** George S. Kaufman
📖 **Book** George S. Kaufman and Morrie Ryskind
🎵 **Music** George Gershwin
♪ **Lyrics** Ira Gershwin
🎭 **Venue** Music Box Theatre, New York
📅 **Date** 26 December 1931

⊙ **Key information**
The original Broadway production, directed by Kaufman, opened in 1931 and ran for 441 performances, gaining critical and box-office success. It has been revived twice on Broadway and in concert stagings in the US and in London. In 1932, *Of Thee I Sing* was the first musical to win the Pulitzer Prize for Drama.

secretary of the contest's top beauty. Wintergreen wins the election and weds Mary, but then has to contend with the jilted pageant loser, who wages a righteous campaign of her own. Hovering in the wings while controversy swirls around Wintergreen is the fumbling nonentity Alexander Throttlebottom, the vice-presidential candidate, played by the popular comedian Victor Moore.

bride for his love-themed campaign, so he conducts a beauty pageant Miss America-style in Atlantic City. However, he falls instead for Mary, the

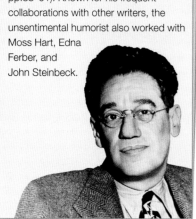
CATCHY TUNES
The play ridicules not only the executive branch, but Congress, the Supreme Court, the Navy, farmers, motherhood, the French, not to mention the American people and musical

WILD PLOT AND CUTTING SATIRE
Beneath *Of Thee I Sing*'s absurd antics and lively tunes lurked searing criticism of a political system and a surprisingly sweet love story. The action centres around John P. Wintergreen, a hapless presidential candidate in search of a platform. As

▶ **High satire**
The Capitol building is the ultimate symbol of American politics. This did not deter the Gershwins in their mockery.

CAST LIST

William Gaxton John P. Wintergreen
Lois Moran Mary Turner
Sam Mann Louis Lippman
Harold Moffet Francis X. Gilhooley
Vivian Barry Maid
Dudley Clements Matthew Arnold Fulton
George E. Mack Senator Robert E. Lyons
Edward H. Robins Senator Carver Jones
Victor Moore Alexander Throttlebottom
George Murphy Sam Jenkins
Grace Brinkley Diana Devereaux
June O'Dea Miss Benson
Tom Draak Vladimir Vidovitch
Sulo Hevonpaa Yussef Yussevitch

comedies in general. If the tone of the musical was unusual for its time, so too was its structure. The Gershwins did not just punctuate the plot with musical numbers, but told their story in the songs' lyrics. In fact, more scenes were sung than spoken. With a nod to the comedy operas of Gilbert and Sullivan, *Of Thee I Sing*'s outlandish situations drove the comic and upbeat libretto. Hits from the show include "Of Thee I Sing, Baby", "Love Is Sweeping the Country", and "Who Cares?". Revivals followed, including a television adaptation in 1972 with Carroll O'Connor, Cloris Leachman, and Jack Gilford, and a radio version in 1984. Other Broadway productions were mounted in 1933 and 1952; in 1990 by a Gilbert and Sullivan troupe; and in 2006 with Victor Garber as Wintergreen. One of the most interesting recent evocations of the title of this show is US President Barack Obama's use of it for a book published in 2010. This version of *Of Thee I Sing* was an illustrated letter to his daughters, in which the president paid tribute to 13 great Americans. There is irony in the fact that Obama used the title in such a different context.

Of Thee I Sing was the first American musical to feature such a consistently satirical tone. Many subsequent musical satires owe much to the Gershwins' fearless and ground-breaking approach to this work.

▶ **National lampoon**
The cover of the sheet music for the vocal score of *Of Thee I Sing*, which was published in 1932.

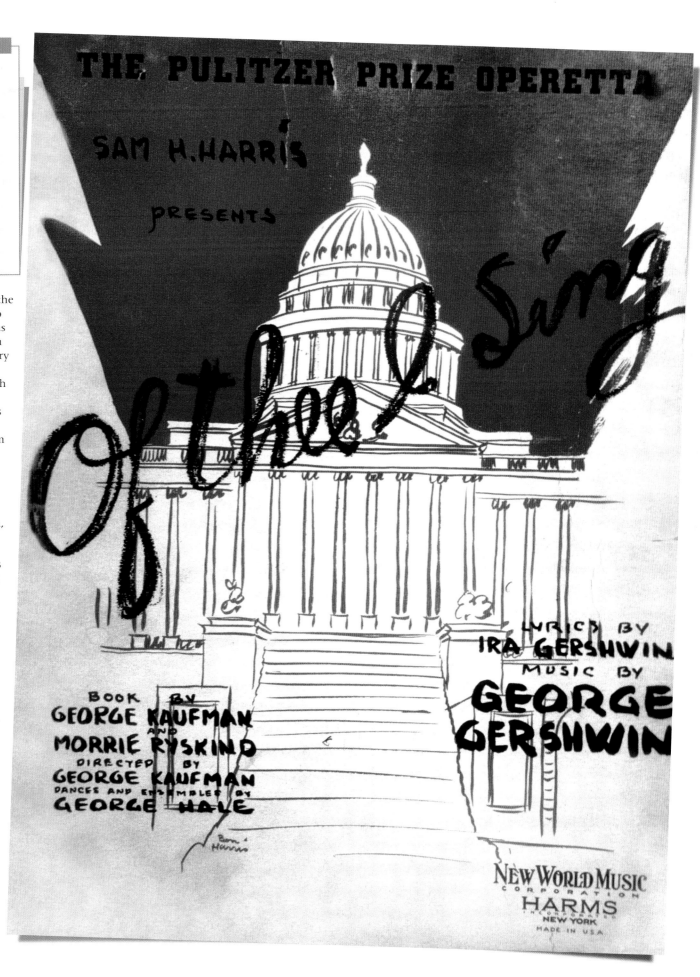

GEORGE AND IRA GERSHWIN

COMPOSERS 1896–1983

George and Ira Gershwin were two halves of a hugely influential and successful song-writing team that dazzled Broadway and Hollywood during the 1920s and 30s.

The brothers Gershwin were born in New York to Jewish immigrant parents of Russian-Lithuanian origin who changed their name from Gershowitz. Ira (who was actually named Israel) was born on 6 December 1896, with George (Jacob) following on 26 September 1898.

Ira showed early literary talent, enrolling at the City College of New York in 1912, while happy-go-lucky George studied piano with a succession of teachers, including the musician and composer Charles Hambitzer, who introduced him to the works of Chopin, Debussy, and Ravel.

FIRST SUCCESSES

At 15, George was showing off remarkable keyboard skills in New York's Tin Pan Alley as a demonstration pianist, "song plugger", and fledgling songwriter. His early melodies were influenced by ragtime, jazz, and contemporary popular music and he

▶ **National treasures**
The US Library of Congress award for songwriting is named after the Gershwin brothers.

impressed the likes of Irving Berlin, composer Jerome Kern, writer P.G. Wodehouse, impresario Florenz Ziegfeld, and Broadway star Al Jolson, who recorded George's song "Swanee" to national acclaim in 1920. Having dropped out of college, Ira was working in a Turkish baths when George asked for help with the lyrics of "The Real American Folk Song (Is a Rag)" for the musical *Ladies First* in 1918. The song was well received and became hugely popular. And so began one of the 20th century's most creative musical partnerships.

A FLOURISHING PARTNERSHIP

Ira's first works, including his 1921 hit *Two Little Girls in Blue* (with Vincent Youmans), were written under the pseudonym Arthur Francis to avoid capitalizing on his brother's reputation. However, after the resounding success, in 1924, of their first musical *Lady, Be Good!* (catapulting Fred and Adele Astaire to stardom), the brothers mainly wrote together. Ira crafted words to fit with George's melodies. In this way they produced a string of songs, musicals, and

▶ **Giants of the genre**
The brothers Gershwin were hugely innovative and influential in the rise of the musical. Individually and together, they wrote a body of work that comprises some of the most popular and enduring songs ever written.

> *"Life is a lot like jazz…*
> *it's best when you improvise."*

GEORGE GERSHWIN

film scores over the next two decades, including the musicals *Oh, Kay!* (for Gertrude Lawrence) and *Girl Crazy*, starring newcomer Ethel Merman (see pp.140–41). Not everything that they produced was successful, however. The daring and, for the time, racially controversial jazz opera *Porgy and Bess* (see p.32), written with DuBose

Heyward, did not impress when it opened in 1935. Later, though, it became the first American opera to enter the classical repertoire and remains a firm favourite with audiences to this day.

PUSHING BOUNDARIES
Ira worked on new and different lyrical styles while George combined classical music with jazz to create original harmonies and rhythms. The song "I Got Rhythm" (from *Girl Crazy*) featured a chord progression that became the basis for later jazz songs. Despite his hectic schedule, George continued studying musical technique and composition. His virtuosity and ability to improvise were dazzling and used to good effect in his jazz piano concerto *Rhapsody in Blue*, which took America by storm in 1924, establishing his credentials as a serious composer. His reputation was strengthened by later concert works – the ambitious *Piano Concerto in F* and *Three Preludes* – while the tone poem *An American in Paris* was inspired by a 1928 trip to Europe when George

▲ **Stars of stage and film**
The film *An American in Paris* was inspired by a 1928 composition by George Gershwin. The Gershwin brothers' music has been adapted for use in many films and for television.

met the composers Joseph-Maurice Ravel, Darius Milhaud, Sergei Prokofiev, Francis Poulenc, and Franz Lehár.

END OF A BRILLIANT RELATIONSHIP
The Gershwins' creative partnership ended abruptly in July 1937 when George died, aged just 38, following an operation to remove a brain tumour. It was three years before a heartbroken Ira resumed work, collaborating with the likes of Jerome Kern (*Cover Girl*, 1944), Harry Warren (*The Barkleys of Broadway* 1949), and Harold Arlen (*A Star is Born*, 1954). Published in 1959, his critically acclaimed book *Lyrics on Several Occasions* brings the lyrics of his most famous songs together with commentaries and anecdotes. He donated the brothers' manuscripts to the Library of Congress, ensuring that their music became part of America's national heritage. Ira died in his Beverley Hills home on 17 August 1983, at the age of 86.

THE GERSHWIN LEGACY
Over two decades the brothers produced extraordinary work that combined Ira's engaging and clever lyrics with George's playful, catchy melodies and jazzy, toe-tapping rhythms that still make listeners of all ages want to dance.

KEY WORKS

Lady, Be Good! ("Fascinating Rhythm"), 1924

Oh, Kay! ("Someone to Watch Over Me"), 1926

Funny Face ("Let's Kiss and Make Up"), 1927

Strike up the Band, 1927

Girl Crazy ("Embraceable You", "I Got Rhythm"), 1930

Porgy and Bess, 1935 (see p.32)

TIMELINE

16 December 1896 Ira is born in Manhattan.

26 September 1898 George is born in Brooklyn.

1912 George begins music lessons with pianist and composer Charles Hambitzer; Ira enters City College of New York.

1918 Their first collaboration, "The Real American Folk Song", is a success.

1920 Al Jolson records George's song "Swanee".

12 February 1924 Premiere of George's *Rhapsody in Blue* at the Aeolian Hall in New York.

1 December 1924 Their musical *Lady, Be Good!* opens at the Liberty Theatre on Broadway, starring Adele and Fred Astaire.

3 December 1925 Premiere of George's *Piano Concerto in F*.

14 September 1926 Ira marries Leonore Strunsky.

4 November 1926 First performance of *Three Preludes for Piano*.

8 November 1926 The musical comedy *Oh, Kay!* opens at Broadway's Imperial Theatre.

1928 George visits France, meeting Ravel, Prokofiev and others.

13 December 1928 Premiere of *An American in Paris*.

NEW YORK STREET SIGN

14 October 1930 *Girl Crazy* opens on Broadway, starring Ethel Merman and Ginger Rogers.

1932 Ira is awarded the Pulitzer Prize for *Of Thee I Sing*.

30 September 1935 *Porgy and Bess* premieres in Boston.

11 July 1937 George dies in Hollywood aged 38.

17 August 1983 Ira dies aged 86 in Beverly Hills.

GOLD DIGGERS
OF 1933

Made in 1933, before the strict enforcement of movie censorship guidelines, *Gold Diggers of 1933* is the archetypal backstage musical, with scantily clad showgirls, great melodies, and the incomparable brilliance of choreographer Busby Berkeley.

Before the film was made, *The Gold Diggers* had already been a 1919 play by Avery Hopwood (who went on to become one of the most successful playwrights of the 1920s), a 1923 silent movie, and a 1929 talkie, *The Gold Diggers of Broadway*. The 1929 movie (now largely lost) featured early Technicolor effects and elaborate song-and-dance numbers, and was a huge success. With Warner Bros spotting an opportunity to exploit the audience's obvious appetite for faintly indecent backstage yarns, their 1933 loose remake kept the basic premise of the previous incarnations – that showgirls may or may not be ready to marry for money. However, they devised a new plot involving four actresses (Polly, Carol, Trixie, and Fay), a rich songwriter and theatrical benefactor, Brad Roberts, his protective brother, J. Lawrence Bradford, and the Bradfords' lawyer, Fanuel H. Peabody.

CAST LIST

Dick Powell Brad Roberts
Warren William Lawrence Bradford
Joan Blondell Carol King
Aline MacMahon Trixie Lorraine
Ruby Keeler Polly Parker
Ginger Rogers Fay Fortune
Guy Kibbee Fanuel H. Peabody
Ned Sparks Barney Hopkins

◀ **Glitz and glamour all the way**
This brightly coloured poster advertising the film made the typically audacious Busby Berkeley claim that the film was "The Biggest Show on Earth". Berkeley was never known for his modesty.

But what really set *Gold Diggers of 1933* apart from its predecessors were the four spectacular song-and-dance sequences devised and directed by Busby Berkeley (see opposite). The 37-year-old choreographer had made his reputation as a highly decorative, often titillating designer of musical production numbers. These usually involved a "parade of faces" (a series of chorus girls presented in adoring close-up) and elaborate symmetrical movements of performers adorned with ostentatious props and costumes. His signature tour de force was the overhead shot in which the coordinated actions of the carefully placed chorus created ornate geometric, almost kaleidoscopic patterns.

ESCAPE FROM REALITY
In the time of the Great Depression, these fantastical escapist displays proved hugely popular, as did defiant, optimistic songs like "We're in the

◀ **Dream-like scenes**
This striking scene, featuring a large troupe of violinists surreally clad in Christmas-tree-like dresses, was typical of Berkeley's excesses.

KEY FACTS

🎬 **FILM**
🎬 **Director** Mervyn LeRoy (drama) and Busby Berkeley (musical sequences)
🎞 **Screenplay** Erwin S. Gelsey and James Seymour
🎵 **Music** Harry Warren
𝄞 **Lyrics** Al Dubin
🕐 **Running time** 96 minutes
📅 **Release date** 27 May 1933

⊙ **Key information**
Gold Diggers of 1933 was one of the top-grossing films of that year. In 2003, it was selected for preservation in the United States National Film Registry by the Library of Congress as being "culturally, historically, or aesthetically significant".

◀ Ginger queen
Ginger Rogers' svelte beauty was ideally suited to a production that revelled in its celebration of Hollywood glamour.

Money", written by Harry Warren and Al Dubin (see pp.28–29). The opening sequence of *Gold Diggers of 1933* features Fay Fortune (played by Ginger Rogers) singing this cheerful ditty amid a bevy of chorus girls fanning and waving giant coins. This spectacle is later outdone by the six-minute setting of "The Shadow Waltz", involving dozens of girls miming the playing of neon-lit violins in configurations that suggest a bird, a flower, a clock, and finally a violin. Berkeley hits a surreally suggestive peak during "Pettin' in the Park". Many courting couples get caught in a rainstorm in Central Park, forcing the ladies to change out of their wet clothes, their silhouettes clearly visible through the backlit screen. Just before a mischievous dwarf (masquerading as a

RELATED WORKS

42nd Street, Harry Warren, Al Dubin, 1933

Floodlight Parade, Harry Warren, Al Dubin, Sammy Fain, Irving Kahal, 1933

Gold Diggers of 1935, Harry Warren, Al Dubin, 1935

Gold Diggers of 1937, Harry Warren, Al Dubin, 1937

Million Dollar Mermaid, Harry Warren, Al Dubin, 1952

Code (sometimes also called the Hays Code), in which revealing attire and sexually provocative situations were strictly forbidden. To avoid trouble with the state censorship boards, Berkeley took to shooting alternative, toned-down versions of some of his numbers, and different edits of the film were made for distribution to sensitive districts.

However, Berkeley didn't always use his talent for overstatement to frivolous purpose. His setting of

"*I wanted to make people happy, if only for an hour.*"

BUSBY BERKELEY, CHOREOGRAPHER

child) raises the screen to reveal their implied nakedness, the ladies emerge clad in metal swimsuits, their voluptuous bodies only accessible to their amorous beaux by a can-opener.

It was this kind of salaciousness that attracted criticism of Berkeley from the Motion Picture Production

"My Forgotten Man" in *Gold Diggers of 1933* – featuring soldiers saying goodbye to loved ones and marching off to war, only to return to hunger, unemployment, and drink – brilliantly and poignantly underlines the accusing, sorrowful tone of Warren and Dubin's score in this Depression-era classic.

BUSBY BERKELEY (1895–1976)

BIOGRAPHY

Though Berkeley's outsized, sexualized conceptions from his 1930s heyday have been analysed for symbolic meaning, he claimed only to be interested in flamboyance for its own sake, attempting to outdo himself with every number. When his inflated style went out of fashion, he became a straight director for both dramas (*They Made Me a Criminal*, 1939) and musicals (*Take Me Out to the Ball Game*, 1949), but reverted to type as choreographer on several Esther Williams watery extravaganzas. His final film as choreographer was for *Billy Rose's Jumbo*, in 1962 (see p.33), though he reprised his signature style for a TV commercial in the 1960s and directed the successful 1971 Broadway revival of *No, No, Nanette*.

HARRY WARREN AND AL DUBIN

{ COMPOSERS/LYRICISTS **1893–1981** }

It is 1933 and America is still in the grip of the Great Depression. A couple of bright and breezy musical movies seem just the tonic the nation needs. Harry Warren and Al Dubin are the men to provide them.

◀ **Shared skills**
Al Dubin (left) and Harry Warren were hugely talented songwriters responsible for many of the most instantly recognizable songs of the era.

It was Warren and Dubin who wrote the wonderfully catchy songs in the musicals *42nd Street* (see pp.222–23) and *Gold Diggers of 1933* (see pp.26–27), such as "You're Getting to be a Habit with Me", "We're in the Money", and "Shadow Waltz". At a difficult time for the United States – a period of depression followed by World War II – they set the entire nation's feet tapping.

Today, these films are regarded as classics and rank among the best musicals ever made. An essential component of their success was certainly the songs written by these two talented men who, over six glorious years, turned out what seemed to be a never-ending stream of hits.

For Harry Warren, it was to be a brief interlude in a four-decade-long career, in which he was one of America's most prolific composers and the first to write primarily for film. But for Al Dubin, it was a six-year period in a life that was tragically cut short by ill health.

The two men came from immigrant families and were born just six months apart, but Warren outlived Dubin by 36 years. He was one of 11 children and he taught himself to play

KEY WORKS

"'Twas Only an Irishman's Dream", 1916, Al Dubin

"Rose of the Rio Grande", 1922, Harry Warren

"Tiptoe Through the Tulips", 1929, Al Dubin

"You're Getting to be a Habit with Me", *42nd Street*, 1932, Warren and Dubin

"We're in the Money", *Gold Diggers of 1933*, 1933, Warren and Dubin

"Chattanooga Choo-Choo", *Sun Valley Serenade*, 1941, Harry Warren

"You'll Never Know (Hello 'Frisco, Hello)", 1943, Harry Warren

"I've Got a Girl in Kalamazoo", *Orchestra Wives*, 1942, Harry Warren

"On The Atchison, Topeka, and the Santa Fe", *The Harvey Girls*, 1946, Harry Warren

accordion, drums, and piano because his family could not afford lessons. At 14 he dropped out of school and did a variety of jobs, including playing the piano for silent movies.

TIN PAN ALLEY

Al Dubin's parents tried to discourage him from following a musical career. But he regularly played truant to see Broadway musicals and visit Tin Pan Alley, where he attempted to sell the songs he had written.

Both men continued their songwriting during their World War I military service, so that by the early 1920s they were beginning to make their names: Warren with his first hit, "Rose of the Rio Grande" with lyrics by Edgar Leslie, and Dubin with "A Cup of Coffee, a Sandwich, and You", written with Joseph Meyer.

GOLDEN BREAKTHROUGHS

Although Warren and Dubin met in 1925, it was not until 1933 that the pair began their collaboration in earnest, contributing four songs to *42nd Street*, which was released in March 1933. The first blockbuster musical film, it became one of the year's most profitable movies.

A few weeks later it was followed by *Gold Diggers of 1933*, which had a similar format and also featured four Warren–Dubin numbers. Busby Berkeley's choreography of the dance routines to "We're in the Money" and "Pettin' in the Park" was lavish. It was also considered saucy for its time, and copies of the movie were distributed with alternative footage to circumvent state censorship issues. Between 1933 and 1939, Warren and Dubin wrote 60 hit songs for over 30 Warner Bros movies, including *Footlight Parade*, starring James Cagney, *Roman Scandals* with Eddie Cantor, and *Go into Your Dance* and

Wonder Bar, both starring Al Jolson. Another Warren–Dubin collaboration, "Lullaby of Broadway", won an Oscar for Best Original Song.

END OF THE PARTNERSHIP

However, by the end of the decade, Al Dubin was in increasingly poor health. For some time his lifestyle had included excessive eating, as well as substantial drink and drug abuse. He became overweight and fell on hard times. Estranged from his wife, Dubin struggled to find work in Hollywood and New York. Eventually, he collapsed from an overdose of prescribed barbiturates and died three days later.

His erstwhile partner, though, had barely reached the peak of a career in which he wrote over 800 songs and published 500. They appeared in 300 films, a third of them for Warner Bros. More than 40 became Top 10 hits.

◀ **Blockbuster**
Dubin and Warren's score for *42nd Street* would, decades later, be reused for the Broadway show hit also called *42nd Street*.

▲ **Censor alert**
Dancers in the movie *Gold Diggers of 1933* performing the catchy song "We're in the Money". Busby Berkeley's choreography was legendary.

Harry Warren also collaborated with lyricists such as Johnny Mercer and Ira Gershwin, and teamed up with Mack Gordon for "Chattanooga Choo-Choo" in 1941. Performed by the Glenn Miller Orchestra, it became the first ever gold record, selling 1.2 million copies.

In the 1950s, Warren composed the theme music for a television series entitled *Wyatt Earp*. Although he continued to write songs for movies throughout the 1960s and 70s, he failed to repeat past successes.

In 1957, Warren received his final Academy Award nomination. *An Affair to Remember* starred Cary Grant and Deborah Kerr and featured a theme song composed by Warren with lyrics by Leo McCarey and Harold Adamson. It was considered to have made a major contribution to the film's success and subsequently became a jazz standard.

Altogether, Harry Warren's songs received 11 nominations and three Oscars. He had more hit songs than Irving Berlin, yet remained virtually unknown. *Time* magazine called him a "Hollywood incognito."

TIMELINE

10 June 1893 Alexander Dubin is born in Zurich, Switzerland, to gynaecologist Simon Dubin and chemist Minna Dubin; the family moved to Philadelphia three years later.

24 December 1893 Salvatore Antonio Guaragna (later renamed Harry Warren) is born in Brooklyn, New York, to Italian immigrants Antonio and Rachel De Luca Guaragna.

1909 Dubin publishes his first two songs, "Prairie Rose" and "Sunray".

1916 "'Twas Only an Irishman's Dream" is Dubin's first hit song.

1922 Warren produces his first hit song, "Rose of the Rio Grande".

1925 Dubin and Warren meet for the first time, but do not form a writing partnership until seven years later.

1929 Now under contract to Warner Bros, Dubin writes "Tiptoe through the Tulips" for *Gold Diggers of Broadway*.

1930 Warren composes music for "Cheerful Little Earful" for the Broadway revue *Sweet and Low*.

1933 Films *42nd Street* and *Gold Diggers of 1933* released by Warner Bros with lyrics by Dubin and music by Warren, marking the first results of their collaboration.

1935 Warren and Dubin's "Lullaby of Broadway" for *Gold Diggers of 1935* wins Oscar for the Best Song.

11 February 1945 Dubin dies in New York.

"REMEMBER ME" BY WARREN AND DUBIN (1937)

1946 Warren receives his third Oscar for "On the Atchison, Topeka, and the Santa Fe", written with Johnny Mercer.

1971 Dubin posthumously inducted into the Songwriters' Hall of Fame.

22 September 1981 Warren dies in Los Angeles.

> "*We're in the money, we're in the money... We've got a lot of what it takes to get along.*"

LYRIC BY **AL DUBIN**, *GOLD DIGGERS OF 1933*, 1933

ANYTHING GOES

{ 1934 }

Full of vitality and drenched in the wit and sophistication of the songs of Cole Porter, *Anything Goes* lifted audiences out of the Great Depression and made a big star of Ethel Merman.

The 1930s was a time of deep economic trouble in the US. For the lucky few, however, it was also the heyday of glamorous ocean travel. So it is no surprise to find the action of *Anything Goes* unfolding on the decks of the SS *American*, en route to London from New York.

RELATED SHOWS

The New Yorkers, 1930, Cole Porter

Gay Divorce, 1932, Cole Porter

Nymph Errant, 1933, Cole Porter

Jubilee, 1935, Cole Porter

Red, Hot and Blue, 1936, Cole Porter

The plot of the original book, by British humourist P.G. Wodehouse and British-American musical comedy writer Guy Bolton, involved the sinking of a ship. Then, two months before *Anything Goes* was due to open, the passenger vessel SS *Morro Castle* sank off the New Jersey coast, with heavy loss of life. The script was hurredly revised to keep the SS *American* safely afloat and good taste intact.

The madcap and inventive plot revolved around the increasingly tortuous efforts of Wall Street stockbroker Billy Crocker to win the heart of Hope Harcourt, who is sailing to London with her fiancé, Lord Evelyn Oakleigh. To win her, Crocker boards the SS *American*, where he is mistaken for gangster Snake Eyes Johnson and

enlists the help of singing evangelist Reno Sweeney and another gangster, Moonface Martin, disguised as the Reverend Dr Moon. After much confusion, Billy and Hope marry.

IT'S A HIT!

When Porter wrote the score to *Anything Goes*, he had one person in mind to play Reno Sweeney – Ethel Merman (see pp.140–41). He gifted her the show-stopping "You're the Top." The show was an immediate success and, inevitably, a film version followed in 1936.

A box-office certainty, the movie star and crooner Bing Crosby was brought in to play Billy and, although Merman still played Reno, the film lost much of the stage show's dazzle – along with the comic brilliance of Gaxton and

Moore (see below) and all but four of Porter's songs. A second film version in 1956 again starred Crosby as Billy. This remake changed the story and included new songs by Jimmy Van Heusen and Sammy Cahn.

KEY FACTS

STAGE

Director Howard Lindsay

Book P.G. Wodehouse and Guy Bolton, revised by Howard Lindsay and Russel Crouse

Music and lyrics Cole Porter

Venue Alvin Theatre, New York

Date 21 November 1934

Key information

Anything Goes was tried out in Boston before moving to Broadway, where it ran for 420 performances, one of the longest runs of any musical in the 1930s. The show opened in London on 14 June 1935, and ran for 261 performances.

> *"By keeping their sense of humor uppermost, they have made a thundering good music show."*
>
> BROOKS ATKINSON, THEATRE CRITIC, *THE NEW YORK TIMES*, 22 NOVEMBER 1934

◀ **Top Performers**
Ethel Merman and Bing Crosby took the lead roles in the 1936 screen version of the musical.

BIOGRAPHY

WILLIAM GAXTON (1893–1963) AND VICTOR MOORE (1876–1962)

Also starring in *Anything Goes* was the comic double-act of suave Gaxton (far right) and hapless clown Moore (right). They were brought together in George and Ira Gershwin's *Of Thee I Sing* in 1933 and became hot Broadway property. They continued to work on stage and in films into the 1940s. Gaxton's ad-libbing once earned him a telegram from director George S. Kaufman: "Am watching from back of house, wish you were here."

TOP HAT

{ 1935 }

If not the greatest of the Astaire and Rogers musicals, *Top Hat* was the most successful and – with its silver-topped canes and top hats – surely the most iconic.

By 1935, Fred Astaire and Ginger Rogers had made several screen appearances together, but *Top Hat* was the first movie that was conceived as a showcase for their dancing partnership. After watching Fred and Ginger steal the show from the ostensible leads (Dolores Del Rio and Gene Raymond) of 1933's *Flying Down to Rio*, and after seeing their success with two pictures adapted from stage shows not really suited to their personalities – *The Gay Divorcee* (1934) and *Roberta* (1935) – RKO chief Merian Cooper insisted that their next project should be shaped around them.

KEY FACTS

🎬 FILM

- 🎬 **Director** Mark Sandrich
- 📝 **Screenplay** Dwight Taylor, Allan Scott
- 📖 **Book** Dwight Taylor
- 🎵 **Music and lyrics** Irving Berlin
- 🕐 **Running time** 101 minutes
- 📅 **Release date** 1935

◉ Key information

Top Hat grossed US$1.7 million at home and US$1.4 million overseas, making it RKO's most profitable film of the 1930s. It was nominated for four Oscars: Best Picture; Art Direction (Carroll Clark and Van Nest Polglase); Original Song ("Cheek to Cheek"); and Dance Direction (Hermes Pan). In 2012, the first stage production opened in London's West End.

▲ **Film poster**
The poster for the film featured the trademark top hat of the title and Rogers' glamorous dress with swirling skirt.

extravagant that it is easy to forget that *Top Hat* was made while the US was midway through the Great Depression – which was, of course, the intention. Watching Astaire relishing the atmosphere of class as he sings in "Top Hat, White Tie and Tails", audiences were treated to a vicarious taste of high living and luxury beyond anything they could reasonably aspire to in that period.

A WINNING SCORE

Top Hat's plot is essentially standard-issue Hollywood musical form. Dwight Taylor and Allan Scott's screenplay is built around the "boy meets girl, girl hates boy, boy dances with girl, girl falls in love" formula of old. But what did mark the film out from its predecessors in the Astaire-Rogers series was its score; the songs weren't just a grab-bag of already existing numbers but were written specifically for the movie. For another, they were the work of Irving Berlin (see pp.76–77), the man Alec Wilder called "the best all-round, over-all song writer America has ever had". Certainly, the only flaw with *Top Hat's* score is that there isn't enough of it. All but one of its songs have gone on to become jazz standards, but the plot arguably lacked the energy of the music. Strangely, Astaire himself may have been partly to blame for this. After reading the first draft of the script, he complained that the story was weak and that his character was "forever pawing the girl or she is rushing into my arms".

▲ **Effortless elegance**
The centrepeice dance numbers of Rogers and Astaire set a standard for Hollywood musicals for decades.

ELEGANT ROMANCE

Astaire has two solo dances in *Top Hat*: the swaggering yet lyrical "No Strings" and the almost aggressively jaunty "Top Hat, White Tie and Tails" (so aggressive it ends with Astaire's feet mimicking the sound of gunfire as he uses his stick to "shoot" at the chorus line). But it is the three numbers featuring Astaire and Rogers together that are the heart of the film. Danced inside a gazebo while the heavens open, "Isn't This a Lovely Day" is a relaxed, will-they-won't-they shuffle. A mickey-take of "The Continental" and "The Carioca", "The Piccolino" is the movie's anticlimactic closing number – anticlimactic because it comes only moments after the lilting, high-romantic grandeur of "Cheek to Cheek", in which Fred and Ginger dance through set designer Carroll Clark's extravagant, Art Deco-inspired take on Venice. The film was so

HERMES PAN (1909–90)

Born in Memphis, Tennessee, Hermes Pan was a choreographer on movies from 1933 to 1981. His most famous working relationship was with Fred Astaire (see pp.42–43), many of whose dances he helped invent (and whose many partners he put through their paces). They met in 1933 on the set of *Flying Down to Rio*, and worked together until Astaire's last major film musical, *Finian's Rainbow* (see p.79).

PORGY AND BESS

{ **1935** }

The ground-breaking "folk-opera" for African-American classical singers blends many musical styles into a towering work of enormous artistry and emotional power.

George Gershwin's reputation as the most bountiful and brilliant popular composer of the early 20th century was earned by his numerous hit songs, Broadway shows (often cowritten with his brother Ira, see pp.24–25), Hollywood films, and concert pieces. Fascinated by DuBose Heyward's 1924 novel *Porgy* about African-American street characters and fishermen set in the tenements of Charleston, South Carolina, Gershwin detected the makings of an opera in its tragic, powerful narrative.

Spending time with Heyward in South Carolina, Gershwin worked with Heyward to compose what he described as "my own spirituals and folksongs… in operatic form".

Like opera, the entire show was sung through, with individual songs threaded together with recitative, or sung, dialogue. There was no spoken dialogue at all. Also like opera, the score called for classical voices.

Unlike classical opera, however, the score featured Gershwin's highly individual musical palette, which along with a Russian classical influence incorporated the flavours of blues, jazz, and Jewish music, plus his own take on traditional African-American forms, all bound together with his rich symphonic orchestrations. In addition, the cast entirely comprised black performers.

◄ **First all-black cast**
American actors Sidney Poitier and Dorothy Dandridge star in the 1959 film production of *Porgy and Bess.*

UNIQUE LOOK AND SOUND
Nothing like *Porgy and Bess* had been heard or seen before on Broadway, and its first run in 1935 (124 performances) suggests that the world wasn't quite ready for it. The show challenged the audience to accept a new form of musical experience, and also challenged America itself, large parts of which still operated policies of racial segregation. When the touring show came to the National Theatre in Washington, D.C. in 1936, the anti-discrimination protestations mounted by members of the cast led to the first ever integrated audience gathering at the venue.

The musical attracted much racial controversy in the United States, not least for the plot, which depicts the African-American characters as poor, feckless, promiscuous gamblers and drug-takers, and fell from favour during the civil-rights era of the 1960s and 70s. These days however, the show is largely accepted as having good intentions and is well received.

"My way of dealing with it was to see that it was really a piece of Americana, of American history"

GRACE BUMBRY, "BESS" IN THE NEW YORK METROPOLITAN OPERA PRODUCTION, 1985

KEY FACTS

🎭 **STAGE**
🎬 **Director** Rouben Mamoulian
🎵 **Music and lyrics** George Gershwin, DuBose Heyward, Dorothy Heyward, Ira Gershwin
🎭 **Venue** Colonial Theatre, Boston
📅 **Date** 30 September 1935

◉ **Key information**
The soundtrack of a 1959 film adaptation won a Grammy. In 2011, the American Repertory Theatre adaptation won two Tony Awards and ran for 322 performances.

ROUBEN MAMOULIAN (1887–1987)

BIOGRAPHY

An Armenian-born theatre and film director, Mamoulian directed two productions of the play *Porgy* (1927 and 1929) and the acclaimed movie *Dr Jekyll and Mr Hyde* (1931) before overseeing *Porgy and Bess* in 1935. He directed the hit shows *Oklahoma!* (see pp.58–61), *Carousel* (see pp.68–69), and *Lost In The Stars* (1949). His final musical was the Fred Astaire movie *Silk Stockings* (1957). He began work on the ill-fated movie of *Porgy and Bess* (1959) but was fired, a fate that also befell him on the films *Laura* (1944) and *Cleopatra* (1963).

JUMBO

{ 1935 }

One of impresario Billy Rose's extraordinarily ambitious extravaganzas, *Jumbo* combined circus spectacle, star turns, and a sparkling Rodgers and Hart score.

Songwriters Richard Rodgers and Lorenz Hart had enjoyed several successful years in Hollywood when, in 1935, they were approached by the well-known impresario Billy Rose.

PART-CIRCUS, PART-MUSICAL

Rose combined the qualities of the flamboyant show producer Florenz Ziegfeld and circus owner P.T. Barnum, especially leading into his latest project, *Jumbo*. All New York was talking about the show, largely because of Rose's relentless promotional campaign and regular newspaper bulletins earlier that year.

For this spectacular part-musical comedy, part-circus, Rose had refurbished the city's Hippodrome Theatre into a one-ring circus (reducing the 5,200 seats to 4,300) at the cost of US$40,000, and negotiated strenuously with Equity to have the show officially categorized as a circus, allowing for ten weeks extra rehearsal time.

The show starred comic actor Jimmy "Schnozzle" Durante and an orchestra led by the self-styled "King of

◄ Larger than life
Jimmy Durante and Doris Day get close to Jumbo in the film adaptation, renamed *Billy Rose's Jumbo* as Rose insisted that he be credited in the title for any film made of the show.

Jazz", Paul Whiteman, along with numerous acrobats, animals, and showgirls plus, of course, Rosie the elephant. Ben Hecht (himself a former circus trapeze artist) and Charles MacArthur, who had cowritten the hit play *The Front Page* (1928), were hired for the book, and Rodgers and Hart agreed to write the songs for the show. Among the reliably memorable of

◄ Jumbo for joy
The colourful circus-inspired poster that advertised the 1962 movie version of the production, made by MGM.

these were "The Most Beautiful Girl in the World", an elegant waltz that featured wickedly ingenious rhymes; the amorous "My Romance"; and the heart-rending "Little Girl Blue".

Jumbo finally arrived at the day of its feverish opening on 16 November 1935, with dozens of celebrity guests in attendance– the Gershwins, Katherine Hepburn, and the mayor – and with accompanying traffic chaos. Playing a gruelling 12 shows a week, it ran until April 1936 and became, along with *On Your Toes*, the longest-running show of the 1935–36 season.

KEY FACTS

☙ STAGE

🎭 **Director** John Murray Anderson and George Abbott

📖 **Book** Ben Hecht and Charles MacArthur

🎵 **Music** Richard Rodgers

A♪ **Lyrics** Lorenz Hart

🎪 **Venue** Hippodrome Theatre, New York

📅 **Date** 16 November 1935

◉ **Key information**
The Broadway run was 233 performances. A movie version of *Jumbo* starred Doris Day – then the biggest US box office draw – and the original star of the Broadway production, Jimmy Durante.

SWING TIME

{ 1936 }

Swing Time is considered one of the most successful confluences of music and dance on the big screen. The duets of "Fred and Ginger" are the best of their career together, but it is their dance routines that really steal the show.

A partnership in perfect harmony
Swing Time was a triumph for Fred Astaire and Ginger Rogers in 1936. It quickly became one of musical cinema's all-time favourite films.

CAST

Fred Astaire Lucky Garnett
Ginger Rogers Penny Carroll
Victor Moore Pop Cardetti
Helen Broderick Mabel Anderson
Eric Blore Mr Gordon
Betty Furness Margaret Watson
Landers Stevens Judge Watson
George Metaxa Ricky Romero

The original title had been planned as either *I Won't Dance* or *Never Gonna Dance*, which ended up as one of the songs. The show's producers had a change of heart when they realized no one would want to see a movie if Fred Astaire might not dance in it. Up to that point, all his movies had been musicals with Ginger Rogers, and Fred and Ginger were now RKO Pictures' biggest stars. The team eventually made ten movies together, *Swing Time* being Rogers' favourite film with Fred Astaire.

The movie was directed by George Stevens, a skilled cinematographer who had never directed a musical before, but who had recently won praise for directing *Alice Adams*, starring Katharine Hepburn. *Swing Time*'s gorgeous art deco sets and innovative lighting and camera work brought glamour and polish to the story of a gambler always trying to get himself out of a jam.

LUCKY AND PENNY
Based on a story by Erwin Gelsey, titled "Portrait of John Garnett", screenwriters Howard Lindsay and Allan Scott created trouble-prone "Lucky" Garnet: dancer, betting man, and good-time Charlie. The movie begins as Lucky prepares for his

wedding to a socialite, played by Betty Furness, a circumstance upsetting to the bride's father, played by Lander Stevens (real-life father of the director). To keep him from breaking up the dance troupe, Lucky's pals convince him he needs cuffs on his tuxedo trousers, which makes him arrive too late on his big day. The bride's father insists that he proves himself by earning $25,000 if he still wants to marry his daughter.

The path to true love takes a turn and begins again when Lucky meets dance teacher Penny, played by Rogers, when he asks for change for a quarter. Lucky returns the favour by getting Penny

Debonair dancer
A typically suave and urbane Fred Astaire brings the fellas round to his way of thinking in a scene from George Stevens' *Swing Time*.

KEY FACTS

FILM

Director George Stevens

Screenplay Howard Lindsay, Allan Scott

♫ **Music** Jerome Kern

Lyrics Dorothy Fields

⏱ **Running time** 103 minutes

Release date 27 August 1936

◎ **Key information**
The number "Bojangles of Harlem" was praised as one of Astaire's most rhythmically imaginative solos. This was the first time Astaire used trick photography to enhance a dance piece. The film won an Academy Award for Best Original Song, "The Way You Look Tonight".

fired from her job, but she can be reinstated if they win a dance contest. Penny also has a previous attachment, with a band leader – that wedding has to be stopped, too, and again, with cuffed trousers. Aiding and abetting the triumphs and travails of Lucky and Penny are their sidekicks, Mabel and "Pop", who supply some of *Swing Time*'s best comic scenes. The wise-cracking Mabel Anderson was played by stage and screen actress Helen Broderick, who also appeared in *Top Hat* with Astaire and Rogers (see p.31).

"WHY DON'T WE SWING IT?"

The musical's composer, Jerome Kern, and lyricist, Dorothy Fields, contributed timeless hits to the pop canon, including the Oscar-winning "The Way You Look Tonight" and "Bojangles of Harlem". When tapper Astaire heard the latter, he commented to arranger and collaborator Hal Borne: "I like the melody and the lyric is just fine, but why don't we swing it?". With choreographer Hermes Pan (see p.31), he created a tap number with three giant shadows of himself dancing along in the background.

▶ **Landmark movie**
Renowned dance critic Arlene Croce said of *Swing Time*: "There never was a more star-struck movie or greater dance musical." It certainly represented a peak for Astaire and Rogers.

GINGER ROGERS (1911–95)

When she first danced on screen with Fred Astaire in *Flying Down to Rio*, his film debut, in 1933, Ginger Rogers already had 25 movie credits to her name. Born in Independence, Missouri, Rogers started her career on Broadway in the 1920s. However, it was her longstanding partnership with Astaire that sealed her fame.

"Of all of the places the movies have created, one of the most magical and enduring is the universe of Fred Astaire and Ginger Rogers."

ROGER EBERT, AMERICAN FILM CRITIC, *CHICAGO SUN-TIMES*

HOLLYWOOD MUSICALS

Screen musicals often celebrate the joy of life on a large scale. A hit movie also offers fans the chance to purchase or rent films, or enjoy movie musicals on television.

Silent films usually showed with musical accompaniment, but with Al Jolson's prophetic words, "Wait a minute, wait a minute! You ain't heard nothin' yet!" in Warner Brothers' 1927 *The Jazz Singer*, movies and music were inextricably joined. In the 1930s, each of the big film studios had their particular style of movie musical. Warner Brothers had the spectacular geometric style of choreographer Busby Berkeley. RKO Pictures had stars Fred Astaire (see pp.42–43) and Ginger Rogers, and choreographer Hermes Pan. Though not out-and-out musicals, Paramount made films with songs performed by crooner Bing Crosby. Goldwyn Studios featured Broadway star Eddie Cantor. Fox had an eclectic stable of musical stars in Shirley Temple, Bill "Bojangles" Robinson, Alice Faye, and Norwegian star skater Sonja Henie.

START OF THE GOLDEN ERA
It was MGM (Metro-Goldwyn-Mayer) studios that consistently made a profit with their *Broadway Melody* series, which

◀ **Iconic logo**
Leo the Lion, the mascot for MGM, features in the production logo. Here, a lion's roar is being recorded for use at the beginning of MGM talking movies.

were all set backstage at fictional Broadway revues, and through their great musicals of the 1930s such as *The Wizard of Oz* (see pp.46–49). In 1939, MGM gave producer Arthur Freed his own production unit to create musicals, which helped to spark the golden age of the movie musical, roughly from 1940–69. The famous Freed unit is responsible for some of the greatest movie musicals, including: *Babes in Arms, Annie Get Your Gun, An American in Paris, Singin' in the Rain*, and *The Band Wagon*.

With the success of the Freed Unit, other movie studios and other film producers jumped on the bandwagon. Film adaptations of successful Broadway musicals were always popular, but by the 1960s they had reached an all-time high with films such as *West Side Story, The Music Man, My Fair Lady*, and *The Sound of Music*. Others were less successful, including *Camelot, Finian's Rainbow, Hello Dolly!, Sweet Charity*, and *Paint Your Wagon*.

By the 1970s, with films such as *Man of La Mancha* and *Mame*, live action (non-animated) movie musicals had gone out of fashion, but they made a marked return in the 2000s with successful films such as *Moulin Rouge!, Chicago, The Phantom of the Opera*, and *Mamma Mia!*.

"Don't try to be different. Just be good. To be good is different enough."

ARTHUR FREED, AMERICAN LYRICIST AND HOLLYWOOD FILM PRODUCER

FOLLOW THE FLEET

{ 1936 }

Setting the standard for the wave of navy musicals to come, *Follow the Fleet* showcases Fred Astaire and Ginger Rogers performing on ship decks and in dance halls.

Their fourth movie, *Follow the Fleet*, was the dancing pair's second highest grossing film. Based on the 1927 Broadway musical *Hit the Deck*, *Follow the Fleet* shared the same basic premise with its precursors: how does a sailor find love in 24 hours? This version, however, was a double romance. The starring couple of Fred Astaire (see pp.42–43) as a sailor and Ginger Rogers as a dance hall singer were joined by Randolph Scott as his buddy and Harriet Hilliard as Rogers' sister.

BAKE AND BILGE
In a twist for the leading pair, Astaire and Rogers took the comic roles of "Bake" Baker and Sherry Martin, former dance partners. However, the star-crossed romance of *Follow the Fleet* centres instead around Sherry's sister, Connie, a shy teacher, and her unrequited love for "Bilge" Smith, Bake's womanizing shipmate. When Bake and Bilge hit the town on shore leave, Bake tries to rekindle the flame with Sherry and Connie yearns for Bilge. Hilliard sings the movie's two ballads: "Get Thee Behind Me Satan"

and "Here I Am, Where Are You?". Not the marrying type, Bilge moves on to one of Sherry's friends, Iris Manning, played by Astrid Allwyn. In the meantime, Bake is unsuccessfully

trying to win back Sherry. Soon it's back to the boat for the two sailors, who are surprised to learn they are to set sail immediately – although they do return.

> "*As a dancer he stands alone, and no singer knows his way around a song like Fred Astaire.*"
>
> **IRVING BERLIN**, *PUTTIN' ON THE RITZ*

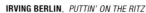

CAST

Fred Astaire "Bake" Baker
Ginger Rogers Sherry Martin
Randolph Scott "Bilge" Smith
Harriet Hilliard Connie Martin
Astrid Allwyn Iris Manning
Betty Grable, Jeanne Grey, Joy Hodges Trio
Harry Beresford Captain Hickey
Russell Hicks Jim Nolan
Brooks Benedict David Sullivan
Ray Mayer Dopey Williams
Lucille Ball Kitty Collins

KEY FACTS

FILM

🎬 **Director** Mark Sandrich
🎞 **Screenplay** Dwight Taylor, Allan Scott
🎵 **Music and lyrics** Irving Berlin
⏱ **Running time** 110 minutes
📅 **Release date** 20 February 1936

◉ **Key information**
In the movie, Ginger Rogers wore a beaded gown so heavy, allowances had to be made for the large swinging sleeves.

FACE THE MUSIC AND DANCE
The musical numbers move from a navy battleship to a dance hall to the schooner Connie is refurbishing for Bilge. The dance competition number, "Let Yourself Go", performed at the Paradise Club, included amateurs recruited by RKO and choreographer Hermes Pan in ballroom contests around Los Angeles. The winning couple, an 18-year-old dishwasher and 20-year-old stenographer, performed in the dance-off sequence with the great pair.

The indisputable masterpiece of *Follow the Fleet* is the haunting duet, "Let's Face the Music and Dance", sung by Astaire. Berlin's beautiful music and the sublime partnering of Astaire and Rogers elevate the play-within-a-play musical number: a potential double suicide attempt turned into a gorgeous duet. The piece was performed for a fundraiser on and for Connie's boat. All glamour and smooth lines, Astaire and Rogers sweep across the ship's deck with uncommon ease.

ME AND MY GIRL

{ 1937 }

The longest-running West End musical of the 1930s, *Me and My Girl* **and its cockney pride delighted a war-struck London with spirited tunes and fun.**

Comedian and music-hall star Lupino Lane commissioned *Me and My Girl* after the success of *Twenty to One*, in which he played a ne'er-do-well gambler, Bill Snibson. The cockney character was so popular that Lane reprised the role, this time in a rags-to-riches musical written by Arthur Rose, who also wrote *Twenty to One*, and Douglas Furber. Songwriter Noel Gay contributed the cheerful score, which introduced the dance phenomenon the "Lambeth Walk".

The show opened to good reviews, but it did not draw big audiences. *Me and My Girl* was on the brink of closing, but serendipity stepped in. BBC Radio needed a show to broadcast in front of

◀ Cockney caper
Audiences loved Lupino Lane's cheeky chappie character Bill Snibson and revelled in the cheerful vulgarity of "The Lambeth Walk".

a live audience at the last minute and chose *Me and My Girl*. Audiences loved the raucous good humour and filled the seats of the Victoria Palace Theatre. The show did not run continuously due to the war, but unlike many productions, it did manage to survive the Blitz.

DOING THE LAMBETH WALK
With its twin *Pygmalion* story lines, *Me and My Girl* follows Snibson and his love from the streets of Lambeth to the halls of Hareford. The illegitimate son of an earl, Snibson becomes the reluctant heir to a title and fortune. He is loathe to leave his gal, Sally, played by Scottish actress Teddie St Denis, and his Lambeth life to mix with the swells of Mayfair. Before he can adopt his lofty perch, his new peers and the Duchess of Hareford must transform him into a "fit and

proper person". Sally doesn't like this turn of events and brings her hometown friends to introduce the Hareford crew to the cocky stroll – the Lambeth Walk. Snibson does find a friend in the family lawyer Sir John Tremayne, played by comedian George Graves, who wants Sally to be accepted at Hareford Hall, too, sparking another class makeover.

It was the cockney anthem "Lambeth Walk" that catapulted *Me and My Girl* to fame. Its jaunty strut ended each refrain with a knee-slapping, thumb to the air, and a shout of Oi! During World War II, the song epitomized the London fighting spirit and caught fire across Europe and beyond. The dance craze arrived in New York nightclubs in 1938, where it vied with Duke Ellington's repertoire for capturing the public's imagination.

A TELEVISION FIRST
Me and My Girl had many revivals over the years after its launch, but one of the most significant was its live telecast on the BBC in May 1939, the first time a musical had been broadcast on television. In 1940, MGM filmed the musical under the title *Lambeth Walk*, capitalizing on the dance sensation, and again starring Lupino

Lane. Years later, in 1984, Noel Gay's son, Richard Armitage, re-created his father's work with actor and writer Stephen Fry, then in his twenties. Their version, starring Robert Lindsay and Emma Thompson, opened in Leicester at the Haymarket Theatre, but moved to London's West End in 1985 for an eight-year run.

Armitage and Fry's revival travelled to the Marquis Theatre in New York in 1986, winning three Tony Awards.

KEY FACTS

STAGE
- **Directors** Gene Gerard, Lupino Lane
- **Book** L. Arthur Rose, Douglas Furber
- **Music** Noel Gay
- **Lyrics** L. Arthur Rose, Douglas Furber
- **Venue** Victoria Palace Theatre, London
- **Date** 16 December 1937

Key information
The musical had a successful original run in the West End in 1937, and was turned into a film in 1939, titled *The Lambeth Walk*, named after one of the show's hit songs.

> "*Here is a show that keeps the audience in the greatest good humour from start to finish.*"
>
> THEATRE WORLD, LONDON, 1937

LUPINO LANE (1892–1959)

Born in Hackney, London, actor and theatre manager Henry William George Lupino started his career as a child performer, later adopting the name Lupino Lane. He was a member of the famous Lupino family: his father Harry Lupino and brother Wallace Lupino, who also appeared in *Me and My Girl*, were music-hall favourites. Celebrated actress and director Ida Lupino was Lane's second cousin. Although primarily a dramatic actress, she appeared in the musicals *Anything Goes* and *Thank Your Lucky Stars*.

SHALL WE DANCE

{ 1937 }

Shall We Dance brings George and Ira Gershwin together with Astaire and Rogers for the first and only time in the history of musicals. It is acclaimed as one of the greatest musical films of this era.

▲ **Flamboyant fun**
A typically bright and classy poster for Astaire and Rogers' latest outing, showing the stars in customary poses and about to set pulses racing.

▶ **Romancing on wheels**
In this unusual story, Astaire's Petrov romances Rogers' character, working hard to persuade her to marry him.

The seventh of ten movies for the Astaire–Rogers team, *Shall We Dance* was their first film with the Gershwins (see pp.24–25), although both performers had worked with them on Broadway. *Shall We Dance* hoped to capitalize on the success of the Rodgers and Hart hit stage musical *On Your Toes* (1936), which also featured a Russian ballet company. Astaire had been asked to star in that production, but declined. *Shall We Dance*, which had working titles of *Stepping Toes* and *On Your Ballet*, also shared a ballet-versus-jazz dance theme. *On Your Toes* choreographer George Balanchine was also asked to create the dance scenes. Even though he was interested, he had already committed to a project with the Metropolitan Opera. Director Mark Sandrich then sought Leonide Massine, another great Russian choreographer, for the ballet sequences, but a relatively unknown New York modern dancer, Harry Losee, was hired instead. As he had done on all of the previous and future Astaire–Rogers movies, Hermes Pan arranged the dance ensembles. Reviews lauded the Gershwin score, but just two months after the premiere, George Gershwin died of a brain tumour at the tragically young age of 38.

KEY FACTS

🎬 **FILM**

🎞 **Director** Mark Sandrich

📧 **Screenplay** Allan Scott, Ernest Pagano

📖 **Book** Lee Loeb, Harold Buchman

🎵 **Music** George Gershwin

🎼 **Lyrics** Ira Gershwin

🕐 **Running time** 109 minutes

📅 **Release date** 7 May 1937

◎ **Key information**

Astaire was no stranger to the Gershwins, having already headlined two of their Broadway shows – *Lady Be Good!* in 1924 and *Funny Face* in 1927. Ginger Rogers first came to Hollywood's attention when she appeared in the "Embraceable You" number, which was choreographed by Astaire, in the Gershwins' *Girl Crazy* of 1930.

PETROV AND LINDA

Shall We Dance begins in Paris with Astaire playing "Russian" ballet dancer Petrov, really Peter P. Peters from Philadelphia, mooning over a photo of Broadway star Linda Keene, played by Ginger Rogers. Petrov tells ballet impresario Jeffrey Baird, played by comedian Edward Everett Horton (see right), that he wants to marry Keene. They book their passage across the Atlantic on the *Queen Anne*, not coincidentally, the same boat Linda is taking. Linda is returning to New York to hang up her dance shoes and marry her fiancé, Jim Montgomery.

While Petrov pursues Linda, ballerina Lady Tarrington sets her sights on Petrov. To throw Lady Tarrington off, Petrov leads her to believe he is married to Linda Keene. To make matters worse, Linda is knitting a sweater for her dog, but the activity is misconstrued and word spreads that she is in fact knitting it for a baby. She is so incensed with Petrov/Pete and her nosy shipmates that she hops on to a mail aeroplane and heads back to New York by this means instead. Linda's manager, Arthur Miller, played by

CAST

Fred Astaire Petrov

Ginger Rogers Linda Keene

Edward Everett Horton Jeffrey Baird

Eric Blore Cecil Flintridge

Jerome Cowan Arthur Miller

Ketti Gallian Lady Denise Tarrington

William Brisbane Jim Montgomery

Harriet Hoctor Herself

▶ Hollywood glamour

Shall We Dance featured the dramatic sets and exotic costumes that were so beloved of movie audiences at that time.

Jerome Cowan, who was known for depicting slick characters, desperately wants her to keep performing. Consequently, Miller conspires to get Linda and Petrov together, with his help. Petrov had vowed to marry Linda when he first set eyes on her and he has not changed his mind.

BALLET MEETS JAZZ

Shall We Dance earned one Academy Award nomination for "They Can't Take That Away from Me". It was the only Oscar nomination George Gershwin ever received. Astaire sings the song to Rogers on a ferry from New Jersey to New York after their characters have secretly married, so that Linda could save face – and now openly divorce. She does not speak a word and they don't dance. When the song was reprised in the 1949 *The Barkleys of Broadway*, the last film Astaire and Rogers did together, they added a sweeping ballroom duet.

Other venues for *Shall We Dance* production numbers include an Art Deco ship engine room for "Slap That Bass", an ocean liner deck for "I've Got Beginner's Luck", a swanky New York nightclub for "They All Laughed", and a rollerskating rink for "Let's Call the Whole Thing Off".

The final dance number brings the ballet-jazz face-off full circle. Ballerinas *en pointe* back up the amazingly limber Harriet Hoctor, who flutters on stage in toe shoes in a flurry of tiny steps. Her signature move is a back arch worthy of a contortionist. Enter Petrov, in Russian costume, who dances a duet with Hoctor accompanied by the ballet corps. In the next sequence, Petrov's transition from ballet dancer to jazz swinger is complete. He enters in a tuxedo, and the dancers, not of the ballet variety this time, all hold masks depicting Linda's face. Linda, witnessing this spectacle, goes backstage to join the jazz dancers and comes out with her own mask. Petrov/Pete has moved from ballet to jazz.

MIXED SUCCESS

The Gershwin melodies did not really catch fire with the public at the time, but numbers such as "They Can't Take That Away from Me" and "Let's Call the Whole Thing Off" are recognized classics that are still popular today.

Regrettably, the Gershwin score of *Shall We Dance* is probably the largest source of the composer's orchestral

works that are now no longer available to the general public. This is due to the fact that some of the instrumental arrangements were only ever recorded for this musical film's soundtrack.

ATTEMPT AT PRESERVATION

On 22 September 2013, it was announced that the Gershwins' full orchestral score will be released at some point in the future. The Gershwin family, working in conjunction with the US Library of Congress and the University of Michigan, launched the Gershwin Initiative to offer "greater insight into the Gershwins' original manuscripts and, in many cases, offer the first performance materials to accurately reflect the creators' vision". The popularity of *Shall We Dance* is such that it is scheduled to be the seventh in the series of scores to be released.

BIOGRAPHY

EDWARD EVERETT HORTON (1886–1970)

Fretful and bumbling, Edward Everett Horton's characters provided comic relief for 50 years of movie-making. He played Fred Astaire's befuddled sidekick in *The Gay Divorcee* and *Top Hat*, in addition to *Shall We Dance*. His long career included work in vaudeville, theatre, radio, and television.

> *"George Gershwin's score contains some of the best things he's done. Its six songs are tuneful and lilting and will be widely played."*
>
> HOLLYWOOD REPORTER, 27 APRIL 1937

FRED ASTAIRE

{ DANCER, ACTOR, SINGER **1899–1987** }

This acclaimed American dancer, actor, and singer delighted audiences on stage, TV, film, radio, and vinyl over seven decades. He's best remembered for his dancing – gliding effortlessly through the 1930s in top hat and tails – with Ginger Rogers.

F red Astaire was born on 10 May 1899 in Omaha, Nebraska, to Johanna Geilus and Austrian-born brewer Frederic Austerlitz. In 1905, the family moved to New York City, changed their name to Astaire, and enrolled young Fred and sister Adele in a theatre school. Adele showed promise as a dancer – by the age of nine she and her seven-year-old brother were seasoned vaudeville performers and he had already donned top hat and tails.

"I suppose I made it look easy, but gee whiz, did I work and worry."

FRED ASTAIRE

THE FRED–ADELE PARTNERSHIP

Long before Astaire became a dancing "item" with the dazzling Ginger Rogers, he and Adele were a highly successful duo. Attractive and vivacious, Adele was regarded as a more natural performer than her perfectionist brother, who spent hours honing his technique. In 1917, the pair made their Broadway debut in the patriotic revue *Over the Top*. During the next 14 years they sang and danced their way through ten stage musicals on both sides of the Atlantic, including *For Goodness Sake* (with music by Astaire's friend George Gershwin), *Stop Flirting*, and the Gershwin brothers' hits *Lady, Be Good!* (1924) and *Funny Face* (1927). Fêted wherever they went, the Astaires became a firm favourite of royalty, which also had unforeseen consequences. In 1932, Adele married Lord Charles Cavendish, the younger son of the Duke of Devonshire, thereby bringing to an end the Astaire siblings' dance partnership.

HOLLYWOOD CAREER

Astaire headed for Hollywood, but his January 1933 screen test by RKO's David O. Selznick was famously damned with faint praise by a studio executive who said, "Can't act. Slightly bald. Also dances". Selznick was won over by Astaire's charm and signed up the dancer. Later that year, Astaire made his first film appearance with new partner Ginger Rogers, dancing "the Carioca" in *Flying Down to Rio*. Their performance stole the show and the pair appeared in eight further movie musicals, including *Top Hat* in 1935 (RKO's most profitable film of the decade, in which Astaire sang Irving Berlin's unforgettable "Cheek to Cheek"), *Swing Time* (1936), and *Shall We Dance* (1937).

◀ **Filial success**
Fred Astaire, pictured with his sister and erstwhile dancing partner Adele in 1932 – the year that she married. This was one of the last times they performed together.

▲ **True virtuoso**
Fred Astaire's dancing was renowned for its grace and invention, but he worked hard to achieve perfection.

In 1939, the pair went their separate ways, reuniting ten years later for the valedictory film *The Barkleys of Broadway*. Although Rogers was exhausted by Astaire's relentless perfectionism, his debonair professionalism and energy perfectly complemented her glamour and exceptional acting talent. Katharine Hepburn memorably said, "Fred gave Ginger class, and Ginger gave Fred sex".

VERSATILE PERFORMER

Fred Astaire continued to make hit musicals with Hollywood's hottest actresses – Judy Garland (*Easter Parade*, see p.87), Audrey Hepburn (*Funny Face*), and Cyd Charisse (*Silk Stockings*, see p.115, and *The Band Wagon*, see p.104). He also carried on recording musical soundtracks by the major composers of the day as well as writing his own compositions. These included "I'm Building Up to an Awful Letdown", with lyricist Johnny Mercer, in 1936, and "It's Just Like Taking Candy from a Baby" with jazz musician Benny Goodman in 1940. Astaire also wrote "If Swing Goes, I Go Too" for the fourth version of the MGM movie *Ziegfield Follies* (1946), but it was later deleted from the movie at his request.

SMALL SCREEN SUCCESS

Astaire began to focus on television work during the 1960s and 70s, guest starring in various popular shows, and presenting musical documentaries. In 1959, he played a cheeky con-man in Victor Canning's TV drama *Man on a Bicycle*, appeared in several episodes of the popular medical series *Dr. Kildare* in 1965, and played the hero's father in the adventure series *It Takes a Thief* four years later. An episode of the 1978 space drama series *Battlestar Galactica* was written specifically in honour of Astaire. Called "The Man with Nine Lives" he plays another conartist – called Chameleon. Astaire also starred in several TV movies, including the 1970 comedy *The Over the Hill Gang Rides Again* and the thought-provoking drama *A Family Upside Down* in 1978.

But it was as a host and presenter that Astaire really shone. *An Evening with Fred Astaire* in 1958 was a highly successful live one-hour TV special. It was also the first television show to be recorded in colour and use innovative production techniques such as dissolves between scenes. It was widely regarded as a comeback for the 59-year-old Astaire, who danced with new partner Barrie Chase (whom he later described as one of his favourite dance partners) in this and three sequels over the next ten years. In 1972, he revisited all the Gershwin greats of his heyday in a nine-minute medley of songs for *'S Wonderful, 'S Marvelous, 'S Gershwin*, an acclaimed musical biography of George Gershwin. Finally, he is also remembered for hosting highly successful musical documentaries such as *That's Entertainment*. MGM's

▲ Enduring success on the big screen
This quirky shot captures a scene from MGM's cult musical hit *The Band Wagon*, in which Fred Astaire starred with Cyd Charisse in 1953.

50th-anniversary compilation was introduced by Astaire and other stars, including Gene Kelly, Mickey Rooney, and Elizabeth Taylor in 1974, with a further instalment presented by Astaire and Kelly two years later.

PERSONAL LIFE

Astaire was devoted to his wife, Phyllis, and their children, Fred Junior and Ava. He also loved breeding and racing horses and briefly "retired" from show business to concentrate on this pastime. However, when Gene Kelly broke his ankle in 1947 and could not partner Judy Garland in *Easter Parade*, Astaire was happy to take his place. This was the first of many comebacks in his long and varied career.

Tragedy struck the Astaire family in 1954 when Phyllis died from cancer. A heartbroken Astaire remained single until 1980 when he married Robyn Smith, a famous jockey 46 years his junior. Continuing to work until his early eighties, he died on 22 June 1987.

◄ Happy hoofer
Fred clowning around on the set of *Roberta*, 1935, with assistant dance director Hermes Pan, who collaborated with Astaire for many years.

TIMELINE

10 May 1899 Astaire is born in Omaha, Nebraska.

November 1905 Astaire and sister Adele join the vaudeville circuit in New York.

28 November 1917 The pair debut on Broadway in *Over the Top*.

1 December 1924 The duo star in the Gershwin musical *Lady, Be Good!*

22 November 1927 The pair star in *Funny Face* on Broadway.

9 May 1932 Adele marries Lord Charles Cavendish.

27 May 1933 Astaire signs with RKO, and dances with Ginger Rogers for the first time in *Flying Down to Rio*.

12 July 1933 Astaire marries Phyllis Baker Potter.

1935 Release of *Top Hat* (see p.31), created to showcase Fred and Ginger's dazzling partnership.

21 January 1936 Birth of Fred Astaire Jr.

27 August 1936 Release of *Swing Time*.

28 March 1942 Birth of daughter Ava Astaire-McKenzie.

8 July 1948 Release of *Easter Parade*.

1949 Astaire wins special Academy Award.

13 September 1954 Phyllis dies of cancer.

13 February 1957 Release of *Funny Face*.

November 1965 Astaire appears in the popular US television series *Dr. Kildare*.

10 December 1974 Release of the blockbuster movie *The Towering Inferno*.

24 June 1980 Astaire marries Robyn Smith.

10 April 1981 Astaire receives a Lifetime Achievement Award from the American Film Institute.

22 June 1987 Astaire dies of pneumonia in Los Angeles, aged 88.

FRED ASTAIRE'S STAR ON HOLLYWOOD'S WALK OF FAME

HELLZAPOPPIN'

{ 1938 }

Broadway critics panned its "antique gags and slapdash buffoonery", but in 1938 *Hellzapoppin'* quickly claimed the top spot as the first real smash of the season.

The show was the brainchild of musical revue entertainers, John Sigvard "Ole" Olsen and Harold Ogden "Chic" Johnson. Both were from the Midwest and went to Northwestern University in Chicago. They met in a Chicago club after they graduated, when they performed together in a band. After the group dissolved, Olsen and Johnson teamed up in 1914 to put together a comedy act and took it on the road. When they hit Broadway in 1938, their vaudeville spirit was displayed in full force.

Hellzapoppin' opened at the 46th Street Theatre in 1938; and its three-year run also included shows at the Winter Garden and Majestic Theatre. A huge success, it ran for a total of 1,404 performances – a record on Broadway at the time.

RAUCOUS HUMOUR

Reviewers panned the show, but audiences relished the lowbrow entertainment. Acts included racy sketches, prop humour, a trick bicycle rider, magic, break-away trousers, acrobatic dance numbers, hulas, and a surprisingly stirring song "Abe Lincoln", with music and lyrics by Earl Robinson and Alfred Hayes. All the while, performers would run through the aisles of the theatre, toss rubber snakes and bananas to patrons, and make comic asides.

To keep the show topical, Olsen and Johnson changed numbers nightly. Running gags such as a man carrying a "growing" tree and an unsuccessful escape artist were mainstays in the line-up. The programme began with a newsreel of Hitler minus the sound, so that actors could supply their own comic monologues.

The classic number "Boomps-a-Daisy" features two performers clapping hands, slapping knees, and bumping behinds – a dance that soon became very popular with the general public. Johnson and Olsen themselves played a variety of characters, including Ninatochka, Chief Odessa, Filthy McNaety, Vladimir Mamlock, and Paul Revere. Film and Broadway composer Sammy Fain (see below) and lyricist Charles Tobias wrote the score, but other musicians, including jazz great Louis Armstrong and Oscar Hammerstein II (see p.99), also provided material. *Hellzapoppin'* did have one virtuoso act – Whitey's Steppers. Also known as Whitey's Lindy Hoppers, they performed a show-stopping dance routine to the jazz song "Jumping at the Woodside". Herbert "Whitey" White's Harlem dancers showcased "queen of swing"

◀ **Riotous fun**
The colourful poster for the film version captured much of the cheerful mayhem that Olsen and Johnson were keen to create. This was a true smash hit.

Norma Miller, who was an award-winning Lindy Hop star of the time.

LIVELY REVIVALS

In 1941, a film version of *Hellzapoppin'*, made by Universal Pictures, retained the Lindy Hop dance number and Olsen and Johnson, but none of the other acts. Comedian Martha Raye and Shemp Howard, one of the *Three Stooges*, starred in the movie.

In other adaptations, a stage play was broadcast in 1972 on the *ABC Comedy Hour* under the same title, starring Jack Cassidy, and Lynn Redgrave. In 1976, a stage revival of *Hellzapoppin'* was planned starring Jerry Lewis and Lynn Redgrave, but never made it out.

BIOGRAPHY

SAMMY FAIN (1902–89)

Fain began his career on the vaudeville circuit in the late 1920s. He went on to collaborate with Paul Francis Webster and together they won two Academy Awards for Best Song: "Love Is a Many Splendored Thing" and "Secret Love". Some of Fain's biggest hits include "Let a Smile Be Your Umbrella", "I Can Dream, Can't I", and "I'll Be Seeing You".

▶ **Laughs all the way**
Mischa Auer clowning as Pepi, in the 1941 film adaptation of *Hellzapoppin'*, which was a notable box-office success.

THE CRADLE WILL ROCK

{ 1938 }

One of the most controversial musicals in Broadway history, *The Cradle Will Rock*'s operetta of class warfare was praised for its biting humour and highly eclectic score.

Composer and writer Marc Blitzstein drew inspiration for *The Cradle Will Rock* from a meeting with German playwright Bertolt Brecht during a visit to New York to oversee his play *Mother*, about the struggles of a working class Russian woman. During their discussion, Brecht encouraged him to write a dramatic treatment showing the corrosive effect of all kinds of prostitution and corruption on society.

The Cradle Will Rock was scheduled to preview on 16 June 1937 and was promoted as "a combination of opera, ballet, dance music, vaudeville, modern jazz, and silly symphony technique". What happened next is the stuff of theatre legend.

GOVERNMENT SHUTDOWN

On the day of the opening at the Maxine Elliott Theatre on 39th Street, leased by the Federal Theatre Project,

> ## *"The best thing militant labour has put into theatre yet."*
>
> THE NEW YORK TIMES, 1938

outside a padlocked theatre. Producer John Houseman and director Orson Welles found another venue, and together the cast and attendees made their way to the new location. In another roadblock, the president of the Actors' Equity union would not allow its members to appear on stage for fear of WPA reprisals. Houseman's solution was to buy tickets for the actors, who then delivered their lines from seats in the audience. Blitzstein sat at a piano on stage, Welles described the scenes, and the chorus sat in the front row with conductor Lehman Engel.

A new backer was found, freeing the production of restraints, although it was still performed without scenery, costumes, or orchestra. The show ran in this mode for 19 performances until 1 July 1937. Finally, after all these tribulations, *The Cradle Will Rock* made its Broadway debut at the Windsor Theatre on 3 January 1938.

BOSS VS WORKERS

The plot of *The Cradle Will Rock* casts all-powerful corporations against union workers in a place called Steeltown, U.S.A. The story focuses on Mr Mister, who controls the town, and his efforts to stop Larry Foreman and Joe Worker from unionizing, depicted in ten cartoon-like vignettes. Characters such as Moll, the prostitute and heroine, and Harry Druggist, an alcoholic who won't stand up to Mr Mister, are portrayed in deliberate stereotypes. A wide range of

the government shut down the show stating WPA financial problems, but many thought the controversial script was the real reason. Theatregoers were left standing

◄ **Contentious fare**
The original cast of the play, with Marc Blitzstein at the piano.

KEY FACTS

🐾 **STAGE**

🎭 **Director** Orson Welles

📖 **Book** Marc Blitzstein

🎵 **Music and lyrics** Marc Blitzstein

🎚 **Venue** Windsor Theatre, New York

📅 **Date** 3 January 1938

⊙ **Key information**
The piece is almost entirely sung through, giving it many operatic qualities, although Blitzstein included popular song styles of the time.

BIOGRAPHY

MARC BLITZSTEIN
(1905–64)

Marc Blitzstein, a piano prodigy, composed music for film, opera, ballet, theatre, and symphony orchestras. A student of Nadia Boulanger and Arnold Schoenberg, Blitzstein's melodies drew inspiration from classical to jazz to show tunes. His deep social conscience shaped the content of his politically themed works.

musical genres – torch song, foxtrot, waltz, church choral music, minstrel show tunes – are paired in unexpected ways with the characters, contributing some of the humour to *The Cradle Will Rock*. Blitzstein described the musical's style as falling somewhere between realism, romance, vaudeville, comic strip, Gilbert and Sullivan, Brecht, and agitprop. Critics lauded Blitzstein's ingenuity in combining a "modernistic musical score with the most sardonic methods of the political cartoonist".

THE WIZARD OF OZ

{ 1939 }

Based on L. Frank Baum's classic children's novel, the movie version of *The Wizard of Oz* is as fresh and vital today as it was the day that MGM released it. It remains one of the most viewed and best-loved movie musicals ever.

It was not surprising that Hollywood saw blockbuster potential in L. Frank Baum's tale of a teenage girl from Kansas and her journey to the land of Oz. When film producer Samuel Goldwyn put the movie rights up for sale in 1938, Metro-Goldwyn-Mayer (MGM) fought, and won, a bitter bidding war.

STRUGGLES WITH THE SCREENPLAY

Mervyn LeRoy, head of production at MGM, was put in charge of the new project, assisted by Arthur Freed (see p.101). No fewer than ten screenwriters worked on the screenplay. The first was fired within a few weeks. American poet Ogden Nash lasted a little longer, but turned in no usable material. Noel Langley, a South African-born dramatist, created much of the framework for the film, but he, too, was sacked in October 1938.

Florence Ryerson and Edgar Allan Woolf, both established MGM writers, had already been brought in to the production over Langley's head. He described what they were proposing as "illiterate mush", but they were neverthess credited for their work. Four directors worked on the film, but Victor Fleming was the only one to make the final credits. LeRoy fired the first after just two weeks because he "didn't quite understand the story". George Cukor lasted less than three days. Fleming shot most of it before he was suddenly loaned to 20th Century Fox, and finally King Vidor was drafted in to finish the film.

◀ **Wicked Witch of the West**
Played by Margaret Hamilton, the witch came to personify evil for a whole generation of children.

KEY FACTS

🎬 **FILM**
🎬 **Director** Victor Fleming
📄 **Screenplay** Noel Langley, Florence Ryerson, Edgar Allan Woolf
📖 **Book** L. Frank Baum
🎵 **Music** Harold Arlen (songs), Herbert Stothart (film score)
A♭ **Lyrics** E.Y. Harburg
🕐 **Running time** 102 minutes
📅 **Release date** 15 August 1939

⊙ **Key information**
In 1939, "Over the Rainbow" won the Oscar for Best Song, and the film's score won Best Original Music. It was also nominated for Best Picture.

> *"I think you turned out a fine picture and you have my congratulations."*
>
> **WALT DISNEY**, WRITING TO LOUIS B. MAYER, 1939

SCORE AND CAST

Composer Harold Arlen and lyricist E.Y. Harburg, an established songwriting team, provided the songs. The duo first tackled "Ding Dong! The Witch is Dead", "We're Off to See the Wizard", and "The Merry Old Land of Oz". Dorothy's ballad, "Over the Rainbow", was nearly axed, but with the approval of renowned American lyricist Ira Gershwin (see pp.24–25), the song was retained.

Herbert Stothart, MGM's house composer, tackled the incidental music. By the time everything was finished, 76 minutes of music had been linked to the songs to create a fully integrated score for the film.

Judy Garland (see left), whom MGM had signed as a child actress in 1935, was the studio's first choice to play Dorothy. Ray Bolger was cast as the Tin Man. Jack Haley took over the part of the Scarecrow from Buddy Ebsen two weeks into shooting. Bert Lahr was the Cowardly Lion. Frank Morgan played the Wizard after the comedian W.C. Fields turned down the role.

ACHIEVING CULT STATUS

Initially, the movie had something of a mixed reception but ultimately went on to conquer the hearts of a global audience. Its rereleases in 1949 and 1955 demonstrated its enduring popularity. And in 1956, CBS showed the film on television, the first step in the rise of *The Wizard of Oz* to the cult status it still enjoys today.

Following the yellow brick road ▶
Dorothy (Judy Garland) skips down the yellow brick road with her three companions, the Scarecrow, the Tin Man, and the Cowardly Lion.

BIOGRAPHY

JUDY GARLAND (1922–69)

Child star Garland became one of MGM's hottest talents, starring in a string of successful films throughout the 1940s. Her filming schedule was punishing, and took a toll on her health. MGM fired her in 1951 and, although Warner Brothers took her on two years later, her movie career languished. She married five times and had two daughters: Liza, with Vincente Minnelli (see p.67), and Lorna, with Sidney Luft, with whom she also had a son, Joseph. She died in London aged only 47.

STORYLINE

Dorothy runs away from home to save Toto, her dog, from being put down at the behest of an ill-tempered neighbour. After an encounter with Professor Marvel, a travelling showman, she returns to her farmstead, only to be swept into the skies – along with the farmhouse – by a tornado, falling back to earth in Oz. After surviving some (often terrifying) adventures, Dorothy wakes up safe in her bed in Kansas.

CAST	
Judy Garland Dorothy	**Billie Burke** Glinda
Frank Morgan Professor Marvel, Wizard of Oz, Gatekeeper, Carriage Driver, Guard	**Margaret Hamilton** Miss Gulch, Wicked Witch of the West
Ray Bolger Hunk, Scarecrow	**Charley Grapewin** Uncle Henry
Bert Lahr Zeke, Cowardly Lion	**Clara Blandick** Auntie Em
Jack Haley Hickory, Tin Man	**Terry the dog** Toto

PLOT OVERVIEW

KANSAS

Orphaned Dorothy Gale lives with Aunt Em, Uncle Henry, and farm hands, Hunk, Zeke, and Hickory. Dorothy's dog, Toto, has bitten Miss Gulch. Dorothy longs for a better home **1**. Miss Gulch arrives with an order to destroy Toto. Dorothy and Toto flee, but then encounters a travelling showman who tricks Dorothy into believing her Aunt Em is ill.

Dorothy hurries home, but is knocked unconscious as the result of a tornado. When she awakens, she finds the house flying in the clouds with odd characters passing her window, including Miss Gulch, who is riding a bike that turns into a broom as she transforms into a witch.

MUNCHKINLAND

The house crash-lands in Munchkinland in the land of Oz. Dorothy and Toto meet Glinda, the Good Witch of the North, who tells Dorothy she has killed the ruby-slippered Wicked Witch of the East by dropping the house on her. Glinda encourages the Munchkins out of hiding **2**.

Dorothy explains the witch's death was accidental **3**.

The Munchkins celebrate the witch's death **4 5 6 7 8 9**.

The Wicked Witch of the West claims the slippers, but Glinda magically puts them on Dorothy. The witch vows revenge. Glinda tells Dorothy only the Wizard of Oz can help her get home and sets her on the yellow brick road to the Emerald City **10 11**.

THE MAGIC RUBY SLIPPERS WORN BY JUDY GARLAND

THE SONGS

1 Over the Rainbow
😊 *Dorothy*

3 It Really Was No Miracle
😊 *Dorothy*

Come Out, Come Out
😊 *Glinda*

5 Ding Dong! The Witch is Dead!
😊 *Munchkins*

We Thank You Very Sweetly
😊 *Munchkins*

6 As Mayor of Munchkin City
😊 *Munchkin*

7 As Coroner I Must Aver
😊 *Munchkin*

9 We Welcome You to Munchkinland
😊 *Munchkins*

Ding Dong! The Witch is Dead (reprise)
😊 *Munchkins*

11 You're Off See the W
😊 *Munchkin*

Follow the Yellow Brick Road
😊 *Munchkins*

⭐ *After the first preview, studio chief Louis B. Mayer ordered "Over the Rainbow" to be cut, but Mervyn LeRoy's indignant protests saved it. He recalled he "almost had to get down on my knees" to Mayer to keep what was to become the film's smash hit.*

THE MUNCHKINS THANK DOROTHY

"*Toto, I've a feeling we're not in Kansas any more.*"

DOROTHY, *THE WIZARD OF OZ* (LANGLEY, RYERSON, AND WOOLF), 1939

DOROTHY AND TOTO

YELLOW BRICK ROAD	EMERALD CITY	HAUNTED FOREST AND WITCH'S CASTLE	EMERALD CITY	KANSAS

Dorothy befriends a Scarecrow **12** **13**, a Tin Man **14** **15**, and a Cowardly Lion **16** **17** who accompany her to see the Wizard. First, an orchard of angry apple trees confronts the group and then they face the Deadly Poppy Fields.

THE TIN MAN

Emerald City is celebrating as Dorothy and her friends arrive **18**. The witch interrupts by skywriting the demand: "Surrender Dorothy". The group gain an audience with the Wizard who will grant their wishes only if they bring him the witch's broomstick.

The group walk through the haunted forest **19**. Dorothy and Toto are carried off by flying monkeys. They take Dorothy to the witch, but while Dorothy lives, the witch cannot obtain the slippers, so she plots to kill her. Toto escapes.

Toto leads the others to the castle **20**. They free Dorothy but the witch and her soldiers catch them. The witch ignites the Scarecrow. Dorothy throws water over him, splashing the terrified witch, who melts. The delighted soldiers, now liberated, give Dorothy her broomstick.

Back in the Emerald City, the Wizard gives the Scarecrow a diploma, the Tin Man a clock as a heart, and the Lion a bravery medal. He explains to Dorothy that he, too, comes from Kansas and arrived in Oz in an escaped balloon. He promises to take her home with him.

Dorothy gets left behind but Glinda encourages her to use the slippers' magic. She awakens in her bedroom and tells everyone her adventures, but they laugh. Dorothy, convinced the journey was real, hugs Toto and assures them all she is now sure that "There's no place like home" **21**.

12 **13** **14** **15** **16** **17** | **18** | **19** **20** | | **21**

We're Off to See the 😊 **Wizard**

We're Off to See the Wizard 😊 (reprise)

We're Off to See the Wizard 😊 (reprise)

The Merry Old Land of Oz
Dorothy, Scarecrow, Tin Man, Cowardly Lion, Citizens of the 😊 *Emerald City*

March of the Winkie Guards 😊 *Winkies*

Over the Rainbow 😊 (orchestral reprise)

If I Only Had a Brain
Scarecrow, 😊 *Dorothy*

If I Only Had a Heart
Tin Man, 😊 *Dorothy*

If I Only Had the Nerve
Cowardly Lion, 😊 *Dorothy*

If I Were King of the Forest
Cowardly Lion, Dorothy, 😊 *Scarecrow, Tin Man*

THE COWARDLY LION'S MEDAL FOR COURAGE

⭐ *"If I Only Had a Brain" was originally shot with an elaborate Busby Berkeley-choreographed dance sequence, but this was dropped from the final version of the film.*

DOROTHY AND HER FRIENDS AT THE GATES OF THE EMERALD CITY

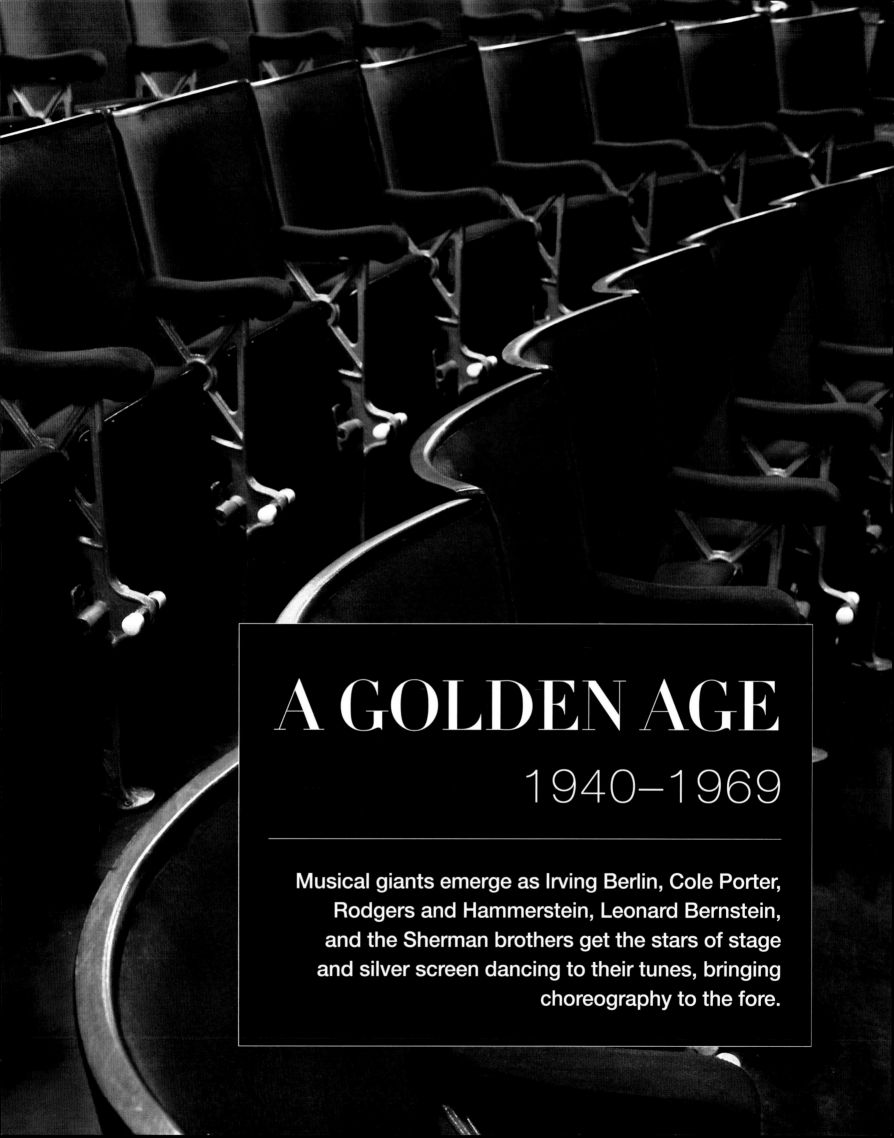

A GOLDEN AGE

1940–1969

Musical giants emerge as Irving Berlin, Cole Porter, Rodgers and Hammerstein, Leonard Bernstein, and the Sherman brothers get the stars of stage and silver screen dancing to their tunes, bringing choreography to the fore.

A GOLDEN AGE

▲ Made for the movies
The success of movie musicals led to Hollywood studios like MGM contracting some of the biggest Broadway stars to create new musicals for film.

The 1940s, 50s, and 60s were a very rich period for musicals both on stage and on the big screen; many classic shows originated in these three decades.

As revolutionary as Kern and Hammerstein's *Show Boat* had been in the 1920s, so Richard Rodgers and Oscar Hammerstein's *Oklahoma!* was in the 1940s. *Oklahoma!* (see pp.58–61) was a thoughtful amalgamation of song, story, and dance; the rich,

Hits by Rodgers and Hammerstein dominated the decades, including *Carousel* (see pp.68–69), *South Pacific* (see p.96), *The King and I* (see pp.98–99), and *The Sound of Music* (see pp.134–37). All of these shows became lavish and successful movies and spawned best-selling cast recordings.

Little wonder that for many, musical theatre was synonymous with Rodgers and Hammerstein.

MUSICAL AMBITION
The Rodgers/Hammerstein scores de-emphasized the jazz influence on Broadway music in favour of a luxuriously melodic style with noble lyrics. It was an approach that was broadly adopted by another hit team of the period, Alan Jay Lerner (1918–86) and Frederick Loewe (1901–88). Together they produced some of the most sumptuous and admired musicals of their time, including *Brigadoon* (see p.86), *My Fair Lady* (see pp.120–21) and *Camelot* (see p.144).

The grand old man of American song – Irving Berlin (see pp.76–77) – continued to make his distinctive mark on Broadway throughout the period with the hits *Annie Get Your Gun* (see pp.72–75) and *Call Me Madam* (1950), both starring the formidable leading lady Ethel Merman (see pp.140–41). However, Cole Porter (see pp.84–85) struggled to match his 1920s and 30s peak until 1948: first with the extravagantly accomplished *Kiss Me, Kate* (see pp.80–83), which was hailed as a

triumphant comeback, and later with *Can-Can* (1953), which made a star of actress-dancer Gwen Verdon.

Kurt Weill (see p.21) produced a string of idiosyncratic, artful Broadway scores, including 1941's *Lady in the Dark* (see p.56), *One Touch of Venus* (1943) and the closest he got to his ambition of a "Broadway opera", *Street Scene* (1947). Conductor-composer Leonard Bernstein (see pp.126–27) explored a dense, fresh musical style that blended elements of classical and modern jazz with the exuberant *On The Town* (see pp.64–65), the lighter *Wonderful Town* (see p.105) and the explosive *West Side Story* (see pp.122–25), a production that was welcomed by some as a landmark in musical theatre.

West Side Story made the names of everyone associated with it, including the lyricist Stephen Sondheim (see pp.220–21), who collaborated with Jule Styne (1905–94) on another Broadway classic *Gypsy* (see pp.138–39) before finally producing both the sophisticated music and lyrics for the hit musical farce *A Funny Thing Happened on the Way to the Forum* (see p.149).

OFF-BROADWAY FLOURISHES
In the 1950s and 60s, Off-Broadway – a community of more intimate New York theatres featuring smaller productions – became a valuable place for new theatrical work to be developed away from the commercial glare of Broadway. Sometimes a huge hit would emerge, including the 1954 modernization by Marc Blitzstein (see

p.45) of Kurt Weill and Bertolt Brecht's *The Threepenny Opera* (see pp.20–21), and *The Fantasticks* (see p.145) by Harvey Schmidt (1929–) and Tom Jones (1928–), which began its 42-year run in 1960 and became the longest-running musical of all time.

CHOREOGRAPHING SUCCESS
Dance was an increasingly important feature. George Balanchine was the first to be credited for choreography in *On Your Toes* (1936), but it was only after the character-illuminating, plot-enhancing work of Agnes de Mille in *Oklahoma!* that choreography became central to the character of a show. Ballet-trained Jerome Robbins (see pp.108–09) made his mark on dozens of shows, including *On The Town* (1944) and *West Side Story* (1957), while Bob Fosse (see pp.200–01) created an unmistakable, idiosyncratic style of his own in *Sweet Charity* (1966).

▲ Theatrical rivals
Filmgoers congregate outside a cinema showing the movie musical *Lady in the Dark* (1944), which was based on the 1941 Broadway show.

melodious score and expressive choreography by Agnes de Mille created a ground-breaking show, heralding the so-called "golden era" of musical theatre – both on stage and on screen – which lasted throughout the 1940s, 50s, and 60s.

▲ Dance directions
Actor and dancer Gene Kelly, seen here with Leslie Caron in *An American in Paris*, was one of the major stars in musicals in the 1940s and 50s.

▲ Integrated musicals
Slick choreography in musicals like *West Side Story* became central to the plot and took the integration of music and dance to a new level.

In the movies, Gene Kelly (1912–96) brought a distinctive athleticism to *An American In Paris* (1951) and *Singin' in the Rain* (see p.101), as did Broadway veteran Michael Kidd (1915–2007) in *Seven Brides For Seven Brothers* (see pp.112–13), among many other films and shows.

MAGICAL MOVIES
During the 1940s, around 30–40 movie musicals were produced annually, including classics like *Meet Me in St. Louis* (1944). However, it was MGM producer Arthur Freed (1894–1973) who ushered in the era of classic movie musicals. In tempting Broadway talent to Hollywood – such as lyricists and librettists Betty Comden and Adolph Green, the team responsible for *On the Town* (see p.64–65) – Freed oversaw a steady stream of creations like *Easter Parade* (see p.87), and *An American in Paris*; remakes such as *Show Boat* (1951); adaptations like *On the Town* (1949); and original shows including *Gigi* (1958). These lavish, Technicolor wonders were high-value vehicles for Gene Kelly, Vera-Ellen, Ann Miller and, in the second phase of his movie career, Fred Astaire (see pp.42–43).

In the 1960s, the various film studios enjoyed some conspicuous hits – *Mary Poppins* (1964) and *Oliver!* (1968) – and a few artistic triumphs like

◀ Cabaret stars
Composer John Kander, lyricist Fred Ebb, and director Harold Prince accept Tony Awards for *Cabaret* (1966).

The Umbrellas of Cherbourg (see pp.164–65), but the relative failure of big budget movie musicals like *Camelot* (1967), *Doctor Doolittle* (1967), and *Star!* (1968) marked the passing of the golden age of silver screen musicals.

WEST END DEVELOPMENTS
British musical theatre was largely overshadowed in the "golden era" by its American counterpart, but the UK continued to produce its own distinctive shows, such as Ivor Novello's *Perchance To Dream* (1945), containing operetta music evoking past eras. There were occasional transatlantic hits: Sandy Wilson's *The Boy Friend* (1953) was a pastiche of early Rodgers and Hart; Julian Slade's unsophisticated but irrepressible *Salad Days* (1954) conjured more innocent times. Lionel Bart's *Oliver!* (see p.142) and Leslie Bricusse and Anthony Newley's *Stop The World I Want To Get Off* (1961) indicated a new, earthy, post-rock vitality in British musicals.

NEW STYLES
Broadway was also evolving as the 1960s dawned. While *Hello, Dolly!* (see pp.160–61) in 1964 continued the traditional blend of jazzy American song incorporating vaudeville, burlesque, and aria tendencies, other musicals signposted a growing diversity in musical styles. *Fiddler On the Roof* (see pp.150–53) had Jewish music inflections; *Man of La Mancha* (see p.162) used Spanish idioms to tell the tale of Don Quixote; and *Cabaret* (see p.166) plundered Weimar-era Kurt Weill. Burt Bacharach and Hal David's *Promises, Promises* (see p.178) introduced cultured pop music, but the watershed was *Hair* (see pp.172–73), which suggested that musical theatre could thrive with a rock-based score.

PAL JOEY

{ 1940 }

Known as the first musical to feature an anti-hero as its main character, *Pal Joey*'s seedy subject matter was not to everyone's taste in 1940. However, today this show is regarded as a classic.

In the late 1930s, *The New Yorker* magazine published a series of expressive but unschooled letters to "Dear friend Ted", a fictitious successful band-leader, from "Pal Joey", an equally fictitious and frustrated drummer, subtly revealed to be duplicitous and manipulative. The author, John O'Hara, already acclaimed for his novels *Appointment in Samarra* (1934) and *Butterfield 8* (1934), offered the pieces to composer Richard Rodgers (see pp.70–71) and lyricist Lorenz Hart as source material for a new musical before gathering them into book form in 1940.

ADAPTING THE MATERIAL

Rodgers and Hart relished the idea of distinguishing between trashy numbers performed as part of the club's entertainment ("That Terrific Rainbow", "The Flower Garden of My Heart") and the more graceful music that expressed the characters' feelings, sincere or otherwise ("I Could Write a Book", "Bewitched, Bothered and Bewildered").

The songwriters were also fascinated by the idea of an amoral, charming heel who was "not disreputable because he was mean", as Rodgers assessed in 1952, "but because he had too much imagination to behave himself, and because he was a little weak". With the help of O'Hara, they turned Joey into an unscrupulous, womanizing dancer/singer who dreams of opening a nightclub, and looked for a performer with the necessary qualities and skills. They found him in Gene Kelly, a 27-year-old dancer/ choreographer turning heads as hopeful hoofer Harry in William Saroyan's Pulitzer Prize-winning play *The Time of Your Life* (1939).

Kelly's dedication to rigorous rehearsal produced flawless work and he dazzled Broadway with his freestyle dancing talent. "I don't believe in conformity to any school of dancing," he said at the time. "I never let technique get in the way of mood or continuity."

A FOUL WELL?

Pal Joey made Gene Kelly a star, and though not a smash hit by today's standards, at 374 performances it was Rodgers and Hart's longest-running musical to date. While some reviews were raves – "Brilliant, sardonic, and strikingly original" wrote the *New York Herald Tribune* – others were not. *The New York Times* called the story "odious", Hart's frankly sexual lyrics in "Bewitched, Bothered and Bewildered" "scabrous", and added, "although *Pal Joey* is expertly done, can you draw sweet water from a foul well?"

The 1952 Broadway revival, with Harold Lang as Joey and Vivienne Segal reprising her role as Vera, found the world a little more ready for *Pal Joey*; the show won three Tonys and 11 Donaldsons (a theatre industry award handed out between 1944 and 1955) and ran for 540 performances.

KEY FACTS

🎭 **STAGE**
🎬 **Director** George Abbott
📖 **Book** John O'Hara
🎵 **Music** Richard Rodgers
🎵 **Lyrics** Lorenz Hart
🎭 **Venue** Ethel Barrymore Theatre, New York
📅 **Date** 25 December 1940

⊙ Key information

The original 1940 Broadway production starred Vivienne Segal and Gene Kelly. Though it received mixed reviews, the show ran for ten months, the third-longest run of any Rodgers and Hart musical. There have been several revivals since, including a 1952 Broadway revival, a 1980 West End production, a 2008–09 Broadway run, and a 1957 film adaptation.

CAST

Gene Kelly Joey Evans
Vivienne Segal Vera Simpson
Leila Ernst Linda English
June Havoc Gladys Bumps
Jean Casto Melba Snyder
Jack Durrant Ludlow Lowell

▲ **Seedy entertainment?**
Gene Kelly and Leila Ernst performed alongside one another in the original Broadway production of the show. *Pal Joey* was a big hit, but it attracted mixed reviews.

> "*In many respects* Pal Joey *forced the musical theatre to wear long pants for the first time.*"
>
> **RICHARD RODGERS**, COMPOSER

THE MOVIE AND BEYOND

When the 1957 movie came to be made, Gene Kelly and Marlon Brando were considered for Joey, but Frank Sinatra ultimately landed the role. For Sinatra fans, the 1957 movie *Pal Joey* represents the perfect cinematic vehicle for the singer's talents, and he

▼ **Looking to the future**
Vivienne Segal (as Vera Simpson) and Harold Lang (Joey) perform in the finale of Act 1 during the 1952 Broadway revival of *Pal Joey*.

won a Golden Globe that year for his performance. For fans of the original show, the film was a watered-down disappointment. The movie, which was subject to the Motion Picture Production Code that did not apply to theatre shows, cleaned up Hart's lyrics and had Joey unfeasibly reform at the end of the film. Also, with Joey now a singer rather than a dancer, several numbers were imported from other Rodgers and Hart shows for Sinatra to perform, while others were totally cut or redistributed with little relationship to their original context or importance to the show.

◀ **Original Joey**
Gene Kelly had his big break in the original Broadway production of *Pal Joey*.

Playwright Richard Greenberg adapted the O'Hara material substantially for the 1992 and 2008 productions, including an unused song from the original score and reintroducing the show's trademark dark tone, to a mixed reception from the critics.

There have been a variety of other revivals and adaptations that have kept the show's profile afloat over the years and continue to make it familiar to contemporary audiences.

LADY IN THE DARK

{ **1941** }

Composer Kurt Weill's fourth US-based musical features a witty, satirical book by Moss Hart – inspired by his own psychoanalysis experiences – and extended dream sequences.

Playwright Moss Hart first began exploring psychiatry and the world of the unconscious in a straight play entitled *I Am Listening*, in which he envisaged dramatic actress Katherine Cornell in the starring role. Moss soon realized that the phantasmagorical, allusive quality he was after needed a wide range of music to convey the right mood. Although very experienced in musical comedy, Hart was uninterested in creating a musical for its own sake. Discussions with the German composer Kurt Weill

KEY FACTS

🎭 **STAGE**

🎫 **Director** Moss Hart

📖 **Book** Moss Hart

🎵 **Music** Kurt Weill

𝄞 **Lyrics** Ira Gershwin

🎭 **Venue** Alvin Theatre, New York

📅 **Date** 23 January 1941

◉ **Key information**

Lawrence's raunchy performance was particularly well received. Subsequent faithful revivals and concert performances have helped re-establish this singular show's reputation.

THE SHOW

The plot concerned Liza Elliott, the prim editor of *Allure*, a fashion magazine, who visits a psychoanalyst for help with panic attacks and depression. Mid-treatment, the scene changes to the "Glamour Dream", in which Liza is hailed by a dozen tuxedoed men as the height of charm ("Oh Fabulous One") and greeted similarly by the patrons of a high-class nightclub ("Girl of the Moment"). Liza awakens from her trance to be told that she is living a contradiction; professionally promoting glamour while personally avoiding it.

"A goddess; that's all."

BROOKS ATKINSON ON GERTRUDE LAWRENCE, *THE NEW YORK TIMES*, 1940

(see p.21), whose contributions to the American musical canon were by no means standard Broadway fare, convinced Hart that he wanted "a show in which music carried forward the essential story and was not merely imposed on the architecture of the play".

With Hart's encouragement, Weill and lyricist Ira Gershwin devised a remarkable and original score. Katherine Cornell was also replaced in the lead role by British actress and singer Gertrude Lawrence (see right).

WEIRD AND WONDERFUL

Other dream-like sequences in the musical include the "Wedding Dream", in which Liza almost marries her soon-to-be-divorced boyfriend, and the "Circus Dream", in which "The Greatest Show on Earth" is presented as a dramatic show of Liza's various neuroses. A series of bizarre episodes follows, including a court room trial.

Lawrence's performance in the starring role was well-received, especially her remarkable bump-and-grind business during "Jenny". However, it was the extraordinary "Tchaikowsky", not to say the flamboyantly camp portrayal of Liza's assistant Russell, that stole the show and made a star of the versatile American actor Danny Kaye.

Lady In the Dark ran for 467 performances with the sophistication of the subject matter and the sublime richness of the score inspiring ecstatic reviews. The *Chicago Daily Tribune* called it as "a high point in the history of the American musical stage", while *The New York Times* dubbed the new musical "a work of theatre art".

The 1944 movie adaptation of *Lady in the Dark* rewrote Hart's book quite extensively and removed most of Kurt Weill and Ira Gershwin's songs, adding comedy drama instead.

◀ **Glamour Dream**
Ginger Rogers in the 1944 film of *Lady in the Dark*, wearing a dress designed by costume designer Edith Head.

GERTRUDE LAWRENCE (1898–1952)

BIOGRAPHY

One of the most revered singer-actresses of her time, Lawrence was born in London. She started performing aged nine, and trained at the Italia Conti drama school. In 1926, she became the first British performer on Broadway in the Gershwins' *Oh, Kay!*. Lawrence appeared in childhood friend Noël Coward's revues and plays throughout the 1920s, 30s, and 40s, and won a Tony Award as Anna in *The King and I* (1951). Julie Andrews starred as Gertie in the biopic movie *Star* (1968).

CARMEN JONES

{ 1943 }

In late 1943, showman Billy Rose and lyricist Oscar Hammerstein II teamed up with an all-black cast to produce one of the biggest hits of the Broadway season.

After seeing a performance of *Carmen* at the Hollywood Bowl in Los Angeles, Oscar Hammerstein II made it his personal mission to transform George Bizet's great 1875 French opera into a modern American setting with an all-black cast. What began in 1934 as a film project saw the light of day as a surprise Broadway hit, *Carmen Jones*, in 1943. He wrote the libretto over eight years and finally found a backer in Broadway impresario Billy Rose. Faithfully set to Georges Bizet's original score, Hammerstein told the story in the colloquial black dialect of a small Southern town. In the original libretto, a gypsy seductress betrays her soldier lover for a bullfighter. Hammerstein's version replaces a cigar factory in Seville, Spain, with a parachute manufacturer during World War II. A star bullfighter is replaced by Husky Miller, a prize-fighting boxer; Don Jose became Joe, a corporal in the US Army. Carmen, no longer a cigarette-maker, is a now a factory seamstress. The "Toreador Song" became "Stan' up an' Fight", and the "Habanera" was now "Dat's Love".

KEY FACTS

STAGE

- **Director** Hassard Short, Charles Friedman
- **Book** Oscar Hammerstein II
- **Music** Georges Bizet
- **Lyrics** Oscar Hammerstein II
- **Venue** Broadway Theatre, New York
- **Date** 2 December 1943

Key information

The original show was a great success, running for 503 performances on Broadway. This was followed by a national tour. *Carmen Jones* was also revived in London in 1991 and 2007.

SINGERS AND DANCERS EVERYWHERE

The work called for more than 100 cast members, a rare opportunity for classically trained black singers to perform in an era in which opera companies were racially segregated. Hammerstein asked jazz expert John Hammond Jr, who had strong ties within the black community, to help him cast the opera. He discovered the soprano Muriel Smith (see right), who shared the role of Carmen Jones with Muriel Rahn, working at a photographic developing laboratory; Luther Saxon, as Joe, worked in the Philadelphia navy yard; and Glenn Bryant, playing Husky Miller, took a leave of absence from the New York Police Department in order to be on the show. It did not matter where the performers came from; if they had sufficient talent, they were cast in the show.

Every part of the production was praised. Renowned director and lighting designer Hassard Short created a different colour palette for each scene and thus reinforced Raoul Pene du Bois' bold costumes. Choreographer Eugene Loring's dance arrangements were praised for their fire and humour.

MOVIE VERSION

The renowned theatre and film director Otto Preminger originally planned to produce a movie version of *Carmen Jones* independently. However, like Hammerstein, he had a difficult time financing the film, but eventually found funding from Darryl F. Zanuck at 20th Century Fox. The setting was similar to Hammerstein's, but Preminger enlisted a new libretto from screenwriter Harry Kleiner. The movie starred Dorothy Dandridge, Harry Belafonte, and Pearl Bailey. Even though Belafonte and Dandridge were popular singers, Preminger dubbed their music with opera singers. Marilyn Horne supplied Dandridge's part as Carmen, but Bailey was one of the few who sang her own songs. Also appearing in the movie were dancers Alvin Ailey and Carmen de Lavallade, jazz drummer Max Roach, and young actress Diahann Carroll. The film earned two Academy Awards

BIOGRAPHY

MURIEL SMITH (1923–85)

A singer from New York, Muriel Smith was the first African-American female to attend the Curtis Institute of Music in Philadelphia. Among her classmates were celebrated composers Leonard Bernstein (see pp.126–27) and Ned Rorem. She performed in other American musicals, including *The Cradle Will Rock* (see p.45), but relocated to London, where she performed in musicals and opera, and recorded a pop hit, "Hold Me, Thrill Me, Kiss Me".

nominations: Best Actress for Dorothy Dandridge and Best Scoring for a Musical. In 1955, it won a Golden Globe for Best Picture.

▶ **Large-scale production**
The members of the cast of the original Broadway production of *Carmen Jones* perform on stage at the Broadway Theatre in 1943. Scenic design for the show was by Howard Bay.

OKLAHOMA!

{ 1943 }

Rodgers and Hammerstein's first musical together created a sensation. The ovation the show received on its first night signalled that this would be a smash hit. "It seemed," said one cast member, "that the applause would never stop."

Promise of fun ▲
Thie original poster for the production heralded a show full of all-American song and dance; audiences were not disappointed.

Richard Rodgers and Oscar Hammerstein II had known each other for years, but *Oklahoma!* was their first musical collaboration. Both men were well-established Broadway writers – Hammerstein mainly collaborating with Jerome Kern (see pp.14) and Rodgers with Lorenz Hart.

The credit for the idea for the show, however, went to producer Theresa "Terry" Helburn, the leading light behind the New York Theatre Guild, who first thought that *Green Grow the Lilacs*, a play by Lynn Riggs, a young Oklahoma-born playwright, "would make a good musical". She invited Rodgers to see the play. He was the first outsider to become involved.

HART OR HAMMERSTEIN?

Rodgers' chief concern was his lyricist partner Hart. By 1942, Hart's drinking problem had become acute and eventually, Rodgers warned him that he was prepared to write the new show with Oscar Hammerstein instead. When Hart dropped out of the project, Hammerstein was available to take over. The composer and his new lyricist immediately settled down to work. Such was their enthusiasm that they did not even ask the Theatre Guild for an advance – not that the Guild was in a position to pay them one at that stage. Helburn was finding it almost impossible to interest backers in the show. Even one of her partners dubbed it "Helburn's folly".

COMPOSING OKLAHOMA!

Rodgers and Hammerstein always worked together in the same way – Hammerstein wrote the lyrics first and sent them to Rodgers to set to music. What emerged was a brilliantly imaginative integrated composition that broke many of the long-established rules of musical theatre of the time. Every aspect of the show was dedicated to fleshing out the characters and advancing the narrative. Star turns that contributed little to the story were ruthlessly rejected – indeed, the cast was full of unknowns. Rodgers and

Hammerstein had vetoed the suggestion that Shirley Temple be cast as Laurey, the heroine, and that Groucho Marx be given the role of the comical character Ali Hakim.

The lack of glamour on stage was picked up by influential newspaper columnist Walter Winchell's secretary, who was sent by her boss to the New Haven preview to scout out the new production. The telegram she sent to him read succinctly: "No legs, no jokes, no chance."

CRAFTING A LASTING HIT

When *Away We Go!*, as *Oklahoma!* was first titled, opened in New Haven and then Boston before finally transferring to New York, its first audiences did not know what to make of it. Following the New Haven first night, Rodgers, Hammerstein, choreographer Agnes de Mille (see p.69), and stage director Robert Mamoulian set to work. Within a few weeks, the show had been

◄ Plain staging
Set designer Lemuel Ayers created sparse sets dominated by vivid backdrops to suggest the wide, open plains of Oklahoma.

KEY FACTS

STAGE

Director Rouben Mamoulian
Book and lyrics Oscar Hammerstein II
Music Richard Rodgers
Venue St James Theatre, New York
Date 31 March 1943

⊙ **Key information**
Produced by Teresa Helburn for the New York Theatre Guild, the original stage show won no major awards, but in 1944 Rodgers and Hammerstein were awarded a Pulitzer Prize (Special Citation). *Oklahoma!* ran for 2,212 performances and was seen by more than 4.5 million paying customers, and eventually grossed more than US$7 million for its backers.

▲ Dancing the dream ballet
This famous and influential sequence was created by one of the leading choreographers of her time, Agnes de Mille.

> *"It takes me ... sometimes three weeks to write the words ... it takes him an hour or two [to write the music]."*
>
> **OSCAR HAMMERSTEIN II** ON SONGWRITING WITH RICHARD RODGERS

extensively revised. The second act's revamp included the transformation of a conventional dance number into a rousing full-company showstopper.

The tinkering continued until an exhausted Rodgers put his foot down. "You know what's wrong with this show?", he said. "Nothing! Now everybody pipe down and let's go to bed!" The make-or-break New York opening lay ahead. It was a triumph. "Helburn's folly" was an even bigger success than she or Rodgers and Hammerstein had ever dared to hope for. No Broadway musical had ever before had such an impact. The Guild sent not one, but two touring companies out on the road. A third company was sent to take the show to the troops in the Pacific war zone. By the time the tour ended, *Oklahoma!* had astonishingly played to an estimated one and a half million US servicemen.

INNOVATIONS ON AND OFF STAGE

Oklahoma! broke new ground in a number of ways. The "dream ballet" dance sequence, entitled "Laurey Makes Up Her Mind", that forms the finale of the first act created a new element in musicals that remained popular during the ensuing two decades. Producer Theresa Helburn commented that with her dream ballet, Agnes de Mille "came into her own as one of America's leading choreographers". The sequence was intended to provide an extra dimension to the plot and characters, and required professionally trained dancers, not simply glamorously costumed performers. The success of this sequence placed the choreographer high up on the list of the talents needed for a hit show.

Such was the show's impact that it became the first-ever musical to be recorded in full by the original cast. Immediately after opening night, Jack Kapp, the head of Decca Records, brought the cast and pit orchestra into the Decca studio on West 57th Street, where he and his brother personally supervised the recording. It was a tricky task – the songs had to be crammed on to single sides of 78rpm 12-inch records with a maximum playing time of not more than five minutes. By the time *Oklahoma!* closed on Broadway, Decca had sold 800,000 complete albums.

BEYOND BROADWAY

The London production that opened in May 1947 at the Theatre Royal, Drury Lane, sold out for the next three-and-a-half years. Millions more viewed the film version, which premiered in 1955.

Australian actor Hugh Jackman landed his first international role when he was cast as Curly in a production of *Oklahoma!* at the National Theatre in London in 1998. This production was directed by Trevor Nunn and featured new choreography by Susan Stroman.

RELATED SHOWS

Show Boat, 1927, Jerone Kern, Oscar Hammerstein II (see pp.14–17)

Annie Get Your Gun, 1946, Irving Berlin (see pp.72–75)

South Pacific, 1949, Richard Rodgers, Oscar Hammerstein II (see p.96)

West Side Story, 1957, Leonard Bernstein, Stephen Sondheim (see pp.122–25)

STORYLINE

The scene is the Indian Territory (about to become the new state of Oklahoma) at the turn of the 20th century, and the plot centres on a love triangle – the rivalry between Curly, a ranch hand, and the villainous farmhand Jud for the affections of Laurey, niece of the owner of an Oklahoma farmstead. The flighty Ado Annie, Will Parker (another cowboy), and the pedlar Ali Hakim make up a second trio, providing light relief.

ALFRED DRAKE AND
JOAN ROBERTS AS
CURLY AND LAUREY

THE FRONT OF LAUREY'S FARMHOUSE

PLOT OVERVIEW

After the overture ❶ the curtain rises. Aunt Eller is churning butter outside her farmhouse. Curly, who has come to invite Laurey to a box-social that evening, sings ❷.

Laurey enters carrying some washing and picks up Curly's song. She pretends to be indifferent to the invitation, when Curly tells her that he is hiring a Surrey to take her to the party in style ❸. When he admits it is a figment of his imagination, she angrily flounces off.

Will Parker enters and describes his recent visit to Kansas City, where he won $50 in a steer-roping contest ❹. He needs the money in order to marry Laurey's friend, Ado Annie, whose father insisted on him earning such a sum before he would consent to the match.

To make Curly jealous, Laurey decides to go to the social with Jud. Ado Annie reveals that her date is pedlar Ali Hakim. She is, she says, the kind of girl who can't refuse a man anything ❺. Curley says he will go with someone else, but Laurey expresses her indifference ❻. Ado's father forces Ali to propose to her, much against his wishes ❼.

Curly and Laurey discuss going to the social together after all but, to avoid gossip, they must behave discreetly ❽. Curly goes to break the news to Jud.

THE SONGS

Overture
😊 *Orchestra*

Oh, What a Beautiful Mornin'
😊 *Curly*

The Surrey With the Fringe on Top
Curly, Laurey,
😊 *Aunt Eller*

Kansas City
Will Parker,
Aunt Eller,
😊 *Male Ensemble*

I Cain't Say No
😊 *Ado Annie*

It's a Scandal! It's a Outrage!
Ali Hakim, Male
😊 *Ensemble*

Many a New Day
Laurey, Female
😊 *Ensemble*

I Cain't Say No (reprise) and Oh, What a Beautiful Mornin' (reprise)
Will, Ado Annie, Curly, Aunt Eller
😊 *Ensemble*

People Will Say We're in Love
😊 *Curly, Laurey*

ANDREW CARNES FORCES ALI
HAKIM TO PROPOSE TO ADO ANNIE

AUNT ELLER AND CURLY

CAST

Betty Garde Aunt Eller
Alfred Drake Curly
Joan Roberts Laurey
Howard da Silva Jud Fry
Celeste Holm Ado Annie
Lee Dixon Will Parker
Joseph Buloff Ali Hakim
Ralph Riggs Andrew Carnes

"Songs, dances, and a story have been triumphantly blended ..."

HOWARD BARNES, THEATRE CRITIC, *NEW YORK HERALD TRIBUNE*, 1 APRIL 1943

THE SMOKE HOUSE

In Jud's gloomy room in the smoke house, Curly starts to flatter Jud, telling him, despite appearances, people really like him and would mourn his death **9** . The scene turns into a confrontation between Curly and Jud about Laurey, and Curly leaves. Now alone, Jud wallows in self-pity **10** .

A GROVE ON LAUREY'S FARM

Laurey dreams of getting married to Curly, but the wedding is broken up by Jud, who beats Curly up and forces her to go off with him **11** . As soon as the dream is over, both men appear. Laurey is frightened by her dream, but is taken to the social by Jud. The bewildered Curly is left alone.

THE SKIDMORE RANCH

An orchestral entr'acte 12 leads into the next scene, where the box-social is in full swing **13** . Curly and Jud vie to outbid each other in an auction for a hamper of goodies prepared by Laurey. Curly wins. Hakim, determined to escape marriage, pays Will $50 for the presents he bought in Kansas City. He and Ado can now plan their future together **14** . Curly and Laurey finally confess their love for each other **15** .

Three weeks later, Curly and Laurey's marriage ceremony is is under way when the drunken Jud storms into the party and threatens Curly with a knife. In the ensuing brawl, Jud falls onto the knife and is killed.

THE BACK OF LAUREY'S FARMHOUSE

In the hasty makeshift trial that follows, Curly is found not guilty of murder as he acted only in self-defence. He and Laurey are free to go off on their honeymoon and start their life together in a brand-new state **16 17** .

9 **10** **11** **12** **13** **14** **15** **16** **17**

9
Pore Jud
is Daid
🙂 *Curly, Jud*

10
Lonely
Room
🙂 *Jud*

11
Out of My Dreams/
Dream Ballet ("Laurey
Makes Up Her Mind")
🙂 *Laurey, "dream figures"*

12
Entr'acte
🙂 *Orchestra*

15
People Will
Say We're in
Love (reprise)
🙂 *Curly, Laurey*

14
All Er Nuthin'
🙂 *Will, Ado Annie*

13
The Farmer and the Cowman
*Andrew Carnes, Aunt Eller, Curly, Gertie
Cummings, Will Parker, Ado Annie, Laurey,*
🙂 *Ike Skidmore, Cord Elam, Ensemble*

17
Oh, What a Beautiful
Mornin' (reprise) and
People Will Say We're
in Love (reprise)
🙂 *Company*

16
Oklahoma
*Curly, Laurey, Aunt Eller, Ike
Skidmore, Cord Elam, Fred,*
🙂 *Andrew Carnes, Ensemble*

⭐ *"Oklahoma", the song that
ultimately gave the show
its name, was not part of
the original score. It was
added just before the show
opened in New York, after
the initial Boston try-out.*

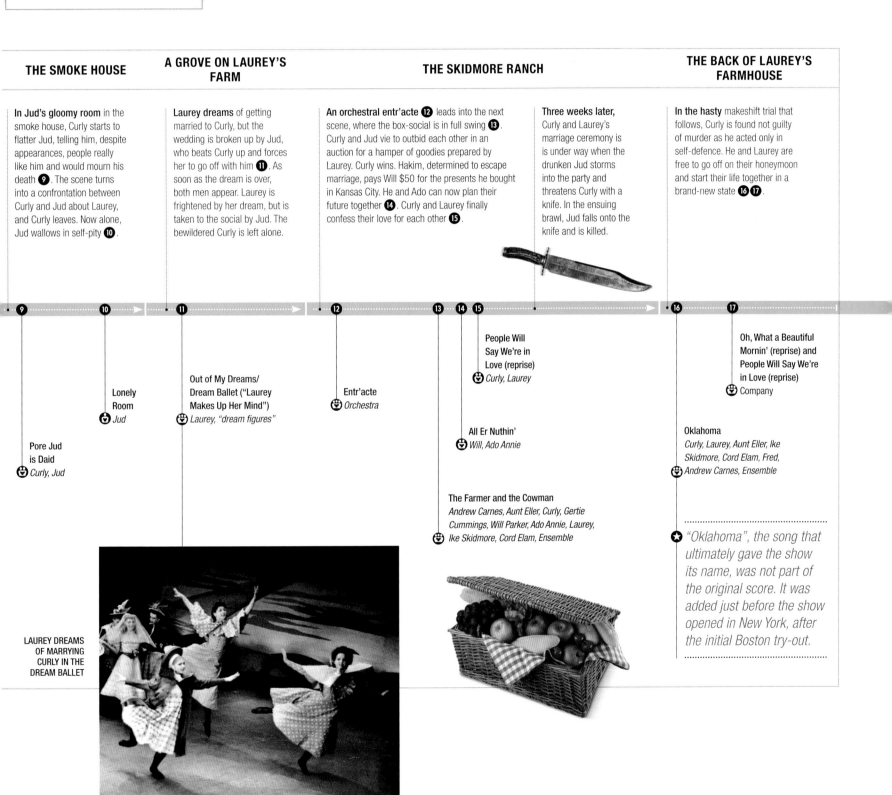

LAUREY DREAMS
OF MARRYING
CURLY IN THE
DREAM BALLET

GOTTA DANCE

In 1943, Agnes de Mille revolutionized the musical by bringing dance routines to the fore – a change that was swiftly embraced by her contemporaries.

Musicals had sparked dance crazes through the 1920s and 30s, but dance was still a minor part of the musical. In 1936, George Balanchine created the ballet "Slaughter on Tenth Avenue", which used dance to further the plot in Rodgers and Hart's *On Your Toes*, but it was *Oklahoma!* in 1943 that changed everything. Its choreographer, Agnes de Mille, was the first to cast her own dancers. Prior to this, producers hired dancers on the basis of their attractiveness rather than their technical abilities. De Mille treated each dancer as an individual, not a decorative object. She gleaned the dancer's unique gifts and used them to flesh out the role they were playing. Every step and gesture showed different facets of the character. For example, the "dream ballet" danced by Laurie at the end of the first act of *Oklahoma!* allowed the audience to witness her complex, subconscious fears as she revealed them through dance.

DRIVEN BY DANCE

After *Oklahoma!*, every choreographer integrated the choreography into the story, and a dream ballet became almost *de rigueur* in every musical.

◀ **Song and dance**
The cast of *Oklahoma!* performs a colourful dance sequence during "The Farmer and the Cowman" in the original Broadway production.

Through the 1940s and 50s, choreographers such as Michael Kidd, Robert Alton, and Donald Saddler refined the model that De Mille had established. In 1957, choreographer Jerome Robbins (see pp.108–09) created an entire physical life for *West Side Story* (see pp.122–25) that drove the narrative from beginning to end. Where Robbins's work was derived from ballet, the choreography of Bob Fosse (see pp.200–01) came from jazz dance infused with vaudeville and burlesque. In 1966, Fosse directed *Sweet Charity* (see p.167), in which he created a physical vocabulary specific to the show. Isolating and moving just one part of the body in an angular way, Fosse's choreography was charged with explicit sexuality. A very different choreographer was Michael Bennett, who created *A Chorus Line* (see pp.204–07). He based much of his choreography on the kind of moves he saw in dance clubs.

All of these choreographers advanced the art form and offered expanded physical vocabularies and new ways of thinking about musical theatre. Today's breed of choreographer – Rob Ashford, Matthew Bourne, John Carrafa, Susan Stroman, Garth Fagan, Twyla Tharp, Graciela Daniele, Andy Blankenbuehler, and others – build on the work of those who came before them, keeping dance routines an integral part of the musical.

> *"When* Oklahoma! *arrived, the theatre – nay, the whole city – shook."*

QUENTIN CRISP, BRITISH WRITER, INTERVIEWED IN *OK: THE STORY OF OKLAHOMA!*, 1993

ON THE TOWN

{ 1944 }

As American forces fought their biggest battles of World War II, back home a new kind of musical opened on Broadway. Brimming with life, *On the Town* was sophisticated, daring, and ready to reflect a changing world.

It seems a simple plot – thee sailors, Gabey, Chip, and Ozzie, are on 24-hour shore leave, determined to make the most of New York. Gabey holds a picture of "Miss Turnstiles", the girl of his dreams, and he is desperate to find her. Chip and Ozzie help Gabey search the city, and each of the three enjoys a romantic encounter – with Ivy ("Miss Turnstiles"), Hildy, and Claire – before they return to their ship. However, the simple plot belied a much more ground-breaking show, suffused with the wit and humanity of Betty Comden and Adolph Green (who also played Claire and Ozzie), the rich orchestrations of Leonard

CAST	
Betty Comden	Claire DeLoone
Adolph Green	Ozzie
Sono Osato	Ivy Smith ("Miss Turnstiles")
Nancy Walker	Hildy Esterhazy
John Battles	Gabey
Cris Alexander	Chip

▼ **Painting the town with joy**
The poster for the 1949 film version of the show promised – and delivered – a fun-filled experience.

> *"... a perfect example of what a well-knit fusion of the respectable arts can provide for the theatre."*

LEWIS NICHOLS, THEATRE CRITIC, *THE NEW YORK TIMES*, 29 DECEMBER 1944

BIOGRAPHY

BETTY COMDEN (1917–2006) **AND ADOLPH GREEN** (1915–2002)

For six decades, New York-born Comden and Green contributed their sharp wit, worldly wisdom, and sensitivity to dozens of Broadway musicals, including *Wonderful Town* (1953), *Bells Are Ringing* (with the unforgettable songs "The Party's Over" and "Just in Time"), and *On the Twentieth Century* (1978). The pair won seven Tony Awards for their stage work and also wrote a number of film musicals, including *The Barkleys of Broadway* (1949) and *Singin' in the Rain* (see pp.100–03).

Bernstein (see pp.126–27), and the ambitious choreography of classically trained Jerome Robbins (see pp.108–09). Robbins had already used the idea of three sailors on leave in his short ballet *Fancy Free* in April 1944, with music by the 26-year-old Bernstein, fresh from his success as conductor of the New York Symphony Orchestra. Robbins was also only in his 20s, as were Bernstein's close friends and revue artists, Comden and Green. Together, they expanded *Fancy Free* into a full-length Broadway musical – one that would tell a simple, honest story but with a blend and depth of character, lyrics, music, and dance that had already proved so successful the year before in the Rogers and Hammerstein musical *Oklahoma!* (see pp.58–61).

URBAN BALLET

Oklahoma! had brought the idea of the "dream ballet" into musicals for the first time, and Robbins followed suit with not one, but two dream ballet

▼ **New York at night**
On the Town captured the glamour, magic, and excitement of New York's neon-lit nightlife in the 1940s.

sequences in *On the Town*. In the first, "Times Square Ballet", at the end of the first act, Gabey, Chip, Ozzie, Hildy, and Claire move into a dance that explores New York's nightlife. The second, "Subway Ride and Imaginary Coney Island", sees Gabey conjure up an imaginary Ivy, who leads him into a dream world. Robbins and Bernstein were to take this intricate fusion of dance and music even further in 1957 in *West Side Story* (see pp.122–25).

WAR AND A NEW WORLD

The team of Bernstein, Robbins, Comden, and Green had all the necessary enthusiasm and talent but needed an older, more experienced hand to guide them. So George Abbott, a man twice their age and a seasoned writer, producer, and director, was brought in to direct. One of the first things Abbott did was to remove any overt references to the ongoing war, although that conflict provided an inescapable backdrop to the action. The characters in *On the Town* try to escape the grim realities of war, to enjoy themselves and let go, if only for a day. The deeply poignant song "Some Other Time" brought this home. As they wait for the subway

train to Coney Island, Chip, Ozzie, Hildy, and Claire muse on their whirlwind 24 hours of excitement and romance. The song captured what many wartime Americans were experiencing – the pain of separation and the need to grasp every fleeting moment of happiness.

On the Town also highlighted the difference the war made to American women. More than two million of them had joined the workforce, often doing the jobs that men had done before. Hildy is a cabdriver, previously a male job, and pursues her man, Chip, with an assertiveness that would have once shocked an audience.

At a time when many Americans were forced to reassess old prejudices, *On the Town* was one of the first musicals brave enough to have a racially integrated cast. The part of Ivy ("Miss Turnstiles") was played in the original production by the Japanese-American dancer Sono Osato, whose father had been held in a US internment camp in 1941. There were six black artists in a cast of 56, who mingled with their white colleagues on stage, something that was unheard of at the time. Everett Lee later took up the baton to become one of the first African Americans to conduct an orchestra in a Broadway show.

THE FILM STEALS THE SHOW

Above all, *On the Town* is a musical about New York, and its noise, brashness, and grandeur were all encapsulated by Bernstein's music. But for the 1949 film version, much of his score for the stage show was rejected. Louis B. Mayer, the head of the MGM studio, found it too demanding and considered the stage version to be vulgar in places. He had Comden and Green rewrite the story and replace all but four of Bernstein's songs. The

film censors also got in on the act, insisting on the change of the word "helluva [town]" in the song "New York, New York" to "wonderful [town]". The film was an instant success, grossing more than US$4 million at the box office and winning an Oscar in 1950 for Best Music.

▲ **On Brooklyn Bridge**
Frank Sinatra (Chip), Jules Munshin (Ozzie), and Gene Kelly (Gabey) prepare to hit the town in the 1949 film *On the Town*.

KEY FACTS

STAGE
🎭 **Director** George Abbott
📖 **Book and lyrics** Betty Comden and Adolph Green
🎵 **Music** Leonard Bernstein
🎭 **Venue** Adelphi Theatre, New York
📅 **Date** 28 December 1944

⊙ **Key information**
On the Town ran for 462 performances, before closing on 2 February 1946 at the Martin Beck Theatre on Broadway.

MEET ME IN ST. LOUIS

{ 1944 }

As wholesome as apple pie, *Meet Me in St. Louis,* with its small-town setting in an idealized American past, brought colour, romance, family togetherness, hope, and heart-warming songs to a war-weary audience.

▼ Ideal home
The comfortable domestic setting for this tale of the relatively minor ups and downs of an idealized all-American family provided a perfect backdrop to this ultimate feel-good movie.

KEY FACTS

📽 **FILM**

🎬 **Director** Vincente Minnelli

📧 **Screenplay** Irving Brecher and Fred F. Finklehoffe

📖 **Book** Sally Benson

🎵 **Music** Roger Edens and Conrad Salinger (score), Hugh Martin and Ralph Blane (original songs)

🕐 **Running time** 113 minutes

📅 **Release date** 1944

◎ **Key information**
A series of stories written by Sally Benson (1897–1972) for *The New Yorker* magazine in the early 1940s was the inspiration for the film. Benson was engaged to produce the screenplay, but her work was discarded and she received a credit only as the writer of the original book.

Released the year after *Oklahoma!* took Broadway by storm (see pp.58–61), *Meet Me in St. Louis* brought to the cinema the same simple but audience-winning appeal of real, believable people bursting into song. World War II had reached a brutal climax in Europe, but the film's sincere expression of American family values and nostalgia for a simpler, less troubled time, before any world wars, proved the perfect escape.

It is the sweet, tender story of the well-to-do but down-to-earth Smith family – father, mother, daughters Rose, Esther, Agnes, and "Tootie", one son, Grandpa, and the maid, Katie – in

▼ The Trolley Song
Surrounded by the colourful dresses of her fellow passengers, Judy Garland as Esther brings a joyous radiance to the screen as she sings of her love in this famous sequence.

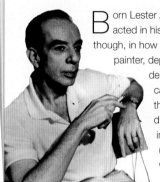

VINCENTE MINNELLI (1903–86)   **BIOGRAPHY**

Born Lester Anthony Minnelli in Chicago, Illinois, as a child Minnelli acted in his parents' theatre company. He was more interested, though, in how things looked and, after serving his time as a billboard painter, department store window dresser, and Broadway set designer and director, he eventually answered Hollywood's call. He continued making films into his 70s, married three more times after splitting from Judy Garland, and died in 1986. In addition to *Meet Me in St. Louis*, his films included *Cabin in the Sky* (1943), *An American in Paris* (1951), *Brigadoon* (see p.89), and *Gigi* (see p.132), for which he won a Best Director Oscar.

▲ **Authentically Western**
The film aimed to appeal to traditional American values and the poster, with its "Wild West" typography, echoed the flavour of the production.

St Louis, Missouri, during the course of a year, as the town gears up for the 1904 World's Fair. Two of the sisters – Esther and Rose – find love. The object of Esther's affections is the boy next door, John Truett – a longing she expresses in "The Boy Next Door" and "Trolley Song", two of the three songs written for the film by the team of Hugh Martin and Ralph Blane. Eldest sister Rose begins the film hoping for a proposal over the telephone from her New York beau, Warren Sheffield, but only receives that proposal at the end. The film moves with the seasons, from summer to spring, and the romance unfolds against the will-they-won't-they backdrop of the family's possible move to New York, announced by the father, Alonzo "Lon" Smith. Eventually, he realizes how distressed his children are, and tells his delighted family they can stay in St Louis.

SONGS OLD AND NEW
Judy Garland (see p.46), in a radiant performance as Esther, steals the show, although she was almost upstaged by the seven-year-old Margaret O'Brien, playing the impossibly cute youngest sister Tootie, a role that won her a Juvenile Oscar in 1945. Garland, though, has the film's best musical moments, including the achingly sentimental "Have Yourself a Merry Little Christmas", which she sings to Tootie to raise her spirits as she worries about the move to New York.

Other than the three Garland showcases written for the film by Martin and Blane, most of the songs in *Meet Me in St. Louis* were rearranged folk songs, such as "Auld Lang Syne" and "Skip to My Lou", or early 20th-century vaudeville numbers, including "Under the Bamboo Tree" and "Goodbye, My Lady Love". The

title song, which reprises several times, including during the film's final scene, was originally a Tin Pan Alley tune written in 1904 to cash in on the World's Fair.

PAINTER AND HIS MUSE
The changing seasons of the musical gave the director, Vincente Minnelli (see above), a golden opportunity to show off his mastery of film colour, or, more precisely, Technicolor. *Meet Me in St. Louis* was his first use of this film process, invented in 1916, and he used its rich, vibrant tones set against more muted colours to paint dynamic scenes with the skill of a master. In the "Trolley Song" scene, for instance, the vivid blues, greens, and reds of the passengers' clothes leap from the screen and perfectly frame Judy Garland in her eye-catching black and white dress.

Minnelli and Garland were both married to other people when they met on the set of the film. At first, they did not get on, but director and actress then fell in love and married in 1945. The couple worked together on two more films, the romantic drama *The Clock* (1945) and the musical *The Pirate* (1948), but the marriage lasted only until 1951. It did, however, produce a daughter, Liza Minnelli, who inherited her mother's powerful singing voice and became the star of film musicals such as *Cabaret* (see pp.166) and *New York, New York* (1977).

> ## *"The Smiths and … their living inspires you like vitamin A."*
>
> **BOSLEY CROWTHER,** FILM CRITIC, *THE NEW YORK TIMES*, 29 NOVEMBER 1944

STRIKING THE RIGHT NOTE
From the moment it opened in cinemas, in November 1944, *Meet Me in St. Louis* was a huge success, grossing more than US$7 million in the US alone. The film became one of MGM's most successful musicals, though it missed out at the Academy Awards, despite being nominated for four Oscars, including Best Music and Best Song. A TV remake was broadcast in 1959 – and again in 1966, but as a non-musical version. Then, in 1989, *Meet Me in St. Louis* reversed the usual stage-to-film tradition when it was turned into a Broadway show – with extra songs. This production ran for 252 performances at the George Gershwin Theatre in New York.

CAST	
Judy Garland	Esther Smith
Margaret O'Brien	"Tootie" Smith
Lucille Bremer	Rose Smith
Joan Carroll	Agnes Smith
Henry H. Daniels Jr	Alonzo "Lon" Smith Jr
Mary Astor	Mrs Anna Smith
Leon Ames	Mr Alonzo "Lon" Smith
Tom Drake	John Truett
Marjorie Main	Katie, the maid
Harry Davenport	Grandpa
Robert Sully	Warren Sheffield

CAROUSEL

{ 1945 }

On the heels of the ground-breaking *Oklahoma!*, *Carousel* stirred audiences with a tragic love story told with beautiful music and sublime dance. It was Richard Rodgers' personal favourite of his many productions.

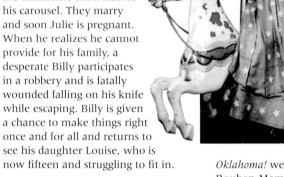

▼ **World-class singers**
Iva Withers (as Julie Jordan) and leading man John Raitt were able to take full advantage of Rodgers and Hammerstein's beautiful music in *Carousel*.

KEY FACTS

🎭 **STAGE**

🎬 **Director** Rouben Mamoulian
📖 **Book** Oscar Hammerstein II
♫ **Music** Richard Rodgers
𝄞 **Lyrics** Oscar Hammerstein II
🎭 **Venue** Majestic Theatre, New York
📅 **Date** 19 April 1945

⊙ **Key information**
The musical was produced by the Theatre Guild. Awards included the 1944–45 New York Drama Critics' Circle Award, with a Special Citation for a Musical. A Broadway production in 1994 won the Tony Award for Best Musical Revival. In 1999, *Time Magazine* named *Carousel* the Best Musical of the 20th Century.

When *Carousel* opened on Broadway, Rodgers and Hammerstein reigned as the kings of musical theatre. *Oklahoma!* (see pp.58–61) was entering its third year and each had had recent hits: Rodgers with *Pal Joey* (see pp.54–55) and Hammerstein with *Carmen Jones* (see p.57).

The idea for *Carousel* came from by the Theatre Guild, a theatrical organization led by Theresa Helburn and Lawrence Langner, producers of *Oklahoma!*. In 1921, the Guild had presented the play *Liliom*, adapted by Benjamin Glazer from the Hungarian play by Ferenc Molnár. The play was a success, so why not a musical? Molnár, who had rejected overtures by Giacomo Puccini and George Gershwin, agreed to let Rodgers and Hammerstein have a go at it after he had seen *Oklahoma!*, of which he approved.

The action in *Carousel* was moved from *Liliom*'s Budapest to Maine, *c.*1873. The story revolves around a charming ne'er-do-well, carnival barker

◀ **West End hit**
A souvenir programme for *Carousel* from the successful London production at the Theatre Royal, Drury Lane, 1950.

Billy Bigelow. Naive mill-worker Julie Jordan falls in love as she observes the handsome showman at his carousel. They marry and soon Julie is pregnant. When he realizes he cannot provide for his family, a desperate Billy participates in a robbery and is fatally wounded falling on his knife while escaping. Billy is given a chance to make things right once and for all and returns to see his daughter Louise, who is now fifteen and struggling to fit in.

OKLAHOMA! TEAM REUNITES
Singer John Raitt, who starred as Curly in the touring production of *Oklahoma!* in 1944, was cast as Billy. His musical talent was such that the seven-minute-long "Soliloquy" was written especially for him by Rodgers and Hammerstein, based on the strength of his audition of opera arias. The role of Julie was played by Jan Clayton, who went on to star in the television show *Lassie*. Bambi Linn, who played daughter Louise, had trained with choreographer Agnes de Mille (see opposite) and made her Broadway debut in *Oklahoma!* at age 17. Many of the creative team for

Oklahoma! were retained for *Carousel*: Rouben Mamoulian directed; de Mille choreographed the dances; and Miles White designed the costumes.

Rodgers' melodies and Hammerstein's lyrics made *Carousel* one of the greatest musicals of all time. The climactic "You'll Never Walk Alone", is sung to Julie by her cousin Nettie Fowler, played by opera singer Christine Johnson, in an effort to comfort her after Billy's death. The now classic song, reprised in the finale by the full company, took on special meaning for audiences at the end of World War II and moved generations to follow with its heartfelt melody and lyrics. Other enduring songs include "If I Loved You", "June Is Bustin' Out All Over",

"Oscar never wrote more meaningful or more moving lyrics, and to me, my score is more satisfying than anything I've ever written."

RICHARD RODGERS, *MUSICAL STAGES: AN AUTOBIOGRAPHY*, 1975

▲ Broadway carnival
The elaborate sets for the original Broadway production of *Carousel* were created by the influential American set designer Jo Mielziner.

and "This Was a Real Nice Clambake". *Carousel* was noted not just for its music but for Agnes de Mille's stunning dance sequences. In Act II, de Mille choreographed a dance number to introduce the troubled Louise – the teenage daughter of Julie and Billy, the father she never knew. The 15-minute dance suite encapsulated her small-town life in one sequence, from childlike play with town boys, to her unhappy relationship with a local family, and a duet with a handsome carnival worker.

MANY REVIVALS AND A MOVIE

Carousel ran for 890 shows at the Majestic Theatre, then travelled around America for two years. The national company returned to New York City in 1949 with a triumphant performance at City Center. *Carousel* saw three more Broadway revivals in 1954, 1957, and 1994. A movie version premiered in 1956. Popular actors and singers Gordon MacRae and Shirley Jones played the lead roles and Henry King directed. Frank Sinatra had originally agreed to take the role of Billy, but he backed out when he heard that extra time would be needed to shoot in what was new film technology at the time, Cinemascope 55.

AGNES DE MILLE (1905–93)

Niece of Cecil B. DeMille and daughter of director and writer William, choreographer and performer Agnes de Mille pioneered an American style of dance that combined modern, ballet, and folk idioms. In addition to *Carousel*, she choreographed the great musicals *Oklahoma!* and *Brigadoon* (see p.86), and the classic ballets *Rodeo* and *Fall River Legend*, still performed today. De Mille was also a writer and memoirist. Her numerous books include *Martha: The Life and Work of Martha Graham*, a lifelong friend. De Mille has been honoured with many awards, among them a Tony and an Emmy.

RICHARD RODGERS

COMPOSER 1902–79

The composer Richard Rodgers gave us many Broadway musicals, over 900 songs, and some memorable film scores. Famous for his partnerships with lyricists Hart and Hammerstein, he won every show business award available.

▶ Long run
Richard Rodgers is pictured holding one of his many musical scores in 1963. Few other composers of musicals have enjoyed such a long, varied, and above all successful career.

In contrast to many of his contemporaries, Richard Rodgers was born into a prosperous New York Jewish family. The boy showed early musical promise, playing the piano at six and composing songs as a teenager. At the age of 16, he met lyricist Lorenz Hart and the duo's debut song, "Any Old Place with You", featured in the 1919 Broadway musical comedy *A Lonely Romeo*.

At Columbia University, Rodgers and Hart, now an established team, co-wrote Varsity shows, some with fellow student Oscar Hammerstein II, who later formed his own highly successful partnership with Rodgers. This happy arrangement continued until 1921, when Rodgers moved to the Institute of Musical Art (now the Juilliard School).

▲ Longstanding legacy
Rodgers' early works with Lorenz Hart stood the test of time. *Garrick Gaieties* spawned a couple of successful sequels in the following years.

THE RODGERS AND HART YEARS

After leaving college, Rodgers worked as a conductor for the comedy actor Lew Fields while continuing to write musicals – such as *Poor Little Ritz Girl* (1920) and *The Melody Man* (1924) – with Hart. Real success proved elusive, however, and a despairing Rodgers briefly considered giving up music to sell children's underwear. Happily – for him and for posterity – audiences loved *The Garrick Gaieties*, a benefit show originally scheduled for just two performances in 1925. It actually ran for 213, and the song "Manhattan" established the duo as serious players. A string of popular Broadway and West End musicals followed – *Dearest Enemy* (1925), *The Girlfriend* and *Peggy-Ann* (1926), and *A Connecticut Yankee* (1927), making hits of such songs as, "Here in My Arms" and "My Heart Stood Still".

Once the Depression took hold, Rodgers and Hart headed to Hollywood, where they wrote scores for such films as the 1932 *Love Me Tonight* (with Maurice Chevalier) and the interestingly named *Hallelujah, I'm A Bum*, starring Al Jolson.

In 1935, the team returned to New York to write the score for Billy Rose's circus extravaganza, *Jumbo* (see p.33), remaining there for the rest of their partnership. They created a number of winning shows – *On Your Toes* (1936), *Babes in Arms* (1937), *Pal Joey* – with

and perfectionist partner to distraction. Rodgers then began writing with Oscar Hammerstein II (see p.99) and they had an immediate hit with *Oklahoma!*, a winning blend of Rodgers' musical comedy genius and Hammerstein's expertise in operetta. The pair become a solid writing team but also formed The Williamson Music Company as a way of controlling the rights to their own work. Hot on the heels of *Oklahoma!* came *Carousel* (see pp.68–69), *South Pacific*, *The King and I* (see pp.98–99), and *The Sound of Music* (1959), which were all later made into star-studded and highly successful films. Who doesn't want to sing along to "Oh, What a Beautiful

▼ **A great partnership**
Richard Rodgers' long partnership with Oscar Hammerstein II brought him his greatest success.

work after Hammerstein's death, collaborating with the likes of Stephen Sondheim (see pp.220–21) and Sheldon Harnick, and winning two Tony Awards for his 1962 Broadway musical *No Strings*.

HAPPY FAMILY LIFE AND LEGACY

In 1930, Richard Rodgers had married Dorothy Belle Feiner, a long-standing family friend and aspiring artist. She proved to be a talented hostess, cook, inventor (of a toilet cleaner, for example), founder of a repair business, and was also the author of *My Favorite Things: A Personal Guide to Decorating and Entertaining*. The couple had three daughters: Mary (a composer and author of the 1972 children's novel *Freaky Friday*), Linda, and a third who died in infancy during the 1930s. Mary and Linda's sons, Adam Guettel and Peter Melnick, themselves became composers of musicals.

Richard Rodgers' prolific and brilliant career spanned six decades. His intensely creative partnerships with Lorenz Hart and Oscar Hammerstein created some of the world's most enduring musicals and film scores, and popular, melodious, and highly characterful songs.

Between them, the three men carefully shaped American musical theatre, transforming the genre from simple collections of songs and sketches into comprehensive works with coherent plots, dialogue, and songs.

"A song is a lot of things. But, first ... a song is the voice of its time."

RICHARD RODGERS

popular and enduring songs that became classics, including "The Most Beautiful Girl in the World", "Little Girl Blue", "My Funny Valentine", "The Lady Is a Tramp", and "Falling in Love with Love". Rodgers and Hart's star was in the ascendant.

RODGERS AND HAMMERSTEIN

By 1943, Hart's health was failing and his all-night partying and drunken binges had driven his disciplined

Mornin'", "People Will Say We're in Love", "Oklahoma" (now the state song of Oklahoma), "If I Loved You", "You'll Never Walk Alone" (adopted by Liverpool football fans in 1963), "Some Enchanted Evening", "My Favorite Things", "Do-Re-Mi", and "Ten Minutes Ago"?

AFTER HAMMERSTEIN

By the time Oscar Hammerstein died of stomach cancer in 1960, the pair had collected 35 Tony Awards, 15 Academy Awards, two Pulitzer Prizes, two Grammy Awards, and two Emmys. Rodgers continued to

◄ **Sweet success**
Richard Rodgers and Oscar Hammerstein pose with Mary Martin, who had starred in *South Pacific* and *The Sound of Music* on Broadway.

ANNIE GET YOUR GUN

{ 1946 }

Bursting with classic Irving Berlin songs, this rollicking 1946 elaboration of the exploits of real-life Wild West sharpshooter Annie Oakley is a witty, spirited, good old-fashioned tune-fest.

American song lyricist Dorothy Fields had a distinguished career, not least through her collaboration with composer Jerome Kern (see pp.14) on the movie *Swing Time* (1936), which starred Fred Astaire. For her idea of basing a musical on the life of exhibition sharpshooter Annie Oakley as a star vehicle for her friend Ethel Merman, she invited Kern to be composer. She also secured the involvement of Richard Rodgers (see pp.70–71) and Oscar Hammerstein (see p.99), fresh from their successes with *Oklahoma!* (see pp.58–61) and *Carousel* (see pp.68–69). In their new roles as Broadway producers of their own and selected outside work, the songwriting pair agreed to work on the show.

After Kern's sudden death in November 1945, Irving Berlin (see pp.76–77), a hugely popular and versatile songwriter and one of the few who wrote both music and lyrics, was invited to compose for the show. To secure Berlin, Fields relinquished her role as lyricist but coauthored the book with her brother Herbert.

HILLYBILLY STUFF
Berlin hesitated for several reasons. First, he knew he wouldn't get his customary above-the-title billing. Secondly, Berlin was aware of Richard Rodgers and Oscar Hammerstein's recent status as masters of the narrative musical and was nervous that his own hit-song style would be unfavourably compared with their approach. He also worried that the "hillbilly stuff" he imagined the show required was beyond his scope. However, he soon realized that the story was about show business and romance, and found the confidence to produce six songs in a single week. During his early score demonstrations, Berlin had presented and then removed his indomitable anthem of the entertainment industry, "There's No Business Like Show Business", convinced his collaborators didn't like it. "I'm crazy about it," said Rodgers, "put it back." The director, Joshua Logan, agreed, assuring the sensitive composer, "We can't scream louder every time we hear it."

Despite his anxiety, Berlin was at his most prolific. It was Logan who suggested that the second act needed another song for Annie and Frank. With the two characters not speaking cordially at this point in the story, it was suggested a "challenge" song might work. Berlin immediately left the meeting and phoned Logan 15 minutes later to sing him "Anything You Can Do", the piece he had devised in the taxi ride back to his hotel.

◀ **Original Annie**
Target shooter Annie Oakley (1860–1926), on whom the show was based, poses with her rifle for this 1899 photograph.

▼ **Shows within shows**
The cast gather on stage for a set-piece tableau in the original stage production of the show.

KEY FACTS

🎭 **STAGE**

🎬 **Director** Joshua Logan
📖 **Book** Dorothy Fields and Herbert Fields
🎵 **Music and lyrics** Irving Berlin
🎭 **Venue** Imperial Theatre, New York
📅 **Date** 16 May 1946

⊙ **Key information**
The show ran for 1,147 performances and Merman played the role throughout. In 1998, the album of the original 1946 Broadway cast recording was added to the Grammy Hall of Fame.

"All the tunes are hits ... Ethel Merman is at her lusty, free and easy best."

VERNON RICE, THEATRE CRITIC, *NEW YORK POST,* 1946

▲ Hit songs
The success of the show was reflected in the demand for sheet music of the songs, such as "I Got the Sun in the Morning".

THE GOON LOOK

Ethel Merman (see pp.140–41) had been away from Broadway for over two years, but seized the role of Annie with gusto, igniting Berlin's songs with her customary fire and creating a memorable character. The legendary moment where she falls in love with Frank, requiring her to "deflate" with desire – a piece of physical comedy dubbed "the goon look" – was the point Logan was convinced they had a hit.

CONFOUNDING THE CRITICS

Logan lost some of his confidence in the production after the opening Broadway audience's muted reaction to the first act. The unruffled Merman reassured her nervous team in the interval. "You may think I'm playing the part, but inside I'm saying 'If you were as good as I am, you'd be up here!'" The second act played to an uproarious reception.

If some of the reviews suggested that the show was a bit of a stylistic throwback compared to the elegant quasi-operatic style of *Oklahoma!* and the recently opened *Carousel* (1945), the huge advance sales and a near three-year run proved *Time* magazine's judgement that this was a "fetch-the-crowds" musical. And Merman's portrayal of Annie Oakley cemented her status as a Broadway's legend. While Betty Hutton took the lead in the 1950 movie (see right), Merman reprised the role of Annie in a 1966 Broadway revival. Other notable productions include a 1986 UK show starring American rock star Suzi Quatro and a 1999 Broadway production starring Bernadette Peters.

CAST CHANGE FOR THE MOVIE

Hollywood never entirely took to Ethel Merman, and it was Judy Garland (see p.46) who was originally cast as Annie in the 1950 MGM movie. However, repeated clashes between Garland and the movie's director, Busby Berkeley, led to her being replaced by Hollywood star Betty Hutton. The film received four Oscar nominations and won the award for the Best Music Scoring of a Musical Picture.

RELATED SHOWS

Call Me Madam, 1950, Irving Berlin

Calamity Jane, 1953, David Buttolph, Howard Jackson

There's No Business Like Show Business, 1954, Irving Berlin

STORYLINE

In Cincinnati, Ohio, in the 1880s, Annie Oakley is an uneducated girl who supports her younger siblings by selling the game she shoots. Her sharpshooting skills are noticed by Buffalo Bill and she joins his Wild West Show. She falls for rival sharpshooter Frank Butler, who loves her but dislikes being outshone by her professionally. He leaves the troupe while she tours Europe with them. Frank and Annie are eventually reunited and love wins the day.

CAST	
Ethel Merman	Annie Oakley
Ray Middleton	Frank Butler
Marty May	Charlie Davenport
Art Barnett	Foster Wilson
William O'Neal	Col William. F. Cody "Buffalo Bill"
Kenny Bowers	Tommy Keeler
Anne Nyman	Winnie Tate

PLOT OVERVIEW

IN AND AROUND CINCINNATI, OHIO

The show's manager and the troupe introduce Buffalo Bill's Wild West Show ❶, while the star of the show, Frank Butler, establishes himself as a good-natured rogue with a song of his many on-the-road romantic conquests ❷.

Annie defends her uneducated, plain-living philosophy with a playful series of anecdotes concerning her family avoiding taxes, stealing chickens, and living to old age ❸.

Frank sings in lilting waltz-time that his favoured female would be "soft and pink as a nursery" dressed in "satin and lace" ❹. The tomboyish Annie, already smitten, is crestfallen ❺. She comically considers whether her sharpshooter skills are of any use in her romantic life.

Having won a shooting contest, Annie is invited into the Wild West Show and joins in with a stirring celebration of the highs and lows of the entertainment life ❻.

IN AND AROUND MINNEAPOLIS, MINNESOTA

Frank, increasingly enamoured of Annie as they work together, assures the starry-eyed girl that love is indeed "wonderful", just as she's heard ❼.

Annie and her cowboy friends sing her siblings to sleep with a lullaby ❽ about the making of illegal "moonshine" liquor.

THE SONGS

❶

❷ **I'm a Bad, Bad Man**
😊 Frank Butler, Girls

Colonel Buffalo Bill
Charlie Davenport,
😊 Ensemble

❸ **Doin' What Comes Natur'lly**
Annie Oakley, Kids,
😊 Foster Wilson

❹ **The Girl That I Marry**
😊 Frank Butler

❺ **You Can't Get a Man With a Gun**
😊 Annie Oakley

❻ **There's No Business Like Show Business**
Frank, Col William F. Cody (Buffalo Bill), Charlie, Annie
😊 Oakley, Ensemble

❼ **They Say It's Wonderful**
Frank Butler,
😊 Annie Oakley

❽ **Moonshine Lullaby**
Annie Oakley, "Moonshine
😊 Lullaby" Trio

ANNIE (ETHEL MERMAN) DOING WHAT COMES NATURALLY

"Moonshine Lullaby" was ★ omitted from the 1950 film, possibly because of references to the illegal brewing of liquor.

ETHEL MERMAN
AS ANNIE

"Hey mister …? Don't you like girls?"

ANNIE TO FRANK, *ANNIE GET YOUR GUN* (FILM), SIDNEY SHELDON, 1950

IN AND AROUND NEW YORK

GOVERNOR'S ISLAND, NEW YORK

The show's knife-thrower, Tommy, and his assistant, Winnie, sing a song to celebrate the value of sharing **9**. Meanwhile, Frank admits his days of philandering are over **10**; Annie has got to him and he confesses to liking it.

Annie performs an impressive shooting trick to surprise Frank and deflect business from Pawnee Bill's rival Wild West Show. His pride stung, Frank storms off to join Pawnee Bill. Meanwhile, Annie becomes a star and is adopted into the Sioux tribe by Chief Sitting Bull **11**.

Buffalo Bill's Wild West Show has no money despite a successful tour of Europe, so plans are made to merge with Pawnee Bill. Annie sings of how she still yearns for Frank **12**. Meanwhile, Winnie and Tommy express their growing commitment to each other **13**.

Annie learns that Pawnee Bill is broke too, so vows to sell her sharpshooter medals in order to finance the merger. She sings a song celebrating her appreciation of the simpler things in life **14**. The reunited Annie and Frank briefly affirm their love for each other **15** before falling out, cancelling the merger, and calling off the wedding.

A final shooting match takes place to determine who has the best shot **16**. To protect Frank's ego and win his heart, Annie deliberately misses her shot **17**.

9 **10** **11** **12** **13** **14** **15** **16** **17**

My Defenses Are Down
Frank Butler,
⭐ *Boys*

I'm an Indian Too
⭐ *Annie Oakley*

Who Do You Love, I Hope
Winnie Tate,
⭐ *Tommy Keeler*

They Say It's Wonderful (reprise)
Annie Oakley,
⭐ *Frank Butler*

There's No Business Like Show Business (reprise)
⭐ *Ensemble*

I'll Share It All With You
Winnie Tate,
⭐ *Tommy Keeler*

Lost in His Arms
Annie Oakley,
⭐ *Ensemble*

Sun in the Morning
Annie Oakley,
⭐ *Ensemble, Dancers*

Anything You Can Do
⭐ *Annie Oakley, Frank Butler*

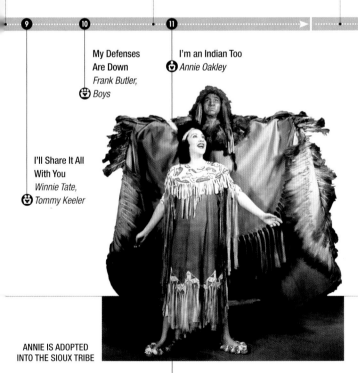

ANNIE IS ADOPTED
INTO THE SIOUX TRIBE

⭐ *Some revisions were made to the libretto and score for the 1999 revival. The changes included the removal of the song "I'm an Indian Too" and other references to Native Americans that were considered insensitive.*

IRVING BERLIN

COMPOSER 1888–1989

"The King of Tin Pan Alley" was a prolific composer, responsible for the immortal "White Christmas" and patriotic anthem "God Bless America". His songs were recorded by many of the greatest musical artists of his day.

▶ **Partial piano player**
Given his extraordinarily prolific output, it is hard to believe that Irving Berlin could not read music and could only play piano in the key of F sharp.

KEY WORKS

"Marie from Sunny Italy", 1907
"Alexander's Ragtime Band", 1911
Top Hat, 1935 (see p.31)
Follow the Fleet, 1936 (see p.38)
White Christmas, 1954
Annie Get Your Gun, 1946 (see pp.72–75)
Call Me Madam, 1950
Mr President, 1962

In 1893, when Israel Beilin was five, his parents fled persecution in Russia, settling with their eight children in New York. The family changed its name to Baline but his father, a former synagogue cantor, struggled to earn a living. When he died, young Israel left school to help support the family, becoming a singing waiter in 1906 and cowriting his first song, "Marie From Sunny Italy" the following year. The publishers misspelled his name – as Berlin – and it stayed that way.

With a new name and burgeoning career as a Tin Pan Alley lyricist, Berlin struck gold in 1911 with the song "Alexander's Ragtime Band". This became an overnight success.

MUSICALS MAESTRO

Berlin wrote both music and lyrics for many popular stage musicals, from *Watch Your Step* in 1913 to numerous revues (collections of songs) and light comedies throughout the 1920s and 30s. The 1946 smash hit *Annie Get Your Gun* starring Ethel Merman (see pp.140–41), is regarded as his best musical score. The upbeat songs "There's No Business Like Show Business" and "Anything You Can Do I Can Do Better" tapped into a huge surge of post-war optimism. *Call Me Madam*, his 1950 collaboration with Merman, was another success.

An astute businessman, Berlin founded the Irving Berlin Music Corporation as early as 1914 to retain control of his copyrights. He also built the Music Box Theatre on Broadway (with producer Sam Harris) to showcase his work. *The Music Box Revue* played there from 1921 to 1925, as did the revue *As Thousands Cheer* in 1933.

PATRIOTIC BERLIN

Berlin was profoundly grateful to America for giving him a home, and when the US entered the war in April 1917, Sergeant Berlin wrote many patriotic songs for the US army. His all-soldier musical, *Yip Yip Yaphank*, opened to huge acclaim in July 1918. The anthem "God Bless America" was

"The toughest thing about success is that you've got to keep on being a success."

IRVING BERLIN

► True patriot
Irving Berlin wrote many patriotic pieces for his adoptive country, the United States. Here, he is seen performing for the troops in 1944.

first sung in 1938 by contralto Kate Smith to mark the 20th anniversary of the Armistice and has since been recorded by many artists. Berlin described the song as "an expression of my feeling toward the country to which I owe what I have and what I am".

During World War II, Berlin's 1942 Broadway stage show *This is the Army* toured army bases around the world raising morale, while the 1943 film of the same name, featuring Ronald Reagan, was also a hit. Together, play and film earned US$10 million in royalties for the US Army.

THE BIG SCREEN

Berlin's first film success came in the 1930s, with a series of light romantic musicals starring Fred Astaire, Ginger Rogers, Alice Faye, Bing Crosby, and Judy Garland. The first was *Top Hat* in 1935 (see p.31), featuring Astaire singing the unforgettable "Cheek to Cheek". This was followed the next year by *Follow the Fleet* (see p.38) and yet another iconic song, "Let's Face the Music and Dance". Others included *Gold Diggers in Paris* (1937), *Holiday Inn* (1942) featuring "White Christmas", and the energetic romp *Easter Parade* (see p.87) in 1948.

SONGWRITING SUCCESS

Berlin wrote songs ranging from love ballads to music for dance crazes, including the bizarre "chicken walk". He aimed to compose at least one a day. "I do most of my work under pressure," he said in a 1916 interview. But it wasn't easy. He "sweated blood", as one of his daughters put it, and at times suffered from writer's block. He could not read music and only played the piano in the key of F sharp, so used a special transcribing piano and paid others to write out and harmonize his songs. Berlin eschewed clever and pompous lyrics in favour of direct and uncomplicated words that appeal to the emotions. His first love song,

"When I Lost You", expresses his overwhelming grief at the loss of his young wife Dorothy Goetz in 1912. He penned many other well-loved romantic ballads – "What'll I Do?", "Always", "Blue Skies" (for his first child in 1926), and "Say It Isn't So". The most popular of all – "White Christmas" – sung by Bing Crosby for *Holiday Inn* (and later in the 1954 picture *White Christmas*) sold 50 million copies and remains the best-selling single of all time.

BERLIN – THE MAN

Berlin knew all about hardship. Having fled persecution in Russia, he grew up in abject poverty in New York. After the death of his first wife, Dorothy, he fell in love again 13 years later with Catholic heiress Ellin Mackay. Her father cast her off in

1926 when she eloped with Berlin, although they were eventually reconciled. The couple had four children and remained happy together until Mackay's death in 1988.

BERLIN'S LEGACY

During a long and fruitful career spanning 60 years, Berlin wrote 19 Broadway shows and music for 18 Hollywood films. He received eight Academy Award nominations, winning in 1943 for "White Christmas".

The complete tally of his songs is staggering: he wrote an estimated 1,500 in total, many of which have been recorded in the decades since by some of the world's greatest singing stars. Berlin's songs reached the top of the American music charts as many as 25 times altogether.

George Gershwin called Irving Berlin "the greatest songwriter that has ever lived", crediting him with creating "a real, inherent American music". Composer Jerome Kern went one better, saying that Irving Berlin "is American music".

◄ Key breakthroughs
The original sheet music for "Alexander's Ragtime Band" and "White Christmas" – both huge hits for Berlin, written more than 30 years apart.

- **11 May 1888** Israel Beilin born in Russia to Jewish parents.

- **1893** The family moves to New York, and changes their name to Baline.

- **1906** Berlin becomes a singing waiter at the Pelham Cafe in Chinatown.

- **May 1907** Publication of "Marie From Sunny Italy". He becomes Irving Berlin.

- **18 March 1911** "Alexander's Ragtime Band" is a hit.

- **February 1912** Berlin marries Dorothy Goetz, she dies in July.

- **July 1918** Opening of *Yip Yip Yaphank* at Camp Upton's Little Liberty Theatre.

- **1921** Berlin co-builds the Music Box Theatre.

- **4 January 1926** Berlin marries Ellin Mackay.

- **1926** Berlin writes "Blue Skies".

- **29 October 1929** Berlin loses fortune in the Wall Street Crash.

- **6 September 1935** Release of *Top Hat*.

- **20 February 1936** Release of *Follow the Fleet*.

- **4 August 1942** Release of *Holiday Inn*.

- **1943** "White Christmas" wins an Academy Award for Best Song.

- **16 May 1946** Broadway opening of *Annie Get Your Gun*.

- **8 July 1948** Release of *Easter Parade*.

- **1954** Berlin receives Congressional Gold Medal for "God Bless America".

- **29 July 1988** His wife Ellin dies.

- **22 September 1989** Berlin dies in New York aged 101.

FILM POSTER, 1954

NIGHT AND DAY

{ 1946 }

A slice of Cole Porter's life as seen through rose-tinted glasses is accompanied by a treasure trove of his great music and memorable songs. The film featured some top stars.

KEY FACTS

FILM

Director Michael Curtiz

Screenplay Charles Hoffmann, Leo Townsend, William Bowers

Music Ray Heindorf (score)

Music and lyrics Cole Porter

Running time 128 minutes

Release date 3 August 1946

⊙ Key information

Highlights include a Cary Grant duet with big band singer Ginny Simms, singing a medley of Porter's songs originally introduced on Broadway by Ethel Merman.

▼ **Focus on the music**
Jane Wyman singing to Cary Grant's piano accompaniment in this tribute to Cole Porter.

The idea to make a biography of Cole Porter's life (see pp. 84–85) came from fellow composer Irving Berlin. He felt Porter's struggle to recover from a brutal leg injury sustained in a horse-riding accident was inspirational, especially for soldiers returning home and recovering from wartime injuries. Berlin called Jack Warner, head of Warner Brothers, and successfully pitched the concept. After several months of negotiation, Porter agreed to Warner's terms and received US$300,000 for the film rights to his life. The title "Night and Day" was taken from Porter's hit song in the 1930s Broadway stage show *The Gay Divorce*, starring Fred Astaire (see pp.42–43).

Night and Day purports to tell the story of Porter's life from 1910–40, beginning with his years at Yale to the height of his success. Because Porter and his wife Linda were still alive, the movie was not a warts-and-all story of his life. Michael Curtiz, of *Casablanca* and *Yankee Doodle Dandy* fame, directed, and Cary Grant and Alexis Smith were cast as the Porters. The production did not go smoothly. It cost US$4 million to mount, a significant portion of that going to writers, of whom there were several. Grant and Curtiz were said to be at odds often. Nevertheless, *Night and Day* attracted audiences and did well at the box office.

FANCIFUL BIOGRAPHY

A showcase for Porter's tunes, *Night and Day* includes two dozen songs from the nearly 1,000 he wrote over a lifetime. The film's drama centres on Porter's polo accident, which destroyed his legs. Against medical advice, Porter refused to have his leg amputated.

What the movie did not address, however, was his homosexuality and marriage of convenience. There are also some inaccuracies, such as his wartime exploits being exaggerated, and Monty Woolley was, in fact, a classmate of Porter's at Yale, not his professor.

◄ **Glamorous tribute**
Cary Grant and Alexis Smith portrayed the Porters' lives in full Hollywood style.

LAVISH PRODUCTION

The production was glamorous and lush. Choreographer LeRoy Prinz, who worked on scores of stage and film musicals, including *Anything Goes* (see p.30) and *Show Boat* (see pp.14–17), created the dance numbers, including the song and dance "Begin the Beguine", against a stylized tropical backdrop.

In one of the film's most popular numbers, Mary Martin reprises her demure striptease with a chorus dressed as Eskimos in "My Heart Belongs to Daddy", originally performed in the Broadway musical *Leave it to Me*, in 1938. Other stars include Jane Wyman as Gracie Harris, one of Porter's friends, and Eve Arden as Gabrielle, a French cabaret singer.

BIOGRAPHY

CARY GRANT (1904–86)

Although not known as a musical star, Cary Grant could sing and dance. Born Archibald Alexander Leach in Bristol, England, he began his entertainment career as a stilt walker at age 16. When he moved to the United States as Archie Leach, he performed in four Broadway musicals from 1923–31. When he left Broadway for Hollywood, he became Cary Grant the movie star, but did appear in several film musicals in the 1930s.

FINIAN'S RAINBOW

{ 1947 }

Mixing make-believe with social commentary, *Finian's Rainbow*'s light touch brought enchantment and social vision to Broadway.

KEY FACTS

🎬 STAGE

🎬 **Director** Bretaigne Windust
📖 **Book** E.Y. Harburg, Fred Saidy
🎵 **Music** Burton Lane
A♭ **Lyrics** E.Y. Harburg
🎭 **Venue** 46th Street Theatre, New York
📅 **Date** 10 January 1947

⊙ Key information

The show was produced by Lee Sabinson and William R. Katzell. It won the 1947 Tony Award for Best Featured Actor in a Musical (David Wayne), among several others.

T wo months before Lerner and Loewe's *Brigadoon* (see p.86) first bowed at the Ziegfeld Theatre in March 1947, another Celtic fantasy had debuted in January, *Finian's Rainbow*. Playwright E.Y. (Yip) Harburg wrote the original story in which a leprechaun pursues the person who stole his pot of gold. Finian McLonergan, the crook in question, has a notion that by burying his treasure near Fort Knox the gold will grow and make him a rich man. Harburg, who wrote "Brother Can You Spare a Dime?" and "April in Paris", was known for his witty lyrics and commitment to social causes. He is most remembered for his work on the 1939 movie musical with composer Harold Arlen, *The Wizard of Oz* (see pp.46–49).

ROMANCE, MAGIC, AND POLITICAL SATIRE

In *Finian's Rainbow*, Yarburg explores racial prejudice in an unlikely world of Irish sprites and crocks of gold.

Described as the most elaborate plot since *War and Peace*, the musical tells the story of Irishman McLonergan and his daughter Sharon and their pursuit of wealth. Finian, after stealing a pot of

▶ Colourful caper
This colourful artwork adorns the cover of the souvenir programme for the 1968 film adaptation of *Finian's Rainbow*.

gold from leprechaun Og, travels to the mythical town of Rainbow Valley in the state of Missitucky: destination Fort Knox. Og, of course, is in hot pursuit – if he doesn't get his gold back he will turn into a human. Into the fray arrives the corrupt and bigoted senator Billboard Rawkins, who Sharon accidentally turns black. She unknowingly made a wish near the magic crock of gold, thereby setting him on a path to redemption.

Finian's Rainbow also has several love stories: Og falls for Sharon; Sharon loves the handsome local Woody Mahoney, who is organizing black workers and sharecroppers against the racist senator; and Susan the Silent, Woody's sister, has her eye on Og. Other characters involved in the search for gold include a sheriff, a preacher, a trio of geologists, and a trio of gospel singers.

TONY AWARDS AND HIT SONGS

Enthusiasm for the musical was robust. *Finian's Rainbow* won three Tonys: David Wayne for his role as Og; Michael Kidd for choreography; and Milton Rosenstock for his role as conductor and musical director. In 1968, Fred Astaire played Finian on the screen, to mixed reviews.

Composer Burton Lane, who later wrote the music for *On a Clear Day You Can See Forever*, created a rich score with recognizable tunes, including "How Are Things in Glocca Morra?", "Ol' Devil Moon", "When I'm Not Near the Girl I Love", "If This Isn't Love", and "Look to the Rainbow". Michael Kidd, choreographing his first Broadway show, earned special praise for his clever dance sequences rooted in his belief that movement be grounded in real life.

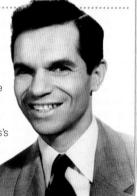

KISS ME, KATE

{ 1948 }

In Cole Porter's first and only fully integrated musical, Baltimore gangsters muscle in on a Shakespearean actor's production of *The Taming of the Shrew*. The show was so good, one critic dared say it was better than the original.

Cole Porter's shows had dominated Broadway throughout the 1930s. But by the mid-1940s, with his health failing and his wife seriously ill, not to mention the back-to-back failures of his shows *Seven Lively Arts* (1944) and *Around the World* (1946), Porter's stock was low.

SELF-DOUBT AND ENVY

Plagued by self-doubt, and envious of Irving Berlin's return to form with *Annie Get Your Gun* (see pp.72–75), he grew to realize that the musical comedy form that had made his name was dead. Thanks to the success of

Rodgers and Hammerstein's *Oklahoma!* (see pp.58–61), the integrated musical had undoubtedly conquered the genre. "Those two," said Porter, "made it much harder for everybody else: the librettos are much better, and the scores are much closer to the librettos than they used to be."

COLE PORTER'S COMEBACK

So Porter crafted an intricate show-within-a-show structure for *Kiss me, Kate*, in which every song (with the exception of the ludicrously catchy "Too Darn Hot") grows organically from the story. On earlier shows, Porter said, he would often have been working on numbers for the second act even as the players were already rehearsing for the first.

MAKESHIFT TEAM

With Porter's reputation in the doldrums, however, he couldn't rely on getting the biggest names to help out, leading to some unconventional appointments: director John C. Wilson was better known as a producer; one of the two producers, Lemuel Ayers, was actually a costume designer; and the other, Saint Subber, was actually a stage manager. The choreographer, however, was Hanya Holm, one of the most influential modern dancers of her time. As for the script, Samuel and Bella Spewack weren't musical writers but straight dramatists. That didn't stop the cynics braying that they weren't classy enough to rewrite Shakespeare, who was in any case considered musical box-office poison. What's more, Porter couldn't get his first choice for the part of Kate: Mary Martin. She was in talks with Richard Rodgers (see pp.70–71) and Oscar Hammerstein (about *South Pacific* (see p.96). So, it's little wonder that *Kiss Me, Kate* found itself opening at the New Century Theatre, not quite Off-Broadway but several blocks north of the musical epicentre of Manhattan.

◀ **Bianca and Lucentio**
Tommy Rall and Ann Miller provided a suitably romantic pairing as Bill Calhoun and Lois Lane.

▲ **Of its time**
Redolent of the aesthetic of the post-war era, this poster for the film production echoed that of the original Broadway production, as the set designs for the film echoed the predominant colours of the original stage design.

VIRTUOSITY AND WIT

Despite all these problems, Porter doesn't seem to have found the writing of the score burdensome. Between February and May 1948, he wrote an astonishing 25 songs full of melodic virtuosity and impish wit. Seventeen of the songs made the final show, many of them marked by the deliciously naughty wordplay he had long made his trademark.

Beneath the light-hearted fun, though, Porter had done some serious composing. To give the show-within-a-show Shakespearean scenes an authentic Italian Renaissance feel, he re-familiarized himself with early Italian musical forms. For example, "Tom, Dick, or Harry" is essentially an unaccompanied madrigal (a type of part song) and, following its bluesy introduction, "Why Can't You Behave?" is based on the style of a Renaissance *pavane* (a stately dance that was popular in courts throughout Europe in the 16th century). For "I Sing of Love", meanwhile, Porter used the hectic rhythm of the *tarantella* (a frenzied dance).

KEY FACTS

🎭 STAGE
- 🎬 **Director** John C. Wilson
- 📖 **Book** Samuel and Bella Spewack
- 🎵 **Music and lyrics** Cole Porter
- 🎫 **Venue** New Century Theatre, New York
- 📅 **Date** 30 December 1948

⊙ Key information
The show ran for 1,077 performances. In 1949, *Kiss Me, Kate* was nominated for, and won, five Tony Awards: Best Musical, Best Author, Best Score, Best Costumes, and Best Producer. It opened in London in 1951, where it ran for 400 performances at the London Coliseum.

RELATED SHOWS

The Boys From Syracuse, 1938, Richard Rodgers, Lorenz Hart

West Side Story, 1957, Leonard Bernstein, Stephen Sondheim (see pp.122–25)

"If there's a better musical than Kiss Me, Kate I haven't seen it."

TERRY TEACHOUT, DRAMA CRITIC, *THE WALL STREET JOURNAL*, 2009

For all its initial travails, *Kiss Me, Kate* was a triumph from the off and is considered by many to be Porter's masterpiece. Indeed, after the first night try-out in Philadelphia on 2 December, it was agreed (almost uniquely in the history of the musical) that the show needed no big changes before moving to Broadway. However, five minutes of dialogue was cut to allow for an encore of the comedy number "Brush Up Your Shakespeare".

REPEATED REVIVALS

After an initial run lasting two years in New York, the show moved to London's West End, where it ran for more than a year. *Kiss Me, Kate* has since been revived on numerous occasions (see right). The Royal Shakespeare Company also produced a popular revival in 1987 at London's Old Vic Theatre.

Every time the show has been mounted it has run for more performances than any production of *The Taming of the Shrew*. But then, as British-born American poet W.H. Auden once provocatively said, *Kiss Me, Kate* is "a wonderfully inventive show – greater than Shakespeare's."

BROADWAY REVIVAL

In 1999, Australian theatre director Michael Blakemore revived the show on Broadway – 40 years after it first opened. This production ran for 881 performances before moving to London in August 2001, where it enjoyed an impressive ten-month run. In 2000, the show was nominated for 12 Tony Awards and won five, including Best Revival of a Musical

▼ **Renaissance splendour**
Inspired by Italian Renaissance painting, the sets and costumes of the show provided a stylish backdrop to an old story with a modern twist.

STORYLINE

A theatre troupe rehearses *The Taming of the Shrew* in a Baltimore theatre. Directing (and playing Petruchio) is Fred Graham. His ex-wife, Lilli Vanessi, plays Katherine (the "Kate" from the title) opposite him. Fred is chasing after Lois Lane, playing Bianca, but Lois is in love with her co-star Bill. An inveterate gambler, Bill has just lost big-time to a gangster, and signed the IOU in Fred's name. So, when the gangster's henchmen arrive demanding money, will the curtain rise?

CAST	
Alfred Drake	Fred Graham/Petruchio
Patricia Morison	Lilli Vanessi/Katherine
Lisa Kirk	Lois Lane/Bianca
Harold Lang	Bill Calhoun/Lucentio
Charles Wood	Hortensio
Harry Clark	First Man
Jack Diamond	Second Man

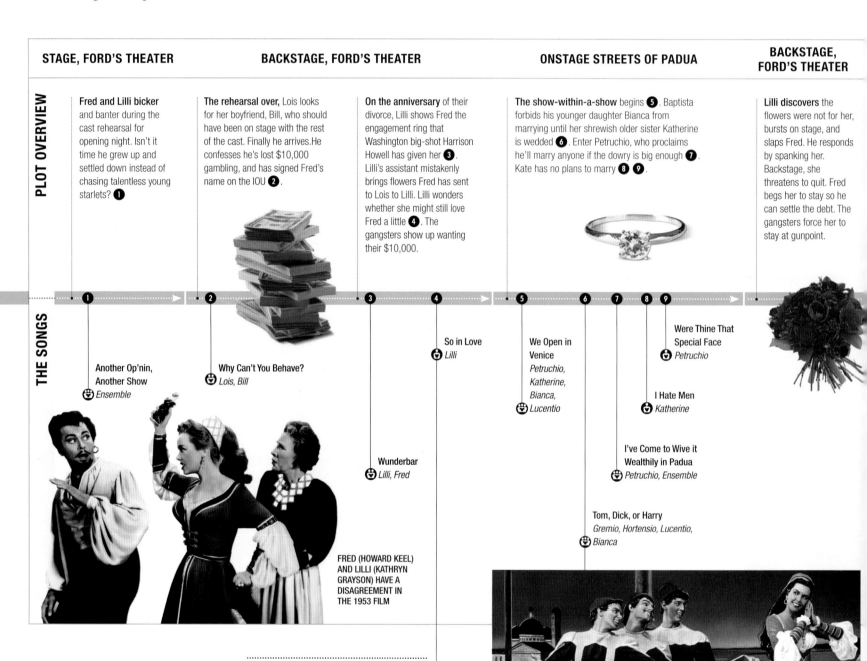

STAGE, FORD'S THEATER

BACKSTAGE, FORD'S THEATER

ONSTAGE STREETS OF PADUA

BACKSTAGE, FORD'S THEATER

PLOT OVERVIEW

Fred and Lilli bicker and banter during the cast rehearsal for opening night. Isn't it time he grew up and settled down instead of chasing talentless young starlets? ❶

The rehearsal over, Lois looks for her boyfriend, Bill, who should have been on stage with the rest of the cast. Finally he arrives. He confesses he's lost $10,000 gambling, and has signed Fred's name on the IOU ❷.

On the anniversary of their divorce, Lilli shows Fred the engagement ring that Washington big-shot Harrison Howell has given her ❸. Lilli's assistant mistakenly brings flowers Fred has sent to Lois to Lilli. Lilli wonders whether she might still love Fred a little ❹. The gangsters show up wanting their $10,000.

The show-within-a-show begins ❺. Baptista forbids his younger daughter Bianca from marrying until her shrewish older sister Katherine is wedded ❻. Enter Petruchio, who proclaims he'll marry anyone if the dowry is big enough ❼. Kate has no plans to marry ❽ ❾.

Lilli discovers the flowers were not for her, bursts on stage, and slaps Fred. He responds by spanking her. Backstage, she threatens to quit. Fred begs her to stay so he can settle the debt. The gangsters force her to stay at gunpoint.

THE SONGS

❶ ❷ ❸ ❹ ❺ ❻ ❼ ❽ ❾

Another Op'nin', Another Show
☺ *Ensemble*

Why Can't You Behave?
☺ *Lois, Bill*

Wunderbar
☺ *Lilli, Fred*

So in Love
☺ *Lilli*

We Open in Venice
Petruchio, Katherine, Bianca,
☺ *Lucentio*

Tom, Dick, or Harry
Gremio, Hortensio, Lucentio,
☺ *Bianca*

I've Come to Wive it Wealthily in Padua
☺ *Petruchio, Ensemble*

I Hate Men
☺ *Katherine*

Were Thine That Special Face
☺ *Petruchio*

FRED (HOWARD KEEL) AND LILLI (KATHRYN GRAYSON) HAVE A DISAGREEMENT IN THE 1953 FILM

A version of "So in Love" recorded ✪
by Patti Page entered the US Billboard charts in February 1949. Peggy Lee and Ella Fitzgerald also recorded the song.

TOM, DICK, AND HARRY COURT BIANCA IN THE SHOW WITHIN A SHOW

HOWARD KEEL AS FRED/
PETRUCHIO IN THE FILM

"Anyone who will rhyme Cressida and ambassador is capable of ... anything."

WOLCOTT GIBBS, CRITIC, *THE NEW YORKER,* 1949

ONSTAGE STREETS OF PADUA	STAGE DOOR, FORD'S THEATER	ONSTAGE PETRUCHIO'S HOUSE	BACKSTAGE, FORD'S THEATER		ONSTAGE
Bianca and Lucentio dance a *tarantella* to cover the scene change while the chorus performs a song **10**. The scene changes and Petruchio and Kate exit a church, newly married **11**, but under the watchful eyes of the gangsters, in costume, close by on stage.	**During the interval,** the male dancers and crew stand around outside the theatre and complain about the heat **12**.	**Unable to tame** the shrewish Kate, Petruchio laments the loss of his bachelorhood and recalls his women-chasing days **13**.	**Harrison Howell arrives** to see Lilli and bumps into his former lover, Lois, who must then reassure Bill that she loves only him **14**. Lilli tells Harrison of the gangster's plot, but he refuses to believe her and wants to talk about their wedding plans. Fred suggests theirs might not be the most passionate of marriages.	**Desperate to hold** on to his relationship with Lois, Bill sings her a love song he has written **15**. Fred tries once more to convince Lilli to stay **16**. She doesn't.	**The gangsters learn** that their boss has been killed, so the IOU is invalid. But they get caught unawares on stage in front of the audience and so improvise a song about the romance of Shakespeare **17**. It's the wedding of Bianca and Lucentio, and Katherine, who has a big speech to deliver, is notably absent. She arrives just in time **18** and, as Bianca and Lucentio ardently kiss, Lilli and Fred silently reconcile **19**.

10 ─── 11   **12**   **13**   **14**   **15 ─ 16**   **17 ─ 18 ─ 19**

Kiss Me, Kate
Katherine,
Petruchio,
😊 *Ensemble*

Where is the Life
That Late I Led?
😊 *Petruchio*

So in Love
😊 *Fred*

Finale
Petruchio, Katherine,
😊 *Company*

Too Darn Hot
😊 *Paul, Ensemble*

Always True to You
in My Fashion
😊 *Lois, Bill*

I Am Ashamed That
Women Are So Simple
😊 *Katherine*

I Sing of Love
Bianca, Lucentio,
😊 *Ensemble*

Bianca
😊 *Bill, Girls*

Brush Up Your Shakespeare
😊 *First Man, Second Man*

LILLI AND FRED HAVE ANOTHER BACKSTAGE
SPARRING MATCH IN THE FILM

⭐ *"Always True to You in My Fashion" was inspired by a line ("I have been faithful to thee, Cynara!") in London-born poet Ernest Dowson's poem "Cynara" (1894).*

COLE PORTER

Years after the death of the man hailed as the greatest popular songwriter of the 20th century, his biographers are still arguing about how he was able to put so much sincerity into his lyrics.

Even though his personal integrity was often questioned, few doubt that Cole Porter wrote straight from the heart. Nevertheless, he had a lifelong reputation for artful rhyming, name dropping, and breezy cosmopolitanism.

Among the more than 800 songs that Porter crafted, many have become standards that are still being recorded to this day, despite their references to passing fads and long-forgotten celebrities. Porter once confided to a friend: "I don't know how I did it."

Enigmatic to the end of his life, Cole Albert Porter was born in a small Indiana town to local pharmacist Sam Porter and his wife, Kate, who was the daughter of a high-powered businessman named James Omar Cole.

▼ If anyone can...
Although he suffered a serious accident halfway through his life, Cole Porter never stopped writing songs, adding spice to musicals such as *Can-Can* right up to the end of his life.

Despite initial misgivings about the unassuming Sam, J.O. Cole ensured the family enjoyed a comfortable life. Porter never had to worry about money during his career and he did not have to struggle for anything, particularly during his early life.

Yet there was no lack of effort from the young boy. From the age of six he studied first the violin and then, two years later, the piano. He abandoned the violin and devoted all his energy to the piano, regularly practising for up to two hours a day.

Often he was joined by his mother, the two performing parodies of the day's popular songs. She also made sure her boy enjoyed his share of the limelight when he performed in public. And so when Porter began to compose, she paid to have his work printed, with copies sent to family and friends.

Porter attended the exclusive Worcester Academy in Massachusetts. While there, Kate decided her son's attainments would look more

impressive if two years were removed from his age. His time at the school was to have a positive influence on his career; one of his instructors, Dr Abercrombie, told him that "words and music must be so inseparably wedded to each other that they are like one".

▶ An easy ability
Not only was Cole Porter one of the most prolific songwriters of all time, he could also play the trumpet to a good standard.

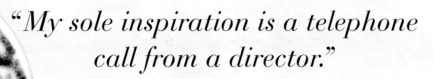

"My sole inspiration is a telephone call from a director."

COLE PORTER

At Yale, Porter wrote musical shows for college friends, turning out more than 300 songs. He subsequently attended Harvard Law School, on his grandfather's insistence, but was advised by the dean that he would be better off pursuing a musical career.

HEROIC DEEDS

Porter's first attempt for the professional musical theatre ended after only 15 performances in 1916, although it did raise his standing in New York society. A year later, Porter left for France, later claiming to have performed heroic deeds with the French Foreign Legion during World War I. The precise nature of his war-time activities remains a mystery, although it seems more likely that he was in fact enjoying Parisian social life.

It was during this time that Porter met and married a prominent socialite. The beautiful divorcee Linda Lee Thomas was 15 years his senior. She was well aware of his homosexuality yet determined to dedicate herself to her husband's career. Indeed, the couple remained together until Linda's death 35 years later.

They enjoyed a glittering social life in Paris, the French Riviera, and Venice. It was said that their home boasted platinum wallpaper and zebra-skin chairs. Porter contributed to a number of shows, including *Hitchy-Koo* (1919) and *Greenwich Village Follies* (1924). Then, an invaluable recommendation from Irving Berlin brought him to the notice of the producers of *Paris*, enabling him to win recognition as a songwriter for the stage.

Between 1929 and 1935, successive Broadway shows ensured Porter enjoyed success after success. But in 1937, he was out riding in Long Island when his horse slipped and fell on top of him. He was gravely injured. The doctors wanted to amputate one, and possibly both, of his legs. Kate and Linda refused to allow it but Porter would have to endure more than 30 operations over the next 20 years, such was the damage caused by the accident.

CROWNING ACHIEVEMENT

Porter refused to give in to his misfortune and soon afterwards was scoring another Broadway musical, *Leave it to Me!* (1938), now best remembered for Broadway newcomer Mary Martin performing a mock striptease while singing "My Heart Belongs to Daddy". He maintained his prodigious work rate and

▲ **Man about town**
Porter was happily married to Linda Lee Thomas for more than 35 years. The pair lived in great style and moved in elevated social circles.

Kiss Me, Kate (see pp.80–83) is now considered to be his crowning achievement in musicals.

Writing songs for films occupied Porter's later years, and there were more triumphs with *Silk Stockings* (see p.115), *High Society* (1956), and *Les Girls* (1957). His health, however, was deteriorating. His right leg was amputated in 1958 and, following the death of his mother and his wife, Porter, the one-time socialite, became a recluse who shunned his own 70th birthday party.

Cole Porter's legacy was a galaxy of songs characterized by wit and sophistication laced with more than a touch of melancholy.

KEY WORKS

"What is This Thing Called Love?", 1928

"You Do Something to Me", 1929

"Night and Day", 1932

"Just One of Those Things", 1935

"I've Got You Under My Skin", 1936

"You'd be so Nice to Come Home to", 1942

"Ev'ry Time We Say Goodbye", 1944

"True Love/Who Wants to be a Millionaire?", 1955

TIMELINE

9 June 1891 Cole Albert Porter is born in Peru, Indiana, to Sam Porter and Kate née Cole.

1913 Graduates from Yale, where classmates vote him the most entertaining member.

1916 First musical *See America First* flops.

1928 Broadway musical *Paris* brings Porter his first major success with five songs, including "Let's Do It (Let's Fall in Love)".

1930 *The New Yorkers* attains instant notoriety, with a song about a streetwalker ("Love for Sale").

THEATRE PROGRAMME, 1930

1932 *Gay Divorce* (1932), starring Fred Astaire, runs for 248 performances and includes numbers like "Night and Day" and "After You Who?".

1934 With a host of stars, *Anything Goes* features memorable numbers like "Anything Goes", "I Get a Kick out of You", and "You're the Top".

1935 *Jubilee* features Porter's biggest hit yet, "Begin the Beguine".

1937 A horse-riding accident causes nervous system damage and ensures Porter will spend the rest of his life enduring numerous operations and constant pain.

1946 Cary Grant plays Cole Porter in a biopic, most of which is fictitious.

1948 *Kiss Me, Kate* scored by Porter opens on Broadway and will run for a remarkable 1,077 performances.

1955 Cole Porter's songs add polish to the film *High Society*, starring Frank Sinatra, Bing Crosby, and Grace Kelly.

15 October 1964 Cole Porter dies in Santa Monica, California, aged 73.

BRIGADOON

{ 1947 }

Celebrated songwriting team Lerner and Loewe score their first hit, inspired by Rodgers and Hammerstein's rural settings and featuring choreography by Agnes de Mille.

P rior to *Brigadoon*, songwriting duo Alan Jay Lerner and Frederick Loewe had enjoyed only modest success with a short-lived Off-Broadway run of their aviator musical *What's Up*, and 167 performances of *The Day Before Spring*, about a high school reunion.

Taking their inspiration from the rural idyll in the Rodgers and Hammerstein's hits *Oklahoma!* and *Carousel*, their next project, *Brigadoon* – possibly named after the popular Scottish tourist attraction Brig O'Doon in Ayrshire –

▼ **Highland scene**
Gene Kelly and Cyd Charisse perform "The Heather on the Hill", a dance number, in the 1947 film, directed by Vincente Minnelli.

repeated the formula with a piece that evoked the country charms of Scotland, its myths and ancient traditions.

The story concerns two male New Yorkers who stumble upon a mythical highland village, which, thanks to a spell, only appears once every 100 years. The men become embroiled in a number of romantic and comic incidents, before one of them falls in love with a local girl, returning later from America to be reunited with her for all time.

ROMANCE AND HIT SONGS
The show's humour comes from the culture clash of city types adapting to a simpler rustic way of living, while its charm comes from a romanticized view of Scottish life. Many of the songs are

achingly beautiful and represent the first mature writing of the team who would go on to have such success with shows such as *My Fair Lady* (see pp.120–21) and *Gigi* (see p.132) on Broadway and in Hollywood. The musical number "The Heather on the Hill" has become a much loved stand-alone song.

BROADWAY SUCCESS
The 1947 Broadway premiere was notable for the choreography of Agnes de Mille (see p.69). For *Brigadoon*, she wove authentic traditional Scottish dances into the choreography, in much the same way she had worked rough and tumble American folk dancing into some of the routines in *Oklahoma!* (see pp.58–61).

Brigadoon also won praise from the critics for the way song and dance was often, although not always, integrated into the dialogue and plotting. This was still a relatively novel idea in the 1940s, but a technique that went on to become the norm in modern musical theatre.

KEY FACTS

STAGE
- **Director** Robert Lewis
- **Book** Alan Jay Lerner
- **Music** Frederick Loewe
- **Lyrics** Alan Jay Lerner
- **Venue** Ziegfeld Theatre, New York
- **Date** 13 March 1947

⊙ **Key information**
The Broadway run of the musical was 581 performances. In 1949, the show opened in London at Her Majesty's Theatre and ran for 685 performances.

EASTER PARADE

{ 1948 }

Irving Berlin's glorious Oscar-winning score gilds Astaire and Garland's most lucrative outing together in cinema. This was a firm favourite with both audiences and critics.

This 1948 film could have been a disaster. The director and two of its stars had to be replaced prior to filming, the plot is flimsy and absurd, and the age difference between its protagonists is almost unbelievably large. Yet, somehow, *Easter Parade* embraced all its problems to become one of the most successful movie musicals of all time.

CAST AND CREW CHAOS
The original plan was that Judy Garland would play opposite Gene Kelly, battling Cyd Charisse for his affections, directed by her husband, Vincent Minnelli. However, just before filming got underway, Kelly broke his ankle playing volleyball, Charisse became unavailable, and Minnelli was replaced, some people claim on the advice of Garland's psychiatrist. Instead, Fred Astaire (see pp.42–43) was coaxed out of one of his many attempts at retirement to be the leading man, new MGM signing Ann Miller was recruited to play his former partner, and choreographer Charles Walters was put in charge of direction.

MUSICAL MASTERPIECES
One thing that remained constant throughout – along with Garland in the

▶ Ragged chic
Fred Astaire and Judy Garland, high-stepping their way to a big box-office success.

female lead – was a set of extraordinary songs and musical numbers by Irving Berlin (see pp.76–77). The songwriter was at the height of his powers and a great number of the film's songs are still well-loved classics.

The story, written by Broadway and Hollywood veterans Frances Goodrich and Albert Hackett and revised by Sidney Sheldon, concerns an ambitious song and dance man (Astaire) whose dance partner (Ann Miller) replaces him professionally and romantically. In a rash moment, he picks out a chorus girl (Garland) to train up as his new partner. The film entangles the three in a series of romantic misunderstandings involving his best friend (Peter Lawford) and professional false starts on their way to true love and success.

Despite the film's 1911 setting, the show-business backdrop allowed Berlin the opportunity to pen a series

▲ Cinematic triumph
The film won the 1948 Academy Award for Best Original Score and the Writers Guild of America Award for Best Written American Musical.

> *"It only happens when I dance with you."*
>
> **DON HEWES**, *EASTER PARADE* (SIDNEY SHELDON AND IRVING BERLIN), 1948

of song and dance numbers that reflected popular songs of the day and recent past, and others that have become synonymous with traditional Easter celebrations in the US. Highlights include the vaudeville number, "I Love a Piano", the mainstay of many a cabaret act ever since, and the uplifting and infectiously catchy "Shakin' the Blues Away". "Steppin' Out with My Baby" is another favourite, as is the haunting ballad "Better Luck Next Time". "A Couple of Swells" saw Astaire and Garland dressed as tramps in a stage routine that has become iconic. The eponymous

"Easter Parade", a song written by Irving Berlin in 1933, had been a huge hit for American actor and singer Bing Crosby.

There have been a number of attempts over the years at turning *Easter Parade* into a stage show, but none have so far been successful.

KEY FACTS

FILM

- **Director** Charles Walters
- **Screenplay** Sidney Sheldon
- **Music** Roger Edens (Score)
- **Music and lyrics** Irving Berlin
- **Running time** 108 minutes
- **Release date** 30 June 1948

⊙ **Key information**
This film was Fred Astaire and Judy Garland's biggest ever earner at the box office. It won the 1948 Academy Award for Best Original Score.

GUYS AND DOLLS

{ 1950 }

Lauded by the choreographer Bob Fosse as "the greatest American musical of all time", this is among the most beloved of its genre. Thanks to its vivid characters, idiosyncratic but memorable dialogue, and perennially appealing Frank Loesser score, the show is revived again and again.

KEY FACTS

STAGE

Director George S. Kaufman
Book Jo Swerling and Abe Burrows
Music and lyrics Frank Loesser
Venue 46th Street Theatre, New York
Date 24 November 1950

Key information
Guys and Dolls won the Best Musical and Best Book Tony Awards in 1951 and ran for 1,200 shows on Broadway over three years. It was selected for the 1951 Pulitzer Prize for Drama.

◄ Song score
The song "A Bushel and a Peck", sung in the original stage show by Vivian Blaine as Miss Adelaide, was omitted from the 1955 film.

Kansas-born newspaperman, Damon Runyan (1880–1940), who was also a baseball reporter, gambler, and associate of mobsters, wrote several short stories in the 1930s. The tales are peopled by hustlers, gangsters, actors, gamblers, and the women in their lives. They speak in a dainty argot combining historic present-tense formality and invented street slang, later dubbed "Runyonese".

NOT A WASTED NOTE OR WORD

Cy Feuer, a former Hollywood composer on the verge of becoming a major theatre producer, was excited by the idea of a musical set in Runyon's world. To adapt Runyon's stories, Feuer and fellow producer Ernest Martin hired the tough-talking composer and lyricist Frank Loesser (see pp.92–93), with whom they were enjoying success on Broadway in 1948

with the musical *Where's Charley?*, and the established Hollywood scriptwriter Jo Swerling.

Using Swerling's early draft as a structure, Loesser quickly produced 14 songs of unusual range and richness. From the ingenious three-way horseplay counterpoint of "Fugue for Tinhorns" through the tone-poem quality of "My Time of Day" and romantic lyricism of "I've Never Been In Love Before" to the dazzling, show-stopping vitality of "Sit Down, You're Rocking the Boat", there was not a wasted note or word. The composer's work was so well received that when radio comedy writer and script doctor Abe Burrows was hired to continue work on the script, he simply followed the flow of Loesser's songs. This procedure resulted in a score that was acclaimed for its refined "integration" with the storyline.

DRAMA BACKSTAGE

In rehearsal, however, Loesser's perfectionism and explosive temper got the better of him on at least

Movie leads ►
Established stars took the four main roles in the 1955 film: Marlon Brando (Sky Masterson), Jean Simmons (Sarah Brown), Frank Sinatra (Nathan Detroit), and Vivian Blaine (Miss Adelaide).

two legendary occasions. Once, frustrated by the slow progress rehearsing "The Oldest Established", he stormed on to the stage to complain about the quality of the singing. When Burrows mediated, Loesser told him to shut up. "You're Hitler," he barked at the unfortunate writer, "I'm the author. You're working for me."

A worse fate befell American actress Isabel Bigley who, like many Sarah Browns to follow her, was struggling to negotiate the large interval between two notes in her song "I'll Know". Loesser's startling and, in 21st-century terms, unacceptable method of "encouragement" was to slap her across the face. He later tried to mollify her with the gift of a bracelet.

RAVE RECEPTION

The show opened in 1950 to rave reviews for all aspects of the production, though Loesser's score was often singled out as *Guys and Dolls'* crowning glory. *The Daily News* observed that the songs were "so right for the show and so completely lacking in banality, that they amount to an artistic triumph", while *The New York Times* praised the show as "a work of art. It is spontaneous and has form, style, and spirit."

FROM STAGE TO SCREEN AND BEYOND

Vivien Blaine (see p.90), the skilled comedy actress for whom the character of Miss Adelaide was created, took her star performance to London's West End in 1953. Along with several original supporting cast members, Blaine also appeared in the 1955 Hollywood movie as did the original choreographer (Michael Kidd).

Though Frank Sinatra (see p.55) was on a powerful career upswing, he couldn't persuade film producer Sam Goldwyn to cast him as charismatic gambler Sky Masterson. That part went to non-singer Marlon Brando, then the biggest movie star in Hollywood, while Sinatra played Nathan Detroit. Established Hollywood stars Betty Grable, Grace Kelly, and Deborah Kerr were all approached to play Salvation Army girl Sarah Brown, a part that eventually went to British film actress Jean Simmons.

Unusually, all the leading actors sang their own roles, and, though adjusted a little, the movie succeeds thanks to the faithful transfer of the show's style, Loesser's score, and the charismatic star performances.

Much of the original show has survived the numerous successful revivals down the years. While London's National Theatre productions of 1982 and 1996 and the Broadway production of 1992 jazzed up the orchestrations and extended some numbers with new music, the essence and much of the atmospheric detail of Loesser's "Runyonland" remains intact in most incarnations of *Guys and Dolls*.

"I'm so happy that I couldn't get Grace Kelly."

SAM GOLDWYN, AFTER VIEWING THE RUSHES OF JEAN SIMMONS, 1950

▼ **Unlikely pairing**
The "goody-goody" screen persona of Jean Simmons contrasted perfectly with the shady underworld character of Marlon Brando's role.

STORYLINE

In 1930s New York, con man and gambler Nathan Detroit has to find a new home for his illegal craps (dice) game. But he doesn't have enough money. To solve this problem he bets Sky Masterson, a high-stakes gambler, that he won't succeed in taking a "doll" chosen by Nathan on a date to Havana, Cuba. Sky agrees to the bet and Nathan chooses Sarah Brown of Broadway's Save-a-Soul Mission. While persuading Sarah to make the trip, Sky falls in love with her.

BIOGRAPHY

VIVIAN BLAINE (1921–95)

Born in Newark, New Jersey, Blaine sang in 1930s dance bands and appeared in several 1940s movies, including Rodgers and Hammerstein's *State Fair* (1945). Her legendary turn as Adelaide in *Guys and Dolls* was her Broadway debut. She later starred in *Say, Darling* (1958), and *Zorba* (1968), and toured in *Gypsy* (1960) and *Company* (1971–73).

IN AND AROUND BROADWAY, NEW YORK

A NIGHTCLUB, HAVANA, CUBA

PLOT OVERVIEW

Gamblers, gangsters, and hustlers wordlessly flurry around the streets in a hive of activity ❶. Three hopeful gamblers discuss the odds on their chosen racehorses ❷. The Save-A-Soul Mission band arrives led by the devout and virtuous Sarah Brown who calls for sinners to repent ❸. She is ignored.

Gambler Nathan Detroit and his cronies discuss the problems of finding a venue for his long-running, floating craps game ❹. To raise a deposit, he bets fellow gambler Sky Masterson that Sky won't be able to persuade a "doll" of Nathan's nomination to go to Havana. Sky accepts and Nathan nominates Sarah Brown.

Sky promises to deliver 12 sinners to the mission if Sarah agrees to accompany him to Havana. Sarah sings of falling for a man with "strong moral fibre". Sky, by contrast, sings of wishing to be surprised by romance ❺.

Miss Adelaide sings a gauche and amusing number at the Hot Box Club ❻. Disappointed by Nathan's continuing unwillingness to marry her, she sings of her perpetual cold symptoms ❼. Nicely and Benny watch Sky and Nathan ingratiating themselves with their respective girls and observe that men in love behave in strange ways ❽.

When threatened with the mission's closure, Sarah succumbs to Sky's Havana scheme. She innocently drinks several rum-laden milkshakes and dances with Sky ❾. Tipsy but happy, Sarah declares her desire to stay with Sky in Havana ❿. Sky, in a rush of conscience, insists they return to New York.

THE SONGS

❶ ❷ ❸ ❹ ❺ ❻ ❼ ❽ ❾ ❿

Runyanland
Orchestra,
😊 *Company*

Follow the Fold
Sarah, Mission
😊 *Band*

I'll Know
😊 *Sarah, Sky*

Fugue for Tinhorns
Nicely, Benny,
😊 *Rusty*

The Oldest Established
Nathan, Nicely, Benny,
😊 *Guys*

A Bushel and a Peck
Miss Adelaide,
😊 *Hot Box Girls*

Adelaide's Lament
😊 *Miss Adelaide*

Guys and Dolls
😊 *Nicely, Benny*

Havana
😊 *Orchestra*

If I Were a Bell
😊 *Sarah*

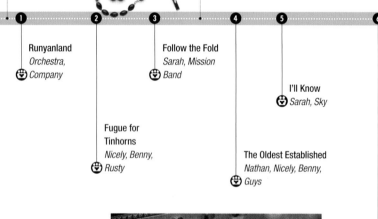

SKY (ROBERT ALDA) AND SARAH (ISABEL BIGLEY)

SARAH AND SKY DRINK RUM-LADEN MILKSHAKES IN CUBA

⭐ *Considered one of the great comic musical theatre songs of all time, "Adelaide's Lament" was conceived to exploit the particular gifts of actress Vivian Blaine and became a reliable showstopper.*

"A work of easy and delightful humor."

ROBERT COLEMAN, CRITIC, *NEW YORK DAILY MIRROR*, 1950

MARLON BRANDO AS SKY ON
SET WITH SOME "DOLLS"

IN AND AROUND BROADWAY, NEW YORK

Back outside the mission at 4am, Sky tells Sarah he's never wanted to share his favourite time of day with anyone else before. They sing of their feelings for each other **11**. A siren sounds and the gamblers from Nathan's craps game flee the mission. Convinced now that she's been duped, Sarah rejects Sky. Miss Adelaide performs another number at the Hot Box club **12**.

Nathan has promised to elope with Miss Adelaide that evening, but he doesn't show up and Adelaide is left to dwell further upon her symptoms **13**.

Sarah's uncle, a member of the mission, sings of his desire to see his niece find her true love **14**. He suspects it might be Sky Masterson. Sky, for his part, reaffirms his promise to deliver 12 sinners to the mission.

A SEWER, NEW YORK

In the sewer, the new location of the floating craps game, the gamblers dance a ballet **15**. Sky challenges the assembly to gamble with their souls; if he loses, everyone gets $1,000. If he wins, everyone attends the Save-A-Soul mission. He sings to Lady Luck to not "blow on some other guy's dice" **16**.

IN AND AROUND BROADWAY, NEW YORK

Sky having won his bet, Nathan meets Miss Adelaide and explains he must attend the mission. She assumes he's lying again. In the face of Adelaide's accusatory distress, Nathan shrugs off his shortcomings and assures her he loves her **17**. An insincere show of remorse from Nicely turns into a zealous prayer meeting **18**.

Nathan admits to Sarah that Sky's Havana trip was for a bet he devised. Sarah accepts that Sky cares for her. Sarah and Miss Adelaide commiserate with each other about their respective love lives, and resolve to gamble with commitment to their men, leaving any needed reforms for the future **19**. The newly married Sky plays in the mission band while Nathan, who has developed flu-like symptoms, accepts his fate **20**.

11

My Time of Day/I've Never Been in Love Before
☺ *Sky, Sarah*

12

Take Back Your Mink
Miss Adelaide,
☺ *Hot Box Girls*

13

Adelaide's Second Lament
Miss
☺ *Adelaide*

14

More I Cannot Wish You
☺ *Arvide*

15

Crapshooters Ballet
☺ *Orchestra*

16

Luck Be a Lady
☺ *Sky, Guys*

17

Sue Me
Miss Adelaide,
☺ *Nathan*

18

Sit Down, You're Rockin' the Boat
☺ *Nicely, Company*

19

Marry the Man Today
☺ *Miss Adelaide, Sarah*

20

Guys and Dolls (reprise)
☺ *Company*

✪ *Don Henley, ex-lead singer of The Eagles, recorded "Sit Down, You're Rockin' the Boat" for the soundtrack of the 1992 film* Leap of Faith.

SKY AND NATHAN PLAY CRAPS IN A NEW YORK SEWER

CAST

Robert Alda Sky Masterson	**Pat Rooney** Arvide Abernathy
Sam Levene Nathan Detroit	**B.S. Pully** Big Jule
Isabel Bigley Sarah Brown	**Tom Pedi** Harry the Horse
Vivian Blaine Miss Adelaide	**Johnny Silver** Benny
Stubby Kaye Nicely-Nicely Johnson	Southstreet

FRANK LOESSER

The multi-talented, award-winning American lyricist and composer Frank Loesser gave us such memorable Broadway hits as *Guys and Dolls* and *How To Succeed In Business Without Really Trying*, as well as 700 songs.

▲ **Popular songs by the dozen**
Frank Loesser's was a songwriting talent well suited to his era. His wartime ditties were huge favourites of the time.

Given his family background, it is no surprise that Frank Loesser was musically gifted. He was born in New York City on 29 June 1910 to German immigrants Henry and Julia Loesser. Henry played and taught piano while his son Arthur (Frank's older step-bother) became a renowned concert pianist. Although he was never formally taught, as a boy Frank Loesser had a remarkable musical ear – he wrote his first song at the age of six, and he also managed to teach himself the piano and harmonica. However, he rejected his family's high-brow, classical tastes in favour of popular music.

EARLY STRUGGLES

His father died suddenly in 1926, and 16-year-old Loesser took various jobs to support the family – newspaper advertisement seller, cartoonist, and editor and writer of sketches and radio scripts. However, his first love remained music, and in 1931 he wrote the lyrics for his first published song, "In Love with the Memory of You".

Workaholic Loesser, who survived on just a few hours' sleep a night, also sang and played the piano at New York nightspot The Back Drop. It was there that he met his first wife, singer Lynn Garland, whom he married in 1936. The newly-weds moved to Hollywood, Loesser having signed a contract with Universal Studios.

FRUITFUL YEARS

Over the next few years Loesser wrote with the good and great – Hoagy Carmichael, Burton Lane, and Alfred Newman, with whom he had his first Hollywood hit, "Moon of Manakoora" for Dorothy Lamour in Paramount Pictures' *The Hurricane* (1937). Two years later, Loesser and Friedrich Hollaender had a runaway success with the spirited "See What the Boys in the Back Room Will Have" for Marlene Dietrich in the film *Destry Rides Again*. During World War II, Loesser wrote morale-boosting songs

◀ **A rare combination of talents**
Not many key players in Broadway history have been able both to write lyrics and compose music with the skill and prolificity of Frank Loesser.

KEY WORKS

Destry Rides Again, 1939

Sweater Girl, 1942

Where's Charley?, 1948

Neptune's Daughter, 1949

"Baby, It's Cold Outside", 1949

Guys & Dolls, 1950 (see pp.88–89)

How to Succeed in Business Without Really Trying, 1961 (see p.148)

"I Believe In You", 1961

and worked on recruitment shows in the US Army's Radio Productions Unit. At this time he started composing music as well as lyrics for popular hits including "Praise the Lord and Pass the Ammunition" (1942) and "The Ballad of Rodger Young" (1943). He also wrote "They're Either Too Young or Too Old", sung by Bette Davis in the star-studded 1943 film fundraiser, *Thank Your Lucky Stars*.

AWARD-WINNING MUSICALS
During the late 1940s, the versatile composer embarked upon the most creative and critically acclaimed period of his career. In 1949 he won an Academy Award for Best Original

works in theatre management, and Susan, author of *A Most Remarkable Fella: Frank Loesser and the Guys and Dolls in His Life: A Portrait by His Daughter*.

Loesser's second wife, Jo Sullivan, whom he married in 1959, starred in his 1956 musical, *The Most Happy Fella*. Sullivan left the stage for several years to care for the couple's two daughters, Emily, now an award-winning musical star, and Hannah, a

talented artist who sadly died in 2007. A life-long chain smoker, Loesser died of lung cancer on 28 July 1969 in New York City, aged just 59.

◀ **Top guys**
Frank Loesser and Marlon Brando hard at work in the rehearsal studio, while preparing for the movie release of *Guys and Dolls* in 1955.

Many of Loesser's musical shows are regularly revived, and a lot of his songs are regarded as classics of the genre. During his life he contributed to more than 50 films, and his songs remain popular choices for modern movies. "Luck be a Lady" in *Payback* (1999); "I've Never been in Love Before" in *The Love Letter* (1999); "Guys and Dolls" in *Artificial Intelligence* (2001); and "Baby, It's Cold Outside" – performed by Will Ferrell and Zooey Deschanel in *Elf* (2003) – are but a few.

> ## "Remember, a song is like a freight train moving across a stage."
>
> FRANK LOESSER

Song for "Baby, It's Cold Outside", written five years earlier and included in the film *Neptune's Daughter*. He also provided the music and lyrics for several phenomenally successful musicals, including *Where's Charley?*, a 1948 arrangement of the drawing-room farce *Charley's Aunt*, followed in 1950 by *Guys and Dolls* (see pp.88–89). The latter won Loesser two Tony Awards. Other hit musicals followed, including *Greenwillow* (1960) and the sensational *How to Succeed in Business Without Really Trying* (see p.148), which won the 1962 Pulitzer Prize for Drama, and, finally, *Pleasures and Palaces* in 1965.

FAMILY LIFE
Loesser's marriage to singer Lynn Garland lasted for 21 years, but eventually ended in divorce in 1957. They had two children – John, who

THE LOESSER LEGACY
Frank Loesser is widely regarded as one of the most prolific and talented composers and lyricists of his generation. Like Cole Porter (see pp.84–85) and Irving Berlin (see pp.76–77), he was one of the few who could both write lyrics and compose successfully and was described by many as supremely confident in his own talents.

Loesser was a self-taught but nonetheless instinctive musician who could utilize clever musical devices and employ classical musical forms when required. His versatility was such that he could create a drawing room farce (*Where's Charley?*) followed by convincing and engaging music and lyrics about subjects as disparate as big business (*How to Succeed in Business Without Really Trying*) and Catherine The Great of Russia (*Pleasures and Palaces*).

▲ **Relaxed genius**
Frank Loesser lights a cigarette while supervising rehearsals of his musical *The Most Happy Fella* at the Coliseum Theatre, New York, 1960.

TIMELINE

● **29 June 1910** Frank Loesser is born in New York.

● **1925** Loesser leaves City College of New York.

● **1931** "In Love with the Memory of You" published.

● **1934** First hit song, "I Wish I Were Twins", published.

● **1935** Loesser starts performing at The Back Drop nightclub.

● **19 October 1936** Loesser marries Lynn Garland and then moves to Los Angeles.

● **29 December 1939** First film that Loesser works on, *Destry Rides Again*, released.

● **13 July 1942** Release of *Sweater Girl* with "I Don't Want to Walk Without You".

● **1942** Publication of "Praise the Lord and Pass the Ammunition".

LOESSER SONG SHEET

● **1944** Daughter Susan born.

● **1949** Loesser wins Academy Award for "Baby, It's Cold Outside".

● **1950** Son John born.

● **24 November 1950** *Guys and Dolls* opens.

● **25 November 1952** Film *Hans Christian Andersen* released.

● **3 May 1956** *The Most Happy Fella* opens.

● **1957** Loesser and Lynn divorce.

● **29 April 1959** Loesser marries Jo Sullivan.

● **8 March 1960** *Greenwillow* opens.

● **14 October 1961** *How to Succeed in Business Without Really Trying* opens.

● **1962** Loesser wins Pulitzer Prize for Drama.

● **22 October 1962** Daughter Hannah born.

● **2 June 1965** Daughter Emily born.

● **28 July 1969** Loesser dies.

BROADWAY'S BRIGHT LIGHTS

Musicals have roots in Greek and Roman theatre, European operetta, and Gilbert and Sullivan – but the heart of the modern musical has always been Broadway.

The Broadway district in New York is the heart of the "city that never sleeps", and Times Square is the heart of the theatre district. Sometimes called "The Crossroads of the World", Times Square is where Broadway intersects 7th Avenue, from 42nd Street to 47th Street. *The Huffington Post* rates the square as the second most visited tourist attraction in the world, with just under 40 million people a year going to see the display of lighted billboards, the TKTS tickets booth where they queue up for discounted tickets to that day's performances, and the 40 Broadway theatres, many of them presenting musicals.

Broadway refers to an area, but a Broadway show is further defined as being produced in a theatre with 500 or more seats.

CENTRE OF THEATRELAND

When the first playhouses were established in New York they were located in the southern end of Manhattan, slowly migrating north as the city expanded. By 1883, Broadway had moved as far north as 39th Street. The theatres in Broadway's current location, between 42nd and 47th Street, were built during the 1920s.

Within easy reach of the Broadway theatres is an entire infrastructure, everything needed to mount all the Broadway musicals – design studios that build sets, costume shops that create costumes, lighting and sound equipment companies, musical instrument rentals, producers' offices, offices for Actors' Equity (the actors' union), IATSE (the stagehands' union), AFM-local 802 (the musicians' union), the Dramatists' Guild, and much more. There is a synergistic effect of having everything needed for production so accessible – it creates the opportunity for production. Nothing grows in a vacuum, including Broadway musicals, which grow in this thriving community.

Theatre companies produce musicals around the globe, with tours replicating original productions regularly crisscross the US, Europe, Asia, and Australia. And yet people travel around the world to see a musical on Broadway. In 2014, US$1.36 billion worth of tickets were sold to Broadway shows.

▶ **The heart of Broadway**
The brightly lit billboards on Times Square advertise a multitude of musicals on show in New York's theatre district.

> *"It wasn't until Broadway came along that I felt I had really made it."*
>
> **JULIE ANDREWS,** BRITISH ACTRESS, 2001

SOUTH PACIFIC

{ 1949 }

No understanding of musical theatre is complete without an appreciation of Rodgers, Hammerstein, and Logan's achievements with *South Pacific*.

This much-loved musical has become such a staple of community theatre and amateur productions that it is easy to forget what an extraordinary and innovative work it originally was when it first appeared back in 1949.

Songwriting team Richard Rodgers and Oscar Hammerstein (see pp.70–71) were searching for new source material for a musical when the director Joshua Logan recommended a popular series of short stories by the American author James Michener, set during World War II in the southern Pacific.

CONTENTIOUS SUBJECT MATTER

The war was fresh in everyone's mind, and yet it was audacious at the time to consider it a subject suitable for song and dance. The realism of Michener's fearless depiction of heroism, discrimination, illegality, insubordination, illicit sex, and death in battle did not initially appear to be suitable fare for a Broadway musical. This was despite the fact that legendary forerunners such as *Show Boat* (see pp.14–17) had dealt with subjects as radical as racism, inter-marriage, and alcoholism as long ago as 1927. In the late 1940s, the United States was also in a state of flux regarding racism, with the Southern states still racially segregated. Could a musical tackle such weighty subjects satisfactorily and turn them into a form of entertainment?

Undaunted, the team threw themselves into development of the piece. It was clear right away that a whole new musical theatre language would need to be conceived to do the subject matter justice.

This was one of the first musicals to tackle controversial subjects for a mainstream audience, and certainly the first to do away with a chorus (everyone on stage is a named character). It was also the first show to overlap staging, so that one scene runs seamlessly into another, and the first show to generate such an extraordinary pre-opening buzz that box offices had to shut down.

FUNNY, MOVING, AND POIGNANT

Theatrically, thematically, and musically, *South Pacific* was an innovation in almost every area of composition, staging, and production. If that were not enough, it also manages to be funny, moving, and poignant to this day, with a raft of exceptional songs that have transcended even classic status to become part of the musical zeitgeist of the 20th century. The plot entwines a number of stories and characters by Michener and concerns an unworldly young female nurse stationed in the South Pacific. She falls in love with an older man, a French plantation owner, and is forced to confront her prejudices concerning the his mixed-race children from a previous relationship. The secondary love story, involving a dashing young American soldier who falls in love with an island girl – despite the prejudices of his dubious contemporaries – marked the first time that a sub-plot romance was not treated comically in musical theatre story structure. Significant comedy in the musical, however, is provided by two unscrupulous traders, one a US marine, the other a ruthless local woman, who are both engaged in a battle of wits to make as much money as possible from the conflict.

AWARDS AND RECORDING SUCCESS

Almost every song in the score of *South Pacific* is a classic, including great comedy and character numbers – "There is Nothing Like a Dame", "Happy Talk" – and some of the most romantic love songs ever written ("Some Enchanted Evening", "I'm in Love with a Wonderful Guy"). There are also achingly poignant anthems of yearning and injustice, such as "You've Got to Be Carefully Taught".

The show has seen regular revivals, and casts over the years featured many theatre greats. *South Pacific*'s huge theatrical success was also matched by its success on screen and on record.

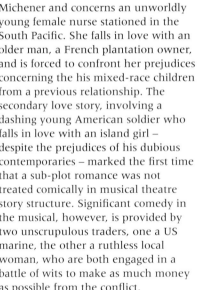

◀ **Conflict of emotions**
Mary Martin in the original show, famously "washing that man right out of her hair", as she decides she is over the idea of falling in love with an older Frenchman.

▲ **Exotic settings, ground-breaking drama**
Enticing publicity for the original UK production. The musical's idyllic setting was counterpointed by series of distinctly controversial themes.

KEY FACTS

🎭 **STAGE**

🎬 **Director** Joshua Logan
📖 **Book** Oscar Hammerstein II, Joshua Logan
🎵 **Music** Richard Rodgers
🎼 **Lyrics** Oscar Hammerstein II
🎭 **Venue** Majestic Theatre, New York
📅 **Date** 7 April 1949

⊙ **Key information**
The original show was performed a total of 1,925 times. It won ten Tony Awards, and in 1950 won the Pulitzer Prize for Drama.

PAINT YOUR WAGON

{ 1951 }

Set in Gold Rush-era California, this gritty musical marked a departure from the usual glamour of musical theatre and was only a modest success for creators Lerner and Loewe.

Their early work on *Paint Your Wagon*, with its grim pioneer setting, seems far removed from the glamour of Lerner and Loewe's later works, including *My Fair Lady* (see pp.120–21), *Camelot* (see p.144), and *Gigi* (see p.132). Despite this, it was a modest hit on Broadway in 1951, in London's West End in 1953, and on film in 1969, even though public taste and younger audiences were turning away from movie musicals.

Perhaps its lack of traditional musical theatre gloss and stars, replaced by a grittier cast and setting, helped it survive against the tide. The film's star, Lee Marvin, even had a chart hit with the song "Wanderin' Star", despite his inability to sing. He simply growls his way through it in a way described by

the wider social picture with more intimate musical soliloquies.

The story is set in 1853 in an isolated, bleak Gold Rush settlement in California, where women are scarce, and introduces a Mormon preacher with two wives. One of these is auctioned off and bought by a grizzled protagonist, whose daughter has helped discover gold. Despite numerous romantic rivalries and complications, love civilizes the men, but the town dies out as most of the inhabitants move on in the hope of

◀ **Unusual departure**
The gritty themes and harsh realism of this unlikely musical did not stop it from becoming a hit.

film, directed by Joshua Logan, whose ability to inject musical theatre with realism had also served Rodgers' and Hammerstein's *South Pacific* (see opposite) so effectively.

REVIVALS OF THE STAGE MUSICAL
There have been two notable and well-reviewed attempts to revamp the musical in a new adaptation, the first of which premiered in Los Angeles

KEY FACTS

STAGE
Director Daniel Mann
Book Alan Jay Lerner
Music Fredrick Loewe
Lyrics Alan Jay Lerner
Venue Shubert Theatre, New York
Date 12 November 1951

⊙ **Key information**
The original Broadway show ran for a total of 289 performances from 1951–53. It transferred to London's West End in 1953. The film version appeared in 1969.

in 2004 with a revised libretto by David Rambo. This was revived with a cast of almost 30 in 2007 by the Pioneer Theatre Company in Salt Lake City. A concert revival of *Paint Your Wagon* was also included in New York's prestigious *Encores!* season in 2015.

> "*Loewe displayed... an uncanny ability to write scores indigenous to the time and locale of the characters and plots.*"

STEVEN SUSKIN, AUTHOR OF *SHOW TUNES*, 2000

the film's co-star Jean Seberg as "like rain gurgling down a rusty pipe".

The Lerner and Loewe song list for both versions of the musical also includes "I Still See Elisa", "Take the Wheels off the Wagon", "Another Autumn", "They Call the Wind Maria", and "I Talk to the Trees".

NEW REALISM
The plot of the film differs considerably from the stage show, but despite its anti-musical theatre feel, both benefit from a traditional structure that alternates chorus numbers reflecting

finding more gold and better fortune elsewhere. Another key incident is the arrival of a group of professional girls, essentially prostitutes, who lift the spirits of the all-male community.

Improbably, the stage version also incorporated ballet sequences by celebrated choreographer Agnes de Mille (see p.69). Dance is not a major element of the

▶ **Big screen stars**
Clint Eastwood, Lee Marvin, and Jean Seberg pictured on the set of the 1969 film adaptation.

THE KING AND I

{ 1951 }

Rodgers and Hammerstein took some persuading to take on *The King and I*. But once they did, they succeeded in transforming the unlikely story of a Victorian governess and an Eastern king at loggerheads into a spectacular and triumphant hymn to hope, tolerance, and fairness.

KEY FACTS

♨ STAGE

🎬 **Director** John Van Druten
📖 **Book** Oscar Hammerstein II
🎵 **Music** Richard Rodgers
𝄞 **Lyrics** Oscar Hammerstein II
🎭 **Venue** St James Theatre, New York
📅 **Date** 28 March 1951

◉ **Key information**
The Broadway show ran for 1,246 performances and won five Tony Awards, including Best Musical. The show has had numerous revivals, including award-winning Broadway productions in 1996 and 2015.

By 1951, composer Richard Rodgers (see pp.70–71) and lyricist Oscar Hammerstein II were well established, basking in the success of their 1949 musical *South Pacific* (see p.96). At this time they were approached on behalf of the English stage star Gertrude Lawrence, who wanted to make, and take the lead in, a musical based on the 1944 novel *Anna and the King of Siam*. Written by American author Margaret Landon, it recounted the memoirs of Englishwoman Anna Leonowens who was employed by King Mongkut of Siam (modern-day Thailand) as a teacher to his many wives, concubines, and more than 80 children.

FORTUNATE FIND

Rodgers and Hammerstein had some reservations about the project at first, not least with the vocal abilities of Lawrence, but also the casting of the key role of the Siamese king.

The latter puzzle was solved by Broadway star Mary Martin, who had played a leading role in *South Pacific*. She introduced the composer and lyricist to a near-unknown Russian-born actor called Yul Brynner. With his Eastern looks, commanding physique and voice, and haughty bearing, 30-year-old Brynner was the perfect fit for the king. And to minimize the problem of her vocal limitations, Gertrude Lawrence was given songs, such as "I Whistle a Happy Tune" and "Getting to Know You", which did not overstretch her vocal range, leaving the more demanding numbers to other members of the cast.

CULTURE CLASHES

The King and I made unconventional use of its two main characters – Anna and the king. Most musicals have romance at their heart, but here was a male–female axis that was largely chaste and based for much of the time on confrontation. The only moment of real

▲ Top billing
The top billing given to Gertrude Lawrence in this poster for the pre-Broadway try-out was merited by her status as one of the top talents of her day. Despite being one of the leads, Yul Brynner is billed alongside the cast in the supporting roles.

sexual tension happens in "Shall We Dance?", where Anna teaches the king how to polka.

There is romance, though, as well as tragedy, in the doomed love affair between the slave girl, Tuptim, a gift to the king of Siam from the king of Burma, and her escort, Lun Tha. They try to elope, but Lun Tha is killed and Tuptim caught. In a key moment, Anna stops the king from whipping Tuptim. The king is now a broken, dying man who, nevertheless, reconciles with Anna on his deathbed.

The cultural tensions between East and West and their often-clashing customs, played out between Anna and the king, are at the centre of the story. Anna embodies Western ideas

◄ Exotic setting
Set in the Royal Court of Siam (Thailand), *The King and I* was the perfect opportunity for lavish sets and colourful costumes, which the exotic backdrop required.

RELATED SHOWS

Kismet, 1953, Alexander Borodin, Robert Wright, George Forrest

Flower Drum Song, 1958, Richard Rodgers, Oscar Hammerstein II

Camelot, 1960, Alan Jay Lerner, Frederick Loewe (see p.144)

> # "On stage I portray the king; he takes me over."
>
> **YUL BRYNNER,** INTERVIEWED IN 1984

of freedom (especially for women) and democracy, while the king represents the stricter, more traditional attitudes of the East.

GLOBAL APPEAL

Rodgers and Hammerstein rightly sensed they had a hit on their hands. This was musical theatre of real depth, with its strong central characters and exotic setting, uplifting and memorable melodies, and strong moral message of tolerance and understanding, which was in tune with post-war sentiments.

The writers were helped by the intricate dance routines staged by the choreographer Jerome Robbins (see pp.108–09), the lavish staging by Jo Mielziner, who had already worked with Rodgers and Hammerstein on *Carousel* (see pp.68–69) and *South Pacific*, and the vibrant silk costumes designed by Irene Sharaff, whose spectacular period dresses had lit up the screen in the film *Meet Me in St. Louis* (see pp.66–67).

The King and I opened on Broadway to rapturous acclaim from both the public and critics. Two years later, it made a triumphant move to London's West End, running for 926 performances at the Theatre Royal, Drury Lane. *The King and I* went on to score similar successes across Europe and as far afield as Australia and Japan.

▶ **Assertive stance**
Yul Brynner as the king adopts his trademark stance in this confrontation with Gertrude Lawrence as Anna in the original stage production of the show.

STARS LOST AND FOUND

Tragically, Gertrude Lawrence did not live to witness the global triumph of the musical. Less than two years into the Broadway run, she died of liver cancer at only 54 years of age.

The show, however, launched on the road to stardom the one person who, more than any other, is associated with *The King and I*, Yul Brynner. He made the role of the king his own, playing it more than 4,600 times over 34 years, including revivals on Broadway in 1977 and 1985. He had the show's costume designer Irene Sharaff to thank for his trademark bald look. When he asked what he should do with his scant head of hair, she told him, "Shave it!" The original

West End production starred Herbert Lom as the king, and Brynner first played the role in the UK at the London Palladium in 1979.

FAITHFUL SCREEN VERSION

Brynner also starred in the 1956 film, this time opposite Scottish-born actress Deborah Kerr. The movie remained largely faithful to the stage version and was an enormous success, grossing more than US$21 million at the US box office. It made no money in Thailand, however, where it was banned for what the Thai government judged to be an inaccurate and disrespectful portrayal of their monarchy. Brynner won an Oscar for his performance in the film, one of only ten actors to win an Oscar and a Tony Award for the same role.

BIOGRAPHY

OSCAR HAMMERSTEIN II
(1895–1960)

Born into a musical New York family, Hammerstein left law studies aged 30. In 1927, he and Jerome Kern wrote *Show Boat* (see pp.14–17). In 1942, he began working with Richard Rodgers on *Oklahoma!* (see pp.58–61), Hammerstein insisting on writing the lyrics before the music was composed. He wrote his final song, "Edelweiss", for *The Sound of Music* (see pp.134–37), and died within a year of the musical's Broadway opening.

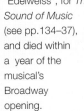

SINGIN' IN THE RAIN

{ 1952 }

Starring Gene Kelly, who sings and dances through the rain after kissing Debbie Reynolds goodnight, this film still tops the all-time-favourite movie list of many critics and fans.

The American Film Institute ranks *Singin' in the Rain* as the number one film musical ever made. Yet, on its release, the film initially evoked only a modest response. Critics were not overly effusive and *Singin' in the Rain* received just two Oscar nominations (see right). Futhermore, the film was not on any critical "top ten" list for the year of its release.

COOL RECEPTION

American film critic and screenwriter Roger Ebert explored this phenomenon in 1998. He wrote that *Singin' in the Rain* was "cobbled together quickly" in order for the studio to capitalize on the massive success of Gene Kelly's musical film *An American in Paris*, made the previous year. But this may have proved the film's greatest strength because, as Ebert suggests, the sense of play and freedom created by the short pre-production period shows up on screen as a natural spontaneity,

◄ **Feverish filming**
This iconic scene for the number "Singin' in the Rain" took two to three days to shoot, with Kelly utterly soaked in a wet wool suit and running a very high fever.

almost as if the scenes had been improvised. It could also be argued that the film's turnaround in popularity was also thanks to Gene Kelly (see p.102). Now considered by many as the greatest musical film star of all time, and honoured in 1985 by The American Film Institute with a lifetime achievement award, he was the right man in the right place. By the time Kelly came to films in 1942, audiences were looking for a likeable guy with whom they could relate – someone who was one of them – and this was the persona Kelly created in the character of Don Lockwood. Kelly's sheer athleticism and insistence on finding the reality of the common man in his dances broke the mould. It not only transformed him into a Hollywood "great" but made that dance in the rain iconic.

◄ **Likeable stars**
The screen characters of Debbie Reynolds and Gene Kelly were likeable and relatable – a winning formula.

BRASH ENERGY

Producer Arthur Freed (see below) brought in the lyricist and screenwriting partnership of Betty Comden and Adolph Green (see p.65) to write a screenplay about Hollywood actors making the transition from silent movies to talkies. The film was to use songs, already in existence, by Nacio Herb Brown (many with lyrics by Freed). The same brash energy and youthful ebullience Comden and Green had displayed in *On The Town* (see pp.64–65), found its way into their screenplay for *Singin' in the Rain*.

The film's female star, American actress Debbie Reynolds, was a fresh-faced 19-year-old without formal dance training. She claims that it was just expected that she would be able to keep up with Gene Kelly and Hollywood dancer, singer, and actor, Donald O'Connor. So, in order to get "up to speed" with her dancing skills, Reynolds went into a period of intensive training with screen dancing

legend Fred Astaire (see pp.42–43) as her teacher. The schedule was punishing, but the execution of the choreography appears so effortless and exuberant on screen that audiences would never know the effort that it had demanded.

KEY FACTS

🎬 **FILM**

🎬 **Directors** Gene Kelly and Stanley Donen

📖 **Screenplay** Betty Comden and Adolph Green

🎵 **Music** Nacio Herb Brown

♪ **Lyrics** Arthur Freed, plus others

🕐 **Running time** 103 minutes

📅 **Date** 11 April 1952

⊙ **Key information**
Donald O'Connor was awarded the Golden Globe for Best Motion Picture Actor – Musical/Comedy. The first stage production was in 1983 at the London Palladium and starred Tommy Steele as Don. There have since been other successful UK productions at the National Theatre and Chichester.

RELATED SHOWS

Anchors Aweigh, 1945, George Stoll

Easter Parade, 1948, Irving Berlin (see p.87)

On the Town, 1949, Leonard Bernstein, Betty Comden, Adolph Green (see pp.64–65)

Take Me Out to the Ballgame, 1949, Adolph Deutsch

An American in Paris, 1951, George and Ira Gershwin

BIOGRAPHY

ARTHUR FREED (1894–1973)

A Jewish-American film producer and lyricist born in South Carolina, Freed started out as a song-plugger and pianist in Chicago. Here, he met Minnie Marx, who brought him into her sons' act as a singer and songwriter. After working as an associate producer at MGM, he was given his own production unit where, during the late 1940s, he helped develop traditional musicals into something new. He died in Los Angeles.

"My feet were bleeding from all that dancing."

DEBBIE REYNOLDS IN A PRESS INTERVIEW, 21 APRIL 2013

STORYLINE

The film is set in Hollywood in 1927, when "talkies" were replacing silent films. Don Lockwood and Lina Lamont are amorous on screen, but Lina is under the illusion that Don loves her for real. The studio is shifting over to talkies and Don has the perfect voice for the songs of a musical he and Lina are starring in. Lina simply cannot make the transition to sound and her voice is to be dubbed. Young actress Kathy Selden lands the voice-over job, and Don falls in love with her.

GENE KELLY AS
DON LOCKWOOD SINGS
AND DANCES IN THE RAIN

	GRAUMAN'S CHINESE THEATRE	OPENING NIGHT PARTY	THE STUDIO	MOVIE MUSICAL MONTAGE	THE STUDIO	
PLOT OVERVIEW	**It is the opening** night of Monumental Pictures' movie *The Royal Rascal*, starring Don Lockwood and Lina Lamont. Don recounts his rise to stardom **1**. During the film's huge ovation, Lockwood and Lamont take a bow but Don doesn't let Lina speak. Backstage we experience her bad temper and worse voice. Lina sadly believes the movie magazine stories about their romance.	**Driving to the party**, Don and his best friend Cosmo get a flat tyre. Don ends up in a convertible driven by Kathy Seldon. She says Don's not a "real" actor, comments that distract Don at the party. Studio head, R.F. Simpson, demonstrates the latest technology, talking movies. Kathy arrives, having been hired to pop out of a cake as entertainment **2**. She runs out in shame.	**Three weeks later**, *The Jazz Singer*, the first full-length talkie opens. Don has not been able to find Kathy and is sad, but Cosmo cheers him up **3**. On the set, Lina has had Kathy fired for her behaviour at the party. Monumental Studios announces they are shutting down all productions to "re-tool" to make talkies.	**We see** a montage of every studio converting over to movie musicals to take advantage of sound **4**.	**Don is delighted** to find Kathy in a small dancing role on the studio lot. Tongue-tied, he takes her to an empty sound stage and sings and dances for her **5**.	**Lina has** a diction lesson. It doesn't go well, while Don and Cosmo's diction lesson leads into a song **6**. Shooting begins on the talking version of *The Duelling Cavalier*.

	1	**2**	**3**	**4**	**5**	**6**
THE SONGS	Fit as a Fiddle 😀 *Don and Cosmo*	All I Do Is Dream of You 😀 *Kathy*	Make 'em Laugh 😀 *Cosmo*	Beautiful Girl 🎵 *Montage*	You Were Meant For Me 😀 *Don, Kathy*	Moses Supposes 😀 *Don, Cosmo*

KATHY POPS OUT OF A CAKE AT THE PARTY

THE DUELLING CAVALIER GOES INTO PRODUCTION

GENE KELLY (1912–96)

Born in Pittsburgh, Pennsylvania, as a boy Kelly enjoyed sports along with his dance lessons. Upon his arrival in New York in 1938, he worked his way from ensemble parts to playing the title role in the 1940 film *Pal Joey* (see pp.54–55). This won him a contract with MGM to star in their movie musicals, a genre that he dominated during the 1940s and 50s. After a series of strokes, he died at home in Beverly Hills aged 84.

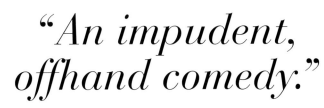

"*An impudent, offhand comedy.*"

BOSLEY CROWTHER, CRITIC, *THE NEW YORK TIMES*, 28 MARCH 1952

GRAUMAN'S CHINESE THEATRE	DON'S HOUSE	ON THE STREET	THE STUDIO	GRAUMAN'S CHINESE THEATRE

The opening night of *The Duelling Cavalier* is a disaster.

Don, Cosmo, and Kathy try to cheer up one another ❼. They come up with the idea of turning *The Duelling Cavalier* into a musical, *The Dancing Cavalier*, using Kathy's voice to replace Lina's.

Don takes Kathy home and kisses her goodnight. On the way home he dances and sings of his joy ❽ even though it is pouring with rain and he gets thoroughly soaked.

Don and Cosmo explain their plan to R.F. Simpson. We see Lina singing the final love ballad, while we hear Kathy's voice ❾. Don explains his idea for the final sequence, a great spoof/tribute to the Busby Berkeley musical numbers of the early sound era, a 14-minute sequence telling the story of a young hoofer coming to New York ❿.

The opening is a big hit, but Lina still tries to keep Kathy under contract to dub her voice without receiving any recognition. Don, Cosmo, and R.F. Simpson refuse to let that happen. Kathy and Don declare their love for each other ⓫.

DECAL FOR GRAUMAN'S CHINESE THEATRE (1941)

❼ Good Morning
Kathy, Don,
Cosmo

❽ Singin' in the Rain
Don

Broadway Rhythm Ballet
Don

Would You?
Kathy, Lina

★ Ironically, Debbie Reynolds did not sing in "Would You?" and "You are My Lucky Star". Both tracks were sung by Betty Noyes.

You Are My Lucky Star
Don, Kathy

CAST

Gene Kelly Don Lockwood
Donald O'Connor Cosmo Brown
Debbie Reynolds Kathy Selden
Jean Hagen Lina Lamont
Millard Mitchell R.F. Simpson
Cyd Charise Gene Kelly's dance partner in "Broadway Rhythm Ballet"
Rita Moreno Zelda Zanders

★ Filming the dance routine for "Good Morning" took a gruelling 14 hours, after which Debbie Reynolds' feet were bleeding and she had to be carried from the set.

THE BAND WAGON

{ 1953 }

Despite making a loss of nearly US$1.2 million, this movie musical comedy is considered by some to be among the finest to emerge from MGM's studios.

The cast of the 1931 Broadway production of *The Band Wagon* included Fred and Adele Astaire (see pp.42–43) in their final show together. It was a successful Broadway revue featuring the songs of composer Arthur Schwartz and lyricist Howard Dietz. From it "Dancing in the Dark", a notably ambitious and philosophical number about "Man and his existence" (as Schwartz had it), was a hit for Bing Crosby in 1931, again for Artie Shaw in 1941, and then inspired a 1949 film of the same name.

THE MOVIE
The songwriters collaborated with other partners and sporadically with each other in the following two decades, before reconvening for the 1953 MGM movie of *The Band Wagon*. The film bore little resemblance to the original revue, but reprised "Dancing in the Dark" and several other songs from the Schwartz/Dietz catalogue, including "By Myself", "I Guess I'll Have to Change My Plan", and "You and the Night and the Music". They also composed the well-known quip-filled anthem "That's Entertainment" especially for the film.

THE TEAM
The movie was written by Adolph Green and Betty Comden, librettists and lyricists for *Singin' in the Rain* (see pp.100–03), and they crafted another satirical backstage story, cleverly

◄ **Rakish style**
The stylish poster for the 1953 movie urged audiences to "get aboard" and made full use of Cyd Charisse's evident physical charms.

pricking inflated egos and artistic pretension. It was directed in a revue style by Vincente Minnelli, with only fleeting regard to narrative sense. Arthur Freed (see p.101), the man responsible for rejuvenating the MGM musical and bringing Fred Astaire out of movie retirement in 1948, was the producer. Astaire was cast in the film as fading song-and-dance man Tony Hunter, while the role of Gabrielle Gerard, the intimidating ballerina who threatens Hunter's authority, went to Cyd Charisse. Oscar Levant provided the wisecracks ("I can stand anything but pain!") and Jack Buchanan played the pompous show director, teaming up with Astaire and comic actress Nanette Fabray for the hilarious and ingenious "Triplets".

ASTAIRE AND CHARISSE
There were sparkling solo features for Astaire ("Shine on Your Shoes") and Charisse ("The Beggars Waltz"), but the highlights were the numbers they performed together. "Dancing in the Dark" was a predictably elegant

moment, with Charisse's formal grace perfectly complementing Astaire's relaxed precision. The 11-minute climax to the movie, "Girl Hunt Ballet (A Murder Mystery in Jazz)", was an artistic tour de force that rivalled the Gershwin/Kelly/Minnelli finale of *An American in Paris* (1951) for movie musical magic. Decades later, pop star/dancer Michael Jackson (who revered Astaire) referenced the piece in his "Smooth Criminal" video.

Encores!, the New York City Center concert series, presented *The Band Wagon* starring Tracey Ullman in 2014.

KEY FACTS

🎬 **FILM**
🎞 **Director** Vincente Minnelli
🎬 **Screenplay** Betty Comden, Adolph Green
📖 **Book** Betty Comden, Adolph Green, Alan Jay Lerner
♫ **Music** Arthur Schwartz
♪ **Lyrics** Howard Dietz
🕐 **Running time** 111 minutes
📅 **Release date** 7 August 1953

⊙ **Key information**
The film version was nominated for several Academy Awards. In 2006, it was also ranked at number 17 in the American Film Institute's list of best musicals. It has been registered as "significant" by the American Library of Congress.

► **Dancing tour de force**
Fred Astaire and Cyd Charisse in full flow during one of *The Band Wagon*'s many popular hits. Their dancing styles were perfectly matched.

WONDERFUL TOWN

{ 1953 }

The tale of two sisters trying to make it in New York – one as a writer, the other as an actress – becomes a rousing and hugely entertaining musical tribute to the city itself.

The story of *Wonderful Town* is based on the play *My Sister Eileen*, by Jerome Chodorov and Joseph A. Fields. The authors were inspired by the autobiographical *New Yorker* short stories of Ruth McKenney, which chronicled the adventures she and her sister experienced when they moved from Ohio to New York to begin their careers. Rosalind Russell starred as Ruth, the quick-witted would-be writer. Russell had already played Ruth in the 1942 film of *My Sister Eileen*. Edie Adams played Ruth's sister, the aspiring actress and man-magnet Eileen.

Director George Abbott and the musical team of composer Leonard Bernstein (see pp.126–127) and lyricists Betty Comden and Adolph Green reunited after their work together on *On the Town* (see pp.64–65). Jerome Robbins (see pp.108–09) had also been part of the creative group, but Donald Saddler (see below) was hired as choreographer for *Wonderful Town*. As it turned out, Robbins was brought in anyway. This was Saddler's first Broadway show as a choreographer and the production was on a breakneck pace

► **New York adventures**
American actress Donna Murphy poses for a publicity shot for the 2003 Broadway revival of *Wonderful Town*.

to finish on time, so they asked Robbins to help out. Several popular songs came out of the musical, including "Ohio", "A Little Bit in Love", and the catchy Irish jig, "My Darlin' Eileen". The setting is Greenwich Village in the 1930s. The two sisters rent a basement apartment, near a subway construction site, frequented by a steady stream of visitors looking for the previous tenant Violet, a lady of the night.

SISTERS IN THE CITY
Although not ideal accommodation, the sisters are surrounded by friendly neighbours, including landlord and artist Appopolus, ex-football player Wreck, his fiancée, and his mother, and a neighbourly police precinct.

Eileen struggles to break into show business, but has no trouble attracting suitors; in fact, she invites three of them – Bob Baker, editor of *Manhatter* magazine; Walgreens manager Frank Lippencott; and newspaperman Chick Clark – to a dinner party. Disaster ensues, but Ruth does eventually get a writing job out of the encounter. After yet more chaos, a story finally results from the mayhem and Ruth lands a permanent job, and a beau, Bob Baker. Eileen is also offered a job, singing in a nightclub, where *Wonderful Town*'s finale takes place.

The 2003 Broadway revival, directed by Kathleen Marshall, was nominated for five Tony Awards.

KEY FACTS

🎭 **STAGE**

🎬 **Director** George Abbott

📖 **Book** Jerome Chodorov, Joseph A. Fields

🎵 **Music** Leonard Bernstein

🎼 **Lyrics** Betty Comden, Adolph Green

🎭 **Venue** Winter Garden Theatre, New York

📅 **Date** 25 February 1953

◎ **Key information**
The musical was choreographed by Donald Saddler, with assistance from Jerome Robbins. It won a total of five Tony Awards in 1953, including Best Actress in a Musical for Rosalind Russell as Ruth.

DONALD SADDLER (1918–2014)

BIOGRAPHY

Before *Wonderful Town*, Donald Saddler was primarily a ballet dancer and in the first corps of the American Ballet Theatre, performing such works as "Giselle", Pillar of Fire", and Jerome Robbins' "Fancy Free". Saddler, born in Van Nuys, California, near Hollywood, was trained in dance at an early age and performed in the chorus of many movie musicals of the 1930s and 40s, including *Wizard of Oz* (see pp.46–49), *Babes in Arms*, and *Strike up the Band*.

THE PAJAMA GAME

A classic Broadway musical with an infectious score, this is a universal favourite. Suddenly, Broadway wasn't about a rural idyll, glamour, or nightclub lowlife. Here was a fresh and sassy show about ordinary people working in an ordinary factory.

Adapted from the 1953 novel *7½ Cents* by American writer Richard Bissell, based on his experience running his family's business, *The Pajama Game* is set in and around a nightwear factory. The show boosts its glamour factor with a famous, if improbable, nightclub sequence.

Long popular with community groups because of its terrific, toe-tapping score, the musical focuses on the stormy relationship between Sid, a new factory supervisor, and Babe, a union organizer, as the workers successfully battle management for a 7½ cent pay rise.

The show begins in the bustling nightwear factory and ends up at a pajama fashion show, visiting Babe's home, a workers annual picnic, a union rally, and an infamous nightspot en route. Mixed up in the mayhem are glamorous secretary Gladys and her jealous boyfriend Hines, who has an amateur knife-throwing act, when he

is not working at the factory. Prez, the union president, factory boss Old Man Hasler, and Sid's feisty personal assistant Mabel also play key roles.

THE TEAM
George Abbott dramatized the story, and Richard Adler and Jerry Ross provided music and lyrics. Some

▶ **On opposite sides**
John Raitt played Sid in the stage and film production of *The Pajama Game* and Doris Day was cast as firebrand union organizer Babe.

people also believe that two of the best songs – the rousing "There Once Was a Man" and the haunting "A New Town is a Blue Town" – were written,

> "*The pedigree of* The Pajama Game *was impeccable – its collaborators were all, or became, the aristocracy of Broadway.*"
>
> **SIR RICHARD EYRE**, DIRECTOR OF THE 2014 WEST END REVIVAL

uncredited, by Frank Loesser, author of *Guys and Dolls* (see pp.88–91). Adler and Ross were protégés of Loesser, and had recently contributed to a successful Broadway review. They went on to write the hit baseball musical *Damn Yankees* (see pp.116–17), before their songwriting partnership was cut tragically short when Ross died of a lung ailment aged just 29.

The Pajama Game's score contains a raft of unforgettable numbers, many of which have become stand-alone classics in their own right. "Hey There" is a great ballad of self-

reflection despite the fact that, bizarrely, when it first appears in the show Sid is dueting with a Dictaphone. "Once a Year Day", sung by staff on a works outing, is a joyous anthem for any special occasion, while "Steam Heat", entertainment at a Union Rally, and "Hernado's Hideaway", celebrating a sleazy nightclub, are showstoppers in any context.

A STAR IS BORN
The first Broadway production won Tony Awards for Best Musical and Best Featured Performance by an Actress in a Musical, awarded to Carol Haney, who played Gladys.

Haney was understudied by the then unknown Shirley MacLaine, who had to take the lead while Haney recovered from an injury. As a result, MacLaine was spotted by Hollywood producer

◀ **Factory scene**
Sid and Babe face off against each other in the Sleep-Tite Pajama Factory and are watched by the other workers.

KEY FACTS

STAGE

🎭 **Director** George Abbott, Jerome Robbins
📖 **Book** George Abbott, Richard Bissell
🎵 **Music and lyrics** Richard Adler, Jerry Ross
🎫 **Venue** St James Theatre, New York
📅 **Date** 13 May 1954

⊙ **Key information**
Choreographed by Bob Fosse, this Broadway hit ran for a total of 1,063 performances from 1954–56. It won three Tony Awards.

This little old world wouldn't be the same without that extra special fun of...

A GEORGE ABBOTT and STANLEY DONEN Production

The Pajama Game

presented by
WARNER BROS.
in **WarnerColor**

ALL THE BOY-CHASES-GIRL-CHASES-BOY ENTERTAINMENT OF THE RECORD-SMASHING BROADWAY HIT SENSATION!

starring

Doris Day as 'Babe' and the wonderful cast of the Broadway play!

John Raitt · Carol Haney · Eddie Foy, Jr.

Hal Wallis, who set her on the path to film stardom.

A third Tony went to the celebrated choreographer Bob Fosse (see pp.200–01), whose iconic dance routines for the show were featured in the choreography compilation tribute *Fosse* (1999).

IN AND OUT OF FASHION

There have been several notable revivals of *The Pajama Game*. In 1957, there was a hit film starring Doris Day and many of the original cast. In 1973, a Broadway revival directed by Abbott flopped; in 2006, it was a New York hit again, starring Hollywood star Harry Connick Jr, but a critically acclaimed West End production struggled to find an audience in 2014.

Whether or not there is enough public demand for tickets to justify major revivals, *The Pajama Game* is a gift for performers and a joy to produce in a noncommercial environment. Unusually for a musical of this period, it is the women who dominate the show. The factory girls are strong, feisty, and drive the plot with some of the best lines, songs, and dance opportunities. Within the central love story, it is Babe who usually captures the audience's heart, and it is the moral dilemmas surrounding her trade union principles that give the show its grit. The secretaries are much more fun than the male bosses they serve. Equally, the exuberance of the girls on the production line is the fire in the belly of any staging, without the need for significant contribution from a male chorus – a characteristic the show shares with other female-led classics such as *Sweet Charity* (see p.167).

◄ **All-American fun**
The play attracted very positive early reviews, and the film adaptation was also successful. The light-hearted and fun nature of the story is reflected in the film poster art.

CAST LIST

Eddie Foy Jr Hines
Janis Paige Babe Williams
John Raitt Sid Sorokin
Marion Colby Brenda
Ralph Dunn Hasler
Carol Haney Gladys
Thelma Pelish Mae
Stanley Prager Prez
Reta Shaw Mabel

JEROME ROBBINS

{ PRODUCER/DIRECTOR **1918–98** }

Legendary dancer, choreographer, producer, and director
Jerome Robbins is best known for the musicals *West Side Story*
and *Fiddler on the Roof*. He also created 60 ballets and
directed or choreographed numerous Broadway and film hits.

It's difficult to imagine young Jerome Robbins enrolling on a chemistry course at New York University. His study was, however, short-lived, as Robbins (born Jerome Wilson Rabinowitz to Jewish immigrants Lena and Harry) soon dropped out. He later studied dance – ballet, modern, Spanish, and folk, as well as composition – and by the age of 21 was dancing in Broadway shows *Keep off the Grass* (choreographed by George Balanchine) and *Stars in Your Eyes*. In 1940, he joined New York's Ballet Theatre, rising in the ranks to dance the lead in Igor Stravinsky's *Petrouchka* and Sergei Prokofiev's *Romeo and Juliet*.

FLEDGLING CHOREOGRAPHER

By 1944, the intensely creative Robbins was choreographing his own work. *Fancy Free*, his ballet about three sailors on leave in wartime New York City, was an overnight sensation. The 25-year-old became a Broadway success that same year, providing the choreography for Leonard Bernstein's musical *On the Town* (see pp.64–65), while another smash hit, *Billion Dollar Baby*, followed in 1945. Two years

▲ **Notorious evidence**
Robbins testifying to the House Un-American Activities Committee. His reluctant evidence meant his personal reputation remained intact.

later, in 1947, he won his first Tony Award for choreography for the Broadway musical *High Button Shoes*.

In fact, Robbins was so prolific that he produced new musicals and ballets each year. After having worked on Irving Berlin's lively musical *Call Me Madam* in 1950, he conceived the dances, including the famous polka "Shall We Dance" and "The March of the Siamese Twins", for Rodgers and Hammerstein's 1951 smash hit *The King and I*. That year also saw the premiere of his daring and thought-provoking ballet *The Cage*, set to Stravinsky's haunting Concerto in D for String orchestra ("Basel Concerto").

Robbins's career was briefly threatened during the early 1950s, when he was suspected of Communist sympathies and called before the House Committee on Un-American

Activities. He resisted naming names for three years but, threatened with public exposure as a homosexual, Robbins reluctantly supplied the names of several actors, film-makers, and playwrights who he believed were Communists. Robbins himself escaped being either blacklisted or outed.

WEST SIDE STORY AND BEYOND

In 1957, Robbins choreographed and directed *West Side Story* (see pp.122–25), a modern musical version of

▶ **Universal man**
Jerome Robbins was unusual in Broadway circles in that he had been an accomplished ballet dancer himself before he began choreographing, composing, producing, and directing. He was a true giant of the arts – a man for all seasons.

Shakespeare's play *Romeo and Juliet*, with music and lyrics by Leonard Bernstein (see pp.126–27) and Stephen Sondheim (see pp.220–21). Robbins won a Tony Award for choreography, and repeated the role of co-director and choreographer for the 1961 film.

Robbins teamed up again with Stephen Sondheim and Arthur Laurents in 1959's *Gypsy*, based on the life of Gypsy Rose Lee and starring Ethel Merman (see pp.140–41). By now known as something of a theatrical trouble-shooter, Robbins managed to pull the 1962 musical farce *A Funny Thing Happened on the Way to the Forum* (see p.149) out of the doldrums and, two years later, did the same with *Funny Girl* (see p.163), which transformed the young Barbra Streisand into a star. That same year,

> *"Dance is like life, it exists as you're flitting through it, and when it's over, it's done."*
>
> **JEROME ROBBINS**

KEY WORKS

Fancy Free, 1944

Billion Dollar Baby, 1945

Common Ground, 1945

The King and I, 1951 (see pp.98–99)

Afternoon of a Faun, 1953

West Side Story, 1957 (see pp.122–25)

Gypsy, 1959 (see pp.138–39)

A Funny Thing Happened on the Way to the Forum, 1962 (see p.149)

Fiddler on the Roof, 1964 (see pp.150–53)

Dances at a Gathering, 1969

the long-running Broadway hit *Fiddler on the Roof* (see pp.150–53) opened to rave reviews and won Robbins Tony Awards for both Best Direction and Best Choreography. His last Broadway show came some time later, in 1989. *Jerome Robbins's Broadway* brought together some of his most successful numbers. It was highly praised and won six Tonys, including Best Musical.

ROBBINS AND HIS BALLETS

Robbins had been a leading performer of the New York City Ballet since 1949, but within a few years he was creating his own ballets. The works *Fancy Free*, *Afternoon of a Faun*, *The Concert*, and *Dances at a Gathering*, set

▲ Enduring choreography
Dancers from the Hamburg Ballet perform Jerome Robbins's *Dances at a Gathering* – set to music by Chopin – at the Hamburg State Opera.

to scores by composers such as Bernstein, Claude Debussy, and Frédéric Chopin, remain to this day in the repertory of the world's major dance companies. He also created works for particular dancers, including 1994's *A Suite of Dances* for the Russian ballet star Mikhail Baryshnikov. In 1972, Robbins became Ballet Master of the New York City Ballet and from then worked almost exclusively in classical dance. His international reputation continued to grow, and in 1981 his Chamber Dance Company toured the People's Republic of China. Robbin's final work was a re-staging of his ballet *Les Noces*. On 29 July 1998, just two months after it premiered, Robbins died at home in New York, following a stroke.

THE MAN, HIS AWARDS AND LEGACY

Robbins was a very private man. Hugely creative, he could also be a harsh and unforgiving perfectionist. A bisexual who counted Hollywood actor Montgomery Clift among his lovers, he never married.

Jerome Robbins's extraordinary work was honoured many times during his lifetime. He won two Academy Awards for *West Side Story*, five Tony Awards, the National Medal of Arts, and many, many others besides. The Jerome Robbins Foundation, established in 1958, still helps to support young theatre and dance talent and, since 1995, offers a prize for outstanding achievement in the field of dance.

(see pp.150–53)

11 October 1918 Jerome Wilson Rabinowitz is born in New York.

1938 Robbins starts dancing in his first chorus roles on Broadway.

9 February 1939 Robbins dances in *Stars in Your Eyes*.

1940 Robbins joins the Ballet Theatre in New York.

1941 Robbins dances in *Giselle*.

18 April 1944 First performance of Robbins's ballet *Fancy Free*.

21 December 1945 *Billion Dollar Baby* opens.

11 September 1950 *Call Me Madam* opens.

29 March 1951 Opening of *The King and I*.

20 October 1954 *Peter Pan* opens.

26 September 1957 *West Side Story* opens.

1958 Jerome Robbins Foundation established.

21 May 1959 *Gypsy*, choreographed and directed by Robbins, opens on Broadway.

18 October 1961 Film version of *West Side Story* is released.

1962 Robbins and Wise receive Academy Award for Best Director for *West Side Story*.

8 May 1962 Opening of *A Funny Thing Happened on the Way to the Forum*.

26 March 1964 *Funny Girl* opens.

22 September 1964 Opening of *Fiddler on the Roof*.

1972 Becomes Ballet Master for the New York City Ballet.

1981 The Jerome Robbins Chamber Dance Company tours the People's Republic of China.

1995 Jerome Robbins Award is established.

ROBBINS WITH BARYSHNIKOV

29 July 1998 Robbins dies in New York.

KISMET

{ 1953 }

Kismet belongs to a small group of Broadway musicals from the 1950s that set lyrics to classical music; in this case, pieces written by the Russian composer Borodin. A film version was released by Metro-Goldwyn-Mayer in 1955.

The team of Robert Wright and George Forrest had already had a hit with the *Song of Norway* – utilizing melodies by Edvard Grieg – and would go on to create *The Great Waltz* (1972), based around Strauss waltzes. Charles Lederer and Luther Davis wrote the book for *Kismet*, based on the 1911 play by Edward Knoblock.

The absurd and complicated plot takes place over one day and one morning and concerns a poet and his daughter in a mythical Baghdad. The father decides to disguise himself as a beggar and promises to lift a curse that deprived a rich man of his son. The reward money he receives pays for such finery for the daughter that she catches the eye of the Caliph and they fall in love. The good times are cut short, however, when the poet, who has been attracting the amorous attentions of the Wazir's wife, is sentenced to have his hand cut off for thieving. All is forgiven when the Wazir turns out to be the missing son, persuading everyone that the poet

must have magical powers. He is then employed to negotiate a tricky marriage contract for the Caliph that would jeopardize his own daughter's hopes of marrying the nobleman. Using a mixture of quick wits and trickery, the poet ensures all ends happily, also allowing him to openly love the Wazir's widow once the Wazir has died.

TELEVISION'S FIRST BROADWAY HIT

The first Broadway production opened during a newspaper strike, so rather than relying on good reviews to sell tickets, the producers were forced to promote the show on television. As a result, the show became a box-office hit, which the late and generally lukewarm reviews did not affect in any significant way. *Kismet* ran for 583 performances, winning the 1954 Tony Award for Best Musical, and was equally as successful in London's West End, where it ran for 648 performances at the Stoll Theatre, starting in April 1955. Two further Tony Awards were won by leading

man Alfred Drake, and the conductor of the show, Louis Adrian.

A film version of the musical followed in 1955. This was directed by Vincente Minnelli and starred Howard Keel, but unfortunately it was not a success and is reported to have lost US$2,252,000. In 1967, a 90-minute made-for-television version was broadcast to moderate acclaim.

STARS AND STRIFE

There have been several notable revivals of *Kismet*, including a retitled, restaging, *Timbuktu*, stripped of its Arabian Nights opulence and relocated to Africa, with a new script by Luther Davis. It starred Eartha Kitt and ran for a healthy 221 performances in 1978. In 1985, the original piece was revived at the New York City Opera, starring George Hearn as the poet, and directed by Frank Corsaro. A 1991 studio cast recording starred Mandy Patinkin and Julia Migenes, and in 2006 there was a concert presentation as part of the New York City Center

Encores! series, starring Brian Stokes Mitchell and Marin Mazzie.

Kismet was revived in London in 2007 by the English National Opera, in an ill-judged and badly timed revival that opened soon after the war had ended in real-life, modern-day Baghdad. Beset with fall-outs and disagreements among the creative team, and featuring a widely derided production concept, it attracted terrible reviews. However, thanks to the enduring

◀ Eastern promise
The poster for the film version of *Kismet* highlighted the show's great love songs, the stunning sets, and lavish costumes.

KEY FACTS

🕮 **STAGE**

🎬 **Director** Albert Marre

📖 **Book** Charles Lederer, Luther Davis

♫ **Music** Alexander Borodin, Robert Wright, George Forrest

𝄞 **Lyrics** Robert Wright, George Forrest

🎭 **Venue** Ziegfeld Theatre, New York

📅 **Date** 3 December 1953

◉ **Key information**
The original production saw a total of 583 performances on Broadway. The show was produced by Charles Lederer and choreographed by Jack Cole. The original cast was comprised of Alfred Drake, Henry Calvin, Joan Diener, Richard Kiley, and Doretta Morrow.

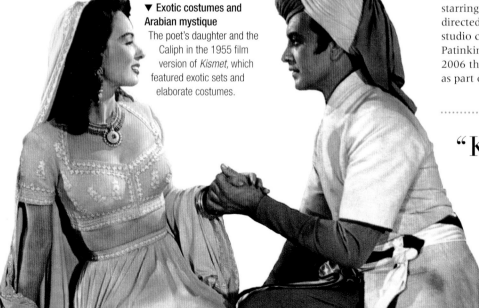

▼ **Exotic costumes and Arabian mystique**
The poet's daughter and the Caliph in the 1955 film version of *Kismet*, which featured exotic sets and elaborate costumes.

> *"Kismet isn't just cheesy; it's the Blue Stilton of Broadway."*

REVIEW OF LONDON'S 2007 REVIVAL, *WWW.WHATSONSTAGE.COM*

أسماك وجبة

popularity of its leading man, West End star Michael Ball, all 16 performances were sold out to appreciative audiences.

BEAUTIFUL HIT SONGS

While revivals of the full show have enjoyed limited success, its most enduring legacy is a fistful of truly beautiful and evocative songs.

Perhaps the most famous is "Stranger in Paradise", which Wright and Forrest based on Borodin's "Gliding Dance of the Maidens", from the Polovtsian Dances in the opera *Prince Igor*. In *Kismet*, the number belongs to two lovers meeting for the first time in a beautiful garden. To begin with they are shy and uncertain, but the sweeping melody and poetry of the

words convince them to arrange a rendezvous and confess to the mutual attraction that they feel. Although performed as a duet in the show, it has been rearranged for many soloists to record out of context, and the beautiful lyrics are a timeless depiction of the power of love to transport the lover to a state of euphoria.

"Stranger in Paradise" was a hit for crooner Tony Bennett – his first in the UK – and the song became so extraordinarily popular that there were six versions in the British charts in 1955. Both The Four Aces and Tony Martin charted at number 6, Bing Crosby reached number 17, Don Cornell number 19, and there was even an instrumental version by Eddie Calvert in the top 20. Since then there

have been a dizzying array of cover versions, from artists as diverse as Sarah Brightman, Sammy Davis Jr, Percy Faith, Isaac Hayes, the Ink Spots, André Rieu, and many more. In 2011, Tony Bennett returned to the song and re-recorded it, this time as a duet with Andrea Bocelli for his album *Duets II*.

"Baubles, Bangles, & Beads" has also proved to have particularly robust appeal, borrowing a tune from the second movement of Borodin's *String Quartet in D*. Peggy Lee had a hit with it in 1954 but she wasn't alone; as with "Stranger in Paradise", simultaneous recordings by other artists also made a strong impression on the record-buying public, and radio listeners, including performances by Lu Ann Simms,

Georgia Gibbs, and Frank Sinatra. The Kirby Stone Four joined the roll call in 1973 with a version that is an easy-listening favourite to this day.

"And This is My Beloved", based on another theme from Borodin's *String Quartet in D*, can also still tug at the heartstrings and was introduced to the wider public, first through a hit recording by actor and singer Mario Lanza in 1956 and then two celebrated television performances by tenor Sergio Franchi, in the UK on *Sunday Night at the London Palladium* and in the US on *The Ed Sullivan Show*.

SEVEN BRIDES FOR SEVEN BROTHERS

{ 1954 }

A charming frontier tale of love and risk in 1850s Oregon, *Seven Brides for Seven Brothers* features unforgettable songs, fabulous choreography, and a genuine chemistry between the two leads, musical veterans Howard Keel and Jane Powell.

The film was a critical and box-office success, something that may have come as a surprise to its MGM producers. *Brigadoon* (see p.86), a Gene Kelly film with music by Alan Lerner and Fritz Loewe, received some of the budget originally intended for *Seven Brides*, as MGM believed that was the musical to put all their weight behind. However, while *Brigadoon* flopped, *Seven Brides* soared, thanks to its fantastic choreography and marvellous acting.

On the surface, the premise was perhaps not promising: a musical, based on the 8th-century BCE Roman legend of the rape of the Sabine women, set in frontier America.

The film follows the fortunes of the seven Pontipee brothers, all hacking out a living together in the Oregon mountains. The first

brother, Adam, seeks a wife in town, shocking people with his cavalier approach to marriage. Luckily, he lands on a hard-working beauty, "sassy as can be". When Milly realizes that marriage has landed her with seven men – rather than one – to look after, she immediately sets about taming them in readiness for courting. Unfortunately, things don't go to

plan, with the outcome being that the brothers are convinced by Adam to kidnap their chosen brides, in the hope that love will grow. Righteous anger follows, but love wins the day with the approach of spring.

To modern sensibilities, the kidnap of six young women is no laughing matter, but the film makes it quite clear that no woman is actually

▲ Ground-breaking format
MGM made much of the fact that their new movie was shot in widescreen Cinemascope and used bright new colour techniques.

coerced into love; in fact, Milly as the female lead does her best to prevent it. Rather, the initial attraction felt in the

> *"Here are these slobs living off the woods … and they're gonna get up and dance? We'd be laughed out of the house."*
>
> MICHAEL KIDD, "OBITUARY", *THE INDEPENDENT*, 29 DECEMBER 2007

◀ Cake anyone?
The main cast, wearing the colourful costumes that were designed both to distinguish the actors and make the most of new film technology.

film's premier number, "Barn Dance", is allowed to strengthen, as the girls get to know the Pontipees better, as they never could if they were living separately in town and country.

VIBRANT COSTUMES
The beautiful costumes were the work of Walter Plunkett, well respected for his work in *Singin' in the Rain* (see pp.100–03), *Annie Get Your Gun* (see pp.72–75), *Show Boat* (see pp.14–17), and *Kiss Me, Kate* (see pp.80–83). The women's costumes were primarily constructed from a stack of old quilts, which Plunkett found in a local thrift store. The lumberjack Pontipees were dressed in bright colours, while the

KEY FACTS

FILM

Director Stanley Donen

Screenplay Albert Hackett, Frances Goodrich, Dorothy Kingsley

Music Gene de Paul, Saul Chaplin

Lyrics Johnny Mercer

Running time 102 minutes

Release date 22 July 1954

Key information

This was a Metro-Goldwyn-Mayer production filmed in the new format, widescreen Cinemascope. In 1955, it won the Academy Award for Music (Scoring of a Musical Picture) and was nominated for four other awards that year: Best Motion Picture; Cinematography (Color); Film Editing; and Writing (Screenplay).

townsmen-rivals were limited to city greys and browns. Finally, Plunkett requested that the actors playing the Pontipees dye their hair bright red, in order to definitively link them together.

It was Michael Kidd's choreography, however, that really shone. At Kidd's insistence, almost all of the leads were professionally trained dancers, with the exception of three of the seven brothers. Howard Keel, a classically trained bass, was required only to sing, and Russ Tamblyn, who went on to star as the leader of the Jets in *West Side Story* (see pp.122–25), managed to get by on his gymnastic skills in the dancing scenes. Benjamin, the second brother, was a former baseball player assigned to the film by MGM; in the dancing scenes he is relegated to the background, due to his relative lack of skills.

EXCEPTIONAL SONGS AND DANCE

Kidd then used the expertise of the remaining 11 to create memorable scenes that were so strong they inspired the songwriters, rather than the other way round. Kidd, for example, thought of "Lonesome Polecat", a rather haunting number

that describes the men's predicament living on the edge of the mountains with no other company. They long for companionship beyond their brothers, and the dance expresses this solitude, even in the midst of seven brothers and one wife.

In "Barn Dance", the athletic dancing had the ultimate showpiece. The film was one of the early adopters of the widescreen format (although also filmed in normal ratio), which allowed the audience to see all of the dancers at once. Additionally, as the six girls switch from dancing with six townsmen and the six Pontipees, the widescreen allows you to not only watch the dancing, but also the expressions on the faces of each set of rejected suitors as the girls continually switch. This level of visual detail, combined with the elegant, balletic couples' dances, was a stroke of genius. In the middle

◀ **Barn dance extraordinaire**
Some of the actors were hired specifically for their athletic skills, which were shown off to best effect in the classic "Barn Dance" scene.

▲ **Love will prevail**
There was a pronounced tenderness between Howard Keel and Jane Powell in the lead roles, which was remarked upon by many critics.

of the scene, the men compete using "traditional" lumberjack activities, such as running on rolling logs and jumping back and forth with axes.

CAST LIST

Howard Keel Adam

Jeff Richards Benjamin

Matt Mattox Caleb

Marc Platt Daniel

Jacques d'Amboise Ephraim

Tommy Rall Frank

Russ Tamblyn Gideon

Jane Powell Milly

Julie Newmar (Newmeyer) Dorcas

Ruta Kilmonis Ruth

Norma Doggett Martha

Virginia Gibson Liza

Betty Carr Sarah

Nancy Kilgas Alice

A STAR IS BORN

{ 1954 }

Judy Garland's vocal fireworks, James Mason's mesmerizing descent into drunkenness, Moss Hart's razor-sharp script, George Cukor's inventive direction, and Harold Arlen's bluesy songs made *A Star Is Born* a great musical drama.

WARNER BROS. PRESENT
JUDY GARLAND
JAMES MASON

We believe there hasn't been before, even once, such performances by motion picture stars, such perfection in motion picture entertainment!

'A Star is Born'
TECHNICOLOR... **CINEMASCOPE**
JACK CARSON · CHARLES BICKFORD TOM NOONAN · MOSS HART

In 1950, the MGM studio dropped Judy Garland (see p.46). With her third husband, the producer Sid Luft, she then started to look for a project to relaunch her Hollywood career. She and Luft persuaded Warner Brothers to create a new, musical version of *A Star Is Born*, based on the 1937 film of the same name. That, in turn, was a retelling of *What Price Hollywood*, directed in 1932 by George Cukor, who was hired to work on the new film.

Cukor wanted film star Cary Grant to play the all-important male lead, Norman Maine, but Grant turned

> "*Everybody's little sister, it would seem, [Judy Garland] has grown out of her braids and into a tiara.*"
>
> *TIME* MAGAZINE, 25 OCTOBER 1954

◀ Garland grows up
The poster for the film conveys the drama of the story – a tale with grown-up themes and a fitting vehicle for an adult star.

the part down, as did British actor Stewart Granger. Eventually, another British actor, James Mason, was hired and shooting began. Garland played Esther Blodgett, a showgirl who encounters Maine, a former matinée idol whose career is in drunken freefall. Maine takes Esther under his wing and promotes her career and a name-change to Vicki Lester. Romance develops, before tensions rise as Lester's career flourishes and Maine declines into alcoholism – and suicide.

STAR TURNS
The plot was melodramatic, but the stars were brilliant. Garland gave her most powerful film performance, intense and vulnerable, reflecting her real-life troubles with drink, drugs, and marriage breakdown. Mason skillfully captured the slow and painful deterioration of a man from the peak of stardom into a booze-soaked, jealous wreck. Garland's singing was at its height of brilliance, her voice packed full of emotion. In one of the film's most spine-tingling moments, she delivers with amazing power the bluesy "The Man That Got Away", in a bar empty except for her band and Mason, watching from the shadows.

TROUBLED MASTERPIECE
The making of *A Star Is Born* was beset with expensive problems, and Garland's mood and weight fluctuated as she struggled with her health. At one point, the studio insisted on the film being re-shot in CinemaScope, a new widescreen format, so Cukor had to start again.

KEY FACTS

FILM

Director George Cukor
Screenplay Moss Hart
♪ **Music** Harold Arlen, Ray Heindorf, Skip Martin
♪ **Lyrics** Ira Gershwin
◉ **Running time** 154 minutes
Release date 29 September 1954

◉ **Key information**
A Star Is Born was nominated for six Oscars in 1954 but won none of them.

The film received rave reviews, but theatre owners complained about its length. Although Warner Brothers cut down the film, discarding two songs and some of the story's coherence, the picture ended up losing money.

BIOGRAPHY

HAROLD ARLEN (1905–86)

Writer of some of the 20th century's most popular songs, including "Stormy Weather" and "It's Only a Paper Moon", Arlen was the son of a synagogue cantor. He wrote several of Judy Garland's most memorable songs, from the innocent "Over the Rainbow", for which he won an Oscar, to the knowing "The Man That Got Away". In the 1940s, he collaborated with lyricist Johnny Mercer to create a roster of hit tunes, but was never able to repeat his earlier successes.

SILK STOCKINGS

{ 1955 }

One of the most expensive musicals of its era, Cole Porter's final stage musical, *Silk Stockings*, while packed with memorable songs, failed to live up to box office expectations.

Loosely based on Ernst Lubitsch's award-winning film comedy *Ninotchka* (1939), the show starred Hildegard Knef as frosty Russian envoy Nina Yaschenko. She is thawed into life after meeting – and dancing with – American theatrical producer Steven Canfield (Don Ameche). Like much American art of the 1950s, *Silk Stockings* was inspired by the Cold War. Its plot centred around Russian agents trying to put a stop to a musical version of Tolstoy's *War and Peace*, with a subplot featuring Peter Boroff, a noted Russia's composer, being wooed by Janice Dayton, an American swimming star. The show was based on the notion that the freedoms inherent in singing and dancing were incompatible with Soviet ideology.

STUTTERING START-UP

The original writers of the book on which the show was based, George S. Kaufman and his wife Leueen MacGrath, were replaced by Abe Burrows, who rewrote the story substantially. And following Kaufman's departure from the project, producer Cy Feuer took over the direction as well. The casting of the three

leads was risky in that none of them had previously performed in a Broadway musical comedy: Knef was a German film and stage actor, Ameche had never sung, and Gretchen Wyler, as Janice Dayton, was making her Broadway debut. But the show had a winning card – its Cole Porter score.

SAUCY SCORE

The score of *Silk Stockings*, having taken him almost two years to complete, turned out to be Cole Porter's (see pp.84–85) musical swan song. Not that the then 64-year-old's talent had run dry. The show boasts one of his greatest love songs ("All of You") and one of his greatest solo dance numbers ("Silk Stockings"). There is also plenty of humour: "Satin and Silk" is a hymn to fine lingerie, and "Stereophonic Sound" is a theatre-lover's assault

on the cinema's abandonment of simple storytelling for technological gimmickry. Even the straight songs have their comic moments. "Paris Loves Lovers" begins as a slow ballad, but soon becomes a showcase for his multi-syllabic rhymes ("Capitalistic", "Pessimistic", "Sensualistic", "Militaristic", "Atheistic", "Imperialistic", "Collectivistic").

MIXED RECEPTION

Porter's score went over well, but critics were less impressed with the show as a whole. The plotting was felt to be weak, and Ameche and Knef – neither of whom had sung or danced professionally before – were judged to be out of their depth. Nevertheless, the show ran on Broadway for just over a year, and subsequently toured in the US.

KEY FACTS

🦋 **STAGE**

🎬 **Director** Cy Feuer
📖 **Book** George S. Kaufman, Leueen MacGrath, Abe Burrows
🎵 **Music and lyrics** Cole Porter
🎭 **Venue** Imperial Theatre, New York
📅 **Date** 24 February 1955

⊙ **Key information**
The show played for 478 performances on Broadway. The movie version of 1957 took two Laurel Awards (Cyd Charisse; André Previn) and was nominated for two Golden Globes.

SILK STOCKINGS, THE MOVIE

A year after *Silk Stockings* closed on Broadway, a movie version of the show was released, directed by Rouben Mamoulian. For the 1957 film, Porter fixed the main structural problem by writing a swinging love song, "Fated to be Mated", for Fred Astaire and Cyd Charisse to pep up the second half. But he also further confused things, by adding a new solo tap number for Astaire – "The Ritz Roll and Rock", a Bill Haley parody whose anti-rock sentiment was rather at odds with the show's anti-Communist theme.

◄ **Staged glamour**
The show was punctuated by lavish set-piece numbers in which Western luxury is displayed to the Russians. The sets were by Jo Mielziner.

DAMN YANKEES

{ 1955 }

Defying theatrical lore that says people who like sport don't go to musicals, and that people who watch shows don't like sport, *Damn Yankees*, a baseball story, was a second hit for the creators of *The Pajama Game*, Adler and Ross.

The musical is based on Douglass Wallop's 1954 novel *The Year the Yankees Lost the Pennant*, and is set in a period of the 1950s when the New York Yankees dominated Major League Baseball. A retelling of Goethe's *Faust* (1808), it is set in Washington, D.C., and centres on a middle-aged fan of the Washington Senators, Joe Boyd, who trades his soul in return for the chance to be a successful young player for the team. The devil, in the form of the urbane Mr Applegate, tries in vain to tempt our hero from his wife with a dancer named "Señorita Lolita Banana" (Lola), and have him prosecuted for fraud. The deal is that Joe can keep his soul if he withdraws from the deception at the last moment, which he manages to do while securing victory for his team.

CELEBRITY CASTING

The colourful characters of Lola and Applegate have attracted a host of big name performers. The part of the devil incarnate was composed so that a comedian or celebrity with only a limited vocal range would be able to master the part. American actor and comic Ray Walston was the first to play the part on Broadway, while cinema stars such as Vincent Price and Jerry Lewis (both on tour and in a West End revival) have made acclaimed appearances in the part.

Notable Lolas include Gwen Verdon in the Broadway premiere, and the Olympic ice skater Gladys Lyne Jepson-Turner, who first played the role in the West

▼ Going for a home run
Ray Walston and Gwen Verdon, playfully looking at each other in a scene from the 1958 film.

▼ Feisty and sexy
Gwen Verdon was hugely popular in the role of Lola in the Broadway production, and when *Damn Yankees* was made into a film, she remained the big drawcard for the movie.

KEY FACTS

🎭 **STAGE**

🎬 **Director** George Abbott
📖 **Book** George Abbott, Douglass Wallop
🎵 **Music** Richard Adler
𝄞 **Lyrics** Jerry Ross
🎭 **Venue** 46th Street Theatre, New York
📅 **Date** 5 May 1955

⊙ **Key information**
The show won seven Tony Awards in 1957
and received another two nominations. The
West End run of the show began in 1957 at
the London Coliseum and lasted for a total
of 1,019 performances.

End. The choreography was by Bob
Fosse (see pp.200–01). Many of his
original routines have become iconic.

Most of the first New York cast
reprised their roles in a 1958 film
version that closely replicates George
Abbott's original production. It was
directed by Abbott and Stanley
Donen and starred singer and actor
Tab Hunter as Joe.

REGRET AND RECOGNITION

This is a highly accessible, fun show
and score. The feeble team's rallying
anthem, "Heart", once heard is never

◀ **Whatever Lola wants**
Gwen Verdon performs the
iconic song "Whatever
Lola Wants", as Lola tries
to seduce Joe.

▶ **The devil and a temptress**
Lola (Gwen Verdon) attempts to seduce
Joe (Tab Hunter) in the locker room on the
instructions of Mr Applegate.

forgotten, and an extended routine in
which Applegate recalls his demonic
historical triumphs is a gift for any
talented and charismatic performer.
"Whatever Lola Wants" has also
become a stand-alone classic.

Tragically, however, the musical
marked the end of Adler and Ross's
promising career. Jerry Ross died on
11 November 1955, from a lung
condition, just after opening night,
at the early age of 29.

In 2009, *Variety* magazine announced
that a film would be made starring
Jim Carrey as Applegate and Jake
Gyllenhaal as Joe. Lowell Ganz and
Babaloo Mandel were reported to
be contemporizing the script, which
would be produced by Craig Zadan
and Neil Meron –the team behind New
Line Cinema's hit film adaptation of
Hairspray (see pp.296–97). The film is
to feature updated choreography and
several new songs, bringing the story
completely up to date and reflecting
the very different milieu in which
professional baseball is played today.

The musical also thrives in small-
scale productions. London has
enjoyed two successful Fringe theatre
revivals. The Bridewell
Theatre helped to
establish its reputation
as a powerhouse for
musical rediscoveries
in the late 1990s when
it revived *Damn
Yankees*. British actor
Peter Gale was a
curmudgeonly, spiteful
Applegate, and the
tender scenes between
Joe and his wife
benefited enormously
from being performed
in close proximity to
the audience.

In 2014, The Landor
Theatre, an even
smaller London fringe
venue above a pub,
staged a critically
acclaimed and popular

production with British actor Jonathan
D. Ellis as an exuberant devil, ten years
after his West End appearance as Prez
in Adler and Ross's *Pajama Game*.

POPULAR WITH ACTORS

Many of the talented people who
have brought the show to life over
the years consider it to be a career
highlight. Although Tab Hunter was
cast in the film for his looks and box-
office appeal rather than his talent as
an actor or singer, he received great
acclaim for his portrayal of Joe, bringing
to the role the perfect combination of
American hero looks and vulnerability.
The success of the stage show and
subsequently the film was also a
landmark in the career of Bob Fosse.
Hunter was not a trained dancer, and
so Fosse himself dances as Joe's alter
ego in his re-creation of some of the
dance solos from the stage show.

As there is not much for the female
chorus to do, the show is the perfect
choice of production for a male-heavy
environment. It is thus a favourite
choice of boys' schools for their
students to perform. *Damn Yankees* is
unique in the musical theatre canon
as a piece in which young performers
can combine their love of sports with
the opportunity to sing and dance.

Although the baseball ethos depicted
in the show is from a gentler, less
business-minded period in the sport's
history, the yearning for success and
the devotion of its fans remains as
pertinent today as it was when it
was first written. There are also few
musicals that depict love between
husband and wife in middle age quite
as poignantly as *Damn Yankees*.

While subsequent revivals have not
enjoyed quite the success of the original,
it is always much nominated for awards.

> *"A work of flossy showbiz*
> *craftsmanship rather than artistry,*
> Damn Yankees *has little more on*
> *its mind than happy diversion."*

CHARLES ISHERWOOD, *THE NEW YORK TIMES,* JULY 2008

MUSICAL DIRECTION

Whether conducting from the orchestra pit or only present through audio and video monitors, the musical director masterminds the show.

Although the choreographer and director may move on to their next project once the musical has been launched (occasionally returning to direct revivals or cast changes), the musical director, who also conducts the show, can remain with a musical from the earliest days of casting until the final performance of the run, keeping the music true to the composer's intentions and sounding as fresh as the opening night.

A DEMANDING ROLE

A musical director must be versatile. He or she is primarily involved with casting, rehearsing, and conducting the shows. However, along with these fundamental roles, a musical director may also be asked to assist with other aspects of the musical, such as composing and arranging the music for the instrumental ensemble, or helping the soloists learn and then interpret their music. On occasion, a music director may even be asked to assist the choreography by selecting and supplying music for the dance routines. During the casting process, the musical director ensures that the lead actors can sing their parts well, and that the ensemble performers are balanced between vocal ranges and blend well.

REHEARSING THE SHOW

Once the cast has been assembled, each of the actors is required to learn their notes by heart – a process that may involve the enrolment of a voice coach, or "répétiteur". The musical director will then help them to polish the music, to get the style and the characterization right, and to ensure that it conforms to the composer's intentions. Crucially, the musical director will determine the articulation, phrasing, and dynamics of each piece so that each performance is repeatable and the ensemble can sing as one.

Then, in performance, he or she coordinates the action on the stage with the instrumental music accompanying it, creating a seamless tapestry of music, song, and dance.

▶ **Giving guidance**
American actress Gwen Verdon works with the musical director, Hal Hastings, on her role as Lola in *Damn Yankees* (see pp.116–17).

"… a good communicator, a good teacher who can be clear and patient with the actors, a good conductor… [and] meticulous about preparation."

STEPHEN SCHWARTZ, AMERICAN SONGWRITER, EXPLAINING THE QUALITIES OF A MUSICAL DIRECTOR, 2010

MY FAIR LADY

{ 1956 }

An elegant rags-to-riches story of a Cockney flower-girl who literally talks her way into the upper crust, *My Fair Lady* featured beautiful costumes by Cecil Beaton and award-winning music by Lerner and Loewe.

▲ **Gaudy yet gracious**
With its jokey wordplays – "loverly" – and vulgar colouring, the poster for the movie version of the show perfectly captured its mood and style.

The musical based on the 1912 play *Pygmalion*, by George Bernard Shaw (1856–1950), took time to be developed. First, the Hungarian producer Gabriel Pascal turned it into a film in 1938, with Shaw's blessing and the kudos of several awards, including the Oscar for Best Screenplay. Pascal also saw *Pygmalion*'s potential as a musical, but waited until Shaw's death, in November 1950, before commissioning any further work.

Pascal approached Alan Jay Lerner, who brought in his collaborative partner, Frederick Loewe (see opposite). Lerner was interested, but struggled to make the musical work without a love story. The project was abandoned until Pascal's death in July 1954, when Lerner decided he had given up prematurely. With Lerner and Loewe back in the picture, music was written and the plot revised. Eliza Doolittle is too uncouth to be employed in an actual flower shop, and therefore forced to sell small bouquets to passers-by. She meets Professor Henry Higgins and his friend Colonel Pickering, who enjoy discussing her accent, but cannot see her as human, merely an object that may perhaps be improved upon. Higgins claims he could fool anyone into thinking her a lady, with only a few months training in upper-class diction and etiquette.

LIVING A LIE
Eliza spends the night contemplating this idea, and the next day arrives at Higgins's door, determined to find a better life for herself through the medium of improved speech and manners. Higgins only agrees to take her on when a bet is proposed between himself and Pickering – can Higgins in fact fool people into thinking that Eliza is indeed a lady? Higgins and Eliza get straight to work, and what follows is scene upon scene of amusing yet, these days, somehow uncomfortable moments as Eliza is challenged to refine and improve herself.

UNDERSTANDING EMOTIONS
These experiments, and the absurdity of being taken for something she is not, begin to affect Eliza's self-esteem. She realizes that by participating in the wager, she is in fact still unfit to work in a flower shop, but now, of course, for the opposite reason: her mode of speech is too refined. The music expresses this longing, both to please Higgins, but ultimately to fit in with the people she grew up with.

Lerner and Loewe's ability to so perfectly capture the feelings of the characters – not only through words

KEY FACTS

🎭 STAGE
🎬 **Director** Moss Hart
📖 **Book** Alan Jay Lerner, based on *Pygmalion* by George Bernard Shaw
🎵 **Music** Frederick Loewe
🎵 **Lyrics** Alan Jay Lerner
🎭 **Venue** Mark Hellinger Theatre, New York
📅 **Date** 15 March 1956

⊙ Key information
My Fair Lady was the winner of six Tony Awards in 1957: Best Musical; Best Performance by a Leading Actor in a Musical; Best Direction of a Musical; Best Scenic Design; Best Costume Design; and Best Conductor and Musical Director. It was also nominated for four others, including Best Performance by a Leading Actress in a Musical and Best Choreography.

CAST LIST

Rex Harrison Henry Higgins
Julie Andrews Eliza Doolittle
Stanley Holloway Alfred P. Doolittle
Cathleen Nesbitt Mrs Higgins
Robert Coote Colonel Pickering
John Michael King Freddy Eynsford-Hill
Philippa Bevans Mrs Pearce
Viola Roache Mrs Eynsford-Hill
Christopher Hewett Zoltan Karpathy

"Why don't we just put all of the lessons together and do 'The Rain in Spain'?"

ALAN JAY LERNER, *MY FAIR LADY*, NATIONAL PUBLIC RADIO, BROADCAST 15 JULY 2000

but also the orchestration – makes *My Fair Lady* one of the greatest musicals of all. Even Higgins's suppressed feelings for Eliza – whether they be for love or mere companionship are debatable – expressed through the mellow tones of "I've Grown Accustomed to Her Face". And this from a man who spends most of the show pretending to all who know him his perfect indifference to almost everything.

Eliza's father, Alfred Doolittle, provides comedic relief. Just when the musical starts to feel a little too heavy, we get a snappy number from Eliza, as she adjures her minor love interest to stop any metaphorical protestations of love, and give her concrete evidence,

in the upbeat "Show Me". This then segues into a song performed by Alfred Doolittle, the hilarious "Get Me to the Church on Time". Forced by an inheritance into respectability, Alfred finds that he must marry his long-term mistress, and join the middle-classes, a problem with which Eliza finds herself in some sympathy.

OUTSTANDING SETS AND COSTUMES

All of this was supported by the wonderful scenic design and brilliant costumes. Oliver Smith, a talented designer and eventual winner of ten Tony Awards, had a legendary memory and strict work ethic, which enabled him to design sets that really worked for the musical in question. An original problem of staging Shaw's *Pygmalion* had been the many different settings, something that Shaw himself

▲ **The dustman and the flower girl**
Stanley Holloway as Alfred P. Doolittle (left) talks to his daughter Eliza Doolittle (Audrey Hepburn) in the film adaptation of *My Fair Lady*.

acknowledged as an issue. So when it came to *My Fair Lady*, Smith used his background in architecture and skill in stage design to make 11 different sliding sets, which enabled the scenes to be changed so quickly that the musical remained uninterrupted.

As costume designer and renowned British fashion, portrait, and war photographer, Cecil Beaton also produced some of his best work, which in turn led to his contribution to the 1964 film. For *My Fair Lady*, Beaton turned to scenes remembered from his childhood, growing up in Hampstead, north London, in

the early 1900s. The costumes told the story, as much as the dialogue and music, of Eliza's transition from a bedraggled flower-seller to pseudo princess. It is this conflagration of elements, plot, music, scenery, and costumes that helped make *My Fair Lady* one of the most beloved musicals of all time.

For the film adaptation of *My Fair Lady*, Rex Harris was cast as Henry Higgins, but Julie Andrews was overlooked for the role of Eliza Doolittle in favour of Hollywood star Audrey Hepburn. Alan Jay Lerner wrote the screenplay for the film, directed by George Cukor, and the film won a total of eight Academy Awards in 1964, including Best Picture, Best Actor (Rex Harrison), Best Director, and Best Costume Design (Cecil Beaton).

◄ **Flowering beauty**
Audrey Hepburn brought a vulnerable glamour to the role of Eliza Doolittle in her acclaimed and widely loved 1964 film portrayal.

ALAN JAY LERNER (1918–86) AND FREDERICK LOEWE (1901–88)

Lyricist Lerner and composer Loewe met in 1942, and continued to work together until 1974. Their work as a team on Broadway was so successful that they brought four musicals from stage to screen with their music – *Brigadoon*, *Camelot*, *My Fair Lady*, and *Paint Your Wagon* – and one the opposite way, *Gigi*. Loewe's patience brought out the best in Lerner; Loewe's melodies finished, Lerner would then spend weeks agonizing over the words.

WEST SIDE STORY

{ 1957 }

◄ Fateful meeting
Maria and Tony meet at the dance in the gym during the original Broadway production.

Set just a few blocks away from Broadway itself, *West Side Story* updates Shakespeare's *Romeo and Juliet* to 1950s New York. For many people, from devoted fans to serious musical critics, it is the greatest show of all time.

The musical came of age with this revolutionary show, yet *West Side Story* was a long time coming. Director and choreographer Jerome Robbins (see pp.108–09) got the idea for the show while watching his friend, Hollywood star Montgomery Clift, playing Romeo in a 1948 production of Shakespeare's classic romance. Planning to turn the play into a musical set in 1950s America, he got together with the conductor and composer Leonard Bernstein (see pp.126–27) and

American playwright Arthur Laurents. "The aim," said Robbins, "was to see if all of us – Lenny who wrote 'long-hair' music, Arthur who wrote serious plays, myself who did serious ballets – could bring our acts together and do them on the pop stage."

JUVENILE DELINQUENCY

Although the three men pushed the idea around a little, it wasn't until six years later, when a gap in Bernstein's hectic schedule opened up, that they actually began the serious work

required. By now it was the mid-1950s, and American newspapers were full of stories about juvenile delinquency. Laurents suggested to Bernstein that they centre the show on gangs in New York City's Spanish Harlem.

Always on the lookout for new inspiration, Bernstein was thrilled with the idea of making use of Latin and South American dance rhythms in his score. As a result, the mambo and cha-cha that the Sharks dance in the gym scene (the equivalent of the Capulet's ball in Shakespeare's original) are Cuban influenced, while the song "America" relies on the rhythms of the Mexican folk dance the *huapango*. In contrast, Bernstein used ideas from bebop jazz for what he called the "self-styled American" Jets. Despite this musical variety, Bernstein used the tune of the opening notes of "Maria" as a unifying musical phrase throughout the show.

TRAINED VOICES REQUIRED

It is a score far more demanding of its singers than the standard musical. In fact, the two leads must be sung by performers with some classical voice training, otherwise they will lack the range and stamina to sing their parts. Indeed, almost three decades after *West Side Story* took Broadway by storm, Bernstein conducted a new version of the score for a CD release, with opera stars Kiri Te Kanawa (singing the role of Maria) and José Carreras (singing the role of Tony). It was not that Bernstein had wanted to write an opera proper. Rather, he wanted to prove that there was no intrinsic difference between a Broadway musical and a serious opera. He

believed that a good musical was just as good as a good opera, and far better than a bad opera.

Originally, Bernstein had planned to write the show's lyrics, too, but when the pressures of work made this impossible, Laurents suggested he hire a young unknown writer who had the advantage of having grown up on New York's Upper West Side. His name was Stephen Sondheim (see pp.220–21), and he became an overnight success for his work on *West Side Story*. Working with Sondheim, Bernstein would later recall, was "like working with an alter ego".

DRIVEN BY DANCE

Sondheim was in turn impressed by Laurents' book. It was one of the shortest in Broadway history and, according to the lyricist, a "miracle" of compression. Tony and Maria "fall in love in eight lines", he once said, "and you believe it". That brevity is largely down to the emphasis *West Side Story* puts on physical communication. No Broadway musical before was as driven by dance. Whole sections of the plot are made clear, not through song, not even through dialogue, but through Robbins"s explosive dance routines. The powerful, nonverbal

---

KEY FACTS

🎭 STAGE

🎬 **Director** Jerome Robbins

📖 **Book** Arthur Laurents

🎵 **Music** Leonard Bernstein

𝄞 **Lyrics** Stephen Sondheim

🎟 **Venue** Winter Garden Theatre, New York

📅 **Date** 26 September 1957

⊙ Key information

West Side Story ran for 985 performances on Broadway (with a national tour midway through its run). It was nominated for seven Tony Awards and won three: Best Musical; Best Choreography (Jerome Robbins); and Best Scenic Design (Oliver Smith). In the UK, the show ran for 1,039 performances from 1958 to 1961.

communication of the dance was reinforced by Bernstein's music and, as *Washington Post* critic Richard Coe put it, "Leonard Bernstein's score makes us feel what we do not understand."

Little wonder *West Side Story* was a success from the moment it opened for its Washington try-out in August 1957 (before moving on to Philadelphia). As Bernstein wrote to his wife: "If it goes as well in New York as it has on the road we will have proved something very big indeed and maybe changed the face of American musical theatre."

There was no "maybe" about it. Together, Bernstein, Sondheim, Laurents, and Robbins redefined the Broadway show. There are musicals before *West Side Story* and musicals after it, and they are not the same thing.

AWARD-WINNING MOVIE
Within a few years, the show had been adapted for the screen. American film director Robert Wise directed the movie but had not yet any experience of directing musicals, so Jerome Robbins directed the musical and

Delinquent ballet ▶
The often balletic choreography of Jerome Robbins (centre) contrasted to stunning effect with the underlying threat of violence throughout the story.

dance scenes. Released in 1961, the film of *West Side Story* was as big a hit as the stage show had been. In total, the film was nominated for 11 Oscars and won ten of them, including Best Picture, Best Director, and Best Actor in a Supporting Role for George Chakiris as Bernardo.

"The most savage, restless, electrifying dance patterns we've been exposed to in a dozen seasons."

WALTER KERR, *NEW YORK HERALD TRIBUNE*, 27 SEPTEMBER 1957

▼ From Jet to Shark
George Chakiris (centre) as the Shark Bernardo in the 1961 film. He had earlier played Riff. leader of the Jets, in the London stage production.

STORYLINE

Two gangs of juvenile delinquents – the Jets and the Sharks – battle for control of the streets of New York's Upper West Side. When Tony, former leader of the Jets, and Maria, the sister of the Sharks' leader, Bernardo, fall in love, both sides violently oppose the match. As the couple continue to meet secretly, their passion deepens. But the gang members become angrier, resulting in tragedy.

TONY AND MARIA
PLAN THEIR WEDDING

	STREETS OF UPPER WEST SIDE, NEW YORK CITY	DOC'S DRUGSTORE	THE GYM	MARIA'S APARTMENT BUILDING	THE ROOFTOP	DOC'S DRUGSTORE	THE BRIDAL SHOP
PLOT OVERVIEW	**Police break up** a street fight between rival gangs ❶, the Jets and the Puerto Rican Sharks. The Jets' leader, Riff, says he will again challenge the Sharks' leader, Bernardo, at the local dance that night ❷.	**Riff tries** to persuade Tony, who founded the gang, to join them in the fight. Tony is reluctant. He then sings of his feelings of expectation ❸.	**The two gangs** engage in a dance contest, with instrumental music including "Blues", "Promenade", "Mambo", "Cha-cha", and "Jump" ❹. Meanwhile, Tony and Bernardo's sister, Maria, lock eyes, share a dance, and fall in love. Bernardo orders his sister home.	**Tony finds his way** to Maria's family home and serenades her from the street below ❺. They unite on the fire escape and declare their love for each other ❻.	**Meanwhile,** up on the roof, Bernardo's girlfriend, Anita, and the other Shark girls celebrate the virtues of life in America ❼.	**The Jets** grow agitated as they await the arrival of the Sharks for a war council ❽. When the Sharks arrive, Tony argues for a fair, weapon-free fight. Disappointed, Riff and Bernardo agree.	**Maria is distraught** when Anita tells her of the planned fight. When Tony arrives, she asks him to call it off. He agrees and, united in hope, they sing of their plan to marry ❾.

THE SONGS

❶ ❷ — ❸ — ❹ — ❺ ❻ — ❼ — ❽ — ❾

Jet Song
Riff, Action, Baby John, A-Rab, Snowboy, Jets

Maria
😊 *Tony*

Prologue
🎵 *(instrumental)*

Something's Coming
😊 *Tony*

Dance at the Gym
🎵 *(instrumental)*

Tonight
😊 *Tony, Maria*

America
😊 *Anita, Shark Girls*

Cool
😊 *Riff, Jets*

One Hand, One Heart
😊 *Tony, Maria*

⭐ *British singer Shirley Bassey* ⭐ *is one of the many stars to have recorded numbers from the show. She included "Something's Coming" in her album 12 Of Those Songs.*

⭐ *For the film, "Cool" was moved to after Riff's death, and the Jets are told to be cool when they agitate for revenge.*

TONY AND MARIA MEET ON THE FIRE ESCAPE

CAST

Larry Kert Tony
Carol Lawrence Maria
Michael Callan Riff
Ken Le Roy Bernardo
Chita Rivera Anita
William Bramley Officer Krupke

"*The sheer visual excitement is breathtaking.*"

WALTER KERR, REVIEWER, *NEW YORK HERALD TRIBUNE*, 27 SEPTEMBER 1957

STREETS OF UPPER WEST SIDE, NEW YORK CITY	THE BRIDAL SHOP	MARIA'S BEDROOM	STREETS OF UPPER WEST SIDE, NEW YORK CITY	MARIA'S BEDROOM	DOC'S DRUGSTORE	PLAYGROUND
The gangs, Anita, Maria, and Tony all anticipate the evening's events **10**. Tony pleads for peace, but is ridiculed by Bernardo. Riff and Bernardo pull knives **11**, and though Tony tries to intervene, Bernardo kills Riff. Distraught with fury, Tony kills Bernardo.	**Unaware** of the tragedy, Maria sings at work of her love for Tony **12**.	**On hearing** that Tony has killed her brother, Maria hides away at home. Tony arrives. Maria expresses her rage against Tony but eventually they agree to run away together because their love must surmount the violence **13**.	**The Jets convene** and work out what to do next, while ridiculing the police and prevailing social attitudes **14**. When they learn that the Sharks are looking for Tony armed with a gun, the gang splits up to find him.	**Anita, grieving,** tells Maria that Tony is no good **15**. But when Maria explains how deeply in love she is **16**, Anita relents and warns her that Tony is in danger of being killed. As the police arrive, Anita agrees to find Tony and tell him to wait for Maria.	**The Jets congregate** at the drugstore, where Tony is hiding in the cellar. Anita arrives to tell Tony to wait for Maria, but the gang molest and insult her **17**. In a rage, she pretends that the Sharks have murdered Maria. Tony rushes off to confront the killers.	**Tony has tracked down** the Sharks, but just as he learns that Maria is alive and well, he is shot. Maria rushes to him, comforting him as he dies **18**. She grabs the gun and threatens to kill everyone, but, overwhelmed with grief, drops it.

10 · **11** · **12** · **13** · **14** · **15** · **16** · **17** · **18**

The Rumble
(Dance) Jets,
🩰 Sharks

**Tonight Quintet
and Chorus**
Anita, Tony, Maria,
Bernardo, Riff,
😊 Jets, Sharks

I Feel Pretty
Maria, Consuelo,
Rosalia, Teresita,
😊 Francisca, Shark Girls

😊 **Somewhere**
Tony, Maria

😊 **Gee, Officer Krupke**
Jets

I Have a Love
😊 Maria

A Boy Like That
😊 Anita

Taunting Scene
(instrumental)
🩰 Anita, Jets

😊 **Somewhere**
(reprise)
😊 Tony, Maria

BERNARDO AND RIFF START TO FIGHT

MARIA THREATENS TO SHOOT

⭐ *In the 2009 Broadway revival, some of the lyrics of "A Boy Like That" were sung in Spanish, although the production later reverted to the original English version.*

LEONARD BERNSTEIN

{ COMPOSER, CONDUCTOR **1918–90** }

No matter that he was a world-class conductor known for his flamboyant style, there are many theatregoers for whom the name Leonard Bernstein will always be associated with the musical stage, and with one production in particular.

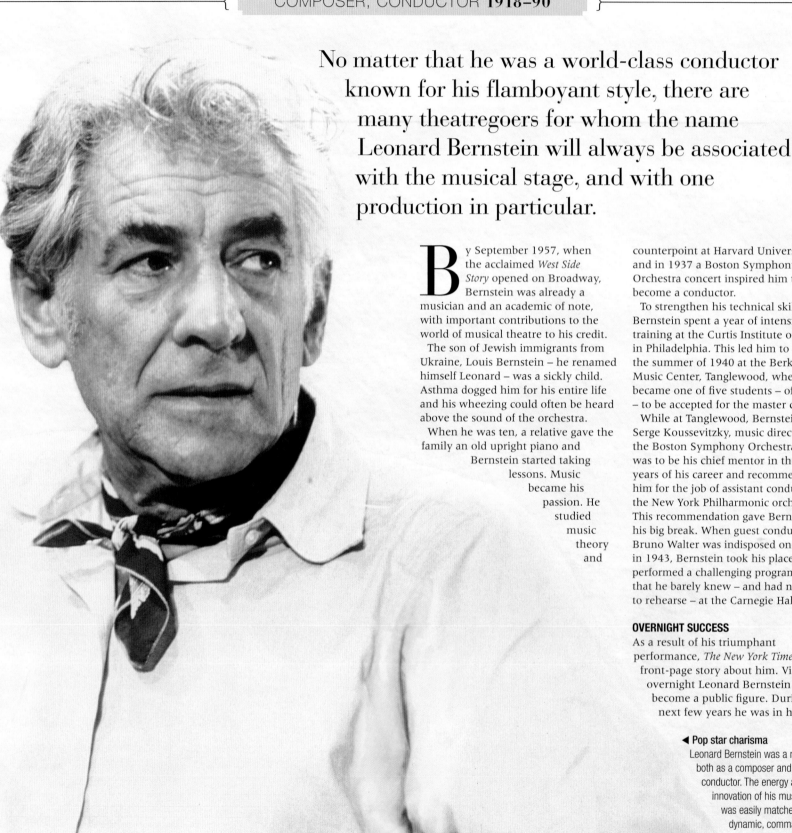

By September 1957, when the acclaimed *West Side Story* opened on Broadway, Bernstein was already a musician and an academic of note, with important contributions to the world of musical theatre to his credit.

The son of Jewish immigrants from Ukraine, Louis Bernstein – he renamed himself Leonard – was a sickly child. Asthma dogged him for his entire life and his wheezing could often be heard above the sound of the orchestra.

When he was ten, a relative gave the family an old upright piano and Bernstein started taking lessons. Music became his passion. He studied music theory and counterpoint at Harvard University, and in 1937 a Boston Symphony Orchestra concert inspired him to become a conductor.

To strengthen his technical skills, Bernstein spent a year of intensive training at the Curtis Institute of Music in Philadelphia. This led him to spend the summer of 1940 at the Berkshire Music Center, Tanglewood, where he became one of five students – of 300 – to be accepted for the master class.

While at Tanglewood, Bernstein met Serge Koussevitzky, music director of the Boston Symphony Orchestra, who was to be his chief mentor in the early years of his career and recommended him for the job of assistant conductor of the New York Philharmonic orchestra. This recommendation gave Bernstein his big break. When guest conductor Bruno Walter was indisposed one night in 1943, Bernstein took his place and performed a challenging programme that he barely knew – and had no time to rehearse – at the Carnegie Hall.

OVERNIGHT SUCCESS

As a result of his triumphant performance, *The New York Times* ran a front-page story about him. Virtually overnight Leonard Bernstein had become a public figure. During the next few years he was in huge

◀ **Pop star charisma**
Leonard Bernstein was a revelation both as a composer and conductor. The energy and innovation of his musicals was easily matched by his dynamic, commanding style when conducting an orchestra.

demand as a guest conductor of every major orchestra in the United States, until he eventually became music director of the New York Philharmonic orchestra in 1958.

Meanwhile, Bernstein was also developing a strong reputation as a composer. His varied repertoire included symphonies, operas, film scores, and work for musical shows. He collaborated with Betty Comden and Adolph Green on *On the Town* (see pp.64–65) and *Wonderful Town* (see p.105). Working with Richard Wilbur, Lillian Hellman, and others, he wrote the operetta *Candide* (1956), which became a hit upon its 1974 revival.

RENOWNED ACHIEVEMENT

For many, though, Bernstein is best known for his work on *West Side Story* (see pp.122–25). A collaboration with the choreographer Jerome Robbins (see pp.108–09) and lyricist Stephen Sondheim (see pp.220–21), its dark theme, sophisticated music, extended dance scenes, and focus on social problems marked a turning point in American musical theatre.

Bernstein's score, characterized by its strong and vivid contrasts between violence and tenderness, determined the show's tone. Many of the numbers became worldwide hits, and included "Something's Coming", "Maria", "America", "Somewhere", "Tonight", "Jet Song", "I Feel Pretty", "A Boy Like That", "One Hand, One Heart", "Cool", and the comic "Gee, Officer Krupke".

The success of this ground-breaking, alternative musical was unexpected. "Everyone told us it was an impossible project," Bernstein recalled later. "And we were told no one was going to be able to sing augmented fourths, as with *Ma-ri-a*... besides, they said, who wanted to see a show in which the first-act curtain comes down on two dead bodies lying on the stage?"

"Life without music is unthinkable... My contact with music is a total embrace."

LEONARD BERNSTEIN, 1967

◀ **Unique style**
Kiri Te Kanawa and Jose Carreras were two of the finest performers ever to sing the parts of Maria and Tony respectively in a 1985 recording.

FRESH SUCCESSES
Bernstein also wrote the score for the Academy Award-winning film released four years later. Yet *West Side Story* was not his first film. He had earlier scored *On the Waterfront*, starring Marlon Brando and directed by Elia Kazan. It was the only film commission that Bernstein accepted: all his other film scores were adapted from stage productions with songs.

As a conductor, Bernstein's energy and emotion roused audiences to a pitch of excitement that sometimes approached frenzy. His regular and highly dramatic television appearances made him the most popular conductor in the United States and brought him worldwide renown.

As a composer, Bernstein continued to break fresh musical ground. For example, in *Mass: A Theatre Piece for Singers, Players, and Dancers*, a large choir performed songs in a variety of styles in an attempt to bridge the gap between Broadway and the concert hall.

Among his many honours were three Tony Awards gained for contributions to *Wonderful Town*, *Candide*, and *West Side Story*. But not all his works were successful. Among Bernstein's rare failures was *1600 Pennsylvania Avenue*, a musical about the White House.

Bernstein was not afraid of attracting controversy for his political views. His criticism of the Vietnam War prompted the FBI to monitor his activities and associations. Yet despite increasingly fragile health, Bernstein maintained an active schedule. In August 1990, he returned to Tanglewood to conduct there for the first time in 50 years. It was to be his last performance.

▼ **A reputation sealed**
Steven Sondheim (at the piano) and Leonard Bernstein rehearsing with Carol Lawrence and the cast of *West Side Story*, New York, 1957.

KEY WORKS

On the Town, 1944 (see pp.64–65)

Peter Pan, 1950

Trouble in Tahiti, 1952

Wonderful Town, 1953 (see p.105)

On the Waterfront, 1954

West Side Story, 1957 (see pp.122–25)

Side by Side by Sondheim, 1976

TIMELINE

25 August 1918 Louis Bernstein is born in Lawrence, Massachusetts, the son of Ukrainian Jewish immigrants Sam Bernstein and his wife Jennie, née Resnick; at 16, he changes his name to Leonard, but is usually known as Lenny.

1928 Starts piano lessons.

1939 Attends the Curtis Institute, Philadelphia, to begin intensive musical training.

1943 Becomes assistant conductor of the New York Philharmonic orchestra, and achieves his first triumph as stand-in conductor for a performance at Carnegie Hall.

1943 Completes first full-scale orchestral work, which he calls Symphony No 1, *Jeremiah*.

1944 Works on first Broadway musical, *On the Town*.

COMMEMORATIVE POSTAGE STAMP, 2001

1945 Conducts New York Symphony Orchestra for the first time.

1953 Becomes the first American to conduct an opera at La Scala, Milan, Italy.

1954 *On the Waterfront* is released, with musical score by Bernstein.

1957 *West Side Story*, with music by Bernstein, opens on Broadway.

1958 Appointed music director of the New York Philharmonic orchestra.

1972 Bernstein is inducted into the Songwriters' Hall of Fame.

1976 *1600 Pennsylvania Avenue* is one of Bernstein's few musical theatre failures.

1985 National Academy of Recording Arts and Sciences awards Bernstein a Lifetime Achievement Grammy Award; one of 11 Grammys won throughout his career.

14 October 1990 Dies in New York of a heart attack brought on by emphysema and other complications.

THE MUSIC MAN

{ 1957 }

As American as musicals come, this wicked but warm tale of a conman infiltrating small-town Iowa in 1912 featured a legendary star turn from Robert Preston and was a big favourite at the 1958 Tony Awards.

▼ Film finale
Professor Harold Hill (Robert Preston) and Marian Paroo (Shirley Jones) lead the Spirit of Troy (the University of Southern California Trojan Marching Band) in the colourful and uplifting finale of the 1962 movie.

> ## "A marvellous show, rooted in wholesome and comic tradition."
>
> **BROOKS ATKINSON,** CRITIC, *THE NEW YORK TIMES*, 1957

By 1948, flautist and musical director Meredith Willson was sufficiently established as a musician and radio personality to produce a memoir, *And There I Stood With My Piccolo*, which detailed the characters and quirks of his hometown of Mason City, Iowa. "I didn't have to make up anything," Willson recalled. "I simply remembered Mason City as closely as I could." Between 1950 and 1956, Willson attempted to adapt his book into a musical. He wrote dozens of drafts and songs until, after being turned down by several producers and burdened by the volume of material he had created, the exhausted Willson approached Franklin Lacey, playwright and renowned play-doctor. Lacey assured

▲ Fearful fraudster
Professor Harold Hill nervously conducts the River City Boys' Marching Band, anxious that he is about to be exposed as a fraud.

Willson, "I can wade you through this jungle overnight," and worked the book into a shape that could be used for a stage show.

UNIMPRESSIVE START
Accountant-turned-producer Kermit Bloomgarden had produced some notable straight theatre, including Lillian Hellman's *Little Foxes* (1939) and Arthur Miller's *Death of a Salesman* (1949), but had also recently achieved musical success with Frank Loesser's *The Most Happy Fella* (1956) and involved himself with another musical with confidence. He approached Moss Hart, the famous Broadway director who had just had a smash with *My Fair Lady* (see pp.120–21). Hart was so unimpressed with the show he almost advised Bloomgarden to drop it. Actor-turned-director Morton DaCosta was hired to direct instead.

STAR SIGNINGS
Casting the lead role of charming, fast-talking conman Professor Harold Hill also proved elusive until the team decided to audition actors as well as musical comedy performers. Robert Preston's rich-toned style of sung-speech captivated them, especially on the patter numbers, and they had their leading man. Barbara Cook, the clear-voiced American soprano who had impressed all who had heard her in *Candide* (1956), was cast as Marian the librarian. The school board,

who were required to sing several tight-knit vocal arrangements, were played by the Buffalo Bills, an award-winning barbershop quartet. From the extraordinary opening number delivered in virtuosic clickety-clack rhythms by salesmen crammed into a train carriage ("Rock Island") to the heart-pumping brass band of the finale, the show packed a genuine wallop and was received rapturously. Critics and audiences were enchanted by the roguish Preston and the winsome Cook and were swept along by the ingenious score. The music combined marching band pomp (as exemplified by the unforgettable "Seventy-Six Trombones") with scattergun wit ("Rock Island", "You Got Trouble", "Pickalittle") and at least one treasured love song ("Till There Was You").

AFTER BROADWAY
After the three-and-a-half year run on Broadway, many of the key players, including Preston, the Buffalo Bills, and Pert Kelton (who played Mrs

Paroo), went on to make the 1962 hit movie. However, Cook was replaced by Shirley Jones, who had become a film star after appearing in *Oklahoma!* (see pp.58–61), *Carousel* (see pp.68–69), and the non-musical *Elmer Gantry* (1960). Unusually, show director DaCosta not only directed the movie, but also produced it, resulting in an uncommonly faithful translation of *The Music Man* from stage to screen.

The Beatles' recording "Till There Was You" on their second album in 1963 did the wider profile of *The Music Man* no harm at all, and the show remains a favourite with school and amateur productions to this day. It was remade as a TV movie in 2003 starring film actor Matthew Broderick and American singer and actor Kristin Chenowith. Though amiable enough, this version was largely lacking the compellingly dangerous quality and infectious energy that Preston had brought to the original piece.

▼ Pied Piper
The 1962 movie of the show was as big a hit as the stage production. The poster emphasized the "pied piper" nature of Harold Hill's impact upon the town of River City.

KEY FACTS

🎭 **STAGE**

🎬 **Director** Morton DaCosta

📖 **Book** Meredith Willson and Franklin Lacey

🎵 **Music and lyrics** Meredith Willson

🎭 **Venue** Majestic Theatre, New York

📅 **Date** 19 December 1957

⊙ **Key information**
The show scored a hit on Broadway and ran for 1,375 performances. It won five Tony Awards in 1958: Best Musical; Best Actor in a Musical (Robert Preston); Best Featured Actor in a Musical (David Burns); Best Featured Actress in a Musical (Barbara Cook); ando for musical director, conductor, and producer Herbert Greene.

MEREDITH WILLSON'S
The MUSIC MAN

STARRING
ROBERT PRESTON · SHIRLEY JONES
CO-STARRING
BUDDY HACKETT · HERMIONE GINGOLD · PAUL FORD
SCREENPLAY BY MARION HARGROVE
MUSIC SUPERVISED BY **RAY HEINDORF**
PRODUCED AND DIRECTED BY **MORTON DaCOSTA**

STORYLINE

Professor Harold Hill, a conman, arrives in River City, Iowa, with the aim of operating a scam. This involves convincing local townsfolk to enrol their young people in a marching band to save them from moral degradation. He then intends to take orders for uniforms and instruments and abscond with the money. But his love for Marian Paroo, the local librarian, saves him, and he redeems himself.

ROBERT PRESTON (1918–87) | **BIOGRAPHY**

Born in Newton, Massachusetts, Preston studied acting at the Pasadena Community Playhouse, in California. His early films were often westerns, though his success in *The Music Man* saw him cast in a string of successful stage musicals, such as *I Do! I Do!* (1965), *Mack And Mabel* (1974), and the films *Mame* (1974) and *Victor/Victoria* (1982). He died in California.

PLOT OVERVIEW

ON A TRAIN FROM ROCK ISLAND, ILLINOIS, TO RIVER CITY, IOWA	MARION'S HOUSE, RIVER CITY	HIGH SCHOOL GYM, RIVER CITY	RIVER CITY	THE TOWN LIBRARY
A group of travelling salesmen discuss their business and the shady activities of fellow salesman Professor Harold Hill ❶. Hill, on the same train and eavesdropping, gets off at River City to discover townsfolk with a proudly uninviting demeanour ❷. Informed by retired conman Marcellus that the local pool hall has taken delivery of a new table, Harold begins preaching against the game's evils and wins the town's trust ❸.	**Town librarian** and piano teacher Marian Paroo arrives home having dismissed Harold's attempts at flirting. She argues with her mother about her impossibly high standards ❹. Marian comforts her piano student, Amaryllis (who has no sweetheart to say goodnight to), by suggesting she say goodnight to "someone" ❺.	**At the high school gym**, Harold preaches the evils of pool, and pitches his idea for a boys' band ❻. Mayor Shinn, owner of the pool hall from which Harold is driving business, wants the school board to investigate Hill's credentials, but Harold distracts them by training them to be a barbershop quartet ❼.	**Harold, rejected once more** by Marian, puts up a brave front to Marcellus ❽. Assorted River City ladies chatter and gossip like pigeons, suggesting to Harold that Marian advocates the "dirty books" of Chaucer and Balzac and made "brazen overtures" to the town's benefactor ❾. Challenged once more by the school board, Harold encourages them to sing once more and makes his exit ❿.	**Harold declares** his love for Marian and leads the library in a jubilant dance. Marian joins in briefly before once more rejecting him ⓫.

THE SONGS

❶ ❷ ❸ ❹ ❺ ❻ ❼ ❽ ❾ ❿ ⓫

(Ya Got) Trouble
Harold Hill,
😊 *Townspeople*

Iowa Stubborn
Townspeople of
😊 *River City*

Rock Island
Charlie Cowell,
😊 *Travelling Salesmen*

Goodnight, My Someone
😊 *Marian*

Piano Lesson
Marian Paroo, Mrs Paroo,
😊 *Amaryllis*

Sincere
😊 *Quartet*

Seventy-Six Trombones
😊 *Harold, Boys and Girls*

Pickalittle (Talk-a-Little)
Eulalie Mackecknie Shinn, Maud Dunlop, Ethel Toffelmier, Alma Hix, Mrs Squires, Ladies
😊 *of River City*

The Sadder-But-Wiser Girl
😊 *Harold, Marcellus Washburn*

Goodnight, Ladies
😊 *Quartet*

Marian The Librarian
Harold, Boys
😊 *and Girls*

"Seventy-Six Trombones" was ✪ played by a 1,1076-piece marching band for the 1971 grand opening of Disney World, Florida.

PROFESSOR HAROLD HILL FLIRTS WITH LIBRARIAN MARIAN PAROO

PROFESSOR HAROLD HILL
LEADS THE BAND

"Ain't no call for a boys' band in this town …"

MARCELLUS WASHBURN, *THE MUSIC MAN* (FILM), MEREDITH WILLSON AND FRANKLIN LACEY, 1962

MARIAN'S HOME

Marian sings to her mother of her desire for a cultured, sensitive man **12**. While the town is excited about the arrival of the delivery wagon containing the band instruments **13**, Marian has found proof that Harold is a fake. But seeing the excitement of her younger brother Winthrop, she destroys the evidence.

HIGH SCHOOL GYM, RIVER CITY

The school board practise their quartet for the upcoming ice-cream social **14** and Marcellus leads a big dance number **15**. Marian dances with Harold and the town ladies, in an about-face, invite Marian to join their dance committee **16**.

On the trail of Harold, the school board are once more led into a quartet and the professor slips away **17**. Sitting on her porch, Marian sings of her love for Harold as the school board quartet continues to sing **18**. Later, Winthrop sings a song to his sister and mother that Harold has taught him **19**.

VARIOUS LOCATIONS, RIVER CITY

Marian sings to Harold of how her love for him has awakened her senses **20**. Harold intends to abscond, but when later he and Marian unknowingly sing a duet **21**, he realizes he loves her.

HIGH SCHOOL GYM, RIVER CITY

As the town closes in on the exposed conman, rather than escape, Harold chooses to stay and sing of his love for Marian **22** and is captured. After the boys' band organized by Marian deliver a ragged but heart-warming recital, Harold is forgiven despite his wrongdoing. Marian and Harold lead a joyful parade **23**.

---

12   **13**

14   **15**   **16**   **17**   **18**   **19**

20   **21**

22   **23**

The Wells Fargo Wagon
Winthrop Paroo,
😊 *Townspeople*

My White Knight
⭐ *Marian*

Shipoopi
Marcellus, Harold, Marian,
😊 *Townspeople*

It's You *Quartet, Eulalie, Maud, Ethel, Alma, Mrs*
😊 *Squires*

Will I Ever Tell You
⭐ *Marian*

Lida Rose
😊 *Quartet*

Pickalittle (Talk-a-Little) (reprise)
😊 *Ladies of River City*

Gary, Indiana
Winthrop, Mrs
😊 *Paroo, Marian*

Seventy-six Trombones/Goodnight, My Someone (reprise)
😊 *Harold, Marian*

Till There Was You
😊 *Marian, Harold*

Finale
😊 *Company*

Till There Was You (reprise)
⭐ *Harold*

⭐ *The Beatles recorded "Till There Was You" on their second album in 1963.*

HAROLD AND MARIAN
DECLARE THEIR LOVE

CAST

Robert Preston   Professor Harold Hill
Barbara Cook   Marian Paroo
Iggie Wolfington   Marcellus Washburn
David Burns   Mayor George Shinn
Helen Raymond   Eulalie Mackecknie Shinn
Pert Kelton   Mrs Paroo
Eddie Hodges   Winthrop Paroo

GIGI

A spectacular celebration of French style and flair and a subtle exploration of the ways in which a girl becomes a woman, Vincente Minnelli's *Gigi* was to charm the world.

Hollywood's longstanding love affair with France was already well under way by the 1950s – Minnelli's own *An American in Paris* had appeared in 1951. Along with Old World elegance, France offered film-makers a suggestion of the *risqué*, which was not unwelcome to an industry chafing under the restrictiveness of the Motion Picture Production Code. The Hays Code, as it was also known – named after the Presbyterian clergyman who had drawn it up in 1930 – had been found irksome from the start and seemed positively prudish to the post-war generation.

The story of a young French girl who is being brought up for a career as a courtesan, but finally finds respectable romance, *Gigi* was very clearly a challenge to the Code.

Producer Arthur Freed was so prepared to make a personal stand against the Code that he paid over the odds for the rights to a work that had already been successfully adapted to the Broadway stage. Adapted by screenwriter Anita Loos, and starring Audrey Hepburn in her début role, this stage production of *Gigi* had come out in 1951. Plans were already afoot for a film: it cost Freed over US$80,000 to buy out this project. With Lerner and Loewe he believed he had the perfect creative team. André Previn provided the score and Joseph Ruttenberg the cinematography.

TRANSATLANTIC TALENTS

British designer Cecil Beaton added a bit more European glamour with his costume designs, but the continental tone was set by the key French members of the cast. Leslie Caron took the title role, and made the perfect French teenager – though this veteran of *An American in Paris* was now 26 and a mother. As Gigi, a tomboyish teenager, she was first to be ignored, then patronized as a "funny, awkward little girl", then exploited, and ultimately adored by Louis Jourdan as Gaston Lachaille. His uncle Honoré Lachaille was played by Maurice Chevalier, who, suave and avuncular as only he could be, lent the whole production a note of the debonair.

QUESTIONABLE ETHICS?

Whilse some "cleaning up" was done for the sake of the US censors, the attitude of moral defiance endures into the final film. Gigi's grandmother and guardian Madame Alvarez (Hermione Gingold) and her sister Alicia (Isabel Jeans) are proud of their pedigree as descendants of a long line of sophisticated courtesans. The toast (if not the chosen wives) of Paris high society, they have enjoyed considerable privilege and esteem

KEY FACTS

🎬 **FILM**

🎞 **Director** Vincente Minnelli

🎬 **Screenplay** Alan Jay Lerner

📖 **Book** Alan Jay Lerner

🎵 **Music** Frederick Loewe, André Previn

𝄞 **Lyrics** Alan Jay Lerner

🕐 **Running time** 115 minutes

📅 **Release date** 15 May 1958

◉ **Key information**

Gigi made Hollywood history in its use of actual Parisian locations, including Maxim's restaurant in the Rue Royale, the Tuileries Gardens, and the Eiffel Tower. It was subsequently adapted for the stage, and opened on Broadway in 1973 and in the West End in 1985.

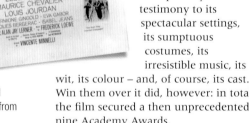

◀ **Understated design**
The simple, demure poster that advertised the film gives no indication of the controversial subject matter.

and are resolved that their young charge should have these too.

That, despite this premise, *Gigi* won over audience and critics so triumphantly is testimony to its spectacular settings, its sumptuous costumes, its irresistible music, its

◀ **French sophistication**
Louis Jourdan and Leslie Caron dressed debonairly for dinner in a classic scene from the international smash hit *Gigi*.

wit, its colour – and, of course, its cast. Win them over it did, however: in total the film secured a then unprecedented nine Academy Awards.

> *"I think I'm quite good in Gigi … Playing a believable little girl when I was 26 and a mother."*
>
> **LESLIE CARON**, *DAILY MAIL*, APRIL 2011

LI'L ABNER

{ 1959 }

The world of *Li'l Abner* could hardly have been more remote from Broadway's bright lights or Hollywood's glitz and glamour. Thanks to the magic of the musical, however, a one-horse Hicksville came to uproarious, irresistible life.

The musical is by its very nature a boundary-busting, hybrid form: it lends itself to crossovers of every kind. Cartoonist Al Capp's *Li'l Abner* comic strip had been running in American newspapers for 22 years by the time the stage musical appeared in 1956; 25 by the time the film version came out. Throughout that time, it had been read by millions – in the United States and far beyond. It had, for better or worse, done a great deal to shape attitudes to the American South as a deeply provincial, hopelessly backward place. Cinemagoers knew very well what they could expect to find in the little town of Dogpatch.

HILLBILLY HIJINKS

Li'l Abner himself (it's part of the joke that he stands six-foot-three) is a shambling, awkward but engaging figure: a simple soul, obliging and naive. He and his idle, feckless father, Pappy Yokum, both find themselves under the thumb of the formidable matriarch, Mammy Yokum. Abner is also relentlessly pursued by the beautiful Daisy Mae, though he is much too ingenuous to understand her interest. His boyish innocence is essential to his charm. Around this central group swirls a horde of subsidiary characters – yokels, idiots, hooligans, politicians, shysters, clowns; each one yet more colourful than the last. The action, like that of the strip that inspired it, is breathlessly frenetic, more or less absurd, and satirical in an easy-going, broad-brush way.

The people of Dogpatch have been told that they are going to have to move to make way for a nuclear test, while an opportunistic tycoon tries to gain the secret formula for Mammy's special Yokumberry tonic. His mistress, the beautiful but sinister Appassionata von Climax, sets out to win Abner's hand, as a way of securing the secret, to Daisy Mae's considerable distress. Their rivalry lends a special edge to the festivities of Sadie Hawkins Day – when, by town tradition, a great running race is held and a woman may marry any man she catches.

FROM STAGE TO SCREEN

The Broadway production had always been intended as the pilot for a film, which was backed by Paramount Pictures. Though a total newcomer to the world of the musical, Peter Palmer never disappointed, winning a Theatre World Award for a performance in which he made the Li'l Abner part his own. And having starred in the Broadway show, he won the title role for the 1959 film.

KEY FACTS

🎥 **FILM**

🎬 **Director** Melvin Frank

🎞 **Screenplay** Norman Panama, Melvin Frank

📖 **Book** Norman Panama, Melvin Frank

🎵 **Music** Gene de Paul, Nelson Riddle, Joseph J. Lilley

♪ **Lyrics** Johnny Mercer

🕐 **Running time** 114 minutes

📅 **Release date** 11 December 1959

◎ **Key information**

Melvin Frank and Norman Panama had been collaborating for the best part of two decades by the time *Li'l Abner* appeared, but the first musical they had worked on together had been *White Christmas* (1954).

▶ **From cartoon-strip to Hollywood**
Stella Stevens, Leslie Parrish, Peter Palmer, Julie Newmar, and the rest of the cast in a scene from the film *Li'l Abner*, featuring Nelson Riddle and Joseph J. Lilley's Oscar-winning score.

THE **SOUND** OF **MUSIC**

{ 1959 }

The 1959 show *The Sound of Music*, the saga of the von Trapp family and their escape to freedom, was the crowning achievement of Rodgers and Hammerstein. The 1965 film was one of the most successful movie musicals in history.

▼ **Broadway success**
Actress Mary Martin (Maria von Trapp) performs a song for the children in the first Broadway production of *The Sound of Music*. Martin won a Tony Award for her performance.

"The Sound of Music ... offered one of the last breaths of innocence in American cinema."

ANTHONY LANE, *THE NEW YORKER*, 1999

▼ **An established singing troupe**
The real von Trapp family embarked on their singing career after the family fortune was lost in the early 1930s, and were already well known in Europe before 1938.

In 1960, 20th Century Fox purchased the rights to adapt the highly successful stage musical *The Sound of Music* for the screen for US$1.25 million. The show, based on a memoir by Maria von Trapp, had opened on Broadway on 16 November 1959 and featured the established Broadway star Mary Martin and actor and singer Theodore Bikel. It was the final collaboration of the award-winning songwriting partnership of Richard Rodgers (see pp.70–71) and Oscar Hammerstein II (see p.99).

INTO PRODUCTION

Ernest Lehman, hired to adapt the script for the screen, championed Robert Wise as director and producer based on their collaboration on the hugely successful film of *West Side Story* (see pp.122–25). After having viewed some footage from the not yet released film of *Mary Poppins* (see pp.154–57). Wise insisted on signing Julie Andrews to play the lead role of Maria.

Many actors were considered for the part of Captain von Trapp. Canadian-born actor Christopher Plummer turned the role down several times, until Wise was able to convince him that they could make the part more

challenging by strengthening and deepening the character for the film. Music and choreography rehearsals began in February 1964, and principal filming began in March in Los Angeles. Shooting on location in and around the Austrian city of Salzburg took place from April to July, and a few final scenes were filmed back in Los Angeles in July. Spending so much time on location was difficult for all concerned, and the weather created havoc with the production schedule.

SLOW WARM-UP

First released in March 1965, *The Sound of Music* had been produced at a cost of US$8.2 million. Despite lukewarm initial reviews, the film was to become a massive international hit. It won five of the nine Oscars for which it was nominated in 1966, and up to the end of 2014 had grossed US$286 million worldwide.

The soundtrack recording of the score was released by RCA and spent more than a year in the record charts in countries around the world. After adjustment for inflation, in terms of box office receipts, it is to date the most successful film musical ever produced, the third highest grossing film in North America, and the fifth highest worldwide.

BEYOND THE CINEMA

The film has continued to enjoy popularity long after the cessation of regular screenings in the cinema. It was first broadcast on American television on ABC in 1976, receiving record ratings. NBC bought the US television rights, airing *The Sound of Music* annually for 21 years from 1979. Since 2002, it has been shown on a yearly basis on television in the US on the ABC family of networks.

The enduring popularity of the film with succeeding generations has led to regular revivals of the stage show over the decades throughout the world in countries as diverse as Sweden, Japan, and Argentina.

In 2000, a London cinema screened a version of the film with subtitled lyrics, encouraging audiences to sing along. "Sing Along Sound of Music" was an almost instant and massive hit on both sides of the Atlantic.

A company called Sing-A-Long-A Worldwide offers packages that include a showing of the film with subtitles, a host to coordinate the event, and lead vocal warm-ups, a costume parade of those audience members who show up in costume, and other participatory activities.

MARIA TURNS POP IDOL

In 2006, *The Sound of Music* entered a new media incarnation. When negotiations fell through with Hollywood star Scarlett Johansson to play Maria von Trapp for the West End revival of *The Sound of Music*, producers Andrew Lloyd Webber and David Ian approached BBC Television about creating a *Pop Idol*-style reality TV show to allow the public to choose who would play Maria. The show went ahead under the title *How Do You Solve a Problem Like Maria?*, and the relatively unknown Welsh actress and singer Connie Fisher won the role. She played the part for well over a year.

▶ **Maria: a problem solved**
After winning a TV competition, Connie Fisher, pictured, played the part of Maria in the 2006 London stage revival of the show.

RELATED SHOWS

Oklahoma!, 1943, Richard Rodgers, Oscar Hammerstein II (pp.58–61)

Carousel, Richard Rodgers, Oscar Hammerstein II, 1945 (pp.68–69)

South Pacific, 1949, Richard Rodgers, Oscar Hammerstein II (p.96)

The King and I, 1950, Richard Rodgers, Oscar Hammerstein II (pp.98–99)

My Fair Lady, 1956, Frederick Loewe, Alan Jay Lerner (pp.120–121)

Mary Poppins, 1964, Richard and Robert Sherman (pp.154–57)

KEY FACTS

🎬 **FILM**

🎞 **Director** Robert Wise
📄 **Screenplay** Ernest Lehman
📖 **Book** Maria von Trapp
🎵 **Music** Richard Rodgers
♪ **Lyrics** Oscar Hammerstein II
🕐 **Running time** 174 minutes
📅 **Release date** 2 March 1965

⊙ **Key information**
The film won five Oscars in 1966, including Best Picture, Best Director, and Best Music. In the same year it also won the Golden Globes for Best Motion Picture and for the Best Motion Picture Actress (Julie Andrews).

STORYLINE

After finding that the life of a nun is not for her, Maria becomes governess to the von Trapp family. Captain von Trapp's grief at the loss of his wife rules their lives, but Maria brings love and song back into the home. Love develops between Maria and the Captain and they marry. The family use the ruse of performing at a local music festival to provide the means of escaping the Nazis after the annexation of Austria to Germany.

MARY MARTIN AND
THEODORE BIKEL

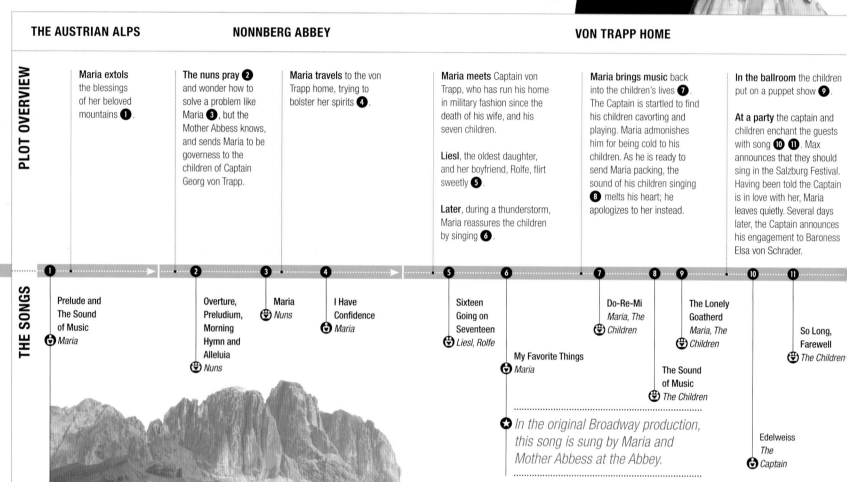

| THE AUSTRIAN ALPS | NONNBERG ABBEY | | VON TRAPP HOME | | |

PLOT OVERVIEW

Maria extols the blessings of her beloved mountains ❶.

The nuns pray ❷ and wonder how to solve a problem like Maria ❸, but the Mother Abbess knows, and sends Maria to be governess to the children of Captain Georg von Trapp.

Maria travels to the von Trapp home, trying to bolster her spirits ❹.

Maria meets Captain von Trapp, who has run his home in military fashion since the death of his wife, and his seven children.

Liesl, the oldest daughter, and her boyfriend, Rolfe, flirt sweetly ❺.

Later, during a thunderstorm, Maria reassures the children by singing ❻.

Maria brings music back into the children's lives ❼. The Captain is startled to find his children cavorting and playing. Maria admonishes him for being cold to his children. As he is ready to send Maria packing, the sound of his children singing ❽ melts his heart; he apologizes to her instead.

In the ballroom the children put on a puppet show ❾.

At a party the captain and children enchant the guests with song ❿ ⓫. Max announces that they should sing in the Salzburg Festival. Having been told the Captain is in love with her, Maria leaves quietly. Several days later, the Captain announces his engagement to Baroness Elsa von Schrader.

THE SONGS

❶ Prelude and The Sound of Music
☺ *Maria*

❷ Overture, Preludium, Morning Hymn and Alleluia
☺ *Nuns*

❸ Maria
☺ *Nuns*

❹ I Have Confidence
☺ *Maria*

❺ Sixteen Going on Seventeen
☺ *Liesl, Rolfe*

❻ My Favorite Things
☺ *Maria*

❼ Do-Re-Mi
Maria, The
☺ *Children*

❽ The Sound of Music
☺ *The Children*

❾ The Lonely Goatherd
Maria, The
☺ *Children*

❿ Edelweiss
The
☺ *Captain*

⓫ So Long, Farewell
☺ *The Children*

✪ In the original Broadway production, this song is sung by Maria and Mother Abbess at the Abbey.

✪ The opening sequence took 12 takes, as Julie Andrews kept being knocked down by the downdraft from the helicopter used to film the scene.

DRESS WORN BY BRIGITTA
AS SHE SINGS "DO-RE-MI"

MARIA AND THE
CHILDREN HAVE FUN

CAST

Julie Andrews Maria
Christopher Plummer
Captain von Trapp
Eleanor Parker The Baroness
Richard Haydn Max Detweiler
Peggy Wood Mother Abbess
Charmian Carr Liesl
Heather Menzies Louisa
Nicholas Hammond Friedrich

Duane Chase Kurt
Angela Cartwright Brigitta
Debbie Turner Marta
Kym Karath Gretl
Anna Lee Sister Margaretta
Portia Nelson Sister Berthe
Ben Wright Herr Zeller
Daniel Truhitte Rolfe Gruber

"You brought music back into the house."

CAPTAIN VON TRAPP TO MARIA, *THE SOUND OF MUSIC* (ERNEST LEHMAN), 1965

NONNBERG ABBEY	VON TRAPP HOME	NONNBERG ABBEY	VON TRAPP HOME	FESTIVAL STAGE	NONNBERG ABBEY
Having retreated to the Abbey, Maria is convinced by the Mother Abbess to face her fears **12**.	**Maria returns**, to everyone's joy **13**. Seeing that the Captain has feelings for Maria, the Baroness leaves him. The Captain and Maria declare their love for each other **14**.	**The wedding** of Maria and Captain von Trapp **15**.	**On their return** from their honeymoon, Maria and the Captain find their home draped with swastika flags, which they rip down. Maria gives Liesl motherly advice regarding her feelings toward Rolfe **16**. **The Nazis** try to conscript the Captain, but to stall he claims that the family is to perform at the Salzburg Festival that evening.	**At the festival**, the von Trapps perform **17 18 19**, and then slip out of the theatre to escape from the Nazis.	**The von Trapp family** hides from the Nazis at the Abbey, but realize they must leave. They escape across Maria's beloved mountains **20**.

12   **13**   **14**   **15**   **16**   **17**   **18 19**   **20**

14
Something Good
Maria,
☻ *The Captain*

15
Processional and Maria (reprise)
☻ *The Nuns*

16
Sixteen Going on Seventeen (reprise)
☻ *Maria, Liesl*

17
Do-Re-Mi (reprise)
Maria, Captain von Trapp, The Children
☻

18
So Long, Farewell (reprise)
The Children, Maria, Captain von Trapp
☻

20
Climb Ev'ry Mountain (reprise)
☻ *The Nuns*

12
Climb Ev'ry Mountain
☻ *Mother Abbess*

13
My Favorite Things (reprise)
☻ *The Children, Maria*

19
Edelweiss
Captain von Trapp, Maria,
☻ *The Children*

MARIA AND THE CAPTAIN ARE MARRIED

★ *Many people believe that "Edelweiss" is a traditional Austrian folk song, but in fact it was an original composition by Rodgers and Hammerstein.*

GYPSY

{ 1959 }

A powerful, multifaceted show about the rise of the celebrity stripper Gypsy Rose Lee, *Gypsy* boasts a melodious, cultured score and one of the great starring roles in musical theatre. A film version of the musical proved just as successful.

Producer David Merrick had acquired the rights to *Gypsy: A Memoir*, the autobiography of striptease artist Gypsy Rose Lee, and was keen to adapt the book into a musical. The story concerned the childhood vaudeville experiences of Louise (Gypsy's real name) and her sister June (herself later a well-known actress), as steered by their ambitious mother Rose, and Louise's eventual route into burlesque performance.

THE TEAM
Well-known writing duo Adolph Green and Betty Comden were invited to adapt the book, but couldn't figure out how to make it work as musical theatre and passed on the project. Jerome Robbins (see pp.108–09) was quickly hired as director and choreographer and insisted on his *West Side Story* (see pp.122–25) colleague, Arthur Laurents, as book writer. Though Laurents had been appalled by Robbins' behaviour on *West Side Story*, when he spotted the inherent theme of the story – "the idea of parents who live their children's lives" as he said – he was on board.

Star performer Ethel Merman (see pp.140–41) had been with the project from

the beginning, but with both Irving Berlin and Cole Porter turning it down, the production struggled to find an established composer. When Jerome Robbins heard the first songs Stephen Sondheim had produced for *A Funny Thing Happened on the Way to the Forum* (see p.149), he recommended the young composer to co-producer Leland Hayward. However, Merman vetoed Sondheim, because his one Broadway credit, *West Side Story*, had been as a lyricist. Though keen to establish himself as both a composer and a lyricist, Sondheim agreed to provide lyrics to Jule Styne's music after Oscar Hammerstein advised it would be good experience to write for a star of Merman's particular qualities.

Though a collaboration of convenience, the Styne–Sondheim partnership proved to be a good one. Styne's profligate melodic facility and instinctive old-school skill blended with Sondheim's sophisticated ambitions and attention to detail to produce a musical score of rare richness and drama. The first act closer, "Everything's Coming up Roses", brilliantly conveys Rose's desperate optimism in the face of disaster (June, the talented daughter,

◀ **Fortune-telling**
Karl Malden and Rosalind Russell share a contemplative moment in the 1962 movie version of *Gypsy*, directed by Mervyn LeRoy.

has just eloped) and is a Merman-shaped classic. The closing number, "Rose's Turn", in which Rose reveals her vulnerability and has the nervous breakdown she's been heading towards for the whole show, was a tour de force for writers and performer alike and a shattering theatrical moment. Reportedly, when Sondheim and Styne first presented it to the cast late into the production, everyone involved broke down and shed tears.

The pivotal role of Herbie, Rose's long-suffering beau, went to actor Jack Klugman, despite the fact that he couldn't sing – something he was all too aware of. He pleaded with the creative team to sack him ("Get a guy in you can write a couple of songs for") but Sondheim assured him that he didn't want a musical voice in the role; "I want someone I can believe," the composer told Klugman.

PRODUCTION STRUGGLES
Robbins struggled to make his mark on the show and resorted to volatile behaviour to assert himself. When the out-of-town try-outs were running long, there was ill-tempered negotiation about what to cut; Robbins wanted less script and Laurents wanted the child vaudeville material trimmed. In the end, both acquiesced. Robbins also wanted to drop the brassy Robert Ginzler-orchestrated overture (see right), since regarded as a classic of its kind. At one point, without warning, he also removed the song "Little Lamb", whereupon Styne threatened to remove the entire score if it was not reinstated; it was.

BROADWAY AND BEYOND
Gypsy opened in 1959 to warm reviews that praised the emotional complexity of the piece, the score, and the performances – especially that of Ethel

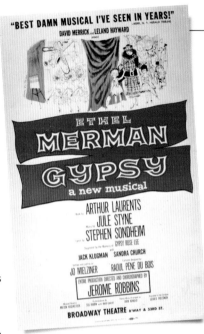

▲ **Another vehicle for Merman**
Ethel Merman secured her place as a Broadway legend with a performance as Gypsy Rose Lee that was universally acclaimed.

BIOGRAPHY
ROBERT "RED" GINZLER
(1910–62)

Acclaimed orchestrator Ginzler was a self-taught trombonist, an early associate of jazz legend Bix Beiderbecke, and a player in the Paul Whiteman and Benny Goodman bands and various Broadway orchestra pits. He began conducting and arranging music, becoming known as a fast producer of upbeat jazzy numbers, notably for *Damn Yankees* (see pp.116–17) and *The Music Man* (see pp.128–31).

KEY FACTS

STAGE

- **Director** Jerome Robbins
- **Book** Arthur Laurents
- **Music** Jule Styne
- **Lyrics** Stephen Sondheim
- **Venue** Broadway Theatre, New York
- **Date** 21 May 1959

Key information

The initial Broadway run was a respectable 702 performances, with Ethel Merman (Rose), Jack Klugman (Herbie), and Sandra Church (Louise) in the leading roles. *Gypsy* is frequently considered one of the crowning achievements of the mid-20th-century's conventional musical theatre art form, often called the "book musical".

Knock on Wood

Natalie Wood certainly looked the part of Gypsy Rose Lee in the 1962 movie, but her singing voice in the film was dubbed.

Merman. The perfect marriage of character and performer ("Rose is dumb, like Ethel," said Laurents, "she doesn't calculate, she just plunders right ahead"), Merman's performance in *Gypsy* became a Broadway legend's finest hour.

MOVIE VERSION

Just as for *Annie Get Your Gun* (see pp.72–75) a decade earlier, Merman was passed over for the 1962 movie, with the role of Rose going to Rosalind Russell. Karl Malden played Herbie Sommers. In the film, which is basically faithful to the show, both Rosalind Russell and Natalie Wood's singing voices are dubbed. Although the film was successful, the views of the critics were mixed. Bosley Crowther of the *The New York Times* memorably commented: "That tornado of a stage mother that Ethel Merman portrayed on Broadway in the musical comedy *Gypsy* comes out little more than a big wind in the portrayal that Rosalind Russell gives her in the transfer of the comedy to the screen."

MEMORABLE MOTHER

The central role of the mother has attracted heavyweight leading ladies in revivals down the years, who have performed with sufficient character and distinction to get Rose out from under the shadow of Merman. These include Angela Lansbury (1973), Tyne Daly (1989), Bette Midler (1993), Bernadette Peters (2003), Patti Lupone (2008), and Imelda Staunton (2014).

"The best damn musical I've seen in years."

WALTER KERR, CRITIC, *NEW YORK HERALD TRIBUNE*, MAY 1959

ETHEL MERMAN

For a generation of stage and screen audiences, the sight and sound of Ethel Merman belting out "There's No Business Like Show Business" and many others truly captured the spirit of musicals.

▲ **Popular movie actress**
Ethel Merman starred as Sally Adams in the 1953 Technicolor musical film *Call Me Madam*, based on the stage play of the same name.

For more than a quarter of a century, it seemed that no Broadway season was complete without a musical featuring the brassy songstress. In her prime, Ethel Merman was the darling of songwriters such as George Gershwin, Irving Berlin, Cole Porter, and Jule Styne. They liked her brash, aggressive personality, shrewd comic sense, and complete lack of nerves.

Merman was also well aware of her talents. "I can hold a note as long as the Chase National Bank," she would say. "I take a breath when I have to."

Born to a middle-class family of German and Scottish descent, Merman derived her love of the theatre from regular Friday night visits to vaudeville shows. She tried to copy the singers, but her parents were against her pursuing a show-business career and she went to work as a stenographer.

But that was her day job – by night she was singing at private parties and performing at night clubs. It was during this period that she shortened her name from Zimmerman to Merman to make it more manageable for publicity purposes.

STAGE TO FILM

As the gigs multiplied, Merman's parents accepted the inevitable and she secured a contract with Warner Brothers. However, after several months of not being offered any film roles, she was allowed to continue her live performances. While Merman was working at the Brooklyn Paramount theatre, news of her talent reached composer George Gershwin (see pp.24–25), who then cast her in *Girl Crazy* (1930).

On the show's opening night, Merman stopped the show with her rendition of "I've Got Rhythm". She held a high C for 16 heroic bars and the audience demanded several encores. After the curtain came down, Gershwin rushed into her dressing room with some advice: "Don't ever let anyone give you a singing lesson. It'll ruin you." Not given to false modesty, Merman recalled later: "When I finished that song a star had been born – me."

When *Girl Crazy* closed she was hired to rescue a shaky edition of the *George White Scandals* in 1931, before stealing *Take a*

◀ **Hoofin' and singin'**
Ethel Merman (left) and Mitzi Gaynor perform "A Sailor's Not a Sailor ('Til a Sailor's Been Tattooed)" in *There's No Business Like Show Business* (1954).

Chance (1932) with her rendition of "Eadie Was a Lady". Film roles followed: *We're Not Dressing* (1934) with Bing Crosby, and *Kid Millions* (1934) with Eddie Cantor.

Back on Broadway, Vinton Freedley's *Anything Goes* (1934) was comprehensively rewritten during rehearsals and Merman used her secretarial skills to type the revised

> "*Broadway has been very good to me. But then, I've been very good to Broadway.*"
>
> **ETHEL MERMAN**

script for the musical. The show was memorable for the Cole Porter (see pp.84–85) numbers performed by Merman, including "Blow Gabriel, Blow", "I Get a Kick Out of You", and "You're the Top".

Ethel Merman also appeared in the film version, although it was clear that movies did not give her particular abilities the scope they deserved. Even so, she appeared in 14 different films, including *Alexander's Ragtime Band* (1938), *There's no Business Like Show Business* (1954), and the zany *It's a Mad, Mad, Mad, Mad World* (1963).

Broadway was where Ethel Merman belonged. Composers knew she would hit every note on the mark, hold it as long as necessary, give it the right shading, and follow the trickiest rhythm flawlessly. Lyric writers could rely on her making every syllable distinct and squeezing every drop of mirth from a comic line.

MEMORABLE SHOWS

The long list of memorable shows featuring Ethel Merman included Cole Porter's *Dubarry was a Lady* and the Jule Styne–Stephen Sondheim musical *Gypsy*. But it was her association with Irving Berlin in *Annie Get Your Gun* (see pp.72–75), *Call Me Madam*, and the film *There's no*

Consummate Broadway star
Ethel Merman's uniquely brash style and ability to hold a high note for a seeming eternity endeared her to Broadway and movie audiences alike.

▶ **Deserved recognition**
Ethel Merman receiving one of the many awards bestowed in her long career. With her (from left) are Hal David, Ginger Rogers, and Lucille Ball.

Business Like Show Business that many saw as representing the peak of Ethel Merman's career.

Her appearance in *Call Me Madam* won her a Tony Award and she followed this up with a Golden Globe for Best Actress in a Musical for the screen adaptation. However, it was her performance as the domineering mother in *Gypsy* that she considered her finest. The critics agreed. The *New York Post* called her "brilliant," while *The Times* thought her performance "indomitable", both as singer and actress. Losing the film role to Rosalind Russell was said to be one of her biggest disappointments.

Yet Merman's presence was still needed in other movies. After her role as a raucous battle-axe in *It's a Mad, Mad, Mad, Mad World* (1963), she appeared in the rather less successful *The Art of Love* (1965). But Merman's belated appearance in *Hello, Dolly!* (see pp.160–61) in 1970, six years after it opened, was a major triumph.

On her return to the New York stage, Merman's opening-night performance was continually interrupted by prolonged standing ovations. The critics were unanimous in their praise.

It was not quite the end of a career studded with success. In addition to her Broadway and film work there were hit records, numerous television appearances, and her own radio show.

When Ethel Merman died, in her Manhattan home in February 1984, all 36 Broadway theatres dimmed their lights in tribute to the star they recognized as the undisputed first lady of the musical comedy stage.

KEY WORKS

Girl Crazy, 1930

"Eadie Was a Lady", 1933

Anything Goes, 1934 (see pp.30–31)

"You're the Top", 1934

"I Get a Kick Out of You", 1935

Annie Get Your Gun, 1946 (see pp.72–75)

Call Me Madam, 1950

"If I Knew You Were Comin' I'd Have Baked a Cake", 1950

Call Me Madam, 1953

There's No Business Like Show Business, 1954

Gypsy, 1959 (see pp.138–39)

TIMELINE

- **16 January 1908** Born Ethel Agnes Zimmerman to accountant Edward Zimmerman and his teacher wife Agnes née Gardner in Astoria, New York.

- **1930** Her first Broadway appearance, in Gershwin musical *Girl Crazy*, brings the house down with her rendition of "I Got Rhythm".

- **1934** Merman's performance in Cole Porter's *Anything Goes* wins critical acclaim.

ETHEL MERMAN

- **1936** Appears opposite Bing Crosby in the screen adaptation of *Anything Goes*, but she feels she is being cast in a supporting role.

- **1939** Appears in two further Porter shows: *Dubarry was a Lady* and *Panama Hattie*.

- **1946** *Annie Get Your Gun* opens at Broadway's Imperial Theatre and runs for nearly three years and 1,147 performances.

- **1950** *Call Me Madam* opens on Broadway; it wins her a Tony Award.

- **1953** Screen adaptation of *Call me Madam* released; Merman's performance wins her a Golden Globe Best Actress Award.

- **1954** Stars in Irving Berlin's *There's No Business Like Show Business*.

- **1959** Wins critical acclaim for her portrayal of a stripper's mother in *Gypsy*.

- **1966** Aged 59 – despite claiming she is four years younger – she returns for a brief revival of *Annie Get Your Gun*.

- **1970** Plays the title role in *Hello, Dolly!* and wins the Drama Desk Award for Outstanding Actress in a Musical.

- **1972** Receives a special Tony Award in recognition of her achievements. This follows three previous Tony Awards for Best Actress.

- **15 February 1984** Dies in New York after undergoing surgery to remove a brain tumour.

OLIVER!

{ 1960 }

Lionel Bart's upbeat, colourful take on a classic novel by Charles Dickens – replete with an unforgettable music-hall-style score – makes for one of the great British musicals.

KEY FACTS

STAGE

- **Director** Peter Coe
- **Book** Lionel Bart
- **Music and lyrics** Lionel Bart
- **Venue** New (now Noël Coward) Theatre, London
- **Date** 30 June 1960

⊙ Key information

The initial West End run was 2,618 performances. The original Broadway production won the 1963 Tony Awards for Best Original Score, Best Conductor and Musical Director, and Best Scenic Design.

Of all Charles Dickens's works, his 1838 novel of underworld London and organized juvenile crime, *Oliver Twist*, inspired the most stage adaptations during the Victorian and Edwardian eras. By the time David Lean's acclaimed 1948 movie was made, *Oliver Twist* had become a streamlined story retaining the author's vivid dramatic scenarios and unforgettable characters.

Though the film may have served as a narrative template, it was the wrapper for Terry's "Oliver Twist" chocolate bar that inspired Lionel Bart's musical adaptation. Bart envisioned a playful show that would convey "the inherent Dickens mood and period atmosphere, translate it into a modern entertainment, creating a new expression of the 'musical' form".

Many were sceptical that Dickens's cruel story of harsh neglect, sinister youth corruption, and brutal violence could be turned into a musical, and Bart struggled to find industry supporters. Finally, the project's potential was spotted by enterprising producer Donald Albery who had, among other ventures, brought Samuel Beckett's *Waiting For Godot* to London.

The production design was by Sean Kenny, whose ground-breaking sets would influence stage design in theatre for many years to come.

The key role of "prostitute with a heart of gold" Nancy went to nightclub singer-turned-actress Georgia Brown, while Fagin was played, despite Bart's initial misgivings, by Ron Moody. Oliver and the Artful Dodger were played by a succession of young boy sopranos – including Phil Collins and Davy Jones.

THE SHOW OPENS

Following a period of development in which Coe and others reshaped Bart's script to include more details from the novel, the show finally opened in

◀ **Dodging to fame**
Mark Lester was charming as Oliver (left) and Jack Wild completely disarming as the Artful Dodger, in the 1968 smash hit movie adaptation of *Oliver!*

▲ **Please, sir, I want some more...**
The characterful theatre programme and posters for the highly successful West End production of *Oliver!* were illustrated by Denis Wrigley.

June 1960 to a tumultuous reception, with a 20-minute standing ovation. Numbers like "Consider Yourself" and "I'd Do Anything" had stopped the show, while the emotional centrepiece "Where Is Love?" and Nancy's defence of an abusive relationship "As Long As He Needs Me" announced themselves as new standards.

ENDURING SUCCESS

Following a remarkable six-year West End run, the Carol Reed-directed 1968 movie immortalized Moody's performance as Fagin.

In 1994, producer Cameron Mackintosh (see pp.232–33) staged a new production, with additional material by Lionel Bart, which ran for four years at the London Palladium. In 2009, this production was reinvented in spectacular style for the Theatre Royal, Drury Lane, with Rowan Atkinson as Fagin.

"It is a very long time indeed since I came out of the theatre whistling the tunes."

BERNARD LEVIN, BRITISH THEATRE CRITIC, *DAILY EXPRESS*, 1960

BYE BYE BIRDIE

{ 1960 }

When *Bye Bye Birdie* opened on Broadway in 1960, it felt like a breath of fresh air, with its youthful cast and upbeat tunes. It remains a favourite with young performers to this day.

No one had heard of composer Charles Strouse and lyricist Lee Adams, who would go on to write *Annie* together, or even the show's star, the unknown Dick Van Dyke, rumoured to have been cast after chatting with Strouse backstage. Yet together they created a hit that has endured as a favourite show for high-school productions.

It's easy to see why it's popular with young performers. Many of the characters are teenagers, the score is not too difficult to sing, and if the lightweight, feel-good show explores anything at all, it is the eternally topical subject of how the generation gap means parents don't understand their kids' taste in music.

ELVIS IMPERSONATOR

The plot was inspired by a time in 1958 when Elvis Presley was drafted into the army and the frenzy that surrounded his military posting to Germany. Before leaving, in a carefully stage-managed photo opportunity, it was arranged that he give "one last kiss" to a carefully selected fan. The event is replicated in *Bye Bye Birdie* when 15-year-old Kim MacAfee from the small town of Sweet Apple, Ohio, is selected to receive a final kiss from the musical's fictional pop star, Conrad Birdie, on *The Ed Sullivan Show.*

Dick Van Dyke played his timid manager, escaping the clutches of a tyrannical mother encouraged by girlfriend Rosie. Subplots and musical numbers dramatize the consequences of Kim's brush with fame for the inhabitants of Sweet Apple, especially Kim's jealous boyfriend, Hugo, who sabotages the publicity stunt live on air. Although much of the humour and pathos is nostalgic and based in the sentiment of 1950s Broadway, there is also an attempt to introduce rock'n'roll music in a couple of the show's numbers.

NO ROOM FOR SATIRE

Despite the show's enduring popularity in high schools, professional productions – including a major tour starring Tommy Tune and a 2009 Broadway revival – were generally not well received by the critics. Commentators have suggested that the sunny tone of the original is hard to reproduce in a more cynical age.

KEY FACTS

STAGE
- **Director** Gower Champion
- **Book** Michael Stewart
- **Music** Charles Strouse
- **Lyrics** Lee Adams
- **Venue** Martin Beck Theatre, New York
- **Date** 14 April 1960

Key information
The original production ran for a total of 607 performances. It was choreographed by Gower Champion and the cast included Dick Van Dyke and Chita Rivera.

▼ The Elvis factor
Jesse Pearson as Conrad Birdie in the movie production of *Bye Bye Birdie*, performing the number "Honestly Sincere".

▲ Bubble-gum fun
Swedish-American actress Ann-Margret played Kim MacAfee in for the 1963 film version of *Bye Bye Birdie*, directed by George Sidney.

CAMELOT

{ 1960 }

Tragedy seemed to dog the creation of *Camelot*, yet the lushly romantic score and the whimsy of Arthurian legend resulted in yet another hit for Lerner and Loewe.

Despite the success of *Brigadoon* (see p.86), *Gigi* (see p.132), and *My Fair Lady* (see pp.120–21), composer Frederick Loewe was not enthusiastic about writing another musical so soon after a heart attack in 1958. He had to be persuaded by his lyricist, Alan Jay Lerner, and director, Moss Hart, to postpone retirement. Lerner and Hart had come up with the idea of writing a musical about King Arthur, based on T.H. White's enchanting novel *The Once and Future King*, which was also to inspire Disney's *The Sword in the Stone* (1963).

EARLY PROBLEMS
With the reluctant composer convinced, the writing then stalled when Lerner's marriage broke down, leaving him too devastated to finish it. However the star-studded cast assembled as planned and slowly, over the course of rehearsals for the try-outs in Toronto and Boston, the show began to take shape.

Film actor Richard Burton starred as King Arthur and was

◀ **Legendary film**
Sumptuous period artwork publicizing the movie version of *Camelot*, which was a big success in 1967.

apparently key to keeping up cast morale through the tortuous rewrites and restaging that were required. Joining him on this journey was Julie Andrews as his queen, Guinevere, and Robert Goulet as Lancelot, his rival in love and best friend.

The first preview ran for four and a half hours, but by the time the show arrived on Broadway, it had shed a considerable 90 minutes.

LAST-MINUTE CHANGES AND TRAGEDIES
The stress took its toll. Lerner was hospitalized with an ulcer for two weeks after the Canadian premiere, and Moss Hart suffered a serious heart attack from which he never really recovered. He died in 1961, at the relatively young age of 57.

The incapacity of two of the leading creatives led to many tussles over who would take over direction. However, eventually Hart was well enough to steer the show through the extensive cuts and revisions to its New York press night. Legend has it that Julie Andrews was only given the song "Before I Gaze at You Again" two days before the first New York preview.

Reviews were mixed, but when the stars appeared on *The Ed Sullivan TV Show*, the box office went crazy and the original cast recording was number one in the album charts for 60 weeks.

Yet it was a national tragedy that turned the piece into an iconic work of musical theatre. When US President John F. Kennedy was assassinated in 1963, word spread that the album had been a favourite of the First Family and the lyric "Don't let it be forgot, That once there was a spot, For one brief shining moment, That was known as Camelot", came to symbolize his thousand days in the White House.

KEY FACTS

🎭 **STAGE**

🎬 **Director** Moss Hart
📖 **Book** Alan Jay Lerner
🎵 **Music** Frederick Loewe
🎼 **Lyrics** Alan Jay Lerner
🎭 **Venue** Majestic Theatre, New York
📅 **Date** 3 December 1960

◉ **Key information**
The original Broadway production ran for 873 performances and won four Tony Awards. A film adaptation followed in 1967, starring Richard Harris as King Arthur and Vanessa Redgrave as Guinevere.

> *"Longer than the 'Götterdämmerung'... and not nearly as funny!"*
>
> ATTRIBUTED TO **NOEL COWARD** DURING EARLY PREVIEWS

▶ **Screen idol**
Vanessa Redgrave played Guinevere in the film of *Camelot*. Her performance was described as "dazzling" by *The New York Times*.

THE FANTASTICKS

{ 1960 }

The original production of *The Fantasticks* enjoyed the longest run of any theatre piece performed continuously in one location and was the world's longest-running musical.

It opened on 3 May 1960 at the Sullivan Street Playhouse, a small Off-Broadway theatre in New York's Greenwich Village, where it was performed for 42 years, until it was no longer financially viable. A new production opened on 23 August 2006 at the Snapple Theater Center, just off Times Square.

SUCCESS THROUGH SIMPLICITY

The show's longevity is thanks in part to the simplicity of its staging requirements (an empty, open stage, a rostra, and a cardboard sun/moon), its small cast, and the fact that it is scored for only two musicians (a pianist and a harpist) – all of which make it economical to mount. Yet, however important those factors are in its success, there is no denying that it continues to enchant people all over the world in community, professional, school, and regional theatre productions.

Conceived at a time when the premiere of American playwright Thornton Wilder's expressionistic drama *Our Town* (1938) had successfully made a virtue of a series of vignettes drawn together by a narrator figure, it is based on *Les Romanesques*, by the late 19th-century French playwright Edmond Rostand. Rostand, celebrated author of *Cyrano de Bergerac*, drew inspiration from Ovid's story of *Pyramus and Thisbe*, Shakespeare's *Romeo and Juliet* and *A Midsummer Night's Dream*, and Donizetti's opera *L'elisir d'amore*. The hit musical adaptation has a score by Harvey Schmidt and a book and lyrics by Tom Jones.

The Fantasticks is an allegorical romance in which two prospective lovers will not be drawn into a relationship, despite their fathers concocting a fake family feud and a staged abduction designed to bring them together. A real life feud follows as a result, during which the lovers go their separate ways, only to discover they do actually love each other, a realization that reunites them and their families.

The show contains a number of much-loved musical numbers, including the hits "Try to Remember", "Soon it's Gonna Rain", and "Once More".

STAGGERING FIGURES

The statistics that surround the show are impressive. More than 11,000 revivals have been staged in over 60 countries across the globe, which have sometimes seen multiple productions. The list of American stars who have appeared in it over the years reads like a roll-call of some of the world's most popular performers. It has also been translated and performed in numerous languages.

Despite its incredible success, the show has sometimes provoked controversy. Issues relating to race and the use of the word "rape" have forced the writers to reshape the material, and a 2010 revival in London's West End was savaged by critics, who found it dated.

▼ A winning formula
Jerry Orbach as El Gallo, Rita Gardner as Luisa, and Kenneth Nelson as Matt in the original production of *The Fantasticks*.

KEY FACTS

⚜ STAGE
🎬 **Director** Word Baker
📖 **Book** Tom Jones
🎵 **Music** Harvey Schmidt
A♪ **Lyrics** Tom Jones
🎭 **Venue** Sullivan Street Playhouse, New York
🗓 **Date** 3 May 1960

◉ **Key information**
Many big American stars of stage, film, and television have appeared in the musical, including Liza Minnelli, Elliott Gould, Jerry Orbach, F. Murray Abraham, David Canary, Robert Goulet, Glenn Close, Keith Charles, Kristin Chenoweth, Richard Chamberlain, John Carradine, and Ed Ames.

CRAFTING SOUND

The sound designer is responsible for everything the audience hears. Each production is different, so he or she must have many skills and capabilities.

Sound design is one of the newer design areas, along with video and projection design, but it is now an essential element in the audience's experience of a musical. The designer and soundboard operator control everything that the audience hears, balancing the band, or orchestra, with the singers. A sound designer ensures that no matter where you are sitting in the theatre you can hear the show properly.

MAKING SOME NOISE

Part of the sound designer's job is to record sound effects for the show, such as a ringing doorbell or telephone, a train passing in the distance, a fog horn sounding, or an angry mob in a rage offstage. But the overall soundscape must also be created, to indicate whether the story takes place in an echoing, cavernous space or a cramped one-bedroom flat. In this way, sound effects sustain the illusion that what we are seeing is real. Carefully placing speakers around the stage or auditorium enables the sound designer to create the impression that the sound is emanating from anywhere.

It was the intrusion of rock'n'roll into musical theatre that created the need for microphones. When the Burt Bacharach musical *Promises, Promises* (see p.178) opened on Broadway in 1968, each singer and instrumentalist was amplified by microphone. In this way, Bacharach could re-create and control the sound he was accustomed to producing in the recording studio.

Legendary Broadway sound designer Abe Jacobs said in a *Playbill* interview in 1971 that "sound was basically set up by the stage manager and an assistant electrician". He described how he brought stagehands out into the house to hear the show from the audience's perspective, and eventually brought trained sound technicians, both designers and board operators, into the mix. His ability to finesse musicals saw him reworking *Hair* and *Jesus Christ Superstar*, and soon earned him the nickname "the Godfather of Broadway Sound Design".

▶ Capturing *The Sound of Music*
A sound designer is able to replicate the same quality of sound on stage that can be achieved in a recording studio, like the one shown here.

"... it involves... an understanding of how that sound will be heard and perceived by the audience... to take them on the journey of the story."

WEBSITE OF THE ASSOCIATION OF SOUND DESIGNERS

HOW TO SUCCEED IN BUSINESS WITHOUT REALLY TRYING

{ 1961 }

From the unlikely source of a self-help book parody, this 1961 smash-hit Frank Loesser musical outperformed every other show of the period, and won a Pulitzer Prize.

Similar in tone to British writer Stephen Potter's 1947 *The Theory and Practice of Gamesmanship (or the Art of Winning Games without Actually Cheating)*, Shepherd Mead's 1952 book *How to Succeed in Business without Really Trying: The Dastard's Guide to Fame and Fortune* satirized both the instructional manual format and the Machiavellian office politics of corporation businesses.

THE CREATIVE TEAM

Though playwrights Willie Gilbert and Jack Weinstock had collaborated on a theatrical adaptation as early as 1955, it remained undeveloped for five years. Seeing its potential as a musical, producers Cy Feuer and Ernest Martin gathered the same creative team who

▼ **Crazy and colourful**
Charles Nelson Reilly as Frump and Claudette Sutherland as Smitty, leading the cast in the famous coffee-break scene from the original show.

had made such a success of *Guys and Dolls* (see pp.88–91), hiring Abe Burrows (see below) to adapt the play and Frank Loesser to write the songs.

THE SHOW

As New York window-cleaner J. Pierrepont Finch reads from his manual *How to Succeed in Business without Really Trying*, the voice of the narrator resounds around the theatre, urging him to apply for a job. He enters the World Wide Wicket Company and finds himself in the mailroom, meeting his future love, secretary Rosemary (who is immediately smitten), and his arch-enemy Bud Frump, the conceited and indolent nephew of Mr Biggley, the company president.

Finch instigates a sequence of book-advised schemes involving myriad secretaries, managers, and executives, eventually becoming Chairman of the Board. Along the way, before an especially important corporate

presentation, he sings the anthem to self-belief into the mirror, "I Believe in You" – the one song from the score that enjoyed a life beyond the show.

A BIG HIT

Though generally considered to be a less distinguished musical effort than *Guys and Dolls* (and conspicuously less popular as a revival or amateur production), Loesser's score skilfully serves the characters and plot. Meanwhile, Burrows' book skims smoothly and wittily through a labyrinthine story of double-dealing, contrivance, and connivance.

The show's blend of humorous song, irreverent farce, and romance proved hugely appealing, and it was a critical and box-office smash, going on to win seven Tony Awards and a Pulitzer Prize.

The 1967 movie adaptation directed by David Swift retained Morse, Vallee, and most of Fosse's choreography, but sadly lost a quarter of Loesser's score.

KEY FACTS

🎭 STAGE
- 🎬 **Director** Abe Burrows
- 📖 **Book** Abe Burrows, Jack Weinstock, Willie Gilbert
- 🎵 **Music** Frank Loesser
- 🎼 **Lyrics** Lorenz Hart, Frank Loesser
- 🎭 **Venue** 46th Street (now Richard Rodgers) Theatre, New York
- 📅 **Date** 14 October 1961

⊙ Key information
The Broadway run lasted for 1,417 performances and won seven Tony Awards in 1962: Best Musical, Best Author (Abe Burrows, Jack Weinstock and Willie Gilbert), Best Leading Actor in a Musical (Robert Morse), Best Featured Actor in a Musical (Charles Nelson Reilly), Best Direction (Abe Burrows), Best Producer (Cy Feuer, Ernest Martin), and Best Conductor/Musical Director (Elliot Lawrence).

BIOGRAPHY

ABE BURROWS (1910–85)

Born in New York, Burrows was a comic performer, author, and director. As a radio writer, he contributed to the popular series *Duffy's Tavern*. After that hit show, Burrows got the reputation as a script doctor ("Get me Abe Burrows" was a Broadway catchphrase when a script wasn't working) and he was credited on the musicals *Can-Can* (1953) and *Silk Stockings* (1955).

A FUNNY THING HAPPENED ON THE WAY TO THE FORUM

{ 1962 }

A fast-paced, bawdy comedy set in ancient Rome, the show featured a skilful cast delivering a witty mix of farce, satire, and vaudeville, plus a sophisticated score by Stephen Sondheim

In 1957, *West Side Story* lyricist Stephen Sondheim (see pp.220–21) approached television writer and director Burt Shevelove to collaborate on a musical that would feature Sondheim's songs, both music and lyrics. Shevelove resurrected an idea he'd had since university of turning the plays of Plautus (251–183 BCE) into a musical, and recruited TV colleague Larry Gelbart to write what Shevelove initially called "A Scenario for Vaudevillians". Eleven re-drafts over a four-year period later and *A Funny Thing Happened on the Way to the Forum* became an intricately plotted, low-comedy farce that reflected the influence of the quick-fire, wise-cracking style of popular American TV shows such as *Sgt Bilko* (1955–59).

Indeed, the original choice for the main character was Phil Silvers, star of the *Bilko* series, though Silvers demurred, unwilling to perform what he called "old schtick". Another contender, TV comedian Milton Berle, was unnerved by all the rewrites and asked for script approval, which was denied. This left the exuberantly dexterous comic actor Zero Mostel to create the memorable role of Pseudolus, the conniving slave who drives much of the action.

In his quest to be free from slavery, Pseudolus manipulates his neighbours and masters – including Lycus the pimp, Senex the ageing lothario, and Miles Gloriosus the braggart soldier – into romantic or lustful situations designed to benefit himself. Inevitably, these situations turn into a comedic pandemonium of classic farce techniques; cross-dressing, room-hopping, and elaborate schemes built on untruths.

STYLISTIC DIFFERENCES

Though Sondheim had written a full-length musical in 1955, he was eager to impress with his first high-profile outing as a composer and delivered a stylish set of songs that seemed to some at odds with the vulgar tone of the show. Shevelove, while recognizing the vaudevillian ingenuity of the saucy "Everybody Ought to Have a Maid", wanted music that was "brassier – from the school of Irving Berlin". While others at the time (and since) recognized that it was the refined score that elevated the show beyond being simply a romp, Sondheim's name was conspicuously absent from the Tony nominations for *Forum* in 1963. Out-of-town try-outs

were disastrous. At George Abbott's insistence, the convolutions of plot had been diluted, and with it, much of the "organized confusion" and fun of the piece. The plot was re-installed, but the creative team by now were falling out; it was only producer Harold Prince's belief in the show that kept it from closing. Overnight, Sondheim produced the rousing "Comedy Tonight", and from that point on, the show was a success.

KEY FACTS

🎭 **STAGE**

🎬 **Director** George Abbott
📖 **Book** Burt Shevelove/Larry Gelbart
🎵 **Music and lyrics** Stephen Sondheim
🎭 **Venue** Alvin Theatre (now Neil Simon Theatre), New York
📅 **Date** 1 May 1962

⊙ **Key information**

In 1963, the show won Tony Awards for Best Musical, Best Author of a Musical, Best Actor in a Musical (Zero Mostel), Best Featured Actor in a Musical (David Burns), Best Direction (Abbott), and Best Producer (Harold Prince).

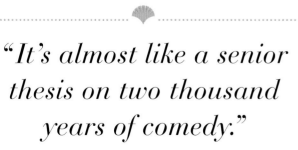

"It's almost like a senior thesis on two thousand years of comedy."

COMPOSER **STEPHEN SONDHEIM** ON SHEVELOVE AND GELBART'S BOOK

◀ **Naughty and silly**
Jack Gilford as Hysterium, camping it up while being playfully pursued by Leon Greene as Captain Miles Gloriosus.

FIDDLER ON THE ROOF

{ 1964 }

The story of Tevye, an impoverished dairyman struggling to uphold cherished Jewish traditions in tsarist Russia as pogroms loom, touched the hearts of people everywhere, and became one of the biggest hit musicals ever.

The worldwide success of *Fiddler on the Roof* can be attributed to the universality of its basic theme – the conflict between traditional values and a changing society. In the story, Tevye's three eldest daughters move further from tradition as each finds a husband. The first, Tzeitel, chooses her own husband rather than leaving it to Yente, the town matchmaker. The second, Hodel, leaves her home to join the man she loves, who has been arrested and imprisoned in Siberia as a dissident. The third daughter marries a non-Jew.

SOCIAL CHANGE AT ONE REMOVE
Fiddler opened in 1964, when social change was in the air. Advocates of women's rights and civil rights, the counter-culture movement, and the sexual revolution all brought the question of traditional values to the forefront of the collective social unconscious. People saw in the story of Tevye, Golde, and their daughters their own stories, but at one step removed. The musical remains potent in the 21st century as we grapple with even bigger social, cultural, and technological challenges.

THE LONG ROAD TO ANATEVKA
By 1964, two Americans, music theatre composer Jerry Bock and lyricist Sheldon Harnick, had already had three musicals produced on Broadway. *The Body Beautiful* (1958)

closed after 60 performances but caught the attention of a renowned American musical producer and director. This was Harold Prince (see pp.210–211), and he produced their next musical, the Pulitzer Prize-winning *Fiorello!* (1959) about New York mayor Fiorello Laguardia. Bock and Harnick's next show, *Tenderloin* (1960), made back its investment but

failed to draw significant audiences. Bock and Harnick had hoped to musicalize a different story by a Yiddish revivalist writer, the Ukrainian-born American Sholem Aleichem (1859–1916), about a travelling theatrical troupe. However, it would have required too large a cast, so they settled on the stories of Tevye and the Jewish village (*shtetl*) of

KEY FACTS

💠 **STAGE**

🎭 **Director** Jerome Robbins
📖 **Book** Joseph Stein
♫ **Music** Jerry Bock
𝄞 **Lyrics** Sheldon Harnick
🎭 **Venue** Imperial Theatre, New York
🗓 **Date** 22 September 1964

⊙ **Key information**
This show became the longest-running production in Broadway history. It won nine Tony Awards. Productions have been seen in North and South America, Europe, Africa, Australia, the Middle East, and Asia.

Bedroom scene ▶
In this famous scene, Tevye recounts a dream to convince his wife that it is acceptable for their daughter, Tzeitel, to marry the man of her choice.

"*Every one of us is a fiddler on the roof.*"

TEVYE, *FIDDLER ON THE ROOF* (SHELDON HARNICK AND JOSEPH STEIN), 1964

Anatevka. Prince was not interested at first, but Bock and Harnick sweetened the pot by offering him their musical *She Loves Me* (1963) at the same time. Young Stephen Sondheim (see pp.220–21) convinced American theatre producer, director, and choreographer Jerome Robbins to join the *Fiddler* project after hearing songs from the show performed in Bock's home. It was Robbins who brought the project together through

▲ Iconic image

The poster for the 1971 film, designed by American artist Tom Morrow, featured a Chagall-inspired silhouette of a lone fiddler playing the violin on a village rooftop.

a series of pre-production meetings in which the themes, metaphors, shape, and structure of the show were developed and refined.

THE STORY OF THE FIDDLER

Fiddler's original set designer, Boris Aronson, took his inspiration from the art of modernist Jewish Russian-French painter Marc Chagall (1887–1985), who came from a similar background to Aronson. The play found its central image in Chagall's portrayals of the Jewish village life of his childhood, in particular that of a fiddler balancing precariously on a rooftop, trying to play without falling off. This powerful image reflects the peril of the poor. In addition, the Hasidic Jews believed that communion with God could be attained through music and dance, so religious ceremonies and festivals never took place without the presence of the fiddler.

BALLET AND THE DANCE OF THE SHTETL

Fiddler on the Roof digs deeply into the practices of Jewish families in that place and time, celebrating the traditions of Hasidic Judaism and watching those conventions being questioned. The opening number, "Tradition", establishes many of these practices and their importance to the cultural fabric of this society. The beautiful "Sabbath Prayer" shows the entire Jewish community of the village of Anatevka lighting the Sabbath candles.

In light of the need to portray these complex cultural interactions, Jerome Robbins, who straddled the worlds of musical theatre and ballet, blended a balletic sensibility with the vocabulary of Jewish folk dance, imbuing *Fiddler on the Roof* with a unique visual style. This combination is so integral to the fabric of *Fiddler* that most major productions around the world are required to re-create Robbins' choreography. As important to the show as the spoken and sung dialogue, is Robbins' staging – particularly of the opening number, "Tradition", with the circle of the community being broken up by the entrance of the Russians, and in the bottle dance at the wedding.

LASTING LEGACY

One of the most frequently produced musicals in the world, *Fiddler on the Roof* has been mounted more than an astonishing 1,300 times in Japan alone and played in parts of the world that had never previously encountered a Broadway musical, and was the first show to run for more than 3,000 performances on Broadway.

The 1971 film, directed by Canadian Norman Jewison and starring the well-known Israeli actor Chaim Topol, who had performed the role in London's West End, enjoyed global success. The acclaimed Soviet-born violinist Isaac Stern recorded all of the violin solos for the soundtrack. Jewison's film won three Oscars, including Best Original Song Score.

▲ Star vehicle

Actors such as the legendary Zero Mostel and Lithuanian-born Israeli actor Shmuel Rodensky (above, right) enjoyed enormous success as Tevye.

RELATED SHOWS

Fiorello!, 1959, Jerry Bock, Sheldon Harnick

She Loves Me, 1963, Jerry Bock, Sheldon Harnick

The Apple Tree, 1966, Jerry Bock, Sheldon Harnick

STORYLINE

Fiddler on the Roof tells the story of Tevye, a Jewish milkman, his wife, and his five daughters. One by one, Tevye's three eldest daughters marry, moving further and further from the traditions of the family and the village community of Anatevka. The story takes place against the backdrop of the persecution of the Jewish communities by the Russian authorities, and concludes with the enforced dispersal of the village and of its inhabitants.

CAST LIST	
Zero Mostel	Tevye
Maria Karnilova	Golde
Bea Arthur	Yente
Joanna Merlin	Tzeitel
Julia Migenes	Hodel
Tanya Everett	Chava
Austin Pendleton	Motel
Bert Convy	Perchik

	ANATEVKA	TEVYE'S HOME	AROUND ANATEVKA	ANATEVKA	MORDCHA'S INN
PLOT OVERVIEW	**Tevye, the milkman,** explains the importance of tradition within the Jewish community in the village of Anatevka ❶.	**Tevye's three oldest daughters,** Tzeitel, Hodel, and Chava, dream of their future husbands ❷.	**Tevye,** pulling his own cart because his horse is lame, wonders what life would be like if he were rich ❸.	**Tzeitel and Motel the tailor** have betrothed themselves to each other without the approval of Yente, the matchmaker, breaking with tradition. Hodel flirts with Perchik, a student just arrived in town offering lessons in exchange for room and board, an even greater break from tradition. Chava has an interest in a Fyedka, a Russian and a non-Jew, the gravest lapse of all. It is a Friday night and the villagers, including Tevye and his family keep the Sabbath ❹.	**After the Sabbath,** Tevye meets with the butcher, Lazar Wolf, who asks for Tzeitel's hand in marriage. Tevye agrees and they celebrate with dancing ❺.

THE SONGS

❶ Tradition
☺ *Tevye, Villagers*

❷ Matchmaker, Matchmaker
Chava, Hodel,
☺ *Tzeitel*

❸ If I Were a Rich Man
☺ *Tevye*

❹ Sabbath Prayer
☺ *Tevye, Golde, Villagers*

❺ To Life
☺ *Tevye, Lazar Wolf, Men*

LAZAR WOLF AND TEVYE CELEBRATE

TEVYE SINGS AS HE DELIVERS MILK

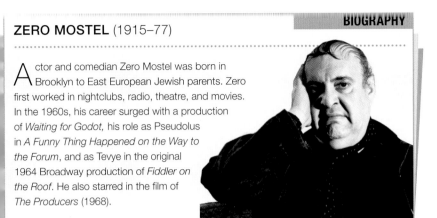

ZERO MOSTEL (1915–77)

Actor and comedian Zero Mostel was born in Brooklyn to East European Jewish parents. Zero first worked in nightclubs, radio, theatre, and movies. In the 1960s, his career surged with a production of *Waiting for Godot,* his role as Pseudolus in *A Funny Thing Happened on the Way to the Forum*, and as Tevye in the original 1964 Broadway production of *Fiddler on the Roof*. He also starred in the film of *The Producers* (1968).

> ## "One of the great works of the American theater."
>
> JOHN CHAPMAN, US THEATRE CRITIC, *NEW YORK DAILY NEWS*, 1964

TEVKA'S HOME

ANATEVKA

Motel tries to convince Tevye to allow him to marry Tzeitel instead **6** . Tevye, impressed by Motel's show of courage, searches his own soul and ultimately agrees to the marriage. Tzeitel and Motel celebrate **7** .

Tevye creates a fictitious bad dream as a sign to Golde, his wife, that they should favour Motel rather than Lazar Wolf **8** .

The wedding is beautiful and the villagers sing of the swift passing of the years **9** **10** .

A group of Russians ride into the village, wreaking destruction.

Perchik proposes to Hodel. He says that he must return to Kiev to work for the revolution, but he will send for her. She accepts. Although Hodel and Perchik feel they don't require Tevye's permission, they ask Tevye for his blessing to wed **11** . He agrees, though he contemplates the changing world **12** .

No longer sure of the world, Tevye asks Golde if she loves him **13** .

A rumour spreads throughout the town that becomes larger with every person who spreads it **14** . Perchik has been arrested and jailed in Siberia for inciting revolution.

Hodel leaves Anatevka to join Perchik in Siberia **15** .

Tevye learns that Chava has secretly married Fyedka, the Russian. This break from tradition Tevye cannot accept. He tells Golde that Chava is dead to them and to go home to take care of the other children. Tevye wonders where he went wrong **16** . An edict comes from the Russian authorities that all Jews must leave Anatevka **17** . The Jews are thrown out of their homes, and cast off into the world **18** .

6 — 7 — 8 —— 9 —— 10 — 11 — 12 — 13 — 14 — 15 —— 16 —— 17 — 18

Tevye's Dream
Tevye, Golde, Grandma Tzeitel, Fruma-Sarah, Villagers

Sunrise, Sunset
Tevye, Golde, Villagers

Now I Have Everything
Hodel, Perchik

Do You Love Me?
Golde, Tevye

Chaveleh Sequence
Tevye

Epilogue
Company

Miracle of Miracles
Motel

The Bottle Dance
(instrumental)

Tradition (reprise)
Tevye

Far From the Home I love
Hodel

Anatevka
Tevye, Golde, Yente, Lazar Wolf, Villagers

Tradition (reprise)

The Rumor (I Just Heard)
Yente, Villagers

THE VILLAGERS PERFORM THE BOTTLE DANCE AT THE WEDDING

⭐ *The 2004 Broadway revival replaced "The Rumor (I Just Heard)" with a song for Yente and two other women called "Topsy-Turvy".*

MARY POPPINS

{ 1964 }

A delightful fantasy about a nanny who helps an Edwardian family, the film features memorable songs, engaging characters, and exhilarating production numbers that blend live action and animation into an enchanting entertainment.

▼ **Family fun**
The Banks family enjoy some time together in the park, flying a kite that George Banks fixed for his children.

KEY FACTS

🎬 **FILM**

🎬 **Director** Robert Stevenson

📖 **Screenplay** Bill Walsh and Don DaGradi

📖 **Book** P. L. Travers

🎵 **Music and lyrics** Richard M. Sherman and Robert B. Sherman

⏱ **Running time** 139 minutes

📅 **Release date** 27 August 1964

⊙ **Key information**

The film won five Oscars, including Best Actress (Julie Andrews) and Best Score (the Sherman brothers).

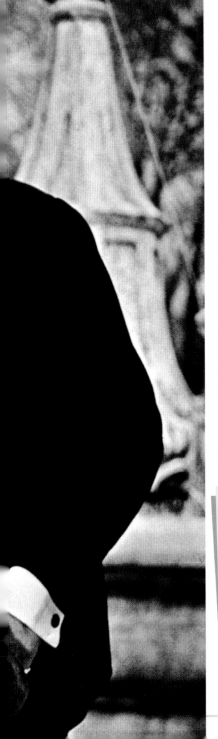

Australian-born author P.L. Travers produced a series of books about a nanny called Mary Poppins from 1934 until 1988. In the stories, Mary is severe, vain, and haughty, but has magical powers to make life better for those around her. Hollywood producer Walt Disney had approached Travers for adaptation rights as early as 1938, but was rebuffed by the author who felt animation (for which Disney was known at the time) would not properly represent her work. Disney eventually managed to secure the movie rights in 1961, though he had to agree to relinquish script approval to Travers.

CONSOLATION PRIZE

Julie Andrews was sought for the key role of Mary very soon after the producers of the movie *My Fair Lady* (see pp.120–21) had cast Hollywood star Audrey Hepburn as Eliza Doolittle, a role Andrews had created on Broadway. Though being offered Mary was some consolation, Andrews initially declined because she was pregnant, but the production waited until she was available.

American comedian, singer, dancer, and actor Dick Van Dyke was cast as Bert, the chimney sweep. Much has been written about the quality of the actor's attempts at a Cockney accent (his accent coach was Irish and, allegedly, couldn't do one either). However, Van Dyke's duet "Chim Chim Cher-ee", sung with Julie Andrews, won an Academy Award for Best Original Song, and the accent did not blemish Van Dyke's endearing portrayal of the role of Bert.

EDWARDIAN MUSIC HALL

For the score, Disney turned to his staff composers, the songwriting brothers Richard and Robert Sherman (see pp.176–77), who had been hired by Disney as staff writers in 1961. When the *Mary Poppins* project came up, the

brothers were already working on four other Disney films. However, tirelessly productive and extremely versatile, they produced a slew of ingenious songs approximating an Edwardian music-hall style. These included "Chim Chim Cher-ee" (for the developed minor character of the chimney sweep), "Let's Go Fly a Kite" (inspired by experiences with their own father), and the tongue-twisting "Supercalifragilisticexpialidocious" (based on a nonsense word recalled from their childhood). They also wrote a beautiful ballad for Mary – "Through the Eyes of Love" – but when Julie Andrews let it be known she would prefer a snappier song, they recovered from their disappointment to produce "A Spoonful of Sugar".

The Sherman brothers' proudest achievement in the production was "Feed the Birds", a plaintive waltz

▲ **High honours**
Pamela Lyndon Travers was made an Officer of the Order of the British Empire by Queen Elizabeth II for her services to literature.

espousing how giving a little extra and caring a little more can make all the difference in the world. It was a sentiment that resonated deeply with Disney, and he was often visibly moved when he heard it.

DISGRUNTLED AUTHOR SNUBBED

Travers and Disney clashed about many aspects of the movie's production. Elements the author objected to included the original songs by the Sherman brothers (she had wanted authentic English songs dating from the Edwardian era), the softening of Mary Poppins's character, and, particularly, the use of animation. When she was apparently snubbed by Disney at the movie premiere, she became an avowed and vocal objector to the film. None of this made the slightest difference to the movie's success. It received rave reviews, won five Oscars, and brought huge box office success to Disney.

However, Travers's continued disapproval of the film scuppered any plans Disney might have had for a movie sequel. She also stipulated that no one associated with the Disney movie could be involved in developing a stage musical of her book. It wasn't until 40 years later that a version produced by Cameron Mackintosh, was launched, going on to captivate audiences worldwide (see left).

OLD AND NEW SONGS

In 1993, Cameron Mackintosh (see pp.232–33) had met Pamela Travers and persuaded her to allow him to do a stage version of *Mary Poppins*. However, it wasn't until 2001 when he met Thomas Schumacher, head of Disney Theatrical, that Mary really started to fly. British songwriters George Stiles and Anthony Drewe independently devised a new song for the project, "Practically Perfect", and were hired to augment the score. The show opened in London at the Prince Edward Theatre in 2004, had a long run on Broadway, and continues to be staged around the world.

LAURA MICHELLE KELLY AS MARY POPPINS IN THE 2004 PRODUCTION

STORYLINE

In Edwardian London, in 1910, a magical nanny arrives from the sky, using her umbrella as a parachute. She has come to live with the Banks family at the request of the children, Jane and Michael. Mary Poppins is the perfect nanny in every practical way and, following a series of fantastical adventures and some words of wisdom – all enhanced by Mary's extraordinary powers – a formerly dysfunctional family is set to rights.

CAST

Julie Andrews Mary Poppins	**Don Barclay** Mr Binnacle
Dick Van Dyke Bert and Mr Dawes Sr	**Arthur Treacher** Constable Jones
David Tomlinson George Banks	**Elsa Lanchester** Katie Nanna
Glynis Johns Winifred Banks	**Marjorie Bennett** Miss Lark
Karen Dotrice Jane	**Arthur Malet** Mr Dawes Jr.
Matthew Garber Michael	**Ed Wynn** Uncle Albert
Hermione Baddeley Ellen	**Jane Darwell** Bird Woman
Reta Shaw Mrs Brill	**Alma Lawton** Mrs Corry
Reginald Owen Admiral Boom	**Marjorie Eaton** Miss Persimmon
	Jimmy Logan Doorman

ABOVE THE ROOFTOPS OF LONDON	THE BANKS'S FAMILY HOME, CHERRY TREE LANE, LONDON	IN AND AROUND LONDON	THE BANKS'S FAMILY HOME

PLOT OVERVIEW

As the titles of the movie unfold over an early morning shot of the rooftops of London, a medley of increasing excitement previews several musical themes. Mary Poppins is seen sitting on a cloud powdering her nose ❶.

Mrs Banks, back from a suffragette protest, sings of "soldiers in petticoats" ❷. Mr Banks, unaware that the nanny has quit and his children are missing, sings of his consistent, ordered life ❸. When a policeman returns the children, Mr Banks calls for a nanny who will impose "tradition, discipline, and rules". His children have different ideas ❹.

Mary Poppins arrives at the Banks' home. She sweetly but assertively secures the position of nanny and astonishes the children with her bottomless bag and her magical way of tidying their nursery ❺.

Mary's friend Bert celebrates being a pavement artist ❻. Bert, Mary, and the children jump into one of Bert's chalk drawings, a magical countryside populated with animated animals. Bert and Mary dance in the air and sing of their mutual regard ❼ before Mary wins a race with a carousel horse. She sings a song introducing a nonsense word ❽.

Mary sings a reverse-psychology lullaby to the children at bedtime when they insist that they're not tired ❾.

THE SONGS

❶ Overture
🎵 Orchestra

❷ Sister Suffragette
🎵 Winifred Banks

❸ The Life I Lead
🎵 George Banks

❹ The Perfect Nanny
🎵 Jane, Michael

❺ A Spoonful of Sugar
🎵 Mary Poppins

❻ Pavement Artist
🎵 Bert

❼ Jolly Holiday
🎵 Bert, Mary

❽ Supercalifragilisticexpialidocious
🎵 Mary, Bert

★ *A song using a nonsense word had been published in 1951 and its writers sued Disney. The suit failed.*

❾ Stay Awake
🎵 Mary

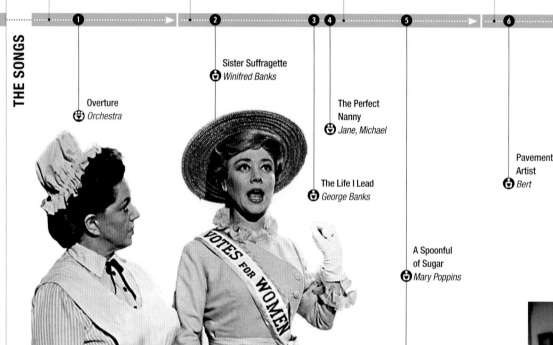

GLYNIS JOHNS AS WINIFRED BANKS, SINGS OF THE SUFFRAGETTE MOVEMENT

★ *Robert Sherman is said to have got the idea for the lyrics of "A Spoonful of Sugar" from his own children receiving their polio vaccines on a lump of sugar. His brother Richard provided the melody.*

MICHAEL AND JANE ARE GIVEN SOME MEDICINE

MR BANKS AND
THE CHILDREN

"*The sets are luxuriant, the songs lilting ...*"

TIME MAGAZINE, 18 SEPTEMBER 1964

IN AND AROUND LONDON	THE BANKS'S FAMILY HOME	FIDELITY FIDUCIARY BANK, LONDON	IN AND AROUND LONDON	THE BANKS'S FAMILY HOME	IN AND AROUND LONDON
The following morning, Bert, Mary, and the children visit Uncle Albert, who is floating in the air with laughter. Bert and the children get caught up in the mood and soon join him on the ceiling. Mary is somewhat vexed **10**.	**Mr Banks stresses** the need for order and tradition. Mary heartily agrees and promises to prepare the children for a day at the bank **11**. That evening, accompanied by dreamlike images of a bird-seller on the steps of St Paul's Cathedral, another Mary Poppins lullaby suggests that tuppence (two pennies) is a small price to pay for a better world **12**.	**In contrast,** Mr Dawes Sr, head of Fidelity Fiduciary Bank, proposes that a better place for their tuppence would be with him **13**. Michael wants to feed the birds with his money and loudly protests when Mr Dawes takes his money away. Panic ensues as customers withdraw their money from the bank.	**Jane and Michael** get lost while escaping the bank but run into Bert who escorts them home. He sings of how lucky he is to be a chimney sweep **14**. Later, Bert and his fellow sweeps, joined by Mary, sing and dance on the rooftops and into the children's house **15**.	**Having received** a summons to the bank to face disciplinary action, Mr Banks regrets the loss of his ordered life and blames Mary **16**. Bert gently reminds him of Mary's good influence and Mr Banks's responsibilities to his fast-growing but adoring children.	**Mr Banks,** fired from the bank yet optimistic, celebrates the pleasures of flying kites and family outings **17**. Informed that Mr Dawes Sr died laughing at the joke Mr Banks told when he was fired, Mr Banks is offered a partnership at the bank. Mary Poppins watches this satisfactory denouement before flying away.

10 **11** **12** **13** **14** **15** **16** **17**

I Love to Laugh
 *Bert, Uncle Albert, Mary*

A British Bank (The Life I Lead)
George Banks, *Mary*

Fidelity Fiduciary Bank
Mr Dawes Sr, George Banks, Bankers

Step in Time
Bert, Mary, Jane, Michael, Chimney Sweeps

Chim Chim Cher-ee
Bert, Jane, Michael

A Man Has Dreams
George Banks, Bert

Let's Go Fly a Kite
George Banks, Bert, Chorus

Feed the Birds (Tuppence a Bag)
 Mary

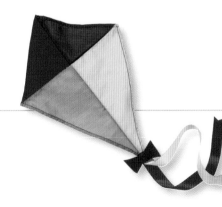

Walt Disney was so emotionally attached to the song "Feed the Birds" that he would often break off meetings to have Richard Sherman play it for him. After Disney died, Sherman relates that he would sometimes visit Disney's old office to play it for him again.

ANIMATED
SONGS

For many people, the first experience of a musical is seeing an animated film as a child, and we continue to hold them close to our hearts for all of our lives.

It will surprise no one that Disney is by far the largest and most successful producer of animated musicals. Just a few of their many classic musicals are: *Snow White and the Seven Dwarfs, Pinocchio, The Jungle Book, Beauty and the Beast, Aladdin, The Lion King, Pocahontas, Mulan,* and *Frozen.*

Disney's cartoon character Mickey Mouse debuted in 1928, in the first cartoon with synchronized sound – *Steamboat Willie*. Animations thrived during the Great Depression and the characters Betty Boop and Popeye were huge favourites at the time. In 1933, Warner Brothers' Studio created its own cartoon division – Merry Melodies. As movie musicals grew in popularity in the 1930s, animated films also began integrating music and songs.

MAKING ANIMATIONS SING

Animated screen musicals spring from any number of sources – a single song, a legend, a play. Generally speaking, once a film studio has decided on a story to animate, writers create a screenplay around it. A composer and lyricist write the songs, and possibly also provide the score. Meanwhile, a team of animators sketch a series of drawings, capturing the visual feel of the film, while a storyboard, created next, details the specific sequence of scenes, on a shot-by-shot basis. Once the voice actors are cast, the studio holds a preliminary video recording session to lay down the dialogue and songs. Animators study these recordings so that their drawings (or computer-generated images) closely mimic the lip movements, facial expressions, and body language of the actor. Sound effects and incidental music enhance the film's narrative and are added towards the end of the process.

HEARD BUT UNSEEN

Animated musicals are so popular that some of the world's busiest actors vie for roles in them, even though only their voice will be heard. Actors such as Idina Menzel and Kristen Bell from *Frozen*, Matthew Broderick, James Earl Jones, and Nathan Lane from *The Lion King*, and Angela Lansbury and Jerry Orbach from *Beauty and the Beast* were already stars when they added their voices to animated characters.

▶ **Animating voices**
Actors are filmed while staging a scene from the 1953 film *Peter Pan* to provide animators with a live-action guide for their illustrations.

"I try to build a full personality for each of our cartoon characters – to make them personalities."

WALT DISNEY, AMERICAN CARTOONIST, ANIMATOR, AND FILM PRODUCER

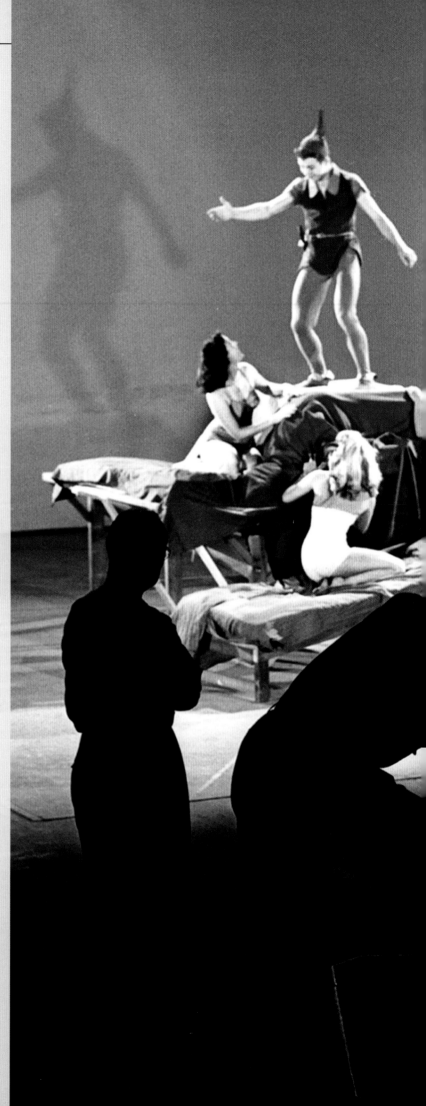

HELLO, DOLLY!

{ 1964 }

Rousing, stylish, and bursting with unforgettable tunes, *Hello, Dolly!* was the first and most successful of a memorable series of Jerry Herman musicals centring on larger-than-life, glamorous women. It was a firm favourite with audiences.

The one-act play *A Day Well Spent* (1835), by British writer John Oxenford, was a comic story of wife-seeking and mistaken identities. This was adapted by Austrian playwright Johann Nestroy in 1842, as *Einen Jux will er sich Machen* (*He Will Have a Good Time*), which was itself turned into an American farce by playwright Thornton Wilder, called *The Merchant of Yonkers* (1938). However, it was Wilder's later revision, called *The Matchmaker* (1955), which was a London and Broadway hit and led to *Matchmaker* producer David Merrick acquiring the rights in order to make a musical adaptation.

PRODUCER AND COMPOSER

Merrick had been impressed with Jerry Herman's score for the Jewish-themed *Milk and Honey* (1961), but was concerned that he was an "ethnic" composer, and "not American enough". To prove to the producer that he was indeed all "apple pie and Abe Lincoln", Herman took away a script marked *Matchmaker Draft #1* and, in a rush of inspiration, produced

◄ **Lavish production**
The 1969 film version of *Hello, Dolly!* starred Barbara Streisand and Walter Matthau. It featured huge sets and was a visual spectacle.

several songs, including "Put on Your Sunday Clothes".

Wilder's *The Matchmaker* had kept the plot of Yonkers shop workers having a farcical and romantic adventure in New York, but greatly expanded the role of widow Dolly Levi, a charismatic meddler and couple fixer-upper. Herman, an untrained musician and instinctive craftsman who had learned his trade by studying the construction of classic songs and shows, established Dolly's character with "I Put My Hand In". This was among the four songs that were demonstrated to Merrick four days after their initial meeting and, though Merrick loved the songs, Herman suspected the producer was even more impressed with the composer's speed; Herman was hired and the musical was under way.

THE CREATIVE TEAM

Michael Stewart, who had written the book for the hit musical *Bye Bye Birdie* (see p.143), was hired as librettist; meanwhile, the director of the same show, Gower Champion, was hired for what had become *Dolly: A Damned Exasperating Woman*. Merrick had always had Ethel Merman in mind for Dolly. Herman, too, had written the songs with her voice in mind, but Merman was determined to spend less time in dressing rooms and turned it down without hearing the songs. Carol Channing, the tall and mezzo-voiced comedy performer who had

made her name in *Gentlemen Prefer Blondes* (1946), was Champion's choice. Herman, initially disappointed at losing Merman, reworked his score to suit Channing's lower vocal range and developed a deep appreciation of Channing's qualities. "It turned out to be a more distinctive show than it would have been with Merman," Herman later judged.

Champion made the most of Channing's comedic gifts and left most of the dancing to the chorus. Employing Herman's vision for Dolly's triumphant return to the opulent Harmonia Gardens Restaurant, inspired by a scene from the Alice Faye movie *Lillian Russell* (1940), Champion crafted a show-stopping number as Dolly is serenaded and celebrated by the waiters singing "Hello, Dolly!".

OUT OF TOWN TROUBLE

The show had a rocky time during its Washington and Detroit try-outs, with Merrick in particularly panicky mood.

"A musical shot through with enchantment."

HOWARD TAUBMAN, CRITIC, *THE NEW YORK TIMES*, 1964

KEY FACTS

🎭 **STAGE**

🎬 **Director** Gower Champion
📖 **Book** Michael Stewart
🎵 **Music and lyrics** Jerry Herman
🎭 **Venue** St James Theatre, New York
📅 **Date** 16 January 1964

◉ **Key information**
The initial Broadway run was 2,844 performances. In 1964, the show won ten Tony Awards, including Best Musical, Best Book of a Musical (Michael Stewart), and Best Leading Actress in a Musical (Carol Channing).

CAST LIST

Carol Channing Dolly Levi
David Burns Horace Vandergelder
Charles Nelson Reilly Cornelius Hackl
Jerry Dodge Barnaby Tucker
Eileen Brennan Irene Molloy
Sondra Lee Minnie Fay
Igors Gavon Ambrose Kemper
Alice Payton Ermengard

"I'm ashamed of these songs," he bellowed at a baffled Herman at one point, before calling in the lyricist Bob Merrill to collaborate on some of the numbers, including "Elegance". Merrick had already changed the show's title to *Call On Dolly*, but when he heard Louis Armstrong's exuberant Dixieland jazz recording of "Hello, Dolly!", he changed the title once more. Armstrong's record went on to sell three million copies around the world and served as a wonderful ambassador for the show. It continues to be a popular recording around the world to this day.

▼ Young pretender
Barbra Streisand brought a very different feel to the eponymous role, as she was far younger than the age of the character.

BROADWAY AND BEYOND

If the initial critical enthusiasm for *Hello, Dolly!* focused on Carol Channing's performance and Gower Champion's staging a little more than it did on Jerry Herman's score, the show was nevertheless a huge success and ran for almost six years on Broadway. A parade of venerable film stars played Dolly when Channing eventually moved on, including Ginger Rogers, Martha Faye, and Betty Grable. Carol Channing returned to the role in the 1978 revival and once more nearly 20 years later in a subsequent 1995 version.

Following her success in the film adaptation of *Funny Girl* (see p.163), casting Barbra Streisand as Dolly in the Gene Kelly-directed movie in 1969 made a lot of commercial sense. However, even the star knew that she was really far too young for the

▶ Flirtatious fun
Louis Armstrong joined Barbara Streisand on screen to perform a duet of the iconic title number in the film *Hello, Dolly!*

role and at one point she actually asked to be replaced. When the request was refused, Streisand asked Herman for two new songs. The composer obliged and this resulted in the dazzling Barbra Streisand archetype "Just Leave Everything to Me". For the film, jazz musician Louis Armstrong made a cameo appearance during the flamboyant title number, and despite the brevity of his part, his unmistakeable voice and unique style makes a lasting impression.

MAN OF LA MANCHA

{ **1965** }

Unusually for a musical, *Man of La Mancha* is based on a television show, though, sadly, one from the days when productions were not recorded. Even the original script has been lost.

Nonetheless, the show made a sufficiently good impression on the viewing public and critics that it was optioned for stage adaptation, first as a play and then as a musical.

Although *Man of La Mancha* draws upon the character of Don Quixote and incidents from the classic novel by Spanish author Miguel de Cervantes, it is not a musical adaptation of the book. Instead, Dale Wasserman, who penned both the original television and Broadway musical version created a "play within a play" scenario in which Cervantes himself, while a tax collector, is arrested during the Spanish Inquisition for foreclosing on a monastery. Cervantes, a former actor, author, and mercenary, is thrown into jail with his manservant and, during a scuffle over his remaining belongings, he strikes a bargain – if he can

demonstrate that a mysterious bundle of manuscripts is of no use to his fellow inmates, he can keep it.

A TRIAL AND TRIBULATIONS
A number of unfortunate incidents follow, including a version of the most famous Don Quixote story, which finds him attempting to fight windmills believing them to be giants. Other misunderstandings involve mistaking a tavern for a mighty castle and a prostitute for a noblewoman whose honour he feels he must defend. Some great songs accompany the action, including "The Impossible Dream", the show's most celebrated musical number. The prison inmates are sufficiently impressed by the entertainment that Cervantes is allowed to keep the manuscript. They are notes for the novel that will one day be *Don Quixote*.

CHANGES TO THE ORIGINAL LINE-UP
The celebrated poet W.H. Auden was initially hired to write lyrics for the musical version, but was later replaced when it was felt his efforts were too literary and satirical. Rex Harrison was originally chosen to play the title role, but despite his phenomenal success as Professor Higgins in *My Fair Lady* (see pp.120–21), the vocal demands were deemed too great and he was replaced by the little-known Richard Kiley. Kiley won a Tony Award for his performance, establishing him as a Broadway star. He would reprise the role in

◀ **Quirky fun**
The comical poster advertising the film and drawing attention to its star-studded cast.

several major productions. Other notable actors who have played Cervantes include Australian actor Keith Michell in the West End premiere (1968) and Spanish tenor Plácido Domingo recorded the role, with Mandy Patinkin as his servant.

The musical first played in a production set entirely in a dungeon, utilizing objects apparently scattered around as the props. This remains the blueprint for most productions.

In 1972, Peter O'Toole starred in the film (but the singing voice was dubbed by Simon Gilbert) alongside James Coco and Sophia Loren.

THE MAN MARCHES ON
There continue to be constant revivals around the world, in many translations. This has led to a large number of cast recordings, but wherever *Man of La Mancha* is performed, the inspiring story of an underdog succeeding against the odds and making the world a better place is always deeply moving.

▲ **The impossible dream**
Don Quixote and his squire, Sancho, set out to find adventures in a scene from the film version of *Man of La Mancha*.

KEY FACTS

🎭 **STAGE**

🎫 **Director** Albert Marre

📖 **Book** Dale Wasserman

🎵 **Music** Mitch Leigh

🎶 **Lyrics** Joe Darion

🎭 **Venue** ANTA Washington Square Theatre, New York

📅 **Date** 30 October 1965

⊙ **Key information**
The original production won five Tony Awards in 1966, including Best Musical and Best Score. The total original New York run of the show amounted to 2,239 performances.

FUNNY GIRL

{ 1964 }

This musical's journey from conception to opening night was almost as eventful as its subject – the rise of a 1920s *Ziegfeld Follies* theatrical star named Fanny Brice.

The film producer Ray Stark had a collection of taped interviews with his mother-in-law, Fanny Brice. At first, he commissioned a book adaptation of the conversations, for which he reportedly paid US$50,000 to have withdrawn from sale. Next, a long line of Hollywood scriptwriters failed to shape the material into a biographical film. When a screenplay eventually met with Stark's approval, it was read by *South Pacific* (see p.96) star Mary Martin, who suggested that the material would make a good musical.

Once he was persuaded by the idea, Stark must have been very tenacious, because the list of big Broadway names who turned down or abandoned the project reads like a roll call of the great and the good. It included Mary Martin, Stephen Sondheim, Anne Bancroft, Dorothy Fields, Eydie Gormé, and Carol Burnett.

Eventually, Jule Styne was signed up as composer, Bob Merrill as lyricist, and Jerome Robbins (see pp.108–09) as director, but they had no star. Robbins knew of Barbra Streisand's work from her first hit show, *I Can Get It For You Wholesale* (1962). She auditioned for Stark and was given the lead, providing her with the first of several iconic roles that have helped define her extraordinary career. Not long after this, Robbins also walked

KEY FACTS

STAGE

🎬 **Director** Garson Kanin
📖 **Book** Isobel Lennart
🎵 **Music** Jule Styne
♪ **Lyrics** Bob Merrill
🎭 **Venue** Winter Garden Theatre, New York
📅 **Date** 26 March 1964

⊙ **Key information**
The original Broadway show enjoyed a run of 1,348 performances over three years. It was nominated for eight Tony Awards, but failed to win any of them.

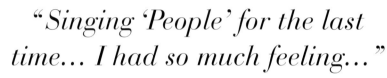

"Singing 'People' for the last time... I had so much feeling..."

BARBRA STREISAND TALKING TO CRITIC GENE SHALIT, 1983

◄ Nobody does it better
Barbra Streisand's comedic talent was perfectly suited for the role of Fanny Brice, and the show was one of the vehicles that made her a huge Broadway star. She also starred in the film.

away from the production, but he returned before the Broadway opening to oversee Carol Haney's choreography.

A REAL-LIFE STORY AND STIRRING SONGS
The main events in *Funny Girl* recall Fanny Brice's early ambitions, her rise to fame, her friendships, and her obsessive love for the charming Nick Arnstein, despite his failed and crooked business ventures. The intensity of Brice's feelings are demonstrated in two extraordinary songs that will long endure as classics of musical theatre. In the song "People", Brice reveals her loneliness and yearning for normality, while "Don't Rain on My Parade" is a stirring anthem to independence.

Even with a creative team and the perfect star in place, the show had a very long first out-of-town try-out. The Broadway opening night was postponed five times, whipping the theatre community into a fever of anticipation.

The show ultimately triumphed, and ran for nearly three years. Streisand reprised her role in the West End revival of 1966 and went on to star in the 1968 film.

OVERWHELMING COMPETITION
Although both the show and the film were critical triumphs, the fates were unkind on both occasions when it came to awards. In most Broadway seasons a show as well received and popular as *Funny Girl* could have expected to sweep the board at the Tony Awards, but in 1964 there was stiff competition from *Hello Dolly!* (see pp.160–01), and so *Funny Girl* lost out. Similarly, in the Best Picture category that year, the musical was beaten by *Oliver!* (see p.142). Despite its original success, *Funny Girl* has not enjoyed a major revival since.

THE UMBRELLAS OF CHERBOURG

{ **1964** }

A startling French musical melodrama that conveys a whole world of its own, this highly individual movie enthrals with its sumptuous sung-through score, intense colour design, and bittersweet storytelling. It is regarded as a Gallic classic.

Though no less artful than the experimental cinema of his New Wave contemporaries, such as Jean-Luc Godard and François Truffaut, the films of French director Jacques Demy betrayed a highly romantic sensibility influenced by, among other things, operetta and classic Hollywood musicals. Indeed, he described his first movie, *Lola* (1961), as a "musical without music".

For his 1964 film *Les Parapluies de Cherbourg* (*The Umbrellas of Cherbourg*), Demy not only made a fully-fledged movie musical, he utilized the operatic recitative technique, to ensure the entire film was sung through, an unprecedented concept in musicals at that time. Demy's musical collaborator was Michel Legrand (see opposite), an ambitious young French composer who was in tune with Demy's vision

◀ **Colourful romance**
The original 1964 movie poster for *The Umbrellas of Cherbourg* conveyed all the French romance that so enthralled cinema audiences.

of a fantasy musical world. A trusted partner, Legrand was at liberty to create ornate jazzy backgrounds and lyrical recitatives to Demy's lyrics/ dialogue along with the distinctively sweeping, sad, melodic music that came so naturally to the composer.

SOCIAL CRITIQUE
The recurring love theme – an aching minor melody that repeatedly soars and rests – dominates the soundtrack; with English lyrics, it became an international hit as "I Will Wait for You". Elsewhere in the score, the melody that would become another standard, "Watch What Happens", is heard and works perfectly in concert with the main theme.

A much gentler commentator than some of his contemporaries, Demy nevertheless fashions an elegant, implicit critique of war and bourgeois standards. Set in 1950s Cherbourg, the story concerns the ill-fated romance of

▶ **Young love**
The young Geneviève and Guy declare their love for each other, with Geneviève promising to wait for Guy when he is called up to the army.

16-year-old Geneviève (Catherine Deneuve) and car mechanic Guy (Nino Castelnuovo), who vow to be true, despite Guy being drafted into service in the Algerian war.

TRAGIC ENDING
With Geneviève pregnant and Guy's letters infrequent, the young girl is persuaded by her mother to receive the overtures of the wealthy jeweller Roland (Marc Michel), whom, after some pressure, she reluctantly marries. In a typical Demy signature, Roland also appeared in his 1961 movie, attempting to woo Lola.

Guy, now a wounded servicemen, returns to find Geneviève gone and seeks solace in the bottle and ultimately the arms of Madeleine

CAST

Catherine Deneuve Geneviève Emery
Anne Vernon Madame Emery
Mireille Perrey Aunt Élise
Ellen Farner Madeleine
Nino Castelnuovo Guy Foucher
Marc Michel Roland Cassard
Jean Champion Aubin
Pierre Caden Bernard
Jean-Pierre Dorat Jean

KEY FACTS

🎬 **FILM**
🎬 **Director** Jacques Demy
🎞 **Screenplay** Jacques Demy
🎵 **Music** Michel Legrand
♭ **Lyrics** Jacques Demy
⏱ **Running time** 91 minutes
📅 **Release date** 19 February 1964

⊙ **Key information**
The Umbrellas of Cherbourg is the middle film in an informal "romantic trilogy" of Demy films that share some of the same actors, characters, and overall look; it followed *Lola* (1961) and preceded *Modelshop* (1967). The film was very successful in France, with a total of 1,274,958 cinema admissions.

RELATED FILMS

Des Demoiselles de Rochefort (The Young Girls of Rochefort) Michel Legrand, Jacques Demy, 1967

Une Chambre en Ville (A Room in Town) Michel Colombier, Jacques Demy, 1982

(Ellen Farner). Six years later, the grown-up and rich Geneviève and garage owner Guy happen upon each other. Guy refuses the chance to meet his daughter and the former couple part for the last time.

PAINT-BOX COLOUR

The daring use of continuous music throughout the film was just one element of this unique cinematic world; the other was the vivid, saturated colour of the movie's cinematography. Filmgoers were entranced by the otherworldly, paint-box colours of the film. Each element – the luminous blue of the rain-soaked cobbles, the shining yellow of Catherine Deneuve's hair and cardigan, the suffocating white of the wedding dress shop – was carefully designed by Demy for maximum visual impact. The effort made in rendering these colours was not lost on marvelling cinema audiences.

The colour faded from the film over time and Demy was hoping to restore the film to its former glory at the time of his passing in 1990. It was left to his wife and fellow film-maker Agnès Varda to complete the job. After a four-month laboratory process using three colour separation masters created by Demy and with a remastered score, the restored movie was reissued in 1996 to rapturous reviews. Christopher Orr in *The Atlantic* wrote: "*The Umbrellas of Cherbourg* takes the mundane and quotidian and elevates them to heartbreaking art, in part through its complete absence of ironic detachment. The film conjures a time and place for the viewer which is both simultaneously familiar and impossible – everyday life glimpsed through the prism of dreams."

THEATRE VERSIONS

Notable attempts to stage *The Umbrellas of Cherbourg* in English include the 1979 New York production at The Public Theatre (with lyrics by Sheldon Harnick) and the West End production directed by Emma Rice, which ran at the Gielgud Theatre from March through May 2012.

> ## "*Jacques wanted to live in a fairy tale world. He wanted to see happiness, smiles, and laughter all around him.*"
>
> COMPOSER **MICHEL LEGRAND** ON DIRECTOR JACQUES DEMY

▲ **French sophistication**
The coolly beautiful French actress Catherine Deneuve was cast as Geneviève Emery in *The Umbrellas of Cherbourg*.

BIOGRAPHY

MICHEL LEGRAND (1932–)

Prodigious and prolific, Legrand moved to Hollywood soon after being nominated for an Academy Award for *The Umbrellas of Cherbourg*. His legendary speed as a composer allowed him to produce over 200 movie scores, including the Oscar-winning song "Windmills of your Mind" from *The Thomas Crown Affair* (1968) and the Oscar-winning scores for *Summer of '42* (1971) and *Yentl* (see p.238).

CABARET

{ 1966 }

Thanks to the award-winning 1972 movie adaptation, this show set in decadent 1930s Berlin is among the most famous musicals of its era and remains a revival favourite.

British author Christopher Isherwood had detailed his experiences living in pre-Nazi Germany with British nightclub singer Sally Bowles in his semi-autobiographical novella *Goodbye to Berlin* (1939). This was adapted into *I Am a Camera* (1951), a play written by the British playwright John van Druten. British composer Sandy Wilson, who had enjoyed a five-year West End run with *The Boy Friend* (1954–59), had independently begun a musical adaptation of Isherwood's book. However, Harold Prince (see pp.210–11) had acquired the rights and hired the book-writer of *She Loves Me* (1963), Joe Masteroff, to adapt. Prince thought Wilson's musical efforts missed the required mood for the piece and hired songwriters John Kander and Fred Ebb to write the songs instead.

Kander and Ebb researched the period carefully, soaking themselves in 1920s German jazz (Kander: "a very rigid kind of rhythmic thing") and the works of the noted composer Kurt Weill (see p.21), producing a distinctive version of German cabaret music, as filtered through a Broadway sensibility. Underlining the connection, Fräulein Schneider was played by Weill's widow, Austrian actress Lotte Lenya.

DECADENT DELIGHTS
The story concerns the doomed love affair between Sally Bowles and Cliff Bradshaw, a young American writer. Conducted in the shadow of the encroaching Nazi regime, their relationship first soars effortlessly towards marriage and emigration to America, but ultimately founders in sadness, abortion, and separation.

The material was freely adapted to centre on the licentious, seedy Kit Kat Club and the lives of its patrons and performers. Sally was played by Jill Haworth, who impressed Prince with her "somewhat off-the-rails" quality, while the ominous, unsettling EmCee was portrayed, in a career-defining performance, by Joel Grey.

The combination of leering debauchery in the songs ("Two Ladies"), satire of racial prejudice ("If You Could See Her"), semi-cathartic refutation of the imminent nightmare of Nazism ("Cabaret"), and Brechtian cynicism ("So What") proved a hit with the critics and public alike.

MOVIE TRANSITION
For the film adaptation, producer Cy Feuer, who had reservations about the original show, required a radical

▲ **Dark menace**
Liza Minnelli and Joel Grey performing "Money" in the film version of *Cabaret*. Grey created a truly creepy monster with his unique "EmCee".

new script (by Jay Presson Allen) and three new songs by Kander and Ebb ("Mein Herr", "Money", and "Maybe This Time").

Though Bob Fosse (see pp.200–01) was generally thought to have fallen short in his direction of the movie of *Sweet Charity* (see opposite), Feuer wanted a sure eye and dark flair for the musical numbers (which were now all set in the Kit Kat Club), and so he took a risk on the volatile director.

◀ **Iconic performance**
In the movie, Sally Bowles was transformed from a semi-professional singer into a mesmerizing performer, with a fully-fledged star turn by Liza Minnelli.

KEY FACTS

🎭 STAGE
- 🎬 **Director** Harold Prince
- 📖 **Book** Joe Masteroff
- 🎵 **Music** John Kander
- 🎼 **Lyrics** Fred Ebb
- 🎭 **Venue** Broadhurst Theatre, New York
- 📅 **Date** 20 November 1966

⊙ Key information
The initial Broadway run was 1,165 performances, and the original show won eight Tony Awards. These included Best Musical, Best Original Score, Best Performance by a Featured Actor (Joel Grey), Best Direction, and Best Choreography.

SWEET CHARITY

{ 1966 }

This vehicle for the 1950s star Gwen Verdon saw the sparkling talents of her choreographer/director husband Bob Fosse come to full fruition on the Broadway stage.

In the late 1950s, star performer Gwen Verdon (see p.198) had enough clout to insist that her latest show, *Redhead* (1959), was choreographed and directed by Bob Fosse (see pp.200–01), a talented dancer-turned-director she had fallen for. After marrying Fosse in 1960, Verdon supported Fosse's choreographic career as muse and assistant, but by 1965 she was keen to return to the stage. A Fosse-written adaptation of *Breakfast at Tiffany's* stalled when author Truman Capote thought Verdon (40) too old to play Holly Golightly (20). Instead, Fosse adapted Federico Fellini's *Nights of Cabiria* (1957), a movie about the luckless efforts of a prostitute in Rome to find true love. Fosse turned Cabiria into a dance hall hostess from New York's Times Square and named her Charity.

Fosse invited Neil Simon to look at his script, which resulted in Simon rewriting it into witty shape and taking sole credit, to Fosse's rumbling chagrin. The story revolves around Charity's up-and-down relationship with Oscar, a shy tax accountant. In a humorous yet completely unsentimental ending, true love does not win the day.

GWEN'S SHOW

The whole show was built around Verdon's singular gifts for dance and vulnerable comedy, and she was given

SWEET CHARITY

A UNIVERSAL PICTURE · TECHNICOLOR° 70MM/PANAVISION° WITH FULL DIMENSIONAL SOUND [G] ⊛

some memorable numbers to work with. "If My Friends Could See Me Now" featured Charity, unable to believe her luck, goofily dancing around the apartment of a film star who has just picked her up; "I'm a Brass Band" was sung and danced in exuberant celebration as she discovers Oscar wants to marry her, even after knowing what she does for a living. With a huskily expressive but limited vocal range, Verdon only wanted one ballad in the show and made Coleman choose from the two he had written for Charity; he chose the poignant "Where am I Going".

SHOWSTOPPERS

The show's jewel in the crown was the cool and brassy "Big Spender". It presented a line of dead-eyed dancers-for-hire singing a seductive customer come-on while striking remarkable insouciant poses, which conveyed sexual taunt and threat in equal measure.

THE MOVIE

Sweet Charity opened to good reviews, and Fosse was chosen to direct the 1969 movie. John McMartin was retained as Oscar, but Gwen Verdon was passed over in favour of the much younger Shirley

> *"You run your heart like a hotel, you get guys checking in and out all the time."*
>
> FELLOW DANCER TO CHARITY, *SWEET CHARITY* (NEIL SIMON), 1966

◀ **Swinging Sixties**
The 1969 poster for the movie version. Fosse received acclaim for his rookie direction, but some critics commented on his obvious inexperience.

Maclaine, a movie star who had got her big break as the understudy to Carol Haney in *The Pajama Game* (see pp.106–07).

Although Maclaine is charming in the leading role and the movie conveys a good deal of the Broadway show's individual style, the flashy camera work and distracting editing betrayed Fosse's inexperience and slight discomfort with the medium of film.

▼ **Leading the band**
Charity Hope Valentine (Shirley Maclaine) leads a band for the number "I'm a Brass Band" in the 1967 film *Sweet Charity*.

THE WAY THEY MOVE

Choreographers spend long hours in solitude in front of a mirror, creating moves that express emotions that are too intense for words.

The choreographer creates the physical life that a musical's characters inhabit. They start with the characters and the story that is being told, and work with the director and writers to determine what moments in the musical would best be served by dance. Musicals can have varying amounts of choreography. Some are danced all the way through, the way others use sung words instead of speech.

CREATING A STYLE

Each different choreographer excels at a range of styles and makes these their trademark. However, few have the distinct, immediately identifiable characteristics of such towering greats of the musical theatre as Agnes de Mille (see p.69), Bob Fosse (see pp.200–01), or Jerome Robbins (see pp.108–09), to name only three.

Once the choreographer has created the individual dance moves, sometimes bearing in mind the unique qualities of the performer who will dance them, he or she works with the musical arranger to develop the full routine. By the time dance rehearsals begin, the choreographer and assistants are ready to teach the dancers the basic dance vocabulary of the show, and to start putting the pieces together. Slowly, painstakingly, literally step by step, each movement is taught,

trained, and drilled until each dancer can execute the routines with the appearance of very little effort. But appearances can be deceiving. These dancers are the ultimate athletes and work harder than most people in the audience imagine to execute the vision of the choreographer.

DRAWN TO DIRECTION

Many of the great choreographers have also had success directing. Agnes de Mille was the first to choreograph and direct at the same time in the 1947 Rodgers and Hammerstein show *Allegro*. Jerome Robbins co-directed *West Side Story* (see pp.122–25). Gower Champion had great success with *Hello, Dolly!* (see pp.160–61) and *42nd Street* (see pp.222–23). Bob Fosse won an Oscar for direction on *Cabaret* (see p.166). Michael Bennett was at the helm of *A Chorus Line* (see pp.204–07) and *Dreamgirls* (see p.225). Tommy Tune brought old-fashioned showmanship to 1980s musical theatre in shows like *The Will Rogers Follies*. And Susan Stroman (see pp.292–93) won a Tony Award for directing *The Producers* (see pp.290–91).

▶ **Man in the mirror**
Bob Fosse, known for his distinctive style of dance, works on a routine at the Broadway Arts Studio, New York, in 1980.

"The truest expression of a people is in its dances and its music. Bodies never lie."

AGNES DE MILLE, CHOREOGRAPHER, *NEW YORK TIMES MAGAZINE*, 1975

MAME

{ **1966** }

The story of an eccentric bohemian lady and her ward, the musical *Mame* has a rebellious heart and a restless, questing soul – as well as some great songs.

When the ingredients are good enough, the story bears repeating: so it seemed with Jerry Herman's *Mame*. This portrait of an eccentric bohemian lady and her long-suffering ward had already gone the rounds by the time the Broadway musical appeared, having started life as American writer Patrick Dennis's novel *Auntie Mame* (1955). Dennis's book had been a bestseller; within a year, Jerome Lawrence and Robert Edwin Lee had turned it into a successful Broadway play, with Rosalind Russell in the title role. In 1958, this stage show became a movie – again, with Russell starring. It was the highest-grossing film of 1959.

By now, the public might have been expected to have had their fill, but Lawrence and Lee believed it would work as a Broadway musical. Jerry Herman's songs, a score by Philip J. Lang, Onna White's choreography, and Gene Saks' direction came together to set the stage for another triumph. The only fly in the ointment was the unavailability of Rosalind Russell, who by now had made the part of Mame very much her own.

LANSBURY LAUNCHED
In the event, this new, musical *Mame* proved the perfect vehicle for Angela Lansbury's Broadway breakthrough. Now 40, the British actress was well respected in the movie world, but never seemingly set to be a star. In *Mame*, she showed exhilarated audiences a different side: irrepressibly energetic and full of fun.

Though Auntie Mame provides the noise and colour (she fanfares her own first entrance, with her nephew Patrick's bugle), Patrick's destiny is pivotal to the drama. He begins as the bemused observer in his guardian's madcap life. Dismayed at the irregularity and unconventionality of Mame's existence, his late father's legal representatives insist that Patrick be sent to boarding school. Time passes, Mame travels the world; is unexpectedly married – to a wealthy plantation-owner – and then, just as abruptly, is left widowed. Returning home to be reunited with Patrick, she finds him changed beyond recognition. The prep school has done its job: Mame finds that no trace of the young bohemian remains and Patrick has instead become impeccably bourgeois – and unbearable.

KEY FACTS

🎭 **STAGE**

🎬 **Director** Gene Saks

📖 **Book** Jerome Lawrence, Robert Edwin Lee

🎵 **Music and lyrics** Jerry Herman, Philip J. Lang

🎫 **Venue** Winter Garden Theatre, New York

📅 **Date** 24 May 1966

⊙ **Key information**
The initial Broadway run for this show was more than 1,500 performances. It was nominated for ten Tony Awards and won in five categories.

TO THE BARRICADES?
In the fight for Patrick's soul, we side with the anarchic Mame against the forces of order. The trustees' victory in having him sent off to school is a clear defeat for decency; the Patrick it produces is an unpleasant stuffed shirt. The mean-spiritedness of his snobbery and the joyless cynicism of his social climbing both contrast starkly with his aunt's ebullient generosity. All this is accompanied by some rousing songs, including the feel-good "My Best Girl", "If He Walked into My Life", which became an international hit, and the American holiday favourite, "We Need a Little Christmas".

▶ **Singing about today**
Lucille Ball assuming a typically madcap and precarious position in the starring role as Auntie Mame in the 1974 film.

THOROUGHLY MODERN MILLIE

{ 1967 }

A musical spoof with satirical notes, *Thoroughly Modern Millie* cheekily covers the Roaring Twenties from a nostalgic Sixties point of view, putting three leading ladies all centre stage.

▼ **Flapping fun**
Thoroughly Modern Millie was Mary Tyler Moore's film debut. She played Dorothy – a naïve and sweet orphan who is befriended by Millie.

Julie Andrews, who had recently appeared in *Mary Poppins* (see pp.154–57) and *The Sound of Music* (see pp.134–37), was a big-name international movie star who was sure to draw in the crowds to this new film. However, as one reviewer put it, it was "hard to say which of the ladies comes out ahead at the end", due to the strong backing performances delivered by Carol Channing and Beatrice Lillie.

Millie Dillmount (Andrews) arrives in New York City from provincial Kansas, determined to leave her curls behind and become a "modern". To this end, she has a haircut, buys flapper dresses, and enrols in stenography (shorthand) school. She takes a room with the malevolent Mrs Meers (Lillie), who is secretly targeting orphaned women to sell on as slave labour.

Into this set-up walks Miss Dorothy Brown (Mary Tyler Moore), a naïve young orphan who wishes to become an actress. Dorothy and Millie become friends, and Millie explains her true aim in coming to New York: to find work as a secretary, fall in love with her boss, and then marry him.

ENLIVENING SONGS
Notable elements of this production included the use of contemporary Twenties songs to beef up the score, such as "Baby Face" and "Jazz Baby". These add to the character of the film, as do the silent movie device of caption cards to tell the audience what Millie is thinking.

In many ways, *Thoroughly Modern Millie* occurred at the close of film's musical golden age. Nevertheless, the film sparkled with fun and fizz, and kept audiences humming.

KEY FACTS

🎥 **FILM**

🎬 **Director** George Roy Hill
🎞 **Screenplay** Richard Morris
🎵 **Music** Elmer Bernstein (score) and various others, including Jimmy Van Heusen and Sammy Cahn
🕐 **Running time** 138 minutes
📅 **Release date** 21 March 1967

◉ **Key information**
This film was the 1968 Academy Award winner for Music (Original Music Score) and was nominated for six others, including Art Direction, Actress in a Supporting Role, and Costume Design.

"The picture was very Twenties – high style, but not high camp."

JULIE ANDREWS

HAIR

{ 1968 }

Many claims are made for shows that may or may not have transformed musical theatre, but in the case of *Hair* the evidence is indisputable. It defined a generation.

Like an explosion of repressed energy, anger, and talent, it can be claimed that *Hair* truly rocked Western culture. Conceived at a time when 1960s America was sharply divided over the validity of a war in Vietnam, it represented the spirit of a "hippie" generation that, in large numbers, refused to conform to the majority view that they should fight and kill because their government ordered them to do so.

Seeds were sown in the early experimental work of New York's theatre scene when the writers James Rado (who had traditional musical theatre aspirations) and Gerome Ragni (a theatrical rebel) became friends while devising and performing in a freely structured Vietnam protest show. The ups and downs of their friendship are reflected in one of *Hair's* central relationships, that of the mild-mannered, romantic Claude and the volatile, reactionary Berger.

The plot and song structure are loose and fluid, and change from major production to production, but,

essentially, the story follows a tribe of young anti-war social dropouts who meet and share their experiences, find new freedom through drugs and sex, and reject the military draft. The tribe evolves when Claude joins the army.

A COLLABORATION OF MAVERICK TALENTS

Apart from Rado and Ragni, it is unlikely the show would have been as phenomenally successful without three other maverick talents.

Composer Galt MacDermot describes himself as relatively "straight" in comparison with the others, but he found an original musical voice for the flower children movement in his merging of rock with funk. *Hair's* Broadway director was the ground-breaking and inspirational Tom O'Horgan, whose rehearsal techniques involved dissolving the traditional cast and creative team hierarchies and instigating the improvisations that resulted in the radical shifts in which the performers switched interpretation of each character's journey between them. Finally, the innovative and courageous producer Joe Papp signed up the show to open his new Public Theatre, despite the surprise and opposition of many of his team.

SHOCK, BEWILDERMENT, AND FEAR

It is hard to draw a line between where the Hippie movement influenced *Hair* and where *Hair* inspired the political and cultural revolution. The two are entwined in such a way that some commentators have stated that no other piece of musical theatre has so powerfully influenced social change. The show marked the first time a

▲ **Flower power on the offensive**
A hippie protest scene from the original Broadway show. Rado and Ragni's radical book outraged many conservative Americans.

story and production were completely racially integrated and the blatant inclusion of nudity, drug-taking, gay sexuality, and disrespect for the American flag drew angry protests and even violence from an outraged American public.

Hair shocked, bewildered, and even frightened conservative America and the older generation of Broadway practitioners. Leonard Bernstein dismissed the songs as "laundry lists" and walked out, Richard Rodgers called the score "one-third music", and even John Lennon is reported to have found it dull. However, it is now widely acknowledged as a classic show, spawning countless revivals – both amateur and professional – around the world, sometimes still provoking passion and sparking protest.

▶ **Tribal love-rock**
The psychedelic artwork that adorned the window card for the original production of *Hair*, staged at the Biltmore Theater in New York in 1968.

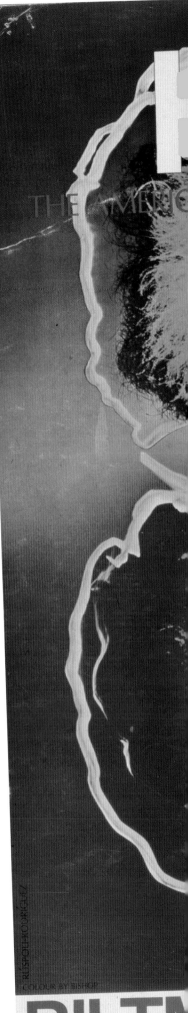

KEY FACTS

🎭 STAGE

📺 **Director** Tom O'Horgan
📖 **Book** Gerome Ragni, James Rado
🎵 **Music** Galt MacDermot
🎶 **Lyrics** Gerome Ragni, James Rado
🎭 **Venue** Biltmore Theater, New York
📅 **Date** 29 April 1968

⊙ Key information

The original production of *Hair* ran for 1,750 performances between 1968 and 1972. The show was choreographed by Julie Arenal. The cast included Lynn Kellogg, Lamont Washington, and a young Diane Keaton.

BUTLER PRESENTS

AIR

BAL LOVE-ROCK MUSICAL

RE THEATER

47TH STREET, 582-5340

◀ **Alternative take**
American actor Will Swenson (centre) as Berger in a production of *Hair* staged at the Gielgud Theatre, London, in 2010.

RECORDING SUCCESS

Several of the songs, notably "Aquarius" and "Good Morning Starshine", have enjoyed chart success in a number of different countries. In 1979, a popular film version was released, and even the adoption of blue jeans as everyday wear has been traced back to the musical's profound influence on every area of post-hippie modern culture in the late 1960s and 70s.

FILM VERSION

As appropriate to a musical in which improvisation and change is actively encouraged, the film differs considerably from the stage show. Directed by Miloš Forman, the mediun of film allowed for the fleshing out of some of the characters to fit with its more naturalistic form. Claude is given a back story

▶ **Show of rebellion**
The assembled cast of the original Broadway production pose for a publicity photo in 1968. A racially integrated cast was a radical move for a Broadway production, even in the open-minded 1960s.

in which he travels to New York from Oklahoma to join the military before getting caught up in the hippie movement, and it is Berger, not Claude, who goes to war and is killed in action. Sheila, the musical's feisty feminist leader, is depicted as a high-society debutante dropping out of a conventional lifestyle to join the tribe. There is also some distillation of the Peace Movements politics and greater emphasis on the free love attitudes of the protagonists.

In order to service this new plot, a number of the songs from the stage shows were omitted. Some only survive as underscoring, as is common practice when musicals make the move from stage to screen.

Notable additions included a new song written by MacDermot, "Somebody to Love". Omissions included "The Bed", "Dead End", "Oh Great God of Power", "I Believe in Love", "Going Down", "Air", "My Conviction", "Abie Baby", "Frank Mills", and "What a Piece of Work is Man". "Manchester, England" and "Walking in Space" remained, but both in condensed form.

> "*Anywhere ... you will see elements of the experimental techniques that* Hair *brought not just to Broadway, but to the entire world.*"

ELLEN STEWART, FOUNDER OF LA MAMMA EXPERIMENTAL THEATRE

CHITTY CHITTY BANG BANG

{ 1968 }

This film musical is based on a story by Ian Fleming, creator of James Bond, adapted by that master of kids' books Roald Dahl, and includes songs by Disney songwriters Richard and Robert Sherman. It's an all-time children's favourite.

▲ **For children of all ages**
The poster advertised the film as "fantasmagorical", and it was certainly that. The boyish charm of Dick Van Dyke and sparkling performances from others ensured its success.

KEY FACTS

🎥 **FILM**

🎬 **Director** Ken Hughes

🎞 **Screenplay** Roald Dahl, Ken Hughes

🎵 **Music and lyrics** Richard M. Sherman and Robert B. Sherman

🕐 **Running time** 144 minutes

📅 **Release date** 16 December 1968

◉ **Key information**
The film was distributed by United Artists. It was a lavish production, which cost US$10 million to make. Despite the success of the movie with audiences, initially it took only US$7.5 million at the box office.

CAST

Dick Van Dyke Caractacus Potts

Sally Ann Howes Truly Scrumptious

Lionel Jeffries Grandpa Potts

Gert Fröbe Baron Bomburst

Anna Quayle Baroness Bomburst

Benny Hill Toymaker

James Robertson Justice Lord Scrumptious

Robert Helpmann Child Catcher

Heather Ripley Jemima

Adrian Hall Jeremy

The film was cowritten and directed by Ken Hughes in 1968. Appropriately, it was produced by Albert R. "Cubby" Broccoli, who had co-produced the James Bond series of films.

It stars Dick Van Dyke as Caractacus Potts, a young widower who invents zany machines to the delight of his children, Jeremy and Jemima, and the exasperation of their grandpa, played by British comic actor Lionel Jeffries.

During a disastrous attempt to sell an invention to a businessman, Lord Scrumptious, Potts becomes smitten with the peer's daughter. Her name is Truly Scrumptious, played by Sally Anne Howes, and she also begins to fall for Potts, despite earlier spiky encounters between the pair. Love begins to blossom.

On a day out with his children and Truly, Potts invents a fantasy in which a car he has renovated, nicknamed Chitty Chitty Bang Bang

▶ **A glorious romp**
Dick Van Dyke, Lionel Jeffries, and Sally Anne Howes lead the children in their riotous fantasy adventures with their flying vehicle, Chitty Chitty Bang Bang.

"A fast, dense, friendly children's musical … None of the audience's terrific eagerness to have a good time is betrayed or lost."

RENATA ADLER, *THE NEW YORK TIMES* REVIEW FOR THE FILM, 1968

after its engine noise, flies them away to adventure. They land in a kingdom in which the bombastic king and queen employ a terrifying Child Catcher, played in an iconic performance by ballet dancer Robert Helpmann, to round up and lock away the country's youngsters. Potts, with the help of Truly and Chitty, rescues them all. During the course of this adventure Truly falls in love with Potts and the couple finally agree to marry.

REPEAT SUCCESS
In 1969, the film was the tenth most popular at the US box office, at a time when cinema was dominated by violent films. Consequently, for many people the arrival of something suitable for family viewing was very welcome indeed.

In the intervening years, *Chitty Chitty Bang Bang* has established itself as a classic through television repeats, often during holiday seasons. The title song was nominated for an Academy Award, and for many who grew up in the 1970s, the songs and melodies of the score stir up evocative memories of childhood, even if the sinister figure of Robert Helpmann's Child Catcher haunted a few early nightmares.

STAGE HITS AND MISSES
In 2002, a stage version was created of the film, with six new songs by the Sherman brothers (see pp.176–77). It was adapted by Jeremy Sams and directed by Adrian Noble, with musical staging by Gillian Lynne. The car "Chitty" used for this production remains the most expensive prop ever in British theatre history.

▶ **Creepy character**
The Child Catcher emerges from his carriage. This scary character did not appear in Fleming's book, but was created for the film by Roald Dahl.

▶ **Clowning around**
Dick Van Dyke's character wears a memorable clown costume to perform the song "Doll on a Music Box", in which he becomes a marionette (a puppet).

The stage show was a hit at the box office, taking £70 million over three and a half years and becoming the longest running show ever at the London Palladium theatre.

A successful and extensive UK tour followed, but, unfortunately, *Chitty Chitty Bang Bang* was not as popular with New York audiences and critics when it transferred to Broadway for a short run in 2005. Successful German and Australian productions followed and these lasted considerably longer. The songs in the film and stage version have attracted little critical acclaim, despite their provenance from the pens of two of Broadway and Hollywood's greatest writers. Even though *Chitty Chitty Bang Bang*'s title song was nominated for an Academy Award, a review in *Time* magazine in 1968 described the score as having" all the rich melodic variety of an automobile horn", and a reviewer for *The New York Times* was only slightly more positive, describing the film's songs as possessing "something of the joys of singing together on a team bus on the way to a game".

ROBERT AND RICHARD SHERMAN

{ COMPOSERS **1925–2012 and 1928–** }

The song "Supercalifragilisticexpialidocious" might sound like incomprehensible nonsense, but there is nothing incoherent about the success it brought to their creators. Like much of the Shermans' music, it defined the film in which it featured.

◀ **Sibling songwriters**
The Sherman brothers are perhaps best known for their work on Disney films, which they invested with highly memorable songs. Their talent lay in combining deceptively simple lyrics with winning, catchy melodies.

This and other 1960s and 70s hits created for Walt Disney came from one of the most prolific, greatly lauded, and long-lasting songwriting partnerships of all time. Robert and Richard Sherman were the sons of a struggling Tin Pan Alley songwriter, Al Sherman, who contributed to vaudeville shows and the *Ziegfeld Follies* and became a sought-after musician himself. But the Sherman brothers would go on to win lasting fame for the film score *Mary Poppins* (see pp.154–57). It secured their place in popular music history and made them multi-millionaires, elevating them far from their humble origins. Their father later admitted that when Robert was born he worried about paying the doctor's bill until he opened an envelope containing a large royalty cheque for one of his songs – "Save Your Sorrow".

Robert displayed a writing talent from an early age. At 16, he wrote a stage play that generated money for war bonds. As a soldier during World War II, he and his squad stumbled on the Dachau concentration camp just after it had been abandoned by the Nazis. He was later wounded in the knee and forced to walk with a stick. Meanwhile, Richard was developing a musical talent, and although it was his ambition to write the Great American Symphony, he teamed up with his brother to write popular songs.

ACCEPTING A CHALLENGE
The brothers were goaded into working together by their father. Richard would later recall: "Dad dropped the gauntlet and said, 'You guys haven't got the capability of writing a popular song.' That started it." Robert added: "When we finally wrote a song we liked, he pointed north-east and said, 'That way is Hollywood, that's where the publishers are, take it and go there.'"
Further advice concerned what Al called "the Three Ss". He told his sons: "Songs have to be simple, singable,

and sincere." The brothers clearly took their father's advice to heart for they wrote several top ten hits, first with teeny-bopper tune "Tall Paul", then with "You're Sixteen", performed by Johnny Burnette in 1960 and Ringo Starr in 1977.

In 1960, Walt Disney hired the brothers as staff songwriters for the big screen. Initially, the Shermans worked on live-action films such as *The Parent Trap*, *In Search of the Castaways*, and *Summer Magic*. They also provided songs for the animated picture *The Sword in the Stone*.

"It's a Small World (After All)" was written for the 1964 World's Fair, and subsequently became a Disney anthem. It made the brothers the obvious choice for scoring *Mary Poppins*. The film's soundtrack album reached number one in the US and stayed in the charts on both sides of the Atlantic for 18 months.

as "I Wanna Be Like You", "Trust in Me", and "That's What Friends are For". The brothers went freelance, but continued to work for Disney on films like *The Aristocats* (1970) and *Bedknobs and Broomsticks* (1971). However, their next Disney production came 28 years later: the 2000 blockbuster *The Tigger Movie*.

The 1968 release of *Chitty Chitty Bang Bang* (see pp.174–75) was the brothers' first non-Disney film. It was scored for James Bond producer Cubby Broccoli, and secured a third Oscar nomination. More Oscar nods followed during the 1970s. *The Slipper and the Rose* (1976) received dual nominations for the Score and Best Song – as did *Bedknobs and Broomsticks*. "When You're Loved",

London Palladium to rave reviews, 34 years after the film was first screened. The Shermans penned six new songs for the show. *Mary Poppins* also made a successful transition to the stage: the joint Disney/Cameron Mackintosh production opened in London in 2004.

▲ **Magical motor**
The iconic flying car from the film *Chitty Chitty Bang Bang*, which was loosely based on Ian Fleming's novel of the same name.

> *"A song has three parts: the music, the lyrics and, the most important, the idea. Everything revolves around the idea."*
>
> **ROBERT SHERMAN**

SUPERCALIFRAGILISTICEXPIALIDOCIOUS!
In 1965, the Sherman brothers achieved Oscar success, winning the awards for Best Original Soundtrack and, with "Chim Chim Cher-ee", Best Song. Altogether, *Mary Poppins* won three other Oscars, including Best Actress for its star, Julie Andrews.

Walt Disney died before the release of *The Jungle Book* in 1967, which featured Sherman-crafted songs such

from *The Magic of Lassie* (1979), was nominated for Best Song, and *Tom Sawyer* (1973) for the Score.

In 1974, the Shermans wrote the hit Broadway show *Over Here!*. Conceived as a vehicle for 1940s icons Patty and Maxene Andrews – the surviving members of the Andrews Sisters trio – it took entertaining troops in wartime as its theme. The show ran for 12 months, and became the biggest-grossing Broadway musical of the year.

In 2002, the West End stage version of *Chitty Chitty Bang Bang* opened at the

Robert relocated to London in 2002; their collaboration continued by fax, email, phone, and regular flights. It was only in 2009 that a documentary film, produced and directed by their sons Gregory and Jeffrey – who did not meet until their 40s – revealed a 50-year estrangement at odds with both their public personas and the sunny optimism of the songs for which the Sherman brothers will be remembered.

◀ **National heroes**
The Sherman brothers were recognized by the US government when they received the National Medal of Arts from George W. Bush in 2008.

KEY WORKS

"It's a Small World (After All)", 1964

Mary Poppins, 1965 (see pp.154–57)

The Jungle Book, 1967

Chitty Chitty Bang Bang, 1968 (see pp.174–75)

The Slipper and the Rose: The Story of Cinderella, 1973

The Tigger Movie, 2000

TIMELINE

19 December 1925 Robert Bernard Sherman born in New York.

12 June 1928 Richard Milton Sherman born in New York.

1937 The family moves to California. The brothers attend Beverly Hills High School, and later Bard College, New York.

1951 The brothers team up to write songs.

1958 Robert forms Music World Corporation as "Tall Paul" becomes the brothers' first top ten hit, performed by Annette Funicello.

1964 Now working for Disney, the brothers write "It's a Small World (After All)" for the New York World's Fair: it becomes the most translated and frequently performed song ever written.

1965 The brothers' score for the movie *Mary Poppins* wins them two Academy Awards, including an Oscar for "Chim Chim Cher-ee".

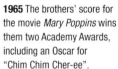
OSCAR®

1967 *The Jungle Book*, featuring songs by the Sherman brothers, is Walt Disney's last film.

1968 The brothers write the score for Albert R "Cubby" Broccoli's *Chitty Chitty Bang Bang*.

1973 *The Slipper and the Rose*, with score and screenplay by the Sherman brothers, is chosen for Royal Command Performance attended by Queen Elizabeth II.

1977 *The Many Adventures of Winnie the Pooh* includes songs that the Shermans wrote for Disney "shorts" in the late 1960s.

2000 The Sherman brothers return to Disney to score *The Tigger Movie*.

2002 Robert Sherman moves to London.

2005 Inducted into the Songwriters' Hall of Fame.

2009 Documentary film *The Boys: The Sherman Brothers' Story* is released.

6 March 2012 Robert Sherman dies in London.

PROMISES, PROMISES

{ 1968 }

A 1968 adaptation of a 1960 movie, *Promises, Promises* combines the wry humour of Neil Simon with the smart pop music of Burt Bacharach and lyricist Hal David.

In the mid-1960s, playwright Neil Simon was at the height of his Broadway success. His comedy plays *Barefoot In The Park* (1963) and *The Odd Couple* (1965) had both been smash hits and, following the success of his book for *Sweet Charity* (see p.167), veteran producer David Merrick wanted another musical from him. Simon suggested adapting Billy Wilder's 1960 movie *The Apartment*, about Chuck Baxter, an office worker who hopes to climb the corporate ladder by letting executives borrow his flat for their extramarital assignations. Simon also suggested hiring two leading pop songwriters, Burt Bacharach and Hal David. Though the songs were cultured and sophisticated, they were not

traditional Broadway fare. Bacharach, for all his pop credentials, felt rather more affinity with the work of Richard Rodgers (see pp.70–71) than with recent musical trends, such as the rock musical *Hair* (see pp.172–73).

WRITING AND REHEARSING

Though they had no set working pattern for this show, Hal David wrote most of the lyrics first and Bacharach composed the music later. In rehearsal, they rewrote extensively to better fit the cast's singing voices, with Jill

◀ Movie inspiration
Billy Wilder's comedy film *The Apartment* had been a huge success and seemed an obvious choice for a spin-off Broadway show.

O'Hara as Fran Kubelik – the hapless mistress of Mr Sheldrake who Chuck falls for – providing special inspiration to the composer. "Her voice, the sound of it," he remembered, "motivated me to go different musically from this cardboard figure in my imagination that I'd been writing for."

KEY FACTS

🏵 **STAGE**

🎬 **Director** Robert Moore

📖 **Book** Neil Simon

🎵 **Music** Burt Bacharach

𝄞 **Lyrics** Hal David

🎭 **Venue** Shubert Theatre, New York

📅 **Date** 1 December 1968

◉ **Key information**
The show won a Drama Desk Award for outstanding music. It played successfully on the West End stage in London in 1969 and was revived on Broadway in 2010.

The score for *Promises, Promises* was a surprisingly intricate maze of complex rhythms and unexpected key changes. Recognizing that giving audiences advance warning of the complicated score might help the show, Bacharach recorded several of the numbers with singer Dionne Warwick months before opening night. Jerry Orbach in the lead role was having particular trouble with the title number and attended the singer's recording of "Promises, Promises", reportedly asking Warwick, "How the hell do you sing this?"

The show was a huge success and ran for 1,281 performances. A recording man through and through, Bacharach had sound engineer Phil Ramone set up the theatre audio system so that the show sounded like a record, and he insisted that everything stay true to the original score, with no variations on interpretations throughout the entire run. However, Bacharach was perhaps too accustomed to working alone, and *Promises, Promises* remained his only musical.

A Broadway revival in 2010 re-created the show with glamour and sensitivity, and added two Bacharach-David greats to the score – " I Say a Little Prayer" and "A House Is Not a Home".

◀ Who's coming to dinner?
Jerry Orbach as a confused-looking Chuck Baxter with the cast of *Promises, Promises* in a huddle, as they plan their secret assignations.

OH! CALCUTTA!

{ 1969 }

This record-breaking show never lost its public appeal, despite consistently scathing reviews. It seemed that the American and British publics' taste for nudity was insatiable.

As a theatre critic, aesthete, and literary manager of the National Theatre, London, Kenneth Tynan was opposed to any kind of censorship in the arts. In 1966, he began exploring the idea of an erotic revue "expressly designed to titillate," as he put it, "in the most elegant and outré way."

The show was to be named after a 1946 painting of a reclining nude by French artist Clovis Trouille entitled Oh Calcutta, Calcutta", a French pun on Oh quel cul t'as, meaning, "What a lovely arse you have".

Tynan imagined stylish burlesque routines interspersed with witty, sexy sketches for a cast of four men and four

Wank", which stayed. Others approached included playwrights Joe Orton and David Mercer, and novelist Edna O'Brien,

Jacques Levy, whose experimental, cool-toned work for the counterculture play American Hurrah (1966) had impressed Tynan, was invited to direct. Hillard Elkins, manager of film star Steve McQueen and producer of the Sammy Davis Jr musical Golden Boy (1964), convinced Tynan that he was the man to produce the show, and he arranged for a New York opening. Michael Bennett was briefly on board as choreographer before changing his mind, whereupon Margo Sappington, his dance captain on Promises, Promises,

replaced him. Though the jazz-rock trio Open Window (Peter Schickele, Robert Dennis, and Stanley Walden) were hired to create the trippy score, the show was never really about music; it was about simulated sex and nudity, an aspect that Levy, perhaps even more than Tynan, was keen to explore. "I always wanted the feeling," Levy said, "that the showing of the whole body was something special."

THE SHOW
When Tynan reviewed Levy's progress, he was disappointed to discover a lack of craftsmanship, and that the exploratory naked workshops had taken precedence over preparation of the sketches. As rehearsals developed and Tynan's favourite pieces were dropped, Tynan threatened to remove his name from the project, fearing the production was descending into a "flesh show". However, he was there on opening night, gamely promoting a piece he perhaps no longer believed in.

Reviews were scathing. Clive Barnes of The New York Times described the show as "innocent and sophomoric", going on to note that it was only suitable for "people who are extraordinarily underprivileged either sexually, socially, or emotionally". The public were intrigued, however, and flocked to see it.

In 1976, Oh! Calcutta! was revived on Broadway. This production was also overseen by Levy and Sappington, and its popularity eclipsed even that of the original show, becoming the longest-running revue in Broadway history.

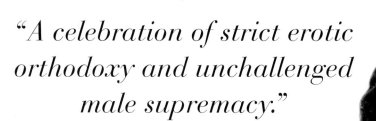

> ## "A celebration of strict erotic orthodoxy and unchallenged male supremacy."
>
> **FRANK RICH**, CRITIC, THE NEW YORK TIMES, ON THE SHOW'S CLOSURE, AUGUST 1989

women. He wrote to various literary and theatrical figures asking for their fantasies and ideas. Anything was permissible, he advised, except for male homosexuality, which was still a criminal act in the UK at the time.

THE TEAM
Among the fellow writers he invited to contribute to the production were playwrights Samuel Beckett and Harold Pinter (whom he also asked to direct), and Beatle John Lennon. Pinter dropped out, but both Beckett and Lennon submitted ideas – respectively "Breathe", later dropped at Beckett's request, and "Liverpool

KEY FACTS

STAGE

Director Jacques Levy

Book Kenneth Tynan, Sam Shepard, John Lennon, Jules Feiffer, others

Music and lyrics Peter Schickele, Robert Dennis, Stanley Walden

Venue Eden Theatre, New York

Date 17 June 1969

Key information
The initial Broadway run of 1,314 performances, and even the West End run of 3,918 performances were eclipsed by the 1976 Broadway revival, which ran for 5,959 shows until 1989.

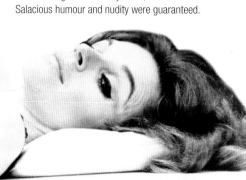

◀ **Trust me, I'm a doctor**
Mark Dempsey and Raina Barrett in a scene from the original Broadway show, 1972. Salacious humour and nudity were guaranteed.

NEW INVENTIONS

1970–1999

Musicals are transformed as imaginative sets and special effects provide spectacular backdrops for powerful rock operas and inspired mega musicals.

NEW INVENTIONS

▲ **Enduring popularity**
The popularity of some of the biggest hit shows from the 1980s and 90s has not decreased, with *The Phantom of the Opera* still in production after three decades.

The 1970s, 80s, and 90s, saw the development of new genres as creators sought new inspiration from popular and world music, and dramatic storylines.

Throughout the 1960s, American musical theatre had remained largely untouched by the ever-changing trends in popular music, maintaining as a staple the tradition of smartly composed, Tin Pan Alley and jazz-influenced dance and song. But the arrival of pop/rock musical language in the scores of *Hair* (see pp.172–73) and *Promises, Promises* (see p.178) heralded a new era of musicals.

It was *Jesus Christ Superstar* (see pp.184–85), by British songwriting team Andrew Lloyd Webber (see pp.270–71) and Tim Rice that set the tone. Beginning life as a rock concept album, the show's grand themes, highly emotional tone, and lack of dialogue led *Superstar* and the similarly biblical *Godspell* (1971) by Stephen Schwartz (1948–) to be dubbed rock operas (see pp.118–19) or rock musicals. Lloyd Webber and Rice repeated the album-to-show model for *Evita* (see pp.208–09), a highly successful musical that blended Latin, classical, and pop styles. Of the other notable shows in the genre, Rice teamed with Benny Andersson (1946–) and Björn Ulvaeus (1945–) of Swedish pop band ABBA to create *Chess* in 1982. A sub-genre of the rock musical featured lighter-hearted shows and 1950s-style rock'n'roll musical scores; these include *Grease* (see pp.212–13), *The Rocky Horror Show* (see pp.192–93), and *Little Shop of Horrors* (see pp.338–39).

POP OPERA

The 1980s saw the rise of the European "pop opera" spectacle, as exemplified by Lloyd Webber's *Cats* (see pp.228–31), *The Phantom of the Opera* (see pp.252–53), and *Sunset Boulevard* (see pp.266–69). These enormously popular, long-running shows featured elaborate staging, dramatic storylines, and loud, dynamic scores with memorable melodic themes that sometimes produced simultaneous hit records.

French songwriting team Alain Boublil and Claude-Michel Schönberg (see pp.258–59) developed a highly intense pop opera style with their adaptation of the Victor Hugo novel *Les Misérables* (see pp.246–49), one

◀ **New breed of success**
Co-produced by Cameron Mackintosh and Andrew Lloyd Webber, *Cats* broke records with long-running productions in London and New York.

of the most successful musicals of all time, and *Miss Saigon* (see pp.256–57). Together with Lloyd Webber's output, these shows, sometimes called mega-musicals (see pp.250–51), dominated the musical theatre landscape around the world in the 1980s and 90s.

Occasionally bucking the trend were smaller scale shows like *Blood Brothers* (see p.339), written and composed by Willie Russell (1947–). This intimate, modestly budgeted nature-versus-nurture tale defied critical indifference to become a genuine people's musical, running for over 24 years (1991–2012) in London's West End.

SONDHEIM

While even composer/lyricist Stephen Sondheim (see pp.220–21) added rock flavours to *Company* (1970), he moved on to explore 1920s and 30s pastiche in *Follies* (1971), Viennese waltz in *A Little Night Music* (see pp.190–91) and elsewhere to create his own customized brand of refined theatre scores. For many, Sondheim represents the artistic conscience of musical theatre; highly literate, profoundly musical, and provocatively creative, with little apparent regard for wide, instant commercial appeal or current

▲ **Dreaming of stardom**
Popular music inspired new musicals, such as *Dreamgirls,* which drew on the glamorous costumes and R'n'B sounds reminiscent of famous Motown bands.

trends. The multi-layered resonance and complexity of pieces such as *Sweeney Todd* (see pp.216–19), *Sunday in the Park with George* (see p.244), and *Into the Woods* (see p.327) ensure that his shows are regularly rediscovered via passionate and inspired revivals, and in the case of *Sweeney Todd* and *Into the Woods*, Hollywood movies.

TRADITIONS SURVIVE

Throughout the modern era of musicals, old-school craftsmen still flew the flag for traditional musical theatre values. Jerry Herman's scores for *Mack and Mabel* (see p.174) and *La Cage Aux Folles* (see p.239) were full of exuberant music reminiscent of another era. The versatile Kander and Ebb wrote *Chicago* (see pp.196–99) in a hot jazz style, while the most successful musical of its era, *A Chorus Line* (see pp.204–07), elegantly combined traditional Broadway swing with rock recitative and catchy pop.

Revivals and vintage adaptations continued to pull the crowds. Successful reworkings of 1930s musicals, including Harry Warren and Al Dubin's *42nd Street* (see pp.222–23), Richard Rodgers and Lorenz Harts's *On Your Toes* (1983), and the Gershwin amalgam *Crazy for You* (see p.262) proved that there remained an enthusiastic audience for old-fashioned shows.

OTHER TRENDS

Dreamgirls (see p.225), a successful backstage musical about a Supremes-style vocal group, continued the

occasional modern trend started by *Raisin* (1973) and *The Wiz* (see p.202) for African-American shows that featured predominantly black music scores. *Bring in 'da Noise, Bring in 'da Funk* (see pp.272–73) was a significantly successful, hip-hop- and funk-infused telling of black history.

Making the most of the great successes of their musical animated features, the Walt Disney Company developed stage versions of *Beauty and the Beast* (1994) and *The Lion King* (see pp.276–79), which were enormous successes, and vital for introducing a new generation to live musical theatre.

Sensing the public's taste for feel-good nostalgia and a good tune was the "musical revue" or "jukebox musical", which threaded a narrative through an existing catalogue of popular songs. These were sometimes biographical; *Elvis* (1977) recounted the rock'n'roll singer's story accompanied by his hits, while others were fictional. *Ain't Misbehavin'* (see p.214) was a polished tribute to the spirit of 1920s and 30s Harlem via the songs associated with singer-pianist Fats Waller, while *Return to the Forbidden Planet* (1989) strung 1950s and 60s pop classics together with a comic science fiction plot. One of the most successful of the jukebox genre was *Mamma Mia!* (see pp.284–85), which wove a romantic storyline set on a Greek island around 22 ABBA songs to spectacular commercial success, and would also contribute to the proliferation of jukebox musicals in the decade following its release.

Contemporary musical composers continued to contribute to the ever-evolving miscellany of musical theatre, often finding young audiences along the way. Jonathan Larson's rock-oriented *Rent* (see p.274) inspired a cult following Off-Broadway before its mainstream success. Jason Robert Brown (1970–) with *Songs for a New World* (1995) and David Yazbek (1960–) in *The Full Monty* (2000) favoured a "smart pop" style, displaying influences from American singer-songwriter Billy Joel to British new wave music.

▲ **Game changers**
Cameron Mackintosh (left) and Andrew Lloyd Webber (right) collaborated on the productions of *Cats* and *The Phantom of the Opera* – shows that would help change the musical genre forever.

ALAN MENKEN (1949–)

New York-born composer for film and stage, Menken's first success was the rock'n'roll pastiche score for *Little Shop of Horrors* (1986), but he is best known for his music on the hugely successful Walt Disney animation movies that introduced a whole new audience to pop-flavoured romantic musical theatre. His films include: *The Little Mermaid* (1989), which was made into a stage show in 2008; *Beauty and the Beast* (1991), a stage show 1994–2007; *Aladdin* (1992), also adapted for the stage in 2011; *Pocahontas* (1995); and *The Hunchback of Notre Dame* (1996).

JESUS CHRIST SUPERSTAR

{ **1971** }

The first "rock opera" to take to the stage, *Jesus Christ Superstar* fired the opening salvo in a European Broadway invasion led by Andrew Lloyd Webber and Tim Rice, and was first in a new era of musicals as global franchises.

O n 21 April 1965, a 20-year-old, pop-loving, trainee solicitor, Tim Rice (see opposite), wrote to a bright and ambitious 17-year-old music student, Andrew Lloyd Webber (see pp.270–71), offering his services as "a 'with it' writer of lyrics for your songs". So began a famous collaboration that six years later would lead to the staging of *Jesus Christ Superstar* and lasting fame for both.

Lloyd Webber and Rice wrote their first musical – *The Likes of Us*, about the philanthropist Thomas Barnardo – that same year, though waited until 1968 for their first taste of musical success when the Colet School in London

commissioned and performed the "pop oratorio" *Joseph and the Amazing Technicolor Dreamcoat* (see p.187), leading to a good review in the *Sunday Times* and an album recording of the show in 1969. The duo now shared a three-year writing contract and the ambition to make a musical based around the New Testament.

Backing for such a potentially controversial subject was not forthcoming, so *Jesus Christ Superstar* appeared first as a "concept album" (see p.189), recorded at London's Olympic Studios. A single, "Superstar", was released late in 1969 and then the album in 1970. The singers and instrumentalists on the album came mostly from the world of rock rather than the theatre.

A BBC ban on the album limited its impact in the UK but it took off in the US, topping the Billboard chart for 1971. Watching this phenomenon was an Australian-born producer and promoter, Robert Stigwood. He saw the potential of *Superstar*, bought the performing rights, and planned its Broadway opening.

GOSPEL READINGS

The musical followed the Gospel versions of the final days of Jesus, but Rice told the story more from the point of view of Judas Iscariot, not least in the dramatic opening song, "Heaven on Their Minds", where Judas wrestles with his doubts about

◀ **Hippy vibe**
The design of this early 70s poster for the London production of the show draws on the "hippie aesthetic" of the period.

KEY FACTS

🎭 **STAGE**

🎬 **Director** Tom O'Horgan
🎵 **Music** Andrew Lloyd Webber
🅰 **Lyrics** Tim Rice
🎭 **Venue** Mark Hellinger Theatre, New York
📅 **Date** 12 October 1971

⊙ **Key information**
Surprisingly, the Broadway production closed after only 711 performances. Opening on 9 August 1972 at the Palace Theatre, London, it ran for eight years and 3,358 performances. The London production grossed about £8 million.

▲ **Human story**
In this scene from the original production, Yvonne Elliman (Mary Magdalene) and Jeff Fenholt (Jesus) conveyed the poignant human story of the show.

Jesus as a divine saviour. Rice also placed particular emphasis on Mary Magdalene's relationship with Jesus ("I Don't Know How to Love Him") and played on the misgivings Jesus himself had over his role as Messiah ("Gethsemane"). This may have been a "rock opera", with music driven by guitar, drum, and bass, but the remarkable versatility of Lloyd Webber's composition style was apparent in grandiose orchestration, set-piece ballads, and the vaudeville comedy of "King Herod's Song".

Tom O'Horgan was hired to direct and bring the same success to *Superstar* that he had brought to the 1968 hippie counterculture show *Hair* (see pp.172–73). O'Horgan's

spectacular and overblown production concept included flying angels, laser beams, dancing dwarves, and a crucifixion set against a golden triangle, all at a cost of US$700,000. Lloyd Webber hated it and has since referred to the New York staging as "a vulgar travesty". Proof of the pudding was in the success of the simpler staging of the original London production that followed.

REVIEWS AND DEMONSTRATIONS

Jesus Christ Superstar opened to mixed reviews, but advances had already brought in more than US$1 million. It was attacked by religious groups, particularly for its sympathetic portrayal of Judas and the suggestion of a less-than-spiritual attraction between Jesus and Mary Magdalene. Many Christians demonstrated outside the theatre, while some Jewish groups were unhappy at what they saw as the anti-Semitic portrayal of some of the Jewish characters, such as the depiction of the priests, Caiaphas and Annas, as Christ-killers.

Yet, other Christian groups praised the musical for bringing the story of Jesus to a new audience. Churches and schools clamoured to put on

BIOGRAPHY

TIM RICE (1944–)

Born in Amersham, England, Rice worked in a legal firm before embarking on a songwriting career. His early success with Andrew Lloyd Webber (see pp.270–77) on *Superstar* was surpassed in 1978 with *Evita* (see pp.208–09), after which the pair split. Rice then helped create the musical *Chess*, with his song "I Know Him So Well" topping the UK singles chart for four weeks in 1985. Rice worked on the film *Aladdin* (1992) and on *The Lion King* (see pp.276–79).

performances, alerting Robert Stigwood to ways in which he could exploit the commercial possibilities of *Jesus Christ Superstar*.

A GLOBAL FRANCHISE

Stigwood saw the potential for licensing a show based on a universally recognized story that could be staged in many countries (sometimes even simultaneously), using the same format, and on long, lucrative runs. A key moment in the history of stage musicals had been reached, with the discovery of a formula for global success that would later be replicated with hit musical franchises such as *Cats* (see pp.228–31), *Les Misérables* (see pp.246–49), and *Mamma Mia!* (see pp.284–85).

Jesus Christ Superstar has since played in more than 40 countries, to date grossing over US$190 million. The show is constantly revived and always on tour somewhere in the world.

Robert Stigwood continued his development of the show's possibilities when he brought *Superstar* to the screen in 1973, using a team of international talent that included Canadian director Norman Jewison, whose previous work included *Fiddler on the Roof* (see pp.150–53), German-American André Previn as conductor, and British novelist and broadcaster Melvyn Bragg as screenwriter. For added authenticity, the film was shot in desert locations in Israel. As with the stage show, the reviews were mixed but the film grossed more than US$24 million in the US alone.

▲ **Costume and set design**
The spectacular designs for sets and costumes of the original production were both nominated for Tony Awards in 1972.

CAST

Jeff Fenholt Jesus Christ
Ben Vereen Judas Iscariot
Yvonne Elliman Mary Magdalene
Bob Bingham Caiaphas, High Priest
Phil Jethro Annas
Barry Dennen Pontius Pilate
Paul Ainsley King Herod

> *"… the biggest all-media parlay in show business history."*
>
> VARIETY, 1971

PIPPIN

{ 1972 }

A surrealist drama about a prince searching for deeper meaning in his life, *Pippin* brought contemporary rock tunes to the stage that kept the audiences humming, supported by the award-winning performance of actor Ben Vereen.

KEY FACTS

🎭 **STAGE**

🎬 **Director** Bob Fosse

📖 **Book** Roger O. Hirson

🎵 **Music and lyrics** Stephen Schwartz

🎪 **Venue** Imperial Theatre, New York

📅 **Date** 23 October 1972

⊙ **Key information**
This unusual musical was the winner of five Tony Awards in 1973: Best Performance by a Leading Actor in a Musical, Best Direction of a Musical, Best Choreography, Best Scenic Design, and Best Lighting Design. It was also nominated for six others.

Loosely based on the life of Pepin the Hunchback, the son of King Charlemagne (c.712–814), the musical was first envisaged by Stephen Schwartz while in college. *Pippin* opened in 1972, a year after *Godspell*, making the 24-year-old Schwartz one of the youngest composer-lyricists in Broadway history to have two shows playing concurrently.

It is Schwartz's youth, perhaps, that colours *Pippin* so deeply. The story follows the prince, Charlemagne's eldest and heir, as he roams the countryside, looking for purpose. He tries conflict, one-night stands, patricide, and home life with a young widow named Catherine and her son, before being lured into thinking of suicide as the ultimate method of living life to the full. Thankfully, at the last moment, Pippin rejects this call, and returns to a quiet, boring but happy life with Catherine.

THE LEADING PLAYER

Throughout it all a mysterious figure, the Leading Player, directs Pippin's actions, like a puppet-master observed by the audience but not always perceived by Pippin himself. Add to this a weird circus troupe, and the audience remains unsure of what is truly real.

This uncertainty is enhanced by Bob Fosse's choreography. The music has a distinctly 1970s feel, featuring pop ballads that recall The Who's famous "Pinball Wizard". The dance pieces also reflect the music of the era, with "jazz hands" – the extension of the performers' hands towards the audience, with fingers splayed – a major feature of the opening number, "Magic to Do". This song also featured the new technique, developed by Fosse, of using lighting during the dances to direct the audience's attention to certain performers, rather than simply placing the most important dancer centre stage.

◄ **Strange and beguiling**
John Rubenstein as Pippin, enjoying the attentions of some of the mystical circus troupe in the original Broadway production.

The troupe's costumes were part of what made the staging feel surreal. But, of course, the final piece of the jigsaw – what took *Pippin* from middling to magnificent – was the strong cast. Especially Ben Vereen, who arrived fresh from his performance as Judas in *Jesus Christ Superstar* (see pp.184–85). With *Pippin*, Vereen took the role of the Leading Player, and used it to beguile the audience into pleasant trust, and then increasing horror as he encourages Pippin to commit suicide with a performer's fiery hoop.

Indeed, the role of the Leading Player is so strong, that in the 2013 Broadway revival, *Pippin* became the first musical to feature actors of different genders winning Tonys for the same role.

> "*Mr Fosse has achieved complete continuity between his staging and his choreography... His dances... swing with life.*"

CLIVE BARNES, *THE NEW YORK TIMES*, 24 OCTOBER 1972

JOSEPH AND THE AMAZING TECHNICOLOR DREAMCOAT

{ 1973 }

The last place most people in the 1960s would have gone looking for a breath of fresh air was the Bible – and the Old Testament at that. *Joseph and the Amazing Technicolor Dreamcoat* came as an utterly exhilarating shock.

KEY FACTS

🎭 **STAGE**

🎬 **Director** Frank Dunlop

📖 **Book** Tim Rice

🎵 **Music** Andrew Lloyd Webber

𝄞 **Lyrics** Tim Rice

🎭 **Venue** Albery Theatre, London

📅 **Date** 6 February 1973

⊙ **Key information**

In bringing *Joseph* to the Albery, producer Michael White was partnered by the Australian-born rock impresario Robert Stigwood. His film adaptation of Rice and Lloyd Webber's *Jesus Christ Superstar* was at this time awaiting its release.

The Rice–Lloyd Webber partnership started small: its first important patron, Alan Doggett, was Head of Music at Colet Court, part of St Paul's, a distinguished English school in West London. However, for Tim Rice and Andrew Lloyd Webber (see pp.270–71), struggling to make a go of musical drama and songwriting, Doggett – a family friend of the Lloyd Webbers – was the perfect connection for the pair at exactly the right time.

In hindsight, moreover, his commission was exactly what they needed artistically. Looking for something his pupils could put on at their end-of-term concert, Doggett had asked them for a "pop cantata" – conjuring into existence a new and liberating musical genre. Casting about for themes, Rice and Lloyd Webber thought about a tale of espionage, before biblical inspiration struck with the Joseph story.

FROM SCHOOL TO STARDOM

And so they wrote a 15-minute show, first performed on 1 March 1968. A second performance was mounted, and in the audience was Derek Jewell, the jazz critic for *The Sunday Times*. He found himself much taken with what he saw. So much so that he mentioned it in his next weekly column, praising its "quicksilver vitality", its "barrier breaking", and its "snap and crackle". On the strength of such acclaim, a record was released.

Not exactly a triumph, then, but enough to embolden the show's young creators, who now went on to find smash-hit success with another biblical offering, *Jesus Christ Superstar* (see pp.184–85). *Joseph* had a second chance, as a follow-up to the New Testament epic – despite having been written two years before. In the 1972 Young Vic show *Bible One*, *Joseph* was preceded by Doggett's adaptation of the Wakefield and York Mystery Plays, dramatizations of scriptural stories that had originally been staged by groups of tradesmen in the 14th century. Their use here, in modernized form, deftly solved the difficulty of setting up Joseph's story for a generation who could no longer be assumed to be familiar with the biblical context.

Ray Galton and Alan Simpson, creators of the British TV comedy *Steptoe and Son*, contributed a prologue, "Jacob's Journey". This detailed the patriarch's birth to Isaac and Rebekah; his quarrel with his brother Esau; his exiling to Canaan; and his marriage and the birth of his sons. Despite some good jokes, though, it was felt to fare no better than Doggett's introduction. For the 1973 West End transfer to the Albery, Rice and Lloyd Webber simply stretched out *Joseph*, reprising several of the best songs.

AMAZING INDEED

The rest is school-music and amateur-dramatics history: over 20,000 productions have now been staged worldwide. Rice's writing, in its wit and humour, struck a chord with an age in which, for growing numbers, nothing could be really sacred. Even religious Christians took to the material. Lloyd Webber was later to be criticized for the "derivativeness" of his music: here, though, as his compositions ran through a range of styles from rock'n'roll through French chanson (art song) to Calypso, his gift for pastiche was an unmixed blessing. Perhaps Rice and Lloyd Webber's most extraordinary achievement, though, was to come up with a work that could coax an entertaining, appealing show out of the most inept performers, and enable average ones to deliver something really quite stunning.

◀ **Technicolor interpretation**
Seldom can there have been such a colourful and lively interpretation of events to be found in the Bible. *Joseph* really was amazing and different.

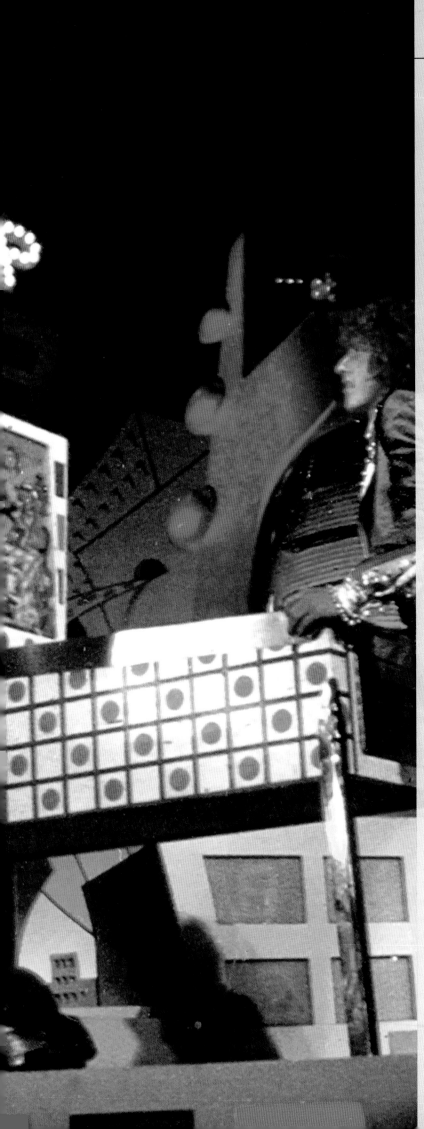

ROCK
OPERA

The rock musicals, particularly rock operas, brought a new generation and a new audience to musical theatre – revitalizing the genre with a new voice.

In the first half of the 20th century, much of the world's popular music came from musicals and was recorded by popular singers in "cover" recordings. By the 1950s, rock'n'roll was outselling all other kinds of music, including the standards that previously came from musicals. New songwriters, writing in new idioms, tried their hand at creating musicals that would speak to a new generation of audience. In 1958, *Expresso Bongo* introduced rock'n'roll to West End audiences, and two years later *Bye Bye Birdie* (see p.143) introduced it to Broadway audiences.

CONCEPT ALBUMS

By the 1970s, composers and lyricists had become quite sophisticated at using rock and roll as a medium for telling stories. However, rock composers frequently found record producers to be more readily accepting of these new pieces than theatre directors, and many rock operas started their lives as concept albums. All of the musical and lyrical ideas in a concept album are unified in the telling of the story.

Since concept albums are, by their very nature, nonstop music, they tend to be easily adapted into the rock operas. Concept rock albums that have been successfully adapted as stage or screen rock operas include: The Who's *Tommy* (1960) and *Quadrophenia* (1973); Pink Floyd's *The Wall* (1979); Andrew Lloyd Webber and Tim Rice's *Jesus Christ Superstar* (1970) and *Evita* (1976); Claude-Michel Schönberg and Alain Boublil's *Les Miserables* (1980) and *Miss Saigon* (1989); and American punk rock band Green Day's *American Idiot* (2004).

Most of the more successful rock musicals that are not operatic in scope tend to have originated on the stage as opposed to the studio. These include: James Rado, Gerome Ragni, and Galt Macdemott's *Hair* (1967); Hal Hester and Danny Apolinar's *Your Own Thing* (1968); Stephen Schwartz's *Godspell* (1971) and *Pippin* (p.186); Richard O'Brien's *The Rocky Horror Show* (pp.192–93); Charlie Smalls' *The Wiz* (p.202); and Elton John's *The Lion King* (pp.276–79), *Aida* (2000), and *Billy Elliot, The Musical* (pp.302–03).

◀ **Pinball wizard**
Elton John appeared in the film version of The Who's *Tommy* in 1975, after the concept album had already formed part of their live performances.

"The allure of the Rock Opera is still vibrant and if you manage to write a great one, people will embrace it with open arms."

SPENCE D., EDITOR, *IGN.COM*, 2006

A LITTLE NIGHT MUSIC

{ 1973 }

This charming comedy of mismatched lovers set in turn-of-the-century Sweden, lush with elegant waltz-time music, was a substantial success and provided Stephen Sondheim with his first hit song – "Send in the Clowns".

KEY FACTS

🎭 STAGE

- 🎬 **Director** Harold Prince
- 📖 **Book** Hugh Wheeler
- 🎵 **Music and lyrics** Stephen Sondheim
- 🎭 **Venue** Shubert Theatre, New York
- 📅 **Date** 25 February 1973

⊙ Key information

The show was nominated for eight Tony Awards and won seven: Outstanding Book of a Musical; Outstanding Music; Outstanding Lyrics; Outstanding Actress; Outstanding Director; Most Promising Performer; Best Musical Show Album. It ran for 601 performances.

Following the financial disaster of *Follies* (1971), the previous theatrical venture that producer-director Harold Prince (see p.210–11) had mounted with composer Stephen Sondheim (see pp.220–21), Prince was keen to produce a romantic musical hit. Sondheim suggested adapting the movie *Smiles of a Summer Night* (1955), directed by Swedish film director Ingmar Bergman – a straight-faced, stylish sex comedy about the amorous entanglements of four pairs of lovers.

Playwright Hugh Wheeler began writing a version where the story was told four times with four different outcomes. He struggled to make the

> ## "Heady, civilized, sophisticated, and enchanting"
>
> **CLIVE BARNES,** *THE NEW YORK TIMES*, FEBRUARY 1973

conceit workable and Sondheim's brooding music was thought too dark, so Prince encouraged a much lighter musical approach, which would allow glimpses of the darkness beneath the surface or, as Sondheim had it, "whipped cream with knives". Ultimately, Sondheim produced an opulent, cultured score largely using waltz rhythms, composed for strings and voices. It was his suggestion to name the show *A Little Night Music*, a translation of the title of a famous serenade for strings by Mozart, *Eine Kleine Nachtmusik*.

◀ Smiles of a Summer Night

Swedish director Ingmar Bergman's 1955 film *Smiles on a Summer Night* was Sondheim's inspiration for the show.

COMPLEX INTERACTIONS

The plot centres around the convoluted interactions of several characters; widowed lawyer Frederik, newly married to 19-year-old Anne who, after eleven months of marriage, still refuses sex; Henrik, Frederik's 20-year-old pessimistic son who is in love with his step-mother Anne; Petra, Anne's sensuous maid; Desiree Armfeldt, an actress who counts Frederik among her many previous lovers; Frederika, Desiree's 13-year-old daughter by Frederik (unbeknownst to him); and Madame Armfeldt, Desiree's mother, a formerly well connected courtesan. Frederik was played by Len Cariou, recently praised for his work opposite screen actress Lauren Bacall in *Applause* (1970), the part of Desiree went to the British star Glynis Johns, and Madame Armfeldt was played by another experienced British theatre and film actress Hermione Gingold.

SEND IN THE CLOWNS

The scenario was rich with song possibilities, and Sondheim made much of them. Musical highlights include the wryly amusing "You Must Meet My Wife", as Frederik explains his marital situation to an outraged Desiree; the heart-breaking "Every Day a Little Death", one of Sondheim's many tart songs about the limitations of marriage; the company-wide choral *tour de force* of "A Weekend in the Country"; and the celebratory "The Miller's Son", as Petra lustily extols the pleasures of pre-marriage freedom. Needing a song near the end of the show when Frederik has refused Desiree's offer to save him from his wife and his life, Sondheim composed "Send in the Clowns", a delicately reflective piece on the farcical mistimings of life. Glynis Johns had a husky singing voice and very limited range, so Sondheim crafted a melody that was easy for her to sing. Though quickly recorded by Frank Sinatra, it was American folk singer Judy Collins who, in 1977, had a Top 20 hit with it.

WIT AND REFINEMENT

The production was praised for its wit, stylishness, and exquisite refinement. As sumptuous and accessible as Sondheim's music was, it was his dazzling lyrics that garnered the most fulsome praise. As well as his celebrated rhyming, his facility for conveying emotional complexity and contradiction was as convincing and involving as ever. Later stage productions have attracted a gallery of notable film and theatre stars to the role of Desiree; these have included Jean Simmons (1974), Judi Dench (1995), and Catherine Zeta-Jones (2009).

◀ **Taylor's turn**
Hollywood legend Elizabeth Taylor is seen here recording songs for the 1977 film version with Stephen Sondheim.

MOVIE STAR CAST

The success of the musical led to a movie version, also directed by Harold Prince. Several leading men dropped out, so Prince called a delighted Len Cariou to reprise his Frederik days before filming began. Desiree was played by screen star Elizabeth Taylor. However, Taylor was unwell during much of the production period so her scenes were largely shot with her in close-up with a double used elsewhere. But the starry cast and several new songs did not prevent the film receiving a poor critical reception.

▼ **Opulence and elegance**
The film version of *A Little Night Music* featured lavish period sets and costumes, as well as the glamour of the star-studded cast.

THE ROCKY HORROR SHOW

{ **1973** }

All the terrors of Transylvania and the space and time shenanigans of science fiction come together to uproarious effect in this great schlock-horror show.

The night is dark, the rain is lashing down, the wind is howling, and a young couple's car has suddenly been brought up short by a flat tyre. The woods are deep and menacing, and the only sign of human habitation to be seen is a forbidding-looking castle. How many hundred horror films have started out this way? Mostly, though, the mad scientist in residence has not turned out to be a transvestite, as Dr Frank N. Furter does in *The Rocky Horror Show*. Nor, in general, have his servants comported themselves like Dr Furter's Transylvanian staff, bursting into grotesquely gothic glam-rock song-and-dance routines.

BRILLIANTLY BANAL
It was in the kinder twilight of a summer's evening that 60-odd people crammed into the tiny Theatre Upstairs at London's Royal Court for the show's

◄ **Beyond camp**
Tim Curry reprised his role as Dr Frank N. Furter for the 1975 film, now called *The Rocky Horror Picture Show.*

opening in 1973. They were in for a considerable shock – though to suggest that they had never seen anything like *The Rocky Horror Show* before would not be strictly true. On the contrary: taken scene by scene, Richard O'Brien's entertainment was nothing more than a farrago of far-too-familiar movie clichés. That, paradoxically, was what made it so enjoyable – that, and the dazzling brilliance with which it had all been woven into a seamless whole.

WILD EXTRAVAGANCE
From the start, the show made play with the very different aesthetics of stage and screen, opening with a cinema-style Usherette, who introduced the evening's offering as a "film". Incongruous juxtaposition was at the heart of O'Brien's entertainment: the unfolding plot veered back and forth between the wilder extravagances of horror and science fiction film. Registers, too, were jumbled unpredictably. While songs like "The Sword of Damocles" depended on the sort of classical allusion traditionally associated with

"I thought we'd have our three weeks of fun on the Royal Court's upstairs stage then move on."

RICHARD O'BRIEN

STAGE

Director Jim Sharman

Book Richard O'Brien

Music and lyrics Richard O'Brien

Venue Royal Court Theatre, London

Date 19 June 1973

Key information

Overall, at its various locations, *The Rocky Horror Show*'s UK run lasted seven years and 2,960 performances. In the United States, it did not fare so well. While in Los Angeles it managed a creditable ten months, on Broadway, in 1975, it folded after just 45 performances.

...igh" culture, "Hot Patootie – Bless [m]y Soul" was a homage to 1950s [ro]ck'n'roll.

Janet's song "Touch-a, Touch-a, [To]uch-a, Touch Me" tilted more at [m]oral taboos, frank as it is in its [ex]pression of frustrated feminine lust [–] not at all what we might have [ex]pected of this seemingly strait-laced [yo]ung lady. Sometimes, it was the [sa]tirical randomness that shocked: the [C]harles Atlas Song", for example, [po]ked fun at the sort of popular [m]agazine advert from the 1970s that [pr]omised anxious young males that [th]ey could "make proper men" of [th]emselves by bodybuilding.

UNIVERSAL CULT

[Lo]ndon audiences loved the stage show; [th]e Americans apparently not so much. [H]owever, when, in 1975, director Jim [S]harman brought out *The Rocky Horror Picture Show*, the tables were turned,

and it was American audiences who took the lead. Experienced the way that student audiences in the United States learned to enjoy it, the film was not an entertainment to be passively consumed. Audiences came dressed as characters, shouted catchlines, heckled, sang – and even acted – along. They brought umbrellas for the rain, party hats for the protagonist's birthday, water bottles to squirt, and rice to throw during the wedding scene.

A "cult" show or movie is by definition a minority enthusiasm,

its fans self-consciously setting themselves apart from all those others who do not appreciate the joke. But *The Rocky Horror Picture Show* was a cult film that found enthusiasts around the world. It has its adherents to this day, with regular sing-alongs assuring the musical's place in history.

IMPROBABLE SUCCESS

The Rocky Horror Show is an improbable mix of material, perhaps, but one that largely works, thanks to its audacious ingenuity, its ebullient energy, and its cumulative emotional force. As silly as its premise may have been, *The Rocky Horror Show* did not stop there but took both its characters and its audience on a real imaginative and moral journey.

The show has enjoyed various revivals and tours. A Broadway revival from 2000 to 2002 saw relative success and was nominated for several Tony Awards. Tours of the United Kingdom (2009), South Korea (2010), New Zealand (2010), and Singapore (2012) followed, with there apparently being no geographical limits to the appeal of the musical's zany humour.

▲ **Zany spectacle**
The poster advertising the film featured artwork that was redolent of the "glam rock" style that proliferated in the mid-1970s.

RICHARD O'BRIEN (1942–)

Born in England but brought up in New Zealand, Richard O'Brien returned to London an aspiring actor. He landed small parts in a number of productions – including musicals such as *Hair* (see pp.172–73) and *Jesus Christ Superstar* (see pp.184–85). However, his real theatrical apprenticeship had been served years before, as a film- and television-viewer. The "resting" periods afforded by an acting career of fits and starts left him time to write his *homage* to drama at its most dire.

◄ **Weird yet wonderful**
Cast members dancing one of the show's most famous numbers, "The Time Warp", in the 1975 movie version directed by Jim Sharman.

GETTING INVOLVED

In Britain, audiences have long been encouraged to participate when watching a musical comedy called pantomime, but this now extends to other musicals too.

In 1954, Peter Pan (Mary Martin) asked Broadway audiences to clap if they wanted Tinkerbell to live, but in the world of the musical, breaking the imaginary fourth wall that separates the audience from the stage began in earnest in the 1960s and 70s with more experimental shows like *Hair* (see pp.172–73). The troupe of players in *Pippin* (see p.186) exhorted the audience to come on stage and take Pippin's place in the spectacular finale as well as offering a sing-along chorus of "Time To Start Living" with lyrics and a bouncing ball. The music hall troupe acting out *The Mystery of Edwin Drood* (1985) had an ongoing relationship with the audience, who were allowed to vote on a variety of plot outcomes. A member of the audience is chosen to participate in *The 25th Annual Putnam County Spelling Bee* (2005). And audiences were given another bouncing ball moment to sing along with "Always Look on the Bright Side of Life" in *Spamalot* (see p.307).

TAKING PART

In our reality show culture, in which anyone can be a star, audiences flock to cinemas in cities around the world that offer screenings of their favourite movie musicals with added subtitles. Audiences not only sing the songs, but often dress up like their favourite characters and bring props to use during the movie. There are even scripts available online indicating what audience members are supposed to shout at the screen during *The Rocky Horror Picture Show* (see pp.192–93).

Gathering together in large communities of fans and belting out the tunes along with the movie stars has proved massively successful. Some movies offered in this format have included: *Frozen* (see p.326), *Grease* (see pp.212–13), *The Sound of Music* (see pp.134–37), *The Rocky Horror Picture Show,* and *Hairspray* (see pp.296–97).

Some aspects of audience interaction has also made its way to the stage productions. For *The Rocky Horror Show,* audiences often dress up, bring props, and shout comments at the actors on stage. And for the jukebox musical *Rock of Ages,* audiences are reminded by the cast that it is a show.

▶ **All the right moves**
Actors dressed as Riff Raff, Columbia, and Magenta perform on stage during a screening of *The Rocky Horror Picture Show.*

"This show feels more like a concert than a musical. They even distribute lighters to flick on during the soulful numbers."

NEWYORK.COM REVIEW OF *ROCK OF AGES,* 2014

CHICAGO

{ **1975** }

An ironic, sexy satire of corrupt justice, press manipulation, and grotesque celebrity culture, this tough, Brechtian vaudeville show opened to muted approval in 1975. But an endlessly running 1996 revival and hit 2002 movie have since seen *Chicago* embraced as a Broadway classic.

▲ **Chicago stars**
A neon-lit "C" for Chicago encircles the three stars – Catherine Zeta-Jones, Richard Gere, and Renée Zellweger – of the screen version.

Before it became a musical, *Chicago* went through several incarnations. It was originally a 1926 play written by Maurine Dallas Watkins, who used her experiences as a crime reporter for the *Chicago Tribune* to satirize the situation in the 1920s where females accused of murder became press celebrities and were rarely convicted. Cecil B. DeMille produced a silent film version of the play in 1927, which was remade in 1942 as *Roxie Hart*.

FROM PLAY TO MUSICAL
It was Gwen Verdon (see p.198), star of *Sweet Charity* (see p.167), who in the early 1960s suggested to her husband, choreographer and director Bob Fosse (see pp.200–01), that the play would make a good musical. Fosse's attempts to acquire the rights were thwarted by

Watkins, who came to regard *Chicago*'s subject matter as unsuitable for musical entertainment. After Watkins died in 1969, Verdon herself bought the rights with Fosse and producer Richard Fryer and, in 1973, persuaded her by-now estranged husband to join the production as co-author and director. Fosse invited Fred Ebb on board as lyricist and co-author, and it was Ebb who came up with the vaudeville setting.

INSPIRATION FROM LIFE
Following Watkins' lead of basing the characters of Roxie Hart and Velma Kelly on real murderesses, Ebb based his musical incarnations on real 1920s vaudeville performers. Roxie (played by Verdon) was broadly derived from the torch singer Helen Morgan; Velma (Chita Rivera) from the abrasive, brassy "queen of the nightclubs" Texas Guinan; lawyer Billy Flynn (Jerry Orbach) from the schmaltzy bandleader Ted Lewis; and Matron "Mama" Morton (Mary McCarty) from the singer and comedian Sophie Tucker – "The Last of the Red Hot Mamas".

A DARK ARTIST
With the Oscar-winning movie *Cabaret* (see p.166), the musical *Pippin* (see p.186), and the TV special *Liza with a "Z"* (all in 1972) recently behind him, and the editing of the movie biopic of the American comedian Lenny Bruce, *Lenny* (1974), sapping his energy, Fosse was in the middle of his most intense

period. He fell ill during *Chicago* rehearsals, which necessitated open-heart surgery and the postponement of the show's opening. Such was the concern over Fosse's health that both the director Harold Prince (see pp.210–11) and director-choreographer Jerome Robbins (see pp.108–09) were discreetly approached as possible replacements.

▶ **Velma and Roxie step out in London**
The critically acclaimed 1979 London production of the show featured Jenny Logan as Velma and Antonia Ellis as Roxie.

KEY FACTS

🎭 STAGE
- 🎬 **Director** Bob Fosse
- 📖 **Book** Fred Ebb and Bob Fosse
- 🎵 **Music** John Kander
- 🎵 **Lyrics** Fred Ebb
- 🎭 **Venue** 46th Street Theatre, New York
- 📅 **Date** 3 June 1975

◉ Key information
Chicago ran for 936 performances on Broadway. Although nominated for 11 Tony Awards in 1976, the show came away empty-handed. The 1996 Broadway revival fared much better, picking up six Tonys. The first London production opened at the Cambridge Theatre in 1979 and ran for more than 600 performances.

▲ Underworld glamour
Bob Fosse's raunchy dance routines played a major role in the original show's success. Here, Ruthie Henshall and Henry Goodman take centre stage in the 1997 London production, which still drew inspiration from Fosse's choreography.

Three months later, however, Fosse was back – but in a palpably darker mood.

Behaving in a way that had Fred Ebb famously dub the director "the Prince of Darkness", Fosse baited composer John Kander ("I'd like Cy Coleman to hear this score"), was condescending to Ebb, sadistic with the dancers, and

had Gwen Verdon (in the role of Roxie) perform grotesquely. His initial staging of "Razzle Dazzle" as a sex orgy on the steps of the courthouse – providing an oblique comment on corrupt justice – was symptomatic of Fosse's increasingly black vision for the show. But after a few previews that confused cast and audiences alike, Fosse was eventually persuaded to restage this key number.

OVERSHADOWED

Chicago opened to moderate reviews and decent business, but was largely overshadowed by the delirious

reception given to *A Chorus Line* (see pp.204–07). Then, two months into the run, Verdon had to leave the show for a throat operation, with Liza Minnelli standing in as Roxie. Minnelli played for five weeks to sold-out houses, and Verdon returned to a hit that was to run on Broadway for almost three years.

THE SHOW GOES ON – AND ON

A London production of *Chicago* opened in 1979. The stars, Antonia Ellis (Roxie) and Ben Cross (Billy), were nominated for Olivier awards for their performances.

In 1996, a Broadway revival, featuring choreography "in the style of Bob Fosse" by Verdon's original replacement, Ann Reinking, found an even more receptive audience and greater critical acclaim. The show was still running on Broadway in 2015, breaking the record for a revival, with more than 7,000 performances, and creating renewed interest in the original show. A film of *Chicago* had been in Fosse's mind in the 1980s, and a hugely successful screen version of the musical was eventually produced in 2002 (see right).

> *"Knock-em-in-the-aisles performances by three stars who glitter like gold dust."*
>
> **CLIVE BARNES**, REVIEWER, *THE NEW YORK TIMES*, JUNE 1975

MOVIE SUCCESS

The 2002 screen version of *Chicago* was directed by Rob Marshall, with the female leads taken by Renée Zellweger (Roxie) and Catherine Zeta-Jones (Velma), and Richard Gere in the role of Billy Flynn. It incorporated aspects of both the revival and original productions, with the late Bob Fosse being given a special acknowledgement in the credits. The film was both a critical success, winning six Oscars, and a financial triumph, grossing more than US$170 million in the US alone.

RELATED SHOWS

Flora the Red Menace, 1965, John Kander, Fred Ebb

Cabaret, 1966, John Kander, Fred Ebb (see p.174)

Woman of the Year, 1981, John Kander, Fred Ebb

Kiss of the Spider Woman, 1992, John Kander, Fred Ebb (see p.260)

The Scottsboro Boys, 2010, John Kander, Fred Ebb

STORYLINE

In 1920s Chicago, chorus girl Roxie Hart kills her lover and, despite Amos, her husband, taking the blame, goes to jail. Here she meets murderess Velma Kelly and prison matron "Mama" Morton. Mama hooks Roxie up with suave lawyer Billy Flynn, who secures her celebrity status. Roxie refuses to join Velma in a vaudeville double act, announces her pregnancy, and prepares for trial. She is acquitted, but Billy and Amos abandon her. Roxie and Velma form a double act.

BIOGRAPHY

GWEN VERDON (1925–2000)

Born in California, Verdon overcame childhood rickets to become one of the most acclaimed Broadway musical performers of the 1950s and 60s. With a tremulous singing voice and tremendous dancing skills, she was a superlative stage performer, winning four Tony Awards: for her cameo in *Can-Can* (1953); and for playing Lola in *Damn Yankees* (see pp.116–17); reformed streetwalker Anna in *New Girl in Town* (1957); and wax modeller Essie Whimple in *Redhead* (1959).

PLOT OVERVIEW

ROXIE'S APARTMENT

On a vaudeville stage, Velma Kelly leads a jazzy number celebrating the sleazy hedonism of the age while Roxie Hart, in her apartment, is seen to shoot her lover dead ❶. When the police attend the scene, Roxie's husband, Amos, cheerfully takes the blame, thinking the man was a burglar. Roxie pays tribute to her loyal husband, but her tone changes from affectionate to disdainful once Amos realizes Roxie lied and gets angry ❷. Roxie is arrested and sent to prison.

COOK COUNTY JAIL

In jail, Velma (who has murdered her husband and sister) and other murderesses justify their crimes ❸. Mama Morton, the corrupt prison warden, explains her system of reciprocal favours ❹ and, on the back of Velma's post-crime fame, promises the murderess a vaudeville tour.

Velma scoffs at Roxie's plan to "tell the truth" at her trial. When Mama suggests that Roxie should hire lawyer Billy Flynn, Roxie sweet-talks Amos into finding the $5,000 to pay him. Flynn is introduced to Roxie at the jail and delivers a slick assurance of his good intentions ❺.

BILLY FLYNN'S OFFICE

Taking on Roxie's case, Flynn presents his plan to get the sympathy of straight-laced "sob-sister" journalist Mary Sunshine ❻ and rewrites Roxie's life story, "from convent to jail". They hold a press conference, where Flynn speaks the carefully prepared answers to the reporter's probing questions, while Roxie dutifully moves her mouth in sync, proclaiming she acted in self-defence ❼.

Back in the jail, Roxie makes plans for her future career in vaudeville ❽. Velma, sensing she is about to be overshadowed as a celebrity murderess, suggests joining forces with Roxie in a double act ❾. The bullish Roxie refuses. In the meantime, as another murderess distracts both Flynn and the press from the plight of Roxie and Velma, they realize they must be self-reliant ❿. Roxie gets full attention once more by collapsing at the jail and announcing her pregnancy.

THE SONGS

When You're Good to Mama
🙂 *Mama Morton*

Cell Block Tango
🙂 *Velma, the Girls*

Funny Honey
🙂 *Roxie Hart*

All That Jazz
Velma Kelly,
🙂 *Company*

All I Care About
🙂 *Billy Flynn, the Girls*

We Both Reached for the Gun
Billy, Roxie, Mary Sunshine, the
🙂 *Reporters*

A Little Bit of Good
🙂 *Mary Sunshine*

I Can't Do It Alone
🙂 *Velma*

Roxie
🙂 *Roxie, the Boys*

My Own Best Friend
🙂 *Roxie, Velma*

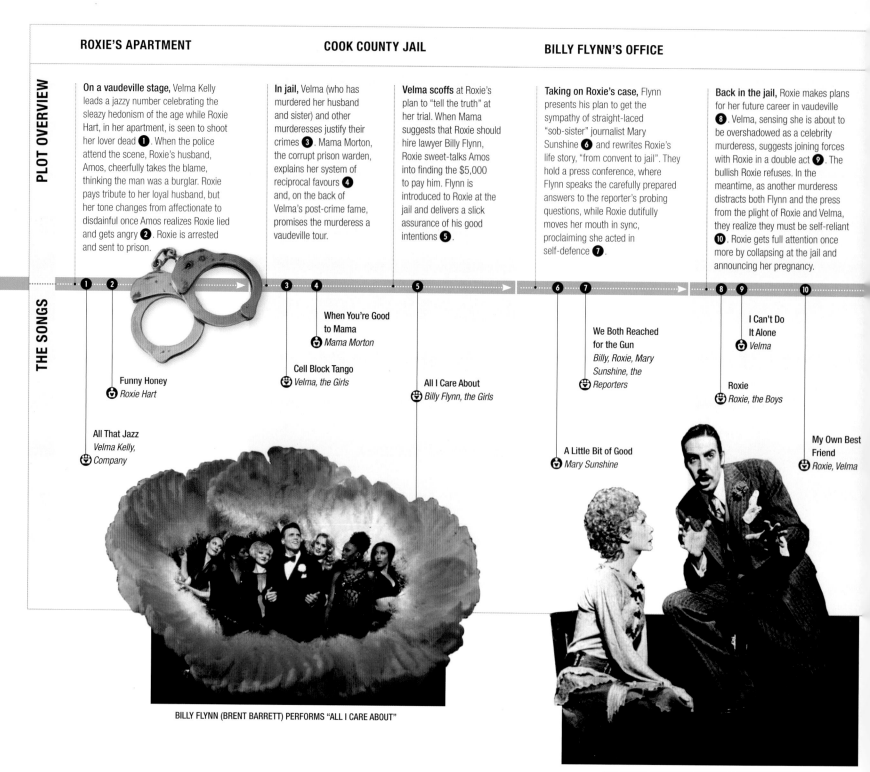

BILLY FLYNN (BRENT BARRETT) PERFORMS "ALL I CARE ABOUT"

BILLY FLYNN (JERRY ORBACH) EXPLAINS HIS PLAN TO ROXIE (GWEN VERDON) IN THE 1975 PRODUCTION

RENÉE ZELLWEGER
AS ROXIE IN
THE 2002 FILM

"Chicago *is cynical and subversive.*"

JAMES LEVE, PROFESSOR OF MUSICOLOGY, *KANDER AND EBB*, 2009

CAST	
Gwen Verdon	Roxie Hart
Chita Rivera	Velma Kelly
Jerry Orbach	Billy Flynn
Barney Martin	Amos Hart
Mary McCarty	Matron "Mama" Morton
M. O'Haughey	Mary Sunshine

COOK COUNTY JAIL

THE COURTHOUSE

Velma compares Roxie's ongoing good luck to her own misfortune ⑪ as Roxie celebrates the approaching birth of her baby ⑫. Amos, assuming he is the father, laments his lack of standing in the world. When Flynn suggests he could not possibly be the father, Amos's self-effacing gloom deepens as he opens his heart to the audience ⑬.

Roxie is unconvinced by Velma's theatrical plans for her courtroom appearance ⑭ and equally unenthusiastic about Flynn's plans for her own trial. She fires him as he warns her that she's a "phoney celebrity" who will be quickly forgotten. Fellow prisoner Kaitlin, who has maintained her innocence throughout, is executed at the jail, and a rattled Roxie reinstates Flynn as her lawyer.

Flynn and Roxie discuss their courtroom tactics, and Flynn insists that the trial is simply a circus; the secret to success is to bamboozle the jury with showbiz flash ⑮.

In court, Roxie spins an elaborate account of the murder and adopts all the tactics originally suggested by Velma, much to the disapproval of Mama and Velma, who feel the world has gone "low-brow" ⑯.

Roxie is acquitted, but even as the verdict is given, the courtroom clears to follow a new story. Flynn abandons Roxie to her fate and, after he hears from Roxie that "there ain't no baby", so does Amos. Nevertheless, Roxie decides that with "jazz", "men", and "booze" everywhere, life is indeed worth living ⑰, and joins forces with Velma to take centre stage in a vaudeville double act ⑱.

⑪ ⑫ ⑬ ⑭ ⑮ ⑯ ⑰ ⑱

Me and My Baby
😊 *Roxie, Company*

I Know a Girl
😠 *Velma*

Mr Cellophane
😞 *Amos Hart*

When Velma Takes
the Stand
😊 *Velma, the Boys*

Razzle Dazzle
😊 *Billy, Company*

Class
Velma,
😊 *Mama Morton*

Nowadays
😞 *Roxie*

Finale: Nowadays/
Keep It Hot
😊 *Roxie, Velma*

GWEN VERDON AS ROXIE IN THE
1975 BROADWAY PRODUCTION

⭐ *Knowing Fosse loved percussive interjections (especially finger-clicks), Ebb encouraged Kander to put in two finger-snaps in the opening riff of the song. Sure enough, "the moment the fingers got snapped", Kander remembered, Fosse "was in heaven".*

⭐ *The original double act closing number, featuring Verdon and Rivera, did not fit the bill, so Kander and Ebb then produced "Nowadays" and, according to Ebb, "the audience's response doubled".*

BOB FOSSE

CHOREOGRAPHER 1927–87

▼ Rebel rouser
A true maverick, the world of musical theatre had never seen anyone like Bob Fosse before.

He may have been versatile and talented enough to try his hand at many different roles, but changing the way audiences viewed dance was Bob Fosse's greatest achievement.

Actor, dancer, choreographer, director, and screenwriter Bob Fosse produced a body of work that was quite unlike anything ever seen before. It was sexually provocative, physically demanding, and highly entertaining, and it found expression in generous finger-snapping, rakishly tilted bowler hats, white gloves, and swivelling hips. And if his dance embraced the full range of human emotions, perhaps that was inevitable in a life fuelled by drink and drugs. That it was cut short by a heart attack came as little surprise to those who knew him as intense and driven as well as visionary.

The youngest of six children, Robert Louis Fosse displayed a precocious talent for dance from an early age. His parents naturally saw their offspring as a child prodigy. Their hopes were to be amply justified. In formal lessons, despite nagging health problems, the boy immersed himself in tap dancing. His dedication was such that by high school he was dancing professionally. At 13, Fosse teamed up with another young dancer to tour local night clubs. Within three years The Riff Brothers (as they

were known) were earning more than US$100 a week. Two years later, Fosse was trying his hand at choreography.

▲ Surreal and compelling
The 1979 musical film *All That Jazz* was directed by Fosse and is a semi-autobiographical fantasy based on elements of his life and career.

"Live like you'll die tomorrow, work like you don't need the money, dance like nobody's watching."

BOB FOSSE

KEY WORKS

The Pajama Game, 1954 (see pp.106–07)

Damn Yankees, 1955 (see pp.116–17)

Redhead, 1959

Sweet Charity, 1966 (see p.167)

Chicago, 1975 (see pp.196–99)

Dancin', 1978

All That Jazz, 1979 (see p.215)

REVOLUTION

In the night clubs, the unrestrained atmosphere of the sleazy vaudeville and burlesque shows, with their dark humour and sexual freedom, made a big impression on the young Fosse. He would soon be using this experience to launch his dance revolution.

Service in the US Navy entertainment unit after graduation from Chicago's Amundsen High School provided a further key influence. "I never knew I could handle anything like that until I tried it on Okinawa," he would recall later. "From then on I knew what I wanted and where I wanted to go."

The early 1950s represented a tumultuous time for Fosse with growing recognition of his talent and the ending of one marriage and the start of a second. It was the time of his Broadway debut in the revue *Dance Me a Song*, and he had also signed an MGM contract. When his Hollywood career stalled, Fosse was hired by legendary Broadway director George Abbott to work out dance numbers for *The Pajama Game* (see pp.106–07).

Choreography was more to Fosse's taste, and he was to find the show an ideal vehicle for his kind of dance. In fact, it won him the first of nine Tony Awards. The second, earned for *Damn Yankees,* arrived on his mantelpiece the following year.

By the end of the decade Fosse had a new dance partner, Gwen Verdon (see p.198), who also became his third

◀ Crazy nights
Shirley MacLaine, John McMartin, and Sammy Davis Jr in a typically wacky and high-energy scene from the film version of *Sweet Charity*.

wife. After a film version of *Damn Yankees,* Fosse created *Sweet Charity* (see p.167) for Verdon, and the pair revelled in the up-tempo "triumph over adversity" theme. Translated to the big screen, the film starred Shirley MacLaine in what was Fosse's first foray into motion picture direction.

FINEST FILM

Despite favourable notices, *Sweet Charity* was not a box office success, but it was followed by what many consider to be Fosse's finest film. *Cabaret* (see p.166) starred Liza Minnelli, Joel Grey, and Michael York and was nominated for a clutch of Oscars, including Best Picture. It won eight. Fosse lifted the Best Director Award.

Now came what was probably his most productive

▲ King of Cabaret
A film classic of the musical genre, *Cabaret* won a host of prestigious awards and made Liza Minnelli a huge international star.

period. There were two more Tonys for choreographing and directing *Pippin* (see p.186) on Broadway, and three Emmys for producing, directing, and choreographing *Liza with a Z* (1972), an unprecedented achievement.

Chicago (see pp.196–99) was another hit, with a two-year Broadway run followed by an extended tour. The musical revue *Dancin'*, three years later, proved to be the high water mark of Fosse's career. He followed it up by cowriting the screenplay of *All That Jazz* (see p.215) a film based on his own life, warts – and heart trouble – and all. It won nine Oscar nominations and enjoyed impressive box office success.

Fosse died of a heart attack in 1987. "I always thought I would be dead at 25," he had announced much earlier. For those who knew him and thought that he had much more to give, it was still a premature departure.

TIMELINE

23 June 1927 Born in Chicago to Norwegian-American vaudeville performer Cyril K. Fosse and his Irish-born wife Sara Alice, née Stanton.

1945 Enlists in the US Navy and is sent to entertain troops in the Pacific.

1949 Marries first wife Mary-Ann Niles.

1950 Broadway debut in revue, *Dance Me a Song*.

1952 Marries dancer Joan McCracken.

1952 Tours in *Pal Joey* (see pp.54–55) revival in title role, having understudied it on Broadway.

YOUNG FOSSE

1953 Signs an MGM contract to dance and sing in three musicals, including *Kiss Me Kate* (see pp.80–83); also appears in and choreographs *My Sister Eileen* (1953).

1954 Choreographs his first musical, *The Pajama Game*, followed a year later by *Damn Yankees*.

1957 Choreographs the film version of *The Pajama Game*.

1959 Directs and choreographs his first Broadway musical, *Redhead*, starring Gwen Verdon.

1960 Third marriage, to actor and dancer Gwen Verdon; their only child, Nicole Providence Fosse, is born three years later.

1966 *Sweet Charity* opens on Broadway.

1969 Directs his first movie, the film version of *Sweet Charity*.

1972 Wins Best Director Oscar for *Cabaret*.

1972 *Pippin* wins two Tony Awards.

1975 *Chicago* opens.

1978 *Dancin'* is last major Broadway hit.

1979 Cowrites screenplay of *All That Jazz*.

COMMEMORATIVE STAMP

23 September 1987 Dies in Washington, D.C.

THE WIZ

{ 1974 }

A unique re-imagining of the film *The Wizard of Oz*, so popular since its release in 1939, *The Wiz* was at the same time something completely new.

In 1974, *The Wiz* opened in Baltimore, not on Broadway: it only arrived in New York the following year. Charlie Smalls, the African-American composer whose idea the whole thing was, explained his thinking in an interview: "*The Wiz* is intended as a new kind of fantasy, colourful, mysterious, opulent, and fanciful. It was also obviously meant to be a fantasy for today – very modern, a dream dreamed by a space-age child." However, Smalls wasn't sure that Broadway audiences were ready for this "new kind" of musical.

SOMETHING NEW
The Wiz's first audiences were indeed the children of the "space age", and they were the children too of an age that had seen a rise in racial consciousness and a mass campaign for civil rights. The wariness with which Smalls sidesteps the most

"*That music – maybe you would call it 'sophisticated funk'…*"

CHARLIE SMALLS, COMPOSER

striking feature of his creation is a reminder of just how audacious a work it was.

With its all-African-American cast, its urban settings, its up-to-the-minute dance rhythms, and its soulful ballads, *The Wiz* worked its own special magic on the Oz of old. *The Wiz* was an audacious piece of appropriation on the part of a group who, though the source of much that was most creative in popular culture, had yet been marginalized in the American showbiz story. That, for many among an overwhelmingly white theatregoing public, *The Wiz* looked "wrong" was, of course, an important part of its makers' point.

KEY FACTS

STAGE

Director Geoffrey Holder

Book William F. Brown

Music Charlie Smalls, Timothy Graphenreed, Harold Wheeler, Luther Vandross

Lyrics Charlie Smalls, Zachary Walzer, Luther Vandross

Venue Morris A. Mechanic Theatre, Baltimore

Date 21 October 1974

Key information
In 1975, the show transferred to the Majestic Theatre, New York, and moved again in 1977 to the Broadway Theatre. It ran for 1,677 performances and won seven Tony Awards, including Best Musical and Best Original Score.

BEST MUSICAL-7 TONY AWARDS

THE WIZ

The new musical version of "The Wonderful Wizard of Oz"

▶ **Broadway hit**
The original Broadway production of *The Wiz* ran for four years and won a total of seven Tony Awards.

A SHOW WITH SOUL
No one could accuse the musical of having been slow to innovate or to move with changing times, but it was hardly the first show to bring African-American themes to the stage. Paul Robeson's performance as Joe captivated audiences of Kern and Hammerstein's *Show Boat* (see pp.14–17) in 1928, and George Gershwin's 1934 opera *Porgy and Bess* (ss p.32) had beaten *The Wiz* to Broadway by 40 years. However, considering the sort of seismic shifts in attitudes that had shaken American society as a whole in the 1960s and 70s, traditionally liberal Theaterland had not

◀ **An alternative take**
Stephanie Mills as Dorothy meets Hinton Battle as the Scarecrow in the original Broadway production of *The Wiz*.

been affected nearly as much as might have been expected. The musical genre is known for responding to cultural shifts, but prior to *The Wiz*, the musicals of the 1960s and early 70s seemed to be mainly responding to shifts in pop music – through rock operas like *Hair* (see pp.172–173), *Tommy*, and *Jesus Christ Superstar* (see pp.184–185). Gospel and soul music were largely left alone.

The Wiz was about to change all that. This was much more than a syncopated version of *The Wizard of Oz*. Just compare the anthem "Home" – an impassioned, gospel-inflected song of yearning – with "Over the Rainbow", the song that it replaced.

While few would argue that *The Wiz* was a greater work than *The Wizard of Oz*, it was a work with more at stake. We can all relate to Dorothy's desire to escape to a more imaginatively rewarding realm beyond the everyday; but this new Dorothy was setting out along a longer, tougher, more important road – leading to equality.

STARMANIA

{ 1979 }

The French rock opera *Starmania* was released as an album a year before its 1979 debut stage performance in Paris. Many of the highly successful songs were therefore already well known.

Pop star
French songwriter, record producer, and influential pop star Michel Berger composed the music for *Starmania*.

Originally conceived in 1975 by French singer and composer Michel Berger, *Starmania* was inspired by the story of Patricia Hearst – the American newspaper heiress who famously came to sympathize with her kidnappers. The character of Cristal, one half of the central love interest, was loosely based on Hearst. Initial attempts to get the venture off the ground failed until Berger teamed up with Québécois lyricist Luc Plamondon (see right) in 1976. The soundtrack of their new musical was released two years later with a stellar cast and to huge acclaim, going gold in both France and, later, in Canada. After this auspicious start, *Starmania* was staged in the Palais des Congrès in April 1979, mainly with the same cast and directed by Tom O'Horgan.

Starmania is a futuristic story of love, violence, jealousy, and betrayal set in Monopolis, a fictitious city full of colourful characters, including robotic waitress Marie-Jeanne, her boyfriend Ziggy, and cross-dressing student Sadia. Three love stories are depicted, but the central one involves a triangle between Sadia who nurses an unrequited passion for Johnny Rockfort, leader of terrorist gang the Black Stars. Johnny loves (and is loved by) Cristal, the host of television show *Starmania*, who joins his gang. A jealous Sadia betrays the pair to shady politician Zéro Janvier and his ex-porn star girlfriend Stella Spotlight.

The soundtrack combines furious energy with expressive melody. There are some beautiful moments – Cristal and Johnny's moving love duet "Besoin D'Amour", Marie-Jeanne's contemplative "Complainte de la Serveuse Automate", and Janvier's "Blues du Business Man". The doomed lovers' determinedly upbeat "Quand on n'a Plus Rien à Perdre" remains a favourite with audiences, as does "Le Monde est Stone", "Monopolis", and "La Chanson de Ziggy".

The original cast included French heart-throb Daniel Balavoine as Johnny Rockfort and France Gall (Berger's wife) as Cristal, with the Canadian singers Claude Dubois as the billionaire and Diane Dufresne as Stella.

Starmania was also released as an English-language album called *Tycoon*, with lyrics by Tim Rice.

KEY FACTS

STAGE

Director Tom O'Horgan
Book Luc Plamondon
Music Michel Berger
Lyrics Luc Plamondon
Venue Palais des Congrès, Paris
Date 12 April 1979

Key information
The original soundtrack of Starmania sold more than 50,000 units in France and 40,000 in Canada upon its release.

BIOGRAPHY

LUC PLAMONDON (1942–)

Born in Saint-Raymond, Canada, Luc Plamondon began writing songs and plays during the 1960s while studying teaching and literature at university. Seeing *Hair* was a turning point: he realized that music should be his career. He has written for many artists, including French Canadian star Diane Dufresne, as well as Céline Dion, and Petula Clark. His other work includes *La Légende de Jimmy* (with Michel Berger), *Suite Rock en Rose* (with Nanette Workman), and *Notre-Dame de Paris* (with Riccardo Cocciante, see p.275).

◀ **Francophone frolics**
French actors France Gall (Cristal) and Daniel Balavoine (Johnny Rockfort) singing in the rock opera *Starmania* at the Palais des Congrès, Paris.

A CHORUS LINE

{ 1975 }

One of the most successful musicals of all time, this portrait of chorus hopefuls or "gypsies" in a dance audition revealed the earthy humanity behind the showbiz sparkle – audiences were illuminated, moved, and thrilled.

▼ Show time
The cast of the original Broadway production (1975–90) perform the climactic routine of the show in their trademark gold costumes.

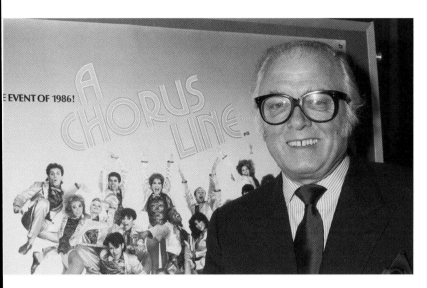

◀ **Attenborough directs**
The film of the show was directed by Richard Attenborough (pictured) and starred Michael Douglas as Zach and Alyson Reed as Cassie.

B eginning life as hours of transcriptions of dancers sharing details of their personal and professional lives in post-rehearsal workshops, the shape of *A Chorus Line* was pulled together over a gruelling series of workshop rehearsals in 1974–75, overseen by choreographer, director, and show visionary Michael Bennett. Supported by Joseph Papp of the Off-Broadway Public Theatre, who borrowed US$1.6 million to produce the musical, rehearsals began on a show that at the start had hours of dialogue and only one song.

YOUTHFUL TEAM
Bennett had hired a young, patient team, willing to help the director fulfil his ambition to portray a dancer's life in his yet-to-be-decided form. The libretto was eventually assembled by former dancer Nicholas Dante and author James Kirkwood, and the songs written by award-winning composer Marvin Hamlisch (see right) and lyricist Ed Kleban.

SINGLE SET STAGING
This team worked towards Bennett's vision of a single-set staging of a dance audition in which songs and dialogue overlapped into a multi-layered whole. Hamlisch had to place his natural proclivity towards strong melody to one side and wrote (in his words), "what the *show* needed". He devised an effective, rhythmically supple score in a variety of styles, from classic Broadway to contemporary soft rock. The big production number, "One", was certainly catchy. However, Hamlisch was concerned the show didn't have a song that would have a life of its own, so he wrote a pop ballad, "What I Did for Love", which became the show's radio hit.

TRUE PERSONAL STORIES
Eight of the original workshop dancers were cast to theatricalize a version of their own stories, including Donna McKechnie as Cassie, the actress and dancer with whom the high-handed director Zach has a personal and professional history. In the show, Cassie and Zach clash about the audition (Zach thinks she's too good for the chorus; Cassie just wants to dance), their fraught on-off romantic relationship mirroring the real-life situation between McKechnie and Bennett. In previews, the creative team sensed that audiences got so involved with Cassie that her failure to get the job was felt to be too harsh. The audition selection was changed so that Cassie was chosen.

RECEPTION AND LEGACY
Though, at first, Hamlisch's score was coolly received, it has since been recognized as an original and unpretentious triumph. "What I finally learned," the composer observed, "is that critics don't know the first time around." What critics did notice, however, was that the show broke new ground in presenting homosexuality as an unsensational part of everyday life, and praised it for its open-heartedness.

KEY FACTS

🎭 **STAGE**
🎫 **Director** Michael Bennett
📖 **Book** James Kirkwood, Nicholas Dante
♫ **Music** Marvin Hamlisch
♪ **Lyrics** Edward Kleban
🎭 **Venue** Public Theatre, New York
📅 **Date** 15 April 1975

⊙ **Key information**
The show transferred to the Schubert Theatre on Broadway in July 1975, where it ran for 6,137 performances until April 1990. It won nine Tony Awards.

BOX OFFICE DISAPPOINTMENT
During the show's Broadway run, Bennett submitted a film-treatment idea in which the gypsies are seen to audition for the movie version of the stage play. When the adaptation was rejected, Bennett declined to assist any screen version. The 1985 film, directed by British actor, film director, and producer Richard Attenborough, was considered a disappointment to many who knew the original. There have been numerous revivals of the stage show, notably when Bob Avian, Bennett's original co-director, brought the show to Broadway in 2006 and to the West End in 2012.

"One of the great glories of modern musical theatre."

ALAN JAY LERNER, *THE MUSICAL THEATRE, A CELEBRATION,* 1989

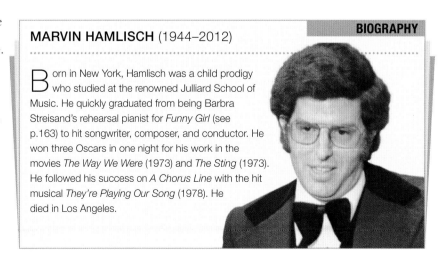

MARVIN HAMLISCH (1944–2012)

BIOGRAPHY

B orn in New York, Hamlisch was a child prodigy who studied at the renowned Julliard School of Music. He quickly graduated from being Barbra Streisand's rehearsal pianist for *Funny Girl* (see p.163) to hit songwriter, composer, and conductor. He won three Oscars in one night for his work in the movies *The Way We Were* (1973) and *The Sting* (1973). He followed his success on *A Chorus Line* with the hit musical *They're Playing Our Song* (1978). He died in Los Angeles.

STORYLINE

A nerve-racking round of auditions for a forthcoming Broadway show is under way. The process has narrowed the dancers down to 17. Only eight are needed, so the director asks the dancers to each share something personal about themselves. Through the musical, each dancer tells their story.

CAST

Scott Allen Roy	**Brandt Edwards** Tom
Renee Baughman Kristine	**Patricia Garland** Judy
Kelly Bishop Sheila	**Carolyn Kirsch** Lois
Pamela Blair Val	**Ron Kuhlman** Don
Wayne Cilento Mike	**Nancy Lane** Bebe
Chuck Cissel Butch	**Baayork Lee** Connie
Clive Clerk Larry	**Priscilla Lopez** Diana
Kay Cole Maggie	**Robert LuPone** Zach
Ronald Dennis Richie	**Cameron Mason** Mark
Donna Drake Trisha	**Donna McKechnie** Cassie

AN EMPTY STAGE IN A BROADWAY THEATRE, NEW YORK

PLOT OVERVIEW

Zach, a brash, arrogant choreographer, is running an audition with many dancers. He efficiently reduces the number to 17 as the dancers sing of their desperation to be selected **❶**.

Zach encourages the dancers to talk more intimately about themselves. Mike begins explaining how he got into dancing by watching his sister's dance class, joining it, and staying "for the rest of my life" **❷**. Bobby goes on to tell some funny, moving anecdotes from his delinquent youth, while other dancers worry about sharing "stories from the past" **❸**.

Sheila displays a provocative, defensive attitude, riling Zach. She then tells of her antagonistic relationship with her family and how she was happy at the ballet where "everything was beautiful". Bebe and Maggie concur, telling similar stories of the ballet being a refuge from unhappy family life **❹**.

The dizzy, nervous Kristine confesses to her inability to sing in tune and demonstrates with the help of her husband Al, who finishes her lines, perfectly carrying the pitch when she fails **❺**.

Mark tells of his early fascination with a medical book with pictures of male and female anatomy and how he mistakes the milky discharge of his "first wet dream" for gonorrhoea. Other dancers share their adolescent traumas (not growing tall, "seeing Mom and Dad doing it") and excitements ("My God, Robert Goulet!") **❻**.

Diana sings of her uninvolving drama course and Mr Karp, a traumatizing teacher, who told her "she'd never be an actress" **❼**. The other dancers' teenage anecdotes come thick and fast: girls practising kissing with girls; boys having permanent erections; Greg and Paul realizing they're gay **❽**.

THE SONGS

❶ Hope I Get It
Zach, Maggie, Tricia, Paul, Company

❷ I Can Do That
Mike

❸ And...
Bobby, Richie, Val, Judy

❹ At the Ballet
Sheila, Bebe, Maggie

❺ Sing!
Kristine, Al, Company

❻ Montage Part 1: Hello Twelve, Hello Thirteen, Hello Love
Mark, Connie, Company

❼ Montage Part 2: Nothing
Diana

❽ Montage Part 3: Mother
Don, Judy, Maggie, Company

CASSIE SINGS TO ZACH

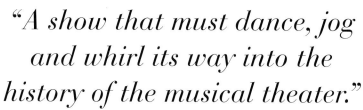

JOHN PARTRIDGE
AND SCARLETT
STRALLEN AS ZACH
AND CASSIE

> *"A show that must dance, jog and whirl its way into the history of the musical theater."*

CLIVE BARNES, *THE NEW YORK TIMES*, REVIEW OF *A CHORUS LINE*, 1975

AN EMPTY STAGE IN A BROADWAY THEATRE, NEW YORK

Richie shares how he nearly became a kindergarten teacher, while the company affirm how they all reached a point where they had to "go to it" **9**. Val laments how her dance talent wasn't enough to get her attention, though cosmetic surgery made all the difference; "Tits and ass can change your life" **10**.

While the dancers are downstairs, Zach asks old flame and aspiring actress Cassie why she's auditioning for the chorus when she's clearly an experienced soloist. Cassie confesses the work isn't coming in ("I can't act!") and that she misses dancing. "Use me, choose me" she pleads, "I'll do you proud". She dances **11**.

Zach coaches the company through their next routine, encouraging perfect unison dancing. The number is rehearsed with all the move instructions recited along with the song **12**. In between the singing, Cassie and Zach argue about the merits of chorus dancing, their frustrated professional ambitions, and the breakdown of their relationship.

Next, the dancers tap dance and start complaining about exhaustion **13**. Paul injures himself and is rushed to hospital. The company reflect how insecure their world is, but agree that they have no regrets. They chose this life because they love it **14**.

Eight dancers are selected, but all seventeen dance in the dazzling finale, taking individual bows, their distinct identities subsumed by the glamorous homogenizing costumes and precisely synchronized dance moves. The lights fade as the chorus line continues kicking. **15**.

9 · **10** · **11** · **12** · **13** · **14** · **15**

Montage Part 4:
Gimme the Ball
Greg, Richie,
😊 *Company*

Dance: Ten;
Looks: Three
🎤 *Val*

The Music and the Mirror
🎤 *Cassie*

⭐ *The original title of Val's song in praise of plastic surgery was "Tits and Ass", but it was changed to "Dance: Ten; Looks: Three" so as not to pre-empt the shock comedy of hearing the phrase in the song for the first time.*

One
😊 *Company*

The Tap
Combination
😊 *Company*

What I Did for Love
😊 *Diana, Company*

One (Reprise)
😊 *Company*

⭐ *"What I Did For Love" was grafted onto the score for its commercial appeal. Hamlisch described the show's signature ballad as "a cheat". Though A Chorus Line benefited from the song's popularity, Hamlisch admitted, "with that song, you always felt a bump in the show".*

THE FINAL EIGHT PERFORM IN STRIKING GOLD COSTUMES

THE DANCERS REHEARSE IN THE 1985 FILM

EVITA

{ 1978 }

Based on the life of one of history's most controversial women, Eva Perón, *Evita* proved to be the final major collaboration of Andrew Lloyd Webber and Tim Rice. Its sung-through, big-themed operatic style came to dominate the musical on both sides of the Atlantic for two decades.

LONG JOURNEY TO THE SCREEN

Paramount Studios acquired the film rights in 1981, and Robert Stigwood stepped up as producer. British director Ken Russell and the American Oliver Stone were approached and rejected before Alan Parker got the job. The American stars Meryl Streep and Michelle Pfeiffer were in the frame for the title role, but eventually the singer Madonna was cast, with Spanish actor Antonio Banderas as Che. The film, released at the end of 1996, was a huge box office success, grossing more than US$141 million worldwide. The song "You Must Love Me", written especially for the film by Andrew Lloyd Webber and Tim Rice, won an Oscar in 1997.

▶ **Forever Eva**
Elaine Paige originated the role of Eva for the West End production and made it her own, with her combination of acting and singing talent.

Young lyricist Tim Rice (see p.185) had immersed himself in the story of Eva Perón (1919–52) after he first heard it on his car radio in 1973. Eva, or Evita as she became known, had risen from humble beginnings to become the wife of the Argentine dictator Juan Perón. Rice travelled to Argentina in 1974 to carry out research and had a flash of inspiration when he realized that Che Guevara, the famous revolutionary, was an Argentinian and a contemporary of the Peróns. Rice decided that Che would make the perfect narrator for his story of Evita – "That way, I could get two icons for the price of one," he later explained.

FROM HIT ALBUM TO STAGE SUCCESS
Tim Rice's composer collaborator Andrew Lloyd Webber (see pp.270–71) agreed to take on the project. The

▲ Film fiction
The poster for the 1996 film implies a relationship between Eva Perón and Che Guevara, whereas, in reality, the two never met.

success of *Jesus Christ Superstar* (see pp.184–85) had been due partly to the release of the album prior to the opening of the show and the interest and expectation this generated. Lloyd Webber and Rice decided to repeat the formula for *Evita*. A double "concept" album appeared in

Film spectacle ▶
Mass rallies with huge casts of extras provided the film with widescreen spectacle to add to the romance and pathos of the core story.

November 1976, with the release a month later of the single "Don't Cry for Me Argentina", sung by the British performer Julie Covington. The single reached number one in the UK charts in February 1977 and sold more than one million copies, much to Rice's surprise – "... who wants to buy a song about a country you've hardly even heard of?"

The *Evita* album generated enough interest to persuade producer Robert Stigwood – the power behind *Jesus Christ Superstar*'s success – to stage it in a theatre. American director Harold Prince (see pp.210–11), responsible for a number of Broadway hits such as *Cabaret* (see p.166) and *A Little Night Music* (see pp.190–91), was brought on board, and the lead role went to actress and singer Elaine Paige (see p.230). After exhaustive auditioning, the other main parts also went to British performers: the actor and pop star David Essex was cast as Che Guevara, and seasoned actor Joss Ackland took the role of Juan Perón.

SUNG THROUGH

Like *Superstar*, but unlike most other musicals, *Evita* is sung through, with no linking dialogue, each song illuminating a particular scene and driving forward the story. The action begins at a Buenos Aires cinema, where the film is stopped for the announcement of Eva Perón's death, while Che Guevara looks on, scathing about the hysterical outpouring of grief ("Oh, What a Circus"). He then narrates Eva's life, from childhood in rural Argentina to her journey to the capital, where she meets ambitious politician Juan Perón ("I'd Be Surprisingly Good for You").

Evita's aspirations are fulfilled as her husband rises to the presidency, but she then struggles to cope with public criticism, the responsibilities of her role, and ultimately life-threatening illness. The showstopping "Don't Cry for Me Argentina" appears early in the second act, as Evita addresses the adoring Buenos Aires crowds from a balcony, full of bravery, defiance, and passion.

NEW MUSICAL DAWN

While *Jesus Christ Superstar* had been billed as a "rock opera", *Evita* was described simply as an "opera", reflecting Lloyd Webber's growing ambitions as a composer and his move

towards a more orchestra-driven, pop-operatic style that would reach its peak in *The Phantom of the Opera* (see pp.252–53). In *Evita*, his increasing versatility embraced Latin-American rhythms, set-piece ballads, hummable pop melodies, and grand orchestral gestures. *Evita* also highlighted the increasing depth and confidence of

Rice's writing, his lyrics capturing the strength, ambition, and vulnerability of a complex heroine.

When *Evita* opened, the reviews were mixed, ranging from "audacious and fascinating" in *The Guardian* to "this odious artefact" from the eminent critic Bernard Levin in *The Times*. Audiences, however, loved it, and the show ran for 3,176 performances and nearly eight years.

The New York production opened at the Broadway Theatre on 25 September 1979. It received a fairly hostile reception, with Lloyd Webber and Rice accused of glorifying the fascist Peróns. But once again, the public disagreed, and the Broadway show had a highly successful run of 1,568 performances.

MOVES TOWARDS A MOVIE

No sooner had *Evita* opened than rumours of a film version began to circulate, but 14 years of negotiations followed the acquisition of the film rights by Paramount Studios before production could actually begin (see opposite). But, ultimately, the success of the film made the wait worthwhile.

> ## "... an experience that compensates for many wasted nights spent watching British musicals."

MICHAEL BILLINGTON, ARTS CRITIC, *THE GUARDIAN*, 22 JUNE 1978

CAST

Elaine Paige Eva Perón
David Essex Che Guevara
Joss Ackland Juan Perón
Siobhán McCarthy The Mistress

RELATED SHOWS

Jeeves, 1975, Andrew Lloyd Webber, Alan Ayckbourn
Tell Me on a Sunday, 1977, Andrew Lloyd Webber, Don Black
Blondel, 1983, Tim Rice, Stephen Oliver
Chess, 1986, Tim Rice, Benny Andersson, Björn Ulvaeus

HAROLD PRINCE

PRODUCER/DIRECTOR **1928–**

Harold Prince is recognized as a towering figure in American theatre for producing or directing some of the most distinctive and influential musicals ever made.

Harold "Hal" Smith Prince has won an unprecedented 21 Tony Awards in six decades of working on Broadway and elsewhere. When he was nine, he was captivated by American actor Orson Welles's (1915–85) great performance in the title role of Shakespeare's *Julius Caesar*. It was, he recalled many years later, "involving, emotional, imaginative".

Prince's parents took him to Saturday afternoon theatre performances and when he was old enough Prince went by himself. Serious drama was his first interest, but the 1945 musical *On the Town* (see pp.64–65) made him realize the potential for music and dance in the American theatre.

In 1947, Prince graduated from the University of Pennsylvania, still determined to pursue a career

KEY WORKS

The Pajama Game, 1954 (see pp.106–07)

West Side Story, 1957 (see pp.122–25)

Fiddler on the Roof, 1964 (see pp.150–53)

Cabaret, 1966 (see p.166)

Evita, 1978 (see pp.208–09)

The Phantom of the Opera, 1986 (see pp.252–53)

in theatre. In a letter to the legendary producer-director George Abbott, Prince offered to work for nothing. Abbott gave him a position as a general assistant.

It was the break Prince needed. After decades in the business, Abbott was still juggling several projects simultaneously and there was no shortage of opportunity for Prince to tweak a script here or manage a touring production there.

By 1952, he was stage managing *Wonderful Town*, with music by Leonard Bernstein (see pp.126–27) and lyrics by Betty Comden and Adolph Green. Then, in partnership with another producer and Abbott protégé, Robert E. Griffith, Prince decided to try his hand as a producer.

The pair acquired the rights to a popular comic novel about a strike in a nightwear factory. Abbott agreed to collaborate with the author in adapting it for the musical stage. Also involved was a budding choreographer named Bob Fosse (see pp.200–01).

◀ Prince by name ...

Harold Prince is revered on Broadway as a legendary producer and director. His varied involvement in so many top shows is unparalleled.

FUN-FILLED

The Pajama Game (see pp.106–07) in 1954 was to be Prince's first big hit, winning the Tony Award for Best Musical. The next fun-filled romp, *Damn Yankees* (see pp.116–17), was based on a novel about an ageing

A demanding perfectionist
Harold Prince is renowned for his high standards and demanding methods. Here, he hammers home a point to the production team of *Evita*.

baseball fan selling his soul to the devil to become a young player leading his team to victory. Unfortunately, it led to a falling out between Prince and Abbott and Fosse, whose choreography they considered a little too raunchy to be suitable for Broadway.

New Girl in Town (1957) enjoyed a modest run, but it made Prince and Griffith realize that it was time for a bigger challenge. Accordingly, they teamed up with Stephen Sondheim (see pp.220–21), Bernstein, and Jerome Robbins (see pp.108–09) on a tale inspired by Shakespeare's *Romeo and Juliet* called *West Side Story*, which opened on Broadway in 1957.

MORE AWARDS
Two years later and there was another Tony Award for *Fiorello*, based on the life of feisty New York Mayor Fiorello H. La Guardia. Unusually for a musical, the play also won a Pulitzer Prize. But in 1961 Griffith died suddenly and Prince went on to make his Broadway directorial debut in 1962 with the non-musical play *Family Affair*.

A Funny Thing Happened on the Way to the Forum (see p.149) found Sondheim and Prince working together again. It was Sondheim's first Broadway musical as a composer.

The 1960s saw yet more successes for Harold Prince, including a first Tony nomination for his direction of *The Shop Around the Corner*. But *Fiddler on the Roof* represented a major departure, with its depiction of life in a Jewish village in pre-Revolutionary

Russia. *Fiddler* proved to be an instant and enduring hit.

Prince's next major project established his record for daring subject matter and unconventional staging. *Cabaret* dramatized Christopher Isherwood's tales of Bohemian life in 1930s Berlin. The set included a huge mirror that enabled the audience to view themselves as patrons of a sordid, decadent nightclub. Prince soon developed a reputation on Broadway for coming up with new and radical concepts such as this.

PINNACLE OF FAME
Soon after, Prince enjoyed more collaboration with Sondheim, with a series of productions that marked a high point in the development of the musical theatre. *Sweeney Todd* is considered to be the pinnacle of this period. Earlier in the 1970s, Prince had also found

a new collaborator in the young British composer Andrew Lloyd Webber (see pp.270–71). Prince applied his dazzling staging to *Evita*, which opened first in London and then in New York, where it broke fresh ground for an American musical, with its dramatic, opera-style presentation.

A brief foray into movie direction soon made it clear that Prince's talents were best suited to live performances on the stage. Subsequently, he found opera to be a more congenial and welcoming arena and directed productions that included *Madama Butterfly* and *Don Giovanni*.

Further collaboration with Lloyd Webber resulted in Prince's biggest success ever. Critics and audiences both in London and New York hailed the lush and romantic re-telling of the gothic horror tale *The Phantom of the Opera*, with Prince's breathtaking staging as the main attraction to a production that simply ran and ran.

LATER WORK
There has been little let-up in Prince's output as he has grown older, and a special Tony Award in 2006 recognized a creative output of more than 50 plays, musicals, and operas. As Prince has famously observed, "the perfect expression of receiving a lifetime award is to be working when they're handing it out".

Prince also believes in a "responsibility to move the musical theatre forward". This he has undoubtedly done. And the one thing audiences have learned to expect from Harold Prince is the unexpected.

▲ **Varied career**
Prince also directed a black comedy film starring Angela Lansbury called *Something for Everyone*. It was known in the UK as *Flowers for the Bride*.

HAROLD PRINCE, *THE NEW YORK TIMES*, 2009

> "*Throwing money at something doesn't really create – forgive me that onerous word – art.*"

30 January 1928 Born in New York City, the son of stockbroker Milton A. Prince and his wife Blanche, née Stern.

1950 Starts military service in the US Army, during which time he serves in Germany, gaining experience that feeds into his subsequent production of *Cabaret*.

1954 Co-produces *The Pajama Game*, which becomes the surprise hit of the season and is followed by another success, *Damn Yankees*.

1957 *West Side Story* opens on Broadway; it will be hailed as a landmark in American musical theatre and a classic of its genre.

1962 Marries Judy Chaplin, daughter of composer Saul Chaplin; they will have two children, director Daisy Prince and conductor Charlie Prince.

1962 Produces *A Funny Thing Happened on the Way to the Forum*, with music by Stephen Sondheim.

1963 *She Loves Me* wins Prince his first Tony nomination for direction.

1964 Prince's production of *Fiddler on the Roof* becomes a sell-out Broadway hit.

1966 *Cabaret* draws on Prince's experience of Germany gained during military service.

1970 Directs first film, *Something for Everyone*; *A Little Night Music* follows in 1977.

1978 Collaborates with Andrew Lloyd-Webber to direct *Evita*.

1979 Directs *Sweeney Todd* on Broadway.

1986 *The Phantom of the Opera*, considered Prince's greatest directorial success, opens in London.

TONY AWARD

2006 Wins special lifetime Tony Award.

2010 Co-directs London premiere of *Paradise Found*.

GREASE

{ 1978 }

A funny take on high-school life in the 1950s, *Grease* has been performed by countless schools in somewhat sanitized versions since the film brought the musical to a worldwide audience. The original, however, has lost none of its bite.

◄ **Hopelessly devoted to you**
Despite being in their mid-20s, Olivia Newton-John and John Travolta both gave convincing performances as love-lorn teenagers.

KEY FACTS

🎬 **FILM**

🎞 **Director** Randal Kleiser

🖥 **Screenplay** Bronte Woodard, Allan Carr

🎵 **Music** Michael Gibson (score)

🎶 **Music and lyrics** Jim Jacobs, Warren Casey, with material by Barry Gibb, John Farrar, Louis St. Louis, Scott Simon, Al Lewis. Richard Rodgers, Lorenz Hart, David White, Jerry Leiber, Mike Stoller, Sylvester Bradford, Sammy Fain.

🕐 **Running time** 110 minutes

📅 **Release date** 16 June 1978

◉ **Key information**
The film version is based on the 1972 Broadway musical *Grease* by Jim Jacobs and Warren Casey. "Hopelessly Devoted to You" was nominated for the 1979 Academy Award for Music (Original Song).

What might surprise is how little experience some members of the cast and crew had, prior to making the film. Director Randal Kleiser had never worked on a feature-length film before, much less a musical, with work in the early 1970s focused on television episodes. Olivia Newton-John, who made Sandy such a memorable character, was also very inexperienced as a screen actress. She had appeared in a single film, *Toomorrow*, which was only released for a week in London before receiving an injunction for non-payment of cast and crew, making *Grease* her American debut. This was to be Newton-John's first experience filming with a Hollywood studio – Paramount Pictures – with a substantial budget and experienced producers, in the form of Robert Stigwood (*Jesus Christ Superstar*, see pp.184–85) and Allan Carr.

THE CREATIVE TEAM
Even the originators of the project, Jim Jacobs and Warren Casey, were new to Hollywood. In fact, they had also been new to Broadway when the original musical opened in 1972. Jacobs and Casey met while acting with the Chicago Stage Guild in the 1960s, and originally developed *Grease* as a play

▼ **Natural performer**
John Travolta's supreme dancing skills were given full rein in the film. He also sang all his own parts throughout the movie.

with music. It was seen by two Broadway producers, Ken Waissman (*Torch Song Trilogy*) and Maxine Fox (*Over Here!*), who – fairytale-like – invited Jacobs and Casey to rework the play into a musical, and bring it to New York. The result was shown Off-Broadway, at the Eden Theatre, but transferred in 1972 to the Broadhurst and was soon after nominated for seven Tony Awards.
To bring the musical from stage to screen, several fundamental changes had to be made. Firstly, the setting of the musical was moved from an unidentified urban area (originally Chicago in the play, then a more generic city on stage) to southern Californian suburbs, a "safer" place that appealed to many nostalgic American viewers. In addition, alterations were

▶ "Summer Nights"
The girl gang, led by the feisty and characterful Rizzo (Stockard Channing), urge Sandy on to embrace summer lovin' with Danny.

made to the music. "Hopelessly Devoted to You" and "Sandy" in particular, have much more of a 1970s sound then that of the 1950s, helping the musical to appeal more greatly to the younger, more contemporary audience of 1978. And, of course, the story of star-crossed lovers never seems to grow old.

SUMMER LOVIN'

Sandy and Danny have enjoyed a summer romance, but even the threat of separation does not convince Sandy of the benefits of becoming lovers.

After parting, Sandy decides to stay in the United States, rather than returning to her native Australia, and enrols in Rydell High School – little realizing that this is also Danny's school. Once discovered, instead of being reunited, they are forced apart by strict social conventions. These separate the "preps" and the "greasers", Danny being a member of the latter group and Sandy very much one of the former. It is only in the final scenes of the film, when Danny reveals he has joined the preps through the acquisition of a track letter jacket, and Sandy wholeheartedly joins the greasers, dressed to kill in leather trousers, that true love wins the day.

Joining the couple are their respective gangs of friends, the T-Birds and Pink Ladies, who supply comic relief and a closer look at problems faced by teenagers, such as dropping out of high school and unwanted pregnancy. Stockard Channing,

as Rizzo, leader of the Pink Ladies, nearly steals the show with her singing, first with the hilarious "Sandra Dee", a satire of "wholesome ingénue" roles portrayed in 1950s films, and "There Are Worse Things I Could Do", a soulfully sung lament about promiscuity and pride.

CRITICAL RECEPTION
Although stars Olivia Newton-John and John Travolta were in their mid- to late 20s, the portrayals they

> "Grease *has some language that would never have been heard in the '50s, though its heart is always pure.*"

VINCENT CANBY, *THE NEW YORK TIMES*, 16 JUNE 1978

gave were generally well received, with at least one critic preferring Travolta's *Grease* to his earlier movie success, *Saturday Night Fever*.

Thus, with its winning songs, some outstanding performances, and a pastiche of 1950s high-school life – all sock hops and malt-shops – *Grease* is still, nearly 40 years after its release, one of the most popular Hollywood musicals of all time. The stage show has also had numerous successful tours and revivals.

A sequel to the film, *Grease 2*, was released in 1982, starring Maxwell

Caulfield and Michelle Pfeiffer. Only a handful of the original cast members reprised their roles, and the film was not as successful as the 1978 film.

◀ *Go, Greased Lightnin'!*
The celebrated car body shop scene, in which Danny and the gang sing about the joys of racing fast cars and dating racy young women.

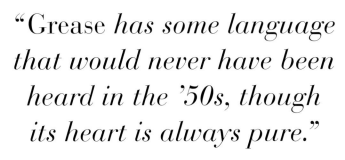

CAST LIST	
John Travolta	Danny Zuko
Olivia Newton-John	Sandy Olsson
Jeff Conaway	Kenickie
Stockard Channing	Betty Rizzo
Barry Pearl	Doody
Didi Conn	Frenchy
Michael Tucci	Sonny LaTierri
Dinah Manoff	Marty Maraschino
Kelly Ward	Roger "Putzie"
Jamie Donnelly	Jan

AIN'T MISBEHAVIN'

{ 1978 }

Not much more than a string of songs, but the rumbustious Fats Waller fest that is the musical *Ain't Misbehavin'* perfectly evokes 1920s and 30s Harlem – a very special time and place.

KEY FACTS

♫ **STAGE**

🎬 **Director** Richard Maltby Jr

📖 **Book** Murray Horwitz, Richard Maltby Jr

♫ **Music** Fats Waller, Luther Henderson

𝄫 **Lyrics** Various writers

♫ **Venue** Longacre Theatre, New York

📅 **Date** 9 May 1978

◉ **Key information**

The Broadway musical was an expanded version of *Ain't Misbehavin'*, a revue put together by Horwitz and Maltby, which was first produced by Manhattan Theatre Club.

In 1926, poet and social activist Langston Hughes, one of the leaders of the African-American movement known as the Harlem Renaissance, wrote, "I too, sing America./I am the darker brother./They send me to eat in the kitchen/When company comes,/But I laugh,/And eat well,/And grow strong".

And grow strong he did with time – ultimately gaining recognition as one of modern America's most important literary voices. Though for America's other "darker brothers" (and sisters), progress has been painfully slow.

Hughes's words still suggest an aspiration more than a self-confident assertion on their part.

Something was assuredly changing, though, at the time when Hughes was writing. The Manhattan district of Harlem was emerging as the capital of a newly proud and self-conscious Black America. What had been a place of banishment, a ghetto, was still for many a sink of deprivation, but it was rapidly acquiring flair and style. Nightclubs and speakeasies were springing up on every street; new rhythms and harmonies were being heard on a fast-evolving jazz scene; and new dance steps and fashions were being seen.

BLACK AND BLUE

So how best to celebrate so complex – and so compromised – patrimony? How better than in the music of jazz pianist and singer Fats Waller? No other performer captured quite so well the energy of Harlem jazz – the richness of its syncopation and its

▲ **Star rhythms**
The Broadway show featured a stellar cast, including Charlayne Woodard (back, left) and Nell Carter (front, right).

bluesy, sophisticated styles – nor its engaging, edgy wit, and the self-confident strut that gave Harlem nightlife so beguiling a buzz.

Such was the thinking behind *Ain't Misbehavin'* – writers Murray Horwitz and Richard Maltby Jr's re-creation of the Harlem Renaissance. There is no story to speak of, and no dialogue – just a medley of songs performed by five star singers and dancers. But the result is that the audience heard this material afresh.

SPREADIN' RHYTHM AROUND

All Harlem life is here: from the sugary romanticism of "Honeysuckle Rose" to the cosy domesticity of "Two Sleepy People", and the leering innuendo of "Find Out What They Like". *Ain't Misbehavin'* also celebrates that strange democracy that (in the age of jazz and Prohibition) brought the party-going class together, across the normal boundaries of social caste. Hence, we are taken to a Harlem house party for "The Joint is Jumpin'", venturing up to the other end of the social scale for "Lounging at the Waldorf" and the "Yacht Club Swing".

◀ **Harlem style**
The cast of *Ain't Misbehavin'* perform a bit of Harlem Swing during this stylish and energetic celebration of Harlem street-life.

ALL THAT JAZZ

{ 1979 }

Its self-indulgence could be irksome, and its self-importance was still harder to stomach. Nevertheless, *All That Jazz* was a hit with the public and won several Academy Awards.

This was a new departure for musical films. Indeed, *All That Jazz* could hardly have been more different from what had gone before it. Loosely autobiographical, the film follows

A HIGH PRICE
Thematically, *All That Jazz* is uncompromisingly "realistic", but it avoids the traditionally realistic mode of narrative, offering instead a fragmentary vision – a montage of

"Live like you'll die tomorrow, work like you don't need the money, and dance like nobody's watching."

BOB FOSSE

perspectives from different times and places, with glances forward to Joe's own deathbed and beyond. He even has an attendant Angel of Death – the beautiful Angelique, played by Fosse's real-life friend and sometime lover Jessica Lange.

Joe himself is played by Roy Scheider, a former athlete and amateur boxer who had the physicality needed to play the role. In the end, Joe passes through the five stages of grief – anger, denial, bargaining, depression, and acceptance – and is finally seen being zipped up in a body bag. At the time, the personal cost of creativity had never been so starkly presented, but the film remains upbeat, and was lauded by Stanley Kubrick as one of the best he had ever seen.

KEY FACTS

🎬 **FILM**

🎬 **Director** Bob Fosse

🎬 **Screenplay** Robert Alan Aurthur, Bob Fosse

🎵 **Music and lyrics** Ralph Burns

🕐 **Running time** 123 minutes

📅 **Release date** 20 December 1979

⊙ **Key information**
All that Jazz won four Academy Awards: Best Art Direction (Philip Rosenberg, Tony Walton, Edward Stewart, and Gary J. Brink); Best Costume Design (Albert Wolsky); Best Editing (Alan Heim); and Best Original Song Score and its Adaptation or Adaptation Score (Ralph Burns).

▼ **Being Bob**
Roy Scheider (right) and Ben Vereen in a still from the movie *All That Jazz*. Scheider captured Fosse's excesses to perfection in a singular biographical performance – directed by Fosse himself.

maverick choreographer and director Bob Fosse (see pp.200–01) through a particularly difficult period of his life, when he was trying to bring the musical *Chicago* (see pp.196–99) to the Broadway stage while also shooting *Lenny* (1974) – a movie about hard-living comedian and satirist Lenny Bruce, who died of an overdose.

DEMONIC BEHAVIOUR
The film's version of Fosse's life is told through the alter ego of Joe Gideon – a frantically chain-smoking, whisky-swigging, dexedrine-popping, compulsively womanizing director and choreographer whose eventual need of a heart operation becomes the mainstay of the show. "To be on the wire is life," says Joe, comparing his existence as a showman to that of a trapeze artist. "The rest is waiting," he bleakly concludes. The film looks deeply into what it is to be someone who only comes alive on stage – who is otherwise only "waiting" – and the picture it paints, although funny, is grim. It turns out that the hardest stage of all is that of ordinary life.

SWEENEY TODD

{ 1979 }

The 1979 stage production of *Sweeney Todd* never went into profit, yet this gruesome tale of a barber's revenge has become Stephen Sondheim's most popular show thanks to many revivals, re-imaginings, a major movie adaptation, and the evolving tastes of audiences.

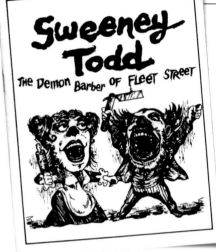

▲ Playbill cover
The poster for the original Broadway production on the cover of Playbill – the free programme given away at all Broadway theatres.

When in London visiting the 1973 West End revival of *Gypsy* (see pp.138–39), for which he wrote the lyrics, Stephen Sondheim (see pp.220–21) saw the production of *Sweeney Todd* at London's Theatre Royal Stratford East. The show was British playwright Christopher Bond's adaptation of the legend of the fictional murderous barber. Sondheim was smitten by the elegant and clever plotting of the melodrama.

In contrast to the callous profiteer of the Victorian version of the character,

Bond's Sweeney is a man driven by a sense of injustice and seeking revenge for the appalling wrongs inflicted by a venal judge on himself and his family. Sondheim found the unfolding of the story and Sweeney's tragic-hero quality most satisfying and, acquiring the rights, brought it to director Harold Prince (see pp.210–11).

A TALE OF THE INDUSTRIAL AGE

Prince was less convinced by the project until he was able to relate Sweeney's rage to the impotence of a working class downtrodden by the rise

> "*[a] muscular partnership of words and music.*"

RICHARD EDER, CRITIC, *THE NEW YORK TIMES*, 2 MARCH 1979

HORROR MOVIE MUSIC

Stephen Sondheim's scores are characteristically rich with detail, wit, and ingenuity, and inspire cult devotion. For *Sweeney Todd*, he drew inspiration from the movie music of American composer Bernard Herrmann, especially the unnerving film score for *Hangover Square* (1945). Sondheim set about composing what he later described as "horror movie" music. He set the entire show to music using sung dialogue and underscoring to create film-like tension. He also incorporated some music from the *Dies Irae* (Day of Wrath), used in the Roman Catholic funeral mass, and peppered the score with recurring musical phrases to give the listener nonverbal clues about the characters. To heighten the sense of grandeur, he scored a few of the characters for voices with some classical vocal training, requiring a strong bass-baritone for Sweeney and a soprano for Johanna. As relief from the heavy, brooding atmosphere, there was

cheery, amoral humour from Mrs Lovett ("The Worst Pies in London"), full-hearted romanticism from young suitor Anthony ("Johanna"), and perverse poignancy in Sweeney's love song to his razors ("My Friends"). For the final climactic 20 minutes, however, with all musical themes established, Sondheim's main compositional aim was simply to be frightening. As he said, "It was just a matter of, 'Okay, let's scare them'."

SONDHEIM'S REGULARS

The star performers were alumni from previous Sondheim shows. Len Cariou (as Sweeney) had been in *A Little Night*

KEY FACTS

♨ STAGE

🎬 **Director** Harold Prince
📖 **Book** Hugh Wheeler
♫ **Music and Lyrics** Stephen Sondheim
🎭 **Venue** Uris Theatre, New York
📅 **Date** 1 March 1979

⊙ **Key information**

The show was nominated for nine Tony Awards and won eight. It was also nominated for 13 Drama Desk Awards, of which it won nine. However, the show closed after only 557 performances.

of a dehumanizing industrial age, and a stage setting of factory walkways and engineering girders was devised to express this. Meanwhile, Sondheim began to write both book and music, but soon realized that his show would have been nine hours long. For editing help he turned to Hugh Wheeler, his book-writing colleague from *A Little Night Music* (see pp.190–91) and *Pacific Overtures* (1976).

▶ London production
Imelda Staunton and Michael Ball took the lead roles in the 2012 London production. The multi-level set evoked the setting, which was updated to the 1950s.

FILMING THE DEMON BARBER

As a student, American film director Tim Burton was entranced by the "sense of the macabre" of the original Broadway show, which he saw umpteen times. Twenty-five years later, he directed the movie adaptation. In the 2007 film, Burton de-emphasized the operatic aspect by casting character actors with no formal musical training while graphically accentuating the "cathartic" violence, as Burton saw it, of the murders. The film is regarded as a financial, critical, and artistic success.

Music, and Angela Lansbury (Mrs Lovett) had starred in the revival of *Gypsy* (1973) and in Sondheim's legendary flop *Anyone Can Whistle* (1964). While both stars were impressed with the quality of the show, neither was convinced that *Sweeney* could be a hit. They were half right.

REVIEWS AND REVIVALS

When the show opened in 1979 on Broadway, critics were largely enthralled and supportive, applauding the piece's scope and ambition, the majesty of the score, and the brilliance of the star performers. Some commentators, however, including *The New York Times*, detected a "confusion of purpose", picking up, perhaps, on the diverging motivations of Harold Prince and Stephen Sondheim.

The many revivals of this show have ranged from full-scale operatic productions to intimate chamber treatments. Scottish stage director John Doyle's stylized West End interpretation (2004) featured ten actor-musicians, who played their instruments on stage. The production transferred to Broadway for a one-year run and tour, and won two Tony Awards. The 2012 London revival, starring British singing actors Michael Ball and Imelda Staunton, was highly acclaimed and won three Olivier Awards. Two productions ran alongside each other in London in 2015: a full orchestral concert staging at the English National Opera and a chamber version in a replica pie shop on Shaftesbury Avenue.

Original stars
Len Cariou (Sweeney Todd) and Angela Lansbury (Mrs Lovett) provided both tragic anguish and humour in the Broadway production of 1979.

STORYLINE

JOHNNY DEPP (SWEENEY) AND ALAN RICKMAN (JUDGE TURPIN) IN THE 2007 FILM

Towards the end of the Industrial Revolution in 1846, a former barber returns to London from unjust exile. In his absence, he is told, his wife committed suicide. A degenerate judge has imprisoned his daughter, lusts after her, and plans to marry her. Under a new identity, the barber takes revenge, using his razors for murderous purposes, and supplying a local pie-maker with human remains for her pies.

	LONDON DOCKS	PIE SHOP, FLEET STREET	JUDGE TURPIN'S MANSION, KEARNEY'S LANE	ST DUNSTAN'S MARKETPLACE	JUDGE TURPIN'S MANSION, KEARNEY'S LANE
PLOT OVERVIEW	**Workers sing** an unsettling ballad of a demon barber ❶. Sweeney Todd bids farewell to Anthony, who saved him from a shipwreck. They dismiss the approaches of a beggar woman ❷. Todd takes his leave, muttering that there is something he "must find out" ❸.	**Todd meets pie-maker** Mrs Lovett ❹, who tells him of the earlier occupants of the room above her shop: a barber, Benjamin Barker, his wife Lucy, now dead by suicide, and daughter Johanna, currently held captive by Judge Turpin ❺. Recognizing Todd as Barker, Mrs Lovett gives him his razors, which she has kept ❻.	**Johanna**, now a young woman imprisoned as Turpin's "ward", sings of the plight of the caged bird ❼. Anthony, overhearing her, is besotted and vows to "steal" her away ❽ ❾. The Judge and the Beadle warn Anthony off.	**Tobias**, assistant to barber Adolfo Pirelli, attempts to peddle a hair-restoring elixir ❿. Todd is among those unconvinced and beats Pirelli in a shaving contest ⓫. Impressed, the Beadle promises to visit Todd's recently opened barber shop above Mrs Lovett's pie shop.	**While lustfully spying** on Johanna, Judge Turpin whips himself into a frenzy of penance and pleasure ⓬. Having composed himself, he proposes marriage to Johanna, who is startled by the idea.

❶ ❷ ❸ ❹ ❺ ❻ ❼ ❽ ❾ ❿ ⓫ ⓬

THE SONGS

No Place Like London
Todd, Anthony,
😊 *Beggar Woman*

Prologue: Organ Prelude, The Ballad of Sweeney Todd 😊 *Company*

The Barber and His Wife 😊 *Todd*

Poor Thing 😊 *Mrs Lovett*

The Worst Pies in London 😊 *Mrs Lovett*

My Friends 😊 *Todd, Mrs Lovett*

Johanna 😊 *Anthony*

Ah, Miss *Anthony,* 😊 *Beggar Woman*

Green Finch and Linnet Bird 😊 *Johanna*

The Contest 😊 *Pirelli, Tobias*

Pirelli's Miracle Elixir *Tobias, Todd, Mrs* 😊 *Lovett, Company*

Johanna (Judge's Song): Mea Culpa 😊 *Judge Turpin*

⭐ *Sung during an act of self-flagellation, "Johanna (Judge's song): Mea Culpa" was cut to trim Act I. Prince confessed, "I didn't know how to stage it because it was so explicit." Sondheim, surprised by Prince's "prudishness", was pleased to see it restored in later productions.*

MRS LOVETT TELLS TODD ABOUT THE BARKER FAMILY

CAST

Len Cariou Sweeney Todd
Angela Lansbury Mrs Lovett
Victor Garber Anthony Hope
Ken Jennings Tobias Ragg
Merle Louise Beggar Woman
Edmund Lyndeck Judge Turpin
Sarah Rice Johanna
Joaquin Romaguera Pirelli
Jack Eric Williams The Beadle

"...artistic energy, creative personality and plain excitement."

RICHARD EDER, REVIEWER, *THE NEW YORK TIMES*, 2 MARCH 1979

BARBER SHOP, FLEET STREET

Todd is impatient for the Beadle's visit. Mrs Lovett advises patience ⑬. Anthony visits Todd's shop, hoping to bring Johanna to hide. Pirelli, revealing himself as a former employee of Todd, whom he recognizes as Barker, attempts blackmail ⑭. Todd kills him.

JUDGE TURPIN'S MANSION/ A LONDON STREET

Anthony and Johanna, nervous of discovery, sing of their mutual passion ⑮. Meanwhile, the Beadle suggests to the Judge that more careful grooming might help his cause in wooing Johanna, and recommends Todd ⑯.

BARBER SHOP, FLEET STREET

While being shaved, the Judge sings with Todd of female delights ⑰. Anthony and Johanna interrupt them, whereupon the Judge storms off with Johanna, immediately mistrustful of the barber. Todd vows vengeance on the human race ⑱ before Mrs Lovett suggests a use for the fresh "meat" ⑲.

Business is thriving ⑳. Todd aches for his daughter, as he slits customers' throats. Anthony too yearns for Johanna. The beggar woman warns of the hellish smoke from the shop ㉑.

Mrs Lovett tries to interest Todd in retiring to the seaside ㉒. Todd helps Anthony disguise himself in order to rescue Johanna from Fogg's asylum ㉓. Hoping to ensnare the Judge, Todd invites him to the shop where he will find Anthony and Johanna ㉔. Tobias, now lodging with Mrs Lovett, expresses protective feelings ㉕.

PIE SHOP, FLEET STREET

Visiting the pie shop to investigate strange smells, the Beadle shares his love of parlour songs with Mrs Lovett ㉖. She sends him upstairs where Todd kills him. The beggar woman appears and Todd kills her in a panic. He then kills the Judge, who has just arrived.

Horrified, Todd recognizes the dead beggar woman as his wife Lucy and blames Mrs Lovett for misleading him into thinking she was already dead. He pushes Mrs Lovett into the oven. As Todd cradles his dead wife, a traumatized Tobias slits Todd's throat ㉗.

---

⑬ ⑭　⑮ ⑯　⑰ ⑱ ⑲　⑳ ㉑ ㉒　㉓ ㉔ ㉕　㉖　㉗

Wait
😀 *Mrs Lovett*

Pirelli's Death
😀 *Pirelli*

Kiss Me
Johanna,
😀 *Anthony*

Ladies in their Sensitivities
😀 *Beadle Bamford*

A Little Priest
Todd,
😀 *Mrs Lovett*

Epiphany
😀 *Todd, Mrs Lovett*

Pretty Women
😀 *Todd, Judge Turpin*

God, That's Good!
Tobias, Mrs Lovett,
😀 *Todd, Company*

Johanna (Quartet)
Anthony, Todd, Johanna, Beggar
😀 *Woman*

By the Sea
Mrs Lovett,
😀 *Todd*

Not While I'm Around
😀 *Tobias, Mrs Lovett*

The Letter
😀 *Quintet from the Company*

Wigmaker Sequence
😀 *Wigmaker, Todd, Anthony*

Parlour Songs
Beadle Bamford,
😀 *Mrs Lovett, Tobias*

Final Sequence
Todd, Mrs
😀 *Lovett, Tobias*

JOHANNA AND ANTHONY FALL IN LOVE

SWEENEY TODD WIELDS HIS RAZOR AS HE SHAVES THE JUDGE

STEPHEN SONDHEIM

{ COMPOSER AND LYRICIST **1930–** }

Over the decades, the American musical has gone through several phases of evolution. Stephen Sondheim is widely acknowledged for moving it in a new and more edgy direction.

It was Sondheim who, at the age of 27, crafted the lyrics for the ground-breaking *West Side Story* (see pp.122–25) in the late 1950s. Yet while it is inevitable that he should be associated with this one production in particular, his career is dotted with landmark shows, characterized by a wide range

It was while he was in Pennsylvania that Sondheim was befriended by the legendary Broadway lyricist Oscar Hammerstein II, who provided tutelage in the craft of musical theatre. Sondheim subsequently worked as an assistant on several of Hammerstein's collaborations with composer Richard Rodgers (see pp.70–71).

> ## *"I'm not writing for myself. I'm writing to entertain, to make people laugh and cry and think."*
>
> **STEPHEN SONDHEIM**

of subject matter, and an unerring relevance to the prevailing mood of audiences.

Musically, Sondheim was a child prodigy, showing an early aptitude for the piano and organ. In 1942, he moved to Pennsylvania, and by the age of 15 he was already writing his first musical. While studying music at Williams College in Williamstown, Massachusetts, he wrote shows for his contemporaries to perform.

By the early 1950s, Sondheim was in Hollywood working on scripts for a television series called *Topper*, after which he returned to New York to work on the incidental music for the play *The Girls of Summer* (1956).

BREAKTHROUGH

Sondheim's big break came the following year, when he met composer Leonard Bernstein (see pp.126–27) and choreographer Jerome Robbins (see pp.108–09), who were looking for a lyricist to work on an adaptation of Shakespeare's *Romeo and Juliet*. The result was *West Side Story*,

KEY WORKS

West Side Story, 1957 (see pp.122–25)

Gypsy, 1959 (see pp.138–39)

A Little Night Music, 1973 (see pp.190–91)

Sweeney Todd, 1979 (see pp.216–17)

Merrily We Roll Along, 1981

Sunday in the Park with George, 1984 (see p.244)

▶ **Leader of the pack**
Stephen Sondheim inherited the mantle of the great musical lyricists of the Golden Age, such as Oscar Hammerstein, and led musical theatre in new and exciting directions.

a seamless blending of words and music that introduced audiences to Sondheim's witty, conversational lyrics and provided late 1950s theatregoers with an exciting new kind of musical. Sondheim had arrived on Broadway, but he had little time to bask in his success. Three months later, he was working on something very different as writer for the CBS TV panel show *The Last Word*, which explored language and its usage. His next theatre project came the following year and marked a return to high-profile projects.

Jule Styne had been hired to compose the music for *Gypsy*, adapted from Arthur Laurent's book, and Sondheim was brought in to write the lyrics. For its time, the subject matter was controversial: a story loosely based on the memoirs of striptease artist Gypsy Rose Lee, focusing on her mother, Rose, who was portrayed as the ultimate show-business parent. The play was widely acclaimed, with one critic even suggesting that it might be the greatest American musical ever produced.

AWARDS AND INSPIRATION

In 1962, Sondheim wrote both the music and the lyrics for *A Funny Thing Happened on the Way to the Forum* (see p.149), a farce based on comedies originally written by the Roman playwright Plautus. The show won a Tony Award for Best Musical, Sondheim's first.

More awards followed in the 1970s, a result of Sondheim's collaborations with producer-director Harold Prince (see pp.210–11). *Company* (1970) was a meditation on marriage and commitment, which won Sondheim his first Grammy Award, while *Follies* (1971) paid tribute to early Broadway shows. The pair's romantic *A Little Night Music* (1973) produced a hit song, and contrasted sharply with their *Sweeney Todd* (1979), a blood-soaked melodrama set in Victorian London.

Throughout this time, Sondheim drew from a wide range of subjects for inspiration. *Pacific Overtures* (1976), for example, was partly a tribute to haiku poetry and Japanese Kabuki theatre, while *Sunday in the Park with George* (see p.244) was inspired by *A Sunday*

Afternoon on the Island of La Grande Jatte, a painting by French pointillist Georges Seurat. The latter was a collaboration with playwright-director James Lapine, with whom he shared the Pulitzer Prize for Drama for the piece in 1985. *Into the Woods* (see p.327) paid homage to traditional fairy tales, while *Assassins* (1990) featured many of the people who have tried (some successfully) to kill the president of the United States – including John Wilkes Booth, who killed Abraham Lincoln, and Lee Harvey Oswald, who shot John F. Kennedy. *Assassins* won five Tony Awards, and in 2014 Sondheim brought the show to London.

BEYOND BROADWAY

Perhaps because of its many influences, Sondheim's work has enjoyed an audience far beyond New York and London. The film version of *West Side Story* was released in 1961, winning an unprecedented ten Oscars, and *Gypsy* appeared the following year. The Harold Prince-directed film of *A Little Night Music* was released in 1978, and many other films have been distinguished by Sondheim's scores.

Anthologies or revues of Sondheim's work, both as composer and lyricist,

▲ Director at work
Sondheim giving direction to performers on the sound stage for the recording of the original Broadway production of *Into the Woods* in 1987.

featuring songs performed and cut from productions, have been staged over the years. Particularly noteworthy were *Side by Side by Sondheim* (1976), directed by Ned Sherrin, *Marry Me a Little* (1980), *You're Gonna Love Tomorrow* (1983), *Putting It Together* (1993), and *Sondheim on Sondheim* (2010).

WORLDWIDE ACCLAIM

Over the past four decades, Stephen Sondheim has set the standard for modern American musical theatre, winning eight Tony Awards – more than any other composer in Broadway history – together with eight Grammy Awards, and that glittering Pulitzer Prize. No doubt this pleases the man who once said: "I want as big an audience as possible."

▲ Unparalleled innovation
Stephen Sondheim has never been afraid to take the themes for his musicals from unlikely sources. The musical *Into the Woods* is based on a collage of different fairy tales.

TIMELINE

22 March 1930 Stephen Joshua Sondheim is born in New York to garment manufacturer Herbert Sondheim and his fashion designer wife Janet, née Fox.

1942 Sondheim's parents' divorce, and this results in a move to Pennsylvania with his mother.

1950 Sondheim graduates from Williams College, where he majors in music.

1956 Composes background music for play *The Girls of Summer*.

1957 Writes lyrics for *West Side Story*, which becomes one of Broadway's most successful productions.

1959 Produces lyrics for *Gypsy*, starring Ethel Merman.

1962 *A Funny Thing Happened on the Way to the Forum* opens for the first of nearly 1,000 performances.

1970 *Company* opens on Broadway, marking the start of over a decade of collaboration with Harold Prince.

1973 *A Little Night Music* opens on Broadway.

1975 Judy Collins' recording of "Send in the Clowns" from *A Little Night Music* enters the Top 40 and will win a Grammy award the following year.

1976 *Side by Side by Sondheim*, an anthology of Sondheim's work, opens in London, moving to Broadway a year later.

1979 *Sweeney Todd* opens on Broadway to rave reviews.

2009 Broadway revives *West Side Story* and *A Little Night Music*.

2010 80th birthday tributes culminate in Broadway's Henry Miller Theatre being renamed the Stephen Sondheim Theatre.

2014 *Assassins*, originally staged Off-Broadway in 1990, opens in London.

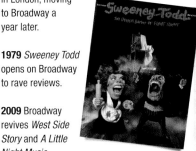

SWEENEY TODD

42ND STREET

{ 1980 }

The stage show of *42nd Street* is so well loved and such a Broadway standard that it may come as a surprise to learn that it has only been around since 1980. It was the brainchild of the legendary showman David Merrick.

For the Broadway show, Merrick raided the 1933 Hollywood musical of the same name, which was based on a book by Bradford Ropes, and the song catalogue of the film's songwriting team, lyricist Al Dubin and composer Harry Warren (see pp.28–29). The result was a spectacular, feel-good musical that is both a depiction of a director creating a hit show during the Great Depression (1929–39) and a reminder that, no matter what, the show must go on.

SALUTING BUSBY BERKELEY

42nd Street's plot is a typical backstage story. Dictatorial director Julian Marsh is at the helm of a sprawling Broadway musical in 1930s New York. The piece introduces us to a host of colourful characters involved in its creation and centres around the star's understudy, Peggy Sawyer. When Peggy's shot at fame and glory arrives, she must find the confidence to rise up, take over the leading role, and make it her own. By the time she does so, Marsh has fallen completely in love with her and, after

▶ **Well-deserved hype**
For once, all the claims about a musical were justified. David Merrick was completely on the money with this Broadway classic.

a couple of setbacks and a near nervous breakdown for Peggy, he resolves to make her a big star.

As originally directed and choreographed by an ailing Gower Champion, the musical is also a salute to old-fashioned Broadway "hoofing", a slang term for dancing in a show. The iconic production opens with the curtain rising slowly on a long chorus line of tap dancing, so that you see the fast-moving feet before the big stage picture is fully revealed. There follows a series of spectacular production numbers that capture the spirit of the breathtaking work of Hollywood choreographer Busby Berkeley during the Great Depression.

During "We're in the Money", the cast dance on huge coins, and in "There's a Sunny Side to Every Situation", the stage fills vertically with the company in individual dressing rooms, switching their mirror lights on and off in syncopation. When Peggy attempts to flee to Broad Street Station, she is lured back to Broadway by "Lullaby of Broadway". The showstopping and spectacular staging of *42nd Street*'s title song reflects the energy, bustle, and glamour of New York theatre's best-known address amid a scenic collage of vintage Times Square lights.

AUDACIOUS PROMOTION
Mirroring Sawyer's journey in the plot, actual understudies from the real-life show have been propelled to stardom while stepping out of the chorus to cover the lead roles. Although this phenomenon seems

◀ **Original cast recording**
Lee Roy Reams, Jerry Orbach, and Joseph Bova (from left to right) in full voice during the recording session the cast recording for RCA Victor, while Wanda Richert listens intently.

kely to have been spun to generate reat publicity, these performers nclude Catherine Zeta-Jones in the riginal London production.

Other legends surrounding the show include Merrick's speech after the first night curtain call, in which he announced the death from cancer of Gower Champion; something he had

kept from even Champion's girlfriend, for maximum dramatic effect. The resulting heady combination of triumph and tragedy ensured spectacular press coverage of the show's launch.

In another typical act of audacity, Merrick also erected a billboard proclaiming *42nd Street* to be "Broadway's Latest Hit", thus alerting

people who were too late to get a ticket for other Broadway shows that they could still get into his show because it started "latest". This cunning ploy ensured many last-minute full houses in the early 1980s.

42nd Street was to be Merrick's last and greatest producing triumph, on Broadway, in the West End, and in several major touring productions. It was the perfect swansong, not only for him but for Gower Champion and the traditional American musical, before the 1980s invasion of British hits such as *Cats* (see pp.228–31) and *Les Misérables* (see pp.246–49).

> # "It's not enough that I should succeed – others should fail."

42ND STREET'S ORIGINATING PRODUCER, **DAVID MERRICK**

KEY FACTS

🎭 **STAGE**

🎬 **Director** Gower Champion

📖 **Book** Michael Stewart, Mark Bramble, and based on Bradford Ropes

🎵 **Music** Harry Warren

🎵 **Lyrics** Al Dubin

🎭 **Venue** Winter Garden Theatre, New York

📅 **Date** 25 August 1980

◉ **Key information**
The original Broadway production won Tony Awards for Best Musical and Best Choreography, and Drama Desk Awards for choreography and costume design. It ran for 3,486 performances.

BARNUM

{ 1980 }

Barnum is a humdinger of a show. Big, brash, loud, and super-spectacular, it delves into the nature of showmanship – and makes legends of its lead performers.

Is a showman necessarily a con artist? Is dressing up a form of deception? Phineas T. Barnum, the 19th century's most famous freakshow, circus, and concert impresario, met this prejudice for most of his life. For decades he accepted this treatment with grace (as well he might: he had immense riches to console him, and there is little doubt that some of his most notorious "freaks" had indeed been hoaxes). But he did eventually come to resent it. No matter what his civic achievements, the showman side of his character and career was never recognized by the US establishment.

Barnum begins with P.T. Barnum singing "There is a sucker born ev'ry minute", introducing Barnum as a man who makes money wherever he

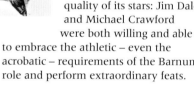

▶ **Talented all-rounder**
Jim Dale's performance in the title role in the original Broadway production left some critics wondering "Is there anything he can't do?".

can – and glories in his gift for getting one over on a gullible public. Against the advice of his wife, Charity, who wants him to settle down, he builds himself a circus, which boasts the oldest woman alive (Joice Heth), the smallest man in the world (Tom Thumb), and the "Swedish Nightingale" soprano Jenny Lind, with whom he tours as her manager for a while. He also runs for political office, but as he acknowledges in his song "The Prince of Humbug", whatever he does, as publisher, philanthropist, or politician, he will only be remembered for one thing – humbug.

SERIOUSLY COMPELLING
And yet we watch, increasingly spellbound, as Barnum builds his entertainment empire and his circus. It is a thoroughly compelling

◀ **Grand spectacle**
The programme cover for P.T. Barnum and Adam Forepaugh's circus, 1887. The musical captures the ambition of the original impresario's shows.

spectacle, and even the most cynical viewer cannot help being won over by the world that Barnum creates – one in which he teams up with James A Baily to create the "Greatest Show on Earth". Both in its initial Broadway run and its subsequent London production, *Barnum* was immensely fortunate in the quality of its stars: Jim Dale and Michael Crawford were both willing and able to embrace the athletic – even the acrobatic – requirements of the Barnum role and perform extraordinary feats.

KEY FACTS

🎭 **STAGE**

🎬 **Director** Joe Layton
📖 **Book** Mark Bramble
🎵 **Music** Cy Coleman
𝄞 **Lyrics** Michael Stewart
🎫 **Venue** St James Theatre, New York
📅 **Date** 30 April 1980

⊙ **Key information**
To prepare for his part as Barnum, Jim Dale spent 12 weeks at the Big Apple Circus School, learning to juggle, tightrope walk, ride a unicycle, and walk on stilts. He won Tony and Desk Drawer awards for his performance.

IN GRAND COMBINATION
P.T. BARNUM & CO'S.
GREATEST SHOW ON EARTH
AND THE GREAT, LONDON CIRCUS
UNITED WITH
ADAM FOREPAUGH'S
NEW AND GREATEST ALL FEATURE SHOW.
CIRCUSES, MENAGERIES, HIPPODROMES
AND ARTIFICIAL LAKE.
MADISON SQUARE GARDEN
COMMENCING MONDAY, MARCH 14TH

> *"There is a sucker born ev'ry minute."*
>
> ATTRIBUTED TO **PHINEAS T. BARNUM**

DREAMGIRLS

{ **1981** }

What do you do when living the dream becomes a nightmare? *Dreamgirls* is a sidelong look at the music business and the true cost of chasing fame.

KEY FACTS

🎭 **STAGE**

🎬 **Director** Michael Bennett

📖 **Book** Tom Eyen

🎵 **Music** Henry Krieger

𝄞 **Lyrics** Tom Eyen

🎭 **Venue** Imperial Theatre, New York

🗓 **Date** 20 December 1981

◎ **Key information**
The original production of *Dreamgirls* ran for 1,521 performances from 1981–85. It was nominated for 13 Tony Awards, of which it won six. It also won five Drama Desk Awards, and two Grammys.

◀ **Glamorous R'n'B**
The Dreams in full flow during a scene from the 2006 film of *Dreamgirls*, which starred Beyoncé Knowles, Jennifer Hudson, and Anika Noni Rose.

etroit, for decades famous as the home of the American automobile industry, became in the 1960s a centre for the mass-production of pop hits. Businessman Berry Gordy Jr referenced his city's manufacturing heritage when, in 1959, he named his new record label "Motown". The label went on to record many notable artists, including the Marvelettes, the Miracles, the Four Tops, Stevie Wonder, Michael Jackson, Marvin Gaye, and the Supremes.

BAD DREAM

Dreamgirls follows an imaginary trio of aspiring singers, called the Dreamettes, who could easily have been the Supremes. Although writers Tom Eyen and Henry Krieger always denied any connection, Curtis Taylor, who takes charge of their career – after discovering them on a talent show – bears an obvious resemblance to Berry Gordy Jr. Likewise, the following travails of the pop-music "family" they all help to build recall those of the historical Motown crowd. Effie is replaced by Deena, just as, in the Supremes, Florence Ballard was sidelined to make way for Diana Ross. Effie struggles to sustain her self-esteem, as Ballard did, and Deena becomes romantically involved with Curtis, just as Diana Ross did with Gordy Jr. As at Motown, their involvement causes jealousy.

"I AM CHANGING"

And so it goes: a steady rise to fame, in which the Dreamettes become the Dreams, and an equally steady descent into rancour. Yet for all the bickering and heartache, the group produce a mesmerizing string of songs. There is the confected Motown-type hit "Cadillac Car" and the soul-searing expressiveness of "And I Am Telling You I'm Not Going". "One Night Only", a song of fleeting love, takes the language of clichéd pop emotion and then digs deeper in its melancholy stoicism, while "I Am Changing" is a moving manifesto of self-redemption and resolve.

The show's popularity took it to numerous stages after its Broadway production, and in 2006 it was made into a critically acclaimed film starring Jamie Foxx, Beyoncé Knowles, Anika Noni Rose, and Jennifer Hudson, who won an Oscar for her portrayal of Effie.

"If you can't feel the emotion of a song, how do you expect anyone else to? It's like a testimony…"

JENNIFER HUDSON, AMERICAN SINGER AND ACTRESS WHO PLAYED EFFIE IN *DREAMGIRLS*, 2014

MADE FOR TELEVISION

Musicals are not exclusive to the stage or big screen. Television musicals have been produced for the small screen as far back as the 1940s.

There are three distinct types of musical represented on television: those written specifically for TV; broadcasts of stage productions; and musical television series.

The first musical written for the small screen was *The Boys From Boise* (1944). Rodgers and Hammerstein's *Cinderella* is one of the most popular TV musicals, airing with Julie Andrews in its initial broadcast in 1957, with Lesley Ann Warren nine years later in 1965, and starring pop stars Brandy and Whitney Houston in the 1997 version.

The most successful musical ever created specifically for the small screen is Disney Channel's *High School Musical* (2006). It has been seen by more than 225 million viewers around the world, and spawned three sequels, a live stage production, an all-skating ice arena production, a series of books, and six games.

Stage musicals have often found a happy second home on television. Some of these productions are strictly recordings of live performances, while others are restaged or adapted for the television camera. *Peter Pan*, which opened on Broadway in 1954, was broadcast live in 1955, 1956, and 1960 – all starring Mary Martin in the title role. In the US, NBC has produced a live broadcast of *The Sound of Music* and *Peter Pan*, and from 2013 initiated a plan to continue producing a new live musical every year.

Television has also offered plot-driven musical series, including shows like *Fame*, *Glee*, *Galavant*, and *Smash*. The most successful of these shows are aired in many countries.

STAR SEARCH

Reality television shows have helped find new stars for major productions. Andrew Lloyd Webber (see pp.270–71) used *How Do You Solve a Problem Like Maria* to find someone to play Maria in his stage production of *The Sound of Music*. To find a new lead for the Broadway production of *Legally Blonde*, MTV produced *Legally Blonde – The Musical: The Search for Elle Woods*.

▶ **Chasing fame**
Fame follows the lives of a group of students studying at the fictional New York High School of Performing Arts in their quest for stardom.

"… NBC is breaking new ground by reviving a tradition from another era: staging a full Broadway musical live on television."

TED CHAPIN, PRESIDENT OF RODGERS & HAMMERSTEIN: AN IMAGEM COMPANY, 2012

CATS

{ **1981** }

Who could have imagined that a poetry collection with neither plot nor story would provide the inspiration for a show that would transform musical theatre forever? *Cats* took this genre to new levels of creativity and success.

As a child, Andrew Lloyd Webber (see pp.270–71) had loved reading *Old Possum's Book of Practical Cats* (1939), a book of poetry by T.S. Eliot (see below), and he began setting Eliot's verse to music in 1977. In order to experience how it felt to set music to pre-existing text, Lloyd Webber worked without a lyricist. However, with the rock musical *Evita* (see pp.208–09) still in development, he kept the Eliot project on the back burner.

GRIZABELLA, THE GLAMOUR CAT
By the summer of 1980, Lloyd Webber was ready to perform some of his Eliot settings at his Sydmonton Festival. At this point, he was still thinking of the project as a possible television concert anthology. Eliot's widow, Valerie Eliot, attended one of the performances, bringing several unpublished pieces to offer Lloyd Webber. It

◄ **Cat's eyes**
Yellow cat's eyes staring out of the darkness, used here on the poster, created an instantly recognizable "identity" for the show.

was this new material, particularly "Grizabella, the Glamour Cat", that made him reconsider the project as a possible stage production.

Lloyd Webber enlisted renowned British theatre director Trevor Nunn as a collaborator to help shape the show, which now included even more new material from Eliot's widow. Nunn, realizing the importance of the spectacle, put together a team that included choreographer Gillian Lynne, set and costume designer John Napier, and lighting designer David Hersey.

INJURED DENCH BOWS OUT
By spring of 1981, rehearsals had begun for the London opening. Judi Dench, a British actor at that time mainly known for her work in Shakespearean roles, was to have played the pivotal character of Grizabella, but she snapped her Achilles tendon during rehearsal and was replaced by British singer and actor Elaine Paige (see p.230). On 11 May 1981, *Cats* opened at the New London Theatre – its record-breaking run had started.

Cats went on to set a new benchmark for success in musical theatre. Prior to *Cats*, most highly successful musicals started on Broadway and then opened productions in other cities after that. *Cats* continued the trend started by *Jesus Christ Superstar* and *Evita*, originating in London and then

> ## *"Cats, now and forever."*
>
> THE SLOGAN ON EVERY POSTER, PRINT, OR TELEVISION ADVERTISEMENT FOR *CATS* WORLDWIDE

► **Top cat**
Elaine Paige originated the part of Grizabella for the original West End production.

transferring to Broadway and the rest of the world. By 2014, *Cats* had been presented in over 300 cities in more than 30 countries worldwide. Translations of the show have been written in Japanese, German, Swiss German, Hungarian, Norwegian, Finnish, Dutch, Swedish, French, Mexican Spanish, Argentinian Spanish, and Italian.

UNIVERSAL APPEAL
But language alone was never at the heart of *Cats*; its success was firmly rooted in the spectacle of scenery, costumes, lighting, make-up, and choreography. For example, the costumes Napier designed, along with the make-up, not only blended huma

KEY FACTS

🎭 **STAGE**
🎬 **Director** Trevor Nunn
🎵 **Lyrics** T.S. Eliot
🎵 **Music** Andrew Lloyd Webber
☑ **Set and costumes** John Napier
🎭 **Venue** New London Theatre, London
📅 **Date** 11 May 1981

⊙ **Key information**
The show won two Olivier Awards: Musical of the Year; and Outstanding Achievement of the Year in a Musical for choreographer Gillian Lynne. The 1983 Broadway production won seven Tony Awards: Best Musical; Best Book of a Musical; Best Original Score; Best Featured Actress in a Musical (Betty Buckley); Best Costume Design; Best Lighting Design; and Best Direction of a Musical.

RELATED SHOWS

Jesus Christ Superstar, 1971, Andrew Lloyd Webber, Tim Rice (pp.184–85)
Joseph and the Amazing Technicolor Dreamcoat, 1973, Andrew Lloyd Webber, Tim Rice (p.187)
Evita, 1978, Andrew Lloyd Webber, Tim Rice (pp.208–09)
Starlight Express, 1984, Andrew Lloyd Webber, Richard Stilgoe (pp.240–41)

▲ **Feline playground**
John Napier's set, with its junkyard props, including dustbins and wrecked cars, created a sense of a parallel cat world.

and cat characteristics, but helped project the distinctive personality of each feline character. Napier's set had very little in the way of magical onstage transitions, but the ambitious environmental setting put the audience in the middle of the action, with the characters moving from among the audience on to the stage. *Cats*, with its strong characters and simple story to follow, transcended all age and language barriers, and non-English-speaking tourists seeing the show in London or New York did not miss out on a moment of the magic. The original West End production ran for an astonishing 21 years and held the record for longest-running London musical until *Les Misérables* (see pp.246–49) overtook it in October 2006. The Broadway production was also a record-breaking success; it ran for 18 years, becoming the longest-running Broadway musical ever, though *The Phantom of the Opera* (see pp.252–253) and the revival of *Chicago* (see pp.196–99) later overtook it. Two generations of musicals fans grew up having *Cats* as their first experience of live theatre.

T.S. ELIOT (1888–1965)

Born and raised in Missouri, Harvard-educated Thomas Stearns Eliot moved to London in 1914, marrying in 1915. While working variously as a teacher and banker, he published his poetry under the mentorship of American expatriate poet Ezra Pound (1885–1972), who nicknamed Eliot "Old Possum". Eliot became a British citizen in 1927. In 1948, he was awarded the Nobel Prize for Literature.

STORYLINE

The theatrical event celebrated in *Cats* is a captivating spectacle set to the evocative poetry of T.S. Eliot, breaking with the long-standing tradition of a musical driven by a plot or story. The action takes place in a "giant playground for cats", which is in fact a rubbish dump, and the scenes are based around the cats' interactions, thoughts, and experiences as described in Eliot's poems.

CAST	
Elaine Paige Grizabella	**Jeff Shankley** Mankustrap
Brian Blessed Old Deuteronomy/Bustopher Jones	**Bonnie Langford** Rumpelteaser
Sharon Lee-Hill Demeter	**Paul Nicholas** Rum Tum Tugger
Sarah Brightman Jemima	
Wayne Sleep Quaxo/Mistoffelees	**Finola Hughes** Victoria

RUBBISH DUMP

PLOT OVERVIEW

The cats gather onstage ❶. They describe how Jellicle cats receive their names ❷, and that tonight is the night that Old Deuteronomy will choose a cat to be reborn in the Heavyside Layer ❸. One by one we are introduced to the various cats of note: Jennyanydots (the old Gumbie Cat) ❹, Rum Tum Tugger ❺, Grizabella ❻, Bustopher Jones ❼, Mungojerrie and Rumpelteazer ❽, and Old Deuteronomy ❾. This is followed by an account of a battle between the "Pekes and the Pollicles" ❿.

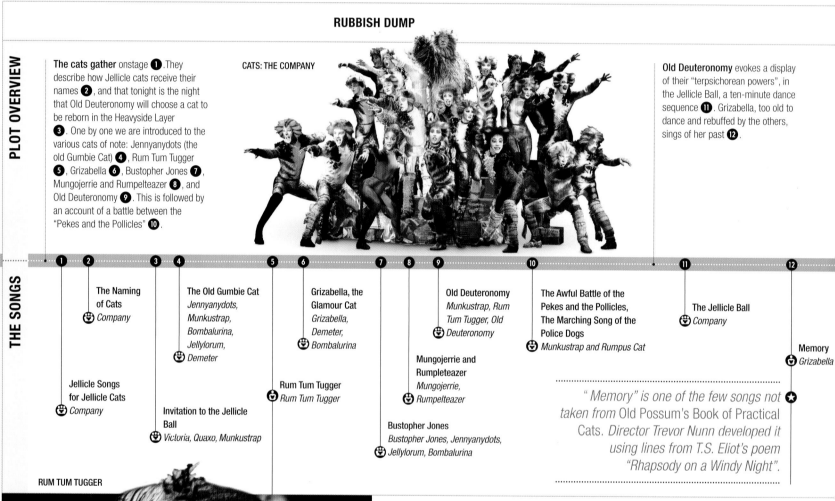

CATS: THE COMPANY

Old Deuteronomy evokes a display of their "terpsichorean powers", in the Jellicle Ball, a ten-minute dance sequence ⓫. Grizabella, too old to dance and rebuffed by the others, sings of her past ⓬.

THE SONGS

❶ Jellicle Songs for Jellicle Cats
Company

❷ The Naming of Cats
Company

❸ Invitation to the Jellicle Ball
Victoria, Quaxo, Munkustrap

❹ The Old Gumbie Cat
Jennyanydots, Munkustrap, Bombalurina, Jellylorum, Demeter

❺ Rum Tum Tugger
Rum Tum Tugger

❻ Grizabella, the Glamour Cat
Grizabella, Demeter, Bombalurina

❼ Bustopher Jones
Bustopher Jones, Jennyanydots, Jellylorum, Bombalurina

❽ Mungojerrie and Rumpleteazer
Mungojerrie, Rumpelteazer

❾ Old Deuteronomy
Munkustrap, Rum Tum Tugger, Old Deuteronomy

❿ The Awful Battle of the Pekes and the Pollicles, The Marching Song of the Police Dogs
Munkustrap and Rumpus Cat

⓫ The Jellicle Ball
Company

⓬ Memory
Grizabella

....

★ "*Memory*" is one of the few songs not taken from Old Possum's Book of Practical Cats. Director Trevor Nunn developed it using lines from T.S. Eliot's poem "Rhapsody on a Windy Night".

....

RUM TUM TUGGER

ELAINE PAIGE (1948 –)

Paige, born Elaine Jill Bickerstaff in North London, made her West End debut in *Hair* in 1968, but *Evita* (see pp.208–09) made her a star. After *Evita*, she continued to work with Andrew Lloyd Webber, originating the role Grizabella in *Cats* and starring as Norma Desmond in *Sunset Boulevard* (see pp.266–69). Paige also worked with Tim Rice on the musical *Chess* (1986). A single from *Chess*, "I Know Him So Well", sung by Paige and Barbara Dickson, remains the top-selling female duet in UK chart history.

NICOLE SCHERZIINGER
AS GRIZABELLA, 2015

"Cats are much like you and me."

T.S. ELIOT, "THE AD-DRESSING OF CATS", *OLD POSSUM'S BOOK OF PRACTICAL CATS*, 1939

RUBBISH DUMP

Old Deuteronomy reminds everyone of the moments of happiness **13**. Asparagus sings of his past as a great theatre cat **14**, and recalls his most famous role, Growltiger **15**.

Skimbleshanks, the railway cat, describes his life **16**. Macavity, the mystery cat, makes his escape in the melee of shorted-out stage lights **17**, but, by great good fortune, the lights are restored by Mr Mistoffelees, the magical cat **18**.

After she sings the full version of "Memory" to the assembled cats **19**, Old Deuteronomy chooses Grizabella to go to the Heavyside Layer **20**. Once there, she rises on a large tyre from the piles of junk on the set **21**.

13

The Moments of Happiness
Old Deuteronomy, Jemima
😊 *(or Sillabub)*

14

Gus: The Theatre Cat
Jellylorum,
😊 *Asparagus*

15

Growltiger's Last Stand
Asparagus, Jellyorum,
😊 *the Crew*

16

Skimbleshanks
😊 *Skimbleshanks*

17

Macavity
Demeter, Bombalurina, Alonzo, Macavity,
😊 *Munkustrap*

18

Mr Mistoffelees
Mistoffelees, Rum Tum Tugger
😊 *Tugger*

19

Memory (reprise)
Victoria,
😊 *Grizabella*

20

The Journey to the Heavyside Layer
😊 *Company*

21

The Ad-Dressing of Cats
😊 *Old Deuteronomy*

OLD DEUTERONOMY SENDS GRIZABELLA TO THE HEAVYSIDE LAYER

RUM TUM TUGGER AND COMPANY

In the original London show, "Growltiger's Last Stand" was a setting of an unpublished T.S. Eliot poem, "The Ballad of Billy M'Caw". For the Broadway show it was replaced by a number in the style of Italian opera. This new version was subsequently incorporated into most productions worldwide.

CAMERON
MACKINTOSH

{ PRODUCER **1946–** }

He may have been described as the world's most successful, influential, and powerful theatrical producer, but even that fails to do full justice to Sir Cameron Mackintosh's career.

◄ West End warrior
Cameron Mackintosh knew from an early age that musicals and the stage would be his life. He has since proved to be one of the most lauded theatre producers of all time.

He owns some of London's most important theatres and is recognized as the producer of some of the most successful shows ever staged. But he is also the man who, more than any other, transformed the musical show into a highly profitable global brand.

Union, were potentially highly lucrative markets. In the process, he demonstrated that collectively such markets could match and even surpass the revenues generated by Broadway or West End productions.

Although he is now a billionaire, Mackintosh insists he has never forgotten queuing up for cheap

"My greatest talent is, providing someone has written something interesting, to be the catalyst to make it work."

CAMERON MACKINTOSH

Mackintosh was the first theatrical producer to recognize that countries where musicals had seldom previously been seen, such as those in the former Soviet

theatre seats. "I realize," he told an interviewer, "that the people who've made my fortune have to budget carefully and want value for money." It is also why he claims the balconies in his theatres are as comfortable "as I can possibly make them". He bought substantial stakes in his first two West End theatres, the Prince of Wales and the Prince Edward, in 1991, having realized that he could best give people what they wanted from his shows by owning and controlling the environment in which they were seen. He has also had a lifelong passion for architecture and

▲ Bringing something new to town
The creative team behind the 1985 production of Schönberg and Boublil's *Les Misérables*, in discussion during a production meeting.

the restoration of old buildings. Mackintosh is now the owner of eight historic West End theatres.

OBSESSION

Cameron Anthony Mackintosh was eight when an aunt took him to a matinee performance of the musical *Salad Days*, written by Julian Slade, in 1954. The boy was hooked: he now knew what he wanted to do with his life. In pursuit of his dream to work in the theatre, Mackintosh spent a year at London's Central School of Speech and Drama before starting work at the Theatre Royal, Drury Lane as a cleaner and stage hand, whilst still only in his late teens. He then became an assistant stage manager and worked on several touring productions.

Mackintosh began producing his own small touring shows before moving back to the West End. His early efforts stumbled, with a revival of *Anything Goes* in 1969 closing after only two weeks. His 1973 production of *The Card* fared better but, after several provincial productions of varying profitability, it was 1976 that brought him his first

KEY WORKS

Side by Side by Sondheim, 1976

Cats, 1981 (see pp.228–31)

Oliver!, 1977, 1994, 2009 (see p.142)

Les Misérables, 1985, 2014 (see pp.246–49)

The Phantom of the Opera, 1986, 2011 (see pp.252–53)

Miss Saigon, 1989, 2014 (see pp.256–57)

Mary Poppins, 2004 (see p.155)

major success with the revue *Side By Side By Sondheim*. Successful London productions of *My Fair Lady* (1978) and *Tomfoolery* (1980) followed and set the scene for the unexpected musical hit of the 1981 theatrical season.

T.S. Elliot's *Old Possum's Book of Practical Cats* was considered unpromising material for a musical, but Mackintosh thought otherwise, and Andrew Lloyd Webber's *Cats* went on to become one of the longest-running shows on both sides of the Atlantic. It was also significant in helping to create a new style of musical production, which could be easily replicated and mounted all over the world.

Mackintosh then approached the French songwriting team Alain Boublil and Claude-Michel Schönberg (see pp.258–59) about bringing an English-language adaptation of their successful concept album *Les Misérables* to the London stage. The show opened at the Barbican Theatre in 1985 before transferring to the West End's Palace Theatre.

Mackintosh had once again seen the potential of interesting material, and *Les Misérables* proved to be a massive hit, with initial tickets sales driven largely by word of mouth. His faith has been fully justified: after 30

▶ Awards galore
The multi-award-winning producer grinning mischievously at the *What's On Stage* awards ceremony in London, February 2015.

years, more than 65 million people in 42 countries have enjoyed the show. Mackintosh's next production, Lloyd Webber's *The Phantom of the Opera*, opened the following year and proved to be another triumph on a similar scale. The New York production has become the longest running Broadway show, with over 11,000 performances.

Producing Boublil and Schönberg's *Miss Saigon* crowned what was proving to be an extraordinary decade for Cameron Mackintosh. A quarter of a century later, *Miss Saigon* would make a return to the West End.

REVIVALS

As the triumphs mounted, Mackintosh was responsible for several West End transfers of National Theatre revivals: *Oklahoma!* (1999), *Carousel* (1993), and *My Fair Lady* (2001).

In 2008, he Cameron Mackintosh revived his own 1994 production of Lionel Bart's *Oliver!*. After a nationwide TV talent search to find an unknown actress to play Nancy, BBC's *I'd Do Anything* crowned Jodie Prenger as its winner. By January 2009, the production had become the fastest-selling show in West End history, with pre-opening sales of £15 million.

◀ King of revivals
In 2008, Mackintosh put on a new production of Lionel Bart's *Oliver!*, with comic actor Rowan Atkinson as Fagin.

Having successfully launched musical shows in previously ignored Eastern Europe, Cameron Mackintosh has recently expressed interest in producing shows in other hitherto neglected areas of the world, such as Asia and Africa.

TIMELINE

17 October 1946 Born in Enfield, near London, to timber merchant and jazz trumpeter Ian Macintosh and Diana, née Tonna, a secretary from Malta of French descent.

1954 Sees the musical *Salad Days* and decides to be a theatrical producer.

1969 Revival of *Anything Goes*, his first London production, closes after two weeks.

1976 Revue *Side by Side by Sondheim* is his first major success.

1981 Teams up with Andrew Lloyd Webber to create *Cats*, which becomes one of the longest-running musicals ever produced.

1985 *Les Misérables* opens in London, with *The Phantom of the Opera* following a year later.

1989 *Miss Saigon* opens at the Theatre Royal, Drury Lane.

1991 Wins an Olivier Award for creative contribution to West End productions; founds Delfont Mackintosh Theatres with Bernard Delfont.

1991 Acquires substantial stakes in his first two West End theatres, the Prince of Wales and the Prince Edward.

1994 *Oliver!* re-launched at the London Palladium; will run for four years.

1996 Knighted for services to British theatre.

MARY POPPINS, 2004

2004 First stage production of *Mary Poppins* is launched at London's Prince Edward Theatre and will run for four years.

2011 Opening of *Betty Blue Eyes*, his first new musical in more than a decade.

2014 Launches a revival of *Miss Saigon* at London's Prince Edward Theatre to mark 25 years since the show's first opening; becomes the first British producer to be inducted into Broadway's prestigious American Theater Hall of Fame.

ANNIE

{ 1982 }

A heart-warming tale set in the era of the Great Depression, the audience can't help but want to cheer on cheeky little Annie as she makes her way from rags to riches.

▼ Cute orphans and hot tunes
Aileen Quinn as the eponymous heroine. Her innocence contrasted interestingly with the film's racy songs "Sign" and "Easy Street".

A dapted from the 1977 Broadway musical, the film version of *Annie* offered new songs and a rearranged plotline that introduced a sense of danger to the climax. The original book was by Thomas Meehan in his Broadway debut; he would go on to write the book for *The Producers* (see pp.290–91), and co-author *Hairspray* (see pp.296–97). For Broadway, the music was by Charles Strouse, famed for his work on *Bye Bye Birdie* (see p.143) in 1960. The lyrics were written by Martin Charnin, an ex-performer who conceived of *Annie* and went on to direct the Broadway version. For the film, Columbia Pictures returned to Meehan, Strouse, and Charnin, with Meehan writing an early version of the screenplay, and Strouse and Charnin hired to write new songs, such as "Sandy", "Dumb Dog", and "Let's Go to the Movies".

A CLASSIC TALE

Annie, an 11-year-old orphan, dreams of the day her parents will come to rescue her from warden Miss Hannigan's dreary establishment. Unlike the other orphans, she was dropped off with a note, explaining that her parents would be back to claim her as soon as they were able. Deciding to act, Annie makes several attempts to run away. On one such adventure she acquires a new friend – fluffy dog Sandy. Back at the orphanage, she awaits punishment when Miss Hannigan is visited by a special guest, Grace Farrell, personal secretary to Oliver Warbucks, a billionaire.

Warbucks has decided to invite an orphan home as a publicity stunt, and Farrell sets her heart on Annie. First Farrell, the servants, and then the mighty Warbucks himself fall in love with Annie, but she doesn't lose sight of her parents,

◄ Plotting against Annie
Lilly (Bernadette Peters), Rooster (Tim Curry), and Miss Hannigan (Carol Burnett) hatch a plot to put themselves on "Easy Street".

and the promise of really belonging to someone. Warbucks offers a reward for Annie's parents to come forward, which leaves her in great danger when Miss Hannigan, her brother, and his girlfriend plot to claim the reward. Annie is eventually secure in the knowledge that she "don't need anyone but" Warbucks himself.

GREAT SONGS, MIXED RECEPTION

This musical is best known for the quality of its thoroughly "singalong" songs, such as the worldwide hits "It's the Hard Knock Life" and "Tomorrow".

Critics were mostly unimpressed, but audiences flocked to cinemas to see it and it became the tenth highest grossing film in the US in 1982.

KEY FACTS

🎬 **FILM**

🎬 **Director** John Huston

📃 **Screenplay** Carol Sobieski

📖 **Book** Thomas Meehan

🎵 **Music and lyrics** Charles Strouse, Martin Charnin

🕐 **Running time** 127 minutes

📅 **Release date** 18 June 1982

⊙ **Key information**
The film version was nominated for two Academy Awards in 1983: for Music (Original Song Score and its adaptation) and Art Direction.

NINE

A story of self-absorption, complex and contorted, becomes a spectacular affirmation of the power of musical theatre to communicate and uplift.

THIS HOLIDAY SEASON BE ITALIAN

▲ Star-studded cast
A film version of *Nine* was released in 2009, starring Daniel Day-Lewis, Judi Dench, Nicole Kidman, and Penélope Cruz.

Stage musicals have routinely been made into movies down the decades; film musicals have frequently been adapted for the stage. It is more unusual, though, to find a successful stage show being made out of a film about a film director failing to make a film. But Federico Fellini is a special case in cinematic history, and his *8½* (1963) had been an instant classic.

The title came from the famous Italian director's own summary CV to date: eight films and one collaboration (hence the "half"). His next film was supposed to have been a sci-fi feature, but struggling to sustain his interest, he had ended up making a movie about himself, his difficulties, and the origins of his artistic vocation.

A LIFE ON TRIAL

Implicitly adding another ½ production to the great director's *8½*, *Nine* brought a version of Fellini's film to the Broadway stage. But this was a show about Maury Yeston too. Long obsessed with the 1963 movie, Yeston had come to see it as the definitive commentary on the creative process – and on his own difficulties in realizing his artistic dreams.

And so we find the Fellini character, the celebrated director Guido Contini, attempting not so much to realize his next vision as to envisage anything at all. The unfolding action flits back and forth across the boundaries between his life and work, between his imagination and the external world. Contini faces challenges in both these spheres – his imminent abandonment by Luisa del Forno, his film star wife, as destabilizing for him as his inability to pull together his next film.

LIFE TRANSFORMATION

A decade on from the film's appearance, the zeitgeist had shifted sufficiently to throw Luisa's loss – and its enormous significance – into relief. This recognition of how prominent – but also how problematic – a role women had in the lives of men was absolutely central to Yeston's vision of *Nine*, he told *The New York Times*. "It took *8½* and became an essay on the power of women."

In "My Husband Makes Movies", Luisa laments that her husband "lives a kind of dream, in which his actions aren't always what they seem". He may need her, but he is "the last one to know" that. Guido in turn thinks that he knows her worth, singing (in "Only With You"), "Being just me is so easy to be when I'm only with you".

As Guido wrestles with the problems in his present life, his memories take him back to his boyhood and his early career. He revisits old relationships and hears voices from his romantic past. His egotism – as man and artist – is on trial, but he is already receiving his punishment, his life now spiralling completely out of control. However, the singing soars; the dancers twist and turn; the orchestra swells; and the lights play. By the end, the pure magic of the musical transfigures a story of selfishness and self-destruction into something beautiful, both affirming and inspiring.

> "*Nine was the thing I really desperately wanted to write – never thinking for a minute that it would ever be produced.*"

GUIDO CONTINI, *NINE* (ARTHUR KOPIT), 1982

KEY FACTS

🪕 **STAGE**

🎬 **Director** Tommy Tune
📖 **Book** Arthur Kopit
🎵 **Music and lyrics** Maury Yeston
🎭 **Venue** 46th Street Theatre, New York
📅 **Date** 9 May 1982

⊙ **Key information**
The Broadway production won five Tony Awards: Best Musical; Best Original Score (Maury Yeston); Best Performance by a Featured Actress in a Musical (Liliane Montevecchi); Best Direction of a Musical (Tommy Tune); and Best Costume Design (William Ivey Long).

MAGICAL
PUPPETS

Puppetry, one of the oldest theatrical techniques known, dates back almost 3,000 years, yet still brings a magical dimension to the musical.

The art of puppetry – taking an inanimate object and imbuing it with life and a personality – is a storytelling tradition that stretches back to ancient Greece and Rome and later extended all across Europe. It is also found in the storytelling traditions of Indonesia, China, Japan, and the Middle East Masks, too, have been used for storytelling since ancient times.

PUPPETS TAKE TO THE STAGE

The 1951 Broadway musical *Flahooley* made extensive use of marionette puppets, designed and controlled by the American puppeteers Bill Baird and Cora Eisenberg Baird. Bill and Cora also performed the puppet show in the film version of *The Sound of Music*. Puppets made another notable appearance in 1961's musical *Carnival*, which featured a crippled puppeteer who could only speak comfortably through his puppets. In 1972, Swiss theatre troupe Mummenschanz began working with masks and costumes, turning

◀ Audrey II, the bloodsucking plant
This puppet was designed by David Farley and created by Artem for the Menier Chocolate Factory production of *Little Shop of Horrors*.

themselves into large, living puppets. Built on a combination of mask-work, puppetry, mime, and choreography, their work opened a whole new world for puppetry in the modern theatre.

Soon afterwards, Howard Ashman and Alan Menken's 1982 *Little Shop of Horrors* featured an offstage singer whose voice was coordinated with an ever-growing, bloodthirsty plant-puppet called Audrey II. In the Off-Broadway musical *Nunsense* (1985) and its sequels, Sister Mary Amnesia's more acerbic side is allowed to come out through a puppet alter ego, Sister Mary Annette.

For *The Lion King* (see pp.276–79), director and puppet designer Julie Taymor (see pp.280–81) created a unique physical and visual vocabulary for the show that brought the animated film to the stage in a way that was suggestive rather than literal. In this, one of the most successful musicals ever, Taymor's highly evocative and poetic imagery has been lauded in productions around the world.

Today, *Avenue Q* (see p.300–01) uses puppets inspired by Jim Henson's television show *Sesame Street*, but whose puppeteers are fully visible on stage – a fact that somehow increases audience sympathy.

"Ms Taymor, a maverick artist known for her bold multicultural experiments with puppetry and ritualized theater, has her own distinctive vision."

BEN BRANTLEY, THEATRE CRITIC, *THE NEW YORK TIMES*, 14 NOVEMBER 1997

YENTL

{ 1983 }

A Yiddish short story offered rich material for transformation into a joyous Hollywood musical. *Yentl* takes its feminist, cross-dressing protagonist straight to viewers' hearts.

▼ **Cross-dressing heroine**
Barbra Streisand in the starring role. After years of delays, she brought *Yentl* triumphantly to the screen, almost single-handedly.

Barbra Streisand first read *Yentl the Yeshiva Boy* by Jewish-American author Isaac Bashevis Singer in 1968, and spent the next 14 years trying to bring it to the screen. In 1973, she bought the film rights for her own production company, and by 1979 decided she wanted to direct as well. In addition, the screenplays crossing her desk simply did not satisfy, so she wrote her own script – which tells the story of a girl born with the soul of a man in the body of a woman. Raised by a doting father who teaches her Jewish scholarship in secret, the girl, called Yentl, escapes her small town after her father's death, cutting off her hair and dressing in his old clothes.

Disguised as a boy and calling herself Anshel, she is able to attend a yeshiva, an institution for religious and Talmudic study open to men only. Here, she befriends Avigdor, sharing everything with him, from hardships to passion for the written word. Little

> *"It might interest you to know that... she has completely captivated us all."*
>
> LETTER REGARDING BARBRA STREISAND FROM
> THE CAST AND CREW OF *YENTL*, TO LEE INTERNATIONAL FILM STUDIOS

KEY FACTS

🎥 **FILM**

🎬 **Director** Barbra Streisand

✉ **Screenplay** Barbra Streisand and Jack Rosenthal

🎵 **Music** Michel Legrand

𝄞 **Lyrics** Marilyn Bergman

🕐 **Running time** 131 minutes

📅 **Release date** 16 November 1983

⊙ **Key information**
The film won the 1984 Academy Award for Music (Original Song Score or Adaptation Score). The song "Papa, Can You Hear Me?" was nominated for Best Original Song.

wonder, then, that Yentl/Anshel begins to have feelings for Avigdor. This leads them both down a strange road, with Avigdor encouraging Yentl/Anshel to marry the woman he loves, Hadass, when he is prevented from doing so himself. Eventually, these tense scenarios are resolved with Avigdor being reunited with Hadass, and Anshel/Yentl leaving for America to start a new life.

A major theme that proceeds from this plot is Yentl's refusal to let being a woman hold her back. Thus we could call *Yentl* a feminist musical; for while other musicals might feature feminist songs, this musical focuses solely on the female lead, with the daring ploy that the only person who sings through the entire show is Yentl, allowing her suppressed feelings a voice.

LA CAGE AUX FOLLES

{ 1983 }

More than a great night out, *La Cage aux Folles* was also a milestone in the journey of gay men on Broadway to find open acceptance in what had long been seen as their secret home.

The success of the film *La Cage aux Folles*, which opened in the United States in 1979, had a significance that went far beyond the arthouse cinemas in which it was seen. Its title translating roughly as "The Cage of Crazy Women" (though *folle* was also a French slang term for "drag queen"), Édouard Molinaro's movie was loosely based on a 1973 play by Jean Poiret. This comedy about the collision of the gay and straight worlds explored in a witty and light-hearted way the tensions between a same-sex couple and the partners' families. This was arguably the closest such issues had ever come to the cultural mainstream.

STAGE ADAPTATION

While it might have been expected to follow almost inevitably, the transition from film to musical was not straightforward – producer Allan Carr could not acquire the rights to the film, so the musical had to be based on Poiret's original play, without Molinaro's modifications. There was additional uncertainty as to how well a gay-themed musical would go down with the theatregoing public, at a time when the AIDS epidemic was raging, in a climate of homophobic mistrust and fear. Director Arthur Laurents was wary, then, but found himself swayed by the passionate commitment of the lyricist Jerry Herman and the writer Harvey Fierstein.

PROUD CONVICTION

Much of this conviction found its way into the songs and texture of a musical drama that transcended the elegant triviality of its original. It is significant that everything started out from the show-stopping anthem "I Am What I Am". Herman had written this one song, Laurents was to recall, before any thought at all had been given to dialogue, music, or overall structure.

However, there is much more to the show than a *cri de cœur* (cry from the heart). The difficult ins and outs of the relationships are alternately amusing and poignant, while the songs – such as "A Little More Mascara" and "Masculinity" – underline the agonizing ironies in the lives of the show's protagonists, Georges and Albin. On the one hand, Albin describes his drag as the transforming persona that enables him to come to terms with himself and helps him "cope again", while "Masculinity" reminds us that the ways of the straight male are a sort of performance in themselves.

KEY FACTS

STAGE

Director Arthur Laurents

Book Harvey Fierstein

Music and lyrics Jerry Herman

Venue Palace Theatre, New York

Date 21 August 1983

Key information

An earlier attempt to bring the film *La Cage aux Folles* to the stage had been made by producer Allan Carr. Called *The Queen of Basin Street*, it was going to transfer the action to New Orleans. Jay Presson was to write the book and Maury Yeston the music, but Carr's new executive producers Fritz Holt and Barry Brown had reservations, wound this production up and started out afresh with the Herman version.

▼ Gay stand
George Hearn in full drag, pleading passionately for his rights as a homosexual man, in the original Jerry Herman-scored Broadway musical.

JERRY HERMAN (1931–)   **BIOGRAPHY**

Brought up in New Jersey, composer and lyricist Jerry Herman attended the University of Miami, where his sketchbook won him campus celebrity. Broadway beckoned for a young man flushed with naive success. Not surprisingly, the Big Apple proved a tougher nut to crack: *Parade* (1960) and *Milk and Honey* (1961, a show about the founding of the state of Israel) fared respectably, but *Madame Aphrodite* (1961) was a fiasco. His luck finally changed in 1964 with *Hello Dolly!* (see pp.160–61), while two years later *Mame* (see p.170) fared even better.

STARLIGHT EXPRESS

{ 1984 }

The ever-evolving hi-tech presentation of Lloyd Webber's 1984 roller-skating rock musical extravaganza has proved unstoppably popular with family audiences for three decades.

When composer Andrew Lloyd Webber (see pp.270–71) became a father in the late 1970s, he was keen to write a musical for his children based on the stories by Reverend W. Awdry about Thomas the Tank Engine and his locomotive friends. Uncomfortable with Lloyd Webber's ideas, Awdry refused the composer permission to adapt his books, whereupon Lloyd Webber devised new characters based upon a Cinderella-style scenario: Rusty is a put-upon steam engine determined to shine, Greaseball and Electra are bullying futuristic locomotives, and Starlight Express is a fairy godmother figure.

ASSEMBLING THE TEAM
The ideas for the show developed into a roller-skating spectacle, and director Trevor Nunn (see opposite), fresh from his triumph and collaboration with Lloyd Webber on *Cats* (see pp.228–31), was engaged. Richard Stilgoe, a musical TV performer who specialized in witty ditties and who had helped with "Jellicle Songs for Jellicle Cats" in *Cats*, was invited to provide the lyrics.

Arlene Phillips, known for her risqué routines with TV dance troupe Hot Gossip, was entrusted with the task of

"*The fastest musical in the universe!*"

ADVERTISING SLOGAN, THE STARLIGHTHALLE, BOCHUM, GERMANY

◀ **Aggressive modernity**
Ken Ard as Electra, the electric train and the embodiment of aggressive modernity, takes centre stage in the Broadway production.

production statistics over the whole run of *Starlight Express* had become part of the legend of the show: 27,600 pairs of skate laces, 27,000 skate wheels, 23,000 toe stops, 5,500 false eyelashes, 750 gallons of paint and varnish, 10 km (6 miles) of timber, two and a half acres of sheet wood, and 60 tonnes of steel.

BEYOND TRADITIONAL VENUES
Starlight Express was less successful on Broadway. It opened in 1987 and ran for 761 performances, but the appeal and longevity of the show lie beyond the traditional theatre venues. With multiple revisions, updated designs, rewrites (involving other collaborators including Lloyd Webber's son Alistair), the show has had multiple tours around the world, several revivals, and a four-year run in Las Vegas. Most astonishing of all, a permanent show of *Starlight Express* is still running in the purpose-built Starlighthalle in Bochum, Germany, and has been seen by over 15 million people since it first opened in 1988.

RELATED SHOWS

Cats, 1981, Andrew Lloyd Webber, Tim Rice (see pp.228–231)

Chess, 1984, Benny Andersson, Björn Ulvaeus, Tim Rice

The Woman in White, 2004, Andrew Lloyd Webber, David Zippel

▲ **Royal approval**
The London cast were introduced to Her Majesty Queen Elizabeth II when she attended the show in 1984.

reating choreography for the skating ast. "I was determined that whatever one could do on their feet as a dancer, one could do it on skates," said

Phillips, "and there's a lot you can do on skates that you couldn't possibly do on your feet."

SYNTHESIZER ROCK
Lloyd Webber used the futuristic setting to explore a range of contemporary, synthesizer-laden rock and disco styles in the score, while also incorporating blues ("Poppa's Blues"), gospel ("Light at the End of the Tunnel"), and melodic pop ("Starlight Express", "Only You").

Cats designer John Napier, a former colleague of Nunn's at the Royal Shakespeare Company and National Theatre, designed a remarkable set in the Apollo Victoria Theatre, London, which had to be specially modified. The skate track swooped through the audience, from the dress circle to the stalls. This was the most extraordinary aspect of a production that went all-out to present a dazzling visual spectacle previously unseen in live theatre. With the technical challenges of set, costume, and special effects mounting, the costs escalated to £2.25 million.

POPULAR APPEAL
The show opened in March 1984 to poor reviews, but awareness of this amazing entertainment spread rapidly among the audience Lloyd Webber was aiming at – ordinary families who were not necessarily regular theatre-goers. The original West End run lasted nearly 18 years. By the time it closed after over 7,000 performances, the

◀ **Disco dazzle**
The costumes and staging were designed to create a look that conjured up the disco-style dazzle of the contemporary dance scene.

SETTING THE SCENE

Like a painter with a blank canvas, the set designer takes an empty space and transforms it convincingly into any time or place, whether real or imagined.

Many months before casting even begins, discussions take place, usually between the director, choreographer, and scenic designer, to decide on the visual aesthetics of the musical. The scenic designer's job is to create a set that evokes the time and place for the unfolding of the story. To enhance this vision and to keep it coherent, he or she communicates with the lighting designer, costume designer, and wig and make-up designer, who use this as the basis for their own designs. In this way, every visual design element pulls together to help create the imaginary world in which the musical takes place.

TRANSPORTING THE AUDIENCE

A set design can be realistic, like the Paris Opera House for *The Phantom of the Opera*; representative, like the moving train tracks of *Starlight Express*, or expressionistic like Boris Aronson's original set for *Fiddler on the Roof*, inspired by the paintings of Russian-French painter Marc Chagall. Realistic or not, the set designer can transport the audience to a show boat travelling up and down the Mississippi River, a Jewish shtetl in turn-of-the-century Russia, a junkyard playground for cats, or the crumbling splendour of a fading Hollywood star's mansion.

ENTER THE PYROTECHNICS

Spectacle has always been a part of musical theatre. In the early days, large sets were often changed behind a curtain, in front of which a small group of actors performed a scene or song – and then the set was revealed. Today, however, when the scene shifts, the change can take place before the audience's eyes, making the transformation another part of the visual drama.

As ticket prices have risen, audiences have demanded more and more for their money. Combined with numerous technological advances, this has brought about a golden age of scenic spectacle. Set designers such as John Napier, who created extraordinary sets for *Cats, Les Misérables, Miss Saigon, Starlight Express*, and *Sunset Boulevard*, have led the way in creating greater and more elaborate visual feasts to help musicals transport their audiences and tell their stories.

At the same time, however, a string of shows, from *The Fantasticks* (1960) to *Once* (2011), has proved that minimal sets can be equally ingenious, and are just as capable of making an emotional impact on an audience.

▶ Spectacular *Starlight* set
The elaborate set required to stage *Starlight Express* has found a permanent home in a purpose-built theatre in Bochum, Germany.

"I wanted to be a set designer when I was young."

DAME JUDI DENCH, BRITISH ACTRESS, *THE GUARDIAN*, 14 OCTOBER 2012

SUNDAY IN THE PARK WITH GEORGE

{ 1984 }

More fun than its reputation would suggest, *Sunday in the Park with George* – a show that ponders the nature of art, love, and life – eventually received considerable critical acclaim.

In the early 1980s, playwright/director James Lapine introduced Stephen Sondheim (see pp.220–21) to *Sunday Afternoon on the Island of La Grande Jatte*, a famous 1884 painting by the French artist Georges Seurat. Sondheim and Lapine speculated on the narrative possibilities of the characters in the painting. Lapine quickly sketched out a fictitious version of the artist's life. Sondheim worked more slowly, but eventually detected musical clues in Seurat's art and began to create what he called "an aural equivalent of Seurat's colour scheme".

DEVELOPING THE IDEA

However, even as the musical ideas flowed, Lapine and Sondheim remained unsure how to proceed. In July 1983, they presented the one act work-in-progress starring Mandy Patinkin and Bernadette Peters at Playwrights Horizon, an Off-Broadway theatre. The show remained in progress right up to the wire, with Sondheim still writing songs only days before its Broadway opening.

SEURAT'S SUNDAY
The story concerns George obsessively painting characters in the park. His long-suffering mistress, Dot, aggrieved at George's absorption in his work, goes off with Louis, the baker, leaving George to himself and his art. Act two features George's great-grandson, also an artist, whose relationship with the contemporary art world is troubled.

FLAWED MASTERPIECE
The majority of the reviews were cool and even the best ones suggested that this was a "flawed masterpiece". Sondheim's shimmering and brilliant score was too rich for most. However, it won the 1985 Pulitzer Prize for Drama, and subsequent revivals and the passage of time have cemented the show's reputation.

KEY FACTS

STAGE

Director James Lapine
Music and lyrics Stephen Sondheim
Book James Lapine
Venue Booth Theatre, New York
Date 2 May 1984

Key information
The original show won Drama Desk Awards (1984) for Outstanding Musical, Outstanding Author, Outstanding Director, Outstanding Lyrics, Outstanding Orchestrations, Outstanding Lighting Design, Outstanding Set Design, and Outstanding Special Effects. It also won two Laurence Olivier Awards: Best New Musical in 1991 for the UK premiere, and Best Musical Revival in 2007. The show ran for a total of 604 performances.

◄ **Re-creating the painting**
Act One ends with a stunning live re-creation of Seurat's painting of *La Grande Jatte*, a scene that has received critical accolades for its design.

> "*Brilliant, deeply conceived, canny, magisterial and by far the most personal statement I've heard from you thus far.*"

LEONARD BERNSTEIN, LETTER TO STEPHEN SONDHEIM, 1983

LINIE 1

{ **1986** }

The most successful German musical ever, *Linie 1* captured the imagination of the German public and has been regularly revived since its first performance in 1986.

The show takes its name from a line on the Berlin metro system. The setting is West Berlin before reunification. At that time, Linie 1 ran from the far west of the city to the south, crossing both poorer and wealthier parts of the city. Linie 1 was popularly known as the Orient Express, because it terminated in Kreuzberg, an area where many Turkish families lived.

A MODERN QUEST

Linie 1 tells the story of a young girl who runs away from her provincial hometown and arrives at the central station in Berlin early in the morning. She is searching for her Prince Charming, a rock musician, who had invited her to come to Berlin but has not given his address. She starts her journey on Linie 1 to find him.

The girl encounters a kaleidoscope of urban characters: punks, prostitutes, office workers, schoolgirls, and old people, strange, sad and happy characters, immigrants, and Nazi widows. Grips Theatre described the essence of the musical in its programme notes: "Her [the girl's] naivety acts as a

"This metro ride is as fresh as on the first day. It is funny and still young at heart."

REVIEW OF THE SHOW'S 1,000TH PERFORMANCE, **BERLINER MORGENPOST**, APRIL 2001

catalyst provoking contacts, actions and reactions, which otherwise would not take place. It's a show, a drama, a musical about living and surviving in a large city, hope and adaptation, courage and self-deception, to laugh and cry at, to dream, and to think about oneself."

ANTI-ESTABLISHMENT MESSAGE

The Grips Theatre was founded in 1972 by Volker Ludwig and others. Ludwig and his friends were part of a left-wing anti-establishment political grouping. They wanted to encourage children and teenagers to express their opinions and fight

for their rights. The journey made by the lead character in *Linie 1* sees the main character overcoming her shyness and making friends with social outcasts and criminals. Not everybody liked this message when the musical was first performed. Conservative politicians and newspapers claimed it would set a bad example to young people. Three decades later, the show has become accepted as one of the best musicals in the German language.

TIMELY SCREENING

In 1988, a film adaptation of *Linie 1* had its premiere in West Germany. One year later, six months before the fall of the Berlin Wall, it was also shown for the first time in East Germany.

The film was directed by Reinhard Hauff, who also wrote the screenplay based on the musical by Volker Ludwig. The story, especially the ending, was reworked and some songs were changed, notably "I Hate You" was replaced by "Berlin, Berlin".

KEY FACTS

STAGE

Director Wolfgang Kolneder

Music Birger Heymann and the band No Ticket

Book and lyrics Volker Ludwig

Venue Grips Theatre, Berlin

Date 30 April 1986

⊙ **Key information**
Grips Theatre toured with an English version – *Line 1* – in Europe, the US, Israel, India, Australia, and Russia. The show has also been performed by more than 70 theatre groups, in Germany and elsewhere. The Korean version was shown over 4,000 times in Korea, as well as in China and Japan.

CAST

Janette Rauch Girl
Dieter Landuris Boy called Bambi, widow, strange boy
Else Nabu Lady, traveller
Petra Zieser Drug-addicted girl called Lumpi, singer
Christian Veit Drunken man, widow, crazy man
Claus-Peter Damitz Pimp, widow, rockstar
Dietrich Lehmann Employee, widow.
Christiane Reiff Old woman, kiosk saleswoman, employee.
Thomas Ahrens Punk, ticket inspector.
Folkert Milster Writer, skinhead,
Ilona Schulz Poor woman called Maria, tourist guide

◀ Urban encounters
The show exposes the rich variety of humanity under the surface anonymity of the archetypal environment of a city metro carriage.

LES MISÉRABLES

{ 1985 }

Les Misérables, one of the most popular and successful musicals ever, initially started out as a French concept album, and ultimately became the longest-running musical in the history of the West End, as well as an international smash hit.

▼ **Broadway hit**
The cast sing "One Day More" during the Broadway production of the show, which ran for 16 years and 6,680 performances from 1987 until 2003.

In 1978, the prolific songwriting team of Claude-Michel Schönberg and Alain Boublil (see pp.258–59) began work on a stage musical adaptation of what is considered to be one of the greatest novels of the 19th century. *Les Misérables*, written in 1862 by French novelist Victor Hugo, is a tale of the struggle of petty criminal Jean Valjean to redeem himself. Boublil had the idea in London while he was watching a West End revival of the musical *Oliver!* He said, "As soon as the Artful Dodger came on stage, Gavroche came to mind." Two years' work yielded first a concept album and then an early production at the Palais des Sports in Paris.

In 1983, shortly after *Cats* (see pp.228–31) opened on Broadway, a copy of the French album of *Les Misérables* landed on the desk of London-based theatre producer Cameron Mackintosh (see pp.232–33). Writing later, he said, "when I first heard the French concept album, a dream of what the show could be flashed through my mind".

KEY FACTS

🎭 STAGE

🎬 **Directors** Trevor Nunn, John Caird

🎵 **Music** Claude-Michel Schönberg

𝄞 **Lyrics** Alain Boublil, Herbert Kretzmer, Jean-Marc Natel

☑ **Set** John Napier

🎭 **Venue** Barbican Theatre, London

📅 **Date** 8 October 1985

⊙ Key information

The show has won three Olivier Awards, including, in 1985, Best Actress in a Musical (Patti LuPone), and in 2012 and 2014, the Audience Award for Most Popular Show. It has also won eight Tony Awards and over 100 major theatre awards worldwide, and been seen on stage by over 70 million people in more than 44 countries. It has been translated into 22 different languages.

In partnership with the Royal Shakespeare Company, Mackintosh then began a development process that took two years to complete.

PICKING THE TEAM

The original French lyrics were written by Alain Boublil and Jean-Marc Natel. Cameron Mackintosh commissioned South African journalist and lyricist Herbert Kretzmer to write the English language lyrics, with additional material provided by librettist and drama critic James Fenton.

The design team included set designer John Napier, whose work had come to define the spectacle-heavy mega-musicals of the 1980s and 90s. Napier's design for *Les Misérables* literally revolved around a large turntable, which provided directors Trevor Nunn and John Caird with wonderfully creative staging opportunities. The turntable in *Les Misérables* reportedly made 25 turns in each performance.

The show continued to develop throughout the rehearsal process. Mackintosh explained in an interview that "'Stars' was written because Roger Allam pointed out that his character, Javert, needed to express why he was so driven." "On my Own" had originally been a song for Fantine called "L'Air de la Misére", but the creators gave the song to Eponine so that Fantine would not sing two ballads in a row just before dying.

Known for her work with the Royal Shakespeare Company, costume

◄ **Owning the role**
Such was his impact that Cameron Mackintosh insisted that Colm Wilkinson play Jean Valjean in the show's first Broadway run.

designer Andreane Neofitou created the costumes for *Les Misérables*. Other members of the creative team included David Hersey (lighting designer), John Cameron (original music supervisor), and Kate Flatt (choreographer).

As well as Roger Allam as Javert, the original London cast featured the Irish tenor Colm Wilkinson as Jean Valjean, skyrocketing him to stardom, and the established American musical star Patti LuPone as Fantine.

STANDING OVATION

Despite a ten-minute standing ovation on opening night, the reviews of that original London production were overwhelmingly negative, referring to the pop-opera as witless, synthetic, and melodramatic. But audiences disagreed; the show proved immediately and overwhelmingly popular with the general public. Cameron Mackintosh recalls the morning after opening, despite being devastated by the reviews, calling in for a report from the box office and being stunned to discover that a record-breaking 5,000 seats had been sold so far that day.

WEST END TRANSFER

The show transferred immediately from the Royal Shakespeare Company's home at the Barbican Centre to the Palace Theatre in London's West End. The show ran just short of 20 years at this prime London venue, before moving to the Queen's Theatre for the next leg of its record-breaking 30-year run, so far. The New York production of *Les Misérables* opened at the Broadway Theatre on 12 March 1987.

BREAKING RECORDS

The show is the longest-running musical ever in the West End, and second longest in the world after *The Fantasticks* (p.145), a musical that opened off-Broadway in 1960 and ran

for 42 years. To celebrate the 25th anniversary in October 2010, three productions ran in the West End simultaneously and the show's production was updated. This updated version spurred revivals and new tours across the world. By the end of 2014, *Les Misérables* had brought in more than US$1.8 billion at the box office.

▲ **Original poster**
The image of a waif-like girl on the original poster captured the public imagination and remains part of the show's identity.

"... a lurid Victorian melodrama produced with Victorian lavishness."

FRANCIS KING, REVIEWER, *SUNDAY TELEGRAPH*, 1985

STORYLINE

Set in 19th-century France, the story follows the life of Jean Valjean, a man imprisoned for stealing bread to feed his family. He rejects a life of crime but his past haunts him as he tries to redeem his life, improve his place in society, and to raise Cosette, a young girl entrusted to him by her dying mother. But he and Cosette become embroiled in the political unrest in Paris with ultimately tragic results.

ÉPONINE SINGS "ON MY OWN"

PLOT OVERVIEW

1815, DIGNE

Having paid his debt to society, Jean Valjean is released from the chain gang he has been serving on, only to realize that the stigma will follow him forever **1**. He steals from the kindly Bishop of Digne, who lies in order to set the re-arrested Valjean free.

1823, MONTREUIL-SUR-MER

Valjean has assumed a different identity and become a successful factory owner, and mayor **2**. His workers demand the dismissal of Fantine, another worker, for having an illegitimate child **3**. To buy food and medicine for her daughter, Fantine sells her hair, her locket, and her body **4**.

Fantine is unfairly arrested, but Valjean has her taken to the hospital, not prison **5**. Arresting officer Inspector Javert suspects he knows Valjean from the chain gang. Valjean promises the dying Fantine to care for her daughter, Cosette **6**, but when Javert arrives to arrest him, Valjean flees.

1823, MONTFERMEIL

Fantine had placed Cosette in the care of the cruel innkeeper and his wife, the Thénardiers **7 8**. Valjean pays for her release and takes her to Paris with him.

1832, PARIS

There is political unrest in Paris. The Thénardiers now lead a street gang and attack Valjean and Cosette, but they are rescued by Javert, who does not recognize Valjean until they have escaped. The Thénardiers' daughter, Éponine, is in love with the revolutionary student Marius, but he loves Cosette.

THE SONGS

Prologue: On Parole
Valjean

I Dreamed A Dream
Fantine

Lovely Ladies
Sailors, Whores, Fantine, Pimp

Who Am I?
Valjean

Fantine's Death: Come to Me
Fantine, Valjean

Master of the House
Thénardier, Madame Thénardier

Castle on a Cloud
Young Cosette

★ *In 2009, Scottish talent-show contestant Susan Boyle sang, "I Dreamed a Dream" on Britain's Got Talent on UK television. The subsequent YouTube recording was watched by millions of people. Worldwide, ticket sales for the musical suddenly spiked.*

At the End of the Day
Fantine, Valjean, Company

THE THÉNARDIERS PERFORM "MASTER OF THE HOUSE"

"*To love another person is to see the face of God.*"

VICTOR HUGO, *LES MISÉRABLES*, 1862

1832, PARIS

Among the revolutionary students ⑨, Éponine agrees to help Marius find Cosette, which she does. She also prevents her father's gang from robbing Valjean's house. Javert discovers Valjean has resurfaced ⑩. Valjean tells Cosette they must flee again.

The students, led by Enjolras, prepare to build the barricade ⑪, ⑫. Marius sends Éponine with a letter for Cosette ⑬, which Valjean intercepts ⑭. The barricade is built ⑮. Éponine grapples with her feelings for Marius ⑯. Javert is revealed as a spy ⑰ thanks to a street child, Gavroche ⑱. Éponine is killed returning to the barricade ⑲. The students prepare for the battle ⑳.

ENJOLRAS MANS THE BARRICADE

Valjean prays to God to protect Marius ㉑. He has a chance to kill Javert, but releases him. During the second attack, Gavroche is shot ㉒; everyone at the barricade is killed except for Marius ㉓. Valjean carries the unconscious Marius into the sewers, where Javert corners him and he pleads for the chance to take Marius to a hospital. Javert relents, having known Valjean's mercy, but unable to reconcile his beliefs, he kills himself ㉔. Marius mourns the death of his friends ㉕.

Nursed by Cosette, Marius recovers and they marry. Marius is unaware that it was Valjean who saved him until the Thénardiers try to blackmail him. Learning the truth, all is revealed to Marius and Cosette before Valjean dies ㉖.

Stars — Javert
ABC Café/Red and Black — Enjolras, Marius, Students,
Do You Hear the People Sing? — Enjolras, Company
One Day More — Company
A Heart Full of Love — Marius, Cosette, Éponine
Javert's Arrival — Javert, Enjolras
On My Own — Éponine
Upon These Stones — Enjolras, Javert, Marius, Eponine, Valjean
Little People — Gavroche
A Little Fall of Rain — Éponine, Marius
Drink With Me — Students, Marius
The Second Attack/Death of Gavroche — Gavroche, Enjolras, Marius, Students
Bring Him Home — Valjean
The Final Battle — Marius, Enjolras, Students
Javert's Suicide — Javert
Empty Chairs and Empty Tables — Marius
Valjean's Death — Valjean
Look Down — Gavroche, Enjolras, Marius, Company

⭐ Gavroche's song "Little People" was dropped from the 1987 Broadway production.

THE PEOPLE SING "LOOK DOWN"

ÉPONINE DIES IN MARIUS'S ARMS

MEGA MUSICALS

The 1980s and 90s were dominated by a new kind of musical. Standing front and centre on the world's stages, the shows were dramatic in nature, highly popular, and changed musical theatre forever.

Often described as "mega muscials", shows such as *Cats*, *Starlight Express*, *The Phantom of the Opera*, *Les Misérables*, *Miss Saigon*, *Chess*, and *Sunset Boulevard* have proved enduringly popular with theatregoers. Many of them have enjoyed exceptionally long runs in the West End, on Broadway, and in major cities around the world.

Although ultimately uplifting, mega musicals tend to draw material from epic tragedies of abandonment, loss, and oppression – but the combination of human endeavour, courage in the face of adversity, romance, and passion gives their stories a timeless appeal. Mega musicals do, in fact, share many of the traits of classical opera. They are often completely or predominantly sung, with little or no spoken dialogue. Dramatic situations are enhanced by highly emotive scores – generally featuring elements of rock or pop – with heart-rending scenes designed to trigger an emotional response. They also push boundaries using high-tech special effects to create iconic moments and move the narrative on. In *Cats* (see pp.228–31), a giant tyre transports Grizabella to the Heavyside Layer, while in *Miss Saigon* (see pp.256–57) a deafeningly realistic helicopter sweeps the Americans away to safety.

INTERNATIONAL ICONS

A high proportion of mega musicals began their life in London; many were written by Andrew Lloyd Webber (see pp.270–71) or the French duo Claude-Michel Schönberg and Alain Boublil (see pp.258–59), whose most popular shows were produced by Cameron Mackintosh (see pp.232–33). Powerful stories, rousing scores, creative sets, and special effects meant there was no need for "names" to attract audiences, and it became possible to mount almost identical shows with the same high production values simultaneously across the world. Strong logos also evolved to promote each show: *Cats* is instantly known by the silhouetted dancers reflected in a pair of cat's eyes; for *Miss Saigon* a helicopter and a young girl's face were artistically combined against a setting sun.

▶ **International recognition**
The image of Little Cosette has become a global symbol for Victor Hugo's classic story of *Les Misérables*.

"Musicals are pleasure machines; vast theatrical mechanisms to generate rapture, exhilaration and joy."

DAN REBELLATO, PLAYWRIGHT, *THE GUARDIAN*, 18 JANUARY 2011

THE PHANTOM OF THE OPERA

{ 1986 }

The story of the hideous but gifted Phantom and his protégée, Christine, is the ultimate Gothic romance. Andrew Lloyd Webber seized on it to create his most operatic work, which has enthralled millions around the world.

This record-breaking show sprung from the long-held desire of Andrew Lloyd Webber (see pp.270–71) to create a romantic piece of musical theatre. In 1984, he contacted producer Cameron Mackintosh (see pp.232–33) after reading a rave review of a version of the story playing at London's Theatre Royal Stratford East.

THE SEARCH FOR A LYRICIST

The first act of *The Phantom of the Opera* was presented to a small invited audience in 1985, with lyrics written by Richard Stilgoe. Lloyd Webber was uncertain Stilgoe was the right person to write all the lyrics for such a romantic piece. He approached Tim Rice, with whom he had collaborated on *Evita* (see pp.208–209), but Rice was too busy with his own new show *Chess* (1986). Lloyd Webber and Mackintosh

▲ **Unmistakable symbol**
The half-mask worn by Ramin Karimloo as the Phantom in 2008. This iconic design has become the unmistakable symbol of the musical.

then approached Alan Jay Lerner, writer of classic musicals such as *My Fair Lady* (see pp.120–21) and *Camelot* (see p.144), who was an old friend of them both. He was very keen to be involved, but three weeks later had to withdraw due to ill heath. Finally, a young unknown called Charles Hart was chosen and finished the lyrics in three months.

TOP TEAM

Harold Prince, who had directed Lloyd Webber's *Evita*, was invited to direct the show and Gillian Lynne, who had worked on *Cats* (see pp.228–31), was the choreographer. For the sets and costumes, Lloyd Webber chose a newcomer to commercial theatre, Maria Björnson, whose staging of William Shakespeare's *The Tempest* for the Royal Shakespeare Company had left a deep impression on Cameron Mackintosh. It was Björnson who had the idea for the Phantom's half-mask. This arose from necessity, as the original design, a full-face mask, blurred the vision and muffled the voice of the actor.

Lloyd Webber chose well-known actors, Michael Crawford and Sarah Brightman, as his two leads. Crawford had won a Laurence Olivier Award for the title role in the London production of the musical *Barnum* (see p.224), and Lloyd Webber knew his versatile voice and athletic acting were ideal for the Phantom. Brightman, who had been a classical soprano, had starred in the original West End production of *Cats* and was married to Lloyd Webber at the time. As he had done with *Jesus Christ Superstar* (see pp.184–85) and *Evita*, Lloyd Webber put out a record of one of the show's songs to test public reaction. The single, "The Phantom of the Opera", was released on 2 January 1986 and reached number seven in the UK charts – enough to spur Lloyd Webber on.

◄ **Crawford and Brightman**
Michael Crawford in his award-winning performance as the Phantom cradles Sarah Brightman as Christine, his protégée, in the original London production.

"Stars, spectacle, score, and story."

JACK TINKER, THEATRE CRITIC, *DAILY MAIL*, 10 OCTOBER 1986

A GOTHIC ROMANCE

The story tells of a horribly deformed composer who haunts the Paris Opera from an underground cavern ("The Phantom of the Opera"), where he writes music for his beautiful protégée, Christine Daaé ("The Music of the Night"). Christine is horrified by the Phantom but feels pity for him ("I Remember/Stranger Than You Dreamt It"). He terrorizes the theatre into promoting Christine ahead of the diva Carlotta, and romance blossoms as Raoul, the patron of the opera house, offers to protect Christine ("All I Ask of You"). She unmasks the Phantom as he appears in his own opera ("The Point of No Return"), whereupon he seizes her, and is pursued by Raoul and the mob. Christine saves the Phantom with a kiss and he disappears, leaving only his mask behind.

THE BIGGEST SHOW IN TOWN

The opening at Her Majesty's Theatre in London received rave reviews and the show immediately became the hit of the season. Its popularity stretched well beyond its opening season and the production reached 11,000 performances on 19 March 2013. *The Phantom of the Opera* has been seen in more than 150 cities and grossed more than US$6 billion worldwide.

A film adaptation of *The Phantom of the Opera* was released in 2004, produced by Lloyd Webber and directed by Joel Schumacher. The cast included famous names, such as Gerard Butler as the Phantom, Emmy Rossum as Christine, Miranda Richardson as Madame Giry, and Minnie Driver as Carlotta. The film was a commercial success, grossing more than US$150 million worldwide.

▶ **Award-winning scenery and staging**
Maria Björnson won a Tony Award for Best Scenery and Costume. Here the Phantom is wearing his Red Death mask for the Masquerade scene.

Butterfly

Most
important
Dancer
'leads'
Chorus

(142)

Phantom of the Opera 'Her Majesties T

Flower

3 Dancers Masquerade 2.1.

(141)

Maria Björnson

LOOKING
THE PART

The work of the costume and makeup designer plays a vital role in bringing a show to life. As aphorist Mason Cooley rightly said, "Clothes make a statement. Costumes tell a story".

The characters backstage in the Paris Opera House at the turn of the century; the lions, hyenas, and other denizens of the African veldt; witches green and white, and other inhabitants of Oz – eight times a week actors around the world transform themselves into these characters and more. Facilitating this transformation is the work of the costume and make-up designer.

Long before the curtain goes up, the actor playing the title role in *The Phantom of the Opera* (see pp.252–53) undergoes a transformation as a bald cap is fitted to his head and adhesive is used to apply prosthetic pieces to his face. These are blended with make-up to match his skin tone. The wires and mouthpiece of his microphone are blended in as well. Once his wig and the famous half-mask are in place, he is ready to be helped into his costume by the wardrobe assistant, or "dresser".

◀ Masquerade
The late Maria Björnson, a highly creative costume designer, was responsible for these evocative designs for *The Phantom of the Opera*.

THE RIGHT LOOK
When creating a look for a character, a costume designer, who must be familiar with every aspect of fashion history, considers how the character would dress. But while costumes help establish character and the setting – whether in the past, present, or future – they do not always need to be realistic. Julie Taymor's evocative costumes for *The Lion King* (see pp.276–79) not only give clues as to the nature of each character, but suggest their emotional state and their relationships with others. Such representational designs send powerful nonverbal messages to the viewer, and enhance the unfolding story. In the same vein, purposely mixing costume styles and eras can bring out themes underlying the show, such as in the "steampunk" production *Spring Awakening* (see pp.308–09).

Some costume designs have become iconic and are inextricably linked with particular shows, such as Irene Sharaff's Tony Award-winning designs for Anna's silk gown in *The King and I* (see pp.98–99), and the flamboyant red dress Sharaff designed for Dolly in *Hello, Dolly!*.

"Theirs is a monumental job, for they must be not only artists, but technicians, researchers, and historians."

AUDREY HEPBURN, BRITISH ACTRESS, THE ACADEMY AWARDS CEREMONY, 1968

MISS SAIGON

{ 1989 }

A tragic romance highlighting the misfortunes and victims of war, *Miss Saigon* was the second major offering of Claude-Michel Schönberg and Alain Boublil. They capitalized on the success of *Les Misérables*, but with a very different story.

In the aftermath of *Les Misérables* (see pp.246–49) it was clear that there was an appetite for musicals with a strong storyline. The source for *Miss Saigon* was Giacomo Puccini's 1904 opera *Madama Butterfly*, the tale of a Japanese geisha abandoned by her American naval officer husband, who later returns for their son. The inspiration for bringing the opera forward to the Vietnam War was a photograph, seen by Schönberg in a French magazine, showing an anguished Vietnamese woman sending her little girl to live with her father in America, presumably never to be seen again, an ending repeated in the plotline of *Miss Saigon*. In this way it was actual, more recent events that inspired the production, and not purely Puccini's famous opera.

Kim is an orphaned young woman, working in a seedy bar owned by The Engineer. On her first day, she meets Chris, a US Marine, who enters her club with a pack of friends. The two pledge their eternal love, but are interrupted by Kim's betrothed, Thuy, who flees with a broken heart. Chris promises to take Kim with him when he leaves Vietnam, but fails to do so.

TRAGIC ROMANCE
Cut to three years later, and Kim is living with her young son Tam, in a Saigon shantytown devoid of hope,

◄ Haunting inspiration
The Vietnam War-era photograph that inspired the development of *Miss Saigon* by Claude-Michel Schönberg and Alain Boublil.

◄ Iconic poster
The original poster for the production at the Theatre Royal, Drury Lane, in London, which opened in late September 1989.

while newly married Chris is living in America. Thuy arrives, offering a way out, but threatens to kill half-American Tam. Kim, frantic for her son, shoots Thuy, fleeing to Bangkok with The Engineer, who hopes to use Tam for a ticket of his own to America. The conclusion is heartbreaking, and reveals everyone to be a victim of the terrible conflict.

The music keeps the plot moving forward as the tragedy unfolds. It vacillates between swanky, gyrating melodies and solitary, haunting songs, with the effect that the audience has nowhere safe to land, rather like Kim herself.

Maverick John Napier's scenic design had an enormous impact on the musical. It was Napier who created *Les Misérables*'s famous barricade, and in *Miss Saigon*, he brought in a new shock tactic: a seemingly real helicopter appearing to land on the top of the American

Embassy in order to airlift the US citizens to safety. Other real-life elements included neon signs among the bars and clubs of Saigon, and an enormous statue of Ho Chi Minh. All this contributed to the feeling that the audience was somehow watching real events, actually taking place before their eyes in real time.

PROBLEMS ON BROADWAY
The concept of "real" took on another meaning with the transfer of *Miss Saigon* to Broadway, and accusations of racism emerged. The Actors' Equity Association (AEA), a powerful American trade union that manages live theatre, refused to allow Jonathan Pryce to perform the role of The Engineer, arguing that the prosthetics and make-up worn by Pryce to make his face more Asian was

◄ Heart-rending scenes
Lea Salonga and David Platt star as the tragic figures of Kim and her son Tam in the original West End production of *Miss Saigon* in 1989.

"Even Les Mis, which is an extraordinary emotional tour de force, doesn't cut you like a dagger in the way that Miss Saigon does."

SIR CAMERON MACKINTOSH, "BEHIND THE SCENES OF THE RECORD-BREAKING NEW *MISS SAIGON*", *THE TELEGRAPH*, 16 MAY 2014

offensive; AEA also pointed out that the role offered the opportunity for a lead role of Asian descent. In the event, AEA bowed to pressure to allow Pryce to perform, but many industry experts believed that the show suffered for it,

winning only three of the 11 Tonys for which it was nominated, although one of these was won by Pryce. In the 2014 revival, in London, the part of The Engineer was played by Filipino actor Jon Jon Briones.

The combination of sensational scenery and stimulating music, combined with a gripping plotline that was at once both old and new left *Miss Saigon*'s audiences both anguished and enthralled.

CAST LIST

Jonathan Pryce The Engineer, aka Tran Van Dinh
Lea Salonga Kim
Simon Bowman Christopher "Chris" Scott
Claire Moore Ellen
Peter Polycarpou John Thomas
Keith Burns Thuy
Isay Alvarez Gigi Van Tranh
Allen Evangelista/Wasseem Hamdan/David Platt Tam

▼ Pyrotechnic effects
"The Morning of the Dragon" scene from Cameron Mackintosh's West End production, staged in 2014 and directed by Laurence Connor.

CLAUDE-MICHEL SCHÖNBERG AND ALAIN BOUBLIL

COMPOSER AND LYRICIST **1941– and 1944–**

The course of musical theatre history was profoundly altered when a French-born singer and songwriter of Hungarian descent met a music publisher from Tunisia. Their creative union was to prove exceptionally fruitful.

It happened quite by chance. For if Alain Boublil had not been driving through Paris with his car radio on that day in 1968, he would not have heard a song written by Claude-Michel Schönberg. And two of the most successful and longest-running musicals ever performed would not have been conceived.

Les Misérables (see pp.246–49), featuring music written by Schönberg and original lyrics by Boublil, has been seen by over 60 million people worldwide. Their second hit, *Miss Saigon* (see pp.256–57) was also internationally acclaimed.

The two men were born three years apart, Boublil in Tunis and Schönberg in Brittany. At the age of 18, Boublil moved to France, where he worked for a music publisher scouting for songwriting talent.

One day in 1968, he heard a song about a young girl bored with her life: *"Tous les jours à quatre heures"*. He tracked down the writer and did a deal to publish the song. "It was the first time anyone had really shown an interest in me as a songwriter," Schönberg told an interviewer three decades later. "I was flattered."

A NEW PARTNERSHIP
The two discovered that they had much in common, on several levels. Both had done economics degree courses, even though they hankered after musical careers. "We spoke the same language about popular music and songs and that's something you find very rarely in a lifetime," Boublil recalled. But it was a production of Andrew Lloyd

Webber's *Jesus Christ Superstar* (see pp.184–85), which Boublil saw in New York, that launched his collaboration with Schönberg. The show fired his desire to write "a through-sung musical in operatic form" and after much thought he conceived the idea of a musical based on the French Revolution.

Schönberg, meanwhile, had been working on his singing and acting career, although he and Boublil remained friends. Now the two started work, with others, to turn Boublil's idea into what was to be the first rock opera in French. Schönberg wrote most of the music for *La Revolution Française*, in which he also played King Louis XVI.

▶ **French force**
The musicals of Schönberg (left) and Boublil were originally written in French, but this has not prevented their shows from receiving worldwide acclaim.

The following year, a song called *"Le Premier Pas"*, written and performed by Schönberg, became a hit in France, selling more than a million copies. Schönberg continued to record albums as a singer until 1985.

KEY WORKS

La Revolution Française, 1973
Les Misérables, 1980 (see pp.246–49)
Miss Saigon, 1989 (see pp.256–57)
Martin Guerre, 1996
The Pirate Queen, 2006
Marguerite, 2008

◀ Perfectionism pays off
Schönberg and Boublil inspect the Cameron Mackintosh set for *Les Misérables* prior to its London opening at the Barbican in 1985.

By the late 1970s, Schönberg and Boublil had moved on to their next project, a musical based on Victor Hugo's story *Les Misérables*. When it opened in its original French-language version, it was savaged by the critics – but audiences absolutely loved it. So

eight Tony Awards, including Best Musical and Best Original Score.

The production was soon in demand around the world, increasing pressure on Schönberg and Boublil to reproduce their success. For their next show, *Miss Saigon* (see pp.256–57),

transferred to Broadway, where the show earned US$24 million in advance bookings before it had even opened, in April 1991. Noted for its high production values, *Miss Saigon* ran for ten years both in London and on Broadway. It was revived in London in 2014 to mark the show's 25th anniversary.

LESSER TRIUMPHS
Schönberg and Boublil's later works have failed to match their earlier block-busting successes. *Martin Guerre* lacked the impact of *Miss Saigon*, but still managed to win an award. The duo's next musical, *The Pirate Queen*, was set in 16th-century Ireland. The show opened on Broadway at the Hilton Theatre in 2006 – but, despite a major marketing campaign, it closed after only 85 regular performances.

Schönberg composed a ballet score for *Wuthering Heights*, which was acclaimed by UK audiences in 2002. His next ballet, *Cleopatra*, also attracted

> ## "There's a kind of complementary relationship between us: I know where we have to go; he shows me the way."
>
> SCHÖNBERG ON BOUBLIL, 1998

lid London producer Cameron Mackintosh (see pp.232–33). He saw the show's potential and negotiated its transfer to London. The English-language production, with lyrics by Herbert Kretzmer, opened in 1985 and won

Schönberg and Boublil were drawn to the story of Cio-Cio San, the tragic heroine of Giacomo Puccini's 1904 opera *Madama Butterfly*. *Miss Saigon* is set in the 1970s during the Vietnam War (1965–73). Directed by Nicholas Hytner, with English lyrics by Richard Maltby Jr, the production premiered in 1989 at the Theatre Royal, Drury Lane. It then

favourable reviews. Yet he credits his collaboration with Boublil as being the most important thing in his life. He told an interviewer: "I achieved what I wanted to do."

▶ Long-running success
The cast of *Miss Saigon* at the 25th-anniversary performance of the show, staged at the Prince Edward Theatre, London, in September 2014.

FILM POSTER FOR LES MISÉRABLES

KISS OF THE SPIDER WOMAN

{ 1990 }

What makes a musical matter? Gritty realism meets movie fantasy in a powerful and searching drama that explores limits in heroic seriousness and human liberation.

S et in an Argentinean prison in the time of the military dictatorship, *Kiss of the Spider Woman* features two very different men who find themselves sharing the same cell. One, Luis Molina, is ostentatiously gay: a window-dresser by trade, he has been convicted of corrupting a minor. Determinedly frivolous, Molina has never in his life, it seems, entertained a serious thought nor questioned for a moment the values of a society that has discarded him as an outcast and a pervert. Escapism has been

his guiding principle: through sex and cinema in the outside world; now through his thoughts of the favourite movies whose plots he exhaustively retells to his cellmate here. As might have been expected, Molina's tastes run to the outlandishly melodramatic and the extravagantly romantic, his exotic imagination knowing no bounds.

The cellmate he regales with all this nonsense could hardly be more different. In some ways,

◀ **Penitentiary passion**
Jeff Hyslop replaced Brent Carver as Luis Molina in the Broadway production. The show was directed by the legendary Harold Prince.

Valentín Arregui is much more obviously admirable. Jailed for revolutionary activities against the government, he is a heroic idealist prepared to die for his beliefs. He has already held out under severe torture by the authorities. But the disgust Molina's decadence inspires in him is a clue to his limitations: his unbending puritanism and unreflecting *machismo*, for a start. Valentín has as much to learn from Luis as Luis – a deeper character than he may in fact first appear – does from him. And so, little by little, as the days go by, they do, in this moving story of mutual- and self-discovery.

KISS OF DEATH – THEN REBIRTH

Kiss of the Spider Woman was unleashed upon the world at the State University of New York's Performing Arts Center, at Purchase, NY. But this first performance was very nearly the show's last. A workshop presentation, never intended for

up to his expectations – and he said so, in no uncertain terms, in the next week's edition of his newspaper.

Kiss of the Spider Woman received the kiss of life when, in 1992, it was revived in Toronto, with Chita Rivera in the Spider Woman role. This proved successful enough to prompt a London

review, it was nevertheless attended by Frank Rich from *The New York Times*, drawn by the scale of the production and the calibre of its director – Harold Prince (see pp.210–11) – and his cast. Unfortunately, the show did not live

West End run later that year. In May 1993, it finally opened on Broadway, with Rivera in a part that she had made her own. In May 1995, a Spanish-language version opened at the Lola Membrives theatre, Buenos Aires.

> *"You're spending half the evening inside of somebody else's fantasy."*
>
> **JOHN KANDER**, COMPOSER

FIVE GUYS NAMED MOE

{ 1990 }

A forgotten chapter of entertainment history, brought back to exhilarating life for a new generation, *Five Guys Named Moe* was a timely reminder that great music never – really – goes out of style.

In 1943, the poster for *Five Guys Named Moe* promised that "The joint never stops jumpin'!", though in truth this musical movie short was quickly forgotten. As, almost, were Louis Jordan and his Tympany Five, despite having been among the most celebrated acts of the 1940s. Jordan's backing musicians had been the "five guys named Moe" of the comic call-and-response song he introduced them with at the start of the show.

Life became more difficult for performers like Louis Jordan. Though black – and proud – the "King of the Jukebox" took pride too in reaching across his country's racial barriers, selling as many records to white buyers as he did to African Americans. Times

changed, though, and as the 1950s wore on and gave way to the 60s, what had been his selling point left him between two stools. Jordan offered cheerful entertainment and gentle humour – but people now wanted something different.

LET THE GOOD TIMES ROLL

Clarke Peters, an American actor based in the UK, put together his own new *Five Guys Named Moe*. He managed to get his show a late-night spot at London's Theatre Royal Stratford East. The theatre's resident director, Philip Hedley, liked it so much that he worked with Peters to put together a full-scale musical. It had the thinnest of plots, involving a character named Nomax. He is broke and his girlfriend has left him, but when he sees five miniature characters named Moe climbing out of his 1930s-style radio to comfort him, things suddenly improve.

The music makes the show: some songs, such as "Saturday Night Fish Fry" and "Ain't Nobody Here But Us Chickens", had never been quite lost from the collective memory. Others were ripe to be rediscovered. Then there was the energy and

resourcefulness of a musical that was so obviously – as much for its cast as for its audience – amazing fun. Cameron Mackintosh was one of those who made the journey east and was responsible for its West End transfer.

▲ A rollicking good time...
The poster for Cameron Mackintosh's production promised great songs and music – and Louis Jordan's back catalogue never disappointed.

KEY FACTS

✺ STAGE

- 🎬 **Director** Charles Augins
- 📖 **Book** Clarke Peters
- 🎵 **Music** Louis Jordan
- 🎵 **Lyrics** Louis Jordan, Clarke Peters
- 🎭 **Venue** Lyric Theatre, London
- 📅 **Date** 14 December 1990

Key information

◉ *Five Guys Named Moe* ran for 464 performances, including previews. It won an Olivier Award for Best Entertainment. Charles Augins, the director/choreographer of the musical's West End run, remained in charge for its opening on Broadway on 8 April 1992.

"I was driving down and Louis Jordan's lyrics seemed to be talking to me."

CLARKE PETERS, LIBRETTIST

CRAZY FOR YOU

{ 1992 }

The Gershwin Brothers came back from the dead to breathe new vitality into the American musical with this show about a show reviving a dying town. And what a resurrection it was.

Many consider George Gershwin (see pp.24–25), whose compositions crossed over between popular and classical styles, to be among the greatest American composers of the 20th century. He is revered not just as a musician but as a fully qualified "composer", fit to be mentioned among the greats of the classical tradition. His lyricist brother Ira is scarcely less distinguished.

Girl Crazy came out as a stage musical in 1930. The show was an undoubted success and was the making both of Ethel Merman and Ginger Rogers. A film version of 1943, featuring Judy Garland and Mickey Rooney, took significant liberties with the plot. In between, an adaptation of 1932 had taken the stage musical's score more or less complete but left little of its action, making instead a raucous vehicle for the American vaudeville double act, Wheeler and Woolsey.

The reuse and reshaping of such material is not unusual in the history of musicals or musical theatre, and all of the variations were popular in their day.

GHOST WRITTEN?

The idea, then, that in 1992 somebody should announce a "new Gershwin musical comedy" is not so strange – even if George had been dead half a century, and Ira for almost a decade. Of *Girl Crazy*'s original 18 numbers, Ken Ludwig had kept only five for *Crazy for You*, though the remaining songs and score were all taken from other Gershwin shows.

FOLLIES BERSERK

In the story, his own dreams of making it in show business having failed ignominiously, Bobby Child is resigning himself to a career in his family's banking business. His first assignment is to go to the town of Deadrock, in Nevada. The town,

apparently in permanent decline and inhabited by a bunch of idle cowboys, lives down to its dismal name. The ironically named theatre, the Gaiety, is failing and Bobby must tell its owner, Everett Baker, that the bank is pulling the plug on its long-term loan. But Bobby falls in love with the place – and with Polly, daughter of the Gaiety Theatre's owner. She loves him too – until she discovers who he is and why he is in Deadrock.

The only way Bobby can think of beginning to redeem himself in her eyes is to save the theatre, and the only way he can think of doing that is to mount a spectacularly successful show, using the local cowboys as his cast. Fortunately, a group of girls from *Zangler's Follies* just happens to be vacationing nearby and Bobby is able to rope them in to help out. Crazy, indeed. But delightfully so, with spectacular choreography and a dazzling plot. The critics loved it.

KEY FACTS

🎭 **STAGE**

🎬 **Director** Mike Ockrent
📖 **Book** Ken Ludwig
🎵 **Music and lyrics** George Gershwin and Ira Gershwin
🎟 **Venue** Shubert Theatre, New York
📅 **Date** 19 February 1992

⊙ **Key information**

Crazy for You won the Tony Award for the Best Musical of 1992; Susan Stroman won the individual honour for Best Choreography. William Ivey Long won for costume design, while the show received nominations in just about every other category.

BIOGRAPHY

BRUCE ADLER (1944–2008)

Bruce Adler, who played Bela Zangler in the Broadway production of *Crazy For You* for the duration of its four-year run, was a living link to the roots of the musical in Yiddish theatre. In the 1940s and 50s, not just his parents but two of his uncles had been major figures in the Lower East Side's thriving scene. Adler made his Broadway debut in the 35th-anniversary production of *Oklahoma!* (see pp.58–61) in 1979. As well as *Crazy For You*, he performed in a number of other Broadway musicals, including *Oh, Brother!* (1981), *Sunday in the Park with George* (1984), *Broadway* (1987), and *Those Were The Days* (1991).

◀ **Spirit of the Thirties**
Crazy for You celebrated George and Ira Gershwin's music for a new generation – with plenty of visual glitz and glamour to boot.

ELISABETH

{ 1992 }

Behind the colourful foray into European politics and history, *Elisabeth* is an exploration of a woman's mind and the disturbing consequences of tragic loss.

History knows her as Elisabeth of Austria (1837–98), the wife of the Emperor Franz Joseph I, which made her the Empress of Austria and Queen of Hungary. To those who loved her she was Sisi, a fresh and affectionate young girl who slowly dwindled into a silent wife, increasingly withdrawn and eventually apparently edging over into madness.

When German lyricist Michael Kunze went into the subject of Elisabeth's life and conceived of it as a musical, he said it was a real intellectual and

Royal wedding
A scene from the 2012 revival staged in Vienna. Elisabeth is pictured with her husband, Franz Josef, at their wedding.

imaginative challenge for him. Here was a woman whose plight made her "Everywoman". Certainly, the ten million and counting theatregoers around the world who have seen *Elisabeth* since its opening have for the most part reportedly found it to be an overwhelming experience, learning much not just about Elisabeth but about themselves.

A MAD LIFE

Neglected by a buttoned-up husband and bullied by his domineering mother, Elisabeth was badly rocked by the death of her beloved daughter, Sophie, just two years old. After wrestling with these difficulties for years, she was derailed completely by the mysterious death of her eldest son, Prince Rudolf, in a seeming suicide pact with his young mistress at the imperial hunting lodge at Mayerling, in the countryside outside Vienna. The random coincidence that placed her in the path of an Italian anarchist looking for a royal to assassinate was just the crowning absurdity of what had come to seem an insane life. Kunze cooks the history books, perhaps, by having his story narrated by Elisabeth's killer, Luigi Lucheni. It makes their collision seem somehow inevitable, her death the logical conclusion to her life. Emotionally, though, it is a clever and convincing touch. With the help of Sylvester Levay's wonderfully atmospheric music, Kunze is able to reconstruct a royal life as it might have been experienced "from the inside" by a sensitive and intelligent woman

KEY FACTS

STAGE

Director Harry Kupfer

Book Michael Kunze

Music Sylvester Levay (including orchestrations)

Lyrics Michael Kunze

Venue Theater an der Wien, Vienna, Austria

Date 3 September 1992

Key information

Elisabeth's initial run, at Vienna's Theater an der Wien, continued for almost five years, until the beginning of 1997. After a nine-month break, the production resumed in the same venue, not finally closing until the end of April, 1998.

▲ **Wagnerian qualities**
Dutch actress Annemieke van Dam in the starring role in the Vienna, 2012. The dramatic sets and atmospheric music of the show were reminiscent of Wagnerian opera.

whose emotional resources and whose reserves of will were ultimately not quite enough to see her through what she was expected to endure.

THE POWER OF MUSIC

It is difficult, perhaps, for English speakers to imagine a German-language musical theatre untroubled by the intimidating precedent of Wagner's uncompromisingly weighty "music dramas". But Wagner understood one thing well: the power of music to plumb the depths of the individual heart and to give expression to the most intimately private feelings.

PUSHING BOUNDARIES

The modern musical's origin is closely linked to vaudeville and dance hall entertainments. Some modern shows build on this connection to combine music and theatre in innovative ways.

Many decades after the original vaudeville shows, a new kind of musical entertainment became popular. Neither book musical nor revue, these entertainments tend to be energetic and highly visual, having little or no reliance on the spoken or sung word, but still employing theatrical devices and visual humour.

In the mid-1980s, a New Age circus troupe called Cirque Du Soleil began in a small town just outside Quebec City in Canada. Cirque has grown and is currently the largest theatrical company in the world. As a character-driven circus show with continuous live music, Cirque has performed extensively around the world. The tremendous success of Cirque du Soleil has inspired a slew of imitators, all featuring a series of circus-like acts (without animals) and a contemporary musical sound.

MUSICAL EXPERIMENTS

In the late 1980s, a movement dubbed "New Vaudeville" began to make its presence felt. The two most prominent practitioners were American comic performers Bill Irwin and David Shiner. Self-named American "disillusionist" magicians Penn and Teller have also tapped into this movement, as have New Age juggling act The Flying Karamazov Brothers, who juggle objects offered to them by the audience, including bowling balls, skillets, and chainsaws.

Since 1991, the award-winning Blue Man Group has played to millions worldwide, with performances in New York, Boston, Chicago, Orlando, Tokyo, Las Vegas, and Berlin, to name but a few. The three Blue Men enthral their audiences with a unique form of entertainment – a mixture of music, comedy, art, and science.

Also in 1991, two percussionists and buskers from Brighton, England, created the choreographed theatrical percussion event *Stomp*, which has been successful around the world. Imitators, such as the Australian show *Tap Dogs*, have combined aspects of musical theatre, contemporary music concert, and street performance in an edgy, often boisterous new form. Likewise, *Riverdance*, a theatrical show consisting of traditional Irish music and dance, has inspired equally successful imitators since it was first performed in Dublin in 1994.

▶ **Thrilling innovation**
The visually stunning and inventive Blue Man Group forgoes spoken language in its highly entertaining musical show.

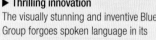

"… a time of newness: new music, new theatre and dance, new vaudeville."

THE NEW YORK TIMES GUIDE TO THE ARTS OF THE 20TH CENTURY, 2002

SUNSET BOULEVARD

{ 1993 }

An Andrew Lloyd Webber musical, *Sunset Boulevard* is based on American filmmaker Billy Wilder's 1950 Academy Award winning film. The stage musical has enjoyed long runs and extensive global tours.

▲ Film poster
The image of twisted celluloid that was used in this poster for the original 1950 film neatly conveys the warped atmosphere of the story.

In the early 1950s, American actress Gloria Swanson, the original star of the film *Sunset Boulevard*, had spent five years working on a stage-musical version with American screenwriter Richard Stapley and American composer/lyricist Dickson Hughs. They first called it *Starring Norma Desmond* and then *Boulevard!*. However, these efforts lapsed in 1957 at the request of Paramount Studios.

IN SEARCH OF A WRITER

In the early 1960s Stephen Sondheim (see pp.220–21) began working on an adaptation with Burt Shevelove but soon shelved the idea. In 1973, after the opening of *A Little Night Music* (see pp.190–91), librettist Hugh Wheeler approached Sondheim about writing *Sunset Boulevard*, for Angela Lansbury with American musical producer and director Harold Prince (see pp.210–11, who held the rights.

Prince had originally planned to work on this project with Andrew Lloyd Webber (see pp.270–71). Lloyd Webber had seen the original film in 1970 or 1971 and had almost immediately started working on a title song. In 1976, after Harold Prince approached him to make it into a musical, Lloyd Webber quickly responded, writing an idea for the moment when Norma Desmond returns to Paramount Studios.

"I am big … it's the pictures that got small!"

NORMA DESMOND, *SUNSET BOULEVARD* (CHARLES BRACKETT AND BILLY WILDER), 1950

Although there were further discussions with the British writer Christopher Hampton, these did not come to anything and the project was put on hold. During the years that followed, Sondheim was approached – and declined – to collaborate on the project, as did the songwriting duo John Kander and Fred Ebb.

LLOYD WEBBER SUCCEEDS

In 1991, working with novice lyricist Amy Powers (and later Don Black), Lloyd Webber composed a version of *Sunset Boulevard* that was performed at his Sydmonton Festival that year.

The Sydmonton Festival is held in a small chapel in Andrew Lloyd Webber's garden and is used to perform small-scale recitals to an audience of family, friends, and theatre acquaintances, to try out new material.

In the following year, a new version was written with lyrics by Don Black and Christopher Hampton. It was first performed at the 1992 festival, starring established American actress and singer, Patti LuPone, who specializes in live music theatre. The show was generally well-received and predictably a West End run followed.

As he had done on shows such as *Cats* (see pp.228–31) and *Les Misérables* (see pp.246–248), British designer John Napier's set provided state-of-the-art spectacle on a massive scale for the production in the Adelphi Theatre. The show's costumes were by Academy Award-winning designer Anthony Powell, who was nominated for a Tony Award for Best Costume Design.

A CRITICAL APPRAISAL

The show opened to mixed reviews in London. The biggest complaint from the critics was that Lloyd Webber had lost the black humour of Wilder's film in favour of the dark mood of the piece. Many critics praised the songs as some of Lloyd Webber's best while holding onto some reservations for the score overall. David Richards summed it up in his New York Times review, saying, "Mr. Lloyd Webber's score is full of rich and swelling melodies, although… when he latches onto an insinuating musical theme, there seems to be no such thing as one reprise too many."

BROADWAY CHANGES

Patti LuPone created Norma in the original West End production. She was contracted to play the lead again in the Broadway show, but Lloyd Webber and his production team brought in film star Glenn Close for the US production. LuPone sued for breach of contract. In the West End production, LuPone was followed by Betty Buckley, Elaine Paige, Rita Moreno, and Petula Clark.

Sunset Boulevard opened in Los Angeles and, when Close moved to New York to open the show on Broadway, Faye Dunaway, best known for her film role as Bonnie in *Bonnie and Clyde* (1967), was brought in to replace Close and keep the Los Angeles production running. However, shortly after rehearsals began the producers announced that Dunaway would not be able to continue with the performance and the production closed.

A US tour in 1998 starred British singer Petula Clark in the lead role. *Sunset Boulevard* also toured the UK in 2001, and in 2008, a fresh, scaled-down production was mounted by the Watermill Theatre in Newbury, UK.

Star turn ▶
The Hollywood star Glenn Close took the part of ageing actress Norma Desmond in the New York production.

KEY FACTS

❧ STAGE

- 🎬 **Director** Trevor Nunn
- 📖 **Book** Don Black, Christopher Hampton
- 🎵 **Music** Andrew Lloyd Webber
- 𝄞 **Lyrics** Don Black, Christopher Hampton
- ☑ **Design** John Napier (sets), Anthony Powell (costume)
- 🎭 **Venue** Adelphi Theatre, London
- 🗓 **Date** 12 July 1993

⊙ Key information

The 1995 Broadway production won seven Tony Awards: Best Musical; Best Original Score; Best Book of a Musical; Best Scenic Design; and Best Lighting Design; Best Performance by a Leading Actress in a Musical (Glenn Close); Best Performance by a Featured Actor in a Musical (George Hearn).

STORYLINE

Norma Desmond, a faded star of silent films, has become a recluse in her once spectacular Hollywood mansion on Sunset Boulevard. She meets a down-on-his-luck screenwriter, Joe Gillis, who sees an opportunity to solve his financial problems by offering to help Norma with a script she is writing. Their evolving relationship sets them on a course towards jealousy and insanity, concluding with the deluded Norma shooting Joe and mistaking the police for fans and film crew.

CAST			
Patti Lupone Norma Desmond		**Michael Bauer** Cecil B. DeMille	
Kevin Anderson Joe Gillis		**Gareth Snook** Artie Green	
Meredith Braun Betty Schaefer		**Harry Ditson** Sheldrake	
Daniel Benzali Max		**Nicolas Colicos** Manfred	

PARAMOUNT STUDIOS

NORMA DESMOND'S MANSION

PLOT OVERVIEW

Joe, a struggling screenwriter, tries to scrounge up work and hits on a pretty young female screenwriter, Betty, who proposes that they collaborate on a script **1**. Joe's car is going to be repossessed, so he flees, running out of gas and hiding his car in the garage of a crumbling old mansion on Sunset Boulevard.

Joe meets the mansion's owner, Norma Desmond **2**, the once great star of silent movies, unable to make the transition to talkies **3**. Her butler and chauffeur, Max, is also in residence.

Not realizing that she has been forgotten by the world, Norma is planning her comeback with a screenplay she has written called *Salome*. Joe convinces Norma to let him edit her script in exchange for room and board **4**. Max explains that Norma is "The Greatest Star of All" **5**.

Joe continues his work with Betty, their relationship turning romantic **6**. At home with Norma, they watch one of her old movies together **7**. Norma, who has been lavishing gifts on Joe, has fallen in love with him, becoming clingy and possessive **8**. Joe attends her New Year's party at which he is the only guest **9**, but becomes angry and storms out to his friend Artie's celebration **10**. On hearing that Norma has attempted suicide, Joe feels guilty and returns to Norma's mansion.

THE SONGS

Let's Have Lunch
Joe, Artie,
😃 *Sheldrake, Betty*

Surrender
😃 *Norma*

With One Look
😃 *Norma*

Salome
😃 *Norma, Joe*

The Greatest Star of All
😃 *Max*

Girl Meets Boy
😃 *Joe, Betty*

New Ways to Dream
😃 *Norma, Joe*

The Lady's Paying
Norma,
😃 *Manfred, Joe*

The Perfect Year
😃 *Norma, Joe*

This Time Next Year
😃 *Artie, Betty, Joe*

Sunset Blvd

THE ENTRANCE TO PARAMOUNT STUDIOS

A RELATIONSHIP DEVELOPS BETWEEN NORMA AND JOE

⭐ *The Los Angeles production included a new song, "Every Movie's a Circus", sung by Betty and Joe.*

"*All right Mr. DeMille, I'm ready for my close-up.*"

NORMA DESMOND, *SUNSET BOULEVARD* (CHARLES BRACKETT AND BILLY WILDER), 1950

ELAINE PAIGE AS
NORMA DESMOND

PARAMOUNT STUDIOS

Time has passed and Joe tries to justify his life as a kept man **11**. Norma is pleased with the arrangement **12**. A call comes from Paramount Studios and Norma is convinced that Cecil B. DeMille wants her and her script.

Norma makes a grand entrance at the studio **13**. Joe agrees to continue working with Betty. Norma and DeMille spend a moment reminiscing about her great career **14**. But Max learns that all the studio wants is use of Norma's car as a prop. He manages to get Norma back home without destroying her delusions.

NORMA DESMOND'S MANSION

Joe's relationship with Betty becomes increasingly romantic **15**. Norma busies herself with getting ready to "shoot her new film" **16**. Joe and Betty admit their feelings for each other **17**. Max threatens Joe that he will never let Norma be destroyed **18**. Norma discovers that Joe is cheating on her with Betty and tries to confront her, but Joe tells Betty that he enjoys being a kept man and to go back to her old fiancé. Joe announces he is through with Hollywood and leaving to return to Ohio. He tells Norma that *Salome* will never be filmed and that the world has forgotten her **19**.

Norma, now completely insane, shoots Joe and mistakes the police who arrive for studio personnel and fans **20**.

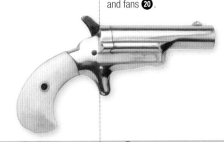

11 **12** **13** **14** **15** **16** **17** **18** **19** **20**

Surrender (reprise) 🙂 *Cecil B. DeMille*

Eternal Youth is Worth a Little Suffering 🙂 *Company*

New Ways to Dream (reprise) 🙂 *Max*

The Greatest Star of All (reprise) 🙂 *Max, Norma*

The Perfect Year (reprise) 🙂 *Norma*

As If We Never Said Goodbye 🙂 *Norma*

Girl Meets Boy (reprise) 🙂 *Joe, Betty*

Too Much in Love to Care 🙂 *Betty, Joe*

Sunset Boulevard (reprise) 🙂 *Joe*

Sunset Boulevard 🙂 *Joe*

⭐ *The title song was originally written in 1971 and parts of it were used in the score for the 1971 film* Gumshoe. *It was reworked for the musical.*

NORMA TAKES A PHOTOCALL AS SHE IS ARRESTED

ANDREW LLOYD WEBBER

COMPOSER AND IMPRESARIO **1948–**

A knighthood, a peerage, seven Tony Awards, three Grammys, seven Olivier Awards, a Golden Globe, an Oscar, and two international Emmys: Andrew Lloyd Webber's achievements are myriad.

◀ **Renaissance man**
Andrew Lloyd Webber, pictured sitting at his piano in 1996. His long career in the West End has seen a plethora of musical hits and popular songs. He continues to be hugely influential.

According to one observer, Andrew Lloyd Webber "has spun a worldwide empire unmatched in the history of musical theatre". Three of his shows – *Jesus Christ Superstar*, *Starlight Express*, and *Cats* – became the longest-running musicals in British theatre history, while *The Phantom of the Opera* has celebrated over 28 years in the West End. His company, the Really Useful Group, owns six London theatres, including the Theatre Royal, Drury Lane, and the London Palladium. Perhaps a career in music was inevitable for a boy born to a musical family. His father was an organist and composer, his mother a music teacher, and his brother Julian became a renowned cellist. However, even though he was a musical prodigy, playing the piano, violin, and French horn from an early age as well as publishing his own compositions at the age of nine, the young Lloyd Webber had another interest.

DIFFERENT DIRECTION

It was this that propelled him to Westminster School as a Queen's Scholar at the age of 13 and later to Magdalen College, Oxford, to read history. His love of music combined with a developing interest in musical theatre would pull him in a new direction.

When he was 17 he received a letter from a 21-year-old law student named Tim Rice (see p.185) who said he believed Lloyd Webber was seeking a partnership with a writer of lyrics. "I wonder if you consider it worth your while meeting me," Rice added. Clearly, Lloyd Webber did, because

"There's a very fine line between success and failure. Just one ingredient can make the difference."

ANDREW LLOYD WEBBER

◀ What's new, pussycat?
Cast members of the record-breaking *Cats*, here seen in their famous furry costumes in the original Broadway production.

the duo's collaboration began with a musical based on the life of Victorian philanthropist Dr Barnardo. Although *The Likes of Us* (1965) was not staged at the time, it led to a 20-minute pop-cantata version of a biblical story that would later become *Joseph and the Amazing Technicolor Dreamcoat* (1968).

Sticking with the biblical theme, their next collaboration was the rock-opera *Jesus Christ Superstar*, which began a tradition of recording an album of music first and then developing the play from it.

Collaboration with British playwright Alan Ayckbourn resulted in *Jeeves* (1974), but it found little success. Two years later, Lloyd Webber and Rice teamed up to create a concept album called *Evita*, which led to a stage show that opened in London in 1978 and on Broadway the following year.

◀ Honoured achievements
At the 29th Kennedy Centre Honours ceremony in Washington, D.C., with (from left to right) Zubin Mehta, Stephen Spielberg, Dolly Parton, and Smokey Robinson.

The 1980s saw the ending of the partnership with Rice, due to "creative tensions and artistic differences", but also the beginning of an era of Lloyd Webber blockbusters. For next came *Cats*, based on T.S. Eliot's *Old Possum's Book of Practical Cats* and produced by Cameron Mackintosh (see pp.232–33). Lloyd Webber had been a fan of Eliot's book of poetry since he was a boy, and was determined to transform its contents into a musical. It ran for 21 years in London to become one of the West End's longest-running musicals.

OVERSHADOWED

Cats has remained popular with audiences ever since, but even that success was overshadowed by Lloyd Webber's next show. *The Phantom of the Opera* (1986). It debuted in London before moving to Broadway, where it celebrated its 10,000th performance in 2012.

Lloyd Webber's 1990s creations included *Sunset Boulevard* (see pp.266–69) and a film version of *Cats*, but the heady days of the 1980s were not replicated. *Whistle Down the Wind* (1998) had its Broadway run cancelled after a dismal opening in

Washington, D.C. But an album of covers from it created a hit for Boyzone with "No Matter What".

Mixed reviews greeted *The Beautiful Game* (2000), and *The Woman in White* (2004). The star of Lloyd Webber's stage production of *The Sound of Music* (see pp.134–37) was discovered via a television reality show – an idea proposed by Lloyd Webber himself – as was that of his adaptation of *The Wizard of Oz*. As well as using the medium of television to find new stage performers, Lloyd Webber also runs the Sydmonton Festival at his Hampshire home, in order to "try out" potential new works. His Really Useful Group licenses alternative productions of his works around the country and is a hot house for developing new shows.

Andrew Lloyd Webber's hard work and success have made him one of the 100 richest people in Britain. Asked if he had any regrets, he admitted to an interviewer in 2013 that he missed not having a long-term working partner. He said: "I was really hoping that the Tim Rice relationship would have gone on but I'm obsessed with theatre and for Tim it's something that he does enjoy doing, is very good at, but it isn't his whole life as it is with me."

▲ **West End stars**
Andrew Lloyd Webber and Tim Rice are pictured with cast members Elaine Paige and Gary Bond at an *Evita* after-show party in 1979.

KEY WORKS

Joseph and the Amazing Technicolor Dreamcoat, 1968 (see p.187)

Jesus Christ Superstar, 1971 (see pp.184–85)

Evita, 1978 (see pp.208–09)

Cats, 1981 (see pp.228–31)

Starlight Express, 1984 (see pp.240–41)

The Phantom of the Opera, 1986 (see pp.252–53)

TIMELINE

22 March 1948 Born in Kensington, London, to William Lloyd Webber, director of the Royal College of Music, and Jean, née Johnstone, a music teacher.

1965 Studies history at Magdalen College, Oxford, but drops out to study music at the Royal College of music.

1965 Meets lyricist Tim Rice, with whom he will collaborate on his most successful shows.

1968 First performance of *Joseph and the Amazing Technicolor Dreamcoat*.

1971 *Jesus Christ Superstar* opens on Broadway; will be released as a film in 1973.

1976 Concept album *Evita* released; as a musical the Broadway production will win seven Tony Awards.

EVITA RECORD COVER

1981 *Cats* opens in London; the Broadway production will win Tony Awards for best musical and best score.

1983 Becomes the first composer to have three musicals playing simultaneously on Broadway and London's West End; he will duplicate the feat in 1988.

1984 *Starlight Express* opens in London.

1986 London premiere of *The Phantom of the Opera*; will become the longest-running musical in Broadway history.

1989 *Aspects of Love* opens.

1992 Knighted by Queen Elizabeth II to become Sir Andrew Lloyd Webber.

1997 Created honorary life peer, as Baron Lloyd-Webber of Sydmonton, in the County of Hampshire.

2015 Lloyd Webber's production of *School of Rock* opens on Broadway.

BRING IN 'DA NOISE, BRING IN 'DA FUNK

{ 1996 }

Bring in 'da Noise, Bring in 'da Funk tells the story of African-American history from slavery to the present day by combining tap dance with song, projection, and commentary. It burned brightly on and off Broadway from 1995–99.

▲ **Get down!**
The dynamic design of the cover of the Playbill for the original Broadway production promises an energetic dance show.

The principal creatives were George C. Wolfe, a major figure in New York theatre who conceived and directed the show, Reg E. Gaines (whose rap lyrics were set to funk and hip-hop rhythms by composers Daryl Waters, Zane Mark, and Ann Duquesnay), and Savion Glover, who provided the celebrated choreography.

Glover showed talent from an early age, soaking up the legacy and technique of tap dancing from a number of teachers, including the legendary Gregory Hines, who went on to claim that Glover is "possibly the best tap dancer that ever lived". For the choreography of *Bring in 'da Noise, Bring in 'da Funk*, Glover used classic tap as a starting point, then he put his own contemporary spin on the steps, a process he described as paying homage to the past masters.

The original cast included tap dancers Vincent Bingham, Jimmy Tate, Baakari Wilder, Dulé Hill (who went on to star in the television series *West Wing*), and Savion Glover himself, drummers Jared Crawford and Raymond King, and Ann Duquesnay, whose jazz-singing character served as a narrator. Successive casts also represented the very best of African-American talent.

DARKNESS AND LIGHT

The show swings between humour and pathos, including many dark moments as appropriate to its depiction of the experience of African Americans and how they inspired the work of pioneering dancers. The staging is often powerfully simple, with locations starkly suggested. It opens with a single beam of light from above picking out a shivering slave in the hold of a ship, chanting the names of the infamous vessels that brought Africans in chains to America. The birth of tap begins with their desire to find solace in moving their bodies to the traditional rhythms of their original culture, first to a drum beat, and then to the percussive sound of dance steps, which become more pronounced to form a prototype of the tap dance we recognize of today.

The story then progresses through how tap as an art form developed via the work of its most celebrated exponents. This development is shown in the context of a variety of landmarks in America's civil rights history. Sequences tell the story of the post-slavery migration from the South to the North, the rise of Harlem, the Black Power movement of the 1960s, and how tap dance slowly introduced black artistic expression into America's mainstream culture, despite the often humiliating way in which it was presented at first.

There are 27 scenes in all, including a one-man scene, titled "Green, Chaney Buster, Slyde", in which Glover pays tribute to the four great influences of his career – while dancing in each of their styles. Another tells the tale of a

◀ **Off-Broadway**
Dancers performing during *Bring in 'da Noise, Bring in 'da Funk*'s original Off-Broadway run at the Public Theater in 1995.

KEY FACTS

🎭 STAGE
- 🎬 **Director** George C. Wolfe
- 📖 **Book** Reg E. Gaines
- 🎵 **Music** Daryl Waters, Zane Mark, Ann Duquesnay
- 🎵 **Lyrics** Reg E. Gaines, George C. Wolfe, Ann Duquesnay
- 🎭 **Venue** Ambassador Theatre, New York
- 📅 **Date** 25 April 1996

⊙ Key information
Based on an idea by George C. Wolfe and Savion Glover, the show ran for nearly three years on Broadway, eventually closing on 10 January 1999 after a total of 1,135 performances. The show won four Tony Awards – for best actress, best director, best choreography, and best lighting design.

Powerful narration

[J]n Duquesnay, who acts as a narrator, tells [so]me of the boys "like it is", in a soulful scene [fr]om the original Broadway production.

[...] an travelling to Chicago, where he [h]as been led to believe life is better for [bl]ack people – only to discover rioting, [po]lice brutality, and death. The [p]enultimate scene, called "Taxi", is [bo]th funny and sad in equal measure.

It depicts four African Americans trying to hail a cab – a futile task, even though one of them has a signed copy of Colin Powell's autobiography and another has a gold credit card.

SPECIALIST DANCE SKILLS
Despite the critical and commercial success of *Bring in 'da Noise, Bring in 'da Funk*, surprisingly the show was not replicated in London's West

End as most Broadway hits are. Neither has it enjoyed significant touring and regional productions. Perhaps the specialist dance skills required to perform the piece presents too much of a challenge for producers and directors and prohibits revivals.

◀ **Tap wizard**
The dynamic and innovative tap-dancing routines of Savion Glover were the foundation for *Bring in 'da Noise, Bring in 'da Funk*.

> "*As dance, as musical, as theatre, as art, as history and entertainment, there's nothing Noise/Funk cannot and should not do.*"

MARGO JEFFERSON IN *THE NEW YORK TIMES*

RENT

{ 1996 }

Rent brought Broadway to a new kind of theatregoer: younger and perhaps less affluent. This new audience would bring something radical and fresh to Broadway too.

Jonathan Larson's *Rent* is generally described as a loose modern adaptation of Italian composer Giacomo Puccini's 1896 opera *La Bohème*. Like the great opera, it traces the tragic fortunes of a group of aspirational artists who have come to the big city, have not yet made it, and must consequently live in poor and cramped conditions in a quarter that, although apparently bright and lively, is also a place of struggle – and sometimes of misery.

In transporting the action from Paris at the end of the 19th century to New York's East Village in the 1990s, Larson was, of course, being enterprising: it made an established classic seem urgently topical at a stroke. Artists attempted to make it here, even if they were living next door to exotic dancers, rather than seamstresses.

PORTRAIT OF THE ARTIST

Born in White Plains, New York, in 1960, the author of *Rent* resembled his characters as the young suburbanite

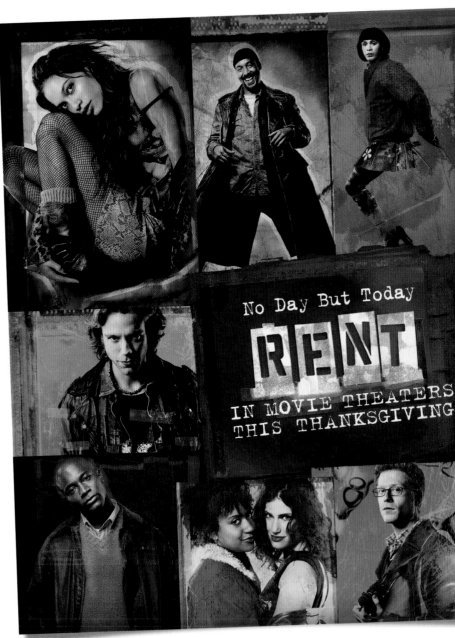

▶ Radical chic
The film poster for *Rent* is similar to the original Broadway poster, with images designed to appeal to a younger, more Bohemian audience.

who had dreamed of the metropolitan creative life and come to New York to find it. Jonathan Larson worked as a waiter while pursuing his "real" career.

DEATH AND DEBUT
Rent changed all that, although Larson was barely to live to see it – and he never knew quite how successful he had been. It was a big, sprawling, and incoherent work when it was taken up by James Nicola of the New York Theatre Workshop, with occasional highlights and innumerable flaws. Gradually, over weeks, they worked together and fashioned it into something like its final form – only for Larson to die suddenly, of an aortic aneurysm, the day before the first preview. This tragedy inevitably attracted unprecedented publicity for a show that was still very much an obscure Off-Broadway production.

That *Rent*'s appeal proved so much more enduring reflected the real depth of Larson's portrayal of his characters as well as the immediacy of the social and cultural crisis he identified. Now his memorial-in-action, *Rent* drew such crowds that it had to move to a bigger theatre. Offering tickets at prices they knew their audience could afford, the producers took over the near-derelict Nederlander Theatre and staged it there.

KEY FACTS

🎭 **STAGE**

🎬 **Director** Michael Greif
📖 **Book** Jonathan Larson
🎵 **Music and lyrics** Jonathan Larson
🎭 **Venue** New York Theatre Workshop
📅 **Date** 25 January 1996

◉ **Key information**
The original Broadway production of *Rent* won a host of prizes in 1996, including the Pulitzer Prize for Drama, four Tony Awards, six Drama Desk Awards, and two Theatre World Awards.

"That isn't our music uptown on Broadway; those aren't our characters;... our stories."

JONATHAN LARSON, COMPOSER

NOTRE-DAME DE PARIS

{ 1998 }

Not for the first time, the work of Victor Hugo brought something special to the French stage. *Notre-Dame de Paris* arguably saved the French musical to fight another day.

With its crazy flying buttresses, its iconic gargoyles, quirky statuary, and shimmering stained glass, a visit to Notre Dame is a highlight of any trip to Paris. It did not always seem so, though. Victor Hugo wrote his 1831 novel *Notre-Dame de Paris* specifically to draw attention to the cathedral's wonderful history at a time when the building had been neglected during what was self-consciously an "Age of Reason" – a period that rejected medieval superstitions – and more or less allowed to go to rack and ruin.

A MUSICAL RENAISSANCE

It would be an exaggeration to suggest that, by the 1990s, the French musical was in quite the state of decay that Notre Dame had come to be in Victor Hugo's day. At the same time, though, despite the strength of the association of France with the form through *Les Misérables* (see pp.246–49), the country's theatreland had been fairly quiet for some years.

Significantly, it was to be from outside France that the impetus for change was at last to come. Luc Plamondon, who wrote the book for the musical of *Notre-Dame de Paris*, is not actually French, but a French-speaking Canadian. As for composer Richard Cocciante, although born to a French mother in what was then Saigon, in the French colony of Indochina (now Vietnam), he had always regarded himself as an Italian, like his father. Between them, the two French-foreigners sensed something that France itself seemingly could not: that the French musical was ready to rise again.

And rise it did, triumphantly. *Notre-Dame de Paris* took France by storm with its passionate lyricism, its colour, and its gigantic scale. The production demonstrated an imaginative ambition that seemed a match for Hugo's own: here, we had "the age of the cathedrals", live on stage. But it wouldn't have been anything without Hugo's colourful cast of original characters – and one of the greatest love stories ever told.

GOTHIC ROMANCE

Gringoire, a poet, is our narrator. He introduces Frollo, Archdeacon of the Cathedral, and the rag-tag crew of beggars and refugees led by Clopin and his teenage ward, Esmeralda – a beautiful gypsy girl who is also Gringoire's muse.

They dance and sing together at the Feast of Fools and, as the highlight of their festivities, select a "King of Fools" – their choice being the deformed bell-ringer Quasimodo.

As far as Frollo is concerned, the Parisian poor are like an invading army threatening the sanctity of what he regards as his own little realm. He orders Phoebus, Captain of the Royal Archers, to take his men in and clear

◄ Cathedral gargoyle
Notre-Dame de Paris' bombastic scale and ambition was a match for both Victor Hugo's paean to a great monument and the cathedral itself.

the cathedral precincts, and Phoebus agrees to do his best. But Phoebus is also smitten by the sight of Esmeralda. Esmeralda is troubled by advances she has absolutely no desire for, but finds an unexpected friend in Quasimodo. Initially fearing him as a predatory monster, she is finally moved by his sufferings and learns to see him as the man of feeling that he is.

A musical never quite succeeds by spectacle alone: songs like "Belle" and "Vivre" tugged at the heartstrings and became smash hits in France.

"It's not difficult... Everyone loves love stories, no?"

GILLES MAHEU, DIRECTOR

KEY FACTS

🦇 **STAGE**
🎬 **Director** Gilles Maheu
📖 **Book** Luc Plamondon
🎵 **Music** Richard Cocciante
♪ **Lyrics** Luc Plamondon
🎭 **Venue** Le Palais des Congrès de Paris, Paris
📅 **Date** 16 September 1998

⊙ **Key information**
According to the *Guinness Book of World Records*, *Notre-Dame de Paris* had the most successful first year of any musical ever. The original costume design was by Fred Sathal, and set design was by Christian Rätz.

THE LION KING

{ 1997 }

Loosely based on Shakespeare's *Hamlet* and set in Africa, *The Lion King* features enchanting animal costumes, masks, and mime. Julie Taymor's spectacularly directed staging of Disney's 1994 film brought an entirely new aesthetic to Broadway.

In 1994, the theatrical division of The Walt Disney Company successfully transferred their animated film *Beauty and the Beast* to the Broadway stage by finding ways to re-create faithfully the film's images. Flush with this success, Disney decided to transfer *The Lion King*, with a score by Elton John (see pp.304–05), from film to stage. They brought in American director Julie Taymor (see pp.280–81), who had extensive experience in non-traditional forms of theatre, to handle the transition.

TAYMOR'S VISION

Taymor's approach was substantially different to the one used so successfully in *Beauty and the Beast*, which brought the movie's imagery to the stage in a literal way. Instead, Taymor chose to use costumes, masks, puppets, mime, dance, and other elements to indirectly evoke the images of *The Lion King* film. Taymor designed the costumes, masks, and puppets herself, in collaboration with her scenic designer Ronald Hudson, lighting designer Donald Holder, and hair and make-up designer Michael Ward. Together, they created a unique visual vocabulary.

STORYTELLING REDEFINED

The masks, puppets, and African and Asian dramatic forms gave *The Lion King* a completely original look and redefined the way Broadway musicals told stories.

The film's original score, by Elton John and Tim Rice (see p.185) included songs such as "Circle of Life", "I Just Can't Wait to Be King", "Be Prepared", "Hakuna Matata", and "Can You Feel the Love Tonight". The stage show saw the addition of several new songs by John and Rice, as well as a substantial helping of traditional African music, arranged and led by South African singer and composer Lebohang (Lebo M) Morake. The Broadway score successfully integrated pop songs, traditional Broadway sounds, African chanting, and parts of the film's soundtrack, written by German composer and music producer Hans Zimmer, to create an aural palette as diverse as the visual one Taymor had developed in her designs for the sets and costumes. The show broke new ground for the musical genre.

> ### "*You can only marvel at the exotic procession of animals before you.*"
>
> **BEN BRANTLEY,** THEATRE REVIEWER, *THE NEW YORK TIMES*, 1997

KEY FACTS

🎭 STAGE

🎬 **Director** Julie Taymor
🎵 **Music** Elton John, Hans Zimmer, and Lebo M
🎶 **Lyrics** Tim Rice
🎭 **Venue** New Amsterdam Theatre, New York
📅 **Date** 13 November 1997

⊙ Key information

Produced by Disney Theatrical Productions, *The Lion King* won six Tony Awards in 1998, including Best Director of a Musical, Best Choreography of a Musical, and all three design awards, and Best Musical.

▼ **Rafiki rules**
South African actress Gugwana Dlamini as Rafiki in the West End production of *The Lion King*.

◀ **Masks and music**
The exotic costumes and culture-crossing score made the show a sure-fire hit around the world.

Of the opening, in his review for *The New York Times*, Ben Brantley wrote, "[the animals are] creatures of air and light and even a touch of divinity … The ways in which Ms Taymor translates the film's opening musical number, 'Circle of Life', is filled with astonishment and surprise."

While Brantley and the other critics raved about the visual imagery of the opening number, they also complained that the style wore short by the end of the production. The consensus was that Taymor's style was arresting and beautiful, but not always successful in driving the narrative forward.

Despite any minor reservations voiced by the press, *The Lion King* became almost immediately an audience favourite and won a host of awards. It became one of the most difficult shows to get a ticket for; any parent who wanted to take their child to the theatre scrambled for tickets to *The Lion King*.

BESTRIDING THE WORLD

In 1999, the show opened at the Lyceum Theatre in London's West End, and was still running at the time of writing. The production was nominated for eight Olivier Awards and won two of these (Best Theatre Choreographer and Best Costume Design). The original French production, mounted in Paris at the Théâtre Mogador, was also hugely successful. It was nominated for, and won, three Molière Awards (Best Musical, Best Costume Design, and Best Lighting design). As well as these hit shows in Paris and London, stage productions of *The Lion King* have been mounted as far afield as Tokyo, Toronto, Los Angeles, Sydney, Melbourne, South Korea, Denmark, Johannesburg, Taipei, Madrid, Mexico City, and Sao Paulo, while tours of the show have continually crisscrossed the world.

◀ **Movie original**
The animated film released by The Walt Disney Company in 1994 was an enormous box office success.

In September 2014, the theatrical trade magazine *Variety* reported that *The Lion King* officially had taken the title of "Top Box Office Title in Any Medium". Up to that date, the stage version of the musical had generated worldwide box office sales of more than an astonishing US$6.2 billion, officially passing the second-highest-grossing musical, *The Phantom of the Opera* (see pp.252–53).

STORYLINE

With some biblical overtones echoing the Old Testament stories of Joseph and Moses, *The Lion King* loosely adapts Shakespeare's *Hamlet* and sets it in the Pride Lands of Africa, recasting the human roles as various African animals. The story follows the life lessons of a lion cub, Simba, as he comes of age and takes the journey to assume his rightful place as king.

CAST			
Jason Raize Simba		**Max Casella** Timon	
John Vickery Scar		**Tom Alan Robbins** Pumbaa	
Samuel E. Wright Mufasa		**Geoff Hoyle** Zazu	
Heather Headley Nala		**Tracy Nicole Chapman** Shenzi	
Tsidii Le Loka Rafiki		**Stanley Wayne Mathis** Banzai	

PLOT OVERVIEW

PRIDE ROCK

Rafiki, the mandrill, summons the animals to Pride Rock to meet the new prince, cub of Mufasa and Sarabi ❶. Mufasa's brother, Scar resents no longer being heir to the throne. Rafiki divines the new prince's name; he will be called Simba.

THE PRIDE LANDS

Mufasa advises Simba to use his position wisely, and warns him never to go beyond the Pride Lands. Mufasa's adviser, Zazu, arrives and delivers the daily news ❷. Scar tempts Simba to visit the forbidden elephant graveyard. Simba invites Nala, a female cub, to accompany him ❸.

ELEPHANT GRAVEYARD

The cubs explore the graveyard, but hyenas threaten them ❹. Mufasa rescues them and admonishes Simba for disobeying. He tells him that the great kings of the past will always guide him ❺. Scar tells his army of hyenas to prepare for Mufasa's death and Scar's ascent to the throne ❻.

THE GORGE

Scar lures Simba to the gorge ❼ and starts a wildebeest stampede. Mustafa saves Simba, but Scar throws Mustafa under the stampede. Scar convinces Simba that he was responsible for his father's death, and so must flee. Scar sends the hyenas to kill Simba, ascends Pride Rock, and takes the throne.

THE SONGS

I Just Can't Wait to Be King
Young Simba, Young Nala, Zazu 😊

Circle of Life
😊 *Rafiki*

The Morning Report
😊 *Zazu, Young Simba, Mufasa*

★ *"The Morning Report" was left out of the Disney film, but was reinstated in the stage musical.*

Be Prepared
😊 *Scar, Shenzai, Banzai, Ed*

They Live in You
😊 *Mufasa*

Chow Down
😊 *Shenzi, Banzai*

Be Prepared (reprise)
😊 *Scar*

RAFIKI SUMMONS THE ANIMALS

THE WILDEBEEST STAMPEDE

> # *"As blockbuster musicals go, this is one with beauty and brains."*
>
> **SARAH HEMMING,** REVIEWER, *THE FINANCIAL TIMES*, 1999

THE PRIDE LANDS

| THE DESERT | THE PRIDE LANDS | THE JUNGLE | | PRIDE ROCK |

Simba has escaped the hyenas but is suffering from heat exhaustion in the desert. Vultures circle over him but Timon, the meerkat, and Pumbaa, the warthog, rescue Simba. They teach him their philosophy **8** and Simba grows to adulthood.

Scar's reign has turned the Pride Lands dry and lifeless **9** . Haunted by the spirit of Mustafa, Scar decides to take Nala as his queen so she can bear him cubs **10** , but she refuses and sets off in search of help **11** .

Simba, Timon, and Pumba search for a resting place **12** . Simba is restless **13** . When Timon needs to be rescued from a waterfall, Simba freezes in fear, recalling his father's death. He sings to evoke the spirit of his dead father watching over him, recovers from his trauma, and rescues Timon.

When a lioness chases Pumbaa and Simba saves him, he recognizes her as Nala **14** . She asks Simba to return to the Pride Lands and restore the circle of life. Rafiki tells Simba he must return home, and the spirit of Mustafa appears to tell him the same **15** .

Simba returns and confronts Scar, who reveals that he was Mustafa's murderer. Simba overpowers Scar, who falls off Pride Rock to the hungry hyenas below. The animals acknowledge Simba's kingship **16** . Rafiki holds up Simba and Nala's newborn cub, completing the circle of life **17** .

8 — **9** — **10** — **11** — **12** — **13** — **14** — **15** — **16** — **17**

Shadowland
😊 *Nala, Rafiki*

They Live in You (reprise)
😊 *Rafiki, Simba*

Circle of Life (reprise)
😊 *Company*

Hakuna Matata
Timon, Pumba,
😊 *Young Simba*

The Madness of King Scar
Scar, Zazu, Banzai,
😊 *Shenzi, Ed, Nala*

Endless Night
😊 *Simba*

One by One
😊 *Company*

The Lion Sleeps Tonight
😊 *Timon, Pumbaa*

Can You Feel the Love Tonight
😊 *Timon, Pumbaa, Simba, Nala*

King of Pride Rock
😊 *Company*

⭐ *Hakuna Matata means "no worries" in Swahili.*

NALA IS CHOSEN TO BE SCAR'S QUEEN

SIMBA BECOMES KING

⭐ *In 2004, the family of South African composer Solomon Linda successfully sued The Walt Disney Company claiming that "The Lion Sleeps Tonight", was based on his 1939 song "Mbube". The song was omitted from productions after this date.*

JULIE TAYMOR

{ DIRECTOR **1952**– }

Although she has directed a wide range of straight plays, operas, and films, Julie Taymor is best known as the creator of musical shows for Broadway and beyond. She remains one of the most influential figures in the business.

Taymor's range is a wide one, reflecting not only the span of her interests but also the breadth of her education. The youngest of three children, Taymor counts herself fortunate that her parents encouraged her to make her own choices from an early age.

At ten, she joined the Boston Children's Theatre Company, before travelling to Sri Lanka and India with the Experiment in International Living Program to add an interest in folklore and mythology to her passion for theatre. At 16, she went to Paris to study mime.

PUPPETS AND MASKS
Graduating from college, Taymor won a fellowship, which enabled her to study theatre and puppetry in Japan, before forming her own theatrical company in Bali. She had planned to be in Indonesia for three months, but ended up staying four years. "I got lost in the culture," she explained later.

On her return to the US, she gained a reputation for her original costumes and masks. A 60-minute version of *A Midsummer Night's Dream* for the Theatre for a New Audience provided valuable experience and was followed by further Shakespearian interpretations.

Taymor's first major success was a dazzling show based on an 18th-century fairy tale, *The King Stag* (1984). She designed the costumes, masks, and giant puppets for the production, which opened in Cambridge, Massachusetts. It was subsequently staged in many other cities in the US and overseas, and has been revived several times since.

In a collaboration with her long-standing partner – composer Elliot Goldenthal – Taymor achieved another creative breakthrough with *Juan Darien: a Carnival Mass*. This multimedia performance was premiered Off-Broadway in 1988 and won numerous awards.

NEW DIRECTIONS
In the early 1990s, Taymor turned her attention to opera, winning an Emmy Award for her directorial interpretation of Stravinsky's *Oedipus Rex*, which premiered in Japan. Then came a major departure for Taymor, when she was

hired to direct Walt Disney's Broadway production of *The Lion King* (see pp.276–79). It is for this show in particular that Taymor is best known. Her highly acclaimed production won two Tony Awards – and is still running. Taymor became the first woman to receive the coveted award for directing a musical. The second award was for her costume design (she co-designed over 100 costumes and animal masks). *The New York Times*

▶ **Unique talent**
Julie Taymor is renowned for the eclecticism of her work and the scale of her personal creativity. She has never been afraid to take on a wide variety of projects nor to try her hand at something new.

KEY WORKS

The Tempest, 1986

Juan Darien: A Carnival Mass, 1988

The Taming of the Shrew, 1988

Fool's Fire, 1992

The Lion King, 1997 (see pp.276–79)

Frida, 2002

The Magic Flute, 2004

Spider Man: Turn off the Dark, 2011

A Midsummer Night's Dream, 2014

◀ Visual power and effects
Taymor's 1999 film of Shakespeare's *Titus Andronicus* was a production full of bold and stark imagery.

by U2 lead singer Bono and guitarist The Edge. But the show was beset with difficulties: as delays mounted, the budget ballooned. The critics lost patience and Taymor fell out with the producers, citing creative differences. In March 2011, she left the production and the parties ultimately reached an out of court settlement.

ENDLESS INNOVATION
The adaptation of the Spider-Man comic books may have turned out to be a creative step too far, but Taymor says she likes doing things that have not been done before and taking people to places they didn't know they wanted to go. This is particularly apparent in her films, which have long proved to be an effective outlet for Taymor's ceaseless inventiveness. Her moody big screen adaptation of Shakespeare's 1588 play *Titus Andronicus* paired motorcycle outriders with marching legionnaires to

create an impression of a Roman empire that had survived into the modern world. The film starred Anthony Hopkins and was largely well received by the critics, but it was her next film, *Frida*, that won Oscars.

For the 2007 musical film *Across the Universe*, which featured over 30 songs by The Beatles, Taymor mixed genres and cultures to tell a love story set in 1960s England, America, and Vietnam.

Shakespeare's plays remain a fertile source of material for Taymor, as she continues to push boundaries. In *The Tempest* (2010), she challenged tradition with her casting of Helen Mirren in a role normally reserved for a male actor, and her *A Midsummer Night's Dream* (2014) was described as "immersive and inventive". Taymor insists she has no plans to stop. She told an interviewer in 2014: "I don't think it's time to stop creating."

▼ Versatile director
Julie Taymor directs Mexican actress Salma Hayek in the 2002 biopic *Frida*, based on the life of the Mexican artist Frida Kahlo. It was lauded by critics and won two Oscars.

ailed *The Lion King* as "the most memorable, moving, and original theatrical extravaganza in years".

Some observers were surprised that Taymor had been prepared to work for a big company like Disney. She explained: "Everyone learned a transforming lesson from *The Lion King*: you don't have to patronize your audience and you can mix art and commerce. You can simultaneously play to the sophisticated 60-year-old theatregoers and to four-year-olds. I wanted *The Lion King* to have elegance, not to be cute."

HIGHS AND LOWS
Taymor's next experience of a major musical show was not quite so happy. *Spider-Man: Turn off the Dark* seemed to be the creative opportunity Taymor had been waiting for. She took full advantage of the opportunity to bring a comic book to life in three dimensions, but ended up with what was described as Broadway's most technically complex show ever. There were moving set-pieces, elaborate costumes, complicated special effects, and tricky aerial manoeuvres. Music and lyrics were

> *"Creativity is a gift, but if you don't know how to use it you might not even know it's there."*
>
> **JULIE TAYMOR**

TIMELINE

● **15 December 1952** Born in Newton, Massachusetts, to gynaecologist Melvin Lester Taymor and political science teacher Elizabeth née Bernstein.

● **1962** Joins the Boston Children's Theatre.

● **1966** Travels to South Asia with the Experiment in International Living Program.

● **1968** Studies at the Jacques Le Coq School of Mime, Paris.

● **1974** Graduates from Oberlin College, Ohio, with a degree in folklore and mythology.

● **1980** Meets composer Elliot Goldenthal, who will be her professional and domestic partner.

● **1986** Makes directing debut in *The Tempest*.

● **1997** *The Lion King* opens on Broadway to great critical acclaim. It wins her two Tony Awards for direction and costume design.

● **1999** Directs film of *Titus Andronicus*.

● **2002** Directs acclaimed feature film *Frida*.

ACROSS THE UNIVERSE (2007)

● **2007** Named as director of ambitious musical based on the Spider-Man comic book character.

● **2010** As director, she casts a woman, Helen Mirren, in a man's role in Taymor's version of Shakespeare's *The Tempest*.

● **2011** Leaves *Spider-Man: Turn off The Dark* after artistic differences with the producers.

● **2013** *Spider-Man* musical closes amid claims that at US$46.5 million, it is Broadway's biggest flop; Taymor settles her legal action, accepting substantial royalty payments.

● **2014** International film premiere of *A Midsummer Night's Dream*, directed by Taymor.

HEDWIG AND THE ANGRY INCH

{ **1998** }

A radically progressive rock musical takes us back to a time in which accepted sexual boundaries went the way of the Berlin Wall: "Now that it's gone, we don't know who we are." This musical presents gender-bending in an entirely new way.

▼ **Shades of** *Cabaret*?
The German connection and sleazy decadence of this musical point to vague links with *Cabaret* (see p.166). Certainly, writer John Cameron Mitchell's intention was to produce something similarly outrageous.

Boy meets girl: the formula has always been pretty much fundamental to the musical, though we have not so often seen the sexes meet in a single person. But this is what a "post-punk neo-glam rock musical" presents us with. When Hedwig, this musical's heroine, tells us "I was born on the other side", she means that she comes from beyond the Berlin Wall, in Communist East Germany – but she is also reminding us that she was born a boy, Hansel.

FRONTIERS

Hedwig has borrowed her mother's passport, and identity – and even her gender – to escape across the Iron Curtain and find freedom in the West with a US soldier, as his wife. In fleeing the country of her birth, she has at the same time sought to find her way "home" to a place of androgynous completion she has dreamed of ever since she was read Plato's *Symposium* as a boy. In that famous Greek philosophical work, the suggestion is made that male and female were originally two halves of a single being that was divided and has since been striving to be whole. Hence the desperation of the sexual drive in men and women – and the tantalizing possibility of a higher state in which the beauties of both genders might be combined forever. Not the usual stuff of musical theatre, perhaps – though it makes a memorable and moving song in "The Origin of Love".

And, as we are quickly reminded, it is really only a short step from ancient Greece to the Glam Rock of the 1970s, and its fascination with the crossing of gender lines. Long-haired men in shiny satin costumes; capes and gauntlets; glitter and sequins; and platform shoes: the Glam aesthetic mocked conventional assumptions about what a man should be. Performers such as Marc Bolan and David Bowie as "Ziggy Stardust" promoted an unmistakably androgynous ideal of male beauty.

IDEAL VS REAL

For Hedwig, though, the realities of the androgynous life have been at the very best underwhelming. Her (genuinely beloved) husband Luther has left her after only a year. The main thing she has to

KEY FACTS

🎭 **STAGE**

🎬 **Director** Peter Askin
📖 **Book** John Cameron Mitchell
🎵 **Music and lyrics** Stephen Trask
🎭 **Venue** Jane Street Theatre, New York
📅 **Date** 14 February 1998

⊙ **Key information**
The first, Off-broadway, production of *Hedwig and the Angry Inch* won the Obie Award with special citations for Stephen Trask and for its cast. A film, adapted and directed by John Cameron Mitchell, was released in 2001.

> # *"I thought we were gonna perform it a couple of times for our friends."*
>
> **STEPHEN TRASK**, COMPOSER

show for her transgender journey, she tells us in the song "Angry Inch", is the functionless disfigurement left her by the clueless surgeon who gave Hansel his vaginoplasty: the "one-inch mound of flesh where my penis used to be, where my vagina never was". An angry inch indeed, it remains with her as a permanent reminder of what she has given up, what she wants so badly, and what she will never have. Not least because Tommy Gnosis, a young man whose successful rock career has been built on her songs, and whom, since losing Luther, she has considered her soulmate, has recoiled on being told her secret. He does not want a woman who was once a man, fully intact or not.

Nevertheless, Tommy continues to fly high, making a fortune from material Hedwig has written for him, while his stagey rock-star posturings of existential angst make a mockery of the very real despair he has left her in.

"The fates are vicious and they're cruel,/You learn too late you've used two wishes/Like a fool," he sings in "Wicked Little Town", lamenting his fate all the way to the bank and winning the adulation of the world.

While Tommy soars to stardom, Hedwig ekes out a living on an endless tour as a minor rock performer, reduced to marrying Yitzhak, the drag queen she travels with. Theirs is a truly toxic relationship, a marriage of resentful outcasts, founded on her angry contempt and his hopeless vulnerability. What unites them, Yitzhak's song "The Long Grift" suggests, is their common feeling of having been comprehensively "grifted" – cheated: by life and by the people they have loved. Will she ever find the peace she craves – and give Yitzhak the acceptance he deserves?

AUTOBIOGRAPHICAL AMBIGUITIES

Born in 1963, John Cameron Mitchell had grown up with the ambiguities of Glam Rock, but he had also had to negotiate a number of other tricky transitions and uncertainties. The son of a senior US army officer, he had been brought up partly in Germany and afterwards in Britain. There, not only was he an American abroad, he was an individual growing up in the gradual realization that he was gay – at the heart of one the most conventionally masculine institutions in the world.

In Stephen Trask, Mitchell was to find a kindred spirit: he was playing as a musician in a New York club when the two men met. They

▲ **Alternative glamour**
The poster for the film shows John Cameron Mitchell as Hedwig. Most of the vocals were recorded live as the scenes were shot.

developed their show through a series of performances in similar small-club settings, anxious to hold on to all the anarchic energy they could until they presented it on stage. In 2015, John Cameron Mitchell won a Special Tony Award for his performance as Hedwig in the Broadway production.

▶ **Drag rock**
Stephen Trask as guitarist Skszp and John Cameron Mitchell as Hedwig, "getting it on" in one of this unusual show's many rock numbers.

MAMMA MIA!

{ 1999 }

Their songs had saturated the 1970s, and scarcely abated since: Swedish pop group ABBA would not be forgotten. A musical should have been superfluous, but *Mamma Mia!* turned out to be exactly what the new century needed.

▲ **Song showcase**
The hugely successful musical and film have immortalized ABBA's songs and enchanted a new generation of listeners.

Asked to play Tanya for a touring production of *Mamma Mia!* in 2015, Shobna Gulati admitted she was "ecstatic". Not so much because she loved the songs, the dialogue, the story, or the structure of the musical so much – though she clearly did – but, as she told the *Liverpool Echo*, "I can't

contain myself because I'm working with my best friend". Sue Devaney, playing Rosie, was equally enthusiastic about working with Gulati as well as several other old friends.

Any actress wants to be working, of course, and working with friends is always a bonus, but it matters especially with *Mamma Mia!*, it appears. "It's so much about the friendship of the women and their journey," explained Gulati. "That kind of female friendship, that bond, that we all have, that's nothing like the bond

men have. It's a very empowering thing to be in, I think." What goes for the cast goes for their audience too – "There's this huge camaraderie in the audience that's reflected on stage. It's just a very heartwarming experience."

NO RESISTING IT

The feelgood rush that surrounds this musical is something special, even by Broadway and West End standards. *Mamma Mia!* is more than just a show: for those who attend, it is a special event. Also striking is the fervour with

which the stage version continues to be greeted, long after it might have been supposed to be superseded by the star-studded movie of 2008.

▼ **Let the good times roll**
The company of the London production performing one of the celebrated party dance scenes in a mocked-up Greek villa.

On the face of it, this enthusiasm is difficult to explain. And whatever the warmth with which the show is greeted wherever it appears, there was perhaps something a little cold and calculating in the musical's inception. Producer Judy Craymer had been carrying the concept of staging an ABBA musical around with her for some years before she found a writer, Catherine Johnson, to execute her vision. Previously known for raw and edgy works of realist drama, Johnson later remarked that she had found constructing the musical like doing a "jigsaw", coming up with the least implausible plot that would allow the most ABBA songs to be brought together – certainly a difficult challenge for any writer for the stage.

Money", "Waterloo", "Mamma Mia" – the stream of well-remembered classic ABBA hits went on and on. If the thematic connections were sometimes tenuous, the narrative twists and turns that linked them together were occasionally laughably artificial, and yet added to the element of fun.

This was a show to be shared, to be seen by groups of friends – especially female friends – to be stamped and sung along and danced-in-the-aisles to before a few glasses of wine and an uproarious journey home. Catherine Johnson had anticipated this sense of camaraderie in drawing up her plot, which – frothy as it may seem – is ultimately a heart-warming celebration of female friendship.

▲ **Friends reunited**
Donning their old costumes, Donna and the Dynamos reform to perform "Super Trouper" at Sophie's hen party.

"It's a requirement of popular culture that you strike an ironic distance. This doesn't... It's visceral and I love that."

MERYL STREEP, *THE GUARDIAN*, 2 JULY 2008

LIGHT ENTERTAINMENT

While in theory it should not have been possible to go wrong in any way with the music, the danger of overfamiliarity was always there. As was that of the songs' superficiality, perhaps. ABBA's music, universally as it has been enjoyed, is not considered to be of any truly great weight or substance.

Yet it was precisely this lightness that made the musical so successful. Johnson's "jigsaw" approach amounted to a recognition not only of the importance of the songs – and how the narrative of each song helped to drive the story – but the overall primacy of fun and friendship. ABBA's work was powerful, not because it spoke to this or that individual at some intimate emotional or deep intellectual level, but because for everyone it had the same associations of exuberance and joy. "Honey, Honey", "Thank You for the Music", "Dancing Queen", "Take a Chance on Me", "Money, Money,

SUPER TROUPERS

Ostensibly, *Mamma Mia!* follows the fortunes of a young woman who – soon to be married – hopes to find her father. Sophie searches her mother Donna's diary and, going through the descriptions of the various dates Donna had around the relevant time, manages to narrow it down to three possible

▼ **Having the time of their lives**
Meryl Streep leads Julie Walters (right), Christine Baranski (left), and a chorus of Greek islanders in a rendition of "Dancing Queen" during the 2008 film.

men. She invites all the candidates to her wedding, which is due to take place on the lovely Greek island of Kalokairi, in Donna's name – but without her mother knowing anything about the plan. A series of predictably farcical incidents ensues, which, however, leaves Sophie none the wiser as to her paternity.

Ultimately, though, her father's identity turns out to be rather less important than the realization that Sophie has never really known her mother either. Not, at least, the woman she finds before her now, reunited with her oldest female friends. Tanya and Rosie have moved in very different directions since the three friends performed together as girl group "Donna and the Dynamos", yet their loyalty to one another has proven sweetly enduring.

FUN-FILLED SINGALONG

The 2008 film was also a runaway success, attracting a stellar cast, including Meryl Streep, Pierce Brosnan, Colin Firth, Julie Walters, and Amanda Seyfried. Although for some it may be hard to disagree with film critic Mark Kermode's verdict that it is "the closest you get to see A-list actors doing drunken karaoke", this, it

appears, is part of its charm. Kermode's remark is a reminder of how far ABBA's music is something we all feel able to sing along to – however ungifted we may be; it is part of a contemporary "folk memory" we all seem to share. Above all, *Mamma Mia!* is such a huge hit because it is so bouncy, so upbeat, and so unstintingly affirmative: its mood is as sunny as the Aegean sky.

Well into its second decade on the stage, *Mamma Mia!* continues to delight audiences around the world. Apart from the hugely successful Broadway and West End productions, the show has also toured extensively and has been played in more than 40 countries on six continents.

KEY FACTS

🎭 **STAGE**

🎬 **Director** Phyllida Lloyd

📖 **Book** Catherine Johnson

🎵 **Music and lyrics** Björn Ulvaeus, Benny Andersson

🎵 **Lyrics** Stig Anderson

🎭 **Venue** Prince Edward Theatre, London

📅 **Date** 6 April 1999

◉ **Key information**
Mamma Mia! was nominated for six major awards and won a Laurence Olivier Award for Jenny Galloway for Best Performance in a Supporting Role in a Musical. Since 2012, the London production has played at the Novello Theatre. The first Broadway production was nominated for five Tonys.

A MUSICAL REVIVAL

2000–PRESENT

Innovation continues as movies are taken to the stage, collections of songs are reinvented as jukebox musicals, and satirical shows become cult hits.

A MUSICAL REVIVAL

In the 21st century, big-budget productions – especially those adapted from movies – continue to thrive, as do jukebox musicals. However, left-field hits indicate there is still plenty of room for invention in musical theatre.

▲ **A return to the big screen**
At the start of a new century, producers once again saw profit in turning stage shows into big screen productions.

With the old regularly taking its place alongside the new on Broadway and in the West End, a bevy of revivals has ensured that classic musical theatre is remembered, rediscovered, and sometimes reimagined in the 2000s. Notable reappearances have included *South Pacific* (2001) and *West Side Story* (2008) from the 1940s and 50s; *Fiddler on the Roof* (2004) and *Hair* (2009) from the 1960s; and *Grease* (2007) and *A Chorus Line* (2013) from the 1970s.

SCREEN TESTS

Of the new hit musicals that emerged, a significant number were inspired by movies or TV shows. Mel Brooks (1926–) adapted his 1968 comedy *The Producers* (see pp.290–91) into a lavish award-winning stage musical (2001) and movie (2005), while Eric Idle (1943–) plundered *Monty Python and the Holy Grail* (1975) and other Monty Python material to bring *Spamalot* (see p.307) to the stage in 2005. Movies such as *Hairspray* (1988), *Ghost* (1990), and *Billy Elliot* (2000), all became hit stage musicals in the 2000s.

Meanwhile, Baz Luhrmann (1962–) proved the movie musical was still a viable commercial proposition with his lavish jukebox production *Moulin Rouge!* (2001). This paved the way for a rash of musical adaptations including

◀ **Box office gold**
An all-star cast, including Nicole Kidman as Satine, and a score featuring popular songs by various artists made *Moulin Rouge!* a huge critical and commercial success during the early 2000s.

JASON ROBERT BROWN (1970–)

The award-winning New York-born songwriter combines a literate pop sensibility with traditional musical theatre skills and is among the most distinctive of modern musical composers. Jason Robert Brown first came to attention with the cult Off-Broadway show *Songs for a New World* (1995), which produced the cabaret favourite "Stars and the Moon". He has won two Tony Awards for Best Score for *Parade* (1999) and *The Bridges of Madison County* (2014), while *The Last Five Years* (2002) is a favourite two-hander – a show with only two main characters – among regional US theatre groups.

Chicago (2002), *The Phantom of the Opera* (2004), *Sweeney Todd* (2007), *Les Misérables* (2012), and *Into the Woods* (2014), all of which were significant box-office hits.

TELEVISION MUSICALS

Perhaps developing the audience that had grown up with Alan Menken's musical theatre pop songs in 1990s Disney movies, television got a firm foothold in the musical genre during the 2000s. The Disney Channel's made-for-TV *High School Musical* (2006) had poor reviews, but its blend of multi-composer original pop songs and Romeo and Juliet-style plot found a huge audience of young teenagers. The show has since been adapted for the stage and has generated several sequels. Trailed as a "post-modern musical", the Fox TV series *Glee* (2009) relies on musical theatre pop-style covers of established repertoire for its jukebox-style soundtrack.

In the UK, with *How Do You Solve a Problem Like Maria?* (2006), the BBC and Andrew Lloyd Webber used a talent show format to search for an unknown leading star in the revival of Rodgers and Hammerstein's *The Sound Of Music*. While making a household name of its winner and creating enhanced demand for the ensuing West End run, the show did much to raise awareness of repertoire, the required performing skills, and the varied styles of musical theatre, both classic and modern. The programme was franchised abroad and follow-up series repeated the successful formula with *Any Dream Will Do* in 2007 for *Joseph and the Amazing Technicolor Dream Coat*; *I'd*

Do Anything for *Oliver!* in 2008; *Over the Rainbow* in 2010 for *The Wizard of Oz*; and *Superstar* for *Jesus Christ Superstar* in 2012.

THE JUKEBOX PLAYS ON

In the wake of the *Mamma Mia!* phenomenon (see pp.284–85), jukebox musicals continued their hold on Broadway and West End theatres. *We Will Rock You* (2002) is a futuristic fantasy linked by Queen's back catalogue; *Jersey Boys* (see p.206) charts the rise of the 1960s vocal group the Four Seasons; and *Rock of Ages* (2009) is an exuberant celebration of 1980s rock songs. These and the revived or perpetual mega-musicals are sometimes seen as tourist attractions rather than a central part of the ever-evolving art of musical theatre.

◀ **Rock show**
A jukebox musical based on the hits of the British rock band Queen, *We Will Rock You* kept West End audiences entertained for over a decade.

CULT HITS

The musical as spectacle returned with a vengeance in the 2000s in shows like The *Lord Of The Rings* (2007) and *Spider Man: Turn Off the Dark* (2011), but their huge budgets were rarely recouped. In an interesting development, these new blockbuster musicals were

▶ **Rich source material**
Roald Dahl's classic children's book *Charlie and the Chocolate Factory* has inspired two musical films (1971 and 2005), as well as a West End stage musical, which opened in 2013.

largely outperformed by modest-budget shows with a surfeit of wit, invention, and irreverence. *Urinetown* (2001), *Jerry Springer: The Opera* (2003), *Avenue Q* (see p.300–01), and *The Book of Mormon* (see p.320) were fresh, satirical, and smart – inspiring devoted support and plenty of controversy. Similarly received were *Spring Awakening* (see pp.308–09), a lusty rock adaptation of German playwright Frank Wedekind's play of sexual discovery, and *Next To Normal* (2008), a rock musical dealing with the uncommon subjects of depression, drug abuse, and psychiatric ethics.

INTERNATIONAL MUSICALS

Traditionally, musical theatre has been considered the province of America – specifically Broadway in New York – and the UK, in London's West End, but recent years have seen the growth of successful shows originating in other English-speaking territories including Australia (*The Boy From Oz*) and Canada (*The Drowsy Chaperone*).

Non-English musicals have also enjoyed success. Austria's German-language pop-rock show *Elisabeth* (see p.263), by Michael Kunze (1943–) and Sylvester Levay (1945–), had worldwide productions throughout the 2000s. Japan has witnessed a trend for live action musicals based on anime and manga films, notably *Tenimyu* (2003), while Hong Kong combines efforts at creating an indigenous modern musical – *Snow. Wolf.Lake* (1997) – in Mandarin and Cantonese, with local language adaptations of Western shows such as *Fame* (2008).

NEW MUSICAL PROSPECTS

Commentators have for several decades suggested that the spectacular mega-musicals and jukebox extravaganzas that are so popular with tourists and out-of-town families indicate a lack of the

▲ **"Hello"**
Host Neil Patrick Harris and the cast of *The Book of Mormon* perform the opening song at the 66th Tony Awards in 2012.

creative vitality that characterized the musical's "golden age", but there are signs for optimism. Off-Broadway continues to produce vibrant new work, including immersive-style shows such as *Natasha, Pierre and the Great Comet of 1812* (2012), and the David Byrne and Fatboy Slim collaboration about Imelda Marcos, *Here Lies Love* (2013). Broadway producer Ken Davenport has successfully attracted younger audiences to hit shows such as *Altar Boyz* (2005) and *Kinky Boots* (2013), while smaller London venues like Greenwich Theatre and St James's Theatre regularly host workshops and small-scale productions by up-and-coming writers. Shows like Green Day's *American Idiot* (2010), and *Once* (see p.321), reveal that the depth and variety of talent engaging with musical theatre has never been larger, with new writers and composers from a range of genres and backgrounds emerging all the time. To paraphrase Oscar Hammerstein, as long as music helps the story to be told, the musical will continue to flourish.

THE PRODUCERS

{ 2001 }

This satirical comedy concerning two Jewish producers trying to outsmart their investors with a musical about a happy Hitler kept critics and audiences laughing. Based on an earlier film, it featured flamboyantly gay directors and a tall, sexy Swede.

For many, *The Producers* was a musical by the industry for the industry. It highlighted the clichés – an accountant dreaming of being a producer, a beautiful wannabe actress working as a "secretary-slash-receptionist" – and also revealed the dirty secrets, such as the wooing of elderly ladies for cash. In fact, Mel Brooks, famous for his droll spoofs, actually knew characters like this in show business.

Brooks explained the inspiration for the story and its characters in a 2004 interview with *The Guardian*. He had worked for a producer – complete with a chicken-fat-stained homburg and a black alpaca coat – who would pounce on little old ladies and make love to them; grateful for his attention, they gave the producer money for his plays. Later in his career, a press agent Brooks knew explained to him how those two producers made money out of failing shows. "I coupled the producer with these two crooks and – BANG! – there was my story."

THE PLOT

The show centres on producer Max Bialystock, the sleazy one played by Nathan Lane in both the Broadway and West End productions, who convinces his new, daydreaming accountant, Leo Bloom (Matthew Broderick), to help him produce a Broadway play with a twist: this play is intended to be a flop.

With enough money raised, and a supposedly loss-making show, they won't have to pay back their investors and can instead retire to Rio forever. Bialystock and Bloom set out to find a terrible play, hire the worst director and actors ever seen, and raise the funds to stage the production.

Bialystock woos with a vengeance, and together he and Bloom find the worst play, *Springtime for Hitler*, written by Franz Liebkind, an ex-Nazi with a passion for bringing Hitler's soft side to the world. Combining this with the antics of Roger de Bris, and his "common-law-assistant" Carmen Ghia, as director, the play is bound to be a sure-fire flop. However, instead of the disaster they expected, *Springtime for Hitler* is a terrific success. Bialystock is arrested and Bloom goes on the run. Only at the end do the partners prove their devotion to each other, with Bloom defending Bialystock at his trial, and the two enjoying prison together.

MERCILESS SATIRE

The antics and satire of the musical are what truly make it special. Nowhere is this more evident than in the music and lyrics, both written by Mel Brooks. He originally tried to engage Jerry Herman, who composed the scores for *Hello, Dolly!* (see pp.160–61) and *La Cage aux Folles* (see p.239), among others. However, Herman turned the tables, pointing out that Brooks's own songs in his movies *Blazing Saddles* (1974), *History of the World Part 1* (1981), and *Robin Hood: Men in Tights* (1993) had all been hilarious and engaging. Thus, Brooks sat down and wrote it all himself. For the score, he turned to Glen Kelly,

KEY FACTS

🎭 STAGE
🎬 **Director** Susan Stroman
📖 **Book** Mel Brooks, Thomas Meehan
🎵 **Music and lyrics** Mel Brooks
🎭 **Venue** St James Theatre, New York
📅 **Date** 19 April 2001

⊙ Key information
At the 2001 Tony Awards, it swept the board, winning Best Musical, Best Book, Best Original Score, Leading Actor (Nathan Lane), Featured Actress (Cady Huffman), Featured Actor (Gary Beach), and the trophies for direction, orchestration, choreography, set design, costume design, and lighting design.

OTHER PRODUCTIONS

The Producers began as a non-musical film, released in 1968. Brooks directed and wrote the screenplay, but it was considered so controversial that few cinemas showed it, leaving it for arthouse cinemas that could take bigger risks. The film came to the attention of a wider audience when it won the 1969 Academy Award for Best Original Screenplay, and word-of-mouth reviews assured its place as a much-loved comedy. Following their success on stage, Matthew Broderick and Nathan Lane reprised their roles in a musical adaptation for the big screen, and the film was released in 2005.

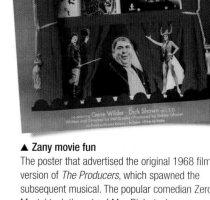

▲ **Zany movie fun**
The poster that advertised the original 1968 film version of *The Producers*, which spawned the subsequent musical. The popular comedian Zero Mostel took the role of Max Bialystock.

for arrangement, and Doug Besterman, who won the Tony for Best Orchestration; they gave the whole work a professional polish and made up for any shortcomings Brook might have had on the musical side. Books had hired Susan Stroman (see pp.292–93) to choreograph the

▶ **Masters of satire**
From left to right, Mel Brooks, Nathan Lane, director Susan Stroman, and Matthew Broderick in a publicity shot for the original Broadway show.

CAST LIST

Nathan Lane Max Bialystock
Matthew Broderick Leopold "Leo" Bloom
Gary Beach Roger De Bris
Roger Bart Carmen Ghia
Cady Huffman Ulla Inga Hansen
Benson Yansen Tallen Hallen Svaden
Swanson Bloom
Brad Oscar Franz Liebkind

▶ **Looney tunes**
Broadway stars Nathan Lane and Matthew Broderick was joined by Uma Thurman for the 2005 film based on the stage show.

show, and Mike Ockrent, Stroman's husband, was to direct it. After Ockrent's death in 1999, Susan Stroman took on the additional task of directing the show. She would also go on to direct the 2005 film version (see opposite) of the stage show.

The Producers won 12 Tonys, breaking the previous record held by *Hello, Dolly!* since 1964. It also set another new record, of winning in every category nominated, the first Broadway musical ever to do so. Altogether, the musical received 15 nominations: Matthew Broderick and Nathan Lane were up against each other for "Leading Actor", while Gary Beach, Roger Bart, and Brad Oscar were all in the running for "Featured Actor".

The talent of the two leads definitely contributed to *The Producers'* enormous success. Broderick and Lane had previously worked together on the original film of *The Lion King* (see pp.276–79), playing (adult) Simba and Timon respectively. The easy camaraderie found in the recording studio translated to the stage, and their amity and sheer delight in the musical was easy to see and highly infectious. In fact, in some ways, their strong skills had an adverse effect on the show's longevity. After playing the roles for a year, from March 2001–02, the two leads left to pursue other work. It had such a detrimental effect on sales that they came back for a limited season, December 2003–April 2004, to renew interest. This had the desired outcome – record ticket sales – and the show then carried on for three more years until April 2007.

Lane would also reprise the role for the West End production in 2004, with British comedian Lee Evans in the taking the role of Leo.

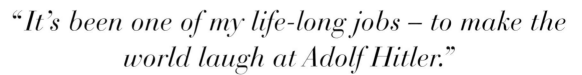

"It's been one of my life-long jobs – to make the world laugh at Adolf Hitler."

MEL BROOKS, CBS NEWS, 12 APRIL 2001

SUSAN STROMAN

CHOREOGRAPHER/DIRECTOR 1954–

As a small child she whirled around the family home making up dances while her father accompanied her on the piano. This was more than just youthful high spirits – she went on to become one of the most respected figures in musical theatre.

KEY WORKS

Flora the Red Menace, 1987
Crazy for You, 1992
Show Boat, 1993
Contact, 2000
The Producers, 2001 (see pp.290–91)
The Scottsboro Boys, 2010
Bullets over Broadway, 2014

Many years later Susan Stroman recalled that her obsession with music was such that "had I not had the outlet to become a choreographer, I probably would have gone crazy". Instead, six decades, five Tony awards, and two Olivier awards later, Stroman has become one of Broadway's most prolific choreographers and directors, renowned for her innovative approach.

It had started when the family watched old musicals on television, with stars like Fred Astaire (see pp.42–43) and Ginger Rogers. "For me," Stroman recalled, "creating to music started when I was five or six." She began taking dancing lessons and creating routines in her head. Her choreography began at high school. She moved to the Academy of the Dance, Wilmington, and specialized in tap, jazz, and ballet. She also took piano and guitar lessons.

Stroman continued to choreograph shows for local community theatres while a student at the University of Delaware. She graduated in English literature in 1976 and then moved to New York to begin her professional show business career.

BROADWAY DEBUT
Initially, Stroman worked as a dancer, touring in the original production of Bob Fosse's *Chicago* (see pp.196–99). Her Broadway debut came in 1979 with the musical *Whoopee!* However, she had now realized that, as foreshadowed two decades earlier by her childhood visualizations, choreography was more satisfying than dancing on stage herself.

The first big break came when director Scott Ellis hired her to choreograph the Off-Broadway revival of Kander and Ebb's *Flora, the Red Menace,* in 1987. When director Harold Prince (see pp.210–11) saw Stroman's work, he engaged her to provide the dance sequences for his New York City Opera production of Mozart's *Don Giovanni.*

In 1992, Stroman collaborated with director Mike Ockrent – whom she married four years later – on *Crazy for You* (see p.262), winning her first Tony Award for choreography. In 1994 she provided the Tony-winning choreography for the revival of *Show Boat* (see pp.14–17), directed by Prince.

▼ **Dancing storyteller**
Susan Stroman is renowned for basing many of her productions around her carefully choreographed routines, telling the story through dance.

"*Ever since I was a little girl I've have had this passion, this obsession. When I hear music I see visions of people dancing.*"

SUSAN STROMAN

John Kander and Fred Ebb's *The Scottsboro Boys*, directed by Susan Stroman at the Garrick Theatre in London's West End, 2014, where it won the 2014 Evening Standard Award for Best Musical.

As choreographer of another revival, this time of *Oklahoma!* (see pp.58–61) in London, Stroman boldly replaced Agnes de Mille's choreography. The *Daily Mail* newspaper hailed her work as "perhaps the biggest star of the night". The production, at the National Theatre, was directed by Trevor Nunn.

In the autumn of 1999, Stroman won another Tony Award for her choreography of *Contact*, a three-part "dance-play". The book for *Contact* was written by the American librettist John Weidman. A broadcast of the show later won an Emmy Award. *Contact* moved to a larger Broadway theatre and was re-classified as a musical.

TRAGEDY AND NEW COLLABORATIONS

However, this success was overshadowed by tragedy. In December of the same year Mike Ockrent lost his battle with leukaemia. Devastated at the loss of her husband, Stroman immersed herself in her work. It was to good effect. Her revival of *The Music Man* (see pp.128–31) involved an imaginative re-telling of the story of a man able to sell anything to anyone. It was well received and won several awards.

Prior to his death, Ockrent had been named as director of the Mel Brooks musical *The Producers*, with Stroman set to choreograph the show. It took months for Brooks to persuade Stroman to take her husband's place as director.

The collaboration was later described by Stroman as among the strongest she had ever experienced. She also said that Brooks had brought the laughter back into her life: for example, as well as dancing and singing during the auditions, the actors had to tell a joke.

The Producers opened to critical acclaim and went on to become a commercial success, scooping a record 12 Tonys, including two for Stroman. This triumph also marked the first time a woman had won the awards for direction and choreography on the same night. The film adaptation of *The Producers*

marked Stroman's debut as director of a feature film, in 2005. It was nominated for four Golden Globe awards.

There was further collaboration with Brooks, when Stroman directed and choreographed the musical *Young Frankenstein* (2007). Two years later she directed and choreographed the musical *Happiness*, collaborating once again with book writer John Weidman.

Now over 60, Stroman shows no sign of hanging up the trademark black baseball cap she wears while working.

▲ Breaking into film
When *The Producers* was adapted for the big screen, Stroman repeated her role as director and worked with many of the original Broadway cast.

► Flying lead
The playbill for Stroman's Broadway adaptation of Woody Allen' film *Bullets Over Broadway*, which she choreographed and directed in 2014.

- **17 October 1954** Born in Wilmington, Delaware, to salesman Charles Stroman and his wife, Frances née Nolan.

- **1976** Graduates from University of Delaware, having majored in English literature.

- **1979** Makes Broadway debut in the musical *Whoopee!*

- **1987** Choreographs Broadway revival of *Flora, the Red Menace*, which becomes a cult sensation and leads Harold Prince to hire her for New York City Opera production of *Don Giovanni*.

- **1992** *Crazy for You* opens on Broadway and will win Stroman's first Tony award.

- **1993** Choreographs *Show Boat* revival, which opens on Broadway.

- **1994** *Show Boat* revival marked by some of Stroman's most innovative ideas, with new dance routines and a revolving door to mark the passage of time.

PUBLICITY FOR STEEL PIER, 1997, CHOREOGRAPHED BY STROMAN

- **1999** London *Oklahoma!* revival wins Stroman her second Olivier award.

- **2000** Stroman co-creates *Contact*, which opens on Broadway.

- **2000** Wins American Choreography Award for Outstanding Achievement in Feature Film for directing *Center Stage*.

- **2001** Collaborates with Mel Brooks on *The Producers*.

- **2010** Directs and choreographs Kander and Ebb's *The Scottsboro Boys*.

- **2014** Works with Woody Allen to direct and choreograph adaptation of his film *Bullets over Broadway* for the musical stage.

- **2015** Inducted into the Theater Hall of Fame in New York City.

MOULIN ROUGE!

{ **2001** }

A great opera re-imagined, a celebrated cabaret evoked, a famous epoch of creativity recalled. Ultimately, *Moulin Rouge!* is a work imagined entirely on its own terms.

The Pigalle district of Paris is the area where the sex shops are to be found: its tone ranges from the raffish through the borderline sleazy to the rather worse. To this day, though, tourists of the utmost respectability turn up by the coachload to see what is on offer at the world-famous cabaret, famed for the giant red windmill on its roof, the *Moulin Rouge*.

Here, raunch takes on a French-accented sophistication. The Moulin Rouge was the last word in 19th-century fin-de-siècle entertainment – with all the extravagant decadence that implies. Its cheeky, racy style was summed up in the swirling petticoats of the high-kicking can-can dancers, immortalized in Henri Toulouse-Lautrec's famous posters.

THROUGH THE MILL

In Australian director Baz Luhrmann's re-imagining, the Moulin Rouge story merges with that of *La Dame aux Camélias* by Alexandre Dumas (1852) and its retelling in the opera *La Traviata* (1853) by Giuseppe Verdi. In the opera and play, a young nobleman meets a courtesan and they fall in love and plan a life together. For his sake, though, she breaks off their relationship and denies her love. Her young lover cannot understand the purity of her motives. He loses her, having doubted her capacity for disinterested love – and his own capacity to inspire it. Realizing too late what he has done, he rushes to her side to find her sickening and dying of tuberculosis and she is taken from him for a second and final time.

Moulin Rouge! follows roughly the same story, though it shifts the action forward half a century to 1900. Christian, the male lead is a would-be writer, portrayed by Ewan McGregor; the beautiful prostitute Satine by Nicole Kidman. The musical chronology is moved forward even further: Luhrmann was determined that his movie should not be experienced as a period piece. However, with hit songs associated with Nat King Cole, Elton John, Randy Crawford, Madonna, the Police, and Queen all featuring, there is no risk of the show being pinned down to any given time in musical history.

ORPHEAN AIRS

Instead, *Moulin Rouge!* attempts to look deep into the eternal sources of artistic creativity. This is why – though only faintly flagged in the unfolding action – the idea of Orpheus is so important to the storyline.

In Greek legend, the original musical genius Orpheus makes the perilous descent into the underworld to fetch back his beloved – but deceased – wife, Euridice. The King of Hades allows the great musician to lead his love back to her home in the world above – so long as he does not at any point look back upon his path out of the abyss. However, as Orpheus reaches the end of his journey, he unthinkingly glances back, and Euridice is snatched back down into hell.

The connection between the Moulin Rouge and the Orpheus myth was vivid: in 1858, the French composer Jacques Offenbach had made the story of *Orpheus in the Underworld* into a satirical operetta. More poetically, though, Baz Luhrmann seems to have seen Christian's walk on the seamy side of Parisian life as a symbolic descent into a social and emotional inferno, from which he was to emerge grief-stricken by Satine's loss.

KEY FACTS

🎥 **FILM**

🎬 **Director** Baz Luhrmann

📖 **Screenplay** Baz Luhrmann, Craig Pearce

📕 **Book** Baz Luhrmann, Craig Armstrong

🎵 **Music and lyrics** Craig Armstrong (and writers of individual songs)

🕐 **Running time** 128 minutes

📅 **Release date** 9 May 2001

⊙ **Key information**
Moulin Rouge!, though lavishly represented in the Oscar nominations for 2001, ultimately only won two, for Best Costume Design (Angus Strathie and Catherine Martin) and Best Production Design (Catherine Martin and Brigitte Broch).

▼ **Opulent fantasy**
Luhrmann's lavish visual style is vividly conveyed in this scene, with the multitude of swirling dancers reminiscent of a Bollywood musical.

WICKED

{ 2003 }

A musical based on a revised reading of *The Wizard of Oz*, beloved since 1939, seems a challenging place to start. Yet *Wicked* manages to both align and differentiate itself.

Stephen Schwartz first read Gregory Maguire's book *Wicked: The Life and Times of the Wicked Witch of the West* while on holiday, and was immediately inspired by the story. After all, it included fairy-tale elements of Munchkins, good witches and bad, all of which make for exciting inspiration for costumes, lighting, and scenery. In addition, the 1939 film of *The Wizard of Oz* (see pp.46–49) is shown virtually every Christmas in both North America and the UK, keeping the story fresh in the minds of viewers, something that few other, if any, films of the same era can claim.

The plot of Maguire's book, similar to L. Frank Baum's original tales, featured a complicated storyline and many characters, and these had to be streamlined for the stage adaptation. In Maguire's book,

all is not what it seems in the world of Oz as we know it from the film. The Wicked Witch of the West, Elphaba, was once a starry-eyed, clever student at Shiz University, discriminated against for her green skin. Her co-star, the future Good Witch of the North, is a fellow university student – pretty, popular, and constantly correcting the mispronunciation of her name Galinda as "Glinda". The two girls initially hate each other, yet reciprocated favours slowly give way to a mutual liking, and eventually a sisterly love.

However, Elphaba's gifts for sorcery make her a target for misuse by the head of the university, Madame Morrible, and the Wizard of Oz himself. Meanwhile, Galinda is promoted to play a role in the public front of the Wizard's government.

The ethical questions thrown up by the plot of the musical are furthered by the songs themselves. "No One Mourns the Wicked" and "No Good Deed" calls the audience's attention to the question of who is really evil and the reasons why.

KEY FACTS

🎭 **STAGE**

🎬 **Director** Joe Mantello

📖 **Book** Winnie Holzman, based on *Wicked: The Life and Times of the Wicked Witch of the West* by Gregory Maguire

♫ **Music and lyrics** Stephen Schwartz

🎭 **Venue** George Gershwin Theatre, New York

📅 **Date** 30 October 2003

◎ **Key information**

Wicked was the winner of three Tony Awards 2004 for Best Actress in a Musical (Idina Menzel), Best Costume Design, and Best Scenic Design. The play was nominated for seven others, including Best Musical, Best Actress in a Musical (Kristin Chenoweth), Best Book of a Musical, and Best Choreography.

> *"Its themes deal with ethical and philosophical questions: What is 'wicked' and what is 'good'…"*

STEPHEN SCHWARTZ, ANSWERING MISCELLANEOUS QUESTIONS ABOUT THE SHOW

▼ **Who's good, who's bad?**
Wicked tells the story of Elphaba, the green-skinned Wicked Witch of the West – seen here played by Margaret Hamilton in the 1939 movie *The Wizard of Oz*.

BIOGRAPHY

STEPHEN SCHWARTZ
(1948–)

Winner of three Oscars and three Grammys, and nominated for six Tonys, Stephen Schwartz is a favourite son of the musical industry. Working since 1969, when he wrote the title song for *Butterflies are Free*, Schwartz has since given us the music and lyrics for *Godspell*, *Pippin* (see p.186), and *Wicked*, as well as the lyrics for Disney's *Pocahontas*, *The Hunchback of Notre Dame*, and *Enchanted*.

HAIRSPRAY

{ **2002** }

In just over a decade, John Waters' *Hairspray* went from being a moderately successful independent film with a cult following to a multi-award-winning smash hit Broadway musical, and then a major Hollywood film.

KEY FACTS

✿ STAGE

- 🎬 **Director** Jack O'Brien
- 📖 **Book** Mark O'Donnell, Thomas Meehan
- 🎵 **Music and lyrics** Mark Shaiman, Scott Wittman
- 🎭 **Venue** Neil Simon Theatre, New York
- 📅 **Date** 15 August 2002

◉ Key information

The original Broadway production ran for a total of 2,642 performances, from August 2002 until January 2009. The many producers of this widely sponsored show included Margo Lion, Adam Epstein, The Baruch-Viertel-Routh-Frankel Group, James D. Stern, Douglas L. Meyer, Rick Steiner, Frederic H. Mayerson, SEL, GFO, and New Line Cinema.

Before *Hairspray*, it is doubtful that anyone would have predicted mainstream success for maverick film-maker John Waters. His previous X-rated movies took delight in pushing at the boundaries of generally accepted good taste. Many starred the extraordinary, avant-garde drag performer Divine. This was the first time Divine played a supporting character, the mother of

revolves around Tracy, a plump teenager in 1960s Baltimore, and her unlikely rise to stardom as a dancer on a local television show. Against a score of 1960s-style dance and R'n'B music, Tracy launches a campaign to racially integrate the show.

With the creative team assembled, Marissa Jaret Winokur was cast at an early stage in the role of Tracy Turnblad and spent two years

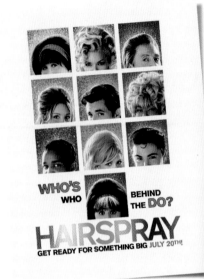

▲ **Sixties fantasy**
The poster for the film perfectly captures all the good-natured kitsch and tongue-in-cheek humour of this acclaimed production.

> *"With a common touch that stops short of vulgarity,* Hairspray *is as sweet as a show can be without promoting tooth decay."*
>
> **BEN BRANTLEY**, *THE NEW YORK TIMES*, 2002

and Direction. Winokur, Fierstein, and Latessa also won in the performance categories.

Like the film before it, the show manages the extraordinary feat of both being nostalgic for the 1960s and feeling completely fresh. It retains tremendous heart through all the high-octane camp and retains its subversive edge, while

a "pleasantly plump" teenager, Tracy. Divine, however, is superb, bringing tremendous heart and character to the role of a struggling suburban housewife and mother.

CREATIVE TEAM AND CAST

In 1998, theatre producer Margo Lion had the idea of turning *Hairspray* into a stage musical and acquired the rights from New Line Cinema. Composer Marc Shaiman and his lyricist and life partner Scott Wittman were hired as songwriters. Rob Marshall initiated direction of the piece, but later handed it over to Jack O'Brien, when he departed to make the film of *Chicago* (see pp.196–99), Jerry Mitchell took over the choreography. The plot

preparing with voice and dance lessons. The producers and creative team were keen to continue the tradition of casting a man as Tracy's mother, Edna Turnblad, so Harvey Fierstein was hired for the role. Dick Latessa was signed to play opposite Fierstein as the sweet but shabby and ineffectual father, Wilbur.

The Broadway production was a massive hit, running for more than six years and receiving 12 Tony Award nominations and winning eight, including Best Musical, Book, Score,

▲ **A star is born**
The previously unknown Nikki Blonsky, starring as Tracy in the 2007 film adaptation of *Hairspray*. Her performance was highly rated by critics.

▶ **Camping it up**
John Travolta was almost unrecognizable in the role of Edna Turnblad (left), mother of Tracy, in the film adaptation of the stage musical.

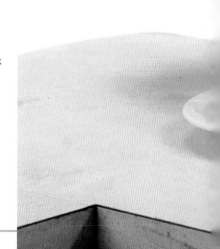

also being an old-fashioned story of family and an underdog succeeding against the odds.

SUCCESS BEYOND BROADWAY

A successful London West End production followed, attracting a record-breaking 11 Olivier Award nominations and winning Best New Musical. There were also acting awards for Best Actress and Actor in a Musical for its new mother and daughter team, Michael Ball (Edna) and Leanne Jones (Tracy).

▶ **Hip-hop Queen**
American actress and hip-hop star Queen Latifah (centre) played Baltimore record-shop owner and radio DJ "Motormouth" Maybelle in the 2007 film.

In 2007, *Hairspray* was adapted for the cinema, resulting in one of the most critically acclaimed and commercially successful musical films of the decade. It was to become the sixth-highest grossing musical film in US cinema history.

After extensive open auditions, the lead role of Tracy went to the unknown and inexperienced Nikki Blonsky. *Grease* star John Travolta was an unusual choice for Edna, but he triumphs in the role encased in a gigantic fat suit and prosthetic make-up. It may not be ground-breaking in style, or herald a new direction for the Broadway musical, but *Hairspray* seems

assured of its place as an enduring classic from early 21st-century Broadway. The show's release for community productions has led to it becoming a favourite piece for high-school revivals throughout the world.

BOLLYWOOD
FLAVOUR

Mumbai, India, is home to Bollywood, which is the centre of the world's largest Hindi language movie industry and one of the largest film production centres in the world.

Just as many different kinds of films are made by Hollywood, there are also many different kinds of Bollywood films. By far the most successful, popular, and internationally influential of these are a kind of film musical that is as distinctive as Hollywood's biggest action/adventure films.

Bollywood musicals are frequently melodramatic, with larger-than-life heroes and villains, and storylines involving characters such as lovers struggling against the wishes of their families and society. The plots are often resolved by the arrival of the gods from above, or amazing coincidences.

However, it is the spectacular song-and-dance routines that stand out the most. These opulently produced sequences do not arise out of character and action in the same way that they would in a Western musical. Frequently, the plot will provide a convenient excuse for a song. Musical numbers in Bollywood films are non-realistic; instead, they are idealized versions of reality that resemble lavish music videos.

CELEBRATED VOICES

Stars are often a driving force behind Bollywood films. Since most of the actors are not exceptional singers, many of the songs in these movies are recorded by professional singers and then lip-synched by the actors onscreen. The recording artists are stars themselves; they are given prominent credit, and can be as much of a featured attraction of the film as the onscreen star.

Choreography in early Bollywood films originally had its basis in classic Indian dance styles, historic dances of northern Indian courtesans, or Indian folk dances. Modern Bollywood dance numbers typically merge this dance vocabulary with contemporary music video choreography and Broadway-style dances.

In the 2000s, Bollywood played a role in the revival of the American musical film genre, with Baz Luhrmann stating that *Moulin Rouge!* (see p.294) was directly inspired by Bollywood musicals.

◀ **Opulent extravaganza**

This scene from the award-winning film *Devdas* shows the lavish costumes and spectacular dance numbers that characterize Bollywood films.

> *"Bollywood stars are versatile; they not only act, but each one has the dance skills of John Travolta in Saturday Night Fever."*

CHRISTIAN LOUBOUTIN, FRENCH FOOTWEAR DESIGNER, 2013

AVENUE Q

{ 2003 }

Couple *Sesame Street* with cynicism and you are left with *Avenue Q*, a satirical take on kids' television and its every-child-a-special-snowflake optimism.

Robert Lopez (see below) and Jeff Marx had both brushed up against the Jim Henson Company – makers of *The Muppets* – before they made their famous puppet musical. Marx had actually worked on *Sesame Street* as an intern for a while, before jumping ship and trying to make programmes of his own. He and Lopez met when they were both struggling songwriters in New York. Deciding to work together, they came up with *Kermit, Prince of Denmark*, a "Muppetization" of Shakespeare's most famous tragedy, though the Jim Henson Company were not finally persuaded of its "kid-appeal". The work they eventually broke through with, though a *Sesame Street*-style drama, in which

Muppet-like puppets and people talk and interact, was very definitely adult fare: "Warning: Contains Full Puppet Nudity; Not Suitable for Children", said the sign on the door of the Vineyard Theatre when it opened.

ALL GROWN UP

"What," asked puppeteer Rick Lyon, another old *Sesame Street* hand involved in the production, "if a cozy, familiar kids' television show had to grow up? Not just the characters, but the subject matter, the songs, the attitude?" As if to underline the absurdity of this idea, Lyon and his fellow puppeteers – Stephanie Abruzzo, Jennifer Barnhart, and John Tartaglia – remained for the most part visible while they manipulated these "characters", even as they chatted with real people live on stage. Since no continuity could necessarily be had over which puppeteer worked which puppet (for some of the more elaborate figures, operation was actually a two-puppeteer job), pretending that they were not there could be hard work.

However, this was nothing compared to the unnerving spectacle of these engaging and profoundly innocent-looking puppets agonizing over the whole gamut of adult issues – from coming out as gay to scratching together rent for their apartments.

The title "Avenue Q", apart from its obvious homage to that of *Sesame Street*, also corresponded with one of

Brooklyn's remotest residential roads – the closest place to the city a young out-of-towner could hope to live. Other troubles include an unfulfilling sex life; the stresses and strains of cohabitation; the temptations of internet pornography; and the appeal of laughing at others' misfortunes.

COLEMAN'S COMPLAINT

To underline the irony, one of the "human" characters portrayed by a living, breathing (although actually female) actor was "Gary Coleman" – named after the former child star of

Diff'rent Strokes. Through the hugely popular television serial that ran in the United States from 1978–86, he had become a household name by the time he was ten years old.

Avenue Q's Gary Coleman, now 33, is working as the janitor of the building in which the action takes place – an exaggeration of the true-life Gary's plight, but not by much. "It Sucks to Be Me," sing all the characters in turn at one point, listing their various grievances and their frustrations in competitive discontent. But all have to agree that it must suck to be Coleman most.

His portrayal comes close to the bone, and seems to have upset its real-life model, who tried to sue. Harsh, but *Avenue Q* does not pull its punches. Coleman might not like it, but he was central to the project. "He's the poster child for what the show is about," Robert Lopez was to explain. "Not feeling special because you're not a kid anymore."

▲ **Surreal success**
Avenue Q has travelled the world, with productions and tours appearing in many cities in more than ten countries.

BILLY ELLIOT

{ **2005** }

One of the most celebrated and successful musicals of the early 21st century, *Billy Elliot* was adapted by writer Lee Hall, director Stephen Daldry, and choreographer Peter Darling from their low-budget British film of the same name.

Despite an understated score by Elton John (see pp.304–05), the staging of this musical is so vivid and the plot about a young boy's unlikely rise from poverty to a career in ballet so uplifting that it has triumphed in productions around the world over the past ten years. One reviewer went as far as saying it was "the greatest British musical" he had ever seen.

The background to Billy's story is the British coal miners' strike of 1984 and its impact on the blue-collar workers in the northeast of England. It is a tough, sometimes brutal environment, in which men were expected to conform to traditional ideas of machismo and where male ballet has no place.

In spite of these obvious disadvantages, our young hero discovers he possesses great skill and appreciation of the art form. His early steps are taken at a local dance class, but when it becomes clear that his developing skill and ambitions could take him further, his family must make considerable sacrifices to send him to a prestigious ballet school. The hardships they face are exacerbated by a lack of income

during a strike to save the local mining industry from the cuts made by Margaret Thatcher's government.

AMBITION TRIUMPHS
Some of the most poignant moments in the production juxtapose gritty depictions of industrial unrest with children's ballet, most notably when a chorus line of young ballerinas dance in front of a line of riot police. Despite the hardships that Billy and his family face, the production gives full expression to his soaring ambitions, including some spectacular aerial work.

The original production opened at The Victoria Palace in London's West End. A plan for it to open in the community where the story is set was abandoned when Newcastle's Tyne Theatre could not finance or accommodate the increasing demands of the staging. The £5.5 million production of the stage show eventually overtook the cost of the film (2000), and includes a spectacular set by Ian MacNeil, which brings scenic elements in from above and deep below the stage.

The stars of the production and the many subsequent stagings around the world are the three boys who alternate in the role of Billy.

The demands of the part, and often local licensing laws, prohibit a single child actor from appearing performance. In order to provide the production with a steady supply of young performers with the necessary acting, singing, and dancing skills, as well as a mastery of the tricky regional accent required, a series of training schemes have been set up wherever *Billy Elliot* is produced.

INTERNATIONAL SUCCESS
Billy Elliot regularly triumphs in theatre awards whenever it is mounted. The original London production won four Laurence Olivier Awards: Best New Musical, Best Actor (awarded jointly to James Lomas, George Maguire, and Liam Mower), Best Sound Design,

KEY FACTS

STAGE
- **Director** Stephen Daldry
- **Book** Lee Hall
- **Music** Elton John
- **Lyrics** Lee Hall
- **Venue** The Victoria Palace Theatre, London
- **Date** 11 May 2005

◉ Key information
The original West End production of this show is still running. Choreographed by Peter Darling, it features sets by Ian MacNeil and costumes by Nicky Gillibrand. The first cast included Liam Mower, James Lomas, and George Maguire (alternating in the roles of Billy), Haydn Gwynne, and Tim Healy.

▼ Picket lines
Billy Elliot is set during the miners' strike of 1984–85. Several scenes depict the picket lines and clashes between the police and striking miners.

▶ Daring to dance
Theatre critic Mark Shenton called *Billy Elliot* "the greatest modern dance musical since *A Chorus Line*."

"*The greatest British musical I have ever seen.*"

CHARLES SPENCER, *THE DAILY TELEGRAPH*

and Best Choreographer. The 2008 Broadway production received a record-equalling 15 Tony Award nominations, winning ten, including the award for Best Musical and Best

Choreography. The role of Billy garnered the three actors sharing the part (David Álvarez, Kiril Kulish, and Trent Kowalik) a joint win for Best Leading Actor in a Musical.

Like all the most successful musical productions, *Billy Elliot* continued to make headlines. When former British Prime Minister Margaret Thatcher died in 2013, the audience was asked to vote on whether a song gleefully anticipating the event should be still performed. It was.

Over the weekend when the stage show was filmed live and broadcast to cinemas, it topped the box office charts in the UK and Ireland, beating the latest Hollywood blockbuster into second place. Regular guest appearances from past, now adult, Billies continue to charm the public

▲ Royal Opera House

The Royal Ballet is based at the Royal Opera House in Convent Garden, London. In *Billy Elliot*, the young Billy is accepted to study at the Royal Ballet School, the Royal Ballet's official school.

and make for reliably popular photo opportunities to mark significant anniversaries in the musical's history.

Notable replicate and touring productions of the show have been big hits across the United States and Canada, in Australia, the Netherlands, and Korea. Meanwhile, the original production continues its triumphant run in the West End.

ELTON JOHN

{ SONGWRITER/COMPOSER **1947–** }

The gifted showman Sir Elton John, CBE, has recorded 51 albums and sold 250 million records worldwide. His influence and involvement in musical theatre has also been great, with award-winning work on such triumphs as *The Lion King*.

Even as a young child, Reginald Dwight (born in 1947 to parents Sheila and RAF trumpet player Stanley), showed extraordinary musical talent. Aged three, he played the piano by ear, and at 11 won a junior scholarship to the Royal Academy of Music in London, attending weekly lessons for four years. While still at Pinner County Grammar School, the young musician played piano on weekends at a hotel under the name of "Reggie", and also on keyboards with local group The Corvettes. They later reformed as Bluesology, with Reginald adopting the stage name "Elton John", taken respectively from the names of Elton Dean (Bluesology saxophonist) and lead singer Long John Baldry. Dwight changed his name legally in 1967.

ELTON AND BERNIE

John, who left school at 17 to pursue his music career, met the teenage lyricist Bernie Taupin in 1967, after both answered a song-writing advertisement by Liberty Records. The pair started writing songs together – by post – and in 1968 left Liberty to join British music publisher Dick James's DJM label. As well as writing material for other artists, they were busy creating and recording songs for John, who was steadily making a name for himself in the UK. He cut his debut album, *Empty Sky*, in 1969 and the next year played in Los Angeles, quite

"Music has healing power. It has the ability to take people out of themselves for a few hours."

ELTON JOHN

▶ **Glittering star**
Elton John performs on Dick Clark's New Year's Rockin' Eve, 31 December 2014, in New York City.

▲ Piano man
Elton John performing at the Dodgers Stadium in Los Angeles in 1975. In this iconic Terry O'Neill image, he is wearing a sequinned baseball uniform.

literally becoming an overnight sensation in the United States.

The 1970s and 80s were intensely creative decades for the song-writing duo, resulting in no fewer than 26 pop-rock albums, 17 during the 1970s alone. Some, like *Duets*, are compilations, but the sheer versatility of the John–Taupin repertoire is breathtaking – heart-rending ballads rub shoulders with vigorous and toe-tapping rock'n'roll numbers. In 1975, John also starred in the musical film *Tommy* based on The Who's 1969 rock opera album of the same name. The 1973 album *Goodbye Yellow Brick Road* is regarded as his best and most popular, featuring the iconic singles "Saturday Night's Alright for Fighting", "Candle in the Wind" (original 1973 version), and "Bennie and the Jets". Who can forget "Rocket Man" (1972), "Don't Go Breaking My Heart" (the chart-topping summer 1976 duet with Kiki Dee), the soulful "Blue Eyes" (1982), or the lively "I'm Still Standing", from the 1983 album *Too Low For Zero*? John's (and the world's) biggest-selling single remains the 1997 version of "Candle in the Wind", adapted as his heart-felt tribute to Princess Diana, who died that year. John and Taupin have continued to pen a succession of well-received albums, including *Peachtree Road* in 2004 and *The Union* (a 2010 collaboration with American musician Leon Russell). Even after nearly 50

Oscar success with *The Lion King*
Elton John and Tim Rice pose with Sylvester Stallone at the 1995 Academy Awards, where the duo won the award for Music (Original Song).

years of successful song-writing, the duo have never physically written a song together – Taupin always writes the lyrics first.

STAGE AND SCREEN
John worked with lyricist Sir Tim Rice (see p.185) on several songs for Disney's 1994 film *The Lion King* and his beautiful rendition of their song "Can You Feel The Love Tonight?" won the Academy Award for Best Original Song the following year. With playwright Lee Hall, John wrote the music for the critically acclaimed and award-winning *Billy Elliot The Musical* (see pp.302–03), which opened in London in 2005. John also wrote the music for the animated Rocket Pictures' film *Gnomeo & Juliet*, co-produced by himself and his husband, David Furnish, in 2011.

THE CHARITIES
Charity work is an important part of John's life. During the early 1990s he established the Elton John AIDS Foundation, which has raised over US$300 million for projects in as many as 55 countries, and is also patron or ambassador to 22 other charities. Sales of the adapted version of "Candle in the Wind" have raised millions for the Diana, Princess

▲ A new partnership
Elton John and Tim Rice formed a highly fruitful songwriting partnership in the late 1990s, when they penned the music and lyrics for *Aida*.

of Wales Memorial Fund. Elton John also endows scholarship funds at The Royal Academy of Music in London and the Juilliard School of Music in New York. In 1998, Elton John was knighted in recognition for "services to music and charitable services".

PRIVATE LIFE
In 1984, Elton John married Renate Blauel, a German sound recording engineer who worked on his album *Too Low for Zero*, but the couple divorced four years later. John formed a civil partnership with Canadian-born David Furnish in 2005, marrying him in 2014. Furnish is chairman of Rocket Pictures and producer of the documentary *Elton John: Tantrums and Tiaras* (1997). The couple have two sons, Zachary and Elijah, born via surrogacy in 2010 and 2013 respectively.

CAREER AND AWARDS
Elton John is a prolific, energetic, and intensely creative songwriter and musician. Over the last 50 years, he has played 3,500 concerts in 80 countries. In 2004, Elton John and his band began a residency with The Red Piano show in Las Vegas, playing there for five years and returning with a new four-year show in 2011. He has also received many awards for his music and charity work, including an Academy Award, 12 Ivor Novello Awards, five Grammy Awards, and a Tony Award, which he won for Best Original Musical Score for *Aida*.

TIMELINE

- **25 March 1947** Born Reginald Dwight, in Middlesex, England.

- **1959–67** Studies at the Royal Academy of Music, London.

- **1965–67** Tours the UK with Bluesology.

- **1967** Changes name to Elton John; begins collaborating with Bernie Taupin.

- **1968** John and Taupin write songs for DJM label.

- **25 August 1970** John's US debut.

- **1973** John founds The Rocket Record Company.

- **19 March 1975** US opening of rock opera *Tommy*.

- **October 1975** Elton John's star unveiled on the Hollywood Walk of Fame.

HOLLYWOOD WALK OF FAME STAR

- **1992** Elton John AIDS Foundation established.

- **15 June 1994** US release of *The Lion King* film.

- **1995** *The Lion King* wins Academy Award for Best Original Score.

- **13 September 1997** Record-selling single "Candle In The Wind" released.

- **24 February 1998** John knighted.

- **8 July 1997** US opening of *The Lion King* musical on Broadway.

- **23 March 2000** US release of *Aida*.

- **2004** John begins residency in Las Vegas.

- **21 December 2005** John enters into a civil partnership with David Furnish.

- **11 May 2005** UK opening of *Billy Elliot The Musical*.

- **25 December 2010** Son Zachary born.

- **2011** John and Furnish co-produce animated film *Gnomeo & Juliet*.

- **11 January 2013** Son Elijah born.

JERSEY BOYS

{ 2005 }

One expects artistic inspiration to flourish in unexpected places – but might not appreciate the true labour it takes to bear fruit. Success brought The Four Seasons glory they could hardly have imagined – but theirs was to be a peculiarly furtive kind of fame.

With their huge hits, "Sherry", "Big Girls Don't Cry", "Rag Doll", and "Bye, Bye, Baby", the rock and pop group The Four Seasons were essential to the Sixties sound. But the boys who were destined one day to find evergreen success as The Four Seasons had to fight every inch of the way to win and then hold on to the success; nor were they quite the clean-cut, effortlessly engaging figures that they appeared to be when they started out.

Francesco Stephen Castellucio – better known now as Frankie Valli – Bob Gaudio, Tommy de Vito, and Nick Massi had all been brought up in an Italian-American community in which organized crime had been an active presence. De Vito and Massi had both been in and out of correctional facilities all their teenage years. It was,

ironically, this chequered history and these gamy gangland connections that ensured that The Four Seasons never stepped out of line. While other stars could afford to flirt with rebellion, experiment with drugs, and take anti-establishment postures, they simply had to stay squeaky clean. "The idea of our story getting out was horrifying to us," Bob Gaudio recalled.

BUILDING SUCCESS

Marshall Brickman and Rick Elice's musical *Jersey Boys* tells their story a season (in both senses) at a time. First, in "Spring", Tommy de Vito describes the early struggles of the band – then just a trio, comprising himself, Frankie, and Nick: the name-changes, the shuffling of the line-up; the seeming successes; the reversals. One of these was De Vito's own spell in New Jersey's Rahway Prison, for passing off

counterfeit money for a friend. The good fortune that had evaded the group this far finally came when they met Bob Gaudio, who takes over the narration for the second section and season, "Summer".

DECLINE AND FALL

The Four Seasons (as they had now called themselves) found success thanks to Bob's songwriting skills and

KEY FACTS

STAGE

Director Des McAnuff

Book Marshall Brickman, Rick Elice

Music and lyrics Bob Gaudio, Bob Crewe

Venue August Wilson Theatre, New York

Date 6 November 2005

Key information

Originally on Broadway, the show also opened in Chicago (2007), London (2008), and Las Vegas (2009). It won four 2006 Tony Awards, including Best Musical, and the 2009 Laurence Olivier Award for Best New Musical.

> *"It took a lot of courage for them to let us put their lives on stage."*
>
> MARSHALL BRICKMAN, CO-AUTHOR OF *JERSEY BOYS*, SEPTEMBER 2010

his collaborations with Bob Crewe: famous hits from "Sherry" to "Walk Like a Man" date from this time. But cracks were already forming beneath the glossy veneer of stardom.

Nick Massi then describes their "Fall" from grace, in the autumn section of the show – Tommy's debts and trouble with the tax man; resentment at Frankie Valli's special stardom.

In "Winter", Frankie himself takes up the tale, describing the strains their life at the top was exacting on the Seasons' personal lives – ultimately, too tough to be endured.

The musical was well received on Broadway and then toured the US. It went on to a West End production and numerous others across the world.

◀ **Seasonal sensations**
John Lloyd Young, Erich Bergen, Vincent Piazza, and Michael Lomenda starred in the 2014 film version of *Jersey Boys*, directed by Clint Eastwood

SPAMALOT

{ 2005 }

Silly songs were always an important part of the Monty Python package, but the first musical – largely the work of Eric Idle – was not actually to appear for three decades.

Spam may have been, as the American GIs joked, the "ham that failed its physical", but for decades it was a staple of the UK diet. Is it so surprising, then, that it should have loomed so large in the imagination of the Pythons, given their respective ages and backgrounds?

It first came welling up like some dark, unsettling monster of the deep unconscious in a famous sketch in 1970, in which Spam is served with every single dish – including lobster. And it came up again when the time came to make a musical of the movie *Monty Python and the Holy Grail* (1975).

LOVELY SPAM

Spam is made by pulping up pork shoulder meat, then mixing it with ham and gelatine before binding the whole mass together with potato starch, salt, and sugar and cooking it in the tin. Some critics found *Spamalot* a similarly unusual mixture. Not only did the musical represent to the public a pre-existing film, which few fans had missed the first time round, but it brought together an enormous range of old Python references – from lumberjacks and the Finland song, to fish-slapping and the Ministry of Silly Walks. What, some wondered, was the point of the thing?

For most of those who flocked to see the show, however, these little acts of homage were pretty much the point: this was a celebration of the Monty Python spirit in all its silliness and over-the-top nonsensicality. Part of the pleasure of Monty Python for its young followers had always been the subsequent recitation (and endless re-recitation)

of extended screeds of dialogue – such as the Dead Parrot sketch, the Restaurant sketch, and the Four Yorkshiremen.

ROMANCING THE SPAM

It goes without saying that any resemblance to the Arthurian legend of English and European tradition is fairly superficial. We do get to see knights in armour roaming round in the time-honoured manner, fighting with swords: there is a "Lady of the Lake", an Excalibur sword, and what at least at first appears to be a damsel in distress. Sir Lancelot turns out to be gay. Then, of course, there is the Holy Grail – an object of chivalric quest since the romances of the Middle Ages, generally assumed to be the sacred chalice used by Christ at His Last Supper. Though sought in vain for

centuries, it finally turns up now – under a seat in one of the theatre's front rows. All this and processed pork as well: in honour of its Broadway opening, making a virtue of necessity, Hormel Foods Corporation, the originators of the product, issued a special tie-in edition of their tins of Spam.

KEY FACTS

STAGE

Director Mike Nichols

Book Eric Idle

Music John Du Prez, Eric Idle, Neil Innes

Lyrics Eric Idle

Venue Shubert Theatre, New York

Date 17 March 2005

Key information

Spamalot won three Tony Awards: Best Musical, Best Direction (Mike Nichols) and Best Featured Actress in a Musical (Sara Ramirez).

▶ Arthurian parody
The film *Monty Python and the Holy Grail*, which starred Graham Chapman, John Cleese, Terry Gilliam, Eric Idle, Terry Jones, and Michael Palin, was the inspiration for *Spamalot*.

SPRING AWAKENING

{ **2006** }

When the musical reworking of Frank Wedekind's 1891 play *Spring Awakening* finally opened on Broadway after seven years in development, it felt like a breath of fresh air amid all the jukebox shows.

The story is set in late 19th-century Germany and deals with the sexual awakening of a group of teenagers. It also addresses the hypocrisy of the adults who will not provide them with a sexual education, yet are horrified at their children's mistakes.

Composer Duncan Sheik and book and lyric writer Steven Sater chose indie rock as the medium with which to tell the story. This unlikely marriage of modern and 19th-century teenage angst proved to be a stroke of genius and allowed young audiences in 2006 to relate to the remarkably similar problems faced by their counterparts on stage.

A "STEAM PUNK" PRODUCTION

With this approach as inspiration, director Michael Mayer, costume designer Susan Hilferty, and set designer Christine Jones also combined a Victorian and modern high school aesthetic to create a "Steam Punk" look for the show. The term attempts to convey the old, Victorian elements ("steam") and the new, contemporary aspects ("punk") of the staging. Props and costumes were, for the most part, from the period of the play (1890s), but this was combined with extreme sculptured hairstyles for the boys and a simple staging, as if the piece were being given a rough-and-ready performance in a school gym. To add to the effect, audience members

---

KEY FACTS

🎭 **STAGE**

🎬 **Director** Michael Mayer
📖 **Book** Steven Sater
🎵 **Music** Duncan Sheik
𝄞 **Lyrics** Steven Sater
🎭 **Venue** Eugene O'Neill Theatre, New York
📅 **Date** 10 December 2006

⊙ **Key information**
The original Broadway production ran for 859 performances in just over two years, closing in January 2009. It was nominated for a total of 11 Tony Awards and won eight. The West End production that followed was nominated for seven Laurence Olivier awards in 2010 and won four.

◄ **Uncomfortable content**
The Playbill for the Broadway show left audiences in doubt as to the explicit nature of the subject matter.

Roundabout Theatre Company. These culminated in a concert at Lincoln Center for the Performing Arts in February 2005 and an Off-Broadway try-out that premiered at the Atlantic Theatre in 2006. That successful run led to a full Broadway transfer, opening at the Eugene O'Neill Theatre on 10 December the same year. Its original cast included Jonathan Groff and Lea Michele, who would both go on to star in the popular television show *Glee*.

Although *Spring Awakening* was a hit with cosmopolitan New York audiences, the edgy production style and subject matter struggled to find an audience in more conservative cities across the country during the national tour.

DISAPPOINTMENT

The piece was equally critically acclaimed and popular when it was remounted at the Lyric Theatre in Hammersmith, an Off-West End venue in London. However, when it transferred to the West End, its limited niche appeal and a hike in ticket prices, which excluded the very young people it was intended for, saw business wither and die. The musical closed early despite winning four Laurence Olivier Awards, including Best New Musical.

A series of international productions followed, including translations into Hungarian, Swedish, Japanese, and Welsh. Beyond Broadway, the show has rarely recaptured the buzz surrounding the original Broadway version. However, a successful new take on the show by Deaf West Theatre premiered in Los Angeles in 2014. Performed in part by deaf actors, it accentuated the show's themes of communication and need for a voice. The Deaf West production eventually transferred to Broadway, opening at the Brooks Atkinson Theatre on 27 September 2015, to much acclaim.

sat on stage around the playing area. The performers alternated between playing naturalistic dialogue and performing the songs into hand-held microphones, as if they were performing at a rock concert. The cast and onstage band were predominantly youthful, but by way of contrast, an older male and female actor played all the adult roles.

Without these brilliant concepts the piece may not have been the success it was, but production, play, and score perfectly meshed into a striking and highly original evening's theatre. Critics were almost unanimous in their view that the conceit worked well.

CONTROVERSY AND ACCLAIM

The Wedekind play has always been controversial for its frank depiction of blossoming sexuality, and the musical did not shy away from explicit references to teenage sexual issues. *Spring Awakening* became the Broadway show that young people begged their parents to take them to see, but it made for rather uncomfortable viewing for any accompanying adult.

NUMEROUS REWRITES

The development process was long and thorough, involving many rewrites and changes to the score through workshops at La Jolla Playhouse, San Diego, California, and the

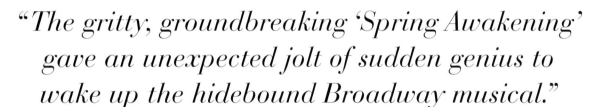

"The gritty, groundbreaking 'Spring Awakening' gave an unexpected jolt of sudden genius to wake up the hidebound Broadway musical."

CLIVE BARNES, THE *NEW YORK POST*

► Multinational appeal
The themes of the show has made it popular for younger audiences around the world. Here, it's being performed in Welsh by the touring Theatr Genedlaethol Cymru in 2011.

JUKEBOX MUSICALS

Using popular music – often from a particular artist or group's back catalogue – as the score, a new form of musical has been bringing in audiences in droves.

Jukebox musicals are a relatively new phenomenon in which full scores for new musicals are taken from catalogues of pre-existing material. Before the 1940s, composers would often take their most popular songs from previous seasons and place them in their new musicals to help ensure success.

NO PLOT NEEDED

In the 1970s and 80s, musical revues became very popular, celebrating the works of great composers and lyricists in an evening of tribute. Some of these included a 1976 revue of the songs of Stephen Sondheim called *Side by Side by Sondheim*, a 1978 revue of Fats Waller's songs named *Ain't Misbehavin'* (see p.214), and *Perfectly Frank* – a 1980 revue of the songs of Frank Loesser (see pp.92–93).

Many contemporary jukebox musicals take the back catalogue of songs from an artist or group and create a full-blown book musical round them. *Jersey Boys*, one of the most successful, took the songs of Bob Gaudio and Bob Crewe written for the band The Four Seasons and used them to tell the story

of that rock group (see p.306). This same format has been used for Carole King (*Beautiful*), Buddy Holly (*The Buddy Holly Story*), and music producer Berry Gordy (*Motown, the Musical*).

FINDING A STORY

Other jukebox musicals place their chosen songs into the context of a story-based book musical. Though some of these book musicals – such as *Mamma Mia!* (see pp.284–85) and *We Will Rock You* – use songs from one set of songwriters, others use a variety of popular songs and chart hits to create the score.

Story-based book musicals include *Return to the Forbidden Planet* (1989), the Rodgers and Hammerstein-based *Crazy For You* (see p.262), *Moulin Rouge!* (see p.294), *Priscilla Queen of the Desert* (2006), and *An American in Paris* (2015), which uses a score of music and songs by George and Ira Gershwin.

▶ **Queen of the desert**
Priscilla Queen of the Desert, based on a cult movie about three performers travelling through the Australian Outback in a brightly coloured bus, uses a host of well-known pop songs for its score.

"I am delighted that producers are still willing to invest in bringing new shows to Broadway and the West End, based on our favourite pop icons."

TOM MILLWARD, *LONDONTHEATRE.CO.UK*, 9 OCTOBER 2014

LEGALLY BLONDE

{ 2007 }

The story of a sorority girl's improbable progress to Harvard Law School makes for a screamingly funny comedy of manners – and a strikingly serious journey of self-discovery.

▶ **Delightfully ditzy**
British actress Sheridan Smith was a huge hit as Elle Woods in the 2009 West End incarnation, also winning an Olivier Award for her performance.

A story of triumph over adversity always goes down well – perhaps especially in the musical theatre where just about any venture seems to start out facing overwhelming odds. But when the difficulty to be overcome is a life of pampered privilege, pink, frothy girliness, sorority society, and non-stop shopping, we know we are dealing with a very special category of disadvantage: that faced by the "legally blonde" Elle Woods. This ditzy-doll-turned-successful-attorney is known to most as the character played by Reese Witherspoon in the 2001 movie.

SOPHOCLES AT SCHOOL

The comedy in *Legally Blonde* walks a fine line between affection and contempt: our first challenge is to take Elle even the slightest bit seriously. As we meet her, she is angst-ridden about the need to find the perfect dress so she can have the perfect celebration of her perfect engagement with her perfect fiancé, Warner Huntington III.

This is our introduction to that peculiar world-within-a-world of the US college sorority and fraternity, which impose their own social caste system on many institutions, each of them known by a collection of Greek letters.

The vapidity of Elle and her friends is matched by Warner's quite astonishing self-importance and pomposity. If one struggles to take Elle seriously at the start, that changes – immediately and irrevocably – when he informs her that he is calling off their engagement because he needs someone more "serious" at his side to take him where he expects to go in life.

If Elle's clear sincerity stirs sympathy, her resolve to get herself into Harvard Law School, and her tireless industry in pursuing that goal, ultimately commands respect.

Along the way, Elle learns to see the law as a means to helping others and making life a little better for everyone she encounters – from her friend Paulette to Vivienne, a former rival who becomes her staunch ally.

KEY FACTS

🎭 **STAGE**
🎬 **Director** Jerry Mitchell
📖 **Book** Heather Hach
🎵 **Music and lyrics** Nell Benjamin, Laurence O'Keefe
🎫 **Venue** Golden Gate Theatre, San Francisco
📅 **Date** 29 April 2007

◉ **Key information**
An MTV recording of *Legally Blonde* in 2007 paved the way for a major reality show when it came to the time for Laura Bell Bundy to be replaced. *The Search for Elle Woods* came up with a clear winner: Bailey Hanks, who took the Broadway role of Elle.

"I've also been a blonde... and I've also been... underestimated."

HEATHER HACH, LIBRETTIST

IN THE HEIGHTS

{ 2008 }

Many blocks from Leonard Bernstein and Stephen Sondheim's West Side, and a million miles away in mood and attitudes, Washington Heights becomes the setting for a very different story.

Beyond Harlem, near the northernmost end of Manhattan Island, is the district of Washington Heights. For decades now, it has been a centre for New York's Hispanic – and especially its Dominican – community. Spanish is spoken; the sound of salsa music (and the smell of Caribbean cooking) fills the air. To white, English-speaking Americans, it can seem strange, exotic – even a bit intimidating – but ordinary decent people here do the best they can to get by from day to day. This is no more the inner-city inferno of caricature than its citizens are the switchblade-clicking gangs of *West Side Story* (see pp.122–25). Lin-Manuel Miranda, who had the idea for this musical as a student at college in Connecticut, hails from the Heights himself and is of Puerto Rican ancestry. And though she was born and brought up, not in New York but in Philadelphia, Quiara Alegría Hudes too has a Puerto Rican background. While the Washington Heights they evoke in their musical certainly moves with a lively Latin beat, it always has the feel of a real place.

DOMINICAN DREAMS

"I am Usnavi," the narrator introduces himself. Named for the inscription his parents saw on the side of a US Navy ship that they saw on their arrival in America, he runs a little local general store, or bodega. Usnavi begins to rap, in the edgy and syncopated style that marks out this show. However, as frenzied as the rap routines may be, as fast and furious as the dancing becomes, life in the Heights has many of the same problems as life elsewhere. A daughter drops out of college, collapsing from the effort of keeping up two jobs to support her studies; her boyfriend dreams of starting his own business; an elderly matriarch helps hold her family together in the new country, but cannot help missing the island world she left behind; and a young hairdresser hankers for the real glamour of the life that she might be able to make downtown.

Not that the less appealing aspects of life in the Heights are glossed over, by any means. There is poverty here; "there are fights and endless debts and bills to pay". The action takes place against the backdrop of a literal, meteorological "long hot summer", prompting some scorn among the elders of these so-called Latins who cannot stand a little heat. When the scorching temperatures cause city-wide power cuts, there are widespread fears of rioting and looting – but the crowd's response is to rally round to help defend the local shops.

▲ **The Heights**
During the 1970s and 80s, the Washington Heights neighbourhood became the centre of New York's Hispanic community.

> *"My earliest memory takes place in a bodega on Dyckman Street in Washington Heights."*
>
> **LIN-MANUEL MIRANDA**, COMPOSER

LUCKY NUMBERS

Overhanging the entire drama, meanwhile, is the general speculation over which of Usnavi's customers is in line for a US$96,000 lottery win, having bought the winning slip in his shop.

Who would not want a ticket out of Washington Heights? The question seems simply rhetorical at first: life here is hard and unrelenting, that much is clear. Usnavi cannot help sharing his mother's dream of a Dominican homecoming – but, as the action unfolds, we start to see the ties that bind him here. These include the loyalties of his extended family, the friendship and support of the community at large, and their pride in what they have built.

KEY FACTS

🎭 STAGE

🎬 **Director** Thomas Kail

📖 **Book** Quiara Alegría Hudes

🎵 **Music and lyrics** Lin-Manuel Miranda

🎦 **Venue** Richard Rodgers Theatre, New York

📅 **Date** 9 March 2008

⊙ Key information

The 2008 Broadway production of *In the Heights* was nominated for 13 Tony Awards. It won four, for Best Musical, Best Original Score, Best Choreography, and Best Orchestrations. In 2009, the show also won the Grammy Award for Best Musical Show Album.

MATILDA THE MUSICAL

{ **2010** }

Few modern musicals have scored a greater success than *Matilda*. Tim Minchin's music and lyrics, Dennis Kelly's book, and Marcus Warchus's direction combined to create a show that was simultaneously funny, moving, and poignant.

Turning Roald Dahl's much-loved children's book *Matilda* into a hit musical was the daunting challenge faced by the Royal Shakespeare Company and its chosen creative team when the decision to go ahead with the project was finally made in 2008. The story of a little girl with a brilliant mind, her uncaring parents, her kindly teacher Miss Honey, and the formidable headmistress, Miss Trunchbull, had been a children's classic since almost immediately after its first publication in 1988. The question was whether a stage adaptation could ever live up to the original story. The project was by no means the first attempt to translate Dahl's prose into other media. There had been two movie versions of *Charlie and the Chocolate Factory* – the first one of which Dahl detested because it focused more on Willie Wonka than on Charlie Bucket himself – and an all-American film version of *Matilda*. The musical was, however, the most ambitious adaptation to date.

DAHL'S PLOTTING PROBLEMS
Dahl himself put in immense efforts to get every detail of *Matilda* right. He got off to a bad start – Stephen Roxburgh, his long-time American editor, described an early draft of the story tersely as "hopeless". For the first time in his long career, Dahl decided to discard everything he had written up until then and start the story afresh. He wrote to Lucy Dahl, his youngest daughter: "The first half is great, about a small girl who can move things with her eyes and about a terrible headmistress who lifts small children up by their hair and hangs them out of upstairs windows by one ear. But I've got now to think of a really decent second half."

It was perhaps not that surprising that Dahl appears to have been struggling. He set himself the highest

◄ **Film poster**
The story had been made into a film in 1996 with American star Danny de Vito, directing, narrating, and taking the part of Mr Wormwood.

possible standards when writing. "You must be a perfectionist," he once said. "That means you must never be satisfied with what you have written until you have rewritten it again and again, making it as good as you possibly can." The composer Tim Minchin (see below) and the writer Dennis Kelly, commissioned by the Royal Shakespeare Company to undertake the task of adapting the book as a musical, were to follow much the same path of seeking perfection when they started working together on *Matilda The Musical*, as their new show was now titled.

◄ **Miss Trunchbull versus Miss Honey**
The archetypal evil headmistress Miss Trunchbull is pitted against the kindly teacher Miss Honey in this scene from the original stage production. Set and costume design is by Rob Howell.

◄ **Celebrating children**
The central character of Matilda embodies and celebrates the natural energy, determination, and sense of justice of children, appealing to family audiences.

FROM PAGE TO STAGE
Tim Minchin had tried to secure the stage rights to Roald Dahl's celebrated story ten years earlier, but had dropped the idea when the Dahl estate asked him to submit a draft "score". Working with director, Matthew Warchus, and writer, Dennis Kelly, who had created the script adaptation, he had his first draft of the score ready by the close of summer 2008, in time for the first workshop production at the RSC's London rehearsal rooms that September. Following that staging, the show was significantly restructured with many more major changes being made over the new year. Some of the innovations that were introduced were radical – originally, for instance, the children's roles were to be played by adults, not by children at all.

MAKING A BLOCKBUSTER
Throughout the creative process, the creative team's aim was clear. "We weren't cynically trying to make a blockbuster," Minchin said in a 2012 interview, "but we did want to tell a story that touched a huge cross-section of people. Kids come out overjoyed and adults come out feeling they've been on an emotional journey."

The quest for perfection continued. Some characters were eliminated, songs were dropped, rewritten, and replaced, and some scenes combined. After a final two-month review of the script, the last workshop production was staged at the end of June 2010. The show went into rehearsal for its major opening at Stratford-upon-Avon three months later.

KEY FACTS

🐝 **STAGE**
- **Director** Matthew Warchus
- **Book** Dennis Kelly
- **Music and lyrics** Tim Minchin
- **Venue** Courtyard Theatre, Stratford-upon-Avon
- **Date** 9 December 2010

◉ **Key information**
The show won a record-breaking seven Olivier Awards in London, including Best New Musical and Best Director. It has won 47 awards since its premiere.

STANDING OVATIONS
Stratford-upon-Avon previews started in November. After final tweaking and fine-tuning, *Matilda The Musical* premiered at the Courtyard Theatre on 9 December 2010. It was, wrote one critic, "a wildly tuneful reimagining" of Dahl's classic tale. Kelly's script had "deepened the emotion of Dahl's story while adding loads of splendid jokes of his own". Minchin's songs "fizzed with humour and great take-home melodies". The audience in the packed auditorium – the show had been sold out for months in advance – gave the show an emphatic seal of approval with its first standing ovation.

The transfer in 2011 to London's West End was even more successful. The next step was obvious. In 2013, *Matilda The Musical* crossed the Atlantic, opening at the Shubert Theatre, New York, in April. The American production won four Tony Awards. At the time of writing, the show is still running in both London and New York, is on tour across America, and and a production also opened in Sydney, Australia, in 2015.

TIM MINCHIN (1975–)   **BIOGRAPHY**

Celebrated anarchic British-born Australian songwriter and stand-up comedy artist Tim Minchin grew up in Perth, Western Australia. His early career included appearances on the Australian stage and TV. But it was not until his 2005 show *Darkside* that he came to public notice. The following year So Rock spawned a successful DVD, So Live. Solo shows in the UK, including the Edinburgh Fringe, drew the attention of director Matthew Warchus, who asked him to write the music for *Matilda The Musical*.

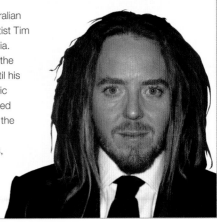

STORYLINE

A precocious and intelligent child, Matilda, who takes refuge in books from her unsympathetic parents, is sent away to school. There she encounters the frightening and cruel Miss Trunchbull, the headmistress, but also the kind and encouraging Miss Honey. Using telekinetic powers, Matilda is able to confront both the cruelty of Miss Trunchbull and the shady business dealings of her father. Eventually, she discovers the means to redress the wrongs inflicted on Miss Honey and is able to engineer a new life for herself.

CAST

Adriana Bertola, Josie Griffiths,
Kerry Ingram Matilda Wormwood
Bertie Carvel Miss Trunchbull
Lauren Ward Miss Honey
Paul Kaye Mr Wormwood
Josie Walker Mrs Wormwood
Peter Howe Michael
Melanie La Barrie Mrs Phelps
Verity Bentham Cook

PLOT OVERVIEW

IN AND NEAR THE WORMWOODS' HOME

A children's chorus sings **1** as obsessed ballroom-dancing and TV addict Mrs Wormwood gives birth to a baby girl. She is more worried about a dancing contest she has missed than her new daughter, while her husband is dismayed that Matilda is a girl and not a boy.

Matilda, now aged five, is unhappy at home with her parents and elder brother. She can read fluently, but the Wormwoods mock Matilda for her gift. She doctors her father's hair oil so that it turns his hair green **2** before seeking refuge in the local library.

CRUNCHEM HALL ACADEMY

As **Matilda** and her classmates arrive for their first day at school, the older children warn them that putting in an effort at Crunchem Hall is a waste of time **3**. Her teacher, Miss Honey, decides to recommend that Matilda be promoted to a higher class **4**. The headmistress, Miss Trunchbull, dismisses the idea, telling her to stick to the rules **5**.

IN AND NEAR THE WORMWOODS' HOME

Matilda's father is annoyed that some wealthy Russians have not bought the decrepit cars he has been trying to sell them. He takes his frustration out on Matilda by tearing up one of her library books. She applies superglue to the rim of his hat in an act of revenge.

CRUNCHEM HALL ACADEMY

Her fellow pupils tell Matilda about Miss Trunchbull's cruel punishments **6**. Miss Trunchbull spins a little girl around by her pigtails and tosses her across the school's playing field.

THE WORMWOODS' HOME

Miss Honey visits the Wormwoods, but Mrs Wormwood mocks Miss Honey for favouring books over television and make-up **7**. Later when alone, Miss Honey reveals how desperate she is to help Matilda **8**.

THE SONGS

1 Miracle
Children, Doctor,
Mrs Wormwood,
Mr Wormwood, Matilda,
Company

2 Naughty
Matilda

3 Pathetic
Miss Honey

School Song
Children

5 The Hammer
Miss Trunchbull

6 The Chokey Chant
Company

Loud
Mrs Wormwood,
Rudolpho

8 This Little G
Miss Honey

MATILDA DOCTORS HER FATHER'S HAIR OIL

"The Chokey Chant" was omitted from ✪ the original cast recording of the Stratford show (2011). It was, however, included in the longer album of the Broadway show released in 2013.

MISS HONEY AND MATILDA HAVING A CUP OF

MATILDA SEEKS SOLACE AMONG
THE BOOKS IN THE LIBRARY

"An exhilarating tale of empowerment."

BEN BRANTLEY, *THE NEW YORK TIMES*, 31 JANUARY 2012

CRUNCHEM HALL ACADEMY	THE WORMWOODS' HOME	CRUNCHEM HALL ACADEMY	THE WORMWOODS' HOME	CRUNCHEM HALL ACADEMY			THE LOCAL LIBRARY
...ce Bogtrotter has ...n a slice of Miss ...chbull's personal ...olate cake. When ...discovers this, she ...s Bruce to eat an ...e cake by himself ...nt of the class, ...bravely ...ort **9**.	**Mr Wormwood reveals** what he believes is the real reason for human success **10**.	**The children sing** about what they think adulthood is like, Miss Honey laments and Matilda resolves to end Miss Trunchbull's cruelty **11**.	**Mr Wormwood is delighted** that he has been able to sell his cars to the Russians after all. Matilda tells him off for his deceitfulness. He retaliates by locking Matilda in her bedroom **12**.	**Miss Trunchbull** forces Miss Honey's class to perform gruelling physical education **13**. She discovers a newt in her water jug, and verbally abuses Matilda, who discovers she has telekinetic powers when she tips over the pitcher **14**.	**Matilda finds out** that Miss Honey has been forced into poverty by her aunt, who turns out to be Miss Trunchbull, and who, so Miss Honey thinks, murdered her father **15**.	**During a spelling** test, Matilda fools Miss Trunchbull into believing that the ghost of Miss Honey's father is writing on the blackboard. The headmistress runs away in panic and the children celebrate **16**.	**Mr Honey's will** has been found. Miss Honey becomes headmistress. The Wormwoods tell Matilda that she has to leave the country with them at once. The Wormwoods agree to Matilda remaining behind with Miss Honey **17**.

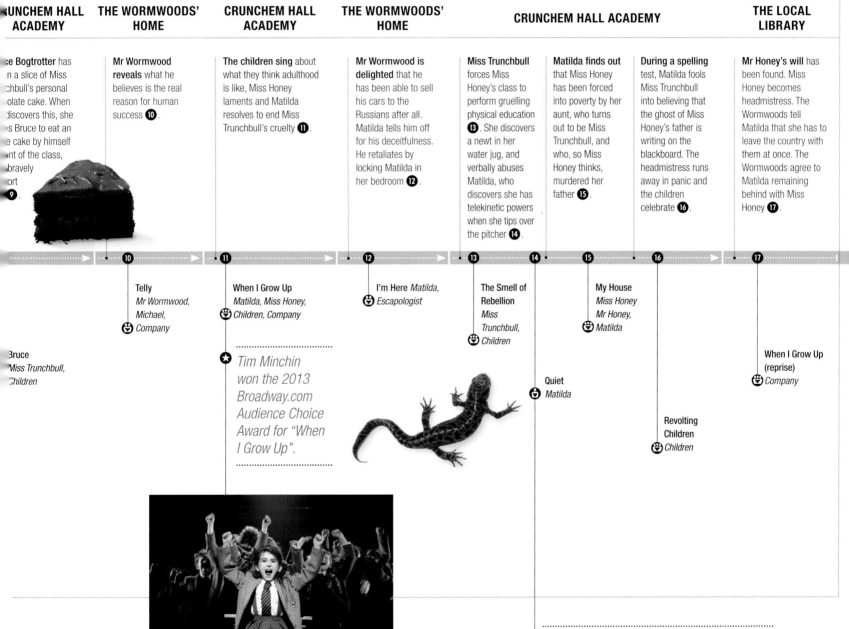

• **Bruce**
Miss Trunchbull,
Children

10
Telly
Mr Wormwood,
Michael,
Company

11
When I Grow Up
Matilda, Miss Honey,
Children, Company

★ *Tim Minchin won the 2013 Broadway.com Audience Choice Award for "When I Grow Up".*

12
I'm Here *Matilda,*
Escapologist

13
The Smell of
Rebellion
Miss Trunchbull,
Children

14
Quiet
Matilda

15
My House
Miss Honey
Mr Honey,
Matilda

16
Revolting
Children
Children

17
When I Grow Up
(reprise)
Company

★ *Minchin originally wrote "Magical" for the scene in which Matilda discovers her telekinetic powers. But it was dropped because Minchin felt it was "too Disney". Eventually, "Quiet" took its place.*

MATILDA AND
THE CHILDREN
CELEBRATE

SHREK THE MUSICAL

{ 2008 }

Shrek The Musical takes a refreshing look at the classic fairy-tale form – while stirring all the old emotions as a good musical should.

From wicked stepmothers to cannibalism, the classic fairy tales are cram-full of "awkward" content. Even so, we like to imagine that these stories somehow embody the innocence of a world of childhood very different from the one we inhabit as grown-ups. William Steig's children's book *Shrek!* (1990) successfully made play with the ironic gaps between these two perspectives, its hero a horrible green ogre who turns out not to be quite so bad after all. When, in 2001, it was made into an animated DreamWorks

▼ Welcome to Duloc
Christopher Sieber originated the role of Lord Farquaad in the original Broadway production. For the role of the diminutive ruler of Duloc, Sieber had to perform the entire show on his knees.

movie, that discrepancy between darkness and innocence was only emphasized and underlined.

The makers of *Shrek The Musical* took things still further, drawing attention to gap between the world on stage and "real life" by highlighting the artificiality of their presentation with topical references and allusions to other Broadway shows.

CREATIVE TEAM
The book and lyrics for *Shrek The Musical* were by Pulitzer Prize-winning playwright David Lindsay-Abaire, and the music was composed by Jeanine Tesori, who joined the production in 2004. For director Jason Moore, it represented a natural progression from his work on the puppet musical *Avenue Q* (see p.300–01).

▶ Waiting for her prince
Young Fiona (Leah Greenhaus), Princess Fiona (Sutton Foster), and Teen Fiona (Marissa O'Donnell) sing about fairy tales and being rescued by a brave prince.

AN OGRE GOES FORTH
Shrek, a misanthropic monster, is quite content in his misery, living all alone in a repulsive swamp. Then, however, his hideous idyll is interrupted by the arrival of a troupe of fairy-tale characters – the Three Bears (and Pigs), Pinocchio, the Wicked Witch, the Big Bad Wolf, along with assorted elves, fairies, and many more. They have all, it seems, been banished from the Kingdom of Duloc, where until now they have been living, by Lord Farquaad, its tyrannical (if tiny) ruler. It is only to secure himself a

quiet life that Shrek agrees to journey to Duloc to confront the dictator. Along the way, he rescues a donkey who goes with him as his guide.

Lord Farquaad agrees to restore his swamp to Shrek in all its solitude if Shrek wins the fair Princess Fiona for Farquaad to be his bride. She is imprisoned in a lonely tower, guarded by a ferocious, fire-breathing dragon, dreaming of the day her handsome prince will come and save her. Instead, her deliverer is the hideous Shrek and her "Prince" is to be the unappealing

Farquaad. As she gets to know him, though, Shrek turns out not to seem quite so ugly and Fiona has her own secret, which is that every night due to a curse she transforms into an ogress.

IMPROBABLE PUPPETS

For the musical, the cast of costumed fairy-tale characters was supplemented by a number of puppets – including a 5 m (17 ft) tall, all-singing, all-stomping dragon under the control of four

> **"Audiences, I think, are slightly sceptical of musicals and love them all at the same time."**
>
> **JASON MOORE,** DIRECTOR OF *SHREK THE MUSICAL*

puppeteers. Incongruous mismatch was essential to the *Shrek* aesthetic. High-flown feelings were whipped up only to be undercut with humour and sweet sentiments soured by lemon-sharp lyrics.

TREMENDOUS FUN

A few older reviewers were grudging in their responses to the show, but, that view was very much in the minority – particularly with younger audiences, who adored *Shrek The Musical*.

◀ Monstrous fun
Brian d'Arcy James (Shrek) in the original Broadway production of *Shrek The Musical*, which was awarded the Tony for Best Costume Design for designer Tim Hatley.

THE BOOK OF MORMON

{ 2011 }

The Mormon Church was among those least offended by an extravaganza of latter-day satire that sent up just about every aspect of American culture, its attitudes, and its role in the wider world.

While the young Mormon Elder Kevin Price is unimpeachably devout, he is naive and profoundly, unreflectingly complacent. He is also completely mismatched with his proselytizing partner, Elder Arnold Cunningham, who has never even read his supposed scripture, *The Book of Mormon*. Even so, it is with the utmost optimism that this eager young pair set off on a mission from Utah for Uganda to do God's work.

Nothing either one has learned in the United States has prepared them for the realities of Africa, a true-life apocalypse of poverty, hunger, violence, and AIDS. Their Church's own senior official in the region, Elder McKinley, is too busy wrestling with his own repressed, and indeed utterly unacknowledged, homosexuality ("Turn It Off" is his simple advice for "fellow sufferers") to have much time for the sufferings of a developing country. The local villagers put on a convincing show of accepting their lot in life, but their joyous song ("Hasa Diga Eebowai") turns out to be obscene and blasphemous.

Struggling to make any spiritual headway in the face of such evils and failing to make their message seem remotely relevant, the young men become disillusioned and part company. While Price gives up completely, Cunningham continues in his ministry, though he is hampered by his unfamiliarity with his sacred text. Reduced to making up his own *Book of Mormon* as he goes along, making do with scraps of science- and fantasy-fiction, he finds to his immense relief that it serves as well as the real thing. So much so that before too long he is making a succession of converts. Price is inspired to take up his cause again.

MISSION ACCOMPLISHED

For the theatregoer, the missionary message is exhilaratingly clear – though it can be confusing in its sheer range and volume. *The Book of Mormon* takes a satirical scattergun to American attitudes in every area of life; the absurdities of religion are just the start. While the arrogance of US foreign policy and the insularity of American public opinion are both obviously targeted, so too are everything from homophobia to popular media and culture.

▶ **Hot ticket**
Despite the distinctly risqué nature of much of the material, *The Book of Mormon* attracted great reviews and quickly became a hot ticket.

"HEAVEN ON BROADWAY. 'THE BOOK OF MORMON' ACHIEVES SOMETHING LIKE A MIRACLE A CELEBRATION OF THE PRIVILEGE OF LIVING INSIDE THAT IMPROBABLE PARADISE CALLED A MUSICAL COMEDY

NEW YORK TIMES BEN BRANTLEY

"In a sense Mormons are the ultimate Americans – we don't have any problem telling you what you should believe."

MATT STONE, COMPOSER AND LIBRETTIST

ONCE

{ 2011 }

Starting life as a low-budget movie with a new approach to musicals, *Once* then transferred to the stage, asking similar questions of theatre audiences.

When is a musical not a musical? The story of the relationship between an Irish busker ("Guy") and the Czech pianist-songwriter ("Girl") who happens to bump into him one day on Grafton Street, Dublin, John Carney's film *Once* was the surprise sensation of 2007. An engagingly small-scale, understated work, long on poignant charm and short on sentimentality, it was set against an appealingly workaday backdrop of modern Irish life. Glen Hansard and Markéta Irglová, who starred as Guy and Girl, had a chemistry as tangible as the talent that shone through in their strong musical performances. A series of lovely, quirky, and often moving songs (which Hansard himself had written) helped advance the action of the film.

And yet, the reviewers of the film agreed, it did not look or feel like a musical. The tone of the piece was too muted; the mood was too intimate; the cinematographic style too naturalistic. At the same time, though, the music was definitely integral to its drama – indeed, it was more or less unthinkable without its songs. The *Los Angeles Times* critic who described it as a "covert musical" perhaps got closest – the phrase may sound clumsy, but it does strike the right note of the clandestine, the contraband. For director John Carney had been frank about the challenge he had faced when he had set about making *Once*: "How do I make a little film that appeals to a younger audience – a musical dressed up in a different way?"

ROMANTIC RESONANCE

His success in finding an answer to that question was borne out triumphantly by the acclaim his movie received. How he had done it is, perhaps, not so clear. That his musician protagonists would naturally be expected to burst into song in the line of daily life and work was one obvious factor; so too was the extent to which the action invested in the whole idea of music and its persuasive power. Their initial attraction notwithstanding, what brings Guy and Girl most closely together in the early stages of the story – both in

◄ **Irish charm**
Glen Hansard (Guy) and Markéta Irglová (Girl) walk down a Dublin street in the 2007 film.

the film and the stage play – is their collaboration on the recording that they hope may win back Marcella, Guy's ex-girlfriend.

STYLISH STAGING

This more-from-less approach is actually quite a theatrical one for such a naturalistically presented a film to take. Normally, this type of approach gives us the impression that (whatever secrets the characters may be keeping) we are seeing everything, in full colour and in high definition detail, working on the assumption that "the camera does not lie".

KEEPING IT SMALL

This is one reason why director John Tiffany and writer Enda Walsh's adaptation of the film for the stage does not seem like a backward step. In cooperation with Bob Crowley's scenic design and Natasha Katz's lighting, Tiffany's stage production doubled down on the movie's minimalism and made a virtue of the necessities of small-scale staging. The actor-musicians also served as the orchestra, sitting on chairs around the periphery of the action, and stepping forward only as their speaking roles required. The onstage bar also sold drinks to theatregoers in the interval.

KEY FACTS

🎭 **STAGE**

🎬 **Director** John Tiffany
📖 **Book** Enda Walsh
🎵 **Music and lyrics** Glen Hansard, Markéta Irglová
🎭 **Venue** New York Theatre Workshop, New York
📅 **Date** 6 December 2011

⊙ **Key information**
The first Off-Broadway production won three Lucille Lortel Awards – Outstanding Musical, Outstanding Choreographer (John Tiffany), and Outstanding Lighting Design (Natasha Katz). It was nominated in a further three categories, and went on to win the New York Drama Critics' Circle Award for Best Musical.

GHOST THE MUSICAL

{ 2011 }

Twenty years after its initial triumph on screen, *Ghost* walked again as a stage musical, in many respects looking just as it had in the cinema.

The 1990 movie *Ghost* is one of the most popular romantic fantasies ever made. It tells the story of a young man who is killed during a botched mugging. However, his love for his partner is so strong that he succeeds in remaining on earth as a ghost, successfully communicating with his true love via a medium. Despite the unchained ardency of the drama, audiences were at the same time deeply moved by the tale of enduring love. Who, after all, would want to argue with a love that, not content with remaining true unto the death, insisted on staying strong, faithful, and protective far beyond? Whatever its shortcomings, *Ghost* still haunts the memory.

▶ **A spirited comeback**
Sharon D. Clarke Oda Mae Brown, Richard Fleeshman as Sam, and Caissie Levy as Molly in the West End production. Set and costume design is by Rob Howell.

GREAT SUCCESS
Normally, the transfer of a work from screen to stage exploits the distinctions between the different media, but here theatre appeared to be aspiring to the condition of cinema. Despite appearing at time when there were numerous film to stage adaptations, *The Guardian*'s senior theatre reviewer, Michael Billington, wrote *"Ghost* is the first I've seen that feels like a film"*. Billington suggested that "the real stars of Matthew Warchus's production are Rob Howell's sets and John Driscoll's video designs".

For many younger theatregoers, though, the lines between "look" and "content" were less clearly drawn – and not because of a lack of sophistication on their part. The musical is by definition a multimedia production and a multi-sensory experience: the richer and more complex that mix, perhaps, the better.

But the way *Ghost* looked and sounded was absolutely central to its message. A story of supernatural visitation, the show had to not only set out a convincing reality in its *mise en scène*, but to hint at a less tangible dimension just beyond. The sets, the video designs – as well as stage

KEY FACTS

🔖 **STAGE**
🎬 **Director** Matthew Warchus
📖 **Book** Bruce Joel Rubin
♫ **Music** Dave Stewart, Glen Ballard
🎵 **Lyrics** Bruce Joel Rubin
🎭 **Venue** Manchester Opera House
📅 **Date** 19 July 2011

◉ **Key information**
Beginning on 28 March 2011, *Ghost The Musical* had a six-week try-out run at the Manchester Opera House before transferring to the West End later that summer. The challenges facing this production were more technical than dramatic: Paul Kieve's illusions had to be exactly right, with full support from lighting, sound, and set design.

magician Paul Kieve's astonishing illusions – were accordingly just as important as the lyrics or the music.

POP SCORE
The show's score, by notable pop creators Dave "Eurythmics" Stewart and Glen Ballard, had an understated feel and also featured The Righteous Brother's "Unchained Melody".

But *Ghost The Musical* had always been intended as a different kind of musical experience and it was in this that its originality was to be found. None of the fine performances could be singled out. Instead, the senses were stunned and the imagination transfixed by a full-spectrum show of language, light, and sound.

GHOSTLY TRAVELS
Ghost The Musical followed its London run with a transfer to Broadway and national tours in the UK and the US. It has since been produced in more than 15 countries around the world, including productions in China, South Korea, and Mexico.

CHARLIE AND THE CHOCOLATE FACTORY

Bewildered, bemused, their senses overwhelmed – like kids in a sweetshop – audiences watched director Sam Mendes's *Charlie and the Chocolate Factory* completely transfixed.

Roald Dahl's 1964 book *Charlie and the Chocolate Factory* remains as compelling to us as adults as it was in childhood. Not just for its inventive ideas, its colourful characters, and its mischievous humour, but also for the way it pins down something that has endured in us from those early times – even if it is simply a love of chocolate. Dahl's classic story hints at a certain childish "innocence" in our most grown-up desires, just as it does the more unedifying aspects of our younger selves. Dahl's character, Charlie Bucket, is twice a winner: first with his golden ticket but then afterwards (and more

▶ A hint of danger
Alex Jennings replaced Douglas Hodge as Willy Wonka in 2014; his performance was compelling and sinister at the same time.

importantly) with his personality – polite, unassuming, and instinctively considerate. The more we can be like him, the better, we understand – though he reminds us, too, how unusual "childlike innocence" actually is in children. Or, rather, his fellow-prizewinners do: the arrogant Veruca Salt; the spoiled and self-willed Mike Teavee; the greedy Augustus Gloop; the attention-voracious Violet Beauregarde.

Sam Mendes's production underlined in its direction what David Greig had already identified in his book as the musical's underlying theme: the struggle within every one of us between good and evil.

A LUXURIOUS CONFECTION
The original Dahl story was choc-full of multicoloured sweets and lollipops. It featured crazy costumes, strangely constructed chutes and silos, and the whirling machinery of Willy Wonka's factory. All these elements combined afforded the possibility of a fantastic visual splurge as uninhibited as any chocolate binge. Just as it was in the two film versions of the novel (1971 and 2005), so it is with the stage musical, whose deeper moral message could never carry through if we were not ourselves utterly transported by the overwhelming abundance before us. "I can resist everything except temptation," said Oscar Wilde.

KEY FACTS

STAGE

🎬 **Director** Sam Mendes

📖 **Book** David Greig

🎵 **Music and lyrics** Marc Shaiman, Scott Wittman

🎭 **Venue** Theatre Royal, Drury Lane, London

📅 **Date** 25 June 2013

⊙ **Key information**
After a slow start caused by technical problems, success came swiftly: the day after its opening, it was announced that the show's run was to be extended by six months. New Year 2014 saw it set a new record for the West End's highest ever take over a week: £1,080,260; a further extension was to follow.

"Deep down, the story is a reassurance that good will always win."

DAVID GREIG, LIBRETTIST

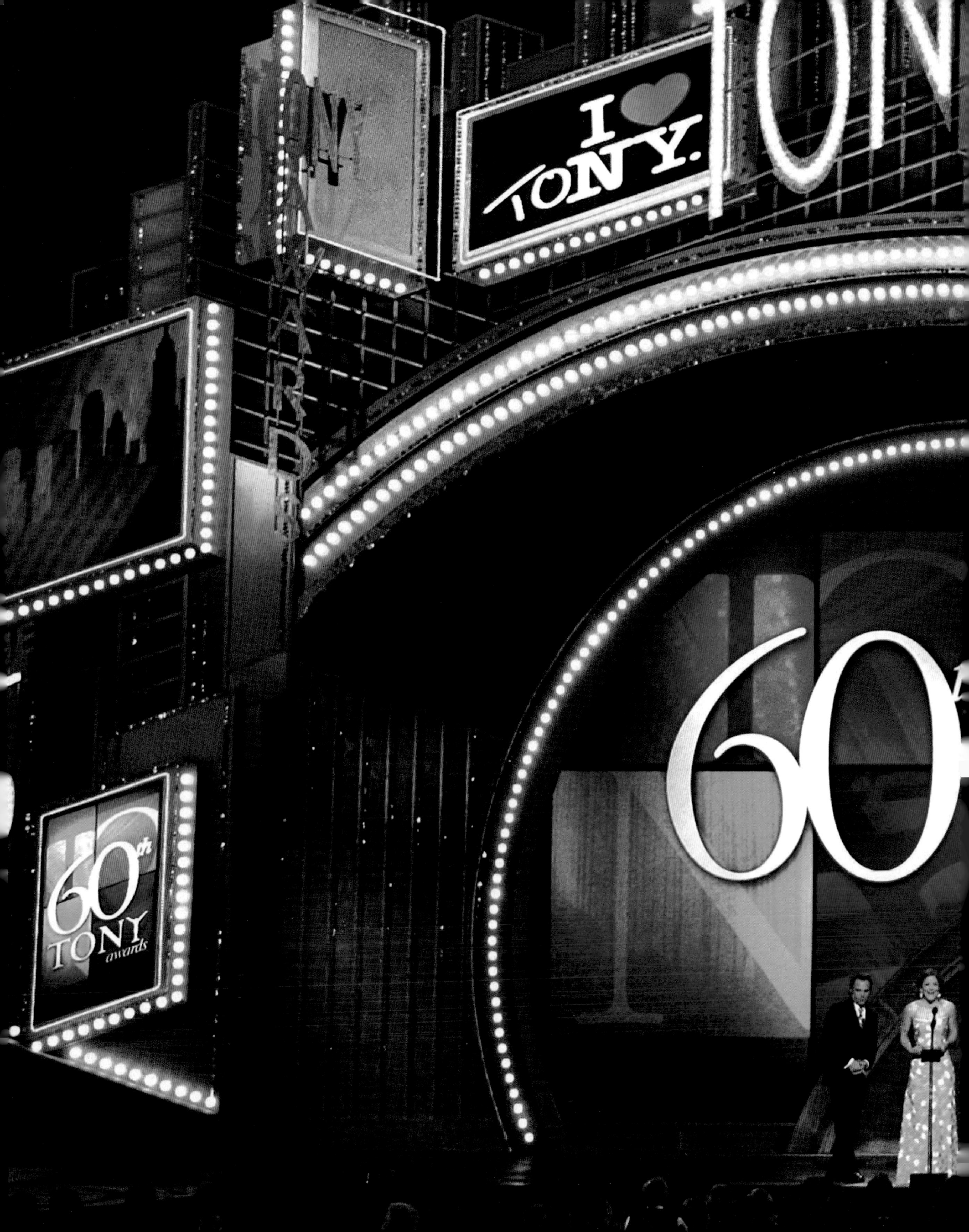
I ♥ TONY.
60th
TONY
awards

AND THE
WINNER IS...

The annual Tony Awards are more than just a celebration of excellence in the Broadway theatre – they are Broadway's biggest advertisement.

In addition to being an actress and a director, Antoinette Perry was cofounder of the American Theatre Wing – an organization dedicated to supporting excellence and education in theatre. The Tony Awards are named for her and were first awarded in 1947 to acknowledge excellence in live Broadway theatre.

For the first three years, the winners received a scroll, cigarette lighter, and articles of jewellery, such as 14-carat gold compacts and bracelets for the women, and money clips for the men. In 1949, scenic designer Herman Rosse entered a contest for the design of a proper award, and his design is the medallion that we know today.

From 1947–56, the ceremony was held at midnight in one of New York's ballrooms and broadcast live over the Mutual Radio Network. In 1956, the award ceremony was broadcast on a local television station for the first

time. In 1967, when the award ceremony, then produced by Alexander Cohen, was aired live on national television, the venue had moved to a Broadway theatre and the awards boasted greater production values.

WINNING BIG
Today, the Tony Awards ceremony is seen on more than seven million television sets. Producers of musicals vie to get the best time slots to present samples of their shows, and revivals of musicals fight for the right to perform a number on the Tony Awards.

A spot on the broadcast can translate directly into sales at the box office. Tony nominations and awards can take a show with marginal sales and make it a hit overnight. For its first eight months, the Broadway production of *Gentleman's Guide to Love and Murder* was experiencing slow sales, but the show's fortunes were revived when success at the Tony Awards brought it to the attention of a wider audience. An award can also take a hit and extend its life, creating a mega-hit.

◀ **Television coverage**
Live television coverage of the ceremony has made the Tony Awards one of the most important marketing opportunities for any Broadway show.

"... [the] producers of Gentleman's Guide (to Love and Murder) *can celebrate the fact that the tuner's Tony wins have at last prodded audiences to take notice of the show."*

GORDON COX, *VARIETY,* 23 JUNE 2014

FROZEN

{ 2013 }

A game-changing plot involving the true love of sisters, as opposed to that of a conventional hero and heroine, *Frozen* transcends expectations of what a fairy tale should look like.

KEY FACTS

🎬 **FILM**

📷 **Director** Chris Buck, Jennifer Lee

✉ **Screenplay** Jennifer Lee

🎵 **Music and lyrics** Robert Lopez, Kristen Anderson-Lopez; Christophe Beck (score)

🕐 **Running time** 102 minutes

📅 **Release date** 27 November 2013

⊙ **Key information**

This film was the winner of two Academy Awards in 2014, for Music (Original Song, "Let it Go") and Animated Feature Film.

The incorporation of two female leads, sometimes in conflict and sometimes in harmony, is reminiscent of *Wicked* (see p.295) and brings the Disney animated feature bang up to date.

Elsa and Anna are the best of friends; their favourite entertainment involves Elsa using her magical powers to create snow, allowing them to throw snowballs at each other. This game unfortunately results in Elsa hitting Anna with an icy blast, freezing her

head. A troll elder provides the cure, but it comes with the warning that Elsa must exercise control, lest she hurt someone more seriously.

Thus begins the key theme of the film: Elsa's attempts to govern her powers, her failure, and the eventual solution that love rather than suppression allows Elsa to use her powers as she wishes. Along the way, of course, there are love stories gone awry, trusty sidekicks who help save the day, and a second, more helpful, contribution from the trolls.

PLOT DEVELOPMENT

The journey to create *Frozen* was a complicated one. As far back as the 1940s, Disney attempted to bring Danish writer Hans Christian Andersen *The Snow Queen* (1844), attracted by the drama of its icy setting. But it was too hard to sympathize with such an evil character. The story was again examined by Disney from 1989–99, a period that produced *Beauty and the Beast*, *Aladdin*, and *The Lion King* (see pp.276–79). Again, the story was shelved. Finally, in 2011, Disney announced *Frozen* would hit cinemas in 2013. The Snow Queen became a casualty of her powers, rather than an abuser, and the role of the girl who defeats the Snow Queen was given to the Queen's own sister.

MEMORABLE SONGS

The music, then, informs and inspires these journeys. It was the song "Let It Go" that first allowed the writers to envision Elsa as a victim rather than a villain. To imagine how it feels to

not hide, and not be frightened any more of hurting someone – by the sad expedient of being completely alone – led the Lopezes to write a song that empowers Elsa, as she lets go of all the fear. It is this song, more

than any other in the film, which the audiences identified with. Other memorable songs include the sad "Do You Want to Build a Snowman?", as well as a hilarious song about relationships, "Fixer Upper".

BIOGRAPHY

IDINA MENZEL (1971–)

Known for her brilliant vocal range, Idina Menzel has been wowing audiences since her first Broadway performance as Maureen in *Rent* in 1996. After this early success, Menzel went on to star in the original Broadway cast of *Wicked* as Elphaba, a role for which she won a Tony and recognition as the "Streisand of her generation" by critics. Beyond Broadway, she reprised her role in *Rent* in a 2005 film adaptation and is also well known for her character in the television drama *Glee*.

▶ **An icy tale**
British illustrator Edmund Dulac's illustration of Hans Christian Andersen's tale *The Snow Queen*. Inspired by Andersen's *The Snow Queen*, the Disney animated musical *Frozen* was a hit with audiences around the world.

INTO THE WOODS

{ 2014 }

This film proves that venturing deep into the woods of life and human consciousness can be surprisingly enjoyable when we are accompanied by some enchanting tales.

In 1938, the Austrian-Jewish psychoanalyst Bruno Bettelheim was arrested by the Nazis and sent, first to Dachau, then to Buchenwald. A lifetime later, in another continent, he was to become world famous as an American scholar of fairy stories, the author of *The Uses of Enchantment* (1976). Bettelheim started out by focusing on the Grimms'

fairy tale forest landscape – and through the plots of several different fairy stories, from *Little Red Riding Hood* and *Rapunzel* to *Jack and the Beanstalk*, *Cinderella*, and *Sleeping Beauty*.

Into the Woods imagines grown-ups being brought into confrontation with a children's world of fairy tale and thereby being compelled to grow up all over again, while dealing with ancient fears.

> *"A studio exec said to me, 'You know, there's an awfully high body count in this movie. Will anybody have to die?'."*

JAMES LAPINE, SCREENWRITER

FOREST OR PARK?

For the Disney film – an admittedly unusual departure for the company – the clock was turned back once again; the world evoked more like that "innocent" one we expect to find in fairy tales – but never actually do. The makers reined back a bit on the sex and violence, though these had not been especially graphic in the original. Inevitably, some critics took exception to these changes, arguing that they robbed the original musical of its essential depth and force – that its wild woods had been thoroughly domesticated, in short. All in all, though, most were in agreement that enough remained of the stage show's spirit (the screenplay had, after all, been written by Sondheim's original collaborator, James Lapine) for the movie to maintain a distinctly enjoyable edge of menace.

Arguably, the first-rate acting made up for any loss of content: the cackling charisma of Meryl Streep's witch won special praise from the

KEY FACTS

🎥 **FILM**
🎬 **Director** Rob Marshall
📖 **Screenplay** James Lapine
📕 **Book** Stephen Sondheim
🎵 **Music and lyrics** Stephen Sondheim
🕐 **Running time** 174 minutes
📅 **Release date** 8 December 2014

⊙ Key information
Efforts to make a film of *Into the Woods* had been going on since the beginning of the 1990s. Francis Ford Coppola's American Zoetrope company had envisaged a version starring Robin Williams and Goldie Hawn. The rights then passed to Sony and Jim Henson Productions, who tried to set up a movie with Billy Crystal and Meg Ryan. This project was last heard of in early 1997.

critics. The British actress Emily Blunt made a wonderfully warm and human baker's wife, while American actor Chris Pine was a big hit as an anything-but-charming Prince.

▼ Dark and disorientating
The cast of a 2014 revival of Stephen Sondheim's *Into the Woods* perform at the Châtelet Theatre, Paris. The film adaptation sparked a renewed interest in the stage show.

collections of fairy tales – closely read, a catalogue of wretchedness – of wicked stepmothers, witches, giants, and monsters. Examining the Grimm brothers' texts more closely, Bettelheim found himself in a bleakly hideous world of symbolic terror – of everything from abandonment to death, from adulthood to sex. The Holocaust might have been unique in the scale of the evil it unleashed on Europe, but in small ways its cruelties and fears had been foreshadowed here.

REGRESSION AND GROWTH

In Stephen Sondheim (see pp.220–21) and James Lapine's 1987 musical *Into the Woods*, a baker and his wife wish they could have a child. The witch who has placed a curse on them continues to harass them as they set off on a life journey that will take them through a

Other musicals

This section celebrates some of the world's most prominent and beloved musicals, arranged chronologically, from the classic stage shows and films of the 1930s to present-day Broadway and West End success stories. Whether performed on a stage or played on the big screen, these musicals have advanced the genre and inspired a love of musical theatre for generations of fans.

Happy End 1929
STAGE

📖 **Book** Elisabeth Hauptmann (German play), Michael Feingold (adaptation)
🎵 **Music** Kurt Weill
♩ **Lyrics** Bertolt Brecht

Happy End is a comedic musical that sets thugs in 1919 Chicago up against members of the Salvation Army, and follows the budding of an unlikely relationship between hardened criminal Bill Cracker and enthusiastic crusader Lillian Holiday. The musical was penned by the team who created the successful show *The Three Penny Opera* (see pp.20–21) and it opened in Berlin in 1929. The political climate in Germany at the time most likely contributed to the show's failure; it was considered a huge flop and closed after just a few days.

The 1977 Broadway production of *Happy End*, which starred Christopher Lloyd and Meryl Streep, had a two-month run at the Martin Beck Theatre. It was nominated for three Tony Awards, including Best Musical. The show includes such well-known songs as "The Bilbao Song" and "Surabaya Johnny".

The New Yorkers 1930
STAGE

📖 **Book** Herbert Fields
♩ **Music and lyrics** Cole Porter

The musical comedy *The New Yorkers*, which ran on Broadway from December 1930 to May 1931, was based on a story by Peter Arno and E. Ray Getz. It takes place during prohibition and features socialite Alice Wentworth's fling with bootlegger Al Spanish.

Cole Porter wrote most of the music and lyrics for the show; Jimmie Durante wrote the songs that he performed himself. But it was Porter's song "Love for Sale", about a prostitute, that gained popularity with audiences – though it was banned from the radio due to its inappropriate lyrics and subject matter.

Three's a Crowd 1930
STAGE

📖 **Book** Howard Dietz
♩ **Music** Arthur Schwartz
♩ **Lyrics** Howard Dietz

Three's a Crowd reunited many of the players from the successful 1929 revue *The Little Show*, including stars Clifton Webb, Fred Allen, and Libby Holman, as well as composer Arthur Schwartz and lyricist Howard Dietz. Also a musical revue, *Three's a Crowd* introduced two extremely notable songs, both performed by Holman: "Something to Remember You By" and "Body and Soul".

Produced by Max Gordon and directed and lit by Hassard Short, *Three's a Crowd* stands in musical theatre history as the first Broadway musical to be staged without footlights; instead, the revue was lit from above with lights hung from the balcony.

Face the Music 1932
STAGE

📖 **Book** Moss Hart
♩ **Music and lyrics** Irving Berlin

To "face the music" means to accept the consequences of one's mistakes or actions – and this was the theme of the 1932 satirical musical *Face the Music*, which successfully combined politics, show business, and the Depression. The show wasn't a huge hit, but Irving Berlin's songs, including "Let's Have Another Cup of Coffee" and "Soft Lights and Sweet Music", won over audiences.

Words and Music 1932
STAGE

📖 **Book** Noël Coward
♩ **Music and lyrics** Noël Coward

Words and Music is a musical revue for which the multitalented Noël Coward wrote all of the songs and sketches, as well as staging the show. It was first presented at the Opera House in Manchester, UK, in August 1932, before transferring to the Adelphi Theatre in London in September. The show ran for 164 performances.

GINGER ROGERS AND FRED ASTAIRE, *THE GAY DIVORCEE*

Some of Coward's most notable songs from *Words and Music* include "Mad Dogs and Englishmen", "Mad About the Boy", and its closing number, "The Party's Over". Coward presented a revised version of *Words and Music* for Broadway; it opened at the Music Box Theatre in January 1939 with a new title, *Set to Music*, and ran until 6 May of that year.

Gay Divorce 1932
STAGE

📖 **Book** Dwight Taylor
♩ **Music and lyrics** Cole Porter

Written as a vehicle for Fred Astaire and based on an unproduced play by J. Hartley Manners, *Gay Divorce* was Astaire's last Broadway show and his only stage appearance without his sister, Adele, who had recently retired.

Gay Divorce follows the story of novelist Guy Holden in his comic attempts to woo not-yet-divorced Mimi Pratt. When Mimi mistakes Guy for the co-respondent hired to help Mimi procure her divorce, Guy plays along and uses his proximity to Mimi to pursue her. The show opened on Broadway at the Ethel Barrymore Theatre in November 1932, closing seven months later after a move to the Shubert Theatre.

In 1934, *Gay Divorce* was made into a film called *The Gay Divorcee*, with screenplay by George Marion Jr, Dorothy Yost, and Edward Kaufman. The movie starred the classic pairing of Astaire and Ginger Rogers. The film retained only one of the original Cole Porter songs, "Night and Day", now a jazz standard that is often

cited as one of the best Porter songs of all time. *The Gay Divorcee* was nominated for five Academy Awards, and "The Continental" by Con Conrad and Herb Magidson won the very first Oscar for Best Original Song.

As Thousands Cheer 1933
🎭 STAGE
📖 **Book** Moss Hart
🎵 **Music and lyrics** Irving Berlin
As Thousands Cheer is a musical revue that was seen as a follow-up to Moss Hart and Irving Berlin's *Face the Music*. Both shows are known for their satirical treatment of current events. *As Thousands Cheer* framed each sketch by pairing it with a newspaper headline. The sketches parodied such notable figures as Josephine Baker, Noël Coward, Joan Crawford, Douglas Fairbanks Jr, Mahatma Gandhi, John D. Rockefeller, and the King and Queen of England. Many songs from the revue became standards, including

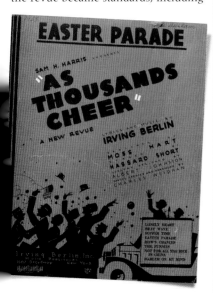

BERLIN WROTE THE MUSIC FOR *AS THOUSANDS CHEER*

"Heat Wave", "Easter Parade", and "Harlem on My Mind". The Broadway production performed at the Music Box Theatre in New York from September 1933 until September 1934 – a total of 400 performances.

Bright Eyes 1934
🎬 FILM
🎬 **Screenplay** William M. Counselman
🎵 **Music and lyrics** Various artists
Bright Eyes is a 1934 American classic film starring Shirley Temple as Shirley Blake, a girl whose pilot father is killed in an plane crash and whose mother is hit and killed by a car on Christmas Eve. A custody battle ensues for the bright-eyed and dimpled little orphan

girl. Temple plays opposite fellow child star Jane Withers; Withers's character, Joy Smythe, terrorizes Blake throughout the picture.

It is in *Bright Eyes* that Temple sings her signature tune "On the Good Ship Lollipop" – which is actually about an aircraft, not a ship. At the age of six, Temple became the first recipient of the special honorary Academy Award for Best Performance by a Juvenile. Future recipients of the award would include Mickey Rooney and Judy Garland. Shirley Temple remains the youngest person to have been honoured by the Academy.

Babes in Arms 1937
🎭 STAGE
📖 **Book** Lorenz Hart, Richard Rodgers
🎵 **Music** Richard Rodgers
🎵 **Lyrics** Lorenz Hart
Richard Rodgers and Lorenz Hart's *Babes in Arms*, choreographed by George Balanchine, opened at the Shubert Theatre in New York in 1937. Ticket sales dipped dangerously low at one point; however, the show survived as competing musicals on Broadway shut down, resulting in *Babes in Arms* becoming the only musical on Broadway for a time in July 1937. The production, with a storyline about a group of teenagers who stage a revue to keep from being sent to work on a farm, ultimately closed in December 1937.

MICKEY ROONEY AND JUDY GARLAND IN THE FILM VERSION OF *BABES IN ARMS*

In 1959, the script was revised by George Oppenheimer, under the supervision of Richard Rodgers for a Broadway revival. The 1939 film version, with screenplay by Jack McGowan and Kay Van Riper, starred Mickey Rooney and Judy Garland; it retained only two songs from the original Broadway production.

Pins and Needles 1937
🎭 STAGE
🎵 **Music and lyrics** Harold Rome
Produced by the International Ladies' Garment Workers Union, *Pins and Needles* is a musical revue about the lives of factory workers. Its humorous songs and skits – updated over the course of the show's run – included light social and political commentary with a progressive slant. Staged at the union's Labor Stage Theatre, the show began as a fun pastime for garment workers, but became so popular that the performers left their day jobs to assume a full performance schedule. In 1939, the show moved to Broadway's Windsor Theatre.

Pins and Needles became the longest running show of the 1930s at 1,108 performances. A special performance was given at the White House in 1938 for President Franklin D. Roosevelt and First Lady Eleanor Roosevelt. The 1962 25th-anniversary recording of *Pins and Needles* featured Barbra Streisand in one of her first recordings.

The Dancing Years 1939
🎭 STAGE
📖 **Book** Ivor Novello
🎵 **Music** Ivor Novello
🎵 **Lyrics** Christopher Hassall
The Dancing Years opened in London's West End in March 1939, and closed at the beginning of September when Britain entered World War II. It went on a national tour in 1940 before returning to the West End from 1942 to 1944. A film version – with screenplay by Ivor Novello, Warwick Ward, and Jack Whittingham – was released in 1950.

The show opens in Vienna, before World War I, and centres on a penniless composer, Rudi Kleber (originated by Novello). Rudi's unwise promise to a young girl ruins his romantic relationship with operetta star Maria Ziegler. Years later, Rudi realizes he is the father of Maria's son as the shadow of World War II encroaches. When Rudi is arrested after the Nazi Occupation, Maria frees him.

Yankee Doodle Dandy 1942
🎬 FILM
🎬 **Screenplay** Robert Buckner, Edmund Joseph
🎵 **Music and lyrics** George M. Cohan
The Warners' film *Yankee Doodle Dandy* tells the life story of American entertainer George M. Cohan. It was originally set to be released on 4 July 1942. Due to Cohan's battle with abdominal cancer – which ultimately took his life in November 1942 – the release date was moved to Memorial Day in May. The night the film premiered at New York City's Hollywood Theatre, Warners sold war bonds instead of tickets to raise money for the war effort.

James Cagney, who portrayed Cohan in the movie, took home the Academy Award for Best Actor; *Yankee Doodle Dandy* also won awards for scoring and sound recording.

Stormy Weather 1943
🎬 FILM
🎬 **Screenplay** Frederick J. Jackson, Ted Koehler
🎵 **Music and lyrics** Various artists
Loosely based on dancer Bill "Bojangles" Robinson's life, *Stormy Weather* was produced and released by Twentieth Century Fox in 1943. In what would be his last film, Robinson plays Bill Williamson, a man who is pursuing his performing career after returning home from World War I.

Lena Horne plays his love interest, Selina Rogers, a beautiful young performer. Cab Calloway and Fats Waller both appear as themselves. Former Cotton Club dance instructor Clarence Robinson choreographed *Stormy Weather*'s all African-American star-studded cast.

Anchors Aweigh 1945
🎬 **FILM**
🎬 **Screenplay** Isobel Lennart
🎵 **Music** George Stoll

Co-starring Gene Kelly and Frank Sinatra, with Kathryn Grayson as the female lead, MGM's song-and-dance extravaganza *Anchors Aweigh* tells the story of two sailors on four-day leave in Hollywood. A memorable scene combined live action and animation for a dance number with Kelly and cartoon character Jerry the Mouse. Animators William Hanna and Joseph Barbera, both at MGM at the time, worked to achieve timing and grace in the magical sequence to "The Worry Song", captivating audiences. The scene took two months to produce.

Nominated for five Oscars – including Best Picture and a nod for Gene Kelly for Best Actor in a Leading Role –

Anchors Aweigh's composer Georgie Stoll took home the award for Best Music, Scoring of a Musical Picture.

Ziegfeld Follies 1945
🎬 **FILM**
🎬 **Screenplay** Ralph Blane, David Freedman, Hugh Martin
🎵 **Music and lyrics** Various artists

Although Florenz "Flo" Ziegfeld Jr was not a musician, singer, or songwriter, he changed the world of musical theatre with his revue format. He hired some of America's most celebrated composers, lyricists, and talent to produce elaborate productions on Broadway, which became known as "Follies". A series of songs, dances, comedy sketches, and beautiful showgirls – known as the Ziegfeld Girls – the *Ziegfeld Follies* increased in splendour throughout the years.

The *Follies* helped launch the careers of a host of major stars, and many of the infectious tunes from his Follies became big hits. After Ziegfeld died in 1932, his widow authorized the use of his name for future productions. While others produced similar revues, Ziegfeld's fabulous Follies proved legendary.

In 1945, MGM premiered a film version of *Ziegfeld Follies*, which featured a collection of acts similar to those seen in the real Ziegfeld shows. The movie starred a long and impressive list of leading talents from stage and screen musicals, including Lucille Ball, Fred Astaire, Judy Garland, Lena Horne, Gene Kelly, and Fanny Brice, who had performed for Ziegfeld in the original Follies.

The Harvey Girls 1946
🎬 **FILM**
🎬 **Screenplay** Edmund Beloin, Harry Crane, Nathaniel Curtis, James O'Hanlon, Samson Raphaelson
🎵 **Music and lyrics** Johnny Mercer, Harry Warren

Based on an original story by Eleanore Griffin and William Rankin and on the novel by Samuel Hopkins Adams, *The Harvey Girls* is a MGM movie musical set in a western town in the late 1800s. The film stars Judy Garland as Susan Bradley, a mail-order bride who upon arriving in town realizes she and her husband-to-be won't work. Instead, she becomes a waitress for the new Harvey House in town. Susan and the Harvey Girls find themselves in conflict with the saloon

ANGELA LANSBURY (CENTRE), IN *THE HARVEY GIRLS*

girls (led by 19-year-old Angela Lansbury), and Susan finds herself falling for the saloon owner (John Hodiak). The film won the Best Music, Original Song Oscar for Mercer and Warren's "On the Atchison, Topeka, and Santa Fe".

The film was inspired by the real-life story of Fred Harvey's restaurant and hotel chain, which pushed west alongside the railroads. The women who went west to be Harvey Girls were subject to a strict code of conduct and had to meet a list of criteria meant to ensure they were of good character.

Words and Music 1948
🎬 **FILM**
🎬 **Screenplay** Fred Finklehoffe
🎵 **Music** Richard Rodgers
🅰️ **Lyrics** Lorenz Hart

No relation to the 1932 show of the same name, the 1948 MGM film *Words and Music* is loosely based on the lives of Richard Rodgers and Lorenz Hart, a legendary team who collaborated on creating hundreds of songs for film and stage. Set in New York in 1919, it tells a fictionalized story of a lyricist searching for a composer. When he finds the perfect match, a friendship and partnership is quickly formed as the duo struggle to land their first contract with a producer.

Words and Music features Tom Drake as Rodgers and Mickey Rooney as Hart. In the movie, a long list of major stars perform Rodgers and Hart's songs – including June Allyson, Judy Garland, Gene Kelly, Mel Torme, Vera-Ellen, Cyd Charisse, Lena Horne, and Dee Turnell.

GENE KELLY AND FRANK SINATRA PLAY TWO SAILORS IN *ANCHORS AWEIGH*

The Inspector General 1949

🎬 FILM

🎞 **Screenplay** Philip Rapp, Harry Kurnitz

🎵 **Music and lyrics** Sylvia Fine

Loosely based on a play by Nikolai Gogol that premiered in St Petersburg in 1836, *The Inspector General* musical comedy was directed by Henry Koster and starred Danny Kaye as Georgi. The film marked Kaye's first and last starring role with Warner Brothers.

The Inspector General is the story of a fool, Georgi, who arrives in Brodny with a medicine show. When the village's corrupt officials mistake him for the cruel Inspector General (in disguise), comedic antics ensue.

Johnny Green, credited for musical direction and incidental score in the movie's credits, was awarded the 1960 Golden Globe Award for Best Motion Picture Score for his work on the film.

Gentlemen Prefer Blondes 1949

🎭 STAGE

📖 **Book** Anita Loos, Joseph Fields

🎵 **Music** Jule Styne

𝄞 **Lyrics** Leo Robin

Set during the twenties and based on Anita Loos's novel and play of the same name, *Gentlemen Prefer Blondes* tells the over-the-top tale of flappers Lorelei Lee and Dorothy Shaw as they make their way to Paris on board the *Ile de France*. According to Loos, the story was inspired by a trip during which a blonde aspiring actress attracted more attention from men than Loos did.

Carol Channing originated the role of Lorelei Lee for the 1949 Broadway production, which opened at the Ziegfeld Theatre in December and ran until September 1951. Her performance was truly a breakthrough moment in her career. Channing reprised her role in the 1973 revised stage version, *Lorelei: Gentlemen Still Prefer Blondes*. In the 1953 movie, Marilyn Monroe played Lorelei, and her performance of "Diamonds Are a Girl's Best Friend" became absolutely iconic.

An American in Paris 1951

🎬 FILM

🎞 **Screenplay** Alan Jay Lerner

🎵 **Music** George Gershwin

𝄞 **Lyrics** Ira Gershwin

This classic Gene Kelly film originated when producer Arthur Freed attended a performance of George Gershwin's *An American in Paris* musical composition, which was inspired by

Gershwin's time in Paris during the 1920s. According to Gershwin, the composition was intended to "portray the impression of an American visitor in Paris as he strolls about the city and listens to various street noises and absorbs the French atmosphere". A stage musical of the same name, with book by Craig Lucas, opened at the Palace Theatre on Broadway in March 2015 to much critical acclaim – particularly for lead actress Leanne Cope of the Royal Ballet in London.

Hans Christian Andersen 1952

🎬 FILM

📖 **Book** Moss Hart

🎵 **Music and lyrics** Frank Loesser

Hans Christian Andersen is a movie musical starring comedian Danny Kaye in what the opening of the film terms a "fairy tale", rather than a biography, about the famous Danish writer. The film follows Hans from his time as a cobbler, telling stories to children, to a time when one of his stories is printed in a newspaper and another is adapted into a ballet. The film also traces Hans's friendship with his assistant, Peter, and his unrequited love for a famous ballerina.

Hans Christian Andersen was a passion project for producer Samuel Goldwyn, who spent over a decade on the film. It was nominated for six Academy Awards, including Best Music, Original Song for Loesser's "Thumbelina". Over the years, a number of stage adaptations have been attempted, though none have made it to Broadway or London's West End.

Calamity Jane: A Musical Western 1953

🎬 FILM

🎞 **Screenplay** James O'Hanlon

🎵 **Music** Sammy Fain

𝄞 **Lyrics** Paul Francis Webster

Calamity Jane follows the title character as she attempts to bring showstopper Adelaide Adams to the Wild West town of Deadwood to entertain the miners – but she accidentally brings Adelaide's maid, Katie Brown, instead. When one of Calamity's love interests, Lieutenant Danny Gilmartin, falls for Katie, Calamity becomes jealous. She turns to her friend and sometimes-rival Wild Bill Hickok and realizes her love for him, ensuring the happy ending.

The 1953 movie musical, which starred Doris Day as Calamity Jane and Howard Keel as Hickok, won an Academy Award for Best Original

DORIS DAY (LEFT) AND ALLYN MCLERIE IN *CALAMITY JANE*

Song ("Secret Love"). It is loosely based on the real-life history of Calamity Jane. The musical was later adapted into a 1961 stage version and a 1963 TV movie starring Carol Burnett in the title role.

Can-Can 1953

🎭 STAGE

📖 **Book** Abe Burrows

🎵 **Music and lyrics** Cole Porter

Can-Can is a musical comedy set in Paris in 1893. It follows the conflict and romance between La Mome Pistache – whose establishment, Bal du Paradis, features can-can dancing – and a young judge, Aristide Forestier, sent to investigate the morality of the club. Love conquers all when Forestier defends Pistache. Notable songs include "I Love Paris" and "C'est Magnifique".

Gwen Verdon, a Broadway newcomer in 1953, was much lauded for her dancing in *Can-Can*, especially in the numbers "The Apaches" and "The Garden of Eden". She was awarded a Tony Award for Best Featured Actress in a Musical. *Can-Can*'s choreographer, Michael Kidd, also took home a Tony for his work on the show. The 1981 stage revival was nominated for three Tony Awards.

A 1960 film, loosely based on the musical and with screenplay by Dorothy Kingsley and Charles Lederer, was directed by Walter Lang and starred Shirley MacLaine, Frank Sinatra, Maurice Chevalier, and Louis Jourdan.

Peter Pan 1954

🎭 STAGE

📖 **Book** J.M. Barrie

🎵 **Music** Mark Charlap

𝄞 **Lyrics** Carolyn Leigh

This full-musical version of *Peter Pan*, the classic J.M. Barrie play, opened on Broadway in October 1954 at the Winter Garden Theatre and starred Mary Martin as Peter Pan. Shortly after, NBC bought the rights for US $500,000 to broadcast the production on television. *Peter Pan*, the story of a boy who refuses to grow up, was broadcast live on NBC's Producers' *Showcase* with the entire Broadway cast on 7 March 1955. Since then, the musical has been presented on stage and screen in many different forms, including the much-loved 1999 Broadway production starring Cathy Rigby, and the 2015 TV version starring Allison Williams broadcast live on NBC in the US.

White Christmas 1954

🎬 FILM

🎞 **Screenplay** Norman Krasna, Norman Panama, Melvin Frank

🎵 **Music and lyrics** Irving Berlin

White Christmas tells the story of entertainers Bob Wallace (Bing Crosby) and Phil Davis (Danny Kaye) as they follow a sister act (Rosemary Clooney and Vera-Ellen) to Vermont. When they arrive, they discover that the inn, owned by their former commanding general, is nearly bankrupt. The foursome, along with Bob and Phil's army buddies, help out their commanding officer by producing

a big musical show to draw a crowd. The show's title song, written by Berlin, was first introduced to the public when Crosby sang the tune in the 1942 film *Holiday Inn*.

The *White Christmas* stage musical, with book by David Ives and Paul Blake, premiered in San Francisco for the 2004 Christmas season. A 2008 production ran at Broadway's Marquis Theatre between November 2008 and January 2009, earning Tony nominations for choreography and orchestration. It returned to the Marquis for 2009's Christmas season.

There's No Business Like Show Business 1954
🎬 FILM

🎞️ **Screenplay** Phoebe Ephron, Henry Ephron
🎵 **Music and lyrics** Irving Berlin

A 1954 movie musical starring Ethel Merman, Donald O'Connor, and Marilyn Monroe, *There's No Business Like Show Business* features husband and wife Terry and Molly Donahue and their three children as The Donahue Five vaudeville act. The family is shaken when one son decides to become a priest and another falls in love with a flashy show girl (Monroe), but the Donahues are reunited in time for the finale after Merman's rousing performance of the title song.

There's No Business Like Show Business was made up of a collection of popular Irving Berlin songs, with the title song drawn from *Annie Get Your Gun* (see pp.72–75), for which Merman had originated the role of Annie Oakley. The film, which was Fox's first Cinemascope musical, was nominated for three Academy Awards.

It's Always Fair Weather 1955
🎬 FILM

🎞️ **Screenplay** Betty Comden, Adolph Green
🎵 **Music** André Previn
🎵 **Lyrics** Betty Comden, Adolph Green

When writers Comden and Green originally got together to write *It's Always Fair Weather*, it was with the intention of developing it as a stage sequel to their smash Broadway hit *On the Town* (see pp.64–65). However, they soon decided not to produce it as a Broadway musical. After receiving approval from Gene Kelly for the storyline, they set out to write the screenplay for MGM instead.

Comden and Green imagined the three service buddies from *On the Town* meeting again ten years later only to

GENE KELLY (CENTRE) IN A SCENE FROM *IT'S ALWAYS FAIR WEATHER*

discover how their lives have changed. Between Kelly, Jules Munshin, and Frank Sinatra – the original three servicemen actors – only Kelly was available for the film. Two other dancers – Dan Dailey and Michael Kidd – were chosen to accompany him.

Ain't Misbehavin' 1955
🎬 FILM

🎞️ **Screenplay** Edward Buzzell, Philip Rapp, Devery Freeman
🎵 **Music** Henry Mancini and others

Based on a story by Robert Carson, *Ain't Misbehavin'* is a movie musical comedy that follows the romance of a poor chorus girl (played by Piper Laurie) and the rich man she marries (played by Rory Calhoun). The young woman's decision to acquire the society polish and manners she thinks her husband desires nearly drives him away. Laurie and Calhoun are supported by Jack Carson, Mamie Van Doren, and Reginald Gardiner.

The title song, "Ain't Misbehavin'", was written in 1929 by Thomas "Fats" Waller, Harry Brooks, and Andy Razaf. It first appeared as part of the 1929 Off-Broadway musical *Hot Chocolates*, by Waller and Razaf. "Ain't Misbehavin'" also became the title for a 1978 revue based on music by Fats Waller.

Bells Are Ringing 1956
🎭 STAGE

📖 **Book** Betty Comden, Adolph Green
🎵 **Music** Jule Styne
🎵 **Lyrics** Betty Comden, Adolph Green

The original production of *Bells Are Ringing* – starring Judy Holliday as phone operator Ella Peterson and Sydney Chaplin (son of Charlie Chaplin) as her love interest, Jeff Moss – opened in November 1956 and enjoyed a run of 924 performances on Broadway. Both Holliday and Chaplin won 1957 Tony Awards for their performances.

Comden and Green specially developed *Bells Are Ringing* to be Holliday's musical-comedy debut, drawing inspiration from real life for many of the show's characters. Peterson, for example, was based on one of Comden's friends, and dentist Dr Kitchell was based on a real songwriting dentist they knew. Holliday herself had worked as a phone operator after graduating from high school.

Holliday reprised her role in the 1960 film version of *Bells Are Ringing*, also starring Dean Martin. The stage show was revived in 2001 and ran for 68 performances at New York's Plymouth Theatre, with Faith Prince playing Ella.

JUDY HOLLIDAY AND DEAN MARTIN IN *BELLS ARE RINGING*

The Most Happy Fella 1956
🎭 STAGE

📖 **Book** Frank Loesser
🎵 **Music and lyrics** Frank Loesser

It took nearly four years for Frank Loesser to write *The Most Happy Fella*, a musical based on the play *They Knew What They Wanted* by Sidney Howard.

The score is often described as operatic; Robert Weede, formerly of the Metropolitan Opera, was cast for the leading role in the three-act Broadway production that opened in 1956.

In the show, an ageing Italian vineyard owner in the Napa Valley proposes marriage via mail to a younger San Francisco waitress. In order to conceal his age, he sends a photo of his young, handsome ranch foreman. The story of their rocky relationship came again to Broadway in 1979 and 1992.

Candide 1956
☙ STAGE
📖 **Book** Lillian Hellman
🎵 **Music** Leonard Bernstein
♪ **Lyrics** Richard Wilbur, John La Touche, Dorothy Parker

Candide, based on the renowned satire by Voltaire, follows the titular young man as he travels across the world in search of his lost love, the beautiful Cunegonde. Ultimately, after desperately clinging to his optimistic belief that everything will work out for the best – as instilled in him by his teacher, Dr Pangloss – Candide returns home, disillusioned.

Infused by Lillian Hellman with a commentary on the House Committee on Un-American Activities, the 1956 production of *Candide* was a flop. But Bernstein's score lived on, and the 1974 revival, which incorporated a new book by Hugh Wheeler and high-concept staging by Harold Prince, was a success.

The 1956 production was nominated for five Tony Awards. The 1974 revival was nominated for seven Tonys and won four, in addition to a Special Award for "outstanding contribution to the artistic development of the musical theatre". A second Broadway revival followed in 1997.

Irma la Douce 1958
☙ STAGE
📖 **Book** Alexandre Breffort
🎵 **Music** Marguerite Monnot
♪ **Lyrics** Julian More, David Heneker, Monty Norman

Irma la Douce is a musical comedy that tells the story of a good-hearted Parisian prostitute and the law student who falls in love with her. The student goes on to lead a double life in an attempt to keep Irma exclusively to himself.

French writer Alexandre Breffort's *Irma la Douce* first opened in Paris in 1956. An English-language version

then opened in London in July 1958. The Plymouth Theatre on Broadway welcomed the same version in September 1960. Elizabeth Seal (the only woman in the cast), Keith Michell, and Clive Revill starred in the West End production and reprised their roles on Broadway. Seal won the Tony Award for Best Actress in a Musical for her portrayal of the title character.

Flower Drum Song 1958
☙ STAGE
📖 **Book** Oscar Hammerstein II, Joseph Fields
🎵 **Music** Richard Rodgers
♪ **Lyrics** Oscar Hammerstein II

Based on C.Y. Lee's novel of the same name and set in San Francisco, *Flower Drum Song* depicts the conflict between the elder and younger generations of Chinese Americans. It follows the romance between Sammy Fong, a nightclub owner, and one of his performers, Linda Low, as Sammy's family work to marry him to a more suitable bride.

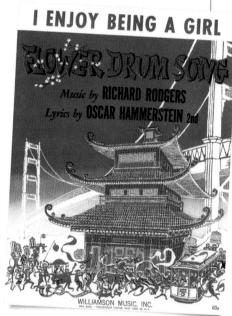

SHEET MUSIC FOR "I ENJOY BEING A GIRL"
FROM THE MUSICAL *FLOWER DRUM SONG*

The original 1958 Broadway production of *Flower Drum Song* is the only Broadway musical Gene Kelly directed. The show was nominated for six Tony Awards and won Best Conductor and Musical Director. The 1961 film – with screenplay by Joseph Fields, who wrote the book for the stage show – was nominated for five Oscars, two Golden Globes, and a Grammy, but it did not win any of the awards.

Fiorello! 1959
☙ STAGE
📖 **Book** Jerome Weidman, George Abbott
🎵 **Music** Jerry Bock
♪ **Lyrics** Sheldon Harnick

Fiorello! is a Pulitzer Prize- and Tony Award-winning musical. The show opened on Broadway at the Broadhurst Theatre on 23 November 1959, where it ran for 796 performances.

The story follows the life of Fiorello H. LaGuardia during his election to the US Congress, his enlistment in the Air Force, and his race for mayor of New York City. Tom Bosley made his Broadway debut in the production and won a Tony Award for his role as Fiorello. The show made history when it tied with *The Sound of Music* for the 1960 Tony Award for Best Musical.

Once Upon a Mattress 1959
☙ STAGE
📖 **Book** Dean Fuller, Jay Thompson, Marshall Barer
🎵 **Music** Mary Rodgers
♪ **Lyrics** Marshall Barer

Once Upon a Mattress was originally written as a short one-act show for a resort in the Poconos where it was performed during the summer of 1958. Later expanded into its popular two-act musical adaptation of the Hans Christian Anderson fairy tale "The Princess and the Pea", *Once Upon a Mattress* made its way to Broadway, receiving two Tony nominations. At the 1960 Tony Awards, Mary Rodgers competed against her father, Richard Rodgers, and his *The Sound of Music* in the Best Musical category.

Notably, comedienne Carol Burnett made her Broadway debut in *Once Upon a Mattress* and earned a Tony nomination for her shenanigans as Princess Winnifred the Woebegone.

Redhead 1959
☙ STAGE
📖 **Book** Dorothy Fields, Herbert Fields, David Shaw, Sidney Sheldon
🎵 **Music** Albert Hague
♪ **Lyrics** Dorothy Fields

Redhead is a musical murder mystery set in the early 1900s at the Simpsons Sisters' Waxworks wax museum in London. When Essie Whimple, who makes the wax models, creates one of a murder victim that offends people who knew the victim, she gets

caught up in the search for the murderer – especially once she falls for Tom Baxter, one of the victim's friends. Over-the-top antics ensue, right up until the end when the murderer is caught.

Originally written for Beatrice Lillie and then rewritten with Gwen Verdon in mind, *Redhead* marked Bob Fosse's debut as a director. The musical, which played at the 46th Street Theatre from February 1959 to March 1960, was nominated for seven Tony Awards and won five, including Best Musical.

The Unsinkable Molly Brown 1960
☙ STAGE
📖 **Book** Richard Morris
🎵 **Music and lyrics** Meredith Willson

The Unsinkable Molly Brown played at the Winter Garden Theatre on Broadway from November 1960 to February 1962. It is loosely based on the life story of Margaret Brown, a legendary survivor of the *Titanic* disaster. The musical, which was Meredith Willson's follow-up to his now-classic *The Music Man* (see pp.128–31), chronicles Brown's rise from her impoverished childhood in Missouri, through her marriage to a lucky Colorado prospector, to her glittering visits to Europe and her voyage on the ill-fated *Titanic*.

Leading actress Tammy Grimes won a Tony Award for Best Featured Actress in a Musical for her turn as Molly Brown. The musical was made into a movie in 1964 (screenplay by Helen Deutsch) starring Debbie Reynolds as Molly, with Harve Presnell, a veteran of the Broadway production, reprising his role as prospector Johnny Brown. The film was nominated for six Academy Awards, including Best Actress in a Leading Role for Reynolds. Reynolds and Presnell reunited for a national tour of *The Unsinkable Molly Brown* in 1989.

Stop the World – I Want To Get Off 1961
☙ STAGE
📖 **Book** Leslie Bricusse, Anthony Newley
🎵 **Music and lyrics** Leslie Bricusse, Anthony Newley

Stop the World – I Want to Get Off debuted in London's Queens Theatre in 1961 and ran for 485 performances. With no costume changes, bleachers inside a circus tent as a set, and just 13 cast members, expenses were very low compared to other productions during that time.

Stop the World is the story of Littlechap, a man who marries his boss's daughter and has affairs with three other women – all of whom are played by the same actress who also plays his wife. In addition to writing and directing the show, Anthony Newley also starred as Littlechap.

The show moved to Broadway in October 1962, where it ran first at the Shubert Theatre and then at the Ambassador Theatre, until closing in February 1964.

No Strings 1962
🐾 STAGE
📖 **Book** Samuel Taylor
🎵 **Music and lyrics** Richard Rodgers
No Strings is the story of an affair between fashion model Barbara Woodruff, who is living in Paris, and David Jordan, a US writer from Maine. Rodgers wrote the role of Barbara specifically for actress Diahann Carroll, and the musical was notable for its portrayal of an interracial couple without race being an issue in the plot. As the title implies, the orchestra, which was seated on stage instead of in a pit, did not include a string section. The title is also a reference to the end of the romance, when the two lovers part without strings.

The Broadway production began its run at the 54th Street Theatre in March 1962 before moving to the Broadhurst Theatre in October. The show closed in August 1963.

No Strings was Richard Rodgers' first musical after the death of writing partner Oscar Hammerstein II. It marked the only musical for which Rodgers wrote his own lyrics. Nominated for nine Tony Awards, *No Strings* won three, in addition to a Special Award for Rodgers.

I Can Get It for You Wholesale 1962
🐾 STAGE
📖 **Book** Jerome Weidman
🎵 **Music and lyrics** Harold Rome
I Can Get It for You Wholesale follows the story of Harry Bogen (Elliott Gould), a young garment maker who will do anything it takes to be successful, even as his actions threaten to alienate his girlfriend, his mother, and other connections. Set during the Great Depression, the musical was based on Jerome Weidman's 1937 novel, which had also been loosely adapted into a 1951 film of the same name.

With the show's first performance at the Shubert Theatre on 22 March 1962, 19-year-old Barbra Streisand made her Broadway debut. She was nominated in the Tony Award's Best Featured Actress category for her performance as Bogen's secretary. Streisand and Gould, who met during the production, were married in March 1963 – and divorced eight years later.

110 in the Shade 1963
🐾 STAGE
📖 **Book** N. Richard Nash
🎵 **Music** Harvey Schmidt
🎵 **Lyrics** Tom Jones
Based on N. Richard Nash's play and the 1956 film *The Rainmaker*, which starred Katharine Hepburn and Burt Lancaster, *110 in the Shade* takes place on Independence Day (4 July) in a small Western town suffering from a drought. Lizzie, a plain young woman who fears she will become an old maid, clashes with newcomer Starbuck, who has convinced the townspeople he can make it rain. Over the course of the day, Lizzie is torn between Starbuck and the local lawman, Sheriff File. Lizzie ultimately chooses File, just as rain begins to fall.

The 1963 stage production was choreographed by Agnes de Mille, and was nominated for four Tony Awards. *110 in the Shade* was revived in 2007, this time receiving five Tony Award nominations – including Best Revival of a Musical and Best Actress in a Musical for Audra McDonald, who is the current record holder for the most Tony Awards won by a performer (six).

Half a Sixpence 1963
🐾 STAGE
📖 **Book** Beverley Cross
🎵 **Music and lyrics** David Heneker
Half a Sixpence, written as a vehicle for British pop star Tommy Steele, is based on the H.G. Wells novel *Kipps*. The musical is set in the Kent town of Folkestone at the turn of the 20th century and centres on the life of a young orphan, Arthur Kipps. Arthur works as a draper's apprentice until he inherits a fortune. When Arthur's money goes to his head, he very nearly marries the wrong girl – but after his wedding to his real sweetheart, Ann, it takes losing his inheritance for Arthur to learn to be truly happy with his life.

Half a Sixpence premiered in London in March 1963 at the Cambridge Theatre and ran for 677 performances.

LESLEY ANN WARREN MADE HER BROADWAY DEBUT IN *110 IN THE SHADE*

A Broadway production opened in April 1965 and was nominated for nine Tony Awards – eight of which went to *Fiddler on the Roof* (see pp.150–53), the big winner that year. *Half a Sixpence* was made into a film in 1967, with a screenplay by the stage show's writer, Beverley Cross, and with Steele reprising his role as Arthur.

She Loves Me 1963
🎭 **STAGE**
📖 **Book** Joe Masteroff
🎵 **Music** Jerry Bock
𝄞 **Lyrics** Sheldon Harnick

She Loves Me is a musical romantic comedy based on *Parfumerie*, a play by Hungarian Miklós László that inspired several other adaptations – notably *The Shop Around the Corner* starring James Stewart and Margaret Sullavan, and the 1998 Nora Ephron film *You've Got Mail* starring Meg Ryan and Tom Hanks.

Set in Europe in 1934, the musical follows the love story of Georg and Amalia, who clash during their day jobs at Mr Maraczek's shop but have been, without knowing it, writing love letters to each other through a lonely hearts advertisement. The original production opened on Broadway in April 1963 at the Eugene O'Neill Theatre, running for 301 performances before closing in January 1964. It was nominated for five Tony Awards, of which it won one: Best Featured Actor in a Musical (Jack Cassidy).

The 1993 revival of *She Loves Me* marked the first Broadway musical for the Roundabout Theatre Company. This time, it was nominated for nine Tony Awards and won Best Actor in a Musical (Boyd Gaines).

Oh! What a Lovely War 1963
🎭 **STAGE**
📖 **Book** Charles Chilton and Theatre Workshop, Inc
🎵 **Music** Alfred Ralston
𝄞 **Lyrics** Lena Guilbert Ford, Stoddard King

The use of period songs was the backbone of the original stage musical of *Oh! What a Lovely War*, which opened in the West End in 1963 and subsequently ran at the Broadhurst Theatre on Broadway from September 1964 to January 1965. A musical revue packed with historical details of World War I, it used irony and satire to communicate the harsh reality of war to the audience. The show received four Tony Award nominations, with Victor Spinelli winning Best Featured

FILM POSTER FOR *OH! WHAT A LOVELY WAR*, DIRECTED BY RICHARD ATTENBOROUGH

Actor in a Musical. A film based on the stage musical, with screenplay by Len Deighton, was released in 1969.

The Jungle Book 1967
🎬 **FILM**
🎬 **Screenplay** Larry Clemmons, Ralph Wright, Ken Anderson, Vance Gerry
🎵 **Music** George Bruns
𝄞 **Lyrics** Richard Sherman, Robert Sherman
♫𝄞 **Music and lyrics** Terry Gilkyon for "Bare Necessities"

Based loosely on the Rudyard Kipling book of the same name, *The Jungle Book* is a 1967 animated musical film produced by Disney Animated Productions. It follows the journey of an orphan boy, Mowgli, growing up and learning to survive deep in the jungle.

The Jungle Book was in production at the time of Walt Disney's death in December 1966, nearly a year before its actual release, making it the last feature film Walt Disney worked on. It was also the first film for which Disney planned a sequel; *Jungle Book 2* was finally released in 2003, more than 30 years after the original.

You're a Good Man, Charlie Brown 1967
🎭 **STAGE**
📖 **Book** Clark Gesner
♫𝄞 **Music and lyrics** Clark Gesner

Charles Schultz's beloved comic strip is brought to life in Clark Gesner's musical *You're a Good Man, Charlie Brown*. Gesner's idea for the show began when he wrote "Peanuts"

songs and recorded them as an album; he was later persuaded to weave the songs into a theatrical production. To do so, Gesner created short scenes, each representing moments in Charlie Brown's life, and strung them together.

You're a Good Man, Charlie Brown opened in 1967 Off-Broadway at the Theatre 80 St Marks. It played for 1,597 performances. This version was revived on Broadway in 1971. A new version appeared on Broadway in 1999, for which Kristin Chenoweth and Roger Bart won Tony Awards for their featured roles as Sally and Snoopy.

Hallelujah, Baby! 1967
🎭 **STAGE**
📖 **Book** Arthur Laurents
🎵 **Music** Jule Styne
𝄞 **Lyrics** Betty Comden, Adolph Green

Hallelujah, Baby!, a meditation on race relations in the first half of the 20th century, opened on Broadway in April 1967 at the Martin Beck Theatre and ran until January 1968. It follows Georgina, a young black woman, her Momma, and her two suitors – Clem, who is black, and Harvey, who is white. As the decades change around them, they do not age. Georgina, who begins as a maid on a plantation, pursues a career as a performer against her mother's wishes and ultimately finds success.

Hallelujah, Baby! was nominated for nine Tony Awards and won five, including Best Musical and a tie for Best Actress in a Musical for star Leslie

Uggams. The musical was originally envisioned as a vehicle for Lena Horne, but when she opted not to take the role, it was rewritten with a lighter sensibility for Uggams.

1776 1969
🎭 **STAGE**
📖 **Book** Peter Stone
♫𝄞 **Music and lyrics** Sherman Edwards

1776 is a stirring yet humorous account of the signing of the Declaration of Independence by the Second Continental Congress. The original Broadway production, which ran from March 1969 to February 1972, was nominated for five Tony Awards. It won three: Best Musical, Best Featured Actor in a Musical (Ronald Holgate), and Best Direction of a Musical (Peter Hunt). The 1997 revival was nominated for three Tonys, including Best Revival of a Musical.

The musical was made into a film in 1972 and starred several actors from the original Broadway production, including William Daniels as John Adams. The most notable change from the stage show to the film was the omission of the song "Cool, Cool,

HOWARD DA SILVA (LEFT) AND WILLIAM DANIELS IN THE 1972 FILM VERSION OF *1776*

Considerate Men" sung by John Dickinson of Pennsylvania and other wealthy conservatives. According to writer Peter Stone, the change was made by producer Jack Warner – allegedly at the request of then-President Richard Nixon. The negatives of this scene were later found and restored in a director's cut released on DVD in 2002.

Coco 1969

STAGE

📖 **Book** Alan Jay Lerner

🎵 **Music** André Previn

🎼 **Lyrics** Alan Jay Lerner

Inspired by the life of iconic fashion designer Coco Chanel, *Coco* premiered on Broadway at the Mark Hellinger Theatre in December 1969 and closed in October 1970. The musical centres on Chanel's endeavour to make a comeback at the age of 71 after 15 years in retirement. Its final number involves a fashion show based on Chanel's most famous designs.

Coco marked Katharine Hepburn's only appearance in a stage musical. Not an accomplished singer, Hepburn was reportedly displeased with her performance as Coco on the Broadway cast album. Regardless, she followed her New York performance with a national tour of the show. *Coco* was nominated for seven Tony Awards and won two, for Best Costume Design and Best Featured Actor in a Musical (René Auberjonois).

Applause 1970

STAGE

📖 **Book** Betty Comden, Adolph Green

🎵 **Music** Charles Strouse

🎼 **Lyrics** Lee Adams

Applause, written by the indomitable team of Betty Comden and Adolph Green, was based on the 1950 film *All About Eve* starring Bette Davis. A longtime friend of Comden and Green, actress Lauren Bacall made her Broadway musical debut as the female lead – despite not being a singer – and took home the Tony for Best Actress in a Musical for her performance. Bacall played the part of ageing legendary Broadway star Margo Channing for four years and never missed a performance, even after suffering a painful knee injury.

Applause went on to win the Tony for Best Musical. Supporting actresses Bonnie Franklin and Penny Fuller were both nominated for the Tony that year, though the award ultimately went to Melba Moore for *Purlie*.

Purlie 1970

STAGE

📖 **Book** Ossie Davis, Philip Rose, Peter Udell

🎵 **Music** Gary Geld

🎼 **Lyrics** Peter Udell

Purlie follows the efforts of a "new-fangled preacher man", as Purlie calls himself, to acquire a church in a small American town in Georgia. To do so he needs to procure a family inheritance from a racist plantation owner, Cap'n Cotchipee. The plan, involving the help of love interest Lutiebelle, goes awry, but eventually Purlie gets his church.

Adapted from Ossie Davis's 1961 play *Purlie Victorious*, the musical's use of over-the-top stereotypes was meant to send up and mock the racial segregation of the time.

Purlie was nominated for five Tony Awards and won for Best Actor in a Musical (Cleavon Little) and Best Featured Actress in a Musical (Melba Moore). The musical, which had a brief revival in 1972, was made into a television movie in 1981.

The Rothschilds 1970

STAGE

📖 **Book** Sherman Yellen

🎵 **Music** Jerry Bock

🎼 **Lyrics** Sheldon Harnick

Set in Europe in the late 18th and early 19th centuries, *The Rothchilds* is based on the true story of the Rothschild family and their rise to prominence. Mayer Rothschild uses his charm and guile to convince Prince William into providing him with a marriage licence so he can marry his sweetheart, Gutele, despite restrictions on Jews marrying in Frankfurt. Mayer's cunning, which his five sons share, serves his family well as their wealth grows and their influence over political matters increases, until it can finally be used to apply pressure for better rights for Jews across Europe.

The Rothschilds was the final musical written by the team of Harnick and Bock, best known for *Fiddler on the Roof* (see pp.150–53) and *She Loves Me*. The original Broadway production ran for 507 performances at the Lunt-Fontanne Theatre between October 1970 and January 1972. It was nominated for nine Tony Awards and won two: Best Actor in a Musical (Hal Linden) and Best Featured Actor in a Musical (Keene Curtis).

Willy Wonka and the Chocolate Factory 1971

🎬 **FILM**

📃 **Screenplay** Roald Dahl

🎵 **Music and lyrics** Leslie Bricusse, Anthony Newley

The 1971 movie *Willy Wonka and the Chocolate Factory* was the first film adaptation of Roald Dahl's 1964 book *Charlie and the Chocolate Factory*. Featuring Gene Wilder in the role of Willy Wonka, the movie certainly did not set any box-office records, but it lives on as a cult-classic favourite.

Willy Wonka and the Chocolate Factory received an Academy Award nomination for its score, and Wilder was nominated for a Golden Globe Award for his performance. In 2014, the Library of Congress inducted the movie into the US National Film Registry, deeming it a film that "harken[ed] back to the classic Hollywood musicals" with its "memorable musical score".

GENE WILDER AS WILLY WONKA IN *WILLY WONKA AND THE CHOCOLATE FACTORY*

Godspell 1971

STAGE

📖 **Book** John-Michael Tebelak

🎵 **Music and lyrics** Stephen Schwartz

Godspell is a musical adaptation of the Gospel of St Matthew. The first act focuses on Jesus building a community of followers and teaching them through parables. The second act portrays Jesus's betrayal by Judas after the Last Supper and his eventual crucifixion. The show is notable for setting traditional hymns to a variety of musical styles, including rock'n'roll, pop, and rap.

Godspell originated as a play, written by John-Michael Tebelak for his master thesis at Carnegie Mellon University (CMU). After a few weeks of performances at NYC's La MaMa Experimental Theatre Club in 1971, Stephen Schwartz, also a former CMU student, was brought on board to turn the show into a musical suitable for what became a very successful Off-Broadway run. The production had included a few songs prior to Schwartz's involvement, but Schwartz scrapped all but one, "By My Side" (music by Peggy Gordon, lyrics by Jay Hamburger).

The Broadway run of *Godspell* opened in June 1976 at the Broadhurst Theatre, ran until September 1977, and received one Tony Award nomination for Best Score. The 1973 movie, adapted by Tebelak and David Greene, starred Victor Garber, of the first Canadian cast, as Jesus.

VICTOR GARBER IN THE 1973 *GODSPELL* FILM

Don't Bother Me, I Can't Cope 1972

STAGE

📖 **Book** Micki Grant

🎵 **Music and lyrics** Micki Grant

Micki Grant not only wrote the book, music, and lyrics for the musical revue *Don't Bother Me, I Can't Cope*, she also starred in it. Grant started working on *Cope*, a collection of music from African-American culture, in 1970. After a brief Off-Broadway run, it opened on Broadway in April 1972 and ran until October 1974.

Grant received many accolades for *Cope*, including a Grammy for Best Score from an Original Cast Show Album. *Cope* was also nominated for four Tonys, including Best Musical. For her playwriting, Grant was deemed an honoured recipient of an NAACP Image Award.

Mack and Mabel 1974

STAGE

📖 **Book** Michael Stewart

🎵 **Music and lyrics** Jerry Herman

Mack and Mabel debuted in San Diego in June 1974, to good, but not great, reviews. The show moved to New York and opened at the Majestic Theatre in October that same year. A biographical musical about the romance of silent film director Mack Sennett and silent film star Mabel Normand, *Mack and Mabel* depicted their love affair until Mabel's tragic death from a drug overdose (though Mack dreams a happier ending).

Much was expected from *Mack and Mabel* and the famed Jerry Herman and Michael Stewart team; in the end, the show was a heartbreaking disappointment that closed after eight weeks and just 66 performances. Despite Herman's wonderful score and Robert Preston and Bernadette Peters in the lead roles, the show was poorly received by audiences and critics.

Shenandoah 1975

STAGE

📖 **Book** James Lee Barrett, Philip Rose, Peter Udell

🎵 **Music** Gary Geld

🎵 **Lyrics** Peter Udell

Set in the Shenandoah Valley of Virginia during the US Civil War, *Shenandoah* is the story of patriarch Charlie Anderson, who strives to keep his family out of the tensions of the war. Charlie is drawn into the conflict when Union soldiers kidnap his youngest son, and as the family searches for the boy, tragedy follows

them. The themes of pacifism and isolationism were especially resonant for audiences, who saw parallels to the then-recent Vietnam War. After more than two years of performances at the Alvin Theatre, beginning in January 1975, the original Broadway production played the last four months of its run at the Mark Hellinger Theatre.

Based on the 1965 film starring James Stewart, *Shenandoah* was nominated for six Tony Awards and won two: Best Actor in a Musical (John Cullum) and Best Book of a Musical. The 1989 revival saw Cullum reprise his role.

Bugsy Malone 1976

🎬 **FILM**

📄 **Screenplay** Alan Parker

🎵 **Music and lyrics** Paul Williams

Bugsy Malone is a movie musical about gangsters, with an all-child cast. Adult singers' voices were dubbed in for the musical numbers. The film stars Scott Baio as Bugsy, Florrie Dugger as Blousey Brown, and Jodie Foster (at age 13) as Tallulah caught in a clash between speakeasy owner Fat Sam (John Cassisi) and his rival, Dandy Dan (Martin Lev). The

Prohibition-era gang warfare is given levity by the child actors – and by their "splurge" guns, which shoot custard.

The film was adapted for the stage by Micky Dolenz, with music by Paul Williams, and opened in the West End in 1983. A young Catherine Zeta-Jones appeared in the West End production, which, like the movie, featured adult singers. The 1997 revival by the UK's National Youth Music Theatre was a true all-child production, with the children providing their own vocals.

The Best Little Whorehouse in Texas 1978

STAGE

📖 **Book** Larry L. King, Peter Masterson

🎵 **Music and lyrics** Carol Hall

The *Best Little Whorehouse in Texas* is a comedic musical about a brothel called The Chicken Ranch, in Texas. Miss Mona, the brothel's madam, has an understanding with the local sheriff, her former lover, that allows the business to operate without trouble from the law – until a local do-gooder TV reporter brings the brothel to the public's attention, thereby forcing The Chicken Ranch to be shut down.

Inspired by the true story of The Chicken Ranch, a brothel that operated for decades outside La Grange, Texas, *The Best Little Whorehouse in Texas* was nominated for seven Tony Awards and won Best Featured Actor in a Musical (Henderson Forsythe) and Best Featured Actress in a Musical (Carlin Glinn). In 1982, the musical was made into a film starring Dolly Parton and Burt Reynolds, with screenplay by the writers of the stage show – Larry L. King and Peter Masterson – as well as Colin Higgins.

Dancin' 1978

STAGE

🎵 **Music and lyrics** Various artists

Dancin', a musical revue, is pure Bob Fosse. Created solely as a vehicle for dance, without a story or book binding together the songs, *Dancin'* was especially popular with international visitors who were pleased to experience a Broadway show without having to worry about understanding the words.

Dancin' opened at the Broadhurst Theatre in March 1978, then moved to the Ambassador Theatre in November 1980 before closing in June 1982. The

CUSTARD-SHOOTING GANGSTERS IN *BUGSY MALONE*

production was nominated for seven Tonys and took home two, including another Best Choreography win for Fosse – his seventh.

Sugar Babies 1978
STAGE
Book Ralph G. Allen
Music Jimmy McHugh and others
Lyrics Dorothy Fields and others
Sugar Babies is a musical revue that celebrates the burlesque and variety entertainment era. The show opened on Broadway in October 1979 and gave Mickey Rooney his Broadway debut at the age of 59. *Sugar Babies* ran for almost three years at the Mark Hellinger Theatre, a total of 1,208 performances – of which Rooney did not miss a single show. Both Rooney and his co-star, Ann Miller, were Tony-nominated for their leading roles.

Tell Me on a Sunday 1978
STAGE
Music Andrew Lloyd Webber
Lyrics Don Black
Tell Me on a Sunday was written as a one-act, one-woman song cycle in 1978. It originally appeared as a BBC television special in 1979 starring Marti Webb. It follows a young English "Girl" who arrives in the States and charts her adventures in search of success and love in New York City.

Over the years, the stage show has undergone various changes. When it opened in London in 1982, *Tell Me on a Sunday* became a two-act show, *Song and Dance*, with an all-singing first act and an all-dancing second half. After a three year run in London, *Song and Dance* arrived in New York. Bernadette Peters was cast as the 27-year-old lead character, but this time, the character was given a name: Emma. Peters won her first Tony Award for Best Actress in a Musical for her performance in this show.

They're Playing Our Song 1979
STAGE
Book Neil Simon
Music Marvin Hamlisch
Lyrics Carole Bayer Sager
They're Playing Our Song is the story of songwriter Vernon and lyricist Sonia, two neurotic artists who come together to explore the possibilities of a writing partnership. They find themselves considering a romantic relationship, hindered by their own personalities and Sonia's inability to cut ties with an ex. While Sonia and

Vernon are the sole characters in the musical, their inner thoughts are voiced by two trios of singers.

Based in part on composer Hamlisch's real-life collaboration and affair with lyricist Carole Bayer Sager, *They're Playing Our Song* was nominated for four Tony Awards, including Best Musical and Best Book of a Musical for Neil Simon. It ran from February 1979 until September 1981 at Broadway's Imperial Theatre.

Fame 1980
FILM
Screenplay Christopher Gore
Music Michael Gore
Lyrics Various artists
The story of students attending New York's High School of the Performing Arts, *Fame* won Oscars for Best Score and Best Song, for "Fame". It was the first time in Academy Award history that two songs from one film ("Fame" and "Out Here on My Own") were nominated in the same category. The film's success resulted in a television series, which premiered in 1982 and starred Debbie Allen.

The stage musical based on the movie – with book by José Fernandez, music by Steve Margoshes, and lyrics by

Jacques Levy – has been put on under two titles: *Fame the Musical* (1988), which premiered at the Coconut Grove Playhouse in Miami, Florida, and *Fame on 42nd Street* (2003), which ran Off-Broadway from 11 November 2003 until 27 June 2004. Many international productions of the musical have also been staged, including a 1995 Laurence Olivier Award–nominated West End production.

A Day in Hollywood, A Night in the Ukraine 1980
STAGE
Book Dick Vosburgh
Music Frank Lazarus; additional songs by Jerry Herman
Lyrics Dick Vosburgh
A Day in Hollywood, A Night in the Ukraine is a pair of one-act musical revues. The first act, which is set in the famous Grauman's Chinese Theater in Hollywood, is a guided tour of movie-musical history, led by singing and dancing theatre ushers. The second act, set in the Ukraine and loosely based on Anton Chekhov's play *The Bear*, is played as if it is a movie by the vaudeville and Hollywood act the Marx Brothers, complete with a Marx Brothers-influenced cast of characters.

The show first opened in the West End in 1979. The original Broadway production of *A Day in Hollywood, A Night in the Ukraine* ran from May 1980 to September 1981 and was nominated for nine Tony Awards. It won for Best Featured Actress in a Musical (Priscilla Lopez) and Best Choreography (Thommie Walsh and director/choreographer Tommy Tune).

Little Shop of Horrors 1980
STAGE
Book Alan Menken
Music and lyrics Howard Ashman
The *Little Shop of Horrors* musical that premiered Off-Broadway in 1982 was based on the 1962 non-musical film that director Roger Corman shot in just two days. Corman was known for making low-budget thrillers; *The Little Shop of Horrors* was no exception. The musical version, by Alan Menken and Howard Ashman, features catchy tunes and puppets designed and operated by Martin P. Robinson. The story centres on a flower-shop assistant, Seymour, who discovers a man-eating plant, Audrey II.

The Off-Broadway production won three Drama Desk Awards, including Outstanding Musical. The 1986 movie musical of the same name, with

THE ORIGINAL FILM VERSION OF *FAME*, DIRECTED BY ALAN PARKER

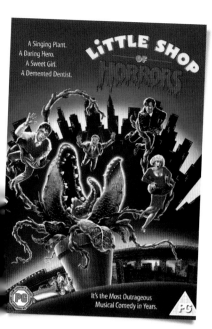

FILM POSTER FOR *LITTLE SHOP OF HORRORS*

screenplay by Ashman and directed by Frank Oz, starred Rick Moranis, Ellen Greene, Steve Martin, and Levi Stubbs as the voice of Audrey II, and became a much-loved cult classic.

Blood Brothers 1983
✦ STAGE
📖 **Book** Willy Russell
♫ **Music and lyrics** Willy Russell

Russell originally wrote *Blood Brothers* as a school play. It was first performed in 1982, with no music or scenery, for an audience of 400 children at a secondary school in a Liverpool suburb. The show eventually moved to London's West End, with music and lyrics also by Russ, in 1983, winning the Laurence Olivier Award for Best New Musical.

Blood Brothers is the story of fraternal twins who are separated at birth; one is raised in poverty, and one is raised in wealth. Later in life, the two brothers meet and fall in love with the same girl, each without knowing the other is his twin.

The 1983 production of *Blood Brothers* went on a national tour, returning to London in 1988 for a revival that ran for 24 years and more than 10,000 performances before closing in 2012. A Broadway production of *Blood Brothers* ran for two years after opening in April 1993; the show was nominated for six Tony Awards.

Big River 1985
✦ STAGE
📖 **Book** William Hauptman
♫ **Music and lyrics** Roger Miller

Miller and Hauptman's *Big River* is a musical adaptation of Mark Twain's timeless classic *The Adventures of Huckleberry Finn*. The show originated when Rocco Landesman – who would eventually go on to produce the show – asked Miller to write a score about *The Adventures of Huckleberry Finn*, Landesman's favourite novel at the time. After writing letters to Miller for about a year, Landesman finally convinced the country singer to take on the project.

With a 1984 try-out at the American Repertory Theatre in Cambridge, Massachusetts, followed by a run in California, *Big River* opened at New York's Eugene O'Neill Theatre in April 1985. Actor John Goodman originated the role Huck's father, Pap Finn – but when Goodman left the show for a major film role, Miller himself took over the part for three months. The production earned seven Tony Awards, including Best Musical, and ran for more than 1,000 performances, closing in September 1987.

The Mystery of Edwin Drood 1985
✦ STAGE
📖 **Book** Rupert Holmes
♫ **Music and lyrics** Rupert Holmes

Originally produced Off-Broadway in August 1985 at the Delacorte Theatre, *The Mystery of Edwin Drood* ran for 27 performances before it transferred to Broadway later in the year. Mid-run, in November 1986, the show's name was changed to simply *Drood*.

Rupert Holmes had a long fascination with Charles Dickens's unfinished novel, inspiring him to create the show. Because Dickens's intended ending is unknown, the audience at each performance of *The Mystery of Edwin Drood* gets to vote on who murdered the unfortunate orphan and see their chosen ending play out.

The musical comedy, with an interactive whodunit twist and witty score, won five Tony Awards, including Best Musical.

Chess 1986
✦ STAGE
📖 **Book** Richard Nelson
♫ **Music** Benny Andersson, Björn Ulvaeus
♫ **Lyrics** Tim Rice

Set in the politically charged environment of the Cold War, *Chess* dramatizes an international chess competition. In it, a fiery, brash American player (loosely based on renowned chess player Bobby Fischer) and his Russian rival find themselves in a love triangle with Florence, a Hungarian-born American. The musical's chess competition is inspired in part by Fischer's match with Boris Spassky in Reykjavik, Iceland, in 1972.

Chess is based on a highly successful 1984 concept album, and the show was a West End hit when it opened in London in 1986. A revised Broadway run in 1988 was less successful and closed after 68 performances. A second revision was done for a 2008 concert at the Royal Albert Hall in London starring Josh Groban, Adam Pascal, and Idina Menzel.

Sarafina! 1988
✦ STAGE
📖 **Book** Mbongeni Ngema
♫ **Music and lyrics** Hugh Masekela, Mbongeni Ngema

Mbaqanga, an upbeat South African rock music genre, is at the heart of *Sarafina!*, which tells the grim story of apartheid through a group of high-school students who are staging a performance to celebrate anti-apartheid visionary Nelson Mandela. Although the show's content is grim, its spirit was described by *The New York Times* as "liberating singing and dancing that nearly raises the theater's roof".

Sarafina! ran at Broadway's Cort Theatre from January 1988 until July 1989 to mixed reviews. In the titular role of Sarafina, Leleti Khumalo received a Tony Award nomination for Best Featured Actress in a Musical, and an NAACP Image Award for Best Stage Actress. She appeared in the 1992 movie musical alongside Whoopi Goldberg.

City of Angels 1989
✦ STAGE
📖 **Book** Larry Gelbart
♫ **Music** Cy Coleman
♫ **Lyrics** David Zippel

City of Angels is set in the 1940s and intertwines the musical-comedy tale of Stine, a detective-story writer, with a film noir storyline that stars Stone, the hardboiled detective featured in Stine's novels.

The original Broadway production opened at the Virginia Theatre in December 1989, running for 879 performances before closing in January 1992. The costumes and set reflected the split between Stine and Stone; the noir characters wore only black, white, and grey on a greyscale set, while Stine's world was designed to be much more colourful. *City of Angels* was nominated for 11 Tony Awards and won six, including Best Scenic Design and Best Musical.

Grand Hotel 1989
✦ STAGE
📖 **Book** Luther Davis
♫ **Music and lyrics** George Forrest, Robert Wright

Set in Berlin in 1928, *Grand Hotel* weaves together the fascinating stories of the guests and staff at the extravagant Grand Hotel. A glittering cast of characters – including a broke baron who turns to thievery, the ageing ballerina he falls for, a young typist who dreams of Hollywood, and many others – contributes to the glamour and intrigue.

The musical is based on Austrian writer Vicki Baum's 1929 novel, which had already been turned into a play as well as a 1932 film starring Greta Garbo, John Barrymore, Lionel Barrymore, and Joan Crawford. Davis, Wright,

(LEFT TO RIGHT) YVETTE LAWRENCE, TIF LUCKENBILL, AND DAVID CASSIDY IN *BLOOD BROTHERS* ON BROADWAY

Forest, and director/choreographer Tommy Tune made a first attempt at the musical in the 1950s under the title *At the Grand*, but after an unsuccessful California try-out, the project was shelved for decades.

Grand Hotel finally opened on Broadway in November 1989. The production ran until April 1992 and won five Tony Awards, including Best Director and Best Choreographer – both for Tommy Tune.

Once on This Island 1990
🎭 STAGE
📖 **Book** Lynn Ahrens
🎵 **Music** Stephen Flaherty
𝄞 **Lyrics** Lynn Ahrens
In 1989, Graciela Daniele choreographed and directed her first Broadway show – which, unfortunately, closed quickly due to poor reviews. Despite the fiasco, Lynn Ahrens and Stephen Flaherty believed in Daniele's talent; they asked her to choreograph and direct their one-act musical, *Once on This Island*, which opened in 1990. This Caribbean fairy tale went on to receive a total of eight Tony nominations. Daniele received two of those nominations, for Best Direction of a Musical and Best Choreography.

The Will Rogers Follies 1991
🎭 STAGE
📖 **Book** Peter Stone
🎵 **Music** Cy Coleman
𝄞 **Lyrics** Betty Comden, Adolph Green
Complete with showgirls, a light-up staircase, and a couple of hundred costumes designed by Willa Kim, *The Will Rogers Follies* opened on Broadway at the Palace Theatre in May 1991. Tommy Tune choreographed and

directed the musical with elaborate production numbers to recount the life and career of cowboy and vaudeville performer Will Rogers and his time with the Ziegfeld Follies.

A Tony darling, *The Will Rogers Follies* won awards for its score, costume design, and lighting design, besides taking home the award for Best Musical. Tommy Tune was also awarded two Tonys for the show – Best Choreography and Best Direction of a Musical.

The Secret Garden 1991
🎭 STAGE
📖 **Book** Marsha Norman
🎵 **Music** Lucy Simon
𝄞 **Lyrics** Marsha Norman
The Secret Garden was adapted from Frances Hodgson Burnett's extremely popular children's novel, which was published in 1911. The story follows spoiled, wilful Mary Lennox, who is brought to England from India after her parents die of cholera. At her uncle Archibald's home in Yorkshire, lonely Mary is neglected by her uncle; he is still in mourning for his wife, Lily, who died ten years earlier giving birth to their bedridden son, Colin. When Mary discovers a secret garden on the grounds and brings it back to life, her efforts impact everyone at the manor.

The Secret Garden was nominated for seven Tony Awards and won three, including Best Featured Actress in a Musical for Daisy Eagan. Eagan, who at age 11 portrayed Mary Lennox, is one of the youngest people to win a Tony Award. The 2001 West End production of *The Secret Garden* involved a revamped book and score.

Falsettos 1992
🎭 STAGE
📖 **Book** William Finn, James Lapine
🎵 **Music and lyrics** William Finn
The Tony Award-winning musical *Falsettos* was originally produced Off-Broadway as two separate one-act shows, *March of the Falsettos* and *Falsettoland*, the last two in a trilogy of Off-Broadway plays (following the first, *In Trousers*). The combined full-length musical with 36 songs is about a man who leaves his wife and son to be with another man, who contracts the AIDS virus. The show, which came at a time when the AIDS crisis was becoming more prominent in America, proved timely.

Falsettos provided humorous and heartbreaking moments in a character-driven show that ran for 486 performances to audiences at the John Golden Theatre in New York. It won Tony Awards for Best Book of a Musical and Best Original Score. A revival is planned for 2016, under the direction of the original Broadway production's director, James Lapine.

The Nightmare Before Christmas 1993
🎬 FILM
🎞 **Screenplay** Michael McDowell, Caroline Thompson
🎵 **Music and lyrics** Danny Elfman
Based on a story and characters by Tim Burton, and directed by Henry Selick, *The Nightmare Before Christmas* is a stop-motion movie musical. When Jack Skellington, the Pumpkin King of Halloweentown, finds his way to Christmastown, he is fascinated by the town's holiday traditions and decides that he'd like to give Christmas a try, even as his friend Sally warns him it's a bad idea. But as Jack and the inhabitants of Halloweentown take on Christmas – and kidnap Santa Claus in the process – their efforts prove a bit too grotesque for the boys and girls of the world.

Chris Sarandon is the voice of Jack, with composer Danny Elfman providing Jack's singing voice. Catherine O'Hara lends her voice to Sally. Since its release, *The Nightmare Before Christmas* has acquired cult-classic status.

The Who's Tommy 1993
🎭 STAGE
📖 **Book** Des McAnuff, Pete Townshend
🎵 **Music and lyrics** Pete Townshend
Based upon The Who's 1969 rock opera concept album, which was made into a film in 1975, *The Who's Tommy*

follows the story of young Tommy, who at age four watches as his father kills his mother's lover. After the experience, Tommy becomes deaf, dumb, and blind. Years pass as Tommy is abused by his family, until, after becoming a pinball wizard, Tommy regains his senses. His miraculous recovery and his pinball skills bring him fame.

Though similar to the album, the musical *Tommy* adds a final reconciliation for Tommy and his family that was not a part of the original album. It also changes Tommy's message to his followers in the song "We're Not Gonna Take It"; in the original album, Tommy suggested his fans attempt to turn off their senses, as he did, but in the musical he advises them against emulating him. *The Who's Tommy* was nominated for 11 Tony Awards and won five, including a tie with *Kiss of the Spiderwoman* (see p.260) for Best Original Score. It ran for more than two years at the St James Theatre, from April 1993 until June 1995.

Beauty and the Beast 1994
🎭 STAGE
📖 **Book** Linda Woolverton
🎵 **Music** Alan Menken
𝄞 **Lyrics** Howard Ashman, Tim Rice
The beloved 1991 animated film by Disney won standing ovations at pre-screenings. *Beauty and the Beast* also became the first animated film to be nominated for the Oscar for Best Picture. It was nominated for six Academy Awards overall and won for Music (Original Score) and Music (Original Song: "Beauty and the Beast"). The film's success inspired Disney to create the 1994 Broadway production, which included several additional songs and marked Disney's first forray into the world of Broadway theatre. It was hugely successful, earning nine Tony nominations (winning one) and boasting a 13-year run – one of the longest in Broadway history.

The story of *Beauty and the Beast* centres on Belle, a young woman who doesn't fit in with small-town life. After Belle's father is taken captive by a beast in an enchanted castle, she offers to take his place as the beast's prisoner. But the beast is really a prince under a curse, and if he can fall in love with Belle and she with him, his curse will be broken.

ROGER DALTREY AS TOMMY IN THE 1975 FILM VERSION OF *TOMMY*

Smokey Joe's Café 1995
🎭 STAGE

📖 **Book** Stephen Helper, Jack Viertel

🎵ₐ **Music and lyrics** Jerry Leiber, Mike Stoller

Smokey Joe's Café is a musical revue featuring a collection of 38 hits from the 1950s and 60s by American songwriting partners lyricist Jerry Leiber and composer Mike Stoller. Leiber and Stoller formed a partnership when they were just 17 years old; within three years, they found success with their first hit song, "Hound Dog", made famous by Elvis Presley. The duo went on to co-write numerous smash hits for major artists, including The Beatles, The Beach Boys, and The Rolling Stones, to name just a few. Leiber and Stoller were inducted into the Songwriters' Hall of Fame in 1985, and the Rock and Roll Hall of Fame in 1987. The Elvis Presley recording of "Hound Dog" was placed in the Grammy Hall of Fame in 1988.

Smokey Joe's Café opened on Broadway on 9 February 1995. It ran for more than 2,000 performances, finishing its run in January 2000. The show received seven Tony nominations, and the cast recording album won a Grammy Award.

ELVIS PRESLEY PERFORMS "HOUND DOG"

Victor/Victoria 1995
🎭 STAGE

📖 **Book** Blake Edwards

🎵 **Music** Henry Mancini; additional music by Frank Wildhorn

Aᴶ **Lyrics** Leslie Bricusse

On 25 October 1995, Julie Andrews returned to the Broadway stage after three decades to star in the stage adaptation of her 1982 film *Victor/Victoria*. Andrews' husband, Blake Edwards, wrote and directed both the film and stage versions of the show.

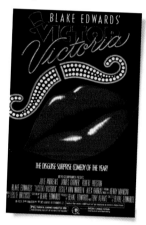

POSTER FOR 1982 FILM OF *VICTORIA VICTORIA*

Based on the career of the titular French entertainer, *Victor/Victoria* is set in Paris in the 1930s. It tells the story of Victoria Grant – a she, playing a he, impersonating a she – who finds fame and love.

Andrews, the only cast member of the show to be nominated for a Tony Award, rejected her nomination for Best Actress in a Musical because she felt the other members of the show had been overlooked. The award that year ultimately went to Donna Murphy for *The King and I*.

Jekyll & Hyde 1997
🎭 STAGE

📖 **Book** Leslie Bricusse

🎵 **Music** Frank Wildhorn

Aᴶ **Lyrics** Leslie Bricusse

Jekyll & Hyde is the musical adaptation of Robert Louis Stevenson's novella *The Strange Case of Dr Jekyll and Mr Hyde*. The story follows a London doctor who, in his attempt to cure his father's mental illness, conducts an experiment on himself that results in him forming an alternate evil personality.

The show debuted at Houston's Alley Theatre in May 1990. After a national tour, the original Broadway production of *Jekyll & Hyde* – starring Robert Cuccioli as the split-personality of Dr Henry Jekyll and Mr Edward Hyde

– opened at the Plymouth Theatre. The production garnered four Tony nominations and ran for nearly three years, boasting 1,543 performances.

Snow.Wolf.Lake 1997
🎭 STAGE

🎵 **Music** Leon Ko, Dick Lee, Iskandar Ismail, Lam Ming Yeung

Aᴶ **Lyrics** Lam Jang Keung, Lam Jik, Sin Man Choo, Jacky Cheung

Pop artist Jacky Cheung, the artistic director of Hong Kong's musical *Snow. Wolf.Lake*, also starred in the 1997 original Cantonese version of the show at the Hong Kong Coliseum. Sandy Lam agreed to play opposite of Cheung in the role of Snow. Kit Chan from Singapore played Snow's older sister in the 1997 version and the subsequent 2005 Mandarin production.

The title of *Snow.Wolf.Lake* comes from the combination of the names of the two lead characters, Snow and Wolf, who in turn name the lake they are boating on after themselves. The modern musical is a tragic love story between a poor gardener and a girl from a rich family.

Bat Boy: The Musical 1997
🎭 STAGE

📖 **Book** Laurence O'Keefe

🎵 **Music** Keythe Farley, Brian Flemming

Aᴶ **Lyrics** Laurence O'Keefe

A 23 June 1992 *Weekly World News* cover story provided inspiration for *Bat Boy: The Musical*. Based on the tabloid's fabricated story about a half-boy, half-bat who was discovered living in a cave in West Virginia, the quirky

musical comedy premiered in Los Angeles on Halloween 1997 prior to its 2001 Off-Broadway debut.

In 2004, American actor Deven May, who played Bat Boy in the Off-Broadway production, reprised his role in London's West End run. Though the show had become an American cult classic, its subject matter didn't translate well to an international audience.

Bat Boy: The Musical won New York's Outer Critics Circle and Lucille Lortel awards for Outstanding Off-Broadway Musical in 2001. Christopher Gatteli received a Lucille Lortel Award for his outstanding choreography, and May took home a Theatre World Award.

Titanic 1997
🎭 STAGE

📖 **Book** Peter Stone

🎵ₐ **Music and lyrics** Maury Yeston

Inspired by the 1912 disaster (and having nothing to do with James Cameron's 1997 blockbuster), *Titanic* recounts the fateful story of the ocean liner from its launch through the sinking and the rescue of survivors. The musical follows the fate of many real-life passengers – including J. Bruce Ismay, managing director of the White Star Line, who in the first act appeals to Captain E.J. Smith to bring the *Titanic* to higher speeds.

Composer and lyricist Maury Yeston and writer Peter Stone had both long been fascinated by the *Titanic* disaster. They decided to write the musical after the ship's remains were discovered by Robert Ballard in 1985. That

THE WHITE STAR LINE'S *RMS TITANIC*

discovery, followed as it was three months later by the *Challenger* explosion in January 1986, highlighted for Yeston and Stone the flaws of technology in a century of technological advancement.

Titanic was nominated for and won five Tony Awards, including Best Musical, Best Book of a Musical, and Best Original Musical Score. It ran for nearly two years after opening at the Lunt-Fontanne Theatre on 23 April 1997.

Violet 1997
🕸 **STAGE**
📖 **Book** Brian Crawley
🎵 **Music** Jeanine Tesori
♪ **Lyrics** Brian Crawley

Violet premiered Off-Broadway in 1997 at Playwrights Horizons, and returned to New York in 2013 as part of the New York City Center's first season of the Encores! Off-Center series, which revives Off-Broadway musicals in concert. The show then moved to Broadway in 2014 and was nominated for four Tony Awards, including Best Revival of a Musical and Best Actress for Sutton Foster in the title role.

Violet, adapted from the short story "The Ugliest Pilgrim" by Doris Betts, takes place in 1964. It follows the journey of a young woman from North Carolina to Oklahoma to see a TV preacher she hopes can heal her. The audience learns as the show progresses that Violet's face was disfigured when her father lost control of his axe blade during her childhood; she aches for the "miracle-working" healer to take away her scar. As Violet rides the bus to Oklahoma, she meets a pair of soldiers – one black, one white – who show interest in her. Her interactions with them, her visit to the preacher, and the journey she has made allow her to confront her past and look towards a new future.

High Society 1998
🕸 **STAGE**
📖 **Book** Arthur Kopit
🎵 **Music** Cole Porter
♪ **Lyrics** Cole Porter; additional lyrics by Susan Birkenhead

The stage production of *High Society* opened on Broadway in April 1998 at the St James Theatre and ran for four months. It featured John McMartin and Anna Kendrick in leading roles, for which they both received Tony Award nominations.

The show was based on the 1956 movie musical of the same name (screenplay by John Patrick), which boasted an all-star cast including Bing Crosby, Grace Kelly, and Frank Sinatra. The film featured original songs by the legendary Cole Porter and marked the last acting role for Grace Kelly before she became Princess of Monaco. In turn, the movie musical was based on Philip Barry's play *The Philadelphia Story*, which opened at the Shubert Theatre on Broadway in 1939.

Ragtime 1998
🕸 **STAGE**
📖 **Book** Terrence McNally
🎵 **Music** Stephen Flaherty
♪ **Lyrics** Lynn Ahrens

Based on E.L. Doctorow's 1975 novel, *Ragtime* follows three families at the turn of the 20th century. The musical contrasts and entwines the lives of a white Protestant family from New Rochelle, NY, a black musician and his lover from Harlem, and a Jewish immigrant and his daughter as they navigate this period of social change in the United States. Their stories are punctuated by appearances by historical figures like Henry Ford, J.P. Morgan, Harry Houdini, Evelyn Nesbitt, and Emma Goldman.

The 1998 Broadway production ran for two years and was nominated for 13 Tony Awards. It won four, including another Best Featured Actress in a Musical Tony for Audra McDonald. The show was a vast spectacle staged to open the new Ford Center for the Performing Arts and featured actual fireworks and a Model T, along with other outsized set pieces. By contrast, the short-lived 2009 revival was a smaller production, with greater focus on character and story.

Contact 1999
🕸 **STAGE**
📖 **Book** John Weidman
♪ **Music and lyrics** Various artists

Conceived, choreographed, and directed by Susan Stroman, *Contact* is a musical in three parts. Each part tells a very different story: the first story is set in a forest glade in the 1700s; the second is set in an Italian restaurant in Queens in the 1950s; and the third is set in New York City in 1999 – or nearly present day, for this 2000 show. The original production moved to Broadway's Vivian Beaumont

Theater, Lincoln Center, in March 2000 after a successful run at the Mitzi E. Newhouse Theater, a smaller Lincoln Center venue. The Tony Awards were kind to *Contact*; it took home four, including Best Musical and Best Choreography. It also received four Drama Desk Awards, including Outstanding New Musical and Outstanding Choreography.

Fosse 1999
🕸 **STAGE**
♪ **Music and lyrics** Various artists

Spanning the career of famed choreographer Bob Fosse, this musical revue strings together dance numbers created by Fosse for the stage (*Chicago*, *Pippin*, *Dancin'*, and others) and screen (*Cabaret*). *Fosse* pays tribute to the late choreographer's unique style and was backed by many of his former colleagues and friends. The idea for the show was conceived by Richard Maltby, Chet Walker, and Ann Reinking. Ralph Burns and Douglas Besterman handled orchestration, while Gordon Lowry Harrell did the musical arrangements.

The revue, which re-created Fosse's steps and distinctive look, was choreographed by Walker, who proposed the idea of a revue to Fosse himself as early as 1986.

FOSSE WAS A REVUE OF THE WORK OF BOB FOSSE

Fosse was nominated for eight Tony Awards and won three, including Best Musical. The production ran at the Broadhurst Theatre from December 1998 to August 2001.

Mozart! 1999
STAGE
📖 **Book** Michael Kunze
🎵 **Music** Sylvester Levay
🎵 **Lyrics** Michael Kunze

Mozart! was inspired by the life of famed composer Wolfgang Amadeus Mozart and follows his life story from his days as a child prodigy through his adult career and death. As Mozart ages, Amadé, the child prodigy that he used to be, stays with him as a symbol of the past from which he cannot free himself and of the genius that drives him. The musical, which premiered in Vienna in 1999, combines Mozart's own music with original modern music in a variety of genres. *Mozart!* has found success around the globe, including productions in the Czech Republic, Germany, Hungary, Japan, South Korea, and Sweden.

Topsy-Turvy 1999
FILM
🎬 **Screenplay** Mike Leigh
🎵 **Music** Carl Davis, W.S. Gilbert, Arthur Sullivan
🎵 **Lyrics** W.S. Gilbert, Arthur Sullivan

Directed and written by British director Mike Leigh, *Topsy-Turvy* is about the writing partnership of the renowned W.S. Gilbert (played by Jim Broadbent) and Arthur Sullivan (played by Allan Corduner). Gilbert and Sullivan created 14 highly popular comic operas, many of which are still performed today.

The film, which includes numbers from a variety of Gilbert and Sullivan operettas, follows the pair from the brink of disaster, when they almost break up after the 1884 failure of *Princess Ida*, through the creation process, rehearsals, and ultimate success of *The Mikado*. The film dives into the background of the show, but also explores the personal lives and relationships of its creators and the creative team behind its success.

Mike Leigh, who is known for his intensive screenwriting process involving creative collaboration with and improvisation by his actors, was nominated for an Oscar for Best Writing, Screenplay Written Directly for the Screen. The film won Oscars for Best Costume Design and Best Makeup.

Les Dix Commandements 2000
STAGE
📖 **Book** Lionel Florence, Patrice Guirao
🎵 **Music and lyrics** Pascale Obispo

Les Dix Commandements, a French-language musical comedy created for the stage by French film director Elie Chouraqui, premiered in 2000 at the Palais des Sports in Paris, marking Chouraqui's first time creating a musical. Three large screens on which images were projected provided the backdrop to the set. As the show's name suggests, the story is biblical. It follows two brothers – Moses, played by Daniel Levy; and Ramses, the Egyptian prince, played by French pop star Ahmed Mouici. The costumes were designed by fashion icon Sonia Rykiel.

The musical was adapted and translated into English, debuting in North America in 2004 at the Kodak Theatre in Hollywood, with Val Kilmer as Moses.

Aida 2000
STAGE
📖 **Book** Linda Woolverton, Robert Falls, David Henry Hwang
🎵 **Music** Elton John
🎵 **Lyrics** Tim Rice

Based on Verdi's opera of the same name, the pop-rock musical *Aida* is the doomed love story of an enslaved Nubian princess, Aida, and an Egyptian captain, Radames, who is engaged to Aida's mistress.

After the success of the film *The Lion King*, Disney was eager to reunite Elton John and Tim Rice for another musical venture. Disney acquired the rights to a children's book adaptation of Verdi's *Aida* – written by soprano Leontyne Price, who had performed the starring role – and suggested that John and Rice write a stage musical based on the book.

Aida opened at the Palace Theatre in New York on 23 March 2000 and ran until September 2004. The production was nominated for five Tony Awards and won four of them, including Best Actress in a Musical for Heather Headley and Best Original Musical Score.

Urinetown 2001
STAGE
📖 **Book** Greg Kotis
🎵 **Music** Mark Hollmann
🎵 **Lyrics** Mark Hollmann, Greg Kotis

Urinetown is a satirical musical about a city in the near future where water has become so scarce, private toilets have been outlawed. Instead, citizens must pay to use the public toilets managed by greedy corporation Urine Good Company. Bobby Strong leads the poor people of the city in a revolution even as he falls in love with Hope Cladwell, daughter of UGC president and villain Caldwell B. Cladwell.

Playwrite Greg Kotis was inspired to write *Urinetown* after a visit to Paris where his budget made it difficult to afford the use of the public conveniences. The show humorously explores government corruption and greed while satirizing and parodying traditional musicals. *Urinetown* was nominated for ten Tony Awards and took home three of them: Best Book of a Musical, Best Director of a Musical, and Best Original Musical Score. Its run at Broadway's Henry Miller's Theatre lasted from September 2001 until January 2004.

A Man of No Importance 2002
STAGE
📖 **Book** Lynn Ahrens
🎵 **Music** Stephen Flaherty
🎵 **Lyrics** Terrence McNally

Set in Dublin in 1964, *A Man of No Importance* centres on the life of Alfie Byrne, a bus conductor and amateur theatre director. Byrne's determination to put on a production of Oscar Wilde's *Salome* at his church complicates an otherwise quiet life and leads to him coming out as homosexual.

Based on the 1994 film of the same name, the show reunited the Tony Award-winning team of Lynn Ahrens, Stephen Flaherty, and Terrence McNally, creators of *Ragtime*. McNally was inspired to adapt *A Man of No Importance* after coming across the film at a video store. After the 2002 Lincoln Center production – which was nominated for seven Drama Desk Awards, including Outstanding Musical, and won the Outer Critics Circle Award for Best Musical – *A Man of No Importance* went on to be staged in Canada and in London's West End.

Movin' Out 2002
STAGE
🎵 **Music and lyrics** Billy Joel

Movin' Out, which features more than two dozen songs by Billy Joel, follows five friends from high school trials in a small town during the Vietnam War and its aftermath. In *Movin' Out*, which has been called a "rock ballet", the five friends and various other characters are portrayed by dancers, while a band and a lead singer/pianist (Michael Cavanaugh in the original Broadway cast) perform the songs from a platform above the stage. After a poorly reviewed 2002 Chicago try-out, director and choreographer Twyla Tharp revamped the production, focusing especially on a problematic first act. The musical opened to strong reviews on Broadway later that year and ran for more than three years – a total of 1,303 performances – at the Richard Rodgers Theatre.

Movin' Out was nominated for ten Tony Awards, with Twyla Tharp winning a Tony for Best Choreography and Billy Joel and Stuart Malina winning for Best Orchestrations.

A PERFORMANCE OF GILBERT AND SULLIVAN'S *THE MIKADO* IN MIKE LEIGH'S *TOPSY-TURVY*

FREDDIE MERCURY'S STATUE WELCOMED
LONDON AUDIENCES TO *WE WILL ROCK YOU*

We Will Rock You 2002
🎭 STAGE
📖 **Book** Ben Elton
🎵 **Music and lyrics** Queen

Created by British writer and comedian Ben Elton, *We Will Rock You* opened at London's Dominion Theatre in 2002 and was produced with Queen's drummer (Roger Taylor) and guitarist (Brian May) as music supervisors.

Set around a group of teenagers living in a future place where rock music is not heard and instruments are banned, the show featured more than 20 of the legendary rock group's biggest hits, including "We Are the Champions", "Another One Bites the Dust", and "We Will Rock You".

Audience members attending the final London performance on 31 May 2014 had a special treat: Taylor and May joined the cast for the encore.

Taboo 2003
🎭 STAGE
📖 **Book** Mark Davies Markham
🎵 **Music** Kevan Frost, Boy George, Richie Stevens, John Themis
🎵 **Lyrics** Boy George

Taboo opened on London's West End in January 2002 at the Venue Theatre – which had, very much in line with the show's themes, been recently converted from a basement dance hall. Set in an abandoned London warehouse, the show pays homage to the evolving 1980s London music and club scene. While most of the songs for the show were newly written, it also included a few of Boy George's hits.

When entertainer Rosie O'Donnell attended a performance of *Taboo*, she fell in love with the show and financed a Broadway production. It opened at the Plymouth Theatre in November 2003 and ran for only 100 performances before closing in February 2004. Though most reviews for the Broadway production were poor, actor Euan Morton – who was brought over from the London production to reprise his role of Boy George – was highly praised by critics for his performance.

Caroline, or Change 2004
🎭 STAGE
📖 **Book** Tony Kushner
🎵 **Music** Jeanine Tesori
🎵 **Lyrics** Tony Kushner

Caroline, or Change is set in Louisiana in 1963, with the Civil Rights Movement and the death of President John F. Kennedy as the story's backdrop. The musical follows Caroline, an African-American woman who is working as a maid to a white Jewish family and struggling to support her children. Caroline's relationship with her employer's son, Noah, becomes complicated when Noah's stepmother suggests that Caroline keep the spare change she finds in Noah's pockets when she does laundry.

Written by Pulitzer Prize winner Tony Kushner, *Caroline, or Change* was partly inspired by Kushner's own childhood in Louisiana. The Broadway production, which ran at the Eugene O'Neill Theatre from May to August 2004, was nominated for six Tony Awards. Anika Noni Rose won a Tony for Best Featured Actress in a Musical for her role as Caroline's spirited daughter, Emmie.

Caroline, or Change was featured in the 2007 documentary *ShowBusiness: The Road to Broadway*, which followed the paths of four 2004 Broadway musicals from creation to the Tony Award ceremony. The documentary also featured *Wicked* (see p.295), *Avenue Q* (see p.300–01), and *Taboo* (see left).

Dirty Rotten Scoundrels 2005
🎭 STAGE
📖 **Book** Jeffrey Lane
🎵 **Music and lyrics** David Yazbek

On 27 April 2005, cast members from Broadway's *Dirty Rotten Scoundrels* signed free copies of their cast album at the Imperial Theatre; fans lined up for blocks. The giveaway, in which 50,000 CDs were distributed between

27 April and 27 May, was a first in Broadway history: the producers of the show, who financed the giveaway themselves, created enough buzz to earn a nomination for the Best Musical Show Album Grammy Award that year.

Dirty Rotten Scoundrels is based on the 1988 film of the same name, with screenplay by Paul Henning, Dale Launer, and Stanley Shapiro. Norbert Leo Butz and John Lithgow headlined the original cast as Freddy and Lawrence, two competing con artists. For his performance, Butz received the 2005 Tony Award for Best Actor in a Musical.

Le Roi Soleil 2005
🎭 STAGE
📖 **Book** Dove Attia, François Chouquet (French), Kamel Ouali (English)
🎵 **Lyrics** Lionel Florence, Partice Guirao

French musical comedy *Le Roi Soleil* ("The Sun King") played at the Palais des Sports in Paris from September 2005 to July 2007. The show's name comes from King Louis XIV's symbol, the sun, which he took to illustrate his status as all-powerful. Based on King Louis XIV's life, *Le Roi Soleil* starred Emmanuel Moire as the King with French pop singer Christophe Maé as his brother, Monsieur.

The Light in the Piazza 2005
🎭 STAGE
📖 **Book** Craig Lucas
🎵 **Music and lyrics** Adam Guettel

The Light in the Piazza is a musical romance that quickly became a classic. When a mother and her daughter, Clara, travel to Italy in the summer of 1953, Clara falls in love with a young Italian man. Clara's mother is opposed to the affair; her reason is gradually revealed to the audience.

The Light in the Piazza won six Tony Awards and achieved a 14-month run and 504 performances at Lincoln Center before closing in July 2006. The show was a visual success; designer Michael Yeargan transported the audience to Florence and Rome through his award-winning set designs.

The show is based on a novella by Elizabeth Spencer that first appeared in *The New Yorker* magazine in 1959. The music and lyrics for the show were written by Adam Guettel, who is the grandson of Richard Rodgers (see pp.70–71).

The 25th Annual Putnam County Spelling Bee 2005
🎭 STAGE
📖 **Book** Rachel Sheinkin
🎵 **Music and lyrics** William Finn

The 25th Annual Putnam County Spelling Bee is a one-act musical based on Rebecca Feldman's improvisational play, *C-R-E-P-E-S-C-U-L-E*. The musical centres on six intelligent, and pretty quirky, middle-school spelling-bee contestants and the adults who administer the bee. During the show, the backstories of the students and the adults are explored as contestants are eliminated one by one.

In keeping with its improvisational roots, the show invites four audience members onstage to compete in the bee during each performance. At a notable performance during Kids' Night on Broadway in 2007, film and stage star Julie Andrews was one of the guest spellers; fittingly, she was eliminated when she misspelled "Supercalifragilisticexpialidocious".

The 25th Annual Putnam County Spelling Bee was nominated for six Tony Awards and won two. The first production outside the US was in Australia, at the Melbourne Theatre Company and then the Sydney Theatre Company.

High School Musical 2006
🎬 FILM
📖 **Screenplay** Peter Barsocchini
🎵 **Music** David Nessim Lawrence

Disney Channel's made-for-television *High School Musical* premiered on 20 January 2006. Shortly after the soundtrack debuted, it rocketed to the top of the Billboard pop chart and went on to become the year's best-selling album in the United States. Successful music video and soundtrack downloads resulted in the movie becoming the first full-length feature film to be available through the iTunes Music Store. The film also made huge stars of some of the actors, such as Zac Efron and Vanessa Hudgens.

A television sequel, *High School Musical 2*, was released in 2007, and a feature-film sequel, *High School Musical 3: Senior Year*, was released in cinemas in 2008. According to an article in *TIME* magazine, the franchise had taken in retail sales of more than US $680 million as of 2008.

A stage show, with book by David Simpatico, is now a popular choice for middle-school and high-school musical productions across America.

The Drowsy Chaperone 2006
❧ STAGE
📖 **Book** Bob Martin, Don McKellar
🎵 **Music and lyrics** Lisa Lambert, Greg Morrison

Narrated by the unnamed "Man in Chair," an opinionated, empassioned musical theatre fan, *The Drowsy Chaperone* harks back to the days of the 1920s musical. Its show-within-a-show format allows Man in Chair to tell his audience all about his favourite musical, *The Drowsy Chaperone* – which in turn tells the story of the wedding of wealthy businessman Robert Martin to starlet Janet van de Graaf, and the ridiculous, over-the-top, classically 1920s shenanigans that almost keep it from taking place.

The Drowsy Chaperone began as a short, humorous piece performed at the stag party of the real-life Bob Martin and fiancée Janet van de Graaf. The creators saw the potential in the project and, with Martin, expanded the piece into a full-length musical, adding the Man in Chair frame story.

The Broadway production of *The Drowsy Chaperone* starred Sutton Foster as Janet van de Graaf when it opened at the Marquis Theatre on 1 May 2006. It was nominated for 13 Tony Awards and won five, including Best Book of a Musical and Best Original Score. The show closed on 30 December 2007, after 674 performances.

Grey Gardens 2006
❧ STAGE
📖 **Book** Doug Wright
🎵 **Music** Scott Frankel
♪ **Lyrics** Michael Korie

Grey Gardens is a musical inspired by Albert and David Maysles' 1975 documentary of the same name. Both follow the lives of Jacquelyn Kennedy Onassis's eccentric aunt and cousin. Set in two key time periods, Grey Gardens shows Edith Bouvier Beale and her daughter, "Little" Edie, at the height of their wealth in 1941, when the Grey Gardens estate was well kept and beautiful, and in 1973 when the estate has begun to crumble around them.

Grey Gardens was nominated for ten Tony Awards and won three: Best Actress in a Musical (Christine Ebersole), Best Featured Actress in a Musical (Mary Louise Wilson), and Best Costume Design of a Musical

CAMP COSTUMES IN *PRISCILLA, QUEEN OF THE DESERT*

for William Ivey Long. It ran at Broadway's Walter Kerr Theatre from November 2006 to July 2007.

Priscilla, Queen of the Desert 2006
❧ STAGE
📖 **Book** Stephan Elliott, Allan Scot
🎵 **Music and lyrics** Various artists

Based on the 1994 film *The Adventures of Priscilla, Queen of the Desert*, the musical follows three drag performers on an adventure together in an old bus named Priscilla through the Australian outback. When his separated wife, Marion, reveals that their young son wants to meet him, Tick convinces fellow performers Bernadette (Tony-nominated Australian actor Tony Sheldon in the Australian, West End, and Broadway casts) and Felicia to come with him on the road.

This camp, flashy jukebox musical features many familiar pop songs, such as "Material Girl", "It's Raining Men", and "I Will Survive". The premiere production opened in October 2006 at the Lyric Theatre in Sydney, and successful follow-up productions were staged around the world.

Xanadu 2007
❧ STAGE
📖 **Book** Douglas Carter Beane
🎵 **Music and lyrics** John Farrar, Jeff Lynne

Set in 1980, *Xanadu* follows a muse named Kira who takes a trip from Mount Olympus to Venice Beach, California, to inspire a young man named Sonny to create the very first roller disco. When Kira falls in love with Sonny, things get complicated in this over-the-top, tongue-in-cheek musical. *Xanadu*

is based on the 1980 movie of the same name, which starred Olivia Newton-John and Gene Kelly.

After the original Sonny, James Carpinello, was injured in a roller-skating incident during previews, Cheyenne Jackson took over the role for the show's opening at the Helen Hayes Theatre on 10 July 2007. Kerry Butler played Kira, and Tony Roberts took on the Gene Kelly character, an investor named Danny Maguire. The show ran for 512 performances, closing in September 2008.

Adding Machine 2008
❧ STAGE
📖 **Book** Jason Loewith, Joshua Schmidt
🎵 **Music** Joshua Schmidt
♪ **Lyrics** Jason Loewith, Joshua Schmidt

Adding Machine is based on Elmer Rice's 1923 expressionist novel. It is a 90-minute black comedy that follows Mr Zero, a book-keeper who murders his boss after being replaced by the titular adding machine. When Mr Zero is executed for his crime and ends up in the afterlife, his assistant, who is in love with him, follows him.

The musical's complex score is performed with piano, synthesizer, and percussion. Bleak yet humorous, the Off-Broadway production of *Adding Machine* won the 2008 Lucille Lortel Award for Outstanding Musical.

Fela! 2009
❧ STAGE
📖 **Book** Jim Lewis, Bill T. Jones
🎵 **Music and lyrics** Fela Anikulapo-Kuti

Fela! celebrates the life of legendary Fela Anikulapo-Kuti, a Nigerian composer, musician, and political activist who pioneered a blend of jazz, funk, and African rhythm and harmonies known as Afrobeat.

In 2000, producer Steve Hendel came across a CD of Anikulapo-Kuti's. He was inspired by his music and message about honest government and justice. In 2004, Hendel brought in Jim Lewis and Bill T. Jones to the write the book for a stage play.

Fela!, which features many of Anikulapo-Kuti's songs, debuted in 2008 Off-Broadway at the 37 Arts Theatre. The award-winning production moved to Broadway in 2009, where it was nominated for 11 Tony Awards and going on to win three. The show also played in London, in a production at the National Theatre.

Sister Act 2009

STAGE

📖 **Book** Cheri Steinkellner, Bill Steinkellner, Douglas Carter Beane

🎵 **Music** Alan Menken

𝄞 **Lyrics** Glenn Slater

Based on the 1992 film of the same name (screenplay by Joseph Howard), the stage version of *Sister Act* repeats the hilarious story of aspiring disco singer Deloris Van Cartier. When Deloris witnesses her gangster boyfriend commit a murder, she is ordered by the police to hide in a convent disguised as a nun – resulting in some unlikely friendships.

Whoopi Goldberg, who played the lead role in the film version, produced *Sister Act* on the London stage in 2009 prior to a slightly revised musical production on Broadway in April 2011. For a period of about two weeks during 2012, Alan Menken had three shows running on Broadway simultaneously: *Sister Act*, *Newsies*, and *Leap of Faith*.

Rock of Ages 2009

STAGE

📖 **Book** Chris D'Arienzo

𝄞 **Music and lyrics** Various artists

Rock of Ages is a jukebox musical set in 1980s Hollywood and centres on a Sunset Strip club called The Bourbon Room. Aspiring rocker/bus boy Drew falls for aspiring actress Sherrie from small town Kansas, while efforts to clean up the town threaten the Strip and The Bourbon Room. The musical includes hits from the era such as "The Final Countdown", "We Built This City", "We're Not Gonna Take It", and "Don't Stop Believin'", and was nominated for five Tony Awards, including Best Musical. Audiences rocked out at the Brooks Atkinson Theatre from April 2009 to January 2011. The show reopened at the

GREEN DAY'S BILLIE JOE ARMSTRONG PERFORMS ON BROADWAY IN THE 2010 SHOW *AMERICAN IDIOT*

THE 2014 WEST END CAST OF *THE SCOTTSBORO BOYS*

Helen Hayes Theatre in March 2011, ending its long run in January 2015.

Rock of Ages was made into a musical film in 2012. It starred Julianne Hough and Diego Boneta as Sherrie and Drew and featured Catherine Zeta-Jones, Russell Brand, Alec Baldwin, Paul Giamatti, Bryan Cranston, Mary J. Blige, Malin Åkerman, and Tom Cruise as part of its ensemble cast.

Memphis 2010

STAGE

📖 **Book** Joe DiPietro

🎵 **Music** David Bryan

𝄞 **Lyrics** David Bryan, Joe DiPietro

Memphis follows a 1950s white radio disc jockey who plays African-American music for his white audience, and a talented black club singer looking for her big break. The musical, with a rock'n'roll score, is loosely based on the legendary DJ Dewey Phillips.

The show won four Tony Awards, including Best Musical and Best Original Score. David Bryan, who wrote the music and co-wrote the lyrics with Joe DiPietro, is no stranger to rock music; Bryan is the keyboard player, songwriter, and founding member of the popular American rock group Bon Jovi.

American Idiot 2010

STAGE

📖 **Book** Billie Joe Armstrong, Michael Mayer

🎵 **Music** Green Day

𝄞 **Lyrics** Billie Joe Armstrong

American Idiot is a rock opera based on punk rock group Green Day's 2004 concept album of the same name and incorporates songs from another

Green Day album, *21st Century Breakdown* (2009). Both albums won the Grammy Award for Best Rock Album in their respective years.

The musical follows three disaffected friends from the suburbs – Johnny, Tunny, and Will – who are about to set off from their empty lives to look for more. Johnny and Tunny leave for the big city, but Will decides to stay behind when he finds out his girlfriend is pregnant. As Johnny is seduced by women and drugs, Tunny enlists and heads off to war.

The musical was a collaboration between Green Day frontman Billie Joe Armstrong, who stepped into the show in the role of drug dealer St Jimmy, and director Michael Mayer, who was a fan of the album and had long been interested in creating a musical based on *American Idiot*. The Broadway production opened in April 2010 and ran for a year, earning a Tony nomination for Best Musical, and winning Tony Awards for Scenic Design and Lighting Design.

The Scottsboro Boys 2010

STAGE

📖 **Book** David Thompson

𝄞 **Music and lyrics** John Kander, Fred Ebb

Set in Alabama in the 1930s, *The Scottsboro Boys* is based on the true story of nine black teenagers falsely accused of raping two white women. The conviction of these innocent teens ultimately provoked a national outrage and was a pivotal moment in the American Civil Rights movement.

The Scottsboro Boys began as a collaboration between composer John Kander and lyricist Fred Ebb,

along with director Susan Stroman, writer David Thompson. Kander and Ebb are well known for their collaborations on *Cabaret* (see p.166) and *Chicago* (see pp.196–99). After Ebb's death in 2004, the project was put on hold for several years, until Kander suggested he could complete the lyrics in Ebb's place.

The show opened on Broadway in October 2010 and it was nominated for 12 Tony Awards, including Best Musical. In 2013, it had an extended run at London's Young Vic, where it won the prestigious Critics Circle Award and was nominated for six Olivier Awards, including Best New Musical. It then moved to the West End, to the Garrick Theatre, where it won the 2014 Evening Standard Award for Best Musical and was nominated for another Olivier Award.

The Bodyguard 2012

STAGE

📖 **Book** Alex Dinelaris

🎵 **Music** Songs recorded by Whitney Houston

Based on the popular 1992 film starring Whitney Houston and Kevin Costner (screenplay by Lawrence Kasdan), *The Bodyguard* is the story of rock superstar Rachel Marron who hires the titular bodyguard, Frank Farmer, to protect her from a stalker. As Frank works to keep Rachel safe, the two fall in love.

The show includes a slew of well-known Houston hit songs, including "Queen of the Night", "I Wanna Dance with Somebody", and "I Will Always Love You", which became a bestselling single after it was used in the movie. The original West End stage production opened in December 2012 and starred Heather Headley as Rachel and Lloyd Owen as Frank.

Newsies The Musical 2012

STAGE

📖 **Book** Harvey Fierstein

🎵 **Music** Alan Menken

𝄞 **Lyrics** Jack Feldman

Newsies is the rousing story of Jack Kelly, a 17-year-old newsboy in 1890s New York City who leads his fellow newsies in a fight for better wages against newspaper giants Pulitzer and Hearst. The stage musical is based on the 1992 Disney movie musical, which starred Christian Bale as Jack Kelly.

The film was a flop at the box office, but it achieved cult classic status on

home video and became the most requested Disney musical not yet adapted for the stage. The ongoing enthusiasm from schools and theatre groups inspired the 2011 Paper Mill Playhouse production in New Jersey. The musical's success at the Paper Mill led to a limited engagement on Broadway at the Nederlander Theatre in 2012, which was ultimately extended and ran for 1,004 performances. *Newsies* was nominated for eight Tony Awards and won two: Best Original Score Written for the Theatre and Best Choreography.

Here Lies Love 2013
STAGE
♫ **Music** David Byrne, Fatboy Slim
♪ **Lyrics** David Byrne

David Byrne of Talking Heads and DJ Fatboy Slim's disco musical *Here Lies Love* opened at the Public Theatre in New York in the spring of 2013. With no seats or intermission in this 90-minute dance party, the audience stands and is encouraged to dance and move with the actors as the story of the political rise and fall of Filipino leaders Imelda and Ferdinand Marcos unfolds. The New York production closed in January 2015, and the show transferred to London for a limited run at the National Theatre's Dorfman Theatre.

A Gentleman's Guide to Love and Murder 2013
STAGE
📖 **Book** Robert L. Freedman
♫ **Music** Steven Lutvak
♪ **Lyrics** Robert L. Friedman, Steven Lutvak

A Gentleman's Guide to Love and Murder is the comedic story of young Monty Navarro who suddenly learns he is merely eight easily murdered relatives away from becoming the Earl of Highhurst. The original Broadway cast featured Tony Award-winner Jefferson Mays in a much lauded, over-the-top turn as all of the members of the D'Ysquith family. In an interview with *Playbill*, Mays revealed the secret to remembering which character he was playing next – early on in the show's run, his dressers would whisper his next character to him during each costume change (some as rapid as three seconds). Having created costumes that were both stunning and could be pulled on and off in a flash, costume designer Linda Cho's Tony Award for the production was well earned.

The musical is based on the 1907 novel *Israel Rank: The Autobiography of a Criminal* by Roy Horniman, which also inspired the 1949 film *Kind Hearts and Coronets*. *A Gentleman's Guide to Love and Murder* was nominated for ten Tony Awards and won four, including Best Musical, Best Book of a Musical, Best Direction of a Musical (Darko Tresnjak), and Best Costume Design for Linda Cho.

The Commitments 2013
STAGE
📖 **Book** Roddy Doyle
♫ **Music and lyrics** Various artists

Adapted by Roddy Doyle from his bestselling 1987 novel of the same name – which also inspired the 1991 film – *The Commitments* is a soul-infused musical set in 1980s Dublin. The show centres on Jimmy Rabbitte, a young working-class Irishman obsessed with soul music who wants to manage a band. After holding auditions, Jimmy manages to bring together a group who make great music, even though their many differences threaten to pull them apart.

The stage musical features a number of classic tunes, including "Mustang Sally", "Heard It Through the Grapevine", "Papa Was a Rollin' Stone", "Night Train", "(I Can't Get No) Satisfaction", and "Try a Little Tenderness". *The Commitments* debuted in London's West End at the Palace Theatre in 2013.

Beautiful: The Carole King Musical 2014
STAGE
📖 **Book** Douglas McGrath
♫ **Music and lyrics** Gerry Goffin, Carole King,
♪ Barry Mann, Cynthia Weil

Beautiful: The Carole King Musical premiered in San Francisco in 2013 before opening on Broadway in January 2014 at the Stephen Sondheim Theatre. The show tells the inspiring true-life story of how Carole King, born Carol Joan Klein, fought her way into the record business as a teenager, wrote songs with her then-husband Gerry Goffin for big-name artists including James Taylor and The Beatles, and launched a successful career as a solo artist.

The show took home two Tony Awards: Best Sound Design of a Musical, and Best Performance by an Actress in a Leading Role in a Musical for Jessie Mueller. *Beautiful* also won a Grammy Award for Best Musical Theatre Album.

Aladdin 2014
STAGE
📖 **Book** Chad Beguelin
♫ **Music** Alan Menken
♪ **Lyrics** Howard Ashman, Tim Rice

One of the first major animated films to feature the voices of well-known movie stars (including that of Robin Williams), The Walt Disney Company's 1992 movie *Aladdin* was immensely popular with both critics and audiences. It was the most successful film of 1992 and won two Academy Awards: Best Music, Original Score, and Best Music, Original Song for "A Whole New World".

The success of the film and popularity of the soundtrack made *Aladdin* a perfect candidate for the Broadway stage. When the Broadway adaption of *Aladdin* opened in 2014 at the New Amsterdam Theatre, it quickly became a hot ticket. For his charming and much lauded performance as the Genie, James Monroe Iglehart won the Tony for Best Performance by an Actor in a Featured Role.

CAROLE KING PERFORMING LIVE

Fun Home 2015
STAGE
📖 **Book** Lisa Kron
♫ **Music** Jeanine Tesori
♪ **Lyrics** Lisa Kron

Adapted from Alison Bechdel's 2006 graphic memoir, *Fun Home* tells the dark yet often humorous story of Bechdel's relationship with her manic, secretive father. In it, a 43-year-old Alison looks back over her life: a childhood spent living in the family's historic home that doubled as a funeral parlour, coming to terms with her sexuality in college, and dealing with the eventual suicide of her father.

After an Off-Broadway run in 2013, the show transferred to Broadway's Circle in the Square Theatre in April 2015 where it was restaged to be performed in the round and won five Tony Awards, including Best Musical and Best Original Score.

Hamilton 2015
STAGE
📖 **Book** Lin-Manuel Miranda
♫ **Music and lyrics** Lin-Manuel Miranda

Hamilton relates the life story of Alexander Hamilton, the "ten-dollar Founding Father". Based on Ron Chernow's doorstopper biography *Alexander Hamilton*, the musical follows Hamilton from his impoverished childhood in the West Indies through his rise to prominence during the American Revolution, subsequent tumultuous political career, and death after a duel with former friend and then vice president Aaron Burr.

Hamilton's writer and star, Lin-Manuel Miranda, also wrote the music and lyrics for and starred in *In the Heights* (see p.313). Like *Heights*, *Hamilton* incorporates a blend of musical styles, from hip-hop to jazz to Broadway. Miranda's vision for the show includes an almost exclusively non-white cast, depicting, as Miranda has said, the "story of America then, told by America now".

Hamilton first opened Off-Broadway at the Public Theater in early 2015 and played to sold-out houses and rave reviews, drawing in celebrities from around the globe. The show extended its run three times before it transferred to Broadway, opening on 6 August 2015, at the Richard Rodgers Theater, and quickly becoming Broadway's hottest ticket.

Index

X

Y

Z

Acknowledgments

Dorling Kindersley would like to thank the following people for their assistance with this book:
Rosy Runciman and Emma Williams at Cameron Mackintosh Ltd.; Deb Saunders at The Really Useful Group Ltd.; Bert Fink and Robin Walton at Rodgers & Hammerstein; Mark Fox for all the help and advice; Mark Shenton and Crispin Lord for additional editorial help; Jo Walton for picture research; and the writers – John Andrews, Linda Bozzo, Chris Bray, Sarah Evans, Autumn Green, Vicky Hales-Dutton, Jeremy Harwood, Nathan Hurwitz, Chris Ingham, Michael Kerrigan, Tina Stadlmayer, Joan Strasbaugh, and Phil Willmott. Special thanks also to Sharon Spencer for design; and Christine Stroyan, Martin Copeland, Myriam Megharbi, Jenny Faithfull, Nic Dean, Sarah Hopper, and Sarah Smithies for additional picture research.

The publisher would like to thank the following for their kind permission to reproduce their photographs:

(Key: a-above; b-below/bottom; c-centre; f-far; l-left; r-right; t-top)

2-3 Alamy Images: theatrepix / www.achoruslinelondon.com. **4 Alamy Images:** Paul Ridsdale Pictures (l). **Getty Images:** Mark Sykes (r). **5 Corbis:** Joho / cultura (r). **Getty Images:** Joshua Blake (l). **6-7 Getty Images:** Ariel Skelley. **8-9 Alamy Images:** Paul Ridsdale Pictures. **10 Corbis:** Bettmann (t, b, t); Bettmann (t, b, t); Underwood & Underwood (c). **Corbis:** Bettmann (t, b, t); Bettmann (t, b, t); Underwood & Underwood (c). **10 Corbis:** Bettmann (t, b, t); Bettmann (t, b, t); Underwood & Underwood (c). **Corbis:** Bettmann (t, b, t); Bettmann (t, b, t); Underwood & Underwood (c). **11 Alamy Images:** Mary Evans Picture Library (l); Pictorial Press Ltd (br). **Corbis:** John Springer Collection (t). **12 Dorling Kindersley:** The George Hoare Theatre Collection at Drury Lane (b); National Music Museum (t). **13 Corbis:** John Springer Collection (tr). **Getty Images:** NY Daily News Archive (tl); Transcendental Graphics (l). **The Kobal Collection:** Warner Bros (br). **14 Corbis:** Bettmann (b). **Dorling Kindersley:** The George Hoare Theatre Collection at Drury Lane (t). **15 Alamy Images:** WorldPhotos. **16 Dorling Kindersley:** The George Hoare Theatre Collection at Drury Lane (bl, br). **17 Dorling Kindersley:** The George Hoare Theatre Collection at Drury Lane (tr, bl, br). **18-19 Dorling Kindersley:** The George Hoare Theatre Collection at Drury Lane. **20 Alamy Images:** Marka (t). **Lebrecht Music and Arts:** Kurt Weill Foundation (b). **21 Corbis:** Bettmann (r). **Lebrecht Music and Arts:** Dee Conway (l). **22 Corbis:** Bettmann (bl). **23 Photofest. 24 The Library of Congress, Washington DC:** (l). **24-25 Lebrecht Music and Arts:** Photofest Inc.. **25 Alamy Images:** Photos 12 (t); Kevin Browne (br). **26-27 The Kobal Collection:** Warner Bros. **26 Getty Images:** GAB Archive / Redferns (t). **The Kobal Collection:** Warner Bros (b). **27 Getty Images:** Santi Visalli (br). **28 Alamy Images:** Pictorial Press Ltd. **29 Alamy Images:** moozic (br); Pictorial Press Ltd (bl). **The Kobal Collection:** Warner Bros (t). **30 Photofest:** (r); Paramount Pictures (l). **31 Alamy Images:** Pictorial Press Ltd (c, tr). **Getty Images:** Hulton Archive (br). **32 Corbis:** Underwood & Underwood (l). **Getty Images:** General Photographic Agency (r). **33 Alamy Images:** AF archive (bl). **Corbis:** Bettmann (br). **Photofest:** MGM (t). **34 Getty Images:** RKO Radio Pictures (r). **The Kobal Collection:** RKO Radio Pictures (l). **35 Corbis:** John Springer Collection (l). **The Kobal Collection:** RKO Radio Pictures (r). **36-37 The Kobal Collection:** MGM. **38 The Kobal Collection:** RKO. **39 Corbis:** John Springer Collection. **Lebrecht Music and Arts:** (t). **40 The Kobal Collection:** RKO (b, t). **41 Corbis:** Bettmann (b). **The Kobal Collection:** RKO (t). **42-43 The Kobal Collection:** MGM / Bull, Clarence Sinclair. **42 Alamy Images:** Everett Collection Historical (l). **43 Alamy Images:** Bildagentur-online / McPhoto-Weber (cr). **The Kobal Collection:** MGM (t). **Photofest:** RKO Radio Pictures (b). **44 Corbis:** John Springer Collection (bl). **The Kobal Collection:** Universal (bc, br). **45 Alamy Images:** Everett Collection Historical (r). **Photofest:** (bl). **46 The Kobal Collection:** MGM / Paul Faherty (Colour) (t). **Photofest:** (b).

47 Alamy Images: Pictorial Press Ltd. **48 Alamy Images:** AF archive (b). **The Kobal Collection:** MGM (l, tr). **49 Alamy Images:** AF archive (br). **Corbis:** 145 / M G Therin Weise / Ocean (bl). **Getty Images:** MGM Studios (tr). **The Kobal Collection:** MGM (cl, cr). **50-51 Getty Images:** Mark Sykes. **52 Corbis:** John Springer Collection (br). **The Kobal Collection:** (l). **Photofest:** MGM (t). **53 Photofest:** (b); (t). **54 Corbis:** CinemaPhoto (tr). **Getty Images:** Ralph Morse / Pix Inc. / The LIFE Images Collection / © Courtesy of The Rodgers and Hammerstein Organization. **55 Photofest:** (tl); As authorised by the Estate of Jo Mielziner / © Courtesy of The Rodgers and Hammerstein Organization. **56 Alamy Images:** Chronicle (r). **The Kobal Collection:** Paramount / Faherty, Paul (Colour) (l). **57 Alamy Images:** Pictorial Press Ltd (t). **Getty Images:** Gjon Mili / The LIFE Picture Collection / © Courtesy of The Rodgers and Hammerstein Organization (b). **58 Alamy Images:** WorldPhotos / © Courtesy of The Rodgers and Hammerstein Organization (t). **Lebrecht Music and Arts:** Photofest / © Courtesy of The Rodgers and Hammerstein Organization (b). **59 Lebrecht Music and Arts:** Photofest / © Courtesy of The Rodgers and Hammerstein Organization (t). **60 Dorling Kindersley:** Dan Bannister (cl). **Getty Images:** George Karger / Pix Inc. / The LIFE Images Collection / © Courtesy of The Rodgers and Hammerstein Organization (bl). **Lebrecht Music and Arts:** Photofest / © Courtesy of The Rodgers and Hammerstein Organization (br). **Photofest:** © Courtesy of The Rodgers and Hammerstein Organization (t). **61 Dorling Kindersley:** Confederate Memorial Hall, New Orleans (t). **Photofest:** © Courtesy of The Rodgers and Hammerstein Organization (bl). **62-63 Photofest:** © Courtesy of The Rodgers and Hammerstein Organization. **64 Getty Images:** GAB Archive / Redferns. **65 Alamy Images:** Pictorial Press Ltd (t). **Corbis:** Bettmann (b). **The Kobal Collection:** MGM (c). **66 The Kobal Collection:** MGM (l). **66-67 Photofest:** MGM. **67 The Kobal Collection:** (tr); MGM (tl). **68 Dorling Kindersley:** The

George Hoare Theatre Collection at Drury Lane (bl). **Photofest:** As authorised by the Estate of Jo Mielziner / © Courtesy of The Rodgers and Hammerstein Organization. **69 Getty Images:** Jack Mitchell (br). **Photofest:** As authorised by the Estate of Jo Mielziner / © Courtesy of The Rodgers and Hammerstein Organization. **70 Alamy Images:** Chronicle (tr). **Lebrecht Music and Arts:** (bl). **71 Alamy Images:** CBW (br). **Getty Images:** Michael Ochs Archives (t). **Photofest:** (b). **72 The Library of Congress, Washington DC:** LC-USZ62-7873. **72-73 Photofest:** © Courtesy of The Rodgers and Hammerstein Organization. **73 Dorling Kindersley:** National Music Museum (t). **74 Fotolia:** Olena Pantiukh (t). **Photofest:** As authorised by the Estate of Jo Mielziner / © Courtesy of The Rodgers and Hammerstein Organization. **75 Corbis:** Bettmann / © Courtesy of The Rodgers and Hammerstein Organization (t). **Dorling Kindersley:** courtesy of the Board of Trustees of the Royal Armouries (br). **Dreamstime.com:** Roman Sotola (br/ target). **Photofest:** As authorised by the Estate of Jo Mielziner / © Courtesy of The Rodgers and Hammerstein Organization. **76 Corbis:** Bettmann. **77 Alamy Images:** Pictorial Press Ltd (br, t). **Dorling Kindersley:** National Music Museum (bl, bc). **78 Corbis:** Underwood & Underwood (br). **The Kobal Collection:** (t); Warner Bros (bl). **79 Corbis:** John Springer Collection (b). **80 Getty Images:** GAB Archive / Redferns (t). **Photofest:** (b). **81 The Kobal Collection:** MGM. **82 Alamy Images:** AF archive (bl); Pictorial Press Ltd (br). **83 Alamy Images:** Pictorial Press Ltd (bl). **Photofest:** MGM (t). **84 Alamy Images:** AF archive (bl). **84-85 Alamy Images:** Pictorial Press Ltd. **85 Alamy Images:** Chronicle (r). **Corbis:** Bettmann (tc). **86 Photofest:** MGM. **87 The Kobal Collection:** MGM (t). **Photofest:** MGM (b). **88 Corbis:** John Springer Collection (r). **Lebrecht Music and Arts:** (l). **89 Corbis:** CinemaPhoto. **90 Corbis:** John Springer Collection (t). **The Kobal Collection:** MGM / Samuel Goldwyn (br). **Photofest:** Courtesy of the Estate of Alvin Colt / All Rights Reserved. / As authorised by the Estate of Jo

Mielziner (bl). **91 Corbis:** Metro-Goldwyn-Mayer Pictures / Sunset Boulevard (t). **Dreamstime.com:** Sven Larsen (c). **Photofest:** Courtesy of the Estate of Alvin Colt / All Rights Reserved / As authorised by the Estate of Jo Mielziner (b). **92 Getty Images:** Buyenlarge (r); Gene Lester (l). **93 Alamy Images:** AF archive (t); mooziic (c). **Rex Features:** ANL (b). **94-95 123RF.com:** Andrey Bayda. **96 Dorling Kindersley:** The George Hoare Theatre Collection at Drury Lane (l). **Photofest:** As authorised by the Estate of Jo Mielziner / © Courtesy of The Rodgers and Hammerstein Organization. **97 The Kobal Collection:** Paramount (b). **98 Alamy Images:** WorldPhotos / © Courtesy of The Rodgers and Hammerstein Organization (r). **Dorling Kindersley:** The George Hoare Theatre Collection at Drury Lane (b). **99 Corbis:** Bettmann (l). **Photofest:** © Courtesy of The Rodgers and Hammerstein Organization (r). **100 The Kobal Collection:** MGM. **101 Corbis:** Bettmann (b). **Getty Images:** Movie Poster Image Art (t). **102 Getty Images:** Movie Poster Image Art (t). **The Kobal Collection:** MGM (bl, br). **103 Corbis:** CinemaPhoto (t); John Springer Collection (b). **Dreamstime.com:** Ffulya (cr). **Getty Images:** Jim Heimann Collection (cl). **104 The Kobal Collection:** MGM (l, r). **105 Photofest:** (b, t). **106 Photofest:** (t);. **107 The Kobal Collection:** (r). **108 Corbis:** Bettmann. **109 Corbis:** Bettmann (br); Didier Olivré (bl). **Hamburg Ballett - John Neumeier:** Holger Badekow (t). **110 Alamy Images:** AF archive (r). **Photofest:** (bl). **111 Photofest. 112 The Kobal Collection:** Paramount (t). **Photofest:** MGM (b). **113 The Kobal Collection:** MGM (t, b). **114 Corbis:** Bettmann (br). **The Kobal Collection:** Warner Bros (l). **115 Photofest:** As authorised by the Estate of Jo Mielziner. **116 The Kobal Collection:** Warner Bros (bl). **Photofest:** Warner Bros (br). **117 Photofest:** Warner Bros (t, b). **118-119 Photofest. 120 The Kobal Collection:** Warner Bros (t). **121 Corbis:** John Springer Collection (br). **The Kobal Collection:** (l); Warner Bros (tr). **122 Photofest:** set design by Oliver Smith (The Oliver Smith Collections is in the Music Division of the Library of Congress, Washington DC), Courtesy of Rosaria Sinisi. **123 Alamy Images:** AF archive (t). **The Kobal Collection:** MIRISCH-7 ARTS / United Artists (b).

124 Photofest: set design by Oliver Smith, Courtesy of Rosaria Sinisi (t, b). **125 Alamy Images:** United Archives GmbH (br). **Dreamstime.com:** Pablo Eder (t). **Getty Images. 126 Corbis:** Annemiek Veldman / Kipa. **127 Alamy Images:** sjvinyl (t). **iStockphoto.com:** Ken Brown (r). **Rex Features:** ITV (b). **128 The Kobal Collection:** Warner Bros. **129 Getty Images:** GAB Archive / Redferns (b). **The Kobal Collection:** Warner Bros (t). **130 Corbis:** John Springer Collection (t). **Photofest:** Warner Bros. Pictures (br). **131 Getty Images:** Warner Brothers (t). **Photofest:** Warner Bros. Pictures (br). **132 Alamy Images:** Pictorial Press Ltd (l). **Getty Images:** Movie Poster Image Art (r). **133 The Kobal Collection:** Paramount. **134 Photofest:** set design by Oliver Smith, Courtesy of Rosaria Sinisi / © Courtesy of The Rodgers and Hammerstein Organization. **135 Getty Images:** Christie Goodwin (br); Popperfoto (t). **136 Alamy Images:** EPA (bc). **Photofest:** © Courtesy of The Rodgers and Hammerstein Organization (t); set design by Oliver Smith, Courtesy of Rosaria Sinisi / © Courtesy of The Rodgers and Hammerstein Organization (br). **137 Photofest:** set design by Oliver Smith, Courtesy of Rosaria Sinisi / © Courtesy of The Rodgers and Hammerstein Organization (bc). **PunchStock:** Stockbyte (br). **138 Myra Kates and Sheila Kieran:** (br). **The Kobal Collection:** Warner Bros (bl). **The Art Archive:** Museum of the City of New York / MCNY41 (tr). **139 Alamy Images:** AF archive. **140 Alamy Images:** Jeff Morgan 07 (tr); Moviestore Collection Ltd (bl). **141 Alamy Images:** ZUMA Press, Inc. (tc). **Corbis:** John Springer Collection (cr). **Getty Images:** Archive Photos (l). **142 Cameron Mackinstosh Limited:** (tr). **Photofest:** Columbia Pictures (b). **143 Getty Images:** Silver Screen Collection (l). **The Kobal Collection:** Columbia (br). **144 Photofest:** Warner Brothers / Seven Arts (r). **145 Photofest. 146-147 Photofest:** Twentieth Century Fox Film Corp.. **148 Corbis:** John Springer Collection (br). **Photofest:** (bl). **149 The Kobal Collection:** United Artists. **150-151 Photofest:** Aronson Family Collection (b). **151 Corbis:** Bettmann / Aronson Family Collection (r). **Getty Images:** Movie Poster Image Art (t). **152 Dorling Kindersley:** Royal Academy of Music (tr, tc). **Photofest:** Aronson Family Collection (bl); Aronson Family Collection (br). **153 Getty Images:**

Gianni Ferrari / Cover (t). **Photofest:** Aronson Family Collection (b). **154-155 Photofest:** © 1964 Disney (b). **155 Cameron Mackintosh Limited:** © Disney / CML. Photo: Michael Le Poer Trench (bc). **Photofest:** (tr). **156 The Kobal Collection:** © 1964 Disney (br). **Photofest:** © 1964 Disney (clb). **157 Photofest:** © 1964 Disney (tr). **158-159 Photofest:** RKO Radio Pictures. **160 The Kobal Collection:** 20th Century Fox / Chenault. **161 Alamy Images:** ClassicStock (b); MARKA (t). **162 Getty Images:** GAB Archive / Redferns (bl). **The Kobal Collection:** United Artists (r). **163 The Kobal Collection:** Columbia. **164 Alamy Images:** Photos 12 (t). **The Kobal Collection:** Parc Films / Madeleine Films (b). **165 Getty Images:** Jean-Regis Rouston / Roger Viollet (b). **Photofest:** Zeitgeist Films / Leo Weisse (t). **166 Getty Images:** Warner Brothers (r). **The Kobal Collection:** ABC / Allied Artists (l). **167 Getty Images:** GAB Archive / Redferns (t). **The Kobal Collection:** Universal (br). **168-169 Getty Images:** Jack Vartoogian. **170 The Kobal Collection:** Warner Bros. **171 Photofest:** Universal Pictures. **172 Photofest. 173 Alamy Images:** Geraint Lewis (tc). **Photofest:** (crb). **The Art Archive:** Museum of the City of New York / MCNY43 (l). **174-175 The Kobal Collection:** Warfield / United Artists. **174 The Kobal Collection:** (cra). **175 The Kobal Collection:** Warfield / United Artists (br). **Photofest:** United Artists (tr). **176 Photofest:** © Disney. **177 Alamy Images:** Motoring Picture Library (t). **Corbis:** Catherine Karnow / © A.M.P.A.S.® (cr). **National Endowment for the Arts:** Presidential Press Corps (b). **178 Alamy Images:** Moviestore collection Ltd (t). **Photofest:** Scenic Design by Robin Wagner (b). **179 Photofest. 180-181 Getty Images:** Joshua Blake. **182 Cameron Mackintosh Limited:** (t). **Photofest:** set and costume designs by John Napier (b). **183 Corbis:** Walter McBride (br). **Getty Images:** Dave Benett (cr). **The Kobal Collection:** Dreamworks / David James (bl). **Rex Features:** Michael Le Poer Trench (t). **184 Lebrecht Music and Arts:** David Edward Byrd, used with permission (l). **Photofest:** (cr). **185 Getty Images:** Ron Henbury / Evening Standard (l); John Olson / The LIFE Picture Collection / Scenic Design by Robin

Wagner (r). **186 Photofest:** Set design by Tony Walton. **187 Getty Images:** Chris Jackson / costume design by Mark Thompson. **188-189 Photofest:** Columbia Pictures. **190 Alamy Images:** Moviestore collection Ltd (b). **191 Getty Images:** Graham Morris / Evening Standard (t). **Photofest:** (b). **192 Alamy Images:** AF archive. **193 Getty Images:** GAB Archive / Redferns (t, br); Michael Ochs Archives (bl). **194-195 Corbis:** Saed Hindash / Star Ledger. **196 Alamy Images:** AF archive / poster & logo by Tony Walton (t). **Rex Features:** Associated Newspapers / set Design by Tony Walton (b). **197 TopFoto.co.uk:** PA / set design by Tony Walton. **198 Getty Images:** Hulton Archive (t). **Photofest:** Set Design by John Lee Beatty (bl, br). **199 Alamy Images:** AF archive (t). **Photofest:** set design by Tony Walton (bl). **200 Alamy Images:** Mim Friday / poster & logo by Tony Walton (r). **Getty Images:** GAB Archive / Redferns (l). **201 Alamy Images:** Photos 12 (bl); StampCollection (br). **Corbis:** John Springer Collection (tr). **Lebrecht Music and Arts:** Interfoto (tl). **202 Getty Images:** Hulton Archive (b). **TopFoto.co.uk:** The Granger Collection (t). **203 Corbis:** Manuel Litran / Paris Match (bl); Eric Robert / Sygma (br). **Getty Images:** Jean-Jacques Bernier / Gamma-Rapho (cl). **204 Photofest:** Scenic design by Robin Wagner. **205 Corbis:** Bettmann (br). **Getty Images:** United News / Popperfoto (t). **206 Alamy Images:** Geraint Lewis / Scenic design by Robin Wagner (bl). **Getty Images:** Jack Mitchell (br). **207 Alamy Images:** theatrepix / Scenic design by Robin Wagner (t, br). **Getty Images:** Stanley Bielecki Movie Collection (bl). **208 Getty Images:** Stewart Cook (bl). **Rex Features:** Reg Wilson (br). **209 Alamy Images:** Pictorial Press Ltd (tr). **The Kobal Collection:** Cinergi Pictures (tl). **210 Alamy Images:** Interfoto. **211 Alamy Images:** AF archive (c). **Photofest:** (br). **Rex Features:** Bill Cross / ANL (t). **212 The Kobal Collection:** Paramount (r, l). **213 The Kobal Collection:** Paramount (bl, t). **214 Alamy Images:** Keystone Pictures USA / set design by John Lee Beatty (b). **Photofest:** set design by John Lee Beatty (t). **215 The Kobal Collection:** 20th Century Fox / Columbia. **216 Lebrecht Music and Arts:** Tristram Kenton / set and costume designs by Anthony Ward (b).

Photofest: set and costume designs by Anthony Ward (t). **217 Photofest:** set and costume designs by Anthony Ward. **218 Alamy Images:** Moviestore collection Ltd (t); theatrepix / set and costume designs by Anthony Ward (bl). **219 Alamy Images:** Geraint Lewis / set and costume designs by Anthony Ward (bl); theatrepix / set and costume designs by Anthony Ward (br). **220 Corbis:** Hulton-Deutsch Collection. **221 Alamy Images:** sjtheatre (br, bc). **Getty Images:** Oliver Morris (t). **222 Photofest:** (bl, tr). **223 Photofest:** set design by Douglas W. Schmidt. **224 Photofest:** (l, r). **225 The Kobal Collection:** Dreamworks/ James, David. **226-227 Photofest:** NBC. **228 Michael Le Poer Trench:** Set and Costumes - John Napier (b). **Photofest:** (t). **229 Corbis:** Bettmann (b). **Photofest:** set and costume designs by John Napier (t). **230 Alamy Images:** Gallo Images / set and costume designs by John Napier (bl); Geraint Lewis / set and costume design by John Napier (t). **Justin Downing:** (br). **231 Alamy Images:** Geraint Lewis / set and costume design by John Napier (t). **Getty Images:** Suhaimi Abdullah. Set and Costumes - John Napier (bl). **NASA:** (cr). **Photofest:** set and costume designs by John Napier (br). **232 Rex Features. 233 Cameron Mackintosh Limited:** Courtesy of the Cameron Mackintosh Archive (c) OPL (c, r); Photograph by Michael Le Poer Trench © Cameron Mackintosh Ltd (t). **Rex Features:** Darren Bell (b). **234 The Kobal Collection:** Columbia, bl). **235 The Kobal Collection:** Lucamar Productons. **236-237 Rex Features:** Alastair Muir / Audrey II, designed by David Farley, created by Artem for the Menier Chocolate Factory production. **238 The Kobal Collection:** MGM / UA. **239 Alamy Images:** Everett Collection Historical (l). **Photofest:** (r). **240 Alamy Images:** dpa picture alliance / STARLIGHT EXPRESS GmbH. **241 Photofest:** set and costume designs by John Napier (t). **Rex Features:** Nils Jorgensen (br); Richard Young (cr). **242-243 Photo Jens Hauer, STARLIGHT EXPRESS. 244 Alamy Images:** Lebrecht Music and Arts Photo Library / set and costume designs by David Farley (t). **Corbis:** Walter McBride (b). **245 © David Baltzer / bildbuehne. de. 246 Photofest. 247 Cameron Mackintosh Limited:** Courtesy of the Cameron Mackintosh Archive (r).

Photofest: Michael Le Poer Trench (t). **248 Photofest:** (br, t). **249 Photofest:** (t, bl, br). **250-251 Cameron Mackintosh Limited:** Courtesy of the Cameron Mackintosh Archive. **252 Photofest:** (br). **253 Photofest. 254-255 Maria Bjornson Archive/ Redcase Ltd. 256 Cameron Mackintosh Limited:** Courtesy of the Cameron Mackintosh Archive (t); Photograph by Michael Le Poer Trench © Cameron Mackintosh Ltd (br); France Soir, 1985 (bl). **257 Corbis:** Robbie Jack. **258 Getty Images:** Photoshot. **259 Corbis:** Jon Furniss / Corbis / Splash News (bc). **The Kobal Collection:** Working Title Films (br). **Cameron Mackintosh Limited:** Photograph by Michael Le Poer Trench © Cameron Mackintosh Ltd (t). **260 Photofest. 261 Cameron Mackintosh Limited:** Courtesy of the Cameron Mackintosh Archive. **262 Photofest:** (r); Joan Marcus / set design by Robin Wagner / Scenic Design by Robin Wagner (l). **263 Getty Images:** Manfred Schmid © VBW / Ralf Brinkhoff / Birgit Mögenburg (l). **© VBW / Ralf Brinkhoff / Birgit Mögenburg:** (r). **264-265 Alamy Images:** Wenn Ltd. **266 Alamy Images:** World History Archive. **267 Joan Marcus. 268 Alamy Images:** trekandshoot (tl). **Photofest:** Paramount Pictures (bl); Craig Schwartz (br). **269 Alamy Images:** AF archive (br). **Donald Cooper / Photostage:** (t). **Dorling Kindersley:** Museum of the Moving Image, London (bl); courtesy of Robin Wigington, Arbour Antiques, Ltd., Stratford-upon-Avon (cra). **270 Photofest. 271 Alamy Images:** sjvinyl (cr). **Corbis:** Hulton-Deutsch Collection (bc); Ron Sachs / Pool / CNP (bl). **Photofest:** set and costume designs by John Napier (t). **272 Corbis:** Susan Johann (bl). **Photofest:** (tr). **273 Photofest:** Michal Daniel (t); (b). **274 The Kobal Collection:** Sony Pictures. **275 PunchStock:** Thinkstock / Ron Chapple. **276 © Disney:** (b). **277 Alamy Images:** Photos 12 / © Disney (t). **© Disney:** (b). **278 Dreamstime.com:** Driescronje (br). **Getty Images:** Leonard Adam / © Disney (bl). **279 Corbis:** Gary Hershorn / © Disney (tr). **© Disney:** (bl, br). **Dreamstime.com:** Tim Schuurbiers (cl). **280-281 Rex Features:** Canadian Press (b). **281 Alamy Images:** AF archive (cb). **The Kobal Collection:** Fox Searchlight (tl); Revolution Studios (cr). **282-283 Rex Features:** Courtesy

Everett Collection (b). **283 Alamy Images:** AF archive (tr). **Photofest:** (br). **284 Littlestar Services:** © Littlestar (t). **Photo by Brinkhoff / Mögenburg:** (b). **285 The Kobal Collection:** Universal / Playtone (b). **Photo by Brinkhoff / Mögenburg:** (t). **286-287 Corbis:** Joho / cultura. **288 Alamy Images:** Moviestore collection Ltd (t). **Photofest:** 20th Century Fox (b). **289 Charlie and The Chocolate Factory:** Photo Johan Persson (b). **Getty Images:** Andrew H. Walker / WireImage for Tony Awards Productions (tr); Walter McBride (tl). **We Will Rock You:** (c). **290 Alamy Images:** Moviestore collection Ltd (t). **Photofest:** (b). **291 Alamy Images:** AF archive. **292 Getty Images:** The Hartman Group. **293 Corbis:** Robbie Jack (t). **Photofest:** set design by Tony Walton (r); (bc); Universal Studios / Andrew Schwartz (c). **294 Photofest:** 20th Century Fox. **295 Corbis:** Neville Elder (br). **The Kobal Collection:** MGM (bl). **296 The Kobal Collection:** New Line (tr); New Line / James, David (bl). **297 The Kobal Collection:** New Line / James, David (b, t). **298-299 The Kobal Collection:** DAMFX. **300 Corbis:** Nancy Kaszerman / ZUMA Press (l). **Cameron Mackintosh Limited:** Courtesy of the Cameron Mackintosh Archive (r). **301 Cameron Mackintosh Limited. 302 Alamy Images:** Matt Ellis (bl); Trinity Mirror / Mirrorpix (br). **303 Corbis:** Franz-Marc Frei. **304 Getty Images:** Andrew H. Walker / Getty Images for dcp. **305 Dreamstime.com:** Biansho (cr). **Getty Images:** Ron Galella, Ltd. / WireImage (b); Terry O'Neill (t). **Photofest:** (c). **306 The Kobal Collection:** GK Films / RATPAC Entertainment / RATPAC-DUNE Entertainment / Warner Bros. **307 The Kobal Collection:** Python Pictures / EMI (b). **308 Rex Features:** Alastair Muir. **309 Alamy Images:** Keith Morris / directed by Lee Blakeley, set designs by Alex Eales (br). **Getty Images:** Bryan Bedder (b). **Photofest:** (tl). **310-311 Corbis:** Walter McBride. **312 Alamy Images:** Geraint Lewis. **313 Corbis:** Michael Yamashita. **314 Rex Features:** Geraint Lewis. **315 Alamy Images:** Moviestore collection Ltd (t). **Corbis:** Robert Wallace / Splash News (br). **Rex Features:** Alastair Muir (bl). **316 © Royal Shakespeare Company:** Manuel Harlan (br, bl). **317 Rex Features:** Alastair Muir (t). **© Royal Shakespeare Company:**

Manuel Harlan (b). **318 Dream Works Theatricals:** © 2008 Dream Works Theatricals (Photo by Joan Marcus) (bl, tr). **319 Dream Works Theatricals:** © 2008 Dream Works Theatricals (Photo by Joan Marcus). **320 Photofest. 321 The Kobal Collection:** Samson Films / Summit Entertainment. **322 Rex Features:** Alastair Muir. **323 Charlie and The Chocolate Factory. 324-325 Getty Images:** Paul Hawthorne. **326 Corbis:** Splash News (bl). **326 Alamy Images:** AF Fotografie (br) © The Estate of Edmund Dulac. All rights reserved. DACS 2015. **327 Getty Images:** François Guillot / AFP / © Marie-Noëlle Robert - Théâtre Du Châtelet, Set Design By Alex Eales And Costumes By Mark Bouman. **328 Getty Images:** Michael Ochs Archives. **329 Dorling Kindersley:** National Music Museum (l). **Getty Images:** Metro-Goldwyn-Mayer (bc). **330 Getty Images:** John Kobal Foundation (b). **The Kobal Collection:** MGM (t). **331 Getty Images:** Warner Brothers. **332 Getty Images:** Metro-Goldwyn-Mayer (b, t). **333 Alamy Images:** WorldPhotos / © Courtesy of The Rodgers and Hammerstein Organization. **334 Photofest:** set design by Oliver Smith, Courtesy of Rosaria Sinisi. **335 The Kobal Collection:** Paramount (t). **Photofest:** (b). **336 Alamy Images:** Pictorial Press Ltd (br). **The Kobal Collection:** Wolper / Warner Bros (t). **Photofest:** (l). **337 Alamy Images:** AF archive. **338 The Kobal Collection:** MGM. **339 Alamy Images:** AF archive (t). **Photofest:** (b). **340 The Kobal Collection:** RBT Stigwood Prods / Hemdale. **341 Getty Images:** NBC Television (bl); Bob Thomas / Popperfoto (br). **Photofest:** (t). **342 Getty Images:** Jack Mitchell. **343 The Kobal Collection:** Thin Man / Grennlight. **344 Alamy Images:** Maurice Savage (t). **345 Alamy Images:** Wenn Ltd. **346 Alamy Images:** Bettina Strenske / theatrepix © Toni-Leslie for Costume Design. **Getty Images:** Kevin Mazur (b). **347 Alamy Images:** Wenn Ltd.

All other images © Dorling Kindersley
For further information see:
www.dkimages.com